Freedom in the World

The findings of the *Comparative Survey of Freedom* and the Map of Freedom include events up to 1 January 1993.

Freedom in the World
The Annual Survey of Political Rights & Civil Liberties 1992-1993

Freedom House Survey Team

R. Bruce McColm
Survey Coordinator

Dale Bricker
James Finn
Charles Graybow
Jonathan D. Karl
Douglas W. Payne
Joseph E. Ryan
George Zarycky

Freedom House

First published in 1993

Cover design and map by Emerson Wajdowicz Studios, N.Y.C.

The Library of Congress has catalogued this serial title as follows:

Freedom in the world / —1978-
New York : Freedom House, 1978-
v. : map; 25 cm.—(Freedom House Book)
Annual.
ISSN 0732-6610=Freedom in the World.
1. Civil rights—Periodicals. I. R. Bruce McColm, et al.   I. Series.
JC571.F66   323.4'05-dc 19   82-642048
AACR 2   MARC-S
Library of Congress   [84101]
ISBN   0-932088-79-1   (pbk.)
         0-932088-80-5 (cloth)

Distributed by National Book Network
4720 Boston Way
Lanham, MD 20706

3 Henrietta Street
London WC2E 8LU England

Contents

Foreword

Freedom House is a non-profit organization based in New York that monitors political rights and civil liberties around the world. Established in 1941, Freedom House believes the effective advocacy of civil rights at home and human rights abroad must be grounded in fundamental democratic values and principles.

The *Comparative Survey of Freedom* is an institutional effort to monitor the political rights and civil liberties in 186 nations and 66 related territories on an annual basis. Freedom House began earlier efforts to record the progress and decline in freedoms during the 1950s in reaction to racial violence in the United States. The first year-end review of freedom was sparked in 1955 by the kidnapping and murder of Emmet Till, a fourteen-year old black in Mississippi. An all-white jury subsequently acquitted the two white men indicted for the crime.

During those early years, the project was called the Balance Sheet of Freedom, and later the Annual Survey of the Progress of Freedom. By the late 1960s, the Freedom House Board of Trustees felt there was a need to create a single standard by which to measure and record the development of freedom around the world.

When Freedom House's *Comparative Survey of Freedom* was finally established in the early 1960s, democracy was in a perilous state both at home and abroad: Spain, Portugal and Greece were under military rule; the world's largest democracy, India, would soon declare martial law; an American president faced the possibility of impeachment; and the prospects for liberalization—not to say democratization—in Eastern Europe, Latin America and Asia were dim. This past decade has seen unprecedented gains in freedom over much of the world.

With the new period of structural change beginning in 1989, the *Survey* project has become a year-long effort produced by our regional experts, consultants, and human rights specialists. The *Survey* derives its information from a wide range of sources.

Most valued of these are the many human rights activists, journalists, editors and political figures around the world who keep us constantly informed of the human rights situation in their countries. Sometimes the mere act of objectively reporting government crackdowns, repression and extra-judicial killings puts these courageous individuals and their families at great risk. At other times, these personalities are cast into the midst of political change and, as prime actors in their nation's life, pay the ultimate price. This year, for example, Jeremias Chitunda, the vice-president of UNITA, the guerrilla in Angola, while attempting to negotiate a ceasefire with the Luanda government, was summarily executed after he and his colleagues fled their offices in the Miramar section of the capital.

Western journalists increasingly play an important role in the movement for human rights by their ability to penetrate inaccessible places where local human rights advocates are either nonexistent or are unable to project their urgent message to the world. Since the spring of 1992, Freedom House has been privileged to receive extensive reporting from American journalists covering the conflicts and practice of "ethnic cleansing" in Bosnia and Croatia. Faced with the usual pressures of covering a war situation, these men and women took the time to provide us and others with specific cases of horrendous human rights abuses and the creation of detention camps. Throughout this past year, European and Latin American journalists offered moral and sometimes personal support to the courageous community of human rights activists on the island of Cuba; without their concern, many of the deteriorating conditions in that society would not have come to light.

Throughout the year Freedom House personnel regularly conduct fact-finding missions to gain more in-depth knowledge of the vast political transformations affecting our world. During these week-to-month long investigations, we make every effort to meet a cross-section of political parties and associations, human rights monitors, religious figures, representatives of both the private sector and trade union movement, academics and the appropriate security forces and insurgent movements where they exist.

During the past year, Freedom House traveled to Afghanistan, Angola, Bulgaria, Canada, Croatia, Czechoslovakia, Dominican Republic, Ecuador, El Salvador, Ethiopia, Guyana, Hungary, Kazakhstan, Kosovo, Kurdistan, Macedonia, Pakistan, Poland, Russia, Turkey, Ukraine and Yugoslavia (Serbia).

The *Survey* project team also consults a vast array of published source materials, ranging from the reports of other human rights organizations to often rare, regional newspapers and magazines.

This year's *Survey* team includes R. Bruce McColm, the project coordinator, Dr. Joseph Ryan, a comparative political scientist, Dale Bricker, James Finn, Charles Graybow, Douglas W. Payne and George Zarycky. The general editor of *Freedom in the World* is Jon Karl; the managing editor and editorial assistant are Mark Wolkenfeld and Pei Koay, respectively. This year's research assistants were Boguslaw Artman, Susanna Corwin, Robin Harper, Mariana Katzarova, Ani Oghali, Christina Pendzola, Elizabeth Szonyi, Audrey Weg Schaus and Karen Salama.

Primary financial support for the *Comparative Survey of Freedom* has been generously provided by The Pew Charitable Trusts, which has provided the main support for the *Comparative Survey of Freedom* over the past twenty years. We also want to thank the Lynde and Harry Bradley foundation for its continued support and assistance in this endeavor. ▬

The Comparative Survey of Freedom 1992-1993: Our Crowded Hour
R. Bruce McColm

"The recognition of historical limits must not lead to a betrayal of cherished values and historical attainments...The difficulty of sustaining the values of a free world must not prompt us to come to terms with tyranny."—Reinhold Niebuhr

The West's failure to respond to Serbian aggression in the Balkans cast a long shadow over the continued expansion of freedom around the world. As Christmas approached, the Bosnian capital of Sarajevo remained surrounded by armed forces and its 400,000 inhabitants faced an icy winter and potential starvation. Over 3 million people have become refugees since the spring, and several hundred thousand have been detained in camps, the results of the Serbian campaign of "ethnic cleansing." The Balkan tragedy is one of the gravest crises in Europe since World War II. The Balkans may be a new generation's Spain, the gruesome laboratory of the future.

On the Horn of Africa, American troops intervened for the first time for purely non-strategic "humanitarian" reasons. The disintegration of Somalia into a land controlled by marauding warlords has raised new questions for the post-Cold War order about the limits of sovereignty and the proper response of the world community to the virtual collapse of a nation-state. Millions of Somalis face starvation and nearly one-third of all children under the age of five have died. Humanitarian interventionism has begun a much-needed debate over the new uses of a nation's military capability and the need for pre-emptive diplomacy to head off such crises before the stage of military intervention.

Nationalism, racism, doubt

The dramatic tragedies of the Balkans and Somalia emphasize a major pattern throughout this year's *Comparative Survey of Freedom*—persistent threats to the multi-ethnic nation-state. Although the world is freer than at any time in history, there are new manifestations of nationalism and brutal civil wars that threaten the progress of the past decade and augur a new cycle of authoritarianism if the community of democracies does not respond adequately to the challenge. The wave of ethnic and religious clashes in the Middle East, Africa and Asia counters the other global trend toward a common culture of market-oriented economies and democratic societies. And even within the developed democracies, the year-long epidemic of extreme nationalism and racism has led to a renewal of doubt about the ability of democracy to cope with the complex problems of the emerging world.

The unprecedented rate of political change registered over the past three years has unleashed many forces that can undermine free societies. The new generation taking office in Washington will confront a world that has undergone a political transformation of biblical proportions but one fraught with Old Testament sins. Since the Central European revolutions of 1989, global change has accelerated hyperkinetically. During that epoch-making year 27 nations changed their ratings in the *Survey* compared with 72 this year. This trend has led to the proliferation of hybrid regimes combining elements of market economies with partially democratic governments controlled by the old authoritarian elites. The challenge to the new Clinton administration will be to articulate the role of the U.S. as the

Freedom in the World—1993

The population of the world this year is estimated at 5.446 billion residing in 186 sovereign states and 66 related territories, a total of 252 places. The level of political rights and civil liberties as shown comparatively by the Freedom House Survey is:

Free: 1,352.2 billion (24.83) percent of the world's population) live in 75 of the states and in 48 of the related territories.

Partly Free: 2,403.3 billion (44.11 percent of the world's population) live in 73 of the states and 6 of the related territories.

Not Free: 1,690.4 billion (31.06) percent of the world's population live in 38 of the states and 12 of the related territories.

A Record of the Survey
(population in millions)

SURVEY DATE	FREE		PARTLY FREE		NOT FREE		WORLD POPULATION
January '81	1,613.0	(35.90%)	970.9	(21.60%)	1,911.9	(42.50%)	4,495.8
January '82	1,631.9	(35.86%)	916.5	(20.14%)	2,002.7	(44.00%)	4,551.1
January '83	1,665.1	(36.32%)	918.8	(20.04%)	2,000.2	(43.64%)	4,584.1
January '84	1,670.7	(36.00%)	1,074.8	(23.00%)	1,917.5	(41.00%)	4,663.0
January '85	1,671.4	(34.85%)	1,117.4	(23.30%)	2,007.0	(41.85%)	4,795.8
January '86	1,747.2	(36.27%)	1,121.9	(23.29%)	1,947.6	(40.43%)	4,816.7
January '87	1,842.5	(37.10%)	1,171.5	(23.60%)	1,949.9	(39.30%)	4,963.9
January '88	1,924.6	(38.30%)	1,205.4	(24.00%)	1,896.0	(37.70%)	5,026.0
January '89	1,992.8	(38.86%)	1,027.9	(20.05%)	2,107.3	(41.09%)	5,128.0
January '90	2,034.4	(38.87%)	1,143.7	(21.85%)	2,055.9	(39.28%)	5,234.0
January '91	2,088.2	(39.23%)	1,485.7	(27.91%)	1,748.7	(32.86%)	5,322.6
January '92	1,359.3	(25.29%)	2,306.6	(42.92%)	1,708.2	(31.79%)	5,374.2
January '93	1,352.2	(24.83%)	2,403.3	(44.11%)	1,690.4	(31.06%)	5,446.0

sole remaining super-power, not simply in terms of its military and economic strength, but also in respect to its moral responsibilities in consolidating a structure of freedom around the world.

President Clinton will inherit a world that stands at the high water mark of freedom in history. Since the end of the Cold War, the idea of democracy has triumphed in a convincing fashion: some 34 countries had adopted it as their political system and others may make the transformation by early 1993. The calamities of Somalia, Bosnia, Angola, Haiti or Cuba should not overshadow the fundamental change that has occurred in the condition and democratic expectations of a huge segment of humanity.

Today's challenge lies in consolidating democratic gains around the world and encouraging the opening of those societies that remain closed. Now that the democratic idea has gained global legitimacy, it is time to assist in the construction of democratic societies. Without an aggressive foreign policy that places democracy and human rights at its center, the United States stands to lose prestige and influence around the world and will face a rash of severe challenges to its national interests. Advocates of an atavistic *realpolitik,* who criticize the promotion of democracy as a form of Wilsonian idealism, overlook the implications of the global trend toward more democratic, open and liberal societies and the potential this holds for a more peaceful and stable world order.

Of the 186 countries Freedom House monitors, 99 are formal democracies. Twenty-three of those are rated *Partly Free,* and another, the Serbian- and Croatian-occupied country of Bosnia, is rated *Not Free.* With the possible addition of new democracies in 1993, there will be 31 democracies where substantial human rights violations occur everyday. In light of these developments, the U.S. will face the delicate problem of assisting democratic transitions in countries where human rights continue to be violated by security forces and, in some cases, insurgents. The Clinton administration will have to foster a new engagement with both the human rights community, which traditionally acts as a pressure group to limit or condition assistance to human rights violators, and our newly democratic allies. This dialogue must produce substantial support for the creation of independent judiciaries and the rule of law, the reform of the armed forces and intelligence agencies that violate human rights, support for the development of alternative delivery systems for American assistance, and expanded aid to democratic political parties and other nongovernmental institutions.

Bipolar into multipolar?

The bipolar world dominated by the Soviet-American rivalry is not likely to be replaced any time soon by a robust multi-polar world capable of taking action in cases such as Somalia and Bosnia. The U.S. remains the only nation with sufficient strength and moral stature to embark on a series of initiatives to maintain the momentum toward greater freedom on the one hand and to demonstrate greater concern on the other for those situations where the violations of human rights imperil both a people's existence and international order.

This year's *Survey* confirms the emergence of a new tripartite pattern in the world. Beyond the survey's "freedom catagories," the governments of the world break down into three basic groups: 1) 99 democracies; 2) 31 hybrid authoritarian regimes making modest gestures of liberalization; and, 3) the anachronistic residue of classical Communist regimes, feudal Middle Eastern kingdoms, military regimes and the deteriorating nation-states of Bosnia, Liberia and Somalia.

The welcomed trend toward democratization has also been marked by various failures in the transition process and the onset of decay in established democracies. This past year, we have seen relatively old democracies such as Venezuela shaken to their foundation, and other newly emergent democracies, such as the Congo, beset by violence against opposition parties. Neo-Communists have returned to power or influence in Lithuania, Romania, Bulgaria, Albania, Slovakia and various former Soviet republics.

In nations such as Angola, Ethiopia and Ghana, democracy has not progressed beyond the holding of elections to ratify the legitimacy of a dominant party already controlling the key government institutions. Throughout the emerging democratic world, IMF-designed programs of shock economic therapy threaten recent democratic gains in Africa, Latin America and the post-Communist countries. Those nations undergoing both economic and political liberalization face a radical deterioration in the standard of living. Economic dislocation and its threat to stability and security have already become the theme song of those on all sides of the political spectrum who claim democracy is an experiment to be limited to certain peoples and cultures and is already antiquated for a world in which the global economy makes sovereignty and self-rule a moot issue.

A freer, post-Cold War world must confront the evil stalking the earth in the form of crimes against humanity in the Balkans and the violence and human degradation of a Somalia. The disintegration of the nation-state and the stark problems of human survival it creates require a new approach to collective security and global responsibility. The Cold War era required the management of an international order so as to avoid a fatal collision of the superpowers. This was basically reactive and negative—the requirement of the most basic sense of defense. The partial re-emergence of multilateral organizations such as the U.N. and the OAS should encourage a reconsideration of humanitarian intervention and a more expansive approach to democratic reconstruction in afflicted nations. Pre-emptive diplomacy and humanitarian assistance can forestall man-made political and humanitarian tragedies. However, when such measures fail, as in the Balkans, the new world requires an honest and bold approach to the use of force to deter both aggression and crimes against humanity. ■

The United States: The Old Guard Changes
James Finn

The United States elections of November 1992 threw into sharp perspective many issues of American life that had preoccupied Americans not only during the preceding months of 1992 but during the last several years. In the process, some events and their attendant personalities were diminished and others were lifted into higher prominence. For the average voter as well as for for the candidates, economic issues far outweighed any others, including the military, as a measure of both United States' strength and its weakness. They ranged from narrowly domestic issues of jobs, worker productivity and the national deficit to the broader matters of international competition, trade regulations and agreements. On the social agenda, the elections allowed interest groups to focus with increased intensity on questions that continue to flow from the Anita Hill-Clarence Thomas Senate hearings. Not as dramatic as the world events that dominated political attention during the preceding three years, the results of these electoral debates altered markedly the political universe in which Americans will work out their future.

The defeat of George Bush and the election of Governor Bill Clinton (Ark.) as the forty-second president of the United States confirmed what was being increasingly sensed: as far as the American voters are concerned, the Cold War and the political leaders who brought it to a successful resolution are already part of history. The conflict that for over four decades provided motivation and direction for much of America's political life, is no longer even a reference point, nor can major American participants in that conflict convert their service, however admirable, into political currency.

This remarkable change is both symbolized and borne out by the passage of the presidency from George Bush (68)—who served actively in the armed forces in World War II and in various high political offices during the ensuing years and reigned over the final disintegration of communism and the Soviet empire—to Bill Clinton (46), who protested against and avoided service in the Vietnam war. The relative youth of the president-elect was reinforced by that of his running-mate, Senator Al Gore (44) of Tennessee, who had gained previous national campaign experience during a notably inept run for the presidential nomination in 1988.

With no big-name Democrat willing to take on the seemingly impregnable incumbent, the field was left open to less well-known or weaker contenders: Paul Tsongas (Mass.), Jerry Brown (Calif.), Tom Harkin (Iowa), Douglas Wilder (Va.), Bob Kerrey (Nebr.), and Bill Clinton of Arkansas. Beset early on by questions about marital infidelity and draft evasion, Clinton had difficulty maintaining balance, consolidating popular support, and raising campaign funds. Against the advice of Democratic leaders, who urged him to drop out of the race, he persevered to break away from the pack and wrest the nomination for himself. (During the course of the campaign the role of Bill Clinton's wife, a person of notably strong, informed views, was muted. But Hillary Clinton, friend and advisor as well as wife, is likely to reassert herself and to establish a new model of an activist First Lady.)

George Bush, who was expected to coast into the nomination cost-free, met unexpected opposition when forces on the right supported the challenge mounted by political commentator Patrick Buchanan. Bush was forced to respond, which he did belatedly. He then damaged his candidacy with excessively generous concessions to the right wing of the Republican Party.

The new campaign style

Both the Bush and the Clinton camps were intermittently unsettled by the entrance of the unorthodox, on-again off-again third party candidacy of the Texas billionaire Ross Perot. With practically unlimited personal funds at his disposal, the self-guided Perot was free to style his campaign to suit his personality.

After a tumultuous and often down-and-dirty campaign, the final results from the 3 November election were as follows: Bill Clinton/Al Gore 43 percent, George Bush/Dan Quayle 38 percent, Ross Perot/James Stockdale 19 percent.

In the course of the campaign the Clinton-Gore team changed the public perception of the Democratic party and its relation to a number of party activists, moving toward the political center without giving way to, or losing touch with, particular interest groups. That same team defied and overthrew the conventional wisdom that the presidential and vice-presidential candidates would represent different backgrounds. Not only are Clinton and Gore of the same generation, but from the same part of the country. The combination strengthened the Democratic party in areas that for years had been safely Republican.

This campaign, and very likely all succeeding presidential campaigns, were also changed by the tactics adopted by Ross Perot. Announcing his candidacy for the presidency almost casually on a TV talk show, Perot returned to that and other TV and radio talk shows to project his message directly to the American people, overleaping the usual media reporters and analysts, whom he frequently disparaged, and gaining wide exposure at minimum cost. The other candidates followed his lead, Bill Clinton appearing on one popular night program replete with dark glasses and saxophone. Not everyone was pleased to see the increasing admixture of politics and entertainment, former presidential candidate Walter Mondale remarking that it belittled the dignity proper to the presidential office. However, the evident effectiveness of the novel approach ensured that it would be a part of presidential campaigns in the future.

A very high proportion of the country watched the debates between the presidential candidates and, when given the opportunity, asked the candidates to stick to substantive issues instead of descending to muckraking, personal attacks. Even more surprisingly, they listened to the half-hour, blackboard economic lectures that Perot presented on purchased TV time. In another departure from recent political elections, the electorate turned out in record numbers, reversing a twenty-year decline. At least for 1992 the charge that voters were apathetic and indifferent was laid to rest.

In his unorthodox third-party candidacy, Ross Perot did more than initiate new campaign techniques, provide comic relief during the debates—"I'm all ears"—and press the national deficit as a high priority national issue. In gaining 19 percent of the popular vote he became the most successful third-party candidate since Theodore Roosevelt, who won 27 percent of the vote when he ran on the Bull Moose ticket in 1912. Perot's share of the vote also allowed those who claimed a strong mandate for Bill Clinton to substantiate their views by pointing to the substantial gap between Clinton and second-place Bush in the popular vote—and for those who disallowed a strong mandate to point out that Clinton received 2.6 percent less of the popular vote than Michael Dukakis did when he lost in a landslide electoral vote in 1988, and that 57 percent of the voters chose to vote for someone other than Clinton.

The United States is too powerful a country not to continue to play a major role in foreign affairs, but for the American electorate who voted in 1992 international relations took a back seat to domestic affairs. In the spring of 1992, polls showed that Americans still believe that it is important to keep a strong military and, if asked by allies, to join them in intervening in trouble spots. Americans are not isolationists. But the same polls also indicated that by a proportion of four to one they believed that we should concentrate more on domestic affairs than international affairs. This necessarily diminished the importance given to President Bush's experience and skill in foreign affairs, the astounding favorable rating (90 percent) that he gained for his performance during the Persian Gulf crises rapidly melting away in the glare focused on a prolonged recession, sluggish growth and continued unemployment. Correspondingly, Clinton's lack of experience in international affairs was brushed aside by those who placed hope in the candidate who promised change, movement and growth in the economy, and restraints on spending in various government agencies and programs.

The 103rd Congress

The 103rd Democratic-controlled Congress that the new president will work with has a number of interesting characteristics. The first point to note is that the chief executive and the Congressional majority will be from the same party, precluding partisan differences as a plausible reason for legislative deadlock. Defying predictions, a very high percentage of incumbents who ran were reelected. Because of retirements and resignations, however, there will be 110 new faces in Congress. Overall, the Democrats lost nine House seats, ending up with 259. The Republicans, gaining nine, will have a total of 175. In the Senate the number of Democrats remained at 57 and the Republicans at 43. The composition of both bodies will have noticeable changes, however. The number of women in the Senate went from two to six, one of whom is the first black woman to be elected to that body. (In a show of independence and ideology several of these women rebuffed Senator Biden's subsequent, warm invitation to serve on the Judiciary Committee, the body they had strongly criticized, partly on the grounds that it was composed entirely of white males, during and after the Anita Hill-Clarence Thomas hearings.) The House increased the number of women from 28 to 47. The number of blacks and Hispanics also increased in the House, where they will be joined by the first American Indian to be elected in sixty years, and the first Korean.

In the gubernatorial races of 1992, Democrats won eight and the Republicans four, for a total of thirty Democratic, eighteen Republican and two Independent governors.

Although the number of incumbents returned to office might seem to indicate that the voters' frustration and even anger at the Washington establishment have abated, this is counter-indicated by initiatives launched in fourteen states to limit the length of time their representatives can serve in Congress. Whatever the outcome of these initiatives, which are presently in Constitutional limbo, they testify to an underlying discontent among American citizens.

America's problems—the familiar & the new

However one measures the strength of his mandate, the president who is inaugurated on 20 January 1993 will face problems with which America has been acquainted for several years: sluggish economic growth, the need for more and more skilled jobs, racial tensions that have erupted into violent riots on both coasts and failed programs to alleviate them, widespread dissatisfaction with the nation's educational system, proposals to reduce welfare roles, a neglected national infrastructure, rising health costs with rising demands for a national program, crime and a growing prison population.

The social agenda also included issues of gender equity and sexual harassment, drug abuse, a high and rising rate of litigation to settle common conflicts, gay rights, about which referenda in Oregon and Colorado sent out conflicting signals, speech codes in schools and universities, and a general loss of national confidence that the political system was responsive to and capable of resolving these matters.

It was a goal of Clinton's campaign to convince the voters that the political system could, in fact, be responsive to these problems and that under his leadership it would. Inevitably some of his large intentions were stated in broad, nonpolicy terms. About some others he was quite specific. He spoke out in favor of pro-abortion rights, against vouchers for educational choice that would include private schools, in favor of keeping the death penalty, and proposed dropping the prohibition against gays in the armed forces.

Although, understandably enough, Clinton emphasized domestic issues in his campaign, as president he will be forced to make some tough foreign-policy decisions early on. He immediately showed not only that he was aware of this responsibility but that he was conscious that leaders of other countries, both allies and hostiles, would try to take his measure early on. The day after his election, the man who ran as the candidate of change took care to assure allies of the U.S. that he had been referring to the domestic scene. To them he said, "Even as America's administrations change, America's fundamental interests do not."

In response to the elections, many world leaders who know President Bush expressed appreciation for his international expertise and hoped that the United States would continue to provide needed leadership during a period of global instability and turmoil in a number of countries. Perhaps the most level headed assessment came from Prime Minister Felipe Gonzales of Spain even before the elections. After noting that he had a very comfortable and fruitful relationship with President Bush, he said, "I think the United States has an interna-tional dimension which appears little in the campaigns. But whoever sits in the White House has no choice but to assume it." Then he added, "the U.S. has to recover economically to reassume its international responsibilities."

On the long list of foreign-policy matters that the chief executive must consider and act on are the number of U.S. troops to remain in Europe and South Korea, Arab-Israeli negotiations, the murderous conflicts in former Yugoslavia, human rights and the continuation of the most-favored-nation status of China, the ongoing famine in the Horn of Africa, Haiti and its flight of refugees, and the internal armed conflict that continues in Angola. Only weeks after his election Clinton was being pressured to express his opinion of the struggle within the European Community that pitted the United States against long-standing subsidies of European farmers, including most prominently the French, who were strenuously resisting EC pressure to reduce such subsidies. He must also deal, nearer to home, with the North American Free Trade Agreement (NAFTA), well advanced by the Bush administration and favored by the leaders of Canada and Mexico. Only days before the end of the year, the U.S. and Russia agreed on a plan to make deep cuts in their nuclear arsenals, reducing the number of warheads by about two-thirds. Some details will be left to the Clinton administration to work out. But even as the total number of nuclear weapons in the world decreases, the number of countries with nuclear weapons capability increases. The new challenges to the U.S. will be different but also formidable.

These issues will press upon the new president, demanding response. Other issues to which he committed himself during the campaign will have to be supported and pushed by the administration. One that, if carried through, promises to transform American life in the 1990s and beyond is the proposal to have the United States government invest heavily in scientific research and technology: in robotics, biotechnology, fiber-optics communications, national computer networks, magnetic levitation trains. If pursued as initially outlined, these ventures would demand funds that would match those of Star Wars and the close collaboration of private and governmental sectors.

The fate of this grand proposal, which would be one of the greatest research efforts ever launched, will reveal the extent to which the Clinton-Gore team will stand by large campaign promises, its ability to overcome strong opposition, and its determination to push aggressively into the future.

Canada

During 1992, the United States neighbor to the north, which it frequently takes for granted, had an important referendum whose results could significantly change the future. During the past year, Canada vigorously debated and then rejected a measure that would have instituted major institutional reforms. Known as the Charlottetown agreement after the city in which it was hammered out, it attempted to respond to long-standing expressions of grievance by Quebec, the largely Francophone province. Eager to circumvent Quebec's threat to secede from Canada, Prime Minister Brian Mulroney, himself a Quebecker, had earlier initiated a process of enquiry leading to the so-called Meech Lake accord, which specifically recognized Quebec as a "distinct society" within the larger confines of Canada. The defeat of that accord in 1990 further aggravated the Quebec Francophone majority and strengthened the forces of those who called for the province's sovereignty.

This was followed, in 1992, by a proposal—the Charlottetown report—to revise the constitution in major ways that would satisfy an uneasy and restless citizenry and minimize the gap between divisive forces. It would have given greater autonomy to Quebec and other provinces; established self-government for indigenous peoples; created a new popularly elected Senate as Canada's upper chamber; realigned the Canadian Supreme Court to guarantee three seats for Quebec and to insure adherence to English common law and also to the Napoleonic Code.

When the voters rejected the agreement in October 1992, the specter of a separate, sovereign Quebec that has periodically haunted Canada took on more of a reality. In 1980, when the *Parti Quebecois* asked voters to vote on the question of sovereignty, 60 percent voted No. In the intervening years, sentiments have noticeably shifted. Canada now must prepare for national elections for the parliament, which will be held by November of 1993, and elections in the province of Quebec by 1994. The outcome of these elections could set the stage for a Quebec referendum on sovereignty.

That possibility is accompanied by a host of serious problems both for the province of Quebec, for the rest of Canada, and for North America. To give only one example, it would complicate such measures as the North American Free Trade Agreement, which is favored by the present heads of government of Canada, Mexico and the United States.

The defeat of the Charlottetown agreement pushes this unresolved conflict and Canada into an uncertain future. ▬

James Finn is senior editor of Freedom Review.

Latin America: Democracy and the Politics of Corruption
Douglas W. Payne

Latin America's leaders gathered in Madrid in July 1992 to "reaffirm our commitment to representative democracy, respect for human rights and fundamental freedoms as the pillars of our community." News of their declaration, however, was practically drowned out by the wave of protests directed at their scandal-ridden governments back home. Over the last decade a majority of Latin Americans gained the right to choose their governments through the ballot box. But most aspiring citizens have found that their nations have yet to advance much beyond what the late Venezuelan writer Carlos Rangel called "air republics," in which laws and institutions are suspended on the winds of unchecked power and corruption.

Corruption in Latin America is rooted in the sixteenth-century Spanish and Portuguese conquest whose principal legacy is a tradition of rule based on power rather than law. Since independence, Latin America has produced hundreds of constitutions, many of them with democratic features. But in most Latin American nations, rulers have operated according to the adage, *se acata pero no se cumple* (laws are accepted but not fulfilled), perpetuating a political culture of violence, corruption and impunity that has endured through intermittent periods of elected rule.

Today in Latin America democracy is nurtured by the spread of democratic ideas through advanced communications and modern transportation. New civic organizations and advocacy groups are appearing every year. They are chiseling away at the tradition of centralized authority, as each in its way is demanding a say in how the rules are made after the votes are counted.

But the region remains in a prolonged economic crisis born of the profligate, statist policies of the past and made more difficult by the need to conform to an unforgiving global economy. Many Latin Americans have displayed a willingness to accept a measure of sacrifice in exchange for the promise of renewed economic growth and development. However, austerity programs, restructuring, and an offensive against organized labor have exacerbated social and economic inequities already unmatched by any other region in the world. The gulf between rich and poor has widened and the middle classes, the anchor of any established democracy, are sliding back toward poverty.

Governments can shift some of the blame to demanding international financial institutions and the protectionist tendencies among developed nations. But Latin America's increasingly hard-nosed journalists have begun exposing the age-old systems of bribery, kickbacks, privileges and institutional corruption that flourish behind the rhetoric of democracy and free markets. With scandals grabbing headlines across the region, the idea has taken hold that politicians are imposing economic adjustments principally as a means to reline their pockets and preserve their elite status. Dampened popular expectations have turned to frustration and finally, in a number of countries in 1992, to outrage.

Some Latin American leaders, notwithstanding the noble sentiments expressed in

Madrid, have responded by reverting to authoritarian ways—ruling by decree, relying on force to stem unrest, and attacking the independent media. Their anti-democratic actions are limited by the expectations of the developed world that the democratic trend in the region will continue. But they are confident their transgressions will be overlooked because their economic reforms have been blessed by the international financial community.

Despite the inherent instability of this scenario, the region's armed forces thus far appear reluctant to initiate a new cycle of military rule. The generals handed responsibility for the economic crisis over to the politicians in the 1980s and they do not want it back. However, mounting popular revulsion over politics-as-usual has emboldened nationalist officers, usually younger men who view economic liberalization and budget-cutting as threats to their careers.

At the same time, the drug-trafficking network continues to spread. Driven by expanding markets in the developed world, it is penetrating political systems in nearly every country in the region, threatening even the relatively solid democracies in the English-speaking Caribbean. The drug trade thrives on the culture of corruption, undermines already weak, politicized judicial systems, fuels political and criminal violence, and provides a pretext for human rights violators both in and out of uniform.

Setbacks in Peru and Venezuela, potentially positive developments in Brazil and El Salvador, and the revival of Chile's democratic political culture after years of military rule indicate that the prospects for strengthening democratic rule vary from country to country. But overall, it can be said that if democracy is to advance, if political rights and civil liberties are to be guaranteed by a rule of law rather than merely tolerated by those in power, then the nature of Latin American politics itself must change.

"Kill Politicians"

Presidents Alberto Fujimori of Peru and Carlos Andres Perez of Venezuela did not attend the Ibero-American summit in Madrid. Fujimori, backed by the military, had dissolved Peru's Congress and suspended the constitution in April and was busy consolidating his *autogolpe* (self-coup). Perez had barely survived an attempted coup by midlevel officers in February and his grip remained shaky (he weathered a second attempt in November).

Perez was supported in Madrid and Fujimori was not, as their colleagues condemned "any attempt to alter the institutional order of democracy." Yet a majority of Peruvians and Venezuelans had made it clear they felt different. Polls in Peru showed that Fujimori's popularity had soared after he put most of Peru's political class out of business and promised to eradicate the Shining Path guerrillas.

Perez, however, whose ratings were near the bottom at the time, was besieged by widespread protests demanding he resign. Oil-rich Venezuela has the highest per capita income in South America, yet half its population lives in poverty. Opinion polls showed that many Venezuelans sympathized with the rebel soldiers and most named corruption as the principal reason for the attempted coup.

An idea frequently expressed in both countries was: Better an honest dictatorship than a corrupt democracy. But those who scrawled "Kill Politicians" on city walls more accurately reflected the nature of people's anger. Polls show that Latin Americans of all classes believe their governments are steeped in corruption. They also indicate that most people do not want to forfeit hard-won democratic freedoms. They do not want a return to dictatorship. They just want their politicians to clean up their act, or make way for a more honest and representative generation.

The election of President Fernando Collor de Mello in Brazil in 1989 seemed to signal that at least in one country a new generation had arrived. Collor, young and telegenic, rode to power on an anti-corruption platform. By 1992, however, he had been caught at the center of a $55 million graft and influence-peddling scheme involving close political associates and members of his family. Two months after returning from Madrid he was suspended by the Brazilian Congress and faced with an impeachment trial.

At first it looked like Collor might buy his way out of trouble by siphoning millions of dollars into pork-barrel projects of swing-vote legislators. There were also ominous noises from a military that had given way to civilian rule only in 1985. But with anti-corruption protests filling the streets of Brazil's major cities and the media spotlighting the Congress's every move, Collor went down in history as the first Latin American president to be removed by constitutional means.

Collor's fall is only a first step toward cleaning up Brazilian politics. After all, he was ousted by legislators who have given themselves salaries of $6,000 per month in a country where minimum wage, for those lucky enough to receive it, is barely $40 per month. But what happened in Brazil suggests that Latin America's political systems can be forced to cleanse themselves if an environment of free expression is maintained, and that the armed forces, traditionally primed to step in during an outbreak of disorder, might be less eager to interfere than in the past.

Argentina next?

The events in Brazil sent tremors throughout the region as the media trumpeted the end of the era of "the untouchables." Nowhere was "Collorgate" watched so closely as in neighboring Argentina where scandals had been swirling around President Carlos Menem since 1991. Menem has not been directly linked to the illicit activities involving his family and close associates. But Argentine journalists continued to peel away the layers of government corruption, even inviting Carl Bernstein of Watergate fame to Buenos Aires for consultation.

Menem's response has been to stretch the limits of democratic rule. Since 1991 he has ruled mostly by decree. He packed the Supreme Court and in 1992 used it to uphold executive orders removing officials mandated to probe official wrongdoing. He also initiated a campaign to entangle journalists and writers in a web of lawsuits, while his aides leveled a steady barrage of verbal attacks. Journalists continue to be killed in Latin America at an alarming rate, particularly in the Andean countries. But the assault on the media in Argentina reflects a newer pattern of more sophisticated intimidation by elected governments caught up in scandal.

Menem scoffed at criticism of his authoritarian style from the Congress and the press, stating just prior to the summit in Madrid, "It doesn't bother me to govern by decree." His self-assurance stemmed from his success in capping inflation and the approval of his economic reforms in international circles. But surveys showed that 90 percent of Argentines believed corruption in Menem's government was "high" or "very high." Given the economic down-turn at the end of 1992 and Argentina's notoriously volatile public opinion, many Argentines were thinking "Menemgate."

Menem's disdain for the concept of separation of powers suggests he is enamored of the Mexican model. Mexico, in fact, is the envy of many governments in the region. President Carlos Salinas has carried out a remarkable overhaul of the Mexican economy, putting his country first in line for a free trade agreement with the United States. But he has had the advantage of virtual one-party rule. In the Mexican system, checks and balances are mostly in the president's head. Modest political reforms in recent years have done little to alter Mexico's status as the most authoritarian state in Latin America outside of Cuba and, now, Peru.

With Mexico's move to a market economy, pressure for democratization is increasing. In Mexico, and indeed throughout Latin America, breaking down commercial barriers has led to the dismantling of psychological barriers of anti-modernity which have helped sustain authoritarian traditions for centuries. Mexico's opening to the world and the experience of greater economic freedom have spawned an array of independent civic organizations that lend weight to mounting opposition demands that the Institutional Revolutionary Party (PRI) loosen its grip on the state and allow free elections. Salinas has laid the economic groundwork for what he promises will be a "modern Mexico." But the longer he resists a transition to democratic rule, the greater the risk his project will run aground.

President Cesar Gaviria of Colombia is one leader who has made a serious attempt to fashion a more honest, representative political system. After his election in 1990, he initiated the writing of a new constitution designed to break the traditional oligarchical grip on government, curtail institutionalized corruption and enhance the independence and powers of the judiciary. It was hoped such reforms would entice left-wing guerrillas to join the political process. Gaviria also sought to reduce narco-terrorism by offering drug traffickers leniency in exchange for turning themselves in.

In 1992, however, Colombia was swamped by yet another wave of guerrilla and drug-related violence. Gaviria's credibility plummeted when drug kingpin Pablo Escobar, who had surrendered in 1991, bribed his way out of a cushy detention compound and unleashed the Medellin cartel's hit squads against judges and police. Then, following the breakdown of peace negotiations, left-wing guerrillas initiated a nationwide offensive. The insurgents, having fought for nearly three decades under a Marxist banner, now appear more interested in preserving a multi-million-dollar kidnapping and extortion racket which in some quarters has earned them the sobriquet, "Guerrilla Inc." For the beleaguered Gaviria, ensuring the survival of the state took precedence over reforming it.

Central America

With the exception of democratic Costa Rica, the nations of Central America are the most politically stunted in the hemisphere. The transition to elected rule remains shaky, corrupt militaries continue to exercise veto power over equally corrupt civilian governments, judicial systems don't function, and more than half the people cannot meet basic food and health needs.

In Guatemala, human rights abuses and political violence are responsible for more deaths than in any other country in Latin America except Colombia and Peru. In Nicaragua, the government of President Violeta Chamorro remains locked in an ill-considered embrace with the Sandinistas, which has allowed Gen. Humberto Ortega to emerge as the nation's strongman in the tradition of the former Somoza dynasty. In Panama, an incompetent, unpopular government depends on the presence of the U.S. Southern Command for its security amid mounting protests and political violence. Opinion polls indicate that a majority of Panamanians do not want the U.S. military to leave.

After twelve years of civil war the people of El Salvador were given at least a reprieve. An agreement brokered by the U.N. between the government and left-wing guerrillas led to a cease-fire in February 1992. The pact called for the guerrillas to disarm and the government to reduce the army by half and purge human rights violators by the end of October. Al-though the deadline passed amid mounting tension and mutual charges of noncompliance, the armed peace was maintained and the U.N. was able to forge a second agreement that extended the timetable until the end of the year. But with the unrepentant army and right-wing extremists making threatening noises, Salvadorans remained wary.

Castro's last stand

Fidel Castro went to the Madrid summit looking for assistance to save Cuba's economy from total collapse. He went so far as to sign the declaration endorsing representative democracy and respect for human rights, a monumentally cynical act even for Castro. But it did not work. He was cold-shouldered by his colleagues and mocked in the Spanish media.

Back home Castro declared, "We revolutionaries prefer death a thousand times" to giving up Cuba's socialist system. The island appeared headed for what Castro calls the "Zero Option," in effect the devolution into a pre-industrial society cut off from the world. It was difficult to determine how long the Cuban people would tolerate a diet of apocalyptic rhetoric, deprivation and repression. Castro seemed intent upon making the final chapter of the Cuban Revolution an ugly episode, a potentially eerie complement to the ongoing tragedy across the Windward Passage in Haiti.

Castro was asked during an interview in 1992 if he still believed history would absolve him. He answered yes, repeating his prediction that capitalist democracy was bound to fail. To make his point, he ranged over the myriad problems that beset Latin America and the recent trends in the region that threaten to undermine the promise of democracy. Castro, himself more a product of Latin America's anti-democratic traditions than Marxist ideology, does not want to believe that those traditions can give way to a new set of democratic values.

But political cultures do evolve, if slowly. Twenty years ago Spain and Portugal were ruled by dictators. It galls Castro that the colonizers of Latin America have become solid, representative democracies. But in Latin America today, ordinary people are further along than their leaders in embracing democratic values. They are organizing peasant federations, worker movements, neighborhood associations, and small business, professional, legal service, and rights groups. Even those in the burgeoning informal economies, the poorest of the poor, are demonstrating an ability to form social and economic units more democratic and efficient than the central governments that shun them. The question is whether the politicians will catch up before cynicism and disillusionment set in. ■

Douglas W. Payne is director of hemispheric studies for Freedom House.

Africa's Missed Opportunities

Michael Johns

The end of American-Soviet rivalries in Africa, combined with a mounting distrust of authoritarian governments by Africans, brought hope of a democratic revolution on that continent several years ago.

However, Africa's move toward freedom and democracy over the past year was sluggish, and in many cases steps towards democracy were incremental and sometimes only cosmetic in nature. As a result, sweeping democratization in Africa now appears less likely than it did two years ago. Since 1990, only five African countries and island nations—Benin, Cape Verde, Congo, Sao Tome and Zambia—have witnessed changes of government as a result of free and fair elections. And in many countries, egregious and systematic human rights violations continue unabated by autocratic governments that continue to buck the global democratic trend.

Angola, Somalia and South Africa

The plights of three African countries—Angola, Somalia and South Africa—garnered substantial Western attention over the past year. In Somalia, longstanding head of state Mohammed Siad Barre was overthrown in January 1991 by anti-government rebels, but the change of government has done nothing to improve the lot of the Somali people. Mass starvation claimed some 300,000 Somali lives this year, including more than 25 percent of Somali children under the age of five. And much of the Western food relief was stolen by armed clans, sometimes with government and military cooperation.

Still, the horror story of mass starvation in Somalia—in terms of sheer numbers, the worst human rights crisis anywhere in the world this year—caught on very late in the West. Said a State Department spokesman during the crisis: "Four government press conferences have been held on Somalia in the last 10 months, but only two reporters attended the first three. When Bush announced the food airlift on 14 August, the press deluge began....50 journalists showed up for the fourth briefing."[1]

By early December, with nearly 2 million Somalis threatened by the famine and warlords blocking Western relief supplies, the United Nations Security Council voted to send an American-led military force to Somalia to facilitate relief missions. The initial announcement promised an American force of 28,000. Bush administration officials stressed that the objective of the operation was exclusively to support relief efforts, not to resolve the civil war or set up a new government.

In the second major African story of the year, South Africa, global expectations for peace and democratic change exceeded the reality as violence—some sparked by the government, some sparked by armed black opposition forces—continued to rock the country. Conflict between South Africa's two most prominent anti-apartheid political parties, the Communist-aligned African National Congress (ANC) and the Zulu-dominated Inkatha Freedom Party, continued unabated.

The conflict between the ANC and Inkatha, combined with the ethnic tensions throughout the country, have raised significant concern that a post-apartheid South Africa may fragment into warring ethnic warlords. There also exists significant concern about the commitment to democracy by the major political players in South Africa—the government, the ANC and Inkatha, though all three of the diverse parties contend they support a "democratic" South Africa.

In Angola, elections were held in September between the Marxist government and the U.S.-backed National Union for the Total Independence of Angola (UNITA). Despite seventeen years of economic mismanagement and sometimes brutal totalitarian rule, the government fared unexpectedly well in the elections, winning 49.57 percent of the vote, forcing a yet-to-be scheduled runoff election between ruling President Jose Eduardo dos Santos and UNITA leader Jonas Savimbi, who garnered 40.07 percent. However, observers differed on the fairness of the electoral process. The U.S. State Department reported that the vote was relatively free and fair. But other observers, including some UNITA supporters, claimed that the government engaged in voter intimidation, control of the media prior to the campaign period, and some voting irregularities that may have swayed the electoral balance. One election observer contended that election fraud included: "...reports of stolen ballots, faceless voter registration cards, the sudden creation of some 100 'mobile' polling stations during the voting without the knowledge of party delegates, the circulation of surplus ballots, reports of Namibians crossing the border to vote, and a curiously large percentage of...nullified ballots."[2]

Also disturbing, following the elections, evidence emerged that Angola might be slipping back toward civil war. The government, on 31 October, launched a coordinated air and ground offensive against UNITA's Luanda headquarters and other UNITA strongholds, killing UNITA's vice-president, other UNITA officials, and some 1,000 civilians. A subsequent government attack against UNITA strongholds in early November was reported to have killed thousands of civilians. In violation of the country's peace accords, the government has continued to arm and train a 30,000-strong "anti-riot" police force, which has been used in the attacks against UNITA. Maintaining its role as a guerrilla force, UNITA also renewed military activity, capturing several provincial capitals.

Famine in the Horn

Beyond these three countries, however, much of the rest of Africa received little Western attention over the past year, even though human rights advancements and violations in these countries often were profound. This year's famine crisis in the Horn of Africa, for instance, spread far beyond Somalia —into Djibouti, Ethiopia, Eritrea, and the Sudan. All in all, some 23 million people were affected by it.

The famine crisis in the Horn was due primarily to economic mismanagement in these countries, to the absence of institutionalized democracy and, of course, to armed conflict. As during the 1984-1985 famine crisis in Ethiopia, food often was used as a weapon by governments seeking to starve out areas of political opposition. This was especially the case in the Sudan, where an autocratic Islamic government continued to seek a military victory over largely Christian rebels, the Sudan People's Liberation Army (SPLA), based in the country's southern tier. It also was the case in Djibouti. There a four-month rebellion by anti-government rebels came to an end in March, but the government has yet to yield to demands for multiparty elections and a release of political prisoners.

East Africa: Democratic steps...

In East Africa, only Ethiopia and Eritrea have taken steps toward democracy. An interim Ethiopian government that assumed power upon the May 1991 overthrow of Ethiopia's Marxist dictator, Mengistu Haile Mariam, has set the stage for a two-year transition to a fully democratic political system. And the government of Eritrea has promised a referendum on independence this April. Should Eritrea vote for independence, as expected, Eritrea's provisional government, the Eritrean People's Liberation Front (EPLF), promises multi-party elections to decide Eritrea's next government.

Of course, it always is possible that these promises may not come to fruition, but at last, following decades of autocratic rule, the prospects for democracy in Ethiopia and Eritrea appear modestly encouraging. One discouraging note in Ethiopia, however: According to international observers, regional elections held last June included widespread intimidation of opposition candidates by the ruling Ethiopian People's Revolutionary Democratic Front (EPRDF) and other armed movements.

...and violence and violations

To Ethiopia's west, in Sudan, violence, autocracy, and rights violations ruled the year. For nine years, war has raged between the Islamic government and the SPLA, and the Sudan now is one of only two African countries (Malawi is the other) that has refused to embrace multiparty democracy even in name. Furthermore, the human rights group Africa Watch charged in July that Sudan had initiated a massive resettlement program, which the government contends is designed to remove the environmental health threat presented by squatter camps around Khartoum. The result was demolition of the homes of about 500,000 Sudanese, without compensation to the owners. According to Africa Watch: "The relocations are often violent; in the worst incident, at least 21 people were killed in a clash between squatters resisting relocation and the army."[3]

Kenya is another East African country rocking with calls for democratic change, though it has been viewed traditionally as a beacon of relative stability and economic prosperity in one of the world's poorest and most combative regions. President Daniel arap Moi, who has ruled Kenya since 1977, promised multiparty elections for president and parliament for early 1993, raising the prospect that democracy may reach Kenya soon. However, Moi traditionally has been extremely skeptical of multiparty democracy, and he is tightly controlling the electoral process. Moi critics, for instance, argue that he is seeking to satisfy foreign and domestic demands for democratic change, while controlling the process in such a way that his Kenya African National Union (KANU) party will maintain its upper hand in Kenyan politics. Meanwhile, ethnic tensions in Kenya remain tense, further complicating Moi's transition process.

Elsewhere in East Africa, in Uganda, human rights violations were egregious over the past year. In September, Amnesty International condemned the Ugandan army for "arbitrarily arresting, torturing and even killing civilians."[4] These violations are nothing new for Uganda, whose post-colonial period has been among Africa's bloodiest. Still, the Amnesty report contends: "Uganda's bloody history should not be allowed to dominate its future."[5] Nearly 200 Ugandans now are in jail on treason charges for nonviolent opposition to the one-party state of Yoweri Museveni. Backed by Mu'ammar al-Qadhafi, Museveni also is engaged in a bloody civil war against an opposition rebel force that seeks the Ugandan dictator's removal. According to the Amnesty report and exile sources, rights violations in these war zones (mostly the north and east) have been worse than any other region in the country.[6]

West Africa: "Controlled democracy"

In West Africa the concept of democracy seems to be gaining support, but democratic institutions, where they exist at all, remain fragile. Furthermore, many West African countries seem to be pursuing the path of "controlled democracy," where elections are held or at least scheduled, but candidates and political parties are screened carefully by ruling parties and elections often are marred by irregularities and fraud.

This was widely believed to be the case in Cameroon last October, where the country's first multiparty elections led to the election of longstanding President Paul Biya. International observers reported widespread voting irregularities in Biya's unexpected victory over opposition leader John Fru Ndi.

Nigeria, Africa's most populous nation and one of its most influential, also has flirted with the controlled democracy path, though prospects for a genuine transition to a legitimate, democratic political system remain highly possible. Two years ago, Nigerian President Ibrahim Babangida placed the country on the democratic path. The plan was scheduled to lead to the inauguration of a new, democratic president in January 1993. But in October, the country's Armed Forces Ruling Council cancelled results from the electoral primaries, and now the country's two parties are forced to start their primaries again from scratch.

The cancellation of the results came after the parties alleged that the electoral process, thus far, has been filled with fraud and vote-rigging. (Following the election, the head of Nigeria's National Electoral Commission, Humphrey Nwosu, contended that nearly all of the 23 candidates had cheated in the election.) Still, some Babangida critics allege that the military government, in a bid to hold on to power, orchestrated the entire episode, using the fraud accusations as an excuse to delay a return to civilian rule.

In the human rights arena, there also has been some concern about recent Nigerian government actions. Africa Watch, in June, reported the arrest of four leading human rights activists, who were charged with conspiracy and treason. The government counters that the rights activists were involved in a conspiracy to "illegally engineer a change" in the government's planned transition to civilian rule.[7]

Still, Nigeria is one of the few countries in Africa that has experimented with democracy in its post-colonial era; for ten of the past thirty-two years, it has been governed by a democratic political system. But the military has ruled for the majority of Nigeria's post-colonial period, and whether it really is prepared to step aside and accept civilian rule is a heatedly debated question. Should the military government not step aside, or should it be perceived as unnecessarily delaying the transition, the volatility of Nigeria makes violence probable. Whatever happens, however, it is likely that the regional and continent-wide importance of Nigeria means that the plight of democracy in Nigeria will have ramifications beyond its border; a successful democratic transition likely will enhance the prospects for democracy in West Africa and elsewhere on the continent.

In Ghana, too, strongman Jerry Rawlings has been pursuing the "controlled democracy" path, seeking to satisfy foreign and domestic demands for democratization while maintaining his grip on power. The ruling party, the Provisional National Defense Council (PNDC), is controlling the timetables and details of the country's proposed transition. A new constitution was drawn up by a committee consisting primarily of PNDC delegates, and subsequent sections, providing immunity for government representatives, were added secretly by the government following the first draft of the constitution. A report by the International Foundation for Electoral Systems (IFES), based on a visit to Ghana between 22 April and 8 May, concluded that there exist numerous barriers to democracy in Ghana, including repressive laws and defective voter registration books.

Rights violations also continued on a massive scale in Liberia, where the December 1989 ouster of Liberian autocrat Samuel K. Doe has not slowed that country's brutal and often seemingly senseless civil war. In October, five American nuns joined the 20,000 Liberians, many civilians, who have died from that conflict. The war includes three rebel movements (some including fighters as young as eleven years old) vying for political power against a seven-nation consortium of West African troops, who have had mixed results in their stated objective of "keeping the peace."

Southern and Central Africa

In Southern and Central Africa, the big story of the year was the continued unfolding of South Africa's delicate transition from apartheid to democracy. But there were other advances and setbacks in the region, too.

In Zaire, longtime head of state Mobutu Sese Seko promised a transition to multiparty democracy in April 1990, but little headway has been made since. Mobutu has appointed various transition governments and commissions since that time; elections have been scheduled, then cancelled, and now there exist considerable doubts about whether this transition will take place at all.

Meanwhile, there are signs of unrest throughout Zaire, including a failed coup last January. Mobutu's promises of democracy have not quelled strikes and protests, which seem to be mounting in both regularity and intensity. These run the risk of promoting confrontations, which some opponents seem eager to exploit in their bid to pull down Mobutu.

In the past, Mobutu's military has responded nervously and defensively to such protests —opening fire on protesting students at the University of Lubumbashi in May 1990, for instance, and shooting again on protesters this past February, killing 13 people.

In Mozambique, after years of significant pressure from donor countries, a peace treaty was signed 4 October between the autocratic government of Joaquim Chissano and the rebel movement, RENAMO, led by Afonso Dhlakama. The agreement is to be monitored by a token twenty-five-person United Nations team, too small to fully observe, much less enforce, the agreement. However, a month after its signing, the peace appeared to be holding for the first time since the civil war began sixteen years ago and, in early December, U.N. Secretary General Boutros Boutros-Ghali proposed a controversial (and inevitably expensive) expansion of this force to include up to 10,000 U.N. troops and civilians. The agreement provides for elections before October 1993, though RENAMO has limited financial resources and questions abound about how they can afford to run a successful campaign without some provision for an equal campaign footing. Should RENAMO feel they are not afforded an equal opportunity, or should the government seek to rig the process, a resumption of armed conflict is possible.

Barriers to freedom

The barriers to the advancement of freedom in Africa remain numerous. First, with a per capita income of only $370 a year, Africa remains the poorest continent on the planet. Second, few countries actually have developed the democratic or educational infrastructure capable of sustaining a democratic political system. And, finally, many African countries continue to be ruled by long-standing one-party or military dictators who either resent democracy and seek to prohibit it, or who seek to implement democracy in a controlled and artificial fashion through which they, or their ruling parties, can maintain strict political control. African opposition figures, too, often use the phrase "democracy" as a cover for their quest for power; many have a dubious commitment to democratic ideas. This raises the risk that elections always can result in "one man, one vote, one time" with opposition parties abandoning their democratic pledges once they take power.

Still, with demands for democracy continuing to mount throughout Africa, the prospects for a considerable advance of political freedom still is possible in the coming year. The most critical factor in whether this occurs likely will be the insistence of Western nations and multinational donors that continued aid to Africa be linked to democratization. The Bush administration, and its Agency for International Development, were correctly making preliminary steps in this direction. However, whether the Clinton administration will continue this policy, or enhance it further, remains to be seen.

What is certain is that in Africa, as elsewhere, there appears to be a clear connection between the implementation of democracy and respect for human rights and economic development. African countries that egregiously violate human rights —Liberia, Somalia, Sudan, Uganda, etc.—also prohibit multiparty democracy. Countries with vastly better track records on human rights—Botswana and Gambia, for instance—have successfully implemented democratic political systems. In the economic arena, Botswana (which has maintained a democratic political system since independence in 1966) tops Sub-Saharan Africa in per capita gross domestic product, suggesting that the economic accountability that accompanies democracy also may give democratic African nations a better shot at economic development. The hope is that these connections, which appear to be increasingly clear to Africans, also will become clear to African governments and their foreign donors. ▬

Michael Johns has written widely on Africa.

NOTES

1. Margaret Calhoun, "Somalia: Feeding the Power-Hungry?," *The World and I*, November 1992, p. 94. For further information, see Michael Johns, "The Tragic Neglect of Africa," *Freedom Review* (Freedom House), August 1992 (Volume 23, No. 4), pp. 26-27.

2. Margaret Calhoun, "Only Fair Elections Can Keep Angola's Peace," the *European Wall Street Journal*, 21 October 1992.

3. "Sudan: Refugees in Their Own Country" (Volume 4, Issue No. 8), *Africa Watch*, p. 2.

4. "Uganda: Time for Action to Safeguard Human Rights," Amnesty International USA press release, 8 September 1992, p. 1.

5. *ibid*, p. 2.

6. *ibid*, p. 3.

7. See "Nigeria: Silencing the Vocal Opposition," (Volume 4, Issue No. 7), *Africa Watch*.

The Middle East: Islam vs. the Established Order
David A. Korn

The mighty tidal wave of democracy that crashed over eastern Europe, Latin America and parts of sub-Saharan Africa in 1989, 1990 and 1991 suddenly spent its force when it reached the Middle East.

That it did is hardly surprising. The area that stretches from the Atlantic across the southern shores of the Mediterranean to the Persian Gulf and the Plateau of Iran has always been peculiarly resistant to the call of democracy. Its first experiments with parliamentary democracy—in Iraq, Egypt and Syria in the 1930s and 1940s—turned out to be woeful failures. When the British and French formally handed over power in those countries they left behind parliamentary regimes modeled after their own. On paper, the ingredients for democratic rule were all there: political parties, elections, parliaments, constitutions, and independent judiciaries. In fact, the wealthy land-owning classes took over the institutions of governance and used them to protect and promote their interests and the continued influence of the colonial power. Parliamentary democracy was never practiced as it was intended to be, and it never implanted itself in Arab soil. The end came quickly for the parliamentary regime in Syria, in 1949. Constitutional monarchy lasted in Egypt only until 1952 and in Iraq until 1958. In each case military dictatorships took over.

Arab nationalism plus socialism

This rejection of parliamentary democracy by the three dominant Arab states of the Levant was also a rejection of the West and of Western values. It was followed by a rush to embrace Arab nationalism (or pan-Arabism) and socialism. The 1950s and the 1960s were the heyday of Arab nationalism and Arab socialism. Both were secular doctrines. They reigned with an explosive virulence in the Levant and moved into North Africa, finding acceptance in Algeria, which gained its independence from France in 1962, and in Libya, after the overthrow of the Senussi monarchy by Mu'ammar al-Qadhafi in 1968.

The 1970s and 1980s witnessed the decline of both doctrines. Socialism (in practice it became statism) proved to be bankrupt as a prescription for economic progress; and pan-Arabist aspirations suffered so many setbacks—beginning in 1961 when Syria threw off its union with Egypt, and then in 1967 with Egypt's stunning defeat at the hands of Israel—that all but its most ardent proponents eventually became disillusioned. The *coup de grace* was rendered to Arab nationalism by one of its main surviving champions, Saddam Hussein and his Baath regime, when Iraq invaded Kuwait on 1 August 1990. The Baghdad Baathists, swollen by their own pan-Arabist rhetoric, never imagined that other Arab governments would join with the West to oppose their take-over of Kuwait.

Iraq's defeat, in February 1991, left two contenders standing on the Middle East playing field: the established regimes, some of which had edged toward greater freedom and adopted a few of the trappings of western style democracy; and a new revolutionary challenger that claims more authentic roots and that clearly enjoys an explosive appeal: Islamic fundamentalism. Islam as a political movement bent on capturing the apparatus of the state and imposing religious dogma—the Koran, the Traditions and the various interpretations—as the supreme law of the land, gathered steam in the late 70s and won its first victory in Iran in 1979. A second takeover of government came in 1989, in Sudan. After that, the battleground between political Islam and the established, largely secular regimes shifted to Algeria. But the struggle has spread also across the length and breadth of the Arab world. Almost no Arab state has been wholly exempt from it.

Algeria

After winning independence from France, Algerian leaders rushed to embrace the dominant mode in Arab thinking of the early 1960s. The new state became virulently Arab nationalist and dedicatedly socialist. Islam became the state religion but government and the law were secular.

The setbacks dealt to pan-Arabism, and the Arab public's subsequent disillusionment, no doubt served to undermine the credibility of the ruling party, the *Front de Liberation Nationale* (or FLN). But the really grave damage was done by the lurch into state socialism. Algeria's large deposits of oil and natural gas and its substantial agricultural and industrial resources should have guaranteed a prosperous future. Instead, the socialist economy produced widespread poverty, particularly among the young whose out-of-work rate runs at some 50 percent. The FLN's long tenure in power and the attendant loss of dynamism and spread of corruption compounded its problems, as did a widening gap (despite the FLN's socialist, egalitarian rhetoric) between rich and poor. In October 1988, rioting erupted throughout Algeria. The FLN was shaken. It agreed to give up single party rule and to compete with other parties in a free and fair election. Algeria seemed launched on a course toward democracy.

Immediately, however, the FLN found itself confronted by a powerful opponent, the fundamentalist *Front Islamique du Salut* (FIS). The FIS offered the Algerian public a potent millenial vision, and it proved surprisingly adept at organizing and campaigning; according to some reports it received assistance in these activities from the Iranians and the Sudanese. It swept the field in municipal elections held in June 1990. The FLN responded by delaying elections for a national legislature and gerrymandering electoral districts in its favor. The tactic failed. A first round of legislative elections, held on 26 December 1991, gave the Islamic party 188 seats and the FLN a mere 15 (although the FLN got 1.6 million votes to the FIS' 3.2 million). The FIS seemed set to win the second round of polling, scheduled for January 1992, and to sweep into office.

At this point the Algerian army, a secularist bastion, stepped in. In January 1992, martial law was declared and President Chadli Benjadid resigned. Mohammed Boudiaf, one of the early leaders of Algeria's struggle for independence, was brought back from exile abroad to take Benjadid's place. In March the top FIS leaders were brought to trial and sentenced to prison terms ranging from four to twelve years. Soon thereafter the FIS was banned and thousands of its members were arrested and held without trial.

Repression called forth the customary response. In July, President Boudiaf was assassinated by an Islamic fundamentalist member of his guard. Throughout the summer and fall of 1992 there were disturbances, bombings and attacks on government offices and police and military installations.

The military's intervention deprived Algeria and the world of the opportunity to learn whether that nation's Islamic party would have been more tolerant of diversity or inclined to respect civil liberties and democratic norms than those that have seized power in Iran and Sudan. Opinion on this point remains rather sharply divided. Some believe the FIS to be a different breed of Islamic fundamentalist. They point to the FIS's eschewal of terrorism and its readiness to seek power exclusively through participation in the electoral process; and to assurances given by certain of its leaders—mainly in private conversations, it should be noted—of dedication to the principles of democracy.

Others are skeptical. They argue that Algeria's fundamentalists are perhaps more sophisticated in their methods but do not differ in their goals from those in Iran or Sudan, where fundamentalist seizure of power resulted in the establishment of theocratic dictatorships; and that no group that holds that sovereignty resides in God and the scriptures—not in the people—is likely to agree that the people should have the right to change either the nature of the state or its leaders. They point to the message of intolerance and hate preached by certain FIS leaders; to the pressures exerted on women to give up employment outside the home, wear traditional dress and conform to traditional Islamic norms; and to the FIS's denunciation of the several hundred thousand people who marched in Algiers in support of democracy in January 1992 as "Jews." And they note that the FIS's win at the polls was less impressive than it seemed, since it got less than half the popular vote (the secular vote was split between the FLN and other secular parties) and the ballots of only one-quarter of Algeria's 13 million registered voters.

While this debate plays out, one thing is certain: Algeria's new-found freedoms and democratic rights are no more. Its march toward democracy now seems shunted onto a long detour.

Jordan

In Jordan, political Islam also has come to the fore through elections, though less strongly than in Algeria. After riots in Jordan's major cities in April 1989, King Hussein, who until then had ruled unrestrained by any elected body, agreed to open up the political process to broader participation. A "redemocratization program" was launched, a National Charter was drawn up and elections were held for an 80-member parliament. Hussein and his advisors expected that the Muslim Brotherhood and other Islamic fundamentalists might win twelve to fifteen seats at the most. They were stunned by the election results; the Brotherhood took twenty seats and allied fundamentalists another twelve, giving them some 40 percent of the votes in the parliament.

The Jordanian monarch has accommodated himself warily to this situation. He has given the fundamentalists positions in government and tried to be conciliatory on issues not central to his programs or his rule; the fundamentalists have, in turn, played pretty much by the rules. This however does not mean that the two sides have no deep differences. The fundamentalists have strongly opposed Hussein's decision to have Jordan participate in the Middle East peace talks. And the king has not hesitated to postpone sessions of parliament, ban fundamentalist rallies and seize newspapers in order to prevent their making an issue of the peace talks.

Jordanian government spokesmen now like to call their country "the Arab world's only democracy." That is a stretch. Jordan does not yet qualify for the title of a democracy. Most martial law restrictions have been lifted, exiles have been allowed to come home, freedoms of speech and assembly are generally respected, passports have been handed back to once blacklisted oppositionists, and during 1992 political parties were legalized. Yet the king appoints and dismisses the prime minister and the ministers and retains vast powers that enable him to ignore or dissolve the parliament if he wishes. As one observer has put it, "in Jordan there is definitely a movement towards achieving the forms of democracy, but substance is another matter."

The parliament elected in 1989 reached the end of its term with the end of 1992. The Islamic fundamentalists are expected to make an all out push to win a majority in the new assembly. Despite their participation in the system, they have made it no secret that their aim, if they gain power, is to restructure both state and society along theocratic lines. A fundamentalist victory in the upcoming elections would set the stage for a confrontation with the monarchy and with secular opinion—a confrontation in which Jordanians' fragile new freedoms would very likely become, as they did in Algeria, the first victim.

And elsewhere

There were high hopes in 1991 that the ability of Western and Arab governments to join in a coalition to oppose Saddam Hussein's takeover of Kuwait, and the coalition's victory over Iraq, were going to bring change to the states of the Arabian peninsula. So far it hasn't happened.

The emir of Kuwait, Sheikh Jabr al-Ahmad al-Sabah, who returned to his country only after the amenities of his palace, wrecked by the Iraqis, had been suitably restored, for over a year largely ignored his wartime promise to open up Kuwait to greater political participation. Heavy international and domestic pressure finally persuaded him to agree to elections and the reestablishment of parliament. Elections held in October 1992 brought an unexpectedly big win by secular and Islamic fundamentalist opposition forces who want the al-Sabah family to give up its exclusive hold on power. Of a total of 50 seats in the new parliament, the fundamentalists and their allies took sixteen altogether, and secular oppositionists won another fifteen. It is too early, however, to say how much this means. Only 81,000 of Kuwait's 606,000 citizens were enfranchised. Women were denied the right to vote and only men over the age of twenty-one whose families had been in Kuwait since before 1921 were allowed to cast ballots. Political parties were banned and candidates had to run as individuals. The Emir remains free to choose his ministers and to ignore or disband the parliament.

One would hardly expect Islamic fundamentalism to be a political force in Saudi Arabia, since Islamic doctrine is already the supreme law of the Saudi state and Saudi society. Nonetheless, it is, and a very powerful one. Islamic fundamentalists sharply criticized the government for allying itself with the West against Saddam Hussein following Iraq's invasion of Kuwait. The Saudi monarchy is taking no chances. King Fahd did agree during 1992 to set up a 60-member unelected consultative council. But he categorically rejected democracy: "The democratic system prevalent in the world is not appropriate for us in this region," the king declared in an interview with a Kuwaiti paper in March. "The election system has no place in the Islamic creed..." That Saudi Arabia remains a dedicatedly theocratic state was reaffirmed in September when the government publicly executed a 23 year old man on charges of apostasy from Islam.

The fundamentalists, however, have made clear that they are not placated. In a 46 page petition presented to the Saudi government in the fall of 1992, 107 fundamentalist clergymen demanded revision of Saudi Arabia's pro-Western defense and foreign policies and the prohibition of dealings with Western financial and cultural institutions.

In Egypt, the largest and most securely established of the Arab states, and one that over the past decade has introduced a measure of democratic practice, political Islam has enjoyed a considerable resurgence. Unlike Jordan and Algeria, Egypt has for the most part not sought to work within the existing political framework. The Muslim Brotherhood, once the violent radical wing of political Islam in Egypt, has been partly co-opted and now leads a semi-legal existence. But other extremist groups have risen in its place and appear to exercise greater appeal. They have launched a kind of guerrilla war both against the Egyptian government and against the country's large Coptic Christian community. Copts have been attacked, killed and intimidated, and in some cases forced to convert to Islam. Islamic fundamentalist terrorists, in an effort to disrupt the country's lucrative tourism trade, have also attacked western tourists in upper Egypt.

The fundamentalists' main objective is the the Egyptian political order itself, which they consider to be "non-Muslim." Their proclaimed aim is to overturn it. Fundamentalist violence and the emergency measures that the government has taken to combat it put newly won Egyptian freedoms at risk.

In Syria, the big confrontation between the Islamic fundamentalists and President Hafez al-Asad's Baath regime came in 1980, when on Asad's orders the Syrian army massacred an estimated 20,000 fundamentalists who had holed up in the northern Syrian city of Hama. The Damascus government nonetheless continues to regard the fundamentalists as a threat and to subject them to severe repression. Even Mu'ammar al-Qadhafi's regime in Libya encounters opposition from Muslim fundamentalists and seeks to suppress them, despite the fact that Qadhafi consistently wraps himself in the banner of Islam.

Morocco, at the western end of the Arab world, has, so far, not been greatly affected by the fundamentalist challenge. Perhaps in part for this reason, Morocco this past year was the Arab nation that made the greatest stride toward democracy. A new constitution, proposed by King Hassan II and adopted in September by referendum, enlarges the powers of the parliament and places limits on those of the monarch. The king may no longer dissolve the parliament, and he is now obliged to choose the prime minister from among the electoral majority. Although critics point out that Hassan still retains vast powers, his move in proposing the changes stands as an example of enlightened self-interest. It was one the monarch could afford to make. Hassan's victory in the long struggle over the Western Sahara has given him an enormous boost in prestige and popularity, and in Morocco the monarch has traditionally been regarded as the nation's highest prelate.

Iraq, at the other end of the Arab world, remains its darkest example of tyranny. Saddam Hussein's very efficient apparatus of repression and reward made it possible for him to cling to power this past year and to repair much of the damage done to Baghdad and other major cities during the January-February 1991 bombing. But the Iraqi public has paid a high price, in spiraling inflation and shortages of food, medicine and other necessities, for the regime's failure to comply fully with U.N. resolutions.

Although Saddam Hussein has often sought to exploit Islamic sentiment, his regime is secular and Arab nationalist at its core. Islamic fundamentalists dislike it at least as much as any other. The Shiite clergy of southern Iraq has been one of the regime's main challengers. But even the Shiite fundamentalists have, for the time being, muted their call for a theocratic state, in the interest of joining forces with secular Arab Sunni and Shiite opposition forces, and with the Kurds, to fight the Baath regime.

The Kurds

The brightest spot of all for freedom this year in the Islamic Middle East turned out to be Iraqi Kurdistan. Since the allied coalition forced Saddam Hussein's army out of Kurdistan in the summer of 1991, the Kurds have enjoyed *de facto* self-government. At the beginning of last year they decided the time had come to put their affairs on a more orderly basis.

In May, they held the first free, open and fair elections in Kurdish history. They did it entirely on their own. The U.S. government, which so eagerly and generously offers financial support for elections all around the globe, not only wouldn't help but tried (unsuccessfully) to keep Americans from going to observe the elections. The campaign was heated but peaceful and wholly free of coercion. A bevy of foreign observers, from Europe and North America, certified that the polls were open to all and the count honest. The two main parties, the Barzani led Kurdistan Democratic Party and the Talabani led Patriotic Union of Kurdistan, swept the field and divided the seats in the new parliament equally between them.

The Iraqi Kurdish experiment faces enormous challenges. After the end of the Iran-Iraq war the Baghdad regime deliberately laid waste to most of the Kurdish countryside, destroying a thriving agricultural economy. The Kurds are now working desperately to re-build villages and replant orchards and fields. In the meantime food and basic necessities are in dangerously short supply.

The Kurds' basic problem is that they are surrounded by neighbors who either oppose and wish to crush them or have no incentive to help them. Iraq maintains an embargo on shipments of fuel and other commodities to Kurdistan and keeps an army of 100,000 poised threateningly on the edge of the Kurdish area. Turkey and Iran allow only meager supplies through to Iraqi Kurds. The survival of the current Kurdish experiment in statehood and democracy depends in the short run on the continued presence of the protective allied umbrella, and in the longer run on the disappearance of Saddam Hussein's regime and its replacement by something a good deal more benign—a development devoutly to be wished but not easily foreseen.

Israel, the territories and the peace talks

Israel continued to be the only state in the Middle East to enjoy the full set of democratic institutions—political parties, a freely elected parliament, an independent judiciary, and effective legal guarantees for basic civil liberties. At the same time, repressive military rule over the occupied West Bank and Gaza—whose citizens enjoy none of the freedoms and protections afforded Israelis—continued to cast a shadow on Israel's overall record. The Palestinian *intifada* largely subsided during 1992, in part from sheer fatigue, in part owing to the peace talks begun late in 1991. U.S. diplomacy managed to keep the talks going during the first half of 1992 despite an almost total absence of substantive progress. In June the election of a Labor government headed by Yitzhak Rabin and prepared to endorse the "land for peace" formula, gave the talks a new impetus, but both Israelis and Arabs were reluctant to engage fully before the results of the U.S. elections were known.

The coming year will be critical for the Middle East peace talks. The Palestinian question—the future of the West Bank and Gaza—will remain the central issue. The Syrian government has declared itself ready in principle to make peace with Israel, but President Hafez al-Asad is unlikely to agree to go it alone, as Sadat did earlier; and King Hussein of Jordan cannot afford to. If a breakdown of negotiations is to be averted, there must be progress toward agreement between Israeli and Palestinian negotiators. On the Palestinian side, the talks face strong opposition from militant Islamic fundamentalists. Hamas, the main Palestinian fundamentalist group, rejects any compromise with Israel. The only solution it finds acceptable is Israel's elimination through *jihad*, and it threatens physical violence against Palestinians who take part in the peace talks. Hamas has muscled out the PLO in Gaza and is now disputing the PLO's dominance in the West Bank.

Paradoxically, Palestinian Muslim fundamentalists are said to have received clandestine support from the Israeli military government during the early 1980s. The aim was to weaken the hold of the PLO (a secular organization) over the Palestinian population, but, apparently, it was also thought that the fundamentalists' religious zeal might serve as an opiate for Palestinian political aspirations.

Most authorities agree that there is no true incompatibility between Islam and democracy. The Turks long ago set the example of a Muslim people striving for freedom and democracy, and the Kurds offered yet another example this past year. In both instances, however, a secular state was the model chosen. The examples of Islamic theocratic rule that we have before us so far, in Iran, Sudan, and Saudi Arabia, offer no encouragement that freedom and democracy could flourish under a fundamentalist government. Neither do the declared intentions of Islamic fundamentalists who seek power elsewhere.

Most of the Islamic Middle East is going through a difficult time sorting out relations between religion and the state. While this process lasts—and it may last decades—militant political Islam is sure to remain a powerful force. Just how powerful will determine, in very large measure, the future of freedom and democracy and, perhaps, even of peace, in the Middle East. ▬

David A. Korn is a writer and former diplomat. He is the author of Stalemate: The War of Attrition and Great Power Diplomacy in the Middle East, 1967-1970 *(Westview Press, 1992).*

Asia:
Progress and Problems   William J. Barnds

The magnitude of recent changes in Asia can be illustrated by putting them in the context of modern Asian history. Asia in the 1930s was almost entirely under the rule of outsiders—primarily Europeans. (Japan and Thailand were the chief exceptions, with China enjoying only limited sovereignty and control of its territory.) Governments everywhere were authoritarian and arbitrary. Except for tiny elites and small middle classes, extreme poverty was the normal condition, and health conditions were bad for these groups as well. Today Asia is no longer characterized by foreign domination, near universal poverty, and lack of popular participation in public life. Indeed, East Asia is the world's most dynamic economic region and prosperity is benefiting most people.

The advance of freedom

As conditions in Asia have changed at an accelerating pace, Asians themselves have actively pressed for greater popular participation in their countries' political affairs, as well as raising demands for more effective government. People generally want governments that respond to the popular will, promote economic progress, provide equity and justice, and reduce corruption rather than rely on ideology and sloganeering to achieve legitimacy and popularity. In recent years these pressures have resulted in substantial progress toward democracy and improvements in human rights across an area that includes South Korea, Mongolia, Taiwan, Pakistan, Nepal, Bangladesh and the Philippines. Even Thailand, which had moved toward a democratic system in the 1980s but experienced a military coup in February 1991, reversed course in 1992.

There are several elements behind the pressures for and progress toward representative government. Authoritarian regimes are less able to accommodate the growing diversity of interests that occur as societies become more complex, which makes political pluralism more attractive. Economic progress and rising levels of education and urbanization have created middle classes determined to have a voice in their country's affairs. Deference to authority has declined, which has weakened the self-confidence of ruling groups that they could continue to restrict power to traditional elites. The communications revolution and advances in transportation have greatly enhanced the flow not only of factual data, but of attitudes and aspirations. Societies which have outward-oriented economies and send thousands of citizens abroad each year can no longer wall off their people from new ideas. Finally, the triumph of Western (and Japanese) economic and political systems in the Cold War has provided important psychological and political encouragement to advocates of democracy and has put authoritarianism on the defensive. Progress has not occurred everywhere—witness China, North Korea, Vietnam, and Burma—but the direction of change has been clear.

Constraints and obstacles

Most of Asia's democracies, new and old, are beset by many strains, which rule out complacency and temper optimism. Corruption is widespread and sustains cynicism and erodes public confidence. Even in an established democracy like Japan, massive corruption and links between the governing Liberal Democratic Party and organized crime dominate the political agenda. Ethnic and religious conflicts are widespread in many societies, with disaffected minorities sometimes willing to resort to arms to seek self-determination—a tendency probably strengthened by events in the former Soviet Union. Such struggles in Kashmir and the Punjab, along with caste conflict and rising Hindu-Muslim conflicts, have made violence endemic in India. The widespread religious/political riots in December 1992, following the destruction of a mosque in northern India by Hindu militants, illustrates the difficulty of keeping communal passions in check and of keeping such outbreaks of violence from sparking retaliatory Muslim attacks on Hindus in Bangladesh and Pakistan. The fact that serious ethnic and religious conflicts are also prominent in Sri Lanka, Malaysia, the Philippines, Indonesia, Burma and China indicates that no system of government has found a way either to suppress or accommodate it.

Other problems flow from the weakness of political institutions and processes in most of Asia. (For example, the Philippines successfully managed a presidential transition in June from Mrs. Aquino to Fidel Ramos, but with seven contenders and no run-off system Ramos' victory with only 23 percent of the vote hardly gives him a clear mandate.) Political parties are often the fiefdoms of individual leaders, lack deep popular roots, and members elected to legislative office often shift parties in return for monetary rewards or cabinet posts. Citizens and politicians alike are still struggling to learn the politics of compromise and the acceptance of the idea of a *loyal* opposition. Independent judiciaries and the rule of law are only gradually taking root. Long entrenched and powerful bureaucracies and politically powerful police and military establishments find it difficult to cede ultimate control to elected officials, who—like the bureaucracies and security forces—often are corrupt and more interested in personal power than national policy. (Pakistan—where the military have also long had first claim on budgetary resources—is a good example of this situation.) Demands for governments to promote economic well-being require accepting greater economic interdependence, which enhances a government's ability to make economic progress but forces it to impose sacrifices on economically inefficient but often politically powerful groups.

In such environments, political leadership is crucial, but its tasks are complex. Too personal a ruling style prevents necessary political institutions from developing their own vitality. Traditional beliefs in a firm and purposeful leader who ensures stability coexist with growing distrust of strongman rule. Economic interdependence and external pressures for more open markets make foreigners a tempting political target, but dependence on foreign markets, capital and technology makes xenophobia a self-defeating response. Women too are pressing for greater social and economic rights as well as a greater role in the political process. These enhance the role of women and enrich countries as well as complicate the tasks of rulers. Strong but subtle and skillful leadership is needed to balance these complex pressures without resorting to simplistic sloganeering or demagoguery.

Underlying these specific problems is an Asian ambivalence about the growing domestic and international pressures for human rights and democracy. The collapse of communism and advance of democratic forces on several continents has led to greater acceptance of the idea that there are some universal political values and ideals even though they first arose in the West. Yet cultural pride and belief in certain core values from their own traditions lead many Asians to reject any mechanical transplant of Western political values and structures. They also fear certain elements of modern individualistic Western culture that appear likely to undermine valued social arrangements such as family solidarity, group cohesiveness and social harmony. Moreover, given their deep internal conflicts many Asian countries believe popular participation must be structured in a manner that does not undermine national unity and stability, without which they believe economic progress would be impossible. Awareness of their own vulnerabilities as well as sensitivities over intrusions on their sovereignty will make most Asian countries reluctant to press their neighbors over human rights abuses.

South Asia developments

India, one of Asia's most enduring democracies, exemplified the many disparate trends affecting the South Asia. Although political violence and a series of weak and ineffective central governments had led many observers in recent years to fear that India was becoming ungovernable, the country continued to demonstrate that it had reserves of strength and resiliency. The country's federal parliamentary system, supported by nonpolitical security forces and civil servants, has so far been able to contain the violence without abandoning democracy except temporarily in certain locales. Lack of any viable authoritarian alternative as well as Indian tolerance for violence probably will keep the country on the democratic path, but the internal conflicts are so many and so basic that India will experience continued turbulence.

The Congress Party, which won a large enough plurality in 1991 general elections to enable it to form a government that introduced market-oriented economic reforms, continued to expand the scope of such reforms in 1992. The steady dismantling of the decades-old stifling bureaucratic control of the economy took political courage, and the government's program offers a possibility that India may over time create a decent life for its people. However, only the initial steps have been taken, and powerful economic and political interest groups will contest the abandonment of bureaucratic socialism every step of the way.

On the political front, progress was made when elections were held in the strife-torn Punjab for the first time in years. Militant Sikhs seeking an independent nation were able to keep many away from the polls in the February elections for national and state office, but the September local elections had a high turnout. Yet Kashmir, under direct rule from New Delhi, remains stalemated. Local Muslim guerrilla groups, who have wide popular support, are seeking greater autonomy or independence by rebelling against years of corruption and violence by local officials who were often puppets of New Delhi. The massive security forces the central government has deployed in the state have resorted to virtually indiscriminate violence against suspected guerrillas and civilian bystanders. India, angered at covert Pakistani support of the guerrillas and fearful that Kashmiris will press for secession unless they are firmly controlled, seems unwilling to offer political reforms or concessions until the security threat has been brought under control. The Kashmiri people have little faith that any promises made by New Delhi will be implemented in a way that gives them real control over their affairs.

If political violence were limited to a few areas the situation would be less threatening. However, in many parts of India not only are Hindus and Muslims in violent conflict, but long-repressed castes and economically deprived people are asserting their legal rights for the first time. Local police (and private bands of thugs) under the control of middle and upper classes and castes are struggling to retain their positions against formerly docile elements. While these struggles do not threaten Indian democracy in a formal sense, they pose a growing danger to the lives and liberties of Indian citizens.

Southeast Asia

Continuity was the most striking characteristic of Southeast Asia—with the notable exception of Thailand. Burma's military regime made a few cosmetic changes, but continued to be characterized by brutality, ineptitude and xenophobia. Indonesia's authoritarian government continued to combine economic progress with firm but somewhat flexible political controls—thus making a government victory in the June national elections preordained. The army's November 1991 killing of 50-100 peaceful demonstrators in East Timor caused an international outcry that continued during 1992, and led President Suharto to take the unusual step of dismissing several military officers. At the same time, Indonesia insisted that the matter was an internal affair and foreign pressure would not be tolerated—partly an assertion of sovereignty and partly an indication of the government's determination that other provinces with grievances or even separatist movements not come to believe that they could mobilize foreign support for their causes.

The encouraging news from Southeast Asia in 1992 was the major steps taken to reduce if not fully eliminate the Thai military's ultimate control of political power and widespread economic privileges. Progress toward a democratic system in the 1980s was interrupted by a February, 1991 military coup. The military claimed their action was due to the corruption of the civilian government, although its attempt to bring the military under civilian control was the underlying cause of the coup. Popular anger at the civilian government's corruption, satisfaction with double-digit economic growth, and the military regime's appointment of widely respected civilian technicians and the promise of elections by April, 1992 combined to facilitate public acceptance of the coup.

However, popular anger gradually developed over the military's domination of the body assigned to write a new constitution and its determination to entrench itself in power by reserving control of key power centers. The national elections held in March 1992 resulted in a strong enough showing by several pro-military parties for military leaders to think the public would accept Army Commander General Suchinda as a nonelected prime minister. This was a colossal miscalculation, and the middle class led massive anti-government protests in Bangkok in May. The army killed scores if not hundreds of demonstrators, and the regime declared a state of emergency. The situation became so dangerous that Thailand's revered King Bhumipol intervened on 20 May and used his moral power to force Suchinda to resign and the military to agree to a revised constitution that curbs the power of the military establishment.

A highly respected civilian was appointed prime minister. He not only removed key hard-line generals from their positions of power but also curtailed military control of lucrative positions in state owned or controlled economic institutions. New national elections were held in September, and the "pro-democracy" parties emerged in a considerably stronger position. However, the parties associated with the military were only weakened, not demolished. Moreover, the multiplicity of parties, the questionable honesty of many elected officials, and the lingering power of a resentful military establishment indicate that while Thailand has taken an important step on the road to democracy the country remains in the early stages of creating a solid democratic system.

In Cambodia some progress was made toward peace and representative government. However, at least one major obstacle remains to implementing the October, 1991 agreement that provides for an expensive, complicated process under U.N. guidance to end Cambodia's long nightmare. The ruthless Khmer Rouge, despite its signing of the October agreement which called for each faction in the civil war to reduce the size of its armed units, has refused to reduce its armed forces. This has led some observers to predict a renewed civil war, while others see the Khmer Rouge's position as a bargaining stance designed to secure a stronger role and test the U.N.'s resolve.

Moreover, the Phnom-Penh regime has also resorted to political repression and violence in order to intimidate its opponents, thus muddying a confused situation further.

East Asian contrasts

The major events in China during 1992 centered on the 88-year-old Deng Xiaoping's efforts to move the country further along toward a market oriented economy without loosening authoritarian political controls. Deng, perhaps realizing 1992 represented his final chance to ensure that his policies would outlive him, began the year with a tour of southeastern China extolling the region's rapid private economic development. At the 14th Congress of the Communist Party in October he succeeded in having the party endorse his economic policies, make personnel shifts that increased the power of the pragmatists relative to the hardliners, and replace several top party-oriented military leaders with more professional types. It was an impressive achievement, but its durability remains an open question.

The government has several major assets. One is the country's rapid economic growth—probably averaging over 8 percent a year during the early 1990s—based heavily on Hong Kong, Taiwanese and overseas Chinese investors. It also benefits from the lack of an organized opposition and the regime's monopoly of the instruments of coercion. Moreover, there is a public fear of new upheavals based upon China's turbulent recent history. Offsetting these will be popular alienation from the party and its ideology, cynicism over corruption and Deng's failure to institutionalize procedures for a peaceful succession of power. The gross inefficiencies of the state industrial sector, combined with the political importance of preserving the jobs of industrial workers, make reform as politically difficult as it is economically important. Beijing's declining control of many provinces as a result of economic decentralization also limits the effective power of the national leaders. The key determinants of China's course are likely to be the quality and cohesion of the next group of leaders, and whether or not rapid economic growth continues and spreads further throughout the country. However, South China's economic prospects are threatened by rising Chinese-British disputes over who decides how Hong Kong affairs will be conducted in the years before the territory reverts to Chinese sovereignty in 1997.

China's leaders have the will and capacity to control political developments in the short term, but high level political conflict rather than cohesion is a recurrent feature in China. Combining economic reform and political repression—as called for by the October 1992 Party Congress—is possible for a few years, but probably not indefinitely.

China's political stagnation stands in sharp contrast to the progress toward democracy in Taiwan. The Taiwanese government has been moving steadily though carefully along the path of political reform in recent years. The Kuomintang (KMT) leadership recognized that rapid economic growth alone was not enough to satisfy a growing popular desire for a voice in public affairs, and began a step-by-step process of dismantling its tight political controls. It abolished martial law, allowed opposition parties to form, and gave the majority Taiwanese more positions of power within the mainlander-dominated KMT as an essential move to become competitive when elections became free. The strategy has been successful if hardly smooth. In basically free elections for the National Assembly (which elects the president and vice-president and amends the constitution) held in December 1991, the KMT won 71 percent of the vote compared to the 24 percent won by the opposition Democratic Progressive Party (DPP). But in elections for the

Legislative Yuan (parliament) in December 1992, the KMT popular vote dropped to 53 percent and the DPP vote rose to 31 percent, but the KMP won over 60 percent of the seats in parliament. Even so, the more fluid political situation will make it more difficult for the factionalized KMT to deal with the contentious political issues remaining to be solved. Yet the pessimists on Taiwan are those who think the remaining obstacles to full democracy will be overcome slowly rather than rapidly.

The Republic of Korea's continued political progress was best demonstrated by the failure of the ruling Democratic Liberal Party to win a clear majority in the 24 March parliamentary elections. While the DLP won a large enough plurality to remain the key party in the legislature, the government's inability to assure a victory demonstrated both the limits of its power and the determination of the voters to make their own decisions about the nation's course. The December 1992 election saw the victory of the ruling party's Kim Young Sam, who will be the first president without a military background in several decades. Yet, absent a major crisis, the military establishment appears to recognize that its years of power are over. Departing President Roh has steadily moved the country toward democracy and greater protection of human rights, maintained rapid economic growth, established diplomatic relations with the USSR and China—thus weakening North Korea's international position—and moved toward normalization of North-South Korea relations. Although widely criticized by many Koreans for not moving even more rapidly to dismantle some of the political controls of previous governments, Korea will be fortunate if Kim Young Sam performs as well as President Roh has done. ━

William J. Barnds has served as president of the Japan Institute of America and as staff director of the Subcommittee on Asian and Pacific Affairs of the House Foreign Affairs Committee.

"Europhoria" Disappears in Western Europe
Wayne C. Thompson

Nineteen-ninety-two was a year of nervousness, crisis, and paralysis in Western Europe. Gone was the "Europhoria" of 1989 and 1990 in the aftermath of the collapse of communism and the Warsaw Pact. The unexpectedly sudden disappearance of a threatening, common enemy created a vacuum. Instead of pulling together, Western European leaders indulged in separate domestic agendas in the face of a continent-wide economic recession and anxious and angry voters. Not a single political leader remained strong at home, and the year witnessed many electoral setbacks for governing parties.

What went wrong?
The numbers of refugees and asylum seekers swelled because of ethnic warfare in former Yugoslavia, where more than 2 million persons were displaced. "Ethnic cleansing" prevents many from ever returning to their homes. The Serbs' successful aggression against Croats and Muslims is a painful reminder of Europe's paralysis and failure to adopt effective common foreign and defense policies. A few European nations sent peace-keeping forces, and in mid-December NATO agreed to help the U.N. plan new military operations the Security Council might authorize. Only after the Americans agreed to take the lead in a relief effort did France and Italy consent to send troops.

Germany, whose asylum law was the world's most liberal, took the brunt of the refugees—about a half million in 1992, double the number in 1991. The explosion of xenophobia there, spearheaded by swastika-waving neo-Nazis, is the most spectacular manifestation of a menacing new mood in Europe.

But there are larger problems than the outrages of the neo-Nazis. In a half dozen countries far-rightist parties with articulate leaders gained ground in elections, such as the Freedom Party in Austria, the Republikaner Party in Germany, the National Front in France, and the Flemish Bloc in Belgium. Their growing appeal is based on the same general messages: white, Christian Europe is threatened by an invasion of mostly poor, non-Christian, and nonwhite foreigners. None of these parties is on the threshold of power, but they influence the mainstream parties, which cannot ignore the articulated discontent in the traditionally homogeneous countries. National Front strategist Bruno Megret watches with satisfaction: "Today they criticize our measures. Tomorrow they will try to borrow them."

In an attempt to harmonize immigration laws, EC cabinet ministers met in London on 30 November and followed a general trend in Western Europe to tighten liberal asylum laws and thereby avoid Germany's plight. But the ministers, most of whom face an ugly upsurge of racism at home, overwhelmingly rejected Germany's proposal to set up a quota system for distributing the refugees more evenly throughout Europe.

Europeans' worries are exacerbated by a world economic recession that has not spared them. Unemployment is growing, especially in the manufacturing sector and for the young.

The only possible European "locomotive" that could pull the other nations out of the recession is Germany. But the staggering costs of unification have caused it to do what its allies are increasingly doing: think of its own problems first. In order to keep inflation low and help pay the costs of its national unity by attracting foreign capital from abroad, Bundesbank raised interest rates to such a high level that Germany's partners in the European Monetary System (EMS) had to follow, grudgingly. In September the tension became so great that a massive monetary meltdown occurred. The panic ended in the devaluation of the British pound, Italian lira, and Spanish peseta and forced Britain and Italy out of the EMS. In November, Spain again devalued its currency, as did Portugal, whose economy continues to grow under the stable control of Anibal Cavaco Silva. The currency crisis called into serious question the possibility of a single European currency, which had been viewed as the centerpiece of a daring set of compromises which were to complete the road toward the United States of Europe.

Initial confidence

Europe's leaders entered 1992 full of confidence about the final steps toward unity. They had already planned to introduce a single market within the EC by 1 January 1993, and they had agreed in December 1991 to take several daring steps further. The "Masstricht Agreement" was a complicated blueprint for greater economic and political unity. It would take the twelve partners beyond the "single-market" free trade zone to create a European currency (by 1999) and common foreign and defense policies. It was a far-sighted and bold plan to be ratified by the end of 1992. Negative voter reaction revealed how isolated Europe's leaders had become from their own publics and how badly they misread their peoples' hopes, wishes and worries. The first warning bell was rung in Denmark, where a slight majority of voters rejected the agreement in a June referendum. The Danes' concerns were to be heard again in other EC countries.

Shocked EC governments opposed any renegotiation of the treaty. But Denmark's long-serving minority prime minister, Poul Schlütter, announced that his citizens could not be asked to vote twice on the same thing. He vowed to present the treaty to his voters again in the spring of 1993, only after Denmark, which assumed the rotating EC presidency for a half year on 1 January, is exempted from the treaty's foreign, defense and single currency obligations. Thus perished any thought of a routine ratification of the original text by all twelve partners in 1992. Worse, if the Danes say No a second time, Masstricht will be finished.

The next stern warning came in France, where an increasingly unpopular President François Mitterand had hoped to prop up his sagging poll figures by holding an unnecessary referendum on what he had thought was a winning issue: European unity. The Socialist government and all the major parties supported the treaty. But the vote in September was taken with an unpopular government and economic uncertainty fueled by more than 10 percent unemployment. The referendum unleashed anxiety over possible German domination, which has festered in France and elsewhere (especially Britain) since 1990. An embarrassing hair-thin majority of 51 percent of French voters voted *Oui* for the Maastricht treaty. The narrowness of the victory in one of the EC's founding nations was a stinging blow to France's political elite.

Europe's leaders, trying to find a way out of the EC's most serious crisis in 35 years, met in Birmingham on 16 October to discuss ways of reducing the growing gulf between the governments and EC bureaucracy and their citizens. They agreed that the EC Commission should consult more people before making proposals and that commissioners should be dispatched to national parliaments to answer questions and hear concerns. In their Edinburgh summit in December they tried to turn these vague promises of openness, democracy, and "nearness" into something more concrete. They also exempted Denmark from its commitment to a single currency and a common European defense. Great Britain, the host government for these two summits, finds itself divided and beleaguered. Contrary to most predictions, the Conservative leader, Prime Minister John Major, won the April parliamentary elections, albeit with a greatly reduced majority in the House of Commons. He was soon challenged by a group powerful enough to humble most prime ministers: coal miners. He was forced to retreat, suspending closure orders on 21 of 31 pits he had decided to shut down.

Major's credibility was further shaken during the currency turbulence in September, when the UK was forced to devalue the pound and leave the EMS. This crisis reopened a split within Major's own Tory party. Threatening to resign if he lost, he put the question of moving ahead with the Maastricht Treaty to the House of Commons. His policy was carried by only a three-vote margin, thanks to the votes of the small Liberal Democratic party. With his approval rating standing at just 16 percent by November, the lowest recorded since 1945, he postponed a final vote on ratification until after the next Danish referendum.

Major's doldrums were shared with the queen and the Anglican Church. In the wake of lurid reports in the popular press about marital breakdowns and infidelity within the royal family, and questions about state payments to a very wealthy family, the role of the monarchy in Britain is being questioned. To quiet the fury, Queen Elizabeth announced that she would pay taxes and finance most members of her family out of her own fortune. On the fortieth anniversary of her coronation she publicly described 1992 as an *annus horribilis*. The Anglican Church had an equally memorable year. After its General Synod voted in November to ordain women, traditionalists threaten to split away from the Church. Finally, the IRA continued its cruel yuletide bombings, this time igniting two bombs in central Manchester, injuring 64 people.

Politics was no less eventful across the Irish Sea. In February, Charles Haughey was finally forced out of the prime minister's office and replaced by Albert Reynolds. Two days after taking office, he entered an ethical mine field which took him to the root of the kind of society Ireland is and aspires to be. With abortion forbidden, his government got a court order to prevent a fourteen-year-old rape victim from going to Britain to end her pregnancy, as thousands of Irish women do annually. This triggered a barrage of international criticism and an emotional national debate, which continued even after the court later lifted the ban on travelling to the UK. After calling his own coalition partner "reckless, irresponsible and dishonest," Reynolds lost a no-confidence vote in November. Voters handed both the big parties, Fianna Fail and Fine Gael, serious setbacks, and they doubled the seats of the moderate and progressive Labour Party, led by Dick Spring, who became the kingmaker in Irish politics. Voters also overwhelmingly decided in same-day referenda to permit women to obtain information and to have abortions abroad, though not in Ireland.

Trade wars

It could not have been a worse year for weakened European leaders to face the prospects of a trade war with the United States. For six years an agreement on the Uruguay Round of the General Agreement on Tariffs and Trade (GATT) has been blocked by France. The issue was state subsidies to farmers, who form a powerful lobby in most EC countries, but especially in France. European prosperity depends upon foreign trade, but the U.S. insisted that trade must be reciprocal.

Backed by two GATT rulings that high farm subsidies in Europe allow EC countries to undersell their competitors on world markets, the U.S. responded to stalled negotiations by threatening to raise duties by 200 percent on such agricultural exports (primarily French) as white wine and cheese. It was a difficult time for European leaders to accept the bitter GATT medicine, which would lower farm incomes and employment even further. But the existing problems of dealing with a global recession made a trade war with the Americans unthinkable. In late November, American and EC trade negotiators reached a compromise that sets the stage for completion of the worldwide Uruguay Round.

This settlement, intended to stabilize the EC, had the opposite effect. French farmers took their tractors and manure to the streets of France, targeting McDonald's and Coca-Cola plants (all of which use only French farm products), the National Assembly, and the European Parliament. Already barely surviving economically, many farmers, who constitute 6 percent of the French population, would be forced off the land and into crowded cities, leaving depopulated regions behind them. The Socialist government of Pierre Bérégovoy and all other major political parties announced that France could not accept the settlement. Bérégovoy threatened to resurrect Charles de Gaulle's 1965 "Luxembourg Compromise." This gave each EC member a veto whenever it considered a national interest to be at stake, but it was implicitly suppressed by the Single European Act in the mid-1980s.

The French government finds itself too weak either to accept or fully reject the compromise. Acceptance would risk open rebellion in the streets. Rejection would trigger a major and deeper crisis within the EC and place unprecedented strain on France's alliance with Germany, which favors a settlement with the United States. This is made worse by the timing of upcoming parliamentary elections. In regional elections in the spring the governing Socialists received only 18.3 percent of the votes, its worst showing in 23 years. It fears that the same will happen in March 1993, when most observers expect a victory by conservative parties and a renewal of "cohabitation."

Germany's test

Perhaps no European country was more in the international spotlight than Germany. This is not only because of its size, economic strength, and continuing drama of unification, but because of events that caused many people to ask whether the old demons could reappear and democracy itself be threatened. Chancellor Helmut Kohl contended that Germany's democratic system was "being put to the test." President Richard von Weizsäcker was no less direct: "Let us entertain no illusions. Something evil is afoot."

The most sinister force to emerge is neo-Nazi, anti-foreigner violence. Many Germans are unwilling to accept the fact that, with 6.3 million foreigners, Germany is no longer a homogeneous country. Sporting swastikas, shouting neo-Nazi slogans and cheered on by some bystanders, right-wing youth gangs attacked an asylum hostel in Rostock on 22 August and battled police for several days. Such attacks continued throughout the autumn. When caught, the perpetrators, often minors, could expect shockingly light sentences. On 14 September, in Frankfurt an der Oder, the first sentences, ranging from two to five years, were passed against right-wing skinheads for beating an African immigrant to death on 25 November 1990.

Perhaps most embarrassing for a country still on parole in the minds of many persons was an outbreak of anti-Semitism. Conscious of Nazi crimes against Jews, Germany had always forbidden any public expression of anti-Semitism. In general, the approximately 40,000 Jews who reside in the FRG have not suffered discrimination and indignity. On 16 September Israeli Prime Minister Yitzhak Rabin visited an exhibition in the "Jewish Barracks" on the oppression of Jews during the Third Reich, in Sachsenhausen in Oranienburg (near Berlin). This was the first time an Israeli leader had ever visited a German concentration camp. Ten days later, the barracks were gutted by arson, becoming the third Berlin-area memorial to Jewish Holocaust victims damaged in a matter of weeks. In October vandals damaged a Jewish cemetery for slave laborers at the Ueberlingen labor camp, a satellite of Dachau near Munich, and the Ravensbrück concentration camp for women was firebombed.

Such racist outrages occur in many European countries. But in Germany the historical memory arouses particular international interest in such things. Although Kohl called the attacks "a disgrace for our land," his government was unable to do much about them.

On 8 November 1992, the eve of the anniversary of both the 1938 Nazi Kristalnacht pogrom against Jews and the 1989 fall of the Berlin Wall, a mass rally in Berlin involving 300,000 persons and Germany's top political leaders attempted to show the world that Germany condemns anti-foreigner violence. When it was brought to a halt by an estimated 500 anarchist protestors, who hurled eggs, paint bombs, and angry chants, the leader of Germany's Jewish community, Ignatz Bubis, screamed at anarchists pelting President von Weizsäcker, who was pleading for tolerance: "I am ashamed of what has happened here. We are not in 1938, but in 1992!" On 6 December a quarter million Munich residents took part in a silent, candlelight demonstration to support a growing nationwide movement against the attacks.

Declaring that it would "use all possible legal measures to fight violence and political extremism," the Kohl government ordered in December a far stronger focus on law enforcement and a broader effort to crack down on forms of racist and neo-Nazi expression. It established a special task force to crack down on rightist extremism, and it raided neo-Nazi hideouts all over Germany, confiscating arms and Nazi paraphernalia. It outlawed the neo-Nazis' main party, German Alternative, and asked the Constitutional Court to apply a never-used constitutional clause and strip two leading neo-Nazis of their rights of expression and assembly. To help stem the influx of asylum seekers, the major political parties agreed to scrap the absolute guarantee of political asylum for refugees and introduce a new law like those of other major Western nations.

In May, Austria improved its international standing by electing a new president, Thomas Klestil, a former ambassador to Washington and No. 2 in the foreign ministry. This brought to an end the embarrassing term of Kurt Waldheim, whose Nazi past had reduced him to a ceremonial pariah. Austria has not seen the kind of rightist anti-foreigner violence that Germany has experienced, although eighty Jewish graves were defiled in Eisenstadt. Nevertheless, the influx of immigrants, including 50,000 from Bosnia alone, propelled the immigration issue to the top of the political agenda. One poll indicated that 79 percent of Austrian respondents do not want more newcomers. Charismatic leader Jörg Haider, whose Freedom Party stood at 17 percent in the polls in November, exploited this resentment. Fearing his appeal, the two main parties passed laws restricting the number of asylum seekers and foreign workers.

Admission to the EC

Austria is one of a growing number of neutral states that have applied for admission to the EC. In 1992 Swiss voters narrowly voted to join the International Monetary Fund (IMF) but in December rejected their country's entry into the European Economic Area (EEA), a link between the EC and the seven European Free Trade Association (EFTA) countries. This latter referendum means that the Swiss government, which formally applied to the EC in May, has to convince especially Swiss-German citizens that Helvitia can remain a unique, adamantly self-ruling country within a unified Europe. The Swiss rejection of the EEA delayed its planned introduction on 1 January 1993, while the details of EEA entry are renegotiated.

The governments of the Nordic countries—Norway, Sweden, and Finland—have also formally applied for admission to the EC, although polls show that their citizens do not necessarily view the EC favorably. The formerly buoyant Nordic economies have been rocked by recession, record unemployment, and political apprehension. All three are in the midst of painful adjustments, having opened their markets to foreign products and services to get ready for EC membership. With its oil and gas wealth, Norway is the least vulnerable. Its parliament voted both to accept EEA and, for the fourth time, to seek entry into the EC. But polls show that most Norwegians remain opposed to the EC and will have a chance to say so in a referendum in 1994 or 1995.

The Swedish Conservative government of Carl Bildt is trying to cope with a collapsed real estate market and a krona which had to be floated in November. Although most Swedes agree that the public sector and some cherished welfare programs must be cut and that the revered "Swedish model" is no longer viable, a November poll revealed that 53 percent oppose EC membership.

Nowhere in the Nordic world is support for the EC as high as in Finland, whose center-right coalition government of Esko Aho applied for admission in the spring. Finland fears isolation from the West and is desperately in need of economic partners who can replace the earlier trade (25 percent of its total, now under 4 percent) it lost when the Soviet Union collapsed.

All European countries are affected by the bloody disintegration of Yugoslavia, but few face such a direct threat as Greece. Greeks fear that Macedonia to the North could make irredentist claims on their province with the same name. This prompted Athens to oppose Macedonia's right to use that ancient Hellenic name when it declared its independence from Yugoslavia. One 1992 poll showed that 98 percent of Greeks support their government's position and, in deference to their ally, the NATO countries have refused to recognize the newly independent republic.

Like some Latin American countries, Italy is fighting to prevent itself from falling under the control of unelected international criminals. After the Mafia murdered two top anti-Mafia judges and other officials, the government deployed 7,000 soldiers to Sicily in July to crack down on the Mafia. This was the most drastic step taken since 1945 against a domestic disorder and the first time troops have been used in a large-scale crackdown on the Sicilian mobsters. In October Italian law-enforcement officials joined Spanish, British, and American police to arrest Italians working with the Cali cocaine cartel, and in November the biggest organized crime sweep in almost ten years put scores of Mafia suspects in jail. Among the arrested were several mayors and three members of parliament. This strengthened embarrassing allegations that Christian Democratic (DC) politicians in Sicily were in collusion with the Mafia.

In April parliamentary elections, the perpetually ruling DC saw its share of vote drop to below 30 percent, its lowest since 1945. Italian politics was deadlocked, and President Francesco Cossiga resigned in disgust, to be replaced by Oscar Luigi Scalfaro in May. Socialist

Giuliano Amato finally glued together a shaky four-party coalition with a slim sixteen-seat majority. Spurred by a battering of the lira on the currency markets, which jolted Italian pride and resulted in a devaluation and exit from the EMS, he set about to salvage the country's economy by reducing pensions and the welfare state as never before. A wave of strikes came as no surprise in the world's fifth richest industrial nation, but Amato asserted that "my government is one of necessity, not popularity." At the same time, the government must deal with a virulent campaign of anti-Jewish and anti-foreigner vandalism and terror. The neo-fascist MSI-DN found a new star in Alessandra Mussolini, granddaughter of the fascist dictator and niece of Sophia Loren.

Spain faces its worst recession in years, with annual growth stalled at 1.5 percent, unemployment expected to rise to 20 percent, and a high number of illegal immigrants. The kind of racial violence that has disfigured the rest of Europe has also emerged in Spain, although opinion polls suggest that Spaniards are more tolerant of outsiders than are most other Europeans. On 13 November, Spain experienced its first serious act of anti-foreigner violence in many years. Four hooded gunmen entered an abandoned discotheque outside Madrid, where three dozen mostly black immigrants from the Dominican Republic were sleeping, and opened fire, killing one woman. Foreign Minister Javier Solana shook his head in regret: "Spain is a country where others have always been taken in with great generosity and solidarity." Many Western Europeans are saying the same thing about their own countries. ▬

Wayne C. Thompson is professor of political science at the Virginia Military Institute.

Russian Democracy: Year One

Paige Sullivan

A year after the crash of Mikhail Gorbachev's government, the world watches anxiously to see if the seeds of democracy can grow in the rocky soil of the former Soviet republics. While there have been significant advances, statehood and profound institutional change have brought their share of chaos, economic misery and frustration.

For pessimists, the situation in Russia toward the end of 1992 brought to mind the situation in Germany during the Weimar Republic. This period in Germany's history was characterized by many destabilizing conditions: 1) defeat after a major political/military confrontation; 2) significant loss of territory; 3) a crippling economic depression; 4) a severe loss of faith in previous political ideals and institutions; 5) the perception of "victimization" within the global economy; 6) lack of experience with democratic governance; and 7) virulent ethnic-based conflicts. In Germany, the result was Nazi dictatorship.

On a more optimistic note, it may be said that the almost inconceivably fast-moving and eventful year of 1992 witnessed progress toward the establishment of basic human rights and something close to normal politics in many ex-Soviet states. The most dramatic signs of progress were the emergence of uncensored media and the establishment of free political organizations at local and regional levels in Russia, Ukraine and the Baltics.

But these were not, in themselves, sufficient to guarantee the consolidation of democratic rule. In fact, the year ended on a solemn note, with Russian president Boris Yeltsin in danger of losing his government and possibly his office. The situation was just as grave in the other former republics, with civil war raging in four of them and many on the verge of economic collapse. Still, parliaments were meeting on a regular basis and a semblance of social order prevailed in many of the former republics. The sense was that the democratic reformers would try even harder to fulfill their ideals in 1993.

New political realities

Western and eastern observers alike believed that the road to democracy in the Soviet successor states would require little more than the liberalization of prices, a rapid privatization program to put property back in the hands of the people, and new national and local elections (which would seat the same democrats that had overturned the Communist order).

But new realities quickly set in. Months after many of these first steps had been taken in several of the nascent states, the results were deeply contradictory. Throughout the former Soviet empire, once-privileged apparatchiks got richer, while average men and women experienced the worst drop in living standards since World War II.

In similar fashion, Popular Front democrats who had expected to determine the direction of post-Communist reform in the internal empire of the Soviet Union, were displaced by the same privileged elite of the former regime. This upper stratum of hardline and reform Communists, nationalists and other conservative-leaning groups continued to dispense power and reap the ill-deserved rewards of an enormous region in terrible and awe-inspiring flux.

The power of the old Communist elite developed into the major reality with which the fragile new states of Europe and Asia had to grapple. It was not easy, or even possible in some cases, to overrule hardline former Communist officials (*nomenklatura*) anxious to maintain their status and power by coopting the democratic process in the parliaments and dragging their feet on reforms.

In each nascent state, members of the old guard who had been elected to republican legislatures in 1989 and 1990 under Gorbachev's liberal electoral law managed to push the democrats who had overturned communism to the back of the political bench. In many cases, new parliaments will not be elected until 1994 or 1995.

Uneven democratization

The pace of democratization in the former Soviet Union has been extremely uneven. The entire region may be roughly divided into three geographic groups: 1) European/Slavic (including the Baltics, Moldova, Belarus, Ukraine and Russia); 2) Central Asian (including Uzbekistan, Tajikistan, Kyrgyzstan, Turkmenistan and Kazakhstan); and 3) Transcaucasian (including Georgia, Armenia and Azerbaijan). These groups have displayed certain generalized transitional traits. In the year just ended, by far the most significant progress toward laying the rudimentary foundation for parliamentary democracy and relatively free markets was made by the European/Slavic states. These states succeeded in establishing multi-party systems with conservative-dominated legislatures, and experimented with far-reaching economic reforms.

With the exception of Kyrgyzstan, the Central Asian states showed less interest in democratization and economic reform than the European and Slavic states. Several Central Asian countries remained single-party states governed by nationalist cult figures, such as Turkmenistan's Sapar Murad Niyazov and Kazakhstan's Nursultan Nazarbayev.

With even less to show for their first year of transition politics, the Transcaucasian states were ripped apart by civil war among ethnic factions. Most civil liberties and democratic change in these war-torn states were suspended.

Yeltsin's dictatorial powers

In Russia, political developments revolved around Boris Yeltsin's governing style and his showdown with the Russian parliament. Yeltsin was widely criticized, even by some of his closest advisors, for his undemocratic, dictatorial and unconstitutional use of power in Russia and in dealings with other former republics. These critics were referring to Yeltsin's frequent use of personal envoys to influence local and regional governments in the Russian Federation; his use of presidential decree; and his reliance on a personally appointed nonparliamentary and nongovernmental Security Council (similar to President Mikhail Gorbachev's President's Council).

Yeltsin's actions as the Russian president were made within the chaotic context of historically unprecedented social, economic and political change. No country in the world has ever made the incredible journey away from seventy-five years of totalitarian communism into parliamentary democracy and free markets. For these reasons, the Bush administration, knowing full well the extent of Yeltsin's use of special powers, let it be known that should Yeltsin be forced to dissolve the Russian Congress, it would be accepted if this was the only means by which Yeltsin could save his bold reform program. The Americans would regard the move as undemocratic, extra-constitutional, and illegal, but would not condemn the action if new elections were held by the following spring.

The Russian Congress gave Yeltsin the power to rule by decree in 1991, soon after he became the first popularly elected president of Russia. This power was to be used to assert the legitimacy of Russian over Soviet law in the affirmation of Russian sovereignty. Yeltsin has issued hundreds of decrees. Typically, they have been designed to speed up the legal process of democratization and reform; to insure the stability of the Russian government; and to carry out controversial decisions related to such matters as personnel, foreign policy, and the national budget.

On 7 July, Yeltsin issued decree number 747, creating a special Security Council responsible for every aspect of state security (especially the security of the Presidency). This council, which is staffed by former commanders in Afghanistan, may bypass the Congress and every Cabinet minister in times of crisis. Its secretary, Yurii Skokov, has broad powers to coordinate and supervise the work of other executive agencies. The Russian parliament nevertheless refuses to recognize the council's legitimacy, calling it a new Politburo.

Yeltsin's envoys to various republics of the Russian Federation have also had the power to deliver and implement presidential decrees. These envoys have played a role similar to those of the Russian Tsars, when they were needed to keep communications flowing between Moscow and the far reaches of its vast empire. They have, however, sometimes confused decision-making at local levels and caused resentment on the part of local leaders.

Despite this rather typical Russian use of authoritarian power, Boris Yeltsin has given the world ample reason to believe that he is committed to Western-style democratization in Russia. He has struggled throughout the year against a Congress that has frequently attempted to compete with the executive and to assume executive powers. In July, for example, conservatives in Congress nearly succeeded in setting up an Oversight Council to control the Russian press. They failed only when Yeltsin appeared before Congress and vigorously defended the freedom of the press. By comparison with the other Soviet successor states, especially in Transcaucasia and Central Asia, Yeltsin's use of dictatorial powers has been minor.

Rise of the Civic Union

Open attacks on Yeltsin's government began in June, organized by the Civic Union—a block of three major political parties in the Russian Congress. They are: 1) the Democratic Party of Russia (DPR) led by Nikolai Travkin (a prominent young reform Communist); 2) the All-Russian Renewal Party, whose unofficial leader is Arkadii Volskiy; and 3) the People's Party of Free Russia (NPSR), led by Vice President Aleksander Rutskoi. Together, these parties represent Russian state enterprise managers, reform and hardline Communists, Vice President Rutskoi's right-of-center nationalists and some military leaders.

This group has managed to accumulate impressive strength in Russia over the past six months. It has also succeeded in starting offshoots in other states, such as the Baltics. It claims to support democratization and a free, open market, but there is good reason to believe that its definitions of "democracy" and "market" diverge in significant ways from those in the West. This is not to give the impression that the Civic Union is monolithic in its views. By November, a significant split had appeared between those prepared to compromise with Yeltsin's government and those with more extremist positions and attitudes. In addition, many factions on economic issues had developed within its membership.

The Civic Union's most vocal and concrete demands have been for the replacement of most of Yeltsin's cabinet ministers and the government's adoption of its alternative "anti-crisis" plan for economic reform. That plan calls for a "gradualist" approach to reform rather than "shock therapy" which acting Prime Minister Yegor Gaidar has been attempting to carry out.

The fate of the Russian democrats

The Civic Union gained strength over the last six months not only as a result of its members' former party and state credentials, but also thanks to the progressive weakening of more radical democratic reform groups. The Democratic Russia movement is a case in point. This group played an important role in the anti-Communist revolution, but fell apart after the collapse of the Communist Party of the Soviet Union (CPSU).

Democratic Russia was initially seen as the nucleus of a "president's party," which Yeltsin needed to support his economic reforms. Indeed, its current leaders continue to offer Yeltsin unwavering support. Nevertheless, the movement suffered a series of splits in its ranks quite early in the year. One such split occurred when Sergei Stankevich, Yeltsin's top advisor and former architect of Democratic Russia joined Aleksandr Rutskoi in August in demanding the return of authoritarian rule to Russia. Stankevich said it was impossible to accomplish the transition to a new state with a full parliamentary democracy.

In February, Democratic Russia organized a system of Public Committees for Russian Reforms (PCRR). These committees were set up in workplaces, civic centers and government ministries, which were ordered to give PCRRs access to official information. The movement was severely criticized for trying make itself an appendage of the executive. Some disaffected members even charged it with creating an unconstitutional, one-party dictatorship.

The Democratic Russia movement made certain costly errors partly in reaction to its perception of the conservative opposition's overwhelming political and economic advantages. Another reason is that the ranks of the "democrats" consist mainly of teachers, doctors, intellectuals and peasants —not experienced politicians. So far, they have not proven to be an equal match for the economic malaise, and the complexity and difficulty of the issues they have had to confront.

The frustrations that splintered Russian democratic forces pushed some of them in more extreme directions. A number of local political leaders formerly devoted to liberal democratic ideals have shifted to blatantly chauvinist allegiances. Valentin Fedorov, for example, administrative head of Sakhalin Krai, was hailed as a leading liberal reformer in 1990. Today he embraces the views of the Russian National Assembly—a union of nationalist parties founded in February 1992. The Assembly's program calls for recreating Russia within the boundaries of the old Soviet Union and asserts that an individual's human rights are secondary to state rights.

At the extreme end of the political spectrum, some Russian politicians such as those in the "National Salvation Front" openly espoused policies strikingly reminiscent of the Nazis in the Weimar Republic, calling for the persecution of minorities and the retaking of lost Russian territory by force. In October, Yeltsin banned this party.

Meanwhile, in the Baltics

Since Yeltsin's recognition of their independence in 1991, bilateral relations between Russia and each of the Baltic states have deteriorated. Baltic demands for the immediate withdrawal of former Soviet troops were stalled, until Yeltsin canceled the Russo-Lithuania agreement for complete troop withdrawal by August 1993. Now the Russians say it will be at least five years before their troops go home. Social tensions have flared, in no small part due to the troops' presence.

These tensions made international headlines when, under the foreign-alien clause of its new electoral law, Estonia denied some 600,000 ethnic Russians the right to vote in its October 1992 presidential election. (The total population of Estonia is 1,581,000) The right-of-center Fatherland Party's Lennart Meri won the election and appointed a government in coalition with other conservative formations. Russia insisted that oil be paid for with hard currency at world prices, bringing the country to the brink of economic collapse and setting the stage for a break in relations.

In a surprise upset, the October-November elections in the most independent-minded Baltic state saw Lithuania take a major step back toward the Russian fold. Evidently more from a need for economic security than out of a deep change of heart regarding independence, a democratic election, according to international observers, saw the former Communist party, now called the Democratic Party of Lithuania, led by former CP boss Algerdas Brazauskas, capture 71 out of 141 seats in the Lithuanian parliament. The liberal democratic Popular Front, which has governed during the past two-and-a-half years under the stewardship of Vytautas Landsbergis, conceded defeat graciously, having won only twenty-five seats.

Although he retains strong links to Russia's former Communists, Democratic Party leader Brazauskas defended his party's commitment to democratization. But he has deeply differed with the Popular Front's liberal economic reforms. His party's program is strikingly similar to that of Russia's military-industrial complex under the Civic Union leadership.

How conditions develop in the Baltics is likely to depend a good deal on how they develop in Russia.

Living standards plunge

For various tough political, economic and social reasons, every post-Soviet state experienced disappointment, frustration and failure in laying the economic foundations for democracy and the empowerment of new elites. The political and economic problems of market-building were much huger than some thought, and the solutions extremely difficult to identify, after the first immediately recognizable steps of price liberalization and preliminary privatization had been taken.

This summer, economies in every state began to stagnate causing the living standards of average men and women to spiral downward. The elderly were hit especially hard. Even in Estonia, which is considered more advanced in entrepreneurial skill than the other former republics, elderly men and women in tattered grey clothes stood outside pension offices for hours to receive stipends that barely kept them alive. Later, monthly stipends were not even being paid regularly.

Meanwhile, the privileged few reaped the spoils of confusion and change. Managers of state enterprises in the Baltic states drive Mercedes, paid for as "business expenses," with state funds. Many of these managers set up parallel private companies to which they have transferred valuable state assets. This practice has been dubbed "spontaneous privatization" by discouraged citizens of the ex-Soviet republics. The parallel companies buy the state enterprise's goods at prices well below cost and then sell the goods to wholesalers at up to ten times the price.

These common activities on the part of state enterprise managers and others with access to state assets, have not been stopped by new state governments. Some close observers have conjectured that the governments have intentionally turned a blind eye to their state manager friends. Besides this, laws passed in 1990 paralyzed the ability of the courts to stop the misappropriation and embezzlement of state funds. These laws have even prevented the state governments from examining enterprise records.

As a result, many people have lost faith in the new governments and the whole reform process. "The thing that makes people angry" says Ago Haan, a civil servant in Estonia, "is that the people getting richer now are the people who profited under the old Communist system."

Throughout the former Soviet Union, people have felt they were rapidly losing control over their lives. Hindrek Meri, Estonian controller responsible for overseeing state enterprises, observed in July that "it all shows that Estonia is like a drunk driver swerving back and forth along the road, hitting one ditch after another."

Corruption has been a major problem in every new state. In Khabarovsk Krai, a typical Russian administrative region numbering about 2 million citizens, people are thoroughly disenchanted with their postcoup leadership. Life has definitely grown darker in the Krai since the collapse of the CPSU. Journalists have described the confusion, inefficiency, corruption and cynicism which have fostered such a state of affairs. In one particularly glaring instance, it was reported that a severe housing shortage had stranded 6,000 families in dilapidated slum dwellings. Nearby, several regional officials, with the use of government funds, built themselves luxury villas with swimming pools and saunas.

The urgent need for a middle class

The development of a new middle class of small and medium-sized business owners and technical professionals has been a major goal in the post-Communist transformation process. The very concept of a business-oriented middle class is foreign to the former Soviet republics, with the possible exception of the Baltics. During seventy-five years of Soviet rule, entrepreneurship was ruthlessly stamped out or driven underground except on tiny garden plots. Profits were forbidden and were cause for the harshest criminal punishments. Members of the Soviet middle class were primarily the intelligentsia, midlevel party and state functionaries and sportsmen—all nourished by the state from cradle to grave. Many of these people now resent the economic individualism which has deprived them of government support.

The post-Soviet states desperately need to build a new middle class that will adopt and perpetuate democratic values. Up to now, the fledgling governments have failed to concentrate on this task, and have the mistaken notion that such a class springs up on its own. Understandably they have been preoccupied with macroeconomic stabilization and the disassembling and sale of state enterprises and all the attendant headaches of social disruption. Meanwhile, the creation and expansion of small and medium firms has received much less attention.

Governments will have to turn more attention to small and medium-sized business in the coming year. Such firms have been stifled by confiscatory taxes, stymied by protecionist trade policies and hamstrung by high interest rates, rudimentary banking systems and socialist property laws. Even though acting Prime Minister Yegor Gaidar has done more in one year to reform the former Communist economy than Gorbachev did in five, he will have to address such problems very soon.

The voucher experiment

Several policies aimed at distributing economic power in 1992 became bogged down in political struggles with entrenched interests. One dramatic experiment to empower the people and give them a vested interest in the government's economic reform program was carried out toward the end of the year. In November, the government distributed investment vouchers to every Russian man, woman and child. Each voucher had a face value of 10,000 rubles. Citizens could use them to purchase shares in designated state enterprises at public auctions.

Unfortunately, most Western observers agreed that the system was badly flawed from the beginning. Inflation had whittled down the value of each voucher to about 7,000 rubles by the time they were distributed. (In Czechoslavakia, where a more complex voucher system was used with more success in 1991, vouchers were given no face value.) Furthermore, many people relinquished their vouchers to former nomenklatura in exchange for cash with which to buy bread and other supplies. (When a kilo of meat costs 200 rubles, 7,000 rubles do not go very far.)

The Russian parliament almost unanimously approved the voucher scheme because enterprise directors were able to maintain control of state firms while supporting the impression that average people were being enfranchised within the new system.

Russians as leaders and colonialists

The atmosphere of confrontation and division that characterized much of the democratic institution-building in the Soviet successor states in 1992 extended to military and human rights issues as well: the tension-ridden issue of the withdrawal of former Soviet troops from the Baltic states, the intervention of the Russian army (not always invited) in armed ethnic struggles in Georgia, Moldova, Armenia and Azerbaijan, recriminations and accusations against the Baltic states for their treatment of sizable ethnic Russian populations within their borders. Nationalism was a significant factor driving events in the first year of post-Communist institution-building.

On the other hand, the Russians acted as leaders in 1992, making significant strides in areas such as municipal law reform, the liberalization of prices, passage of foreign investment laws, the opening of "stock exchanges" to replace the old command distribution system, and the working out of difficult political compromises with old guard Communists.

Nineteen-ninety-two was a year of explosive potentialities. The beginning of the social and political transformation of an area equal to one-sixth of the earth's surface provided an historical moment of profound significance. Although nothing is yet assured, the democratic experiments being carried out in eastern Europe and the former Soviet Union made it to a second year. ▄

Paige Sullivan is a research associate at the Center for Strategic and International Studies, Washington, DC.

East-Central Europe: Post-Communist Blues

George Zarycky

Few observers will ever forget the riveting images of 1989, the year Central and East Europe dramatically ousted the last aging standardbearers of Soviet-imposed orthodoxy. In East Germany, Eric Honecker was out, and jubilant Germans celebrated atop the rubble of the Berlin Wall, once the primitive symbol of totalitarian hubris. In Czechoslovakia, dissident playwright Václav Havel addressed euphoric throngs in Prague's Wenceslas Square where two decades earlier Soviet tanks had brutally quashed East Europe's modest try at trickle-down reform. The snow-covered corpses of Nicolae and Elena Ceausescu, Romania's monstrous first couple, were the exclamation point, taking on the symbolic significance that Mussolini and his mistress hanging upside down did for the generation that saw the fall of fascism. Communism was dead, and triumphalism ran rampant from the White House to Madison Avenue. Even today, Sunday morning news shows pause as General Electric hails its historic partnership with the Hungarian lighting company, Tungstrum. Between quick-cuts of a luminescent Budapest, a young man declares: "Freedom is all that matters."

From light bulbs to *lebensraum*

Three years after these images, it is clear that freedom is but one essential step along the anfractuous path to building genuinely pluralistic, free-market societies and new foreign policies from the rubble of the old order. From the Baltic to the Balkans, post-Communist societies are grappling with the Augean task of buttressing fragile democratic gains against the tide of reaction swelled by the destabilizing consequences of systemic economic restructuring, combustible ethnic animosities, political polarization, resurgent nationalism, nascent authoritarianism and a recalcitrant Communist apparatus that doggedly refuses to accept the end of history.

Throughout the region, albeit in varying degrees, the Party priviligentsia has used the old-comrade network to become the new entrepreneurial elite, spurring resentment among economically hard-pressed citizens cynically spoon-fed classless society egalitarianism for over four decades. In some cases, hardline Communists have made common cause with ultranationalist extremists in an effort to tap social discontent and derail economic reforms they blame for unemployment, crime, poverty and corruption.

In Hungary, a bellwether of a smooth transition, a leader of the ruling Hungarian Democratic Forum (MDF) touched a popular nerve by warning that the country was being victimized by of Jews, liberals, the International Monetary Fund and foreign bankers, and questioning the Trianon peace treaty—the territorial settlement after World War I which cost Hungary 60 percent of its land area and left 3.5 million ethnic Hungarians living in neighboring states. He also dangled the tantalizing vision of *lebensraum* in a "Greater Hungary" from Transylvania to Vojvodina. In Romania, the re-election as president of Ceausescu crony Ion Iliescu of the Democratic National Salvation Front (DNSF) coupled with his party's failure to win a parliamentary majority, portends alliances with nationalist parties who blame the country's ills on Hungarians, Gypsies and Jews.

In what used to be East Germany, skinheads and neo-Nazis are terrorizing immigrants and refugees, compelling a jittery government to rethink its asylum policies and send Romanian Gypsies back to their homeland. Gypsies have also been targeted by skinheads in Prague and Hungary, while in Poland young right-wing toughs have attacked Germans and immigrants, and anti-Semitism is reportedly on the rise.

Regional hot spots

Casting a shadow over political, social and economic concerns is the specter of heightened regional and ethnic tensions epitomized by the violent disintegration of Yugoslavia. Bosnia has become a charnel house on the verge of partition by Serbia and Croatia. Elsewhere, ancient ethnic tensions have been exacerbated by tens of thousands of Balkan refugees throughout a region where nativism and xenophobia are endemic and fragile economies make absorption difficult. Perhaps fittingly, the death of Alexander Dubcek, architect of the Prague Spring, coincided with the death of Czechoslovakia, where the promise of the "Velvet Revolution" became a messy Czech-Slovak divorce.

Irredentism and revanchism, long suppressed by Soviet power, have seeped from the fringes into the mainstream, heightening fears that existing crisis points could erupt into open conflicts with broad regional and geopolitical implications. In the Balkans, Macedonia is an ethnic timebomb. The 500,000-strong Albanian minority has been pushing for greater autonomy in regions bordering Albania, raising the prospects of civil and territorial strife. Serbs see Macedonia as an extension of Greater Serbia, while Macedonians view themselves as a distinct ethnic group. Greece has staked a claim on the name Macedonia, imposed an economic embargo and blocked Western attempts to formally recognize the new state. Bulgaria, one of the few countries to recognize the former republic, once controlled Macedonia, though radical Macedonian claims on Bulgarian lands could lead to friction.

In Bulgaria, the Turkish minority, whose 24 representatives in parliament represent a swing block, has reported growing resentment of its political power and an increase in anti-Turkish feelings that under the Communists led to severe repression and expulsion in the late 1980s.

Continued Serbian repression of the 2 million-strong Albanian minority in Kosovo, the ancient seat of Serbian nationhood, could ignite genocide against outgunned Albanians, leading to confrontations with Albania and the Muslim world. And while the situation in Vojvodina, the former autonomous Yugoslav region with a large Hungarian minority, has remained relatively calm, it has strained Serbian-Hungarian relations.

Potential flashpoints are not limited to the Balkans. Romanian demands for restitution of parts of Moldova, a predominantly Romanian area, parts of which were ceded to Ukraine under the 1939 Hitler-Stalin pact, could lead to conflicts with Ukraine and Russia, particularly in light of the armed Slavic uprising in the Trans-Dniester area. Romania formally protested Hungary's use of the historic term Transylvania in official relations. Bucharest's churlishness is rooted in Hungary's traditional links to the region and the Democratic Union of Hungarians in Romania's call for self-administration for the area's 2 million Hungarians. With the election of rabid nationalist Gheorghe Funar of the Party of Romanian National Unity (PRNU) as mayor of the Transylvanian city of Cluj, the type of anti-Hungarian violence that erupted last year could explode again. For its part, Hungary has expressed concern about the 600,000-strong Hungarian minority in Slovakia after the Czechoslovak breakup.

Even Poland is not entirely free from potential ethnic problems, domestic and foreign. Continued political instability and economic hardships could exacerbate tensions with the 350,000 Ukrainian minority and ethnic Germans, estimated at 300,000. The fate of Polish minorities in western Ukraine, Lithuania and Russia could further complicate relations with these states.

Thus far, full-scale upheaval has been limited to former Yugoslavia. But the absence of a collective security apparatus and the deep emotional, economic and historic roots of nationalism, could push shaky governments to move from brinksmanship to belligerence. Throughout the history of East-Central Europe, jingoism and scapegoating have been used by besieged governments to divert attention from failed policies, and playing the nationalism card remains a dangerous game from Serbia to Romania.

The authoritarian temptation

How is democracy doing in a region that, even before the advent of Bolshevism, had a baleful track record in institutionalizing genuine pluralism and maintaining democratic institutions? While it is risky to generalize about an area as diverse as East-Central Europe, most nations face certain fundamental challenges: often weak and underdeveloped non-Communist political parties, decommunization of governmental and nongovernmental institutions, the establishment of the rule of law, effective governance in the face of growing resistance to radical free market reforms, the burden of rebuilding statist economies, and weeding out corruption and lawlessness.

In some cases, a democratic transition has been rendered more difficult by renewed vigor of ex-Communist and new-left parties and a political ethos informed by 40 years of intrusive government bureaucracy and cumbersome state planning. This notion of government's omnipotent (if not omniscient) role permeated not only the mindset of ruling elites, but also the ruled and, to some extent, dissidents working for change, many of whom found themselves in positions of authority. Moreover, in virtually all the countries there is a marked dichotomy between urban and rural areas, with the former generally progressive and better-informed and the latter more conservative and suspicious of change, fertile ground for opportunistic ex-Communists and ultranationalists. Increased voter apathy, as unrealistic expectations of democracy's quick-fix solutions have faded, has tempted some post-Communist governments to flirt with reflex authoritarianism. Three years ago, social democratic Scandinavia, where capitalism is tempered by social safety nets and broad civil liberties, was held up as a possible model; today, one often hears references to Pinochet's Chile.

There is a widening gulf between citizens, many of whom naively equated democracy and free-markets with overnight, universal access to affordable consumer goods, food, etc., and frustrated reformers unable to convince them that prosperity and social stability are a long-term proposition requiring sacrifice and psychological readjustment. Because civil society, the traditional buffer between government and the governed, is still in a toddler stage, civic education, objective information, and the articulation of a new social compact need to be broadly accepted if democracy is to be firmly anchored.

In the main, political party systems remain weak or fragmented, riven by ideological and personality squabbles and often outmatched by better disciplined ex-Communists reorganized as *soi-disant* socialist successor parties. From Czechoslovakia to Poland, many former multi-party opposition coalitions forged immediately after the fall of Communist regimes are either defunct, badly splintered or ineffective. In Bulgaria, President Zhelev of the umbrella UDF narrowly defeated Socialist Party (ex-Communist) Velko Vakanov 53 to 46.5 percent in presidential elections, reflecting the lingering appeal of socialist positions and growing disillusionment with the UDF's often confrontational style of governance. After surviving several nonconfidence attempts, the government of UDF Prime Minister Dimitrov was toppled in October 1992, brought down by a temporary alliance of the SP and the Turkish-based Movement for Rights and Freedom (MRF). The UDF will likely be able to recobble a ruling coalition, but political uncertainty has discouraged foreign investment and the inflow of private capital.

In Albania, the Democratic Party (DP) handily beat the Communist party in March 1992 elections under a new system that intentionally decreased the importance of rural, pro-Communist areas. But President Sali Berisha, the first non-Communist president since World War II, was beset by widescale corruption, a vitiated economy and dramatic upsurge in crime and anti-government protests. By June, the DP was badly split, and many moderates were subsequently purged amid growing accusations that the government was becoming more authoritarian. By July, the Socialists swept local elections, pointing to growing public discontent with the scope, pace and character of change. In response, Socialists faced persecution and intimidation. Meanwhile, Albanians continued to vote with their feet; in 1992 thousands tried to join the hundreds of thousands who had already fled.

A similar scenario was played out in Romania. In local elections in February, the ruling DNSF was trounced in Bucharest and other cities, but in September's presidential and parliamentary vote the eighteen-member opposition coalition, Democratic Convention, again fared poorly in the countryside. With a fragmented parliament, President Iliescu already has announced his government will roll back economic reforms, an obvious pitch to potential rightist coalition partners. Romanians, too, voted with their feet; 2 million are believed to have emigrated since 1989, including young professionals.

In Serbia, hard-line neo-Communist Slobodan Milosevic has managed to cow a defensive and fractious opposition and forestall a democratic transition. The Democratic Party of Serbia has split into at least two factions, with one group siding with Prime Minister Milan Panic and President Dobrica Cosic of the rump-Yugoslavia. The Serbian Renewal Movement under formerly ultranationalist Vuk Draskovic has lost a number of supporters. The umbrella Democratic Movement of Serbia (DEPOS) coalition and the intellectuals grouped in the Civic Alliance, have been unable to muster much support outside Belgrade. Milosevic has obstructed a new election law, and used police crackdowns, restricted access to independent sources of information, and manipulated ethnic antagonisms to hold onto power.

In Croatia, President Franjo Tudjman and his Croatian Democratic Union (HDZ) were re-elected in 1992. To dampen dissent, the government began to show authoritarian tendencies. Mid- and high-level officials not loyal to the HDZ were purged from the federal and many local governments. Pressure was put on media considered too critical of the regime. Croatia's 1990 constitution accorded the president significant powers, and Tudjman has relied on government institutions he had appointed, though the necessity for strong central leadership has been accepted by beleaguered Croatians.

Hungary, which began political reforms from the top and much sooner than other countries, appears to have a relatively effective and democratic multiparty system. But the ruling MDF coalition is feeling internal pressure from its suddenly vocal nationalist right-wing. And while the democratic Alliance of Free Democrats and FIDESZ remain a formidable opposition, the Hungarian Socialist Party (HSP), made up largely of prominent reform Communists, is a viable force. In a 1992 parliamentary by-election, the HSP finished second behind FIDESZ, with the MDF third. Given Hungarians' traditional pessimism, deepening economic recession and the influx of 50,000 Balkan refugees, it remains to be seen if the MDF will give in to the authoritarian temptation.

Poland suffers from a surfeit of parties. In 1992, some 29 bickering parties gridlocked parliament, forcing the resignation of two prime ministers and exasperating President Lech Walesa. In August, parliament adopted the so-called "little constitution," a compromise that confirmed Poland's presidential-parliamentary system and clearly delineated the duties of the executive and legislature. Nevertheless, without a new, post-Communist constitution, fears persist that the "special powers" granted the Sejm to issue decrees in certain areas and Walesa's commitment to a strong presidency leave ample room for future conflict. The country's virulent anti-Communism makes the re-emergence of a unified, neo-Communist left highly unlikely (though not impossible if the economy remains anemic over the next several years).

In 1992, Czechoslovakia moved to peacefully dissolve the 74-year-old union of Czechs and Slovaks. The results of June national and republic elections underscored irreconcilable political differences between Czechs and Slovaks, and often bitter negotiations focused on bringing an end to the country by 1 January 1993. The elections virtually wiped out the post-Communist elite that formed the heart of the now defunct Civic Forum, and the victories of pro-market technocrat Vaclav Klaus in the Czech lands and Vladimir Meciar's separatist-nationalist Movement for a Democratic Slovakia sealed the federation's fate. Meciar's rise to power raised the prospects of increased authoritarianism in Slovakia, as he reined in the opposition press, called for self-censorship and restricted some rights of the large Hungarian minority.

Today, neo-Communists remain at the helm in Serbia, Romania, and Slovakia. In Bulgaria, they constitute a major parliamentary block, and have won local elections in Albania. Communist-nationalist-populism remains a potent mix in rural areas throughout the region. To avoid fates like Lithuania's where reconstituted Communists, capitalizing on economic chaos, public anxiety, and inexperienced leadership, won a large majority in November 1992 elections, governments must accelerate decommunization, stamp out graft and systemic corruption and implement the rule of law.

De-communization, corruption and the rule of law

Virtually all emerging democracies are wrestling with the moral and legal conundrum of establishing the rule of law while decommunizing society, a process often at loggerheads with democratic principles and procedures. Paradoxically, only Bulgaria and Romania have new, post-Communist constitutions (though the latter includes some dubious provisions and both were implemented by neo-Communist governments), while other countries have muddled through on amended Communist documents, some of which include language and provisions unchanged since the 1950s. In a sense, some governments exist in a legalistic grey zone three years after the fall of old-line regimes. As to decommunization, governments are wary of treading a fine line between removal of Communist leaders who actually took part in serious crimes, and witch hunts, particularly since many government functionaries are former Party members.

In Poland, President Walesa and parliament managed to block rightists' calls for an across-the-board housecleaning, apparently acknowledging the Party's role in accepting the inevitability of a transition and keeping Soviet tanks at bay. Hungarians appear to view the Party as an early advocate of economic and political change that exchanged political reform for qualified prosperity under "goulash communism" after the 1956 revolution. Czechoslovakia has banned former senior Communists from public jobs (though not parliament) for five years, though in March 1992, more than 90 deputies opposed to the so-called *lustrace* law petitioned the Constitutional Court to examine the statute's constitutionality.

Bulgaria's privatization law bars Communists from holding any position in a private sector bank for five years. Attempts have also been made in Bulgaria to purge intelligence services and the military of Communists. Former leader Teodor Zhivkov was convicted and sentenced to seven years for corruption and embezzlement, and former Prime Minister Lukanov was arrested for graft.

In Romania, the ruling DNSF has, for obvious reasons, avoided a systemic purge of Communists, choosing instead to put several lower-echelon Ceausescu toadies in the dock. It has also been difficult to ferret out all former hardliners and KGB agents from security services.

On the upside, most East-Central European nations have taken steps toward institutionalizing the rule of law. Bulgaria, Czechoslovakia, Poland, Hungary and Romania have created Constitutional Courts as a final arbiter of constitutionality. They have been relatively effective in settling issues such as presidential power in Hungary and Poland. Because of the region's dearth of liberal traditions, there has been a temptation to put the rule of law on hold in favor of strong executives (Serbia, Croatia, Slovakia, Romania, et al), but pressures from growing civil society groups—as well as Western lenders and investors—have compelled post-Communist states to try and overcome such obstacles as a lack of qualified jurists and lawyers and institute independent judiciaries. But throughout the region, the creation of modern judicial systems from politicized institutions left by communism has proved daunting. Given the ongoing potential for political instability throughout the region, the lack of coherent, fully functional post-Communist constitutions that define the prerogatives of the different centers of power and guarantee basic human and civil rights is in itself a destabilizing factor.

Another destabilizing factor is ongoing corruption in government, particularly relationships between the nomenklatura and private business. Public discontent at the exploitation of power and privilege by the new elite could lead to social unrest and demands for law and order. In Albania, black-marketeering and corruption are rampant. In Bulgaria, former secret police officers and foreign trade companies siphoned off millions of dollars and spirited them abroad. Illegal drug trafficking and arms sales, though not as pervasive as under the old regime, still exist. Ill-defined privatization laws have led to a Wild West capitalism and profiteering throughout the region from Poland to sanction-busters in Serbia. Since many of the new capitalists are members of the nomenklatura, they form a stubborn obstacle to initiatives aimed at curbing their influence and power. As IMF Structural Adjustment Programs make aid and loans contingent on bottom-line cutbacks, citizens feeling the squeeze could constitute a potent political force, willing to scuttle reforms for cradle-to-grave safety nets that once kept everyone beholden to a paternalistic government.

Prospects: more gloom than doom

While some issues discussed above seem to portend an ominous turn in East-Central Europe's democratic transition, there are many encouraging signs that at least some of the nations will succeed. A year-old Freedom House poll in Czechoslovakia, Hungary and Poland did find a degree of pessimism as people looked ahead to the next five years, but few expressed a desire for a return to totalitarianism. And while many felt that a measure of authoritarianism might be needed—a strong central government to guide the dramatic social and economic changes—others saw the need for strengthening political parties and other institutions.

It is difficult to imagine citizens liberated from Communist constraints want to return to the stultifying drabness of socialist bromides about productivity quotas, and life without the right to speak openly. The genie is out of the bottle, and technology has made the world too small to rebuild Berlin Walls, real or figurative. Perhaps most encouraging, from Romania to Poland the last three years have seen a deepening of the civil society: nongovernmental human rights groups, lawyer associations, businessmen's groups, religious institutions, independent media watchdog groups, think-tanks, and independent polling organizations. As these gain strength, influence and acceptance, they cement the very foundation of democratic societies. Measured progress has been made in human rights and the rule of law. Even more significantly, a number of East-Central European nations are seeking to reintegrate into Europe, to form the kind of security and economic interdependencies that provide mechanisms for averting conflict.

But there is always a to-be-sure clause. Nondemocratic traditions and a history of intolerance are difficult to overcome. In a cauldron of nationalities and ethnic groups, it is too easy to stir up hatred and instability. It is foolhardy to expect people not to be shell-shocked by skyrocketing prices, no job security, and basic goods and services suddenly out of reach. Gloom has shrouded much of East-Central Europe, but prescriptions of doom are certainly premature. But to preclude regression—not to mention the spread of the Balkan war— the West must also be prepared, through NATO, the CSCE, the U.N. or other organizations to guarantee the collective security of a region that, after the collapse of the Warsaw Pact, lies at the mercy of its own often bloody history. ▬

George Zarycky is Central European specialist for Freedom House.

The Survey 1993—
The Year in Review

Since the *Survey* was placed on a comparative basis twenty-two years ago, the difficulties in evaluating the state of freedom have multiplied. Since the end of the Cold War in 1989, the rate of political change has accelerated each year, spinning off new permutations and hybrids of political systems and leading to a democratic renaissance.

Few of the repressive regimes from the 1970s exist today. That era's remnants are: five classical Communist regimes, the most significant being the People's Republic of China (PRC); and a few one-party states, military governments and traditional monarchies. The number of democracies has grown from 44 in 1972 to 57 in 1983 to 99 this year. Other countries may become formal democracies in early 1993. In addition, 31 countries with authoritarian systems are at various stages of liberalization.

The *Survey* for 1993 is a snapshot of the world at a juncture where democracies may continue to consolidate or suffer a series of setbacks.

23 Countries that changed categories

Country	1992	1993
Algeria	Partly Free	Not Free
Angola	Partly Free	Not Free
Bhutan	Partly Free	Not Free
Burkina Faso	Not Free	Partly Free
Burundi	Not Free	Partly Free
Estonia	Free	Partly Free
Georgia	Not Free	Partly Free
Ghana	Not Free	Partly Free
Guinea	Not Free	Partly Free
Kenya	Not Free	Partly Free
Kuwait	Not Free	Partly Free
Latvia	Free	Partly Free
Mali	Partly Free	Free
Oman	Not Free	Partly Free
Seychelles	Not Free	Partly Free
Sierra Leone	Partly Free	Not Free
Tajikistan	Partly Free	Not Free
Tanzania	Not Free	Partly Free
Turkmenistan	Partly Free	Not Free
United Arab Emirates	Not Free	Partly Free
Uzbekistan	Partly Free	Not Free
Venezuela	Free	Partly Free
Yugoslavia	Not Free	Partly Free

New Countries Rated Previously as Part of Another Country

Bosnia-Herzegovina	Not Free
Macedonia	Partly Free

New Territories Rated Previously as Part of A Country

Aland Islands (Finland)	Free
Kosovo (Yugoslavia)	Not Free
Kurdistan (Iraq)	Partly Free
Svalbard (Norway)	Free
Vojvodina (Yugoslavia)	Not Free

Nineteen-ninety-two showed a startling increase in the number of countries whose ratings have changed. In 1989, an unprecedented 27 nations changed ratings, and in 1991, 58 changed, indications of radical political change in the world. These record numbers continued in 1992, with 23 countries changing categories and another 50 changing within categories. Thirty-nine countries improved their human rights situations, the same figure as in 1991, while 31 registered declines, nearly double that of the previous year. The previous year saw 6 more countries changing their categories than in 1992.

At the beginning of 1993, there are 75 *Free*, 73 *Partly Free,* and 38 *Not Free* countries. There was a net loss of one *Free* country and four *Not Free* countries, and a gain of eight *Partly Free* countries. There are 48 *Free* territories, 12 *Not Free* and 6 *Partly Free.* With regard to population, there is very little change from last year, one-quarter of the earth living in *Free* countries and 31 percent in *Not Free* countries. Forty-Four percent of the world live in *Partly Free* countries undergoing rapid political change.

Free countries

Within the community of *Free* countries, the changing demographics of Europe and the aging of developed democracies heralded an era of increased ethnic and racial fragmentation, corruption and the rise of neo-Nazi associations.

The 12 Worst Rated Countries

Burma (Myanmar)
China
Cuba
Haiti
Iraq
North Korea
Libya
Saudi Arabia
Somalia
Sudan
Syria
Vietnam

The 3 Worst Rated Related Territories

East Timor (Indonesia)
Kosovo (Yugoslavia)
Tibet (China)

Last January, **Austria** arrested several right-wing extremists, including would-be Fuehrer Gottfried Kuessel. The unification of the Federal Republic of **Germany** was marred by an epidemic of far-right violence against immigrants from Romania, Turkey and the Balkan countries. The number of anti-foreigner attacks exceeded 1,600, with eleven deaths. The Baltic City of Rostock was rocked in August by a week-long attack against Gypsy refugees from Romania and Vietnamese "guest workers." The extreme right-wing Republikaner Party and the German People's Union (DVU) gained votes in state legislature elections in Baden-Wuertemberg and Schleswig-Holstein. In March, German legislators formed a commission chaired by Rainer Eppelmann, a former opposition leader in East Germany, to investigate forty years of Communist rule. Information concerning the collaboration by many prominent East German politicians with the former secret service, STASI, affected several leaders, including Brandenberg Prime Minister Manfred Stolpe.

In **France**, several local authorities banned National Front rallies and prohibited its use of public forums. Italy's rating declined this year because of the tremendous rise in Mafia violence. The revelation of widespread corruption linking **Japan**'s Liberal Democratic Party and organized crime dominated that country's public debate.

Canada's electorate rejected a major constitutional reform package—the Charlottetown agreement—by a wide margin in an October referendum, perhaps paving the way for Quebec's withdrawal from the dominion. Throughout the presidential election year in the **United States**, voters registered dissatisfaction with their elected representatives and gave billionaire and amateur politician Ross Perot the largest third party showing since early in the twentieth century.

After becoming a full member of the United Nations in March, the world's oldest republic, **San Marino**, is included in the *Survey* as a country. This year **Liechtenstein** represents the unusual case of a free country having been mistakenly invaded by another free country-**Switzerland**—during a military exercise.

The democracies of the post-Communist world were confronted with the problems of rapid economic reform, withdrawal of Soviet assistance, and fragile, political institutions.

The neo-Communist Democratic Labor Party was returned to power in **Lithuania** with

26 Gains in Freedom without changing category

Afghanistan
Albania
Armenia
Bahamas
Belarus
Cape Verde
Comoros
Congo
El Salvador
Equatorial Guinea
Ethiopia
Fiji
The Gambia
Guyana
Jordan
Kyrgyzstan
Lebanon
Mexico
Namibia
Niger
Romania
Rwanda
Slovenia
Suriname
Thailand
Yemen

21 Declines in Freedom without changing category

Argentina
Brunei
Croatia
Djibouti
Egypt
Gabon
Guatemala
Iran
Italy
Kazakhstan
Mauritius
Moldova
Morocco
Nicaragua
Panama
Peru
Qatar
Russia
Saudi Arabia
Singapore
Tunisia

Gains and Declines in Freedom Without Changing Category

Laos, Malawi, and Mongolia both gained and declined in the ratings. Laos, rated 6,7 in 1992, changed to 7,6 in 1993. Malawi, rated 7,6 in 1992, changed to 6,7 in 1993. Mongolia, rated 2,3 in 1992, changed to 3,2 in 1993.

an overwhelming electoral victory. Lithuanians also approved by referendum a presidential/parliamentary system of government. A backlash against radical economic reforms brought the neo-Communist People's Revolutionary Party back to power in **Mongolia**. The democratic parties protested the former Communists' advantages of funding, gasoline rations and training by the Chinese. **Poland** weathered political uncertainty and the largest wave of labor unrest since the fall of communism in 1989.

Czechoslovakia moved to peacefully dissolve its union of Czechs and Slovaks after the victory of nationalist, neo-Communist Vladimir Meciar's Movement for a Democratic Slovakia. Meciar reined in the opposition press, called for self-censorship and restricted some rights of Slovakia's Hungarian minority, raising the specter of increased authoritarianism in an independent Slovakia.

The year saw **Hungary**'s Prime Minister Jozef Antall under pressure by the nationalist wing of his ruling Hungarian Democratic Forum and the comeback of the former Communists, the Hungarian Socialist Party. In March, the Constitutional Court overturned a law that would have allowed the government to try former Communists who committed human rights violations during four decades of Communist rule.

Bulgaria held its first direct presidential elections and re-elected President Zhelyu Zhelyev to a five-year term. One year after the Union of Democratic Forces (UDF), the coalition of pro-democracy groups in the country, won elections to parliament, UDF Prime Minister Filip Dimitrov was forced to resign after a no confidence vote. The UDF accused the neo-Communist

Bulgarian Socialist Party of preparing a coup to overthrow the government. The government also set about reorganizing the Bulgarian intelligence services and investigating its notorious past.

Slovenia consolidated its newly won independence by strengthening its governmental institutions and electing a moderate government.

Latin American democracies began their democratic maturing process with widespread discussions over presidential powers and with the initiation of economic reforms.

Scandals involving both financial and political corruption swirled around President Carlos Menem in **Argentina**. He packed the Supreme Court during the year and used it to uphold executive orders that removed officials given the mandate to investigate political wrongdoing.

In **Bolivia**, four factions of the army and navy issued anonymous communiqués against military spending and government corruption, while supporting the coup-plotters in Venezuela.

The 1989 election of President Collor de Mello in **Brazil** signaled that a new generation had arrived in that country's politics. He was soon caught, however, at the center of a multi-million dollar graft and influence-peddling scheme involving close political associates and members of his family. The Brazilian Congress suspended him in September and he later attained the dubious distinction of being the first Latin American president removed by the constitutional means of an impeachment process.

The Coalition for Democracy led by President Patricio Aylwin won a decisive victory in the first municipal elections held in **Chile** in two decades. Throughout the year there were allegations that the armed forces were spying on politicians. General Augusto Pinochet placed the army on alert and initiated sedition charges against the state television station and an independent newspaper. But the Coalition may soon achieve the two-thirds legislative majority needed to subordinate the armed forces to civilian rule.

In the Central American country of **Honduras**, Congress shied away from a proposed bill to place the armed forces under control of the elected civilian government. Sporadic left-wing violence and political killings by the military increased this past year. Sixto Duran Bullen won the July elections in **Ecuador** but soon faced a wave of protests and criminal activity because of his economic restructuring package. After twenty-five years of political control and patronage in the **Bahamas**, Prime Minister Lynden O. Pindling and his ruling Progressive Liberal Party were swept from power in August by the Free National Movement.

On the Asian subcontinent, **Bangladesh** continued a smooth democratic transition under Prime Minister Khaleda Zia but continued to be plagued by the longstanding insurgency in the Chittagong Hill Tracts and the influx of 265,000 refugees from Burma's military regime.

The island democracy of **Papua New Guinea** saw a record number of incumbents defeated in the parliamentary elections. While the government declared victory in its three-year battle with secessionists on Bougainville Island, it faced possible new revolts on the out islands after it proposed closing down provincial governments.

In the Middle East, the first Labor Party victory over Likud in fifteen years marked a shift in **Israel** to greater flexibility in the peace negotiations with the Arabs.

In Africa, the Alliance for Democracy in **Mali** won the April elections. Its victory culminated the process begun last year with the overthrow of General Moussa Traore, the country's ruler of twenty-three years and moved Mali into the *Free* category. **Benin**'s President Nicephore Soglo fended off a military uprising at mid-year and brought corrupt officials to trial. The first year of **Zambia**'s multi-party system saw students and trade unionists protesting against the Chiluba government's implementation of an austerity economic program. Faced with the withdrawal of South African economic support and an economic depression, **Namibia** continued the consolidation of its democracy and SWAPO pulled ahead of other parties in local elections. Clashes between army troops and paramilitary police marred **Sao Tome**'s first year since free elections. President Miguel dos Anjos Trovoada dismissed the government of Prime Minister Daniel dos Santos Daio in what critics termed a "constitutional" *coup d'etat* because of popular resistance to the new structural adjustment program.

Partly Free countries

Three nations rated *Free* last year, fell to *Partly Free* this year—**Estonia, Latvia** and **Venezuela**. Since the fall of the Perez Jimenez dictatorship in 1958, Venezuela has justifiably been viewed as a model of a federal democracy for Latin America. Sadly, for the first time since the *Survey* adopted comparative ratings, the country has fallen into the *Partly Free* category after several coup attempts against the administration of Carlos Andres Perez and often violent resistance to his economic programs. Perez, a genuine hero for his role in the country's democratic revolution, narrowly escaped several assassination attempts.

The Baltic countries of Estonia and Latvia adopted steps to restrict citizenship and exclude Russian-speaking inhabitants. After Estonia passed its citizenship laws, largely disenfranchising 600,000 Russian-speakers, the Russian parliament retaliated with the suspension of the 1991 interstate treaty and economic and trade sanctions. During the summer, tensions led to the eruption of armed clashes between the Estonian Defense Union and Russian troops.

Latvia's first full year of independence after a half century of Soviet occupation saw the expulsion of Russian-speaking deputies from parliament and the disclosure of the names of former Communist party members who had appealed to Moscow the previous year to institute Soviet presidential rule over the country. A parliamentary committee was founded to investigate these activities by anti-independence organizations. In March, the Supreme Court appointed a special commission to investigate crimes against humanity in the Nazi and Communist eras. The question concerning restrictive citizenship laws remains unresolved.

Within the *Partly Free* category, twenty-three formal democracies, as well as a large number of other countries, are transforming their political systems.

Older democracies such as Colombia and India continued their recent slide into corruption, insurgencies and ethnic or religious strife. **Taiwan** and **Paraguay** made rapid strides toward becoming freer societies.

Eleven of the republics that once composed the Soviet Union remained *Partly Free* because of the ongoing influence of hardliners and security forces, the rash of conflicts between subnationalities and the remaining fragility of new political institutions.

Within the category, fourteen African countries improved their ratings and another five declined.

In the Middle East, three nations—**Kuwait, Oman** and the **United Arab Emirates**—changed categories from *Not Free* to *Partly Free*. **Jordan, Lebanon** and **Yemen** improved their numerical ratings, while **Egypt** declined. In the Western hemisphere, gains were registered in **El Salvador, Guyana, Mexico** and **Suriname**. The Central American countries of **Guatemala, Nicaragua** and **Panama** continued to be marred by serious human rights violations, and the situation in Peru deteriorated as the constitutional order was suspended.

After new charges of corruption and the coalescense of the opposition, eighty-one-year old Prime Minister Vere Bird of **Antigua and Barbuda** announced he would step down after completing his term in 1994. The dramatic October elections in **Guyana** brought to an end twenty-eight years of authoritarian rule by the People's National Congress (PNC).

The victor, Cheddi Jagan of the People's Progressive Party (PPP), made rapid steps to end the influence of the military and police in the government.

The administration of Ronald Venetiaan in **Suriname** made significant progress toward the restoration of democratic rule. A peace accord was signed in August between the government and the Jungle Commando and the indigenous-based Tucuyana Amazonas. The role of the military was severely curtailed with the abolition of the People's Militia and conscription. The National Assembly unanimously approved constitutional amendments restricting the role of the military to national defense and combating "organized subversion," forcing former dictator Desi Bouterse to resign as head of the army.

Former Soviet Union and Baltic States

Country	1992	1993
Armenia	5,5 Partly Free	4,3 Partly Free
Azerbaijan	5,5 Partly Free	5,5 Partly Free
Belarus	4,4 Partly Free	4,3 Partly Free
Estonia	2,3 Free	3,3 Partly Free
Georgia	6,5 Not Free	4,5 Partly Free
Kazakhstan	5,4 Partly Free	5,5 Partly Free
Kyrgyzstan	5,4 Partly Free	4,2 Partly Free
Latvia	2,3 Free	3,3 Partly Free
Lithuania	2,3 Free	2,3 Free
Moldova	5,4 Partly Free	5,5 Partly Free
Russia	3,3 Partly Free	3,4 Partly Free
Tajikistan	5,5 Partly Free	6,6 Not Free
Turkmenistan	6,5 Partly Free	7,6 Not Free
Ukraine	3,3 Partly Free	3,3 Partly Free
Uzbekistan	6,5 Partly Free	6,6 Not Free

Former Yugoslavia Countries

Bosnia-Herzegovina	--	6,6 Not Free
Croatia	3,4 Partly Free	4,4 Partly Free
Macedonia	--	3,4 Partly Free
Slovenia	2,3 Free	2,2 Free
Yugoslavia	6,5 Not Free	6,5 Partly Free

Territories

Kosovo	--	7,7 Not Free
Vojvodina	--	6,5 Not Free

Gubernatorial elections were held in the key Mexican states of Michoacan and Chihuahua in July, with the Salinas government allowing the conservative PAN party to win the border state, while the PRI attempted to crush the opposition left-wing PRD. The Mexican government amended the constitution to restore the legal status of the Catholic Church and other religious organizations.

Human rights abuses and political violence in **Guatemala** were responsible for more deaths than in any other Latin American country with the exceptions of Colombia and Peru. Negotiations to end the decades-long guerrilla war remained stalemated and terror and street crime increased. In early 1992, hardline officers attempted to destabilize the Serrano administration with a wave of bomb attacks throughout the capital. The military high command made it clear it would not reduce the size of armed forces or dismantle the 500,000 member Civilian Self-Defense Patrols.

In **Nicaragua**, the government of Violetta Chamorro faced a situation where General Humberto Ortega emerged as the nation's strongman in the tradition of the former Somoza dynasty. Since 1991, **Panama**'s government of Guillermo Endara has faced nearly a dozen coup attempts by the pro-Noriega 20 December Movement and continues to rely on American presence for stability. The military was formally abolished this year and a government human rights office was established.

After twelve years of civil war **El Salvador** finally enjoyed a reprieve with a U.N. supervised ceasefire in February. The Cristiani government purged the military of the most flagrant human rights violators by November, leading to the FMLN guerrillas to start disarming in December.

After a serious effort at political reform, President Cesar Gaviria's government in **Colombia** faced a breakdown in peace negotiations with left-wing guerrillas who began a nationwide offensive against a background of increased drug-related violence.

In **Paraguay** the 1993 presidential elections will be the crucial test for the consolidation of democracy. The 1989 military coup that ended the thirty-five-year-old dictatorship of General Alfredo Stroessner led in June to the adoption of a new constitution and the preparation of cleaner electoral rolls for the future.

A major event in Latin America was the astonishing *auto-golpe* by President Alberto Fujimori in **Peru** and his subsequent capture of Abimael Guzmán, the leader of the Shining Path.

Throughout Asia, there have been improvements in human rights practices and significant progress toward democracy. The **Philippines** experienced its first peaceful transition of power in twentyseven years when Fidel Ramos succeeded Corazon Aquino in June. **Taiwan** relaxed its sedition law and held direct legislative elections. In May, **Fiji** held competitive elections under a constitution that ensures ethnic Fijians a perpetual majority in parliament. Wracked by religious and regional strife, **India** managed to hold elections in the Punjab for the first time in years. **Thailand**'s King Bhumipol intervened on 20 May and forced Prime Minister Suchinda to resign and the military to agree to a revised constitution curbing their powers.

There were setbacks, however. In **Malaysia,** opposition leader Lim Kit Siang was suspended from parliament after it adopted restrictive measures. There was a concerted government policy of sharp cutbacks in development funds for opposition-controlled states. After the ruling Golkar Party handily won the June elections in **Indonesia**, President Suharto announced he would seek a sixth term this year. Throughout the year, opposition meetings were banned. Nongovernmental organizations such as Legal Aid Institute and the Institute for the Defense of Human Rights interested in the East Timor situation were prohibited from accepting Dutch assistance.

Sri Lanka's President Premadasa survived a series of no-confidence motions and rejected opposition charges he had become too authoritarian. Tamils continued fighting in the north and east of the island, while India began repatriating some 200,000 Tamil refugees who had fled to the southern Indian State of Tamil Nadu to escape the fighting.

Throughout the Middle East this year there were contradictory trends of liberalization and repression. This was the bloodiest year in **Egypt** since the assassination of Anwar Sadat in 1981, as Muslim fundamentalists attacked Coptic Christians in the south. Reports that Hasan al-Turabi's movement was training guerrillas in the **Sudan** sparked new antiterrorist legislation. There were reports of torture, extra judicial round-ups and detention by the state security apparatus. Known for its relatively unfettered press, Egypt imposed an unprecedented degree of censorship.

The **Tunisian** government also continued its extensive crackdown on fundamentalists, especially the banned al-Nahda party. A very restrictive law on association passed in February 1992 effectively limited the work of the famous Tunisian Human Rights League, which finally chose to disband in June rather than obey the new statute.

At the beginning of the year, a leading theologian in **Bahrain** was arrested after delivering a lecture in Kuwait arguing for elected parliaments, freedom of expression and curbs on the Al-Khalifah family.

There were a few bright spots. **Jordan**'s King Hussein abolished the remnants of martial law in effect since 1967 and allowed the formation of political parties for the first time in thirtysix years. **Kuwait** re-established its parliament and held elections in October that unexpectedly led to a large victory for parties opposing the al-Sabah family. An historic moment occurred in May, when **Kurdistan** held its first open and fair elections and parliamentary seats were divided equally between the Barzani-led Kurdistan Democratic Party and the Talabani-led Patriotic Union of Kurdistan. **Morocco** adopted a new constitution that enlarges the powers of parliament and places limits on King Hassan II. The constitution says the monarch can no longer dissolve parliament and must choose the prime minister from among the electoral majority. King Hassan II, however, continues to play a dominant role in the country's political affairs.

Last December, **Oman** launched a twoyear experimental Majlis Al-Shura, or consultative council, with candidates elected popularly in each of the country's 59 provinces. The **United Arab Emirates** marginally improved and the rulers of each emirate now address citizen grievances and opinions in consultative councils. The country also has a budding woman's movement.

Within the *Partly Free* category, fourteen African nations improved their ratings, while another six declined, as the continent continued along its troubled path to multiparty systems. Seven subSaharan nations moved up from the *Not Free* into the *Partly Free* category.

Burkina Faso saw opposition figures included in the government cabinet and relatively clean legislative elections in May. **Burundi** made a cautious political opening. Yet, while the people of Burundi approved a multi-party constitution in March, the Special Investigation Police Brigade did not let up on its practice of murdering civilian opponents of the regime. **Ghana** conducted its first ever multiparty presidential and legislative elections in November and December, resulting in a victory for Flight Lieutenant Jerry Rawlings. International observer teams noted numerous electoral irregularities and restrictions on the opposition.

In **Guinea**, the pace of democratization accelerated when opposition parties were legalized on 3 April and a new constitution went into effect. **Kenya**'s President Daniel arap Moi, who has ruled the country since 1977, finally held multiparty elections for both the presidency and the parliament at the end of December. The people of the **Seychelles** rejected a government-sponsored constitutional proposal in the late 1992 referendum. The Revolutionary Party of **Tanzania** allowed opposition parties to form and operate, while deciding to maintain its twenty-seven-year rule until the 1995 elections.

The first ever multi-party election in the **Congo** was won by Pascal Lissouba of the Pan African Union for Social Democracy but gains toward a full democratic system were thwarted by military resistance to the changes and open attacks on opposition figures in December. After last year's commitment to establish a multi-party democracy, the government of the **Central African Republic** resisted significant reforms proposed by the opposition United Forces Coalition (UFD). In **Nigeria**, the Armed Forces Ruling Council cancelled the results of the electoral primaries, which the political parties alleged had been marred by fraud and vote-rigging. The military also arrested and charged human rights activists with conspiracy and treason in June. Throughout the year, political parties in **Niger** were legalized and the nomadic Tuaregs demanded an independent investigation into accusations of human rights abuses.

Madagascar's political transition degenerated toward civil war as the military made a bid for power and declared some coastal regions as self-governing. President Didier Ratsiraka's attempt to extend his eighteen-year rule over the country ended with his defeat in this year's election. In **Lesotho**, dethroned monarch King Moshoeshoe II was allowed to return from exile and the regime recognized the right of assembly for competing political parties. **Gabon** made hesitant progress toward competitive elections in 1993 but the government escalated its attacks on the opposition.

Ethiopia's muchanticipated democratization faltered when the postMengistu regime excluded the opposition from the June elections, in a vote international observers termed as highly irregular. **Eritrea** promised a referendum on the issue of independence in April 1993 and the Eritrean People's Liberation Front (EPLF) committed itself to multi-party elections.

South Africa's transition to a multiracial, multiparty democracy stalled as the negotiating parties disagreed over the percentages required to approve a new constitution and the issue of a minority veto. Violence continued to rock the country as the African National Congress (ANC) and the Inkatha Freedom Party (IFP) strongly contested the KwaZulu/Natal region, and South African security forces sought to weaken the ANC through a series of calculated attacks on its followers and smear campaigns aimed at discrediting political and military leaders.

Former Communist countries

The transitional post-Communist regimes that spun out of the former Soviet Union and Yugoslavia faced the tremendous challenges of creating democratic structures amid ethnic strife and resistance to economic reforms.

Russia's Boris Yeltsin, empowered last year to rule by decree, faced strong opposition from hardliners and state enterprise managers to roll back reform. The emergence of the conservative Civic Union as a powerful bloc in Congress threatened to bring more intense challenge to his rule by the end of the year. **Georgia**'s President Gamsakhudia fled office in January 1992 and was replaced by Eduard Shervadnadze. Some forty-six parties participated in the October elections for parliament. Ethnic conflicts continued in South Ossetia, which voted to join North Ossetia in Russia, and Abkhazia unilaterally declared its independence in July, provoking continued armed conflict. **Azerbaijan** saw the rise and fall of the Mutalibov government, as the country asserted direct rule over Nagorno-Karabakh. President Nursultan Nazarbaev of **Kazakhstan** remains reluctant to give up his authoritarian powers too rapidly, fearing an explosive ethnic conflict with the large ethnic Russian population. **Kyrgyzstan**'s "silk revolution" led by President Askar Akaev consolidated its democratic gains while administering an IMF-supported shock therapy program of economic reform. **Belarus** adopted a series of radical legal reforms and approved the first draft of a democratic constitution. The Kravchuk government in **Ukraine**, under pressure from the democratic opposition, named Leonid Kuchma as the country's new prime minister and empowered him to make sweeping market reforms.

Croatia's President Franjo Tudjman and his Democratic Union were reelected in 1992, enabling him to show strong authoritarian impulses and purge officials not loyal to his party. The country was engulfed in fighting throughout the region, absorbing nearly 580,000 refugees from the fighting in Bosnia and parts of Croatia. The government conducted sweeps rounding up Bosnian refugees, forcing them back to Bosnia for forced induction into the militias fighting the Serbs. In March, President Sali Berisjha became the first non-Communist president to rule **Albania** since World War II. Yet, after a series of antigovernment protests over economic policy, the neo-Communist Socialist Party swept the local elections. Two million people have left **Romania** since 1989. President Iliescu announced upon his re-election that his government would slow down the country's market reforms.

Not Free countries

The most flagrant violators of political rights and civil liberties are among the thirty-eight *Not Free* societies, as well as a number of societies controlled by royal dynasties, Communist parties and military juntas. This year's events in **Somalia** and the continuing civil war in **Liberia** dramatized the emerging phenomenon of nation-states disintegrating into anarchy.

U.N.-supervised elections in **Angola** led to a victory by governing party MPLA over UNITA. Before a required runoff between the two competing leaders, President Eduardo dos Santos and Dr. Jonas Savimbi, UNITA and the other smaller parties charged the government with voter intimidation and a pattern of voter irregularities they claimed disenfranchised their supporters. The breakdown in the ceasefire agreements led to a government-initiated air and ground offensive against UNITA's headquarters and strongholds in Luanda. Government troops summarily executed a UNITA negotiating team led by Vice-President Jeremias Chitunda. The year ended with UNITA returning towns it captured to government control and promising participation in a national unity government.

Major events in **China** centered around eighty-eight-year old Deng Xiaoping's efforts to move the country further toward a market-oriented economy without any major political adjustments. During the 14th Congress of the Chinese Communist Party, the armed forces received greater representation within the Central Committee, virtually precluding any political opening. Both **Vietnam** and **Laos** loosened central controls over their economies but maintained tight political controls. There were reports of acute shortages of food throughout **North Korea**, where an estimated 150,000 are said to be jailed as political prisoners.

The ruling military junta of **Burma** released political prisoners, reopened universities and lifted martial law but there was little movement toward an eventual transfer of power to civilian rule. In **Cambodia**, the complicated step-by-step peace process organized by the United Nations faced the single outstanding obstacle of the intransigence of the Khmer Rouge, which launched new offensives in Kompong Thom and Siem Riep provinces.

Faced with pressures created by regional liberalization, both **Bhutan** and **Brunei** embarked on new campaigns to legitimize royal rule. The government of King Wangchuk continued the process of "Bhutanization" by expelling some 100,000 ethnic Nepalese. The Sultanate of Brunei began to stress the policy of Malay Muslim monarchy, which upholds the king as the defender of Islam and promulgates a social order imbued with traditional Malay and Islamic values.

The long-awaited downfall of the Najibullah regime in **Afghanistan** did not lead to a peaceful transition of power. Competing guerrilla forces have stalled the reconstruction of a society in which 1 million people were killed during the conflict, 6.5 million people are refugees, and 2 million are internally displaced.

Authoritarian crackdowns marked the first years of independence for the former Soviet Central Asian republics of **Uzbekistan, Turkmenistan** and **Tajikistan.**

Algeria's much heralded transition to a multiparty system collapsed with the cancellation of the second round of elections after the Islamic Salvation Front (FIS) swept the December 1991 polls. The military forced the resignation of President Chadli Benjedid and dissolved the National Assembly and the Constitutional Council. Virtually all constitutional rights were suspended as the situation deteriorated into a year of assassinations and unrestricted detention.

Iraq's President Saddam Hussein continued to violate Gulf War ceasefire agreements by attacking Kurds in the north and Shiites in the far south. There were reports of conflicts between various security forces after a reported coup attempt by a brigade of the Republican Guard. U.N. Inspector Max van der Stoel said hundreds of thousands of Shiites, Kurds and political prisoners are in danger of execution and detention and that "scarcely a day passes without executions or hangings." Although Iran held its first parliamentary elections in four years, the Revolutionary Guards were used throughout the year to crush antigovernment protests. In March, King Fahd of **Saudi Arabia** put forth his plan to introduce a consultative council and some type of constitution, while encouraging a crackdown on behavior deemed anti-Islamic.

Sub-Saharan Africa

Despite improvements throughout subSaharan Africa, the continent remains the focus for serious human rights abuses and the suppression of freedom. A consortium of West African troops have had mixed results in maintaining peace in **Liberia** where 20,000 have died in a civil war between three guerrilla movements. Despite last year's promise of a political opening, the **Chad** government of

The Global Trend

	Free	Partly Free	Not Free
1983	55	76	64
1992	76	65	42
1993	75	73	38

Idris Deby dissolved the National Assembly and suspended the constitution. Military conflicts with the followers of deposed president Hissein Habre continued. In July, the **Sudan** government initiated a massive resettlement program, destroying nearly 500,000 homes.

Democratic transitions were reversed in a number of African countries. In **Sierra Leone** the military overthrew President Joseph Mompoh, dissolved the parliament and suspended the 1991 democratic constitution. The military restored order in **Cameroon** after President Paul Biya was unexpectedly declared the winner of the October elections, which the opposition charged were fraudulent. International observers claimed the first multi-party elections in **Mauritania** were marked by vote-buying, intimidation and the falsification of voter registration cards and lists, and security forces raided the opposition party's headquarters in Nouyakchott. There remain 100,000 Mauritanians who are personal slaves. By October, ninety-one-year-old Hastings Banda of **Malawi** announced he would hold a referendum to determine the popularity of multi-partyism. During the year the Catholic Bishops circulated a pastoral letter criticizing the regime's human rights record. Subsequently, the archbishop and six bishops were arrested, sparking massive student protests at the University of Malawi, which were suppressed by the military. **Togo**'s year was marked by several assassination attempts against prominent opponents of the Eyadema regime. After allowing cosmetic liberalization, **Equatorial Guinea** jailed opponents who returned from exile in Spain and France on a guarantee of amnesty.

Mass starvation claimed some 300,000 **Somali** lives in 1992, including more than 25 percent of Somali children under the age of five. By early December, with nearly 2 million Somalis threatened by famine and warlords blocking Western relief supplies, the United Nations Security Council voted to send an American-led military force to Somalia to facilitate relief missions.

In the Western Hemisphere, the two *Not Free* nations—**Cuba** and **Haiti**—showed no signs of improvement. Fidel Castro cracked down on dissidents and installed a Single Vigilance and Protection System that coordinates all the security forces against internal and perceived external threats. The regime continues to stonewall the United Nations Representative on human rights in Cuba.

Freedom House's concern

The *Survey* underscores Freedom House's concern that human rights and the enhancement of democratic institutions and movements abroad be central concerns of American citizens. We urge the new Clinton administration in Washington to assert that a world that observes human rights is consistent with American national interests. There must be heightened efforts by humanitarian agencies and nongovernmental organizations to support those risking their lives for a freer and more peaceful world. ▬

The Map of Freedom—1993

(Numbers refer to the map, pages 68-69)

FREE STATES

9	Argentina	40	Chile	89	Iceland	131	Mongolia
10	Australia	49	Costa Rica	94	Ireland	180	Namibia
11	Austria	51	Cyprus (G)	96	Israel	135	Nauru
13	Bahamas	223	Czecho-Slovakia	97	Italy	136	Nepal
15	Bangladesh	53	Denmark	99	Jamaica	137	Netherlands
16	Barbados	55	Dominica	100	Japan	141	New Zealand
18	Belgium	56	Dominican Rep.	104	Kiribati	148	Norway
19	Belize	58	Ecuador	106	Korea (S)	153	Papua New Guinea
20	Benin	66	Finland	113	Liechtenstein	224	Poland
23	Bolivia	67	France	229	Lithuania	159	Portugal
25	Botswana	71	The Gambia	114	Luxembourg	166	St. Kitts-
26	Brazil	72	Germany	121	Mali		Nevis
29	Bulgaria	76	Greece	122	Malta	167	St. Lucia
33	Canada	78	Grenada	123	Marshall Islands	169	St. Vincent and
35	Cape Verde Isls.	86	Honduras	126	Mauritius		the Grenadines
		88	Hungary	129	Micronesia	170	San Marino

171	Sao Tome & Principe
243	Slovenia
177	Solomon Isls.
181	Spain
186	Sweden
187	Switzerland
195	Trinidad & Tobago
199	Tuvalu
203	United Kingdom
204	United States
206	Uruguay
140	Vanuatu
212	Western Samoa
217	Zambia

FREE RELATED TERRITORIES

249	Aland Isls. (Fin.)	36	Cayman Isls. (UK)	68	French Guiana (Fr)	124	Martinique (Fr)
4	Amer. Samoa (US)	157	Ceuta (Sp)	69	French Polynesia (Fr)	158	Melilla (Sp)
5	Andorra (Fr-Sp)	39	Channel Isls. (UK)	222	French Southern &	130	Monaco (Fr.)
7	Anguilla (UK)	43	Christmas Is. (Austral.)		Antarctic Terr. (Fr.)	132	Montserrat (UK)
138	Aruba (Ne)	44	Cocos (Keeling Isls.)	75	Gibraltar (UK)	139	Ne. Antilles (Ne)
12	Azores (Port)		(Austral.)	77	Greenland (Den)	225	New Caledonia (Fr)
21	Bermuda (UK)	48	Cook Isls. (NZ)	79	Guadeloupe (Fr)	145	Niue (NZ)
27	Br. Vir. Is. (UK)	57	Rapanui (Easter Is.)	80	Guam (US)	146	Norfolk Is. (Austral.)
34	Canary Isls. (Sp)		(Chile)	95	Isle of Man (UK)	147	No. Marianas (US)
		63	Falkland Is. (UK)	117	Madeira (Port)	17	Palau (Belau) (US)
		64	Faeroe Isls. (Den)	127	Mahore (Mayotte) (Fr)	220	Pitcairn Islands (UK)

160	Puerto Rico (US)
162	Reunion (Fr)
165	St. Helena and Dependencies (UK)
165a	Ascencion
165b	Tristan da Cunha
168	St. Pierre-Mq. (Fr)
250	Svalbard (Norway)
192	Tokelau (NZ)
198	Turks & Caicos Isls. (UK)
210	Virgin Isls. (US)
211	Wallis & Futuna Isls. (Fr)

PARTLY FREE STATES

2	Albania	60	El Salvador	235	Kyrgyzstan	155	Peru
8	Antigua	230	Estonia	228	Latvia	156	Philippines
	& Barbuda	62	Ethiopia	109	Lebanon	163	Romania
237	Armenia	65	Fiji	110	Lesotho	201	Russia
238	Azerbaijan	70	Gabon	246	Macedonia	173	Senegal
14	Bahrain	239	Georgia	116	Madagascar	174	Seychelles
233	Belarus	74	Ghana	119	Malaysia	176	Singapore
205	Burkina Faso	81	Guatemala	128	Mexico	179	South Africa
31	Burundi	82	Guinea	234	Moldova	182	Sri Lanka
37	Central African	83	Guinea-Bissau	133	Morocco	184	Suriname
	Republic	84	Guyana	134	Mozambique	185	Swaziland
45	Colombia	90	India	142	Nicaragua	42	Taiwan (China)
46	Comoros	91	Indonesia	143	Niger	189	Tanzania
47	Congo	98	Ivory Coast	144	Nigeria	190	Thailand
244	Croatia	101	Jordan	150	Oman	193	Tonga
59	Egypt	240	Kazakhstan	151	Pakistan	196	Tunisia
		103	Kenya	152	Panama	197	Turkey
		107	Kuwait	154	Paraguay	231	Ukraine

202	United Arab Emirates
208	Venezuela
73	Yemen
215	Yugoslavia
218	Zimbabwe

PARTLY FREE RELATED TERRITORIES

52	Cyprus (T)
232	Eritrea (Ethiopia)
87	Hong Kong (UK)
248	Kurdistan (Iraq)
115	Macao (Port)
245	Northern Ireland (UK)

NOT FREE STATES

1	Afghanistan	38	Chad	118	Malawi	241	Turkmenistan
3	Algeria	41	China (PRC)	120	Maldives	242	Uzbekistan
6	Angola	50	Cuba	125	Mauritania	200	Uganda
22	Bhutan	54	Djibouti	161	Qatar	209	Vietnam
247	Bosnia-	61	Equatorial Guinea	164	Rwanda	216	Zaire
	Herzegovina	85	Haiti	172	Saudi Arabia		
28	Brunei	92	Iran	175	Sierra Leone		
30	Burma (Myanmar)	93	Iraq	178	Somalia		
102	Cambodia	105	Korea (N)	183	Sudan		
32	Cameroon	108	Laos	188	Syria		
		111	Liberia	236	Tajikistan		
		112	Libya	191	Togo		

NOT FREE RELATED TERRITORIES

24	Bophuthatswana (SA)
219	Ciskei (SA)
214	East Timor (Indo.)
226	Irian Jaya (Indo.)
227	Kashmir (India)
251	Kosovo (Yugo.)
149	Occupied Territories (Isr.)
213	Tibet (China)
194	Transkei (SA)
207	Venda (SA)
252	Vojvodina (Yugo.)
221	Western Sahara (Mor.)

The Map of Freedom is based on data developed by Freedom House's *Comparative Survey of Freedom*. The *Survey* analyzes factors such as the degree to which fair and competitive elections occur, individual and group freedoms are guaranteed in practice, and press freedom exists. In some countries, the category reflects active citizen opposition rather than politcal rights granted by a government. More detailed and up-to-date *Survey* information may be obtained from Freedom House.

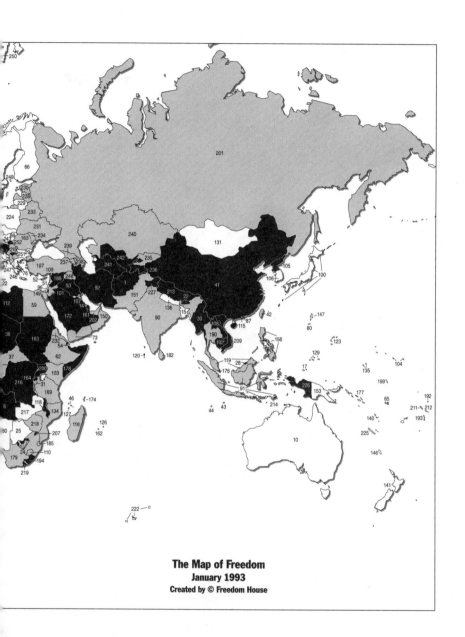

The Map of Freedom
January 1993
Created by © Freedom House

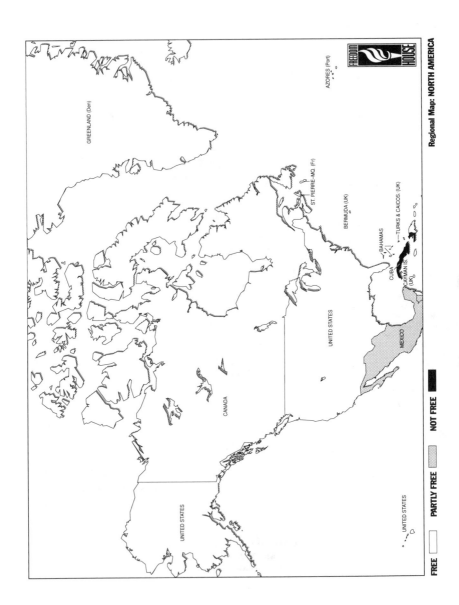

Regional Map: **NORTH AMERICA**

FREE ☐ PARTLY FREE ▨ NOT FREE ■

MEXICO

TURKS & CAICOS. (UK)

CUBA

CAYMAN IS. (UK)

HAITI

PUERTO
RICO (US)

VIRGIN IS. (US)

ST. KITTS–
NEVIS

GUATEMALA

BELIZE

JAMAICA

DOMINICAN REP.

BR. VIRGIN IS. (UK)

ANTIGUA & BARBUDA

MONTSERRAT (UK)

HONDURAS

NE. ANTILLES (Ne)

ANGUILLA (UK)

DOMINICA

NICARAGUA

ARUBA (Ne)

GUADELOUPE (Fr)

ST. LUCIA

MARTINIQUE (Fr)

EL SALVADOR

GRENADA

ST. VINCENT AND
THE GRENADINES

BARBADOS

COSTA RICA

TRINIDAD
& TOBAGO

PANAMA

VENEZUELA

GUYANA

COLOMBIA

SURINAME

FRENCH GUIANA (Fr)

ECUADOR

PERU

BRAZIL

BOLIVIA

RAPANUI/EASTER IS. (Chile)

PITCAIRN IS. (UK)

CHILE

PARAGUAY

URUGUAY

ARGENTINA

FALKLAND IS. (UK)

FREEDOM HOUSE

FREE   PARTLY FREE   NOT FREE

Regional Map: SOUTH AMERICA

SVALBARD
(Norway)

ICELAND

FAEROE IS. (Den)

FINLAND

SWEDEN

NORWAY

ALAND IS. (Fin.)

ESTONIA

RUSSIA

LATVIA

DENMARK

LITHUANIA

ISLE OF MAN (UK)

NORTHERN
IRELAND (UK)

BELARUS

IRELAND

NETHERLANDS

UNITED KINGDOM

POLAND

CHANNEL IS. (UK)

BELGIUM

GERMANY

UKRAINE

LUXEMBOURG

CZECHO-SLOVAKIA

SWITZERLAND

LIECHTENSTEIN

AUSTRIA

HUNGARY

MOLDOVA

ROMANIA

FRANCE

SLOVENIA

VOJVODINA
(Yugo.)

SAN MARINO

CROATIA

AZORES (Port)

ITALY

YUGOSLAVIA

BULGARIA

MONACO (Fr)

KOSOVO (Yugo.)

MACEDONIA

PORTUGAL

SPAIN

ANDORRA (Fr–Sp)

GREECE

TURKEY

ALBANIA

BOSNIA–
HERZEGOVINA

GIBRALTAR (UK)

MELILLA (Sp)

MALTA

CYPRUS(T)

MADEIRA (Port)

CEUTA (Sp)

CYPRUS (G)

FREEDOM
HOUSE

FREE PARTLY FREE NOT FREE

Regional Map: EUROPE

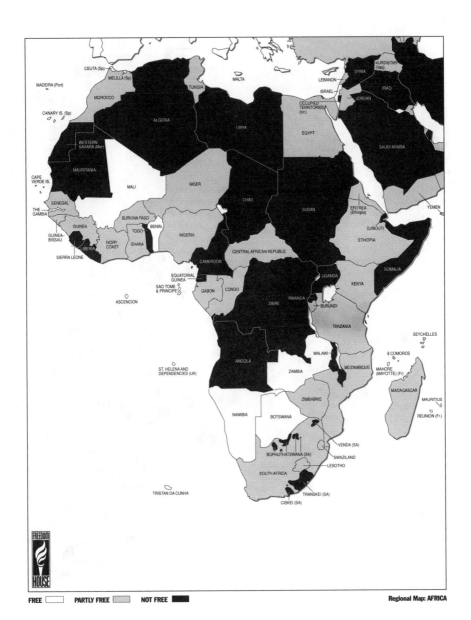

CEUTA (Sp)
MELILLA (Sp)
MADEIRA (Port)
CANARY IS. (Sp)
MOROCCO
WESTERN
SAHARA (Mor)
MAURITANIA
CAPE
VERDE IS.
THE
GAMBIA
SENEGAL
GUINEA-
BISSAU
GUINEA
SIERRA LEONE
LIBERIA
IVORY
COAST
BURKINA FASO
TOGO
BENIN
GHANA
NIGERIA
EQUATORIAL
GUINEA
SAO TOME
& PRINCIPE
ASCENCION
GABON
CONGO
ST. HELENA AND
DEPENDENCIES (UK)
ANGOLA
TRISTAN DA CUNHA
NAMIBIA
BOTSWANA
BOPHUTHATSWANA (SA)
SOUTH AFRICA
CISKEI (SA)
MALTA
TUNISIA
ALGERIA
MALI
NIGER
CHAD
LIBYA
EGYPT
SUDAN
CENTRAL AFRICAN REPUBLIC
CAMEROON
ZAIRE
RWANDA
BURUNDI
UGANDA
TANZANIA
MALAWI
ZAMBIA
ZIMBABWE
MOZAMBIQUE
VENDA (SA)
SWAZILAND
LESOTHO
TRANSKEI (SA)
LEBANON
ISRAEL
OCCUPIED
TERRITORIES
(Isr.)
SYRIA
KURDISTAN
(Iraq)
IRAQ
JORDAN
SAUDI ARABIA
ERITREA
(Ethiopia)
DJIBOUTI
ETHIOPIA
YEMEN
SOMALIA
KENYA
SEYCHELLES
COMOROS
MAHORE
(MAYOTTE) (Fr)
MADAGASCAR
MAURITIUS
REUNION (Fr.)

FREEDOM HOUSE

FREE ☐   PARTLY FREE ▒   NOT FREE ■

Regional Map: AFRICA

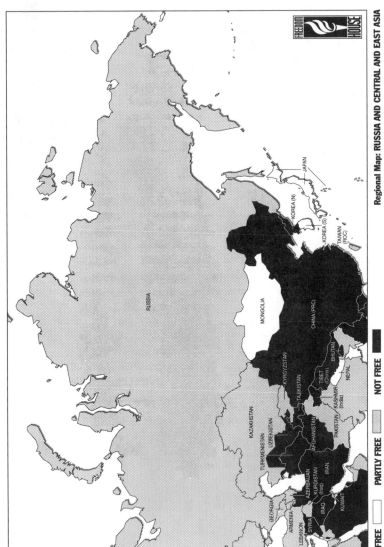

Regional Map: RUSSIA AND CENTRAL AND EAST ASIA

FREE PARTLY FREE NOT FREE

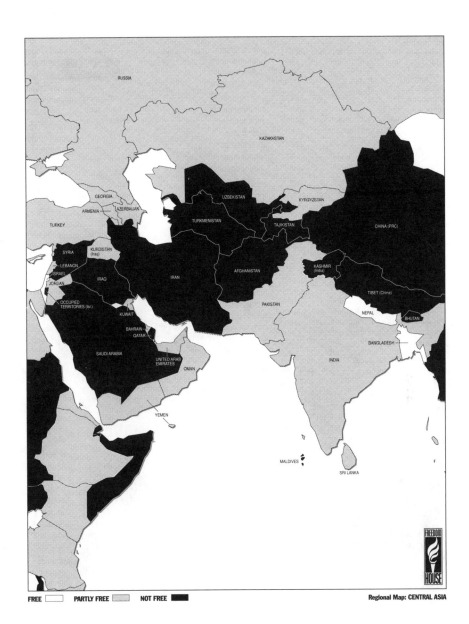

RUSSIA

KAZAKHSTAN

GEORGIA

ARMENIA AZERBAIJAN

TURKEY

UZBEKISTAN

KYRGYZSTAN

TURKMENISTAN

TAJIKISTAN

CHINA (PRC)

SYRIA

KURDISTAN
(Iraq)

LEBANON

ISRAEL

JORDAN

IRAQ

IRAN

AFGHANISTAN

KASHMIR
(India)

TIBET (China)

OCCUPIED
TERRITORIES (Isr.)

KUWAIT

PAKISTAN

NEPAL

BHUTAN

BAHRAIN

QATAR

BANGLADESH

SAUDI ARABIA

UNITED ARAB
EMIRATES

OMAN

INDIA

YEMEN

MALDIVES

SRI LANKA

FREE ☐   PARTLY FREE ▨   NOT FREE ■

Regional Map: CENTRAL ASIA

FREE   PARTLY FREE   NOT FREE

Regional Map: SOUTHEAST ASIA

The Comparative Survey of Freedom—1992-1993 Survey Methodology

Joseph E. Ryan

The purpose of the *Comparative Survey of Freedom* since its inception in the 1970s has been to provide an annual evaluation of political rights and civil liberties everywhere in the world.

The *Survey* attempts to judge all places by a single standard and to point out the importance of democracy and freedom. At a minimum, a democracy is a political system in which the people choose their authoritative leaders freely from among competing groups and individuals who were not chosen by the government. Putting it broadly, freedom is the chance to act spontaneously in a variety of fields outside the control of government and other centers of potential domination. Normally, Westerners associate the adherence to political rights and civil liberties with the liberal democracies, such as those in North America and the European Community. However, there are also Third World democracies such as Costa Rica and Botswana. In another case, Western Samoa combines political parties and competitive elections with power for the *matai*, the heads of extended families.

Freedom House does not view democracy as a static concept, and the *Survey* recognizes that a democratic country does not necessarily belong in our category of "free" states. A democracy can lose freedom and become merely "partly free." Sri Lanka and Colombia are examples of such "partly free" democracies. In other cases, countries that replaced military regimes with elected governments can have less than complete transitions to liberal democracy. El Salvador and Guatemala fit the description of this kind of "partly free" democracy. (For an explanation of the designations "free," "partly free," and "not free," see the section on The Map of Freedom below.)

Just as democracy is not a static concept, the *Survey* itself adapts to changing conditions. Readers of the previous editions of the *Survey* will note that the ratings of many countries and related territories have changed since 1989. Events have changed some ratings, but other changes reflect methodological refinements developed by the *Survey* team.

Definitions and categories of the *Survey*

The *Survey*'s understanding of freedom is broad and encompasses two sets of characteristics grouped under political rights and civil liberties. **Political rights** enable people to participate freely in the political process. By the political process, we mean the system by which the polity chooses the authoritative policy makers and attempts to make binding decisions affecting the national, regional or local community. In a free society this means the right of all adults to vote and compete for public office, and for elected representatives to have a decisive vote on public policies. A system is genuinely free or democratic to the extent that the people have a choice in determining the nature of the system and its leaders.

Civil liberties are the freedoms to develop views, institutions and personal autonomy apart from the state.

The *Survey* employs checklists for these rights and liberties to help determine the degree of freedom present in each country and related territory, and to help assign each entity to a comparative category.

The checklist for Political Rights

1. Is the head of state and/or head of government or other chief authority elected through free and fair elections?

2. Are the legislative representatives elected through free and fair elections?

3. Are there fair electoral laws, equal campaigning opportunities, fair polling and honest tabulation of ballots?

5. Do the people organize freely in different political parties or other competitive political groupings of their choice, and is the system open to the rise and fall of these competing parties or groupings?

6. Is there a significant opposition vote, *de facto* opposition power, and a realistic possibility for the opposition to increase its support or gain power through elections?

7. Does the country have the right of self-determination, and are its citizens free from domination by the military, foreign powers, totalitarian parties, religious hierarchies, economic oligarchies or any other powerful group?

8. Do cultural, ethnic, religious and other minority groups have reasonable self-determination, self-government, autonomy or participation through informal consensus in the decision-making process?

9. Is political power decentralized, allowing for local, regional and/or provincial or state administrations led by their freely elected officials? (For entities such as tiny island nations, the absence of a decentralized system does not necessarily count as a negative in the *Survey*.)

Additional discretionary political rights questions

A. For traditional monarchies that have no parties or electoral process, does the system provide for consultation with the people, encourage discussion of policy, and allow the right to petition the ruler?

B. Is the government or occupying power deliberately changing the ethnic composition of a country or territory so as to destroy a culture or tip the political balance in favor of another group? (Note: This question appears for the first time in the 1992-93 *Survey*.)

When answering the political rights questions, Freedom House considers the extent to which the system offers the voter the chance to make a free choice among competing candidates, and to what extent the candidates are chosen independently of the state. We recognize that formal electoral procedures are not the only factors that determine the real distribution of power. In many Latin American countries, for example, the military retains a significant political role, and in Morocco the king maintains significant power over the elected politicians. The more people suffer under such domination by unelected forces, the less chance the country has of getting credit for self-determination.

Freedom House does not have a culture-bound view of democracy. The *Survey* team rejects the notion that only Europeans and those of European descent qualify as democratic. The *Survey* demonstrates that, in addition to those in Europe and the Americas, there are free countries with varying kinds of democracy functioning among people of all races and religions in Africa, the Pacific and Asia. In some Pacific islands, free countries can have competitive political systems based on competing family groups and personalities rather than on European- or American-style parties.

The checklist for Civil Liberties

1. Are there free and independent media, literature and other cultural expressions? (Note: In cases where the media are state-controlled but offer pluralistic points of view, the *Survey* gives the system credit.)

2. Is there open public discussion and free private discussion?

3. Is there freedom of assembly and demonstration?

4. Is there freedom of political or quasi-political organization? (Note: This includes political parties, civic associations, ad hoc issue groups and so forth.)

5. Are citizens equal under the law, do they have access to an independent, nondiscriminatory judiciary, and are they respected by the security forces?

6. Is there protection from unjustified political terror, imprisonment, exile or torture, whether by groups that support or oppose the system, and freedom from war or insurgency situations? (Note: Freedom from war and insurgency situations enhances the liberties in a free society, but the absence of wars and insurgencies does not in itself make an unfree society free.)

7. Are there free trade unions and peasant organizations or equivalents?

8. Are there free professional and other private organizations?

9. Are there free businesses or cooperatives?

10. Are there free religious institutions and free private and public religious expressions?

11. Are there personal social freedoms, which include such aspects as gender equality, property rights, freedom of movement, choice of residence, and choice of marriage and size of family?

12. Is there equality of opportunity, which includes freedom from exploitation by or dependency on landlords, employers, union leaders, bureaucrats or any other type of denigrating obstacle to a share of legitimate economic gains?

13. Is there freedom from extreme government indifference and corruption?

When analyzing the civil liberties checklist, Freedom House does not mistake constitutional guarantees for the respect for human rights in practice. For tiny island countries and territories and other small entities with low populations, the absence of unions and other types of association does not necessarily count as a negative unless the government or other centers of domination are deliberately blocking association. The question on equality of opportunity also implies a free choice of employment and education. Extreme inequality of opportunity prevents disadvantaged individuals from enjoying a full exercise of civil liberties. Typically, desperately poor countries and territories lack both opportunities for economic advancement and the other liberties on this checklist. We have a question on gross indifference and corruption, because when governments do not care about the social and economic welfare of large sectors of the population, the human rights of those people suffer. Government corruption can pervert the political process and hamper the development of a free economy.

The *Survey* rates political rights and civil liberties separately on a seven-category scale, 1 representing the most free and 7 the least free. A country is assigned to a particular category based on responses to the checklist and the judgments of the *Survey* team at Freedom House. The numbers are not purely mechanical; they also reflect judgment. The team assigns initial ratings to countries by awarding from 0 to 2 points per checklist item, depending on the degree of compliance with the standard. The only exception to this is the discretionary question on cultural destruction and deliberate demographic change to tip the political balance. In that case, we subtract 1-2 points depending on the situation's severity. The highest possible score for political rights is 18 points, based on up to 2 points for each of nine questions.

The highest possible score for civil liberties is 26 points, based on up to 2 points for each of thirteen questions.

After placing countries in initial categories based on checklist points, the *Survey* team makes minor adjustments to account for factors such as extreme violence, whose intensity may not be reflected in answering the checklist questions. These exceptions aside, in the overwhelming number of cases, the checklist system reflects the real world situation and is adequate for placing countries and territories into the proper comparative categories.

The map on pages 68-69 divides the world into three large categories: "free," "partly free," and "not free." The *Survey* places countries and territories into this tripartite division by averaging the category numbers they received for political rights and civil liberties. Those whose category numbers average 1-2.5 are considered "free," 3-5.5 "partly free," and 5.5-7 "not free." The dividing line between "partly free" and "not free" falls within the group whose category numbers average 5.5. For example, countries that receive a rating of 6 for political rights and 5 for civil liberties, or a 5 for political rights and a 6 for civil liberties, could be either "partly free" or "not free." The total number of raw points is the factor which makes the difference between the two. Countries and territories with combined raw scores of 0-14 points are "not free," and those with combined raw scores of 15-29 points are "partly free." "Free" countries and territories have combined raw scores of 30-44 points.

The differences in raw points between countries in the three broad categories represent distinctions in the real world. There are obstacles which "partly free" countries must overcome before they can be called "free," just as there are impediments which prevent "not free" countries from being called "partly free." Countries at the lowest rung of the "free" category (category 2 in political rights, category 3 in civil liberties) differ from those at the upper end of the "partly free" group (category 3 in both). Typically, there is more violence and/ or military influence on politics at 3,3 than at 2,3 and the differences become more striking as one compares 2,3 with worse categories of the "partly free" countries.

The distinction between the least bad "not free" countries and the least free "partly free" may be less obvious than the gap between "partly free" and "free," but at "partly free," there is at least one extra factor that keeps a country from being assigned to the "not free" category. For example, Bahrain (6,5) has a system of consultation between ruler and subjects, and rights of petition. These are examples of aspects that separate this country from its "not free" neighbor, Iraq (7,7). The gap between "partly free" and "not free" is easier to see if one compares Zimbabwe (5,4) with Somalia (7,7). Zimbabwe has some independent political parties and nongovernmental institutions that function peaceably, while Somalia has violently destructive, competing "governments" that have left the country a wasteland of starving people and broken institutions.

Freedom House wishes to point out that the designation "free" does not mean that a country has perfect freedom or lacks serious problems. As an institution which advocates human rights, Freedom House remains concerned about a variety of social problems and civil liberties questions in the U.S. and other countries that the *Survey* places in the "free" category. Similarly, in no way does an improvement in a country's rating mean that human rights campaigns should cease. On the contrary, we wish to use the *Survey* as a prod to improve the condition of all countries.

The approach of the *Survey*

The *Survey* attempts to measure conditions as they really are around the world. This approach is distinct from relying on intense coverage by the American media as a guide to which countries are the least free. The publicity given problems in some countries does not necessarily mean that unpublicized problems of other countries are not more severe. For example, while U.S. television networks are allowed into Israel and El Salvador to cover abuses of human rights, they are not allowed to report freely in North Korea, which has far less freedom. To reach such comparative conclusions, Freedom House evaluates the development of democratic governmental institutions, or lack thereof, and also examines the quality of civil society, life outside the state structure.

Without a well-developed civil society, it is difficult, if not impossible, to have an atmosphere supportive of democracy. A society that does not have free individual and group expressions in nonpolitical matters is not likely to make an exception for political ones. As though to prove this, there is no country in the *Survey* that places in category 6 or 7 for civil liberties and, at the same time, in category 1 or 2 for political rights. In the overwhelming majority of cases in the *Survey*, countries and territories have ratings in political rights and civil liberties that are within two categories of each other.

Readers should not necessarily interpret the ratings as a commentary on the intentions of particular governments. Rather, the ratings represent Freedom House's evaluation of the countries' and territories' situations, which are formed by both governmental and nongovernmental factors.

The *Survey* rates both countries and related territories. For our purposes, countries are internationally recognized independent states whose governments are resident within their officially claimed territories. In the unusual case of Cyprus, we give two ratings, since there are two governments on that divided island. However, in the 1992-93 *Survey,* we have changed Turkish Cyprus from a country to related territory. By having participated in negotiations (albeit unsuccessful ones) to reach a settlement with the Greek Cypriots through the U.N. in 1992, the Turkish Cypriot government acknowledged implicitly that its unrecognized status is untenable. In no way does the listing of Turkish Cyprus as a related territory imply that Freedom House endorses Cypriot division. We note only that neither the predominantly Greek Republic of Cyprus nor the Turkish-occupied, predominantly Turkish Republic of Northern Cyprus is the *de facto* government for the entire island. An internationally recognized state, Monaco, counts as a related territory here, due to its officially dependent relationship with France and its lack of full U.N. membership. With that exception, related territories consist mostly of colonies, protectorates, occupied territories and island dependencies. Although many countries recognize the PLO as the government of Palestine, we do not count Palestine as an independent country, because the PLO does not govern a Palestinian state. Since the publication of our 1991-92 yearbook, Freedom House has carried separate ratings for the republics of the former Soviet Union and for Slovenia and Croatia, the first two internationally recognized republics of the former Yugoslavia. This edition of the *Survey* adds Bosnia-Herzegovina and Macedonia to the list of independent countries rated. The new Yugoslavia (not including the territories of Kosovo and Vojvodina), as rated in the *Survey*, is comprised of Montenegro and Serbia. We have designated Kosovo and Vojvodina as related territories, in order to call attention to their human rights situations and issues of self-determination. Similarly, Iraqi Kurdistan becomes a related territory this year, because the area has distinct human rights problems, held regional elections, and instituted self-government in 1992. Svalbard, a Norwegian Arctic territory with a Russian majority, and the Aland Islands, a Finnish territory with a Swedish majority, also become new related territories. Northern Ireland gained separate status as a related territory in our 1991-92 yearbook and is so designated in *Freedom Review* for the first time. Due to their increasing international recognition and full U.N. membership, Liechtenstein and San Marino change status from related territories to independent countries in this *Survey*.

The *Survey* excludes uninhabited related territories and entities such as the U.S.-owned Johnston Atoll, which has only a transient military population and no native inhabitants. Since most related territories have a broad range of civil liberties and some form of self-government, a higher proportion of them have the "free" designation than do independent countries. ▬

The Tabulated Ratings

The accompanying Table of Independent Countries (page 620) and Table of Related Territories (page 621) rate each country or territory on seven-category scales for political rights and civil liberties, and then place each entity into a broad category of "free," "partly free" or "not free." On each scale, 1 represents the most free and 7 the least free.

Political rights

In political rights, generally speaking, states rated 1 come closest to the ideals suggested by the checklist questions, beginning with free and fair elections. Those elected rule. There are competitive parties or other competitive political groupings, and the opposition has an important role and power. These entities have self-determination or an extremely high degree of autonomy (in the case of related territories). Usually, those rated 1 have self-determination for minority groups or their participation in government through informal consensus. With the exception of such entities as tiny island countries, these countries and territories have decentralized political power and free subnational elections.

Countries and territories rated 2 in political rights are free, but are less free than those rated 1. Such factors as violence, political discrimination against minorities, and foreign or military influence on politics are present, and weaken the quality of democracy.

The same factors that weaken freedom in category 2 may also undermine political rights in categories 3, 4, and 5. Other damaging conditions are at work as well, including civil war, very strong military involvement in politics, lingering royal power, unfair elections and one-party dominance. However, states and territories in these categories still have some elements of political rights such as the freedom to organize nongovernmental parties and quasi-political groups, reasonably free referenda, or other significant means of popular influence on government.

Typically, states and territories with political rights rated 6 have systems ruled by military juntas, one-party dictatorships, religious hierarchies and autocrats. These regimes allow only some minimal manifestation of political rights such as competitive local elections or some degree of representation or autonomy for minorities. A few states in category 6 are traditional monarchies that mitigate their relative lack of political rights through the use of consultation with their subjects, toleration of political discussion, and acceptance of petitions from the ruled.

Category 7 includes places where political rights are absent or virtually nonexistent, due to the extremely oppressive nature of the regime or extreme oppression in combination with civil war.

Civil liberties

States and territories rated 1 in civil liberties come closest to the ideals of freedoms of expression, assembly and demonstration, religion and association. They also do the comparatively best job of protecting the individual from political violence and from harms inflicted by courts and security forces. Entities in this category have free economic activity and tend to strive for equality of opportunity. There is no such thing as complete equality of opportunity, but free places tend to come comparatively closer to the ideal than less free ones. In general, these countries and territories are comparatively free of extreme government indifference or corruption.

The places in category 2 in civil liberties are not as free as those rated 1, but they are still relatively free. In general, these countries and territories have deficiencies in three or four aspects of civil liberties. In each case, the country would be generally free otherwise.

Independent countries and related territories with ratings of 3, 4 or 5 have progressively fewer civil liberties than those in category 2. States in these categories range from ones that are in at least partial compliance with virtually all checklist standards to those which have partial compliance with only eight standards. Some countries have a mixture of good civil liberties scores in some areas and zero or partial credit in others. As one moves down the scale below category 2, the level of oppression increases, especially in the areas of censorship, political terror and the prevention of free association. There are also many cases in which groups opposed to the state carry out political terror that undermines other freedoms. That means that a poor rating for a country is not necessarily a comment on the intentions of the government. The rating may simply reflect the real restrictions on liberty which can be caused by nongovernmental terror.

Typically, at category 6 in civil liberties, countries and territories have a few partial rights. For example, a country might have some religious freedom, some personal social freedoms, some highly restricted private business activity, and relatively free private discussion. In general, these states and territories restrict expression and association severely. There are almost always political prisoners and other manifestations of political terror.

At category 7, countries and territories have virtually no freedom. An overwhelming and justified fear of the state's repressive nature characterizes the society.

The accompanying Tables of Combined Average Ratings average the two seven-category scales of political rights and civil liberties into an overall freedom rating for each country and territory. ▄▄

Introduction to Country and Related Territory Reports

The *Survey* team at Freedom House wrote reports on 186 countries and 66 related territories. This yearbook is the first with separate reports on all former Soviet and Yugoslav republics. The Yugoslav regions of Kosovo and Vojvodina appear under the section on related territories.

The largely Greek Republic of Cyprus appears as a country, while Turkish-occupied Cyprus is a related territory. Iraqi Kurdistan, Svalbard (Norwegian), and the Aland Islands (Finnish) appear as related territories for the first time. Liechtenstein and San Marino join the country reports section in this edition. The information in the reports is accurate through 31 December 1992. Czecho-Slovakia, which split into the Czech Republic and Slovakia on 1 January 1993 appears here as a united country for the last time.

Each report begins with brief political, economic, and social data. This information is arranged under the following headings: **polity, economy, political rights, civil liberties, status, population, purchasing power parities (PPP), population, life expectancy,** and **ethnic groups.** More detailed information follows in an **overview** and in an essay on the political rights and civil liberties of each country.

Under **polity,** there is an encapsulated description of the dominant centers of freely chosen or unelected political power in each country. In some cases, the polity combines elected and unelected elements or freely and unfreely chosen branches of government. Most of the descriptions are self-explanatory, such as Communist one-party for China or parliamentary democracy for Ireland. Such non-parliamentary democracies as the United States of America are designated presidential-legislative democracies. European democratic countries with constitutional monarchs are designated parliamentary democracies, because the elected body is the locus of most real political power. Only countries with powerful monarchs (e.g. the Sultan of Brunei) warrant a reference to the monarchy in the brief description of the polity. Dominant party polities are systems in which the ruling party (or front) dominates government, but allows other parties to organize or compete short of taking control of government. There are other types of polities listed as well. Among them are various military and military-influenced or -dominated regimes, transitional systems, and several unique polities, such as Iran's clergy-dominated parliamentary system. Countries with genuine federalism have the word "federal" in the description.

The reports label the **economy** of each country. Non-industrial economies are called traditional or pre-industrial. Developed market economies and developing economies with a modern market sector have the designation capitalist. Mixed capitalist countries combine private enterprise with substantial government involvement in the economy for social welfare purposes. Capitalist-statist economies have both large market sectors and government-owned productive enterprises, due either to elitist economic policies or state dependence on key natural resource industries. Mixed capitalist-statist economies have the characteristics of capitalist-statist economies plus major social welfare programs. Statist systems have the goal of placing the entire economy under direct or indirect government control. Mixed statist economies are primarily government-controlled, but also have significant private enterprise. Developing economies with a government-directed modern sector belong in the statist category. Economies in transition between statist and capitalist forms may have the word "transitional" in the economy description.

Each country report mentions the category of **political rights** and **civil liberties** in which Freedom House classified the country. Category 1 is the most free and category 7 is the least free in each case. **Status** refers to the designations "free," "partly free," and "not free" which Freedom House uses as an overall summary of the general state of freedom in the country.

Each entry includes a **population** figure which is sometimes the best approximation available. For all cases in which the information is available, the *Survey* provides **life expectancy** statistics.

Freedom House obtained the **Purchasing Power Parities (PPP)** from the U.N. Development Program. These figures show per capita gross domestic product (GDP) in terms of international dollars. The PPP statistic adjusts GDP to account for real buying power. For some countries, especially for newly independent countries, tiny island states, and those with statist economies, these statistics were unavailable.

The *Survey* provides a listing of countries' **ethnic groups**, because this information may help the reader understand such questions as minority rights which the *Survey* takes into account.

Each country summary has an **overview** which describes such matters as the most important events of 1992 and current political issues. Finally, the country reports contain a section on **political rights** and **civil liberties.** This section summarizes each country's degree of respect for the rights and liberties that Freedom House uses to evaluate freedom in the world. These summaries include instances of human rights violations by both governmental and non-governmental entities.

Reports on related territories follow the country summaries. In most cases, these reports are comparatively brief and contain fewer categories of information than in the country summaries. ▬

Afghanistan

Polity: Transitional **Political Rights:** 6
Economy: Statist **Civil Liberties:** 6
Population: 16,862,000 **Status:** Not Free
PPP: $710
Life Expectancy: 42.5
Ethnic Groups: Pashtun, Tajik, Uzbek, Hazara

Overview: The Soviet-installed government of President Mohammad Najibullah fell in April 1992, but civil war continued to ravage Afghanistan as the seven resistance groups that made up the anti-Communist *Mujahideen* fought each other for control of the country.

The Soviet Union's 1979 invasion of Afghanistan followed the 1978 coup led by Hafizullah Amin, leader of the Khalq faction of the Communist People's Democratic Party of Afghanistan (PDPA). The Soviets replaced Amin with his rival, Babrak Karmal, leader of the Parcham faction of the PDPA. Unable to crush the resistance, despite having more than 100,000 troops in Afghanistan, the Soviets replaced Karmal with Najibullah, the head of Afghanistan's secret service at the time, in May 1986. The Soviets hoped that Najibullah would be more effective against the mujahideen. However, under his leadership, fierce fighting continued between resistance forces and government troops.

A decade of Soviet military intervention, Communist rule, and internecine violence has made Afghanistan a world leader in misery and deprivation. More than one million people (mostly civilian) have died since the 1979 invasion. Afghanistan has the lowest life expectancy in the world, the second-highest child-mortality rate (300 per 1,000 live births), the largest refugee problem (6.5 million internationally, mostly in Pakistan and Iran, 2 million internally) and the worst disability rate (2 million, 20 percent of which are from land mines left from the war). More than 5 million land mines seeded throughout the country continue to complicate any economic development and prevent many refugees from returning home.

United Nations initiatives for a peaceful transition from Najibullah's regime to democratic government spurred the dramatic events of 1992. Najibullah's willingness to consider the plan was a sign of his government's declining position.

As the government's control over the provincial cities ebbed, and as Soviet assistance ceased in January, Najibullah, a Pashtun, tried to replace non-Pashtun commanders with members of his own ethnic group. The replacements provoked Uzbeks and Ismailis, including Uzbeck General Abdul Rashid Doestam, to leave the government and join mujahideen forces. On 18 March 1992, after combined opposition forces captured Mazar-i-Sharif, a northern stronghold, Najibullah announced that he would turn over power to the Afghan Interim Government (AIG). Throughout the country, government garrison commanders allied with local mujahideen along clan lines, ceding control of regional centers to the resistance. By 23 April, only Kabul and Jalalabad were not in mujahideen hands.

With mujahideen assistance, vice-presidents of Najibullah's Watan (Homeland) Party (the former Parcham faction of the PDPA) ousted him in a political coup on 15 April. Inter-ethnic group fighting continued as all the mujahideen groups poised to attack Kabul. Foreign Minister Abdul Wakil tried to dissuade the mujahideen by negotiating with the two most powerful commanders: Ahmad Shah Masood, the Tajik, moderate Islamic Jamiat-i-Islami commander, and Gulbaddin Hekmatyar, the hardline Islamic fundamentalist, Pashtun nationalist Hezb-i-Islami leader. Masood agreed not to attack Kabul, but Hekmatyar demanded an unconditional surrender by government forces.

U.N. envoy Benon Sevon redoubled diplomatic efforts to salvage any hope for peaceful transition. Although the Americans and the Russians remained largely disengaged, both Pakistan and Iran continued to wield influence over the various warring factions. Pakistan, seeking trade with the former Soviet Central Asian Republics, cut off aid to the resistance in January and pressured Sunni mujahideen (especially Hekmatyar, Pakistan's longtime ally) for peaceful settlement. Iran continued to influence the Shiite Hezb-i-Wahadat Party and pushed for Shiite representation in all negotiations, while encouraging all groups to form an Islamic republic.

On 24 April, a majority of mujahideen groups agreed to a three-stage plan. During stage one, a 51-member Islamic Jehad Council (IJC) would take power in Kabul for two months of immediate transition. The Council would be composed of a leader, 30 mujahideen commanders, 10 clergy and 10 intellectuals. The negotiators voted for a compromise leader, a Pashtun cleric, Sigbatullah Mojaddidi, head of the moderate Pashtun Afghan National Liberation Front. (Mojaddidi had remained in Pakistan throughout the war. The more powerful, competing Islamic forces found him inoffensive.) During stage two, Mojaddidi would pass power for four months to Burhanuddin Rabbani, leader of the Jamiat-i-Islami Party and head of the AIG. (The AIG operated in exile in Peshawar, Pakistan, for several years.) The final transition stage called for Afghanistan's first democratic elections to determine the permanent government.

Initial reactions to the plan varied. Hekmatyar disapproved of the plan, but conceded as Masood's military strength increased in Kabul. Fearing insufficient representation, the Shiites withheld support. Kabul fell to mujahideen forces on 25 April. Masood's troops faced little resistance, as he had already allied with the government forces, most notably, General Doestam. Fighting ensued between Hekmatyar and Masood's forces. Hekmatyar finally accepted the post of prime minister for one of his trusted Hezbi members, Usted Farid. Masood became minister of defense. On 28 April, the Islamic Republic of Afghanistan was established, with Mojaddidi as its head of state.

Even though his own party held the premiership, Hekmatyar attacked the new government's troops. During a brief respite between Hezbi and Jamiat, Hekmatyar threatened to destroy Kabul if Mojaddidi remained in power. Abdul Rasul Sayyaf, leader of a fundamentalist, Pastun-dominated party, Ittehad-i-Islami (Islamic Union for the Liberation of Afghanistan), also criticized the government for not implementing Islamic practices, and for accepting former Communists and non-practicing Muslims in the government and the military. To quell the fighting, Rabbani, Masood's political leader, demanded that all forces leave the city and that a neutral force composed of all factions be put in place. Rebel leaders refused Rabbani's plea and the fighting continued.

Surprisingly, all parties remained in the government despite the violence. Citing instability, Mojaddidi threatened not to relinquish his post by the agreed date of 28 June. Instead, he advocated a *Loya Jirga* or Council of Elders to convene and decide the fate of the nation. Critics maintained Mojaddidi was afraid to face elections. Despite the threats, Mojaddidi did transfer power to Rabbani on 28 June. Rabbani's first move was to include practicing Muslims in the armed forces. (Previously, Communists filled most of the ranks.) Unsuccessfully, he ordered all militias out of Kabul on 2 July. Despite several cease-fires, the fighting continued. Attacks on civilians escalated. The new central government held no sway with the troops in Kabul, but peace prevailed generally in the countryside.

Throughout the summer and fall, fighting also raged between the Sunni Muslim Ittehad-i-Islami group that Saudi Arabia backed, and the Shiite Hazara Hezb-i-Wahadat group that Iran backed.

While the mujahideen government gave lip service to the protection of minorities, Sunni fundamentalists schemed to disenfranchise the Shiites, Hindus and Sikhs; they demanded that only members of the Sunni Muslim majority participate in government. Sunni fundamentalists do not consider the Shiites proper Muslims.

The fragile government coalition began to break down in August. Younis Khalis, leader of a splinter faction of the hardline Hezb-i-Islami party, left the government, claiming that the inclusion of former Najibullah government officials meant the regime was not adhering to Islamic principles. Hekmatyar also declared the government un-Islamic and closed the airport, claiming that the facility reinforced Doestam's troops.

The central government's inability to contain street fighting among the various militias rendered Kabul's residents helpless, displaced and disenchanted by the mujahideen take-over. Hekmatyar's rocket attacks confined citizens of Kabul to their homes. In late August, 3,000 people were killed in Kabul during one day of rocket attacks. As the security situation in Kabul worsened, over 600,000 people left the city. Many poured into Jalalabad and Peshawar, creating both an internal refugee crisis and a serious strain on the extensive Pakistani refugee management system. Conversely, as peace overtook the countryside, more than 90,000 families returned to their bombed-out houses and mine-strewn fields, preferring an uncertain future at home to refugee life elsewhere.

Hekmatyar reiterated demands for elections, a militia-free zone, imposition of a security force and the release of prisoners. In response, Rabbani ousted Hezbi officials from the government while Hekmatyar's designated Prime Minister Farid was out of the country. Afghanistan's North-South split became more acute as Doestam and Masood, entrenched in the North, engineered alliances with other minority groups, while Hekmatyar shored up support with Pashtun hard-liners in the South. Civil war raged, despite occasional cease-fires.

In September, the government dissolved the Communist party, and banned the secret service, the National Assembly and the Senate. The government reviewed all treaties and annulled several for non-Islamic content. The government seized the assets of the PDPA Parcham and Khalq factions and banned discussions of communism under criminal penalty. Ministries attempted to Islamize their structure. The government continued unsuccessful efforts to clear Kabul of militias.

All parties agreed to participate in a Council of Elders in November to decide the fate of the country. Lacking consensus, the leaders extended Rabbani's term until mid-December. Opposition leaders charged him with packing the council that would choose a successor. In December, General Doestam's forces battled the government to force

Rabbani's resignation. On 30 December, most mujahideen leaders boycotted Rabbani's re-election.

Najibullah remained in internal exile at a U.N. compound throughout the year. Former government workers, fearing retribution, applied *en masse* for exit visas. On 29 April, the Interim government offered amnesty to all former government members except Najibullah.

Afghanistan's Muslim neighbors continued their involvement in the war-torn country. Pakistan feared the creation of a separate Pashtun state out of Afghan territory, while Iran feared encroaching Afghan violence, a permanent refugee problem and Sunni oppression of Afghanistan's Shiite minority. Both Pakistan and Iran urged their historical mujahideen partners and the opposing Afghan forces to take part in a peaceful transition. Iran sought additional influence in Afghanistan by opening two uninvited consulates. The government closed both by force, but they were reopened.

Political Rights and Civil Liberties: Incessant violence renders Afghans incapable of changing their government democratically. Afghans recounted stories of both Sunni and Shiite kidnapping, torture, looting, assassination and rape in 1992. The government purged jails of Najibullah's political prisoners.

The state controls the media and journalists are frequently threatened. The government removed anti-Islamic literature from libraries in 1992. Censors screen all media for sexually explicit and politically or religiously objectionable themes.

In September, a Council of Elders drafted an interim constitution based on Islamic law that provides for freedom of movement, association and expression. However, the promises of law do not always square with the violent and restrictive Afghan realities. The permanent government will decide the fate of the constitution.

Justice Minister Ayatollah Asif Mohseni, leader of the Harakat-i-Islami Party, repealed Mojaddidi's amnesty for former government workers. The ministry permitted extra-judicial "people's courts" to try those workers for crimes that allegedly break national or Islamic law. These courts are beyond Rabbani's control.

Since its inception, the government has held public executions. Some prisoners were convicted in private without formal charges. In May, Islamic courts began imposing Koran-approved punishments of stoning, amputation, public whipping and execution.

Women suffer increasing gender inequality. The new constitution guarantees female suffrage in accordance with Islamic law and Afghan culture. However, women must limit interaction with men. They must quit their jobs if they do not work in single-sex offices. Despite the appallingly few schools, girls may not attend co-ed classes. By law, females must wear traditional, full-body coverings. Women in Kabul had not worn these for 30 years. Gangs attack (and sometimes kill) women for lack of modesty.

Afghans are free to conduct business or agricultural pursuits, but their efforts are limited by the existence of active land mines. Afghanistan is the world's largest producer and exporter of opium, but the state punishes drug traffickers with death.

Albania

Polity: Presidential-
parliamentary democracy
Economy: Statist
(transitional)
Population: 3,285,000
PPP: $4,270
Life Expectancy: 72.2

Political Rights: 4
Civil Liberties: 3
Status: Partly Free

Ethnic Groups: Albanians (two main ethnic linguistic
groups: Ghegs, Tosks, 96 percent), Greeks (2.5 percent)

Overview:

In 1992, Albanians voted out the former Communist government, but new President Sali Berisha faced social unrest, political polarization and a devastated economy as the country struggled to rebuild after the collapse of what had been an isolated, Stalinist state.

Situated between Greece and Serbia on the southern Adriatic coast of the Balkan peninsula, this small, predominantly Muslim nation was established as a one-party Communist regime in 1946 and was ruled by Enver Hoxha until his death in 1985. During his reign, all religion was outlawed, most mosques and churches were razed and the government rejected all other Communist nations, including China, as "revisionist" traitors to the true faith. In 1985, Ramiz Alia succeeded Hoxha as first secretary of the Albanian Party of Labor (Communist). In 1990, following the collapse of Communist regimes in Eastern and Central Europe, Alia was elected president as head of the renamed Socialist Party in elections marred by irregularities. In late 1991, the government of Premier Ylli Bufi resigned after the opposition Democratic Party withdrew from the governing coalition. President Alia asked nonpartisan intellectual Vilson Ahmeti to form an interim government.

The March 1992 elections were preceded by months of intense social unrest as an already impoverished economy all but collapsed. In February, shootings, robberies and thefts reached epidemic proportions. In the city of Rogzhine, 700 armed looters made off with 30 tons of Western food and medical aid. Government services had disappeared or were sporadic. Violence and crime rocked the capital, Tirana, in the face of growing unemployment, poverty and chronic shortages of food, fuel and medicine. Since 1990, some 200,000 Albanians had fled to Greece, Italy and other countries in Europe.

The 1992 vote for the People's Assembly was conducted under a new election system that decreased the importance of rural areas. Two years earlier, President Alia and the Socialists, while losing to the Democratic Party in all major cities, won the election because rural areas were overrepresented; it took far fewer votes to elect a deputy from the countryside than from the cities. The system was changed to elect at least 40 of the 150 deputies by proportional representation.

After multiparty elections and runoffs on 22 and 29 March, the Democratic Party (DP) won 92 seats and the Socialists 38. The Social Democratic Party led by Fatos Nano picked up 7 seats, the Union for Human Rights (which drew its support from the estimated 400,000 Greek Albanians), 2, and the right-wing Republican Party, 1. Approximately 90 percent of eligible voters turned out; the Democratic Party won over

62 percent of the vote and the Socialists won 27 percent. More than 500 candidates ran in direct district elections for 100 parliamentary seats, with 40 to 50 filled by proportional representation from national party lists. Non-Socialist parties won more than the necessary two-thirds majority needed to amend the constitution. Other parties not represented in parliament included the centrist Agrarian Party and the Party of National Unity; and the far-right, monarchist Albanian Democratic Union.

On 3 April, President Alia resigned, and less than a week later, lawmakers elected Sali Berisha president by a margin of 96 votes to 35. Berisha, a 47-year-old heart surgeon, became Albania's first non-Communist president since World War II. Alexander Meksi was named prime minister.

The new president took over a nation at an economic standstill. Inflation had soared to 800 percent and agricultural output declined by 75 percent. Industrial output plummeted by over 50 percent. The country survived largely on international relief aid and remittances from workers abroad. Unemployment hovered at 50 percent and factories remained idle. Workers were guaranteed 80 percent of their wages when enterprises shut down, but this attempt to maintain social stability also put pressure on an already hard-pressed government. Black-marketeering and corruption thrived.

In late April, parliament approved the government's plans to launch an economic package on 1 July aimed at reassuring the International Monetary Fund (IMF) and other potential lenders that the country's transition to a market economy was under way. The Socialists abstained from the vote. The first measure would cut the 80 percent unemployment benefits to idle workers. Under the plan, wage subsidies would be reduced by 10 percent a month until eliminated. Other aspects of the plan included price liberalization, which caused the cost of basic essentials to skyrocket. The proposal also included complete land privatization; gradual but full privatization of most state enterprises as well as of trade, transportation and the fishing and mining industries; and the selling of state homes to inhabitants.

The government's program touched off another wave of would-be refugees. In the southern port of Vlora, police in early June battled to disperse thousands of people attempting to flee by ship. Disturbances also flared up in Tirana.

Also in June, serious rifts resurfaced in the ruling Democratic Party. Economist Gramoz Pashko, a DP co-founder who was critical of the party's withdrawal from the government coalition in December 1991, was ousted from the party's parliamentary group after he implied that party Deputy Chairman Hajdari's departure for the United States to study was actually a defection. Pashko argued that the party had no legal right to expel him. On 29 June, the parliamentary group issued an official declaration sharply condemning Pashko and saying that the Hajdari affair was not an isolated incident and that in the past Pashko had made similar serious errors. The party's press launched a fierce attack on its co-founder reminiscent of the Communist era.

As public discontent grew, diplomats and opposition leaders charged that the new government was becoming more authoritarian. On 14 August, the Democrats purged six moderate leaders from their party, calling them "extreme leftists," "deviationists" and "traitors." Some were threatened with removal from parliament, an action illegal under current Albanian law. After the Socialists won a majority of seats in local elections in July, local DP officials refused to distribute international food aid to towns where the former Communists won. Employees of state enterprises and offices were fired without cause or access to appeal. Police reportedly harassed and detained members of the Socialist opposition.

On 26 August, the IMF announced it had approved its first-ever loan to Albania. The $29 million loan was designed to support the government's economic and financial restructuring. The government also signed an agreement with a group of foreign oil companies to begin on-shore exploration along the Adriatic coast. The government also hoped that foreign investors would rebuild the chromium mining and processing industries.

In other issues, Albanian relations with neighboring Serbia deteriorated as Serbs continued to crack down in Kosovo, the overwhelmingly Albanian enclave that was once an autonomous region within Yugoslavia. Albanians in newly independent Macedonia, where they make up a sizable minority, agitated for greater autonomy. In March, Albanian officials complained to the Greek ambassador that "chauvinist and nationalist" pamphlets were being distributed illegally in southern Albania to influence Greek Albanian voters.

Political Rights and Civil Liberties: In 1992, Albania held direct, multiparty elections for a 150-seat People's Assembly. Unlike the 1991 vote, there were few reports of irregularities and fraud, and the opposition Democratic Party won a majority of the seats, defeating the Socialist (formerly the Communist) Party.

Political parties, civic organizations, independent trade unions and student groups have the right to organize, but in late summer there were persistent allegations from diplomats that the new government was infringing on the rights of the Socialist Party through harassment, detentions and the withholding of food aid to areas where Socialists won in the year's local elections. The independent press is, in large part, controlled by political parties. The only daily newspaper in the country is the Socialist Party's *Zeri i Popullit*, although the Democratic Party's *Rilindja Demokratike* comes out four times a week. Radio, television and other official news media are nominally under parliamentary control. The judicial system remains weak, not fully independent and reflects a lack of legal expertise. Laws banning religion were lifted in 1990, and 1992 saw a continued rebirth of the Muslim, Eastern Orthodox and Catholic faiths. The independent Confederation of Independent Trade Unions of Albania (BSPSh) operates with a minimum of government interference.

Algeria

Polity: Civilian-military
Economy: Statist
Population: 26,041,000
PPP: $3,088
Life Expectancy: 65.1
Ethnic Groups: Arabs (75 percent), Berbers (25 percent)

Political Rights: 7
Civil Liberties: 6
Status: Not Free

Overview: Political crisis in 1992 pushed Algeria to the brink of civil war as an oppressive military regime replaced the long-ruling National Liberation Front (FLN).

Algeria's scheduled transition to a democratic system came to an abrupt halt with the cancellation of the second round of national elections that had been scheduled for

15 January 1992. In the first round, on 26 December 1991, 49 parties competed for the 430 seats in the National Assembly. The fundamentalist Islamic Salvation Front (FIS) won 188 seats and more than 50 percent of the ballots cast. The Socialist Forces Front (FFS) won 26 seats, the FLN won 16 seats and independents won 3 seats. Voter turnout was approximately 50 percent. Reportedly, 200,000 people demonstrated against these results on 2 January 1992. The demonstrators included Algeria's largest trade union, several women's associations and secularist parties that called for the cancellation of the second round. They feared and opposed the FIS's plans to introduce "Shari'a" (Islamic law) as the highest law of the land; to ban the consumption and production of alcohol (one of Algeria's industries); to segregate men and women in the workplaces and schools; and to reduce the status of women to that of "homemakers." Muslim fundamentalists have repeatedly blamed the high unemployment rate on women in the workplace.

The crisis began as the army canceled the second round of elections and forced President Chadli Benjedid, who had been in power since 1979, to resign. The army also dissolved the National Assembly. Upon Benjedid's resignation, the Constitutional Council would have been the only institution to legally replace the president until the next elections. Nonetheless, the army replaced the Constitutional Council with the High Security Council, an advisory committee consisting mainly of army and police officers.

On 14 January 1992, the army replaced the High Security Council with the Higher State Council headed by Mohammad Boudiaf, a 72-year old veteran of the war of independence who been in exile since 1964. The Council postponed elections indefinitely. The Council, which included Mohammad Boudiaf as president and Sid Ahmed Ghozali as prime minister, will apparently be Algeria's highest authority until at least the end of 1993.

On 9 February 1992, the Council imposed a year-long state of emergency under which virtually all constitutional rights were suspended. The decree allowed for unrestricted detentions, curfews, press censorship and bans on public gatherings. The normal daily routine in Algeria became one of riots, arrests, killings and trials of Muslim fundamentalists.

In February, after weeks of violence between troops and fundamentalists, Mohammad Boudiaf introduced a program to encourage economic stability. Algeria is plagued with a $25 billion foreign debt, 30 percent unemployment, 40 percent inflation, and severe shortages of health services, housing and schooling.

On 4 March 1992, an Algerian administrative court banned the Islamic Salvation Front (FIS), accusing the party of using violence to achieve political ends. Prosecutors argued that the party violated constitutional provisions which forbid political parties to form based on religion or race. In April, the Supreme Court of Algeria upheld that decision. The FIS went underground as military pressure grew on its members and leaders.

On 22 April 1992, the government swore in an unelected consultative body to provide advice on economic and political matters. In addition, the new regime brought three opposition figures into the Cabinet as an attempt to appease the fundamentalists. Fraud investigators also began an inquiry of corruption and embezzlement charges against some top Algerian officials.

The crisis escalated once again on 29 June 1992, when a member of the security forces assassinated President Mohammad Boudiaf in the port city of Annaba. The government kept news of the assassination under strict control. There were conflicting reports on the number and identity of the perpetrators. While some pointed the finger at the fundamentalists, others reported that the assassins were Boudiaf's security guards and charged that the assassination was instigated from within the government. A 26-year-old sub-lieutenant in the special anti-terrorist unit, Lembarek Boumaarafi, was arrested and charged with the assassination. The special commission set up to investigate the assassination later speculated that Boumaarafi acted as part of a conspiracy involving Islamic movements and in September 1992, two more members of Algeria's presidential guard were charged with Boudiaf's assassination.

A week later, Prime Minister Sid Ahmed Ghozali resigned and Belaid Abdessalam replaced him. Ali Kafi replaced Boudiaf as head of state.

Another major development in 1992 was the trial of the FIS leaders Abassi Madani and Ali Belhaj. Former Prime Minster Ghozali, former National Assembly Speaker Belkhadem and FLN Secretary-General Abdelhamid Mehri testified in favor of the FIS leaders. The defense argued that the government, and not the FIS leaders, was responsible for the violence following the protests in June 1991 during which at least 55 people were killed. On 15 July 1992, the military court sentenced the two leaders to 12 years in prison. Madani was convicted of fomenting rebellion against the state, while Belhaj was convicted of kidnapping, detention and torture. Five other FIS leaders were also convicted and sentenced to four to six years in prison.

After the Boudiaf assassination, the government took a more extreme line towards the Islamic fundamentalists. Violence between state security officers and fundamentalists continued, despite warnings from President Ali Kafi and Defense Minister Nezzar.

In October, the government established special courts for terrorist cases. The judges are anonymous and verdicts are final. On 1 November, the government executed two fundamentalist soldiers. After the killing of policemen in an Algiers suburb, the state put 90 soldiers on trial. By December, the ruling council imposed an all-night curfew in the Algiers area.

Political Rights and Civil Liberties:

Algerians lost their right to change their government democratically in January 1992, when the army canceled the second round of the national elections and placed the military-led Higher State Council in control of the country.

The state of emergency, declared on 9 February 1992, reinforced the powers of the security forces to shoot, kill and arrest civilians. In addition, there had been an extensive crackdown on all citizens, specifically FIS members and leaders. The Council banned all political gatherings and replaced most of the pro-FIS imams at mosques with others approved by the Ministry of Religious Affairs. Police arrested other imams. Reportedly, the FIS controlled 8,000 of Algeria's 10,000 mosques. The crackdown resulted in hundreds of deaths and approximately 10,000 imprisonments. The government seized power from the FIS-controlled local governments and halted all economic aid programs previously run by the FIS.

The Council suspended freedoms of speech, press and association. Since the declaration of the state of emergency, the state has arrested journalists and subjected publications to either suspension or confiscation. The state ordered ten foreign journalists to leave the country. The publisher and two editors of *AL-KHABAR* were prosecuted after publishing an advertisement placed by the leader of FIS, Abdelkader

Hachani. The advertisement urged military personnel to disobey orders. The new press law placed extensive controls over publications and freedom of the press.

There have been reports of torture and brutal treatment of prisoners by police. The current constitution prohibits any discrimination on birth, race, sex, opinion or other personal or social conditions or circumstances. However, unlike the 1976 constitution, it omits the specific guarantees for women's rights. While laws prohibit discrimination against the Berbers, there have been many restrictions placed on the Berber language, schools and culture. The state postponed the implementation of the Arabization law, which would have prohibited the use of any language other than Arabic, especially in the government.

Under legislation passed in 1990, Algerian workers have the right to form and be represented by trade unions of their choice as long as these unions do not associate with political parties. The unions are forbidden to receive funds from abroad and could be suspended by the government if they violate the law. In accordance with the state-of-emergency decree, the state closed down the headquarters of an Islamic trade union in the capital. In addition, the government took control of state-owned property which it had once placed in the hands of the political parties.

Islam is the official religion, but there are no Islamic courts, and the tiny Christian and Jewish communities are allowed free religious practice. Women cannot obtain a divorce and are legally under the guardianship of their husbands, fathers or brothers.

Algerians are free to travel within the country, although traveling abroad is made difficult by strict currency controls.

Angola

Polity: Dominant party
Economy: Statist
Population: 8,902,000
PPP: $1,225
Life Expectancy: 45.5
Ethnic Groups: Ovimbundu (38 percent), Kimbundu (25 percent), Bakongo (17 percent), other

Political Rights: 6
Civil Liberties: 6
Status: Not Free

Overview: After Angola's first national election in September 1992, allegations of electoral fraud and ethnic violence threatened to derail the country's transition to democracy. At the end of the year, it was unclear whether Angola would successfully complete its democratic transition or return to civil war.

A former Portuguese colony located on the Atlantic coast of southwest Africa, Angola gained independence in 1975 after fourteen years of guerrilla war led by three independence movements: Holden Roberto's National Front for the Liberation of Angola (FNLA), operating primarily in the north among the Bakongo people and militarily moribund since the late seventies; the Marxist-Leninist, Soviet-backed Popular Movement for the Liberation of Angola (MPLA), headed by the poet Agostinho Neto, and dominant in and around the capital of Luanda in a region largely populated by the Kimbundu; and the National Union for the Total Independence of Angola (UNITA), led by Dr. Jonas Savimbi and most active in the central highlands among the Ovimbundu.

Between the departure of the Portuguese and the 1992 multi-party elections, the MPLA regime based in Luanda and led by Eduardo Dos Santos had obtained widespread international recognition as the *de jure* government of Angola. Meanwhile, UNITA, led by Jonas Savimbi, sustained a guerrilla war against the government, operating as the sole *de facto* authority within the southeastern one-third of the country. An estimated 350,000 Angolans died and a million and a half were displaced as a direct result of the war. On 31 May 1991, the Angolan regime and UNITA signed an agreement intended to finally end the country's sixteen-year civil war. The Bicesse Peace Accord provided for a permanent cease-fire supervised by MPLA and UNITA representatives with international military observers. The agreement also called for multi-party elections by the last quarter of 1992 and the eventual merger of MPLA and UNITA troops into a single national armed force. For over a year, the agreement kept the peace in most of Angola.

In early March 1992, two senior UNITA officials defected from the organization, implicating it in the recent disappearance of two former UNITA representatives abroad. Miguel N'Zau Puna, the party's interior minister, and Tony da Costa Fernandes, its foreign secretary, charged that Savimbi had sanctioned UNITA's execution of Tito Chingunji and Wilson dos Santos for having challenged his leadership of the organization. In response, UNITA spokesmen asserted that N'Zau Puna had ordered the two men's murders while Savimbi was abroad. The spokesmen also alleged that Fernandes had tried to extort $15 million from UNITA. The defectors were further accused of being paid agents of the MPLA, sympathizers of an armed secessionist movement in the oil-rich Angolan enclave of Cabinda and directly involved in an assassination plot against Savimbi.

The National Electoral Commission was not set up by the Dos Santos government until 10 May. Critics charged that the over-extended MPLA regime was devoting its time to embezzlement on a massive scale and pre-election politicking rather than organizing the election. The Electoral Commission announced that the two-day parliamentary and presidential elections would begin on 29 September.

As the election approached, both UNITA and the MPLA accused each other of hindering political activity in their respected territories, failing to demobilize troops, and using violence to force the cancellation of the election. In the month before the election, approximately 40 people were killed in politically related violence. Until the last day of voting, the two movements each declared with certainty that they would win. Savimbi asserted that only fraud would allow an MPLA victory. However, in early September, representatives from the U.S., Portugal and Russia—the countries monitoring the peace process—announced in Luanda that leaders of both UNITA and the MPLA had agreed to form a coalition government after the balloting, whatever the final vote count. News of the agreement somewhat lessened widespread apprehension over what might happen in the aftermath of the election.

The two days of voting on the 29 and 30 of September were largely incident-free, with a reported turnout of 90 percent of registered voters. Initial election projections released by the MPLA showed Dos Santos with a commanding lead in the presidential vote and the MPLA with a lead in the legislative vote. Before official results were released, however, UNITA fiercely denounced the MPLA's premature election projection as fraudulent. International observers, however, declared the election generally free and fair, with only minor irregularities. Among other allegations, UNITA charged that ballot boxes had been tampered with, ballots had not been delivered to anti-MPLA areas, voter registration lists had intentionally not been made available for inspection by the opposition, and falsified vote counts were conveyed from polling places to Luanda's national tabulation center. UNITA claimed it led both presidential and parliamentary results in every province. Alternately threatening a renewal of war and hinting that UNITA would accept the election results, Savimbi's posture brought a government offer to allow both a recount and an independent probe of the charges of rigging. The official results of the recount had Dos Santos with 49.57 percent of the vote and Savimbi with 40.07 percent. In the parliamentary balloting, MPLA candidates won 53.74 percent of the vote and 129 seats compared to 34.10 percent and 70 seats for UNITA candidates.

Rejecting Savimbi's allegations of fraud as "blackmail," Dos Santos called for a presidential run-off (which was necessary because no candidate won a simple majority of votes). The regime also invited UNITA to join a government of national unity. However, its formation was made conditional on UNITA's immediate disarmament and its acceptance of a decisive MPLA victory in the legislative elections. Having earlier left Luanda for a UNITA redoubt in southern Angola in order to avoid a possible assassination attempt, Savimbi remained unresponsive to government calls for him to return to the capital and negotiate. UNITA announced within the week that it was willing to enter into arbitration by the U.N. Meanwhile, UNITA forces reportedly withdrew from the partially unified national army and prepared to take provincial capitals throughout the country.

Fierce exchanges of gunfire erupted sporadically between UNITA and MPLA forces in various parts of the country during the tense weeks following the election, but despite affirmations by UNITA that it would participate in a run-off, the situation seemed to spiral rapidly out of control. On 30 October, after UNITA troops reportedly seized control of several provinces, the regime's newly formed paramilitary "anti-riot" police and armed MPLA supporters began a methodical hunt for UNITA supporters. Over a thousand UNITA loyalists were killed in Luanda during the next four days as the regime snuffed out all resistance. The victims included civilian supporters and the core of UNITA's political leadership, including Vice President Jeremias Chitunda. As the smoke cleared, the MPLA's Dos Santos accused UNITA of trying to usurp power and demanded that it withdraw from captured territory.

In November, UNITA stepped up its attacks against government military bases, capturing two key towns in northern Angola. At the same time, Savimbi again stated his willingness to abide by the election results, provided the MPLA release UNITA leaders arrested in the October anti-UNITA crackdown.

On 27 November, the parliament convened for its first session, which was boycotted by the 70 UNITA representatives. The MPLA-dominated parliament named Maurcelius Moco prime minister. In December, the new prime minister offered UNITA one ministerial post as a gesture of "good will." At the same time, however, Moco described UNITA as a terrorist organization that should be declared illegal.

Political Rights and Civil Liberties: Despite elections that international observers declared essentially free and fair, significant charges of electoral fraud and renewed political violence derailed Angola's transition to democracy in 1992.

During Angola's seventeen-year-old civil war, both the MPLA government and UNITA allegedly committed severe human rights violations, including political killings, torture, disappearances, indefinite detention and intimidation. Despite recent vows to desist from such behavior, reports of abuses by both sides continued in 1992. The campaign styles of both the MPLA and UNITA were frequently characterized by recriminations, threats to renew warfare, and the use of partisan violence to neutralize political activity by opponents. Criminal activity has skyrocketed throughout Angola since the 1991 cease fire, as many demobilized MPLA and UNITA forces were forced to fend for themselves.

During its last session in 1991, the MPLA's National Assembly abolished capital punishment, established *habeus corpus*, guaranteed trade union independence, and guaranteed the right to assembly. The parliament also formally established judicial independence, but the MPLA has dominated the judiciary since the Portuguese left Angola in 1975.

In the past, freedom of speech was restricted in both MPLA- and UNITA-dominated areas of Angola. With rare exception, the MPLA-controlled government media has reflected official party policy, while that of UNITA reflects that party's own official policy. One month before the September election, the MPLA granted each opposition party only ten minutes of television air-time per day and twenty minutes on the radio. A number of the smaller under-funded parties were unable to pay for campaign spots.

Antigua and Barbuda

Polity: Dominant party
Economy: Capitalist-statist
Population: 74,000
PPP: $3,940
Life Expectancy: 72.0
Ethnic Groups: Black (89 percent), other (11 percent)

Political Rights: 3
Civil Liberties: 3
Status: Partly Free

Overview: In March 1992, following new charges of corruption and a unity agreement among political opponents, 83-year-old Prime Minster Vere Bird announced he would step down after completing his term in 1994. But calls for his immediate resignation continued, while ruling party figures, including his son Lester, jockeyed for position to succeed him.

Antigua and Barbuda is a member of the British Commonwealth. The British monarchy is represented by a governor-general who acts as ceremonial head of state. The islands became self-governing in 1969 and gained independence in 1981. Formally a parliamentary democracy, Antigua and Barbuda has been dominated by Prime Minister Bird and his Antiguan Labour Party (ALP) for over two decades.

In the 1989 general election, which was marred by irregularities and fraud, the

ALP maintained its control of the parliament, retaining fifteen of seventeen seats in the House of Representatives. The United National Democratic Party (UNDP) won one seat and the Barbuda People's Movement (BPM) won the Barbuda seat. Also competing was the leftist Antigua Caribbean Liberation Movement (ACLM) and a number of smaller parties. In separate elections two weeks later, the BPM took all five Barbuda Council seats.

As in previous elections, the opposition charged that the ALP exerted undue influence over the nominally independent electoral supervisor and used bribery and intimidation at polling time. In response to a petition filed by UNDP, a high court annulled the results in one constituency. Before it could rule on six other contested constituencies, ALP members holding the contested seats resigned, the government announced by-elections, and the ALP named a new election supervisor. The UNDP boycotted the by-elections, stating that they would not participate until reforms were made in the electoral system.

Following the 1989 elections, the ALP confronted a looming succession crisis as Vere Bird, Jr. and Lester Bird competed for the party mantle held by their aging father. Papa Bird favored Bird Jr., but that changed after the Israeli arms scandal in 1990.

In April 1990, the government of Colombia protested that Israeli arms had been sold to the Antiguan government and shipped to the Medellin drug cartel in Colombia with the knowledge of Bird Jr., the minister of public works and national security advisor. Bird Jr. denied the allegation, but his brother Lester, the deputy prime minister and foreign minister, convinced his father to permit an independent judicial inquiry.

A commission headed by prominent British jurist Louis Blom-Cooper implicated Bird Jr. and the chief of the 90-member Antiguan Defense Force. The report, issued at the end of 1990, concluded that the country faced being "engulfed in corruption" and had fallen victim to "persons who use political power as a passport to private profit."

To defuse opposition calls for his resignation, Bird banned Bird Jr. from politics for life. In 1991, after a series of mass demonstrations, Lester announced he had been given a mandate to "devise and lead a political and economic recovery program."

But the exposure in January 1992 of a scheme in which Bird had siphoned public funds into his personal account led to a new round of opposition protest and demonstrations demanding that he step down. In February, the UNDP, the ACLM and the Progressive Labour Movement (PLM) united to form the United Progressive Party (UPP). Baldwin Spencer, holder of the UNDP seat in the parliament, became the UPP leader.

At the end of March, just prior to a widely successful general strike called by the UPP, Bird announced he would not run in the general election due by 1994. In May, the ruling ALP held a convention to determine a new party leader, with Lester Bird and information minister John St. Luce the main candidates. But both received 150 votes from the gathered delegates and the convention ended in a deadlock.

In the aftermath, Lester seemed despondent and suggested he might give up politics. St. Luce and other ALP figures talked about holding a second convention. But by the end of 1992, the question of Bird's successor remained up in the air.

Political Rights and Civil Liberties: Technically, citizens are able to change their government democratically, but elections are tainted by serious irregularities and undue influence exerted by the ruling party on the electoral authorities.

The political system has a bicameral parliament consisting of a seventeen-member House of Representatives elected for five years and an appointed Senate. In the House of Representatives, there are sixteen seats for Antigua and one for Barbuda. Eleven senators are appointed by the prime minister, four by the parlia-mentary opposition leader, one by the Barbuda Council and one by the governor-general. Barbuda has limited self-government through the separately elected Barbuda Council.

Political parties, labor unions and civic organizations are free to organize and an independent Industrial Court mediates labor disputes between unions and the government. Religious freedom is respected.

In February 1992, a peaceful opposition demonstration outside parliament was dispersed by police using tear gas and rubber bullets. In March, a number of arson attacks were carried out, including the fire-bombing of the home of the Speaker of the House. No one claimed responsibility and opposition parties accused the government of instigating the attacks as a pretext for declaring a state of emergency. The government denied the charges and the attacks stopped.

The judiciary is relatively independent and there is an inter-island court of appeals for Antigua and five other former British colonies in the Lesser Antilles. There are no political prisoners.

Newspapers are associated with political parties and include the outspoken leftist weekly, *Outlook*. Some publications have been subject to systematic legal harassment by members of the ruling ALP. Radio and television are either owned by the state or members of the Bird family; the opposition charges both with favoritism. Such charges were lent weight in 1990 as the Antigua Broadcasting Service declined to provide coverage of the arms scandal inquiry, despite the approval of the jurist heading the investigation.

Argentina

Polity: Federal presiden-tial-legislative democracy
Economy: Capitalist
Population: 33,100,000
PPP: $4,310
Life Expectancy: 71.0
Ethnic Groups: Europeans (mostly Spanish and Italian), mestizos, Indians, Arabs

Political Rights: 2
Civil Liberties: 3
Status: Free

Overview: Midway through his six-year term, President Carlos Menem faced mounting criticism for his authoritarian style of governing, and for a spate of government corruption scandals involving close political associates. Undeterred, he appeared intent upon overturning a constitutional ban on presidential re-election.

The Argentine Republic was established after achieving independence from Spain in 1816. A federal constitution was drafted in 1853. In this century, democratic governance has frequently been interrupted by military takeovers. The end of authoritarian rule under Juan Peron (1946-55) led to a period of instability marked by left-wing violence and repressive military regimes. After the military's defeat by the British in the 1982 Falkland/Malvinas war, Argentina returned to elected civilian government in December 1983.

In 1983, most of the constitutional structure of 1853 was restored. The president and vice-president are designated for six-year terms by a 600-member electoral college. The electoral college is chosen on the basis of proportional representation, with each of the 23 provinces and the federal district of Buenos Aires having twice as many electors as the combined number of senators and deputies. The legislature consists of a 254-member Chamber of deputies directly elected for six years, with half the seats renewable every three years, and a 48-member Senate nominated by the legislatures of each of the 23 provinces for nine-year terms, with one-third of the seats renewable every three years. Two senators are directly elected in the Buenos Aires federal district. Provincial and municipal governments are elected, with the exception of the mayor of Buenos Aires, who is appointed by the president.

Menem won the presidency on 14 May 1989, defeating Eduardo Angeloz of the incumbent party, the moderate-left Radical Civic Union (UCR). Menem's predecessor, Raul Alfonsin (1983-89), had overseen the prosecution of former military leaders for gross human rights violations during the "dirty war" against leftist guerrillas, and had weathered three military rebellions led by the nationalist *carapintada* (painted face) faction of the army. President Menem was inaugurated in July 1989, the first time in 61 years that one elected civilian had succeeded another.

Menem campaigned as a populist in the traditional Peronist manner. But after taking office amid the country's worst economic crisis, he stunned many followers by initiating a market-based economic reform program. By early 1991, Menem was besieged by corruption scandals involving government officials and members of his family. But inflation had been reduced to 2 percent a month and voters showed their approval as the Peronists retained a working congressional majority during the round of legislative elections in 1991.

However, with even some Peronists opposing his program to dismantle Argentina's statist economy, Menem increasingly resorted to implementing policy by decree. Since 1990, he has invoked emergency laws to issue over 100 "decrees of necessity and urgency." His predecessor issued only eight during his entire term. Attempts by legislators to challenge Menem in court have been blocked since 1990, when Menem pushed a bill increasing the number of Supreme Court justices from five to nine through the Peronist-controlled Senate and appointed six politically loyal judges.

Menem also has used the packed Supreme Court to uphold decrees removing the comptroller general, whose main function is to investigate executive wrong-doing, and other officials mandated to probe government corruption. A number of top prosecutors have been removed and replaced with officials who had been targets of their investigations. At the same time, with a new wave of scandals commanding headlines in 1992, Menem approved an interior ministry campaign to target journalists investigating official corruption with libel suits.

Menem brushed aside criticism that he was ruling undemocratically, stating in July 1992, "It doesn't bother me to govern by decree." His self-assurance, rooted in the favorable response to his economic policies from international financial institutions and popular relief over the capping of inflation, had evolved into a quest for re-election.

Menem announced in 1991, "I'm going to try to be president again." Although he appeared to reverse himself in 1992, Peronist operatives continued scheming to reverse the constitutional prohibition on re-election. The Peronists, lacking the two-thirds majority in both the Senate and the Chamber of Deputies necessary to amend the constitution, made various overtures to the UCR. The Radicals refused to cooperate. The idea of a holding a plebiscite to intimidate opposition legislators was shelved when the social costs of Menem's economic reforms started taking a toll on his popularity ratings.

In October 1992 Menem reportedly signed off on a plan to replace the proportional representation system in the Chamber with a uni-nominal system. Many analysts agreed it would help the Peronists win more seats in the next round of legislative elections scheduled for September 1993.

Re-election has obsessed Argentina's civilian presidents, including Menem's predecessor, whose attempt to change the constitution was blocked by the Peronists. The only leader to secure re-election was Peron. But if Menem was dreaming of becoming the second, the dimming economic outlook at the end of 1992 and Argentina's notoriously volatile public opinion looked to weigh against him.

Political Rights and Civil Liberties: Citizens are able to change their government through elections. Constitutional guarantees regarding the right to organize political parties, civic organizations and labor unions are generally respected. However, the constitutional separation of powers has been undermined by President Menem's propensity to rule by decree and his manipulation of the judiciary.

The political landscape is dominated by two parties, but there are dozens of others, from Communist and Trotskyist on the left to fascist on the right.

The nation's Catholic majority enjoys freedom of religious expression. However, the Jewish community, numbering around 300,000, has been targeted in recent years by anti-Semitic vandalism. In 1992, the Israeli embassy in Buenos Aires was blown up in a bomb attack. Islamic Jihad, the fundamentalist Muslim group, took credit, claiming it was in retaliation for an Israeli cross-border attack into Lebanon.

Newspapers are privately owned and vocal. There are numerous independent dailies reflecting a wide variety of viewpoints. Television and radio are both private and public. Since 1991, there have been an increasing number of incidents of media intimidation by security forces and shadowy groups apparently linked to orthodox Peronist factions. Those most frequently targeted were journalists and publications investigating official corruption. In 1992, in an atmosphere of increasing government hostility toward the media, the interior ministry initiated a libel-suit campaign against investigative journalists and critical media outlets. Also, a court imposed a prior restraint order on a satirical television show; it was the first such order handed down since the return to civilian rule. In November, anonymous attackers bombed the offices of the weekly *Noticias*.

Labor is well organized. The nation's 3 million organized workers are dominated by the Peronist General Confederation of Labor (CGT). But union influence has diminished in recent years because of corruption scandals, internal divisions, and restrictions on public sector strikes decreed by Menem to pave the way for his privatization program.

The human rights community, well organized and consisting of numerous groups dating back to the 1970s, played an influential role in the prosecution of military officers during the Alfonsin administration. Since condemning Menem's 1990 pardon of officers convicted for human rights violations, rights groups have received anonymous threats and been subject to various forms of intimidation.

After the urban food riots in 1989-90, Menem issued a decree giving responsibility for internal security to the military for the first time since the return to civilian rule. Amid a sharp increase in street crime, there have been frequent reports of arbitrary arrests, torture, ill-treatment by police during confinement, and at least one death. But police brutality cases rarely go anywhere in the criminal justice system due to regular intimidation of witnesses and judges.

The judiciary is nominally independent and some judges proved to be effective in handling the numerous human rights and criminal cases brought against military officers during the Alfonsin administration. Under Menem, however, the judicial system has been made into a political instrument of the president. It also remains riddled with the corruption endemic to all branches of the government. In September 1992, the justice minister resigned in protest after Menem announced the president would personally appoint the members of what was to be an independent penal appeals court. Menem replaced the minister with his legal affairs secretary.

Armenia

Polity: Presidential-par-
liamentary (transitional)
Economy: Statist
transitional
Population: 3,504,000
PPP: na
Life Expectancy: 69
Ethnic Groups: Armenians (93 percent), others

Political Rights: 4
Civil Liberties: 3
Status: Partly Free

Overview:

Fallout from the intensifying war in the predominantly Arme-nian Nagorno-Karabakh region of Azerbaijan threatened to derail Armenia's transition to democracy in 1992. The influx of thousands of refugees and a rail blockade exacerbated Armenia's severe economic problems, leaving much of the country without heat and electricity during the winter.

Armenia officially declared independence on 23 September 1991, two days after 92 percent of the population voted for independence in a national referendum. A unicam-eral, 260-member parliament was created following multi-party elections in May 1990. Levon Ter-Petrossian's umbrella Armenian National Movement (ANM) won 56 seats. Opposition parties in the Supreme Soviet included the Armenian Revolutionary Party (ARF) with 11 members and the Armenian Democratic Liberal Party of Armenia (Ramgavar) with 14. Most members of parliament, which is elected for a five-year term, do not officially belong to any party.

On 16 October 1991, ANM Chairman Ter-Petrossian was elected president, getting over 80 percent of the popular vote. With the collapse of the Soviet Union, Armenia became a member of the Commonwealth of Independent States (CIS) on 21 December 1991 and a formal member of the United Nations on 2 March 1992. It was later admitted to the International Monetary Fund (IMF) and the World Bank.

Attempts by the international community and regional countries to bring a peaceful solution to the four-year-old Nagorno-Karabakh conflict ended without significant progress. Sectarian violence intensified in 1992 and spread to border zones between Armenia and Azerbaijan, which was supported by Turkey and Iran. Hundreds of people were reported killed and thousands forced to flee their homes in renewed fighting that has led to at least 2,000 deaths in four years. Both sides were accused of civilian massacres and other atrocities, as Karabakh self-defense forces expelled almost all Azeri military from the enclave by late May. Fierce fighting resumed in June, as Azeri armored units sought to retake key areas in the northeastern region of the region.

President Ter-Petrossian refused to recognize the independence of Nagorno-Karabakh, where residents overwhelmingly approved an independence referendum on 10 December 1991. In March 1992, President Ter-Petrossian described Nagorno-Karabakh as "Azerbaijan's internal affair," insisting that Armenia had no territorial claims in Azerbaijan. He asserted that "any decision on Nagorno-Karabakh must be adopted by the Azerbaijan leadership and the elected leaders of the Nagorno-Karabakh republic." Ter-Petrossian faced intense political opposition to his stand on Nagorno-Karabakh. Most opposition parties demanded that the region be granted official diplomatic recognition as an independent country.

The volatile issue spurred a spate of demonstrations in June, as the ARF and other opposition groups in parliament criticized the government for failing to assist Armenians in Nagorno-Karabakh. The ARF called for the government to resign. In response, President Ter-Petrossian appeared on nationwide television on 29 June and accused the ARF of "attempting to undermine the government." He also made unsupported claims that Hrair Maroukhian, an ARF bureau representative, was working for the KGB. Maroukhian was ordered by the president to be deported within 48 hours or face criminal proceedings. The president also accused Maroukhian of financing and arming anti-government groups in Nagorno-Karabakh.

Anti-government rallies became more frequent in mid-August. The president survived a no-confidence move by insisting that, should a public referendum support his leadership, the opposition-majority parliament would be dissolved. After lengthy deliberations, the opposition backed down.

Although Armenia was one of the first among the former Soviet republics to fulfill privatization programs, the war in Nagorno-Karabakh crippled the economy. Privatization of agriculture, manufacturing and light industry has been implemented, but Azerbaijan's two-year-old energy and rail blockade of Armenia impeded economic reform and led to the closings of industries and schools. Since January, fuel prices jumped 70-fold. By September 1992, Armenia was only receiving 25 percent of its energy requirements. Economic problems were exacerbated by the influx of approximately 300,000 Armenian refugees from Azerbaijan and the lingering effects of the 1988 earthquake, which destroyed half of Armenia's schools, 30 percent of its industry, and left 500,000 homeless. The IMF estimated that in 1991 the economy contracted by at least 12 percent.

Official corruption and a wave of criminal activity created further problems in

Armenia. In addition to bureaucrats demanding bribes, merchants complained that organized criminal gangs were demanding protection money.

Political Rights and Civil Liberties: Armenians can change their government democratically, but throughout 1992 the opposition accused the government of becoming increasingly authoritarian. The Armenian Parliament had its first elections in 1990, when the Armenian National Movement (ANM) won a majority.

Political parties were allowed to form as long as they did not receive funding from abroad. However, all the opposition parties in Armenia continued to be funded from abroad without government interference until the Maroukhian incident in June. The president directed the Justice Ministry to "begin an investigation of the activities of all parties functioning in Armenia" to verify whether parties followed Armenian law. After a hiatus, the Communist Party of Armenia was officially registered in April 1992.

Judicial reform has not yet been implemented and checks on corruption are practically non-existent. Parliament has not been able to create an independent judiciary.

Freedom of the press is generally respected. Opposition papers publish their views without government interference. The ARF publishes more than 10 newspapers in Armenia. Television and radio are state-owned, and access by certain political parties has been limited. Television and radio were also affected by the severe energy shortage, broadcasting only three hours a day. There are no restrictions on freedom of speech and cultural expression.

Freedom of assembly and demonstration are respected. Propositions by the defense minister to declare martial law, ban opposition parties and restrict public rallies were rejected by the government, and he subsequently resigned. Freedom of religion is respected. In addition to the Armenian Apostolic Church, religions movements have proliferated, including Jehovah's Witnesses, Pentecostals, Nazarenes, Mormons and Hari Krishnas.

Independent trade unions exist and on 14 May 1992, metro-locomotive drivers in Yerevan went on strike over demands for higher pay.

Australia

Polity: Federal parliamentary democracy
Economy: Capitalist
Population: 17,782,000
PPP: $15,266
Life Expectancy: 76.5
Ethnic Groups: European (95 percent), Asian (4 percent), aborigines (1 percent)

Political Rights: 1
Civil Liberties: 1
Status: Free

Overview: Australia's unemployment rate rose to over 11 percent in the summer of 1992 as the economy remained at its worst since the Great Depression. A September poll showed low confidence in the leaders of both major parties, but projected a big victory for the opposition in next year's national election.

The British claimed Australia in 1770 and initially used the Botany Bay area as a penal colony. In January 1901, six states formed the Commonwealth of Australia, adding the Northern Territory and the capital city of Canberra as territorial units in 1911. As a member of the British Commonwealth, the Queen of England is the nominal head of state in this multi–party democracy.

Since World War II political power has alternated between the center-left Australian Labor Party (ALP) and a conservative coalition of the Liberal Party and the smaller National Party. Led by Bob Hawke, the ruling ALP captured four consecutive national elections between 1983 and March 1990. In the 1990 election for the House of Representatives, the ALP won 78 seats, the Liberal Party 55, and the National Party 14, along with 1 independent. In the balloting for the Senate, which has 12 members from each state and 2 from each of the territories, the ALP won 31 seats, the Liberal Party 30, the left-of-center Australian Democrats 8, and the National Party 5, along with 2 independents.

In December 1991, Treasurer Paul Keating became prime minister after beating Hawke in a no-confidence vote among Labor MPs. Keating won by deriding Hawke's defense of Aboriginal and conservationist causes over business interests in a time of economic hardship. Few MPs felt the once-popular Hawke could win over a skeptical electorate by the next election, which must be called by July 1993. At the time of the no-confidence vote, Labor trailed the conservative opposition by 18 points in the polls, unemployment was 10.5 percent, and the party appeared to lack a coherent strategy for dealing with the recession.

In February 1992, Hawke quit parliament and retired from politics. The 11 April by-election for his Melbourne seat, located in an area dominated by manufacturing interests, was a fiasco for both major parties. Popular football coach Phil Cleary shocked the establishment by winning as an independent. He opposed both the government's attempts to scale back tariffs and industrial regulation and the opposition's plan to introduce a goods-and-services tax. While Keating said the district's high industrial base made it a unique case, and continued to emphasize the need to deregulate the economy, the ALP's left-wing argued that the party should not abandon its protectionist roots. Although voters returned the party to office in the state of Queensland in September, the Liberal/National coalition scored a landslide against the incumbent ALP government in Victoria in October. The 6 percent swing in Victoria was well above the 1.4 percent swing the opposition will need at the national level.

To win, the Labor Party will need a sharp economic upswing. As treasurer, Keating had reduced tariffs and deregulated the financial sector to boost the country's competitiveness. However, many blame his tight fiscal policy for the current recession. On 18 August, treasurer John Dawkins announced an $865 million spending plan to help create 160,000 new jobs. Opposition leader John Hewson continued to call for a goods-and-services tax along with a fiscally austere budget, greater mineral mining, and less stringent labor laws, all with the goal of making the country competitive with its Asian neighbors.

In addition to the economic problems, a series of major resignations has weakened public confidence in both parties. In May, Graham Richardson quit as transport and communications minister following charges of connections with a businessman accused of fraudulent dealings in the Marshall Islands. In September, South Australia premier John Bannon of the ALP resigned to take responsibility for $2.1 billion in losses by the State Bank of South Australia. The Liberal Party's Nick Greiner resigned on 24 June as premier of New South Wales after the state's Independent Commission Against Corruption ruled he had improperly appointed a former politician to a top environmental job. In addition, in October two former Labor premiers in Western Australia were criticized by a Royal Commission for corrupt business dealings.

To reflect the country's new focus away from Europe and towards its Asian neighbors, many favor ending the Queen of England's ceremonial role as head of state and formally establishing Australia as an independent republic. Public pressure is also growing to remove the British Union Jack from the Australian flag. Prime Minister Keating fueled the debate by treating Queen Elizabeth II disrespectfully during her February visit. In April, he told Indonesian President Suharto that the proposed changes would break his country's remaining colonial vestiges and ease Australia's political and economic integration as the "odd man in" in the region.

Political Rights and Civil Liberties: Australians regularly change their government in free and fair elections. Although there is no formal constitution, fundamental freedoms are respected in practice, and the judiciary is fully independent of the government.

The country's major human rights issue, the treatment of its Aboriginal minority, drew heavy attention in 1992. In March, the Australian Broadcasting Corporation aired a two-year-old amateur video showing raucous police officers in blackface mocking the police-related deaths of two Aboriginals, Lloyd Boney and David Gundy. A week earlier the network had broadcast a documentary showing police verbally abusing Aboriginals in Sydney.

In April, the government announced plans to improve the treatment of Aboriginals in the justice system. A study released in 1991 had found that Aboriginals are incarcerated at 29 times the rate of the general population, often after being unable to afford a fine or having been denied bail for minor offenses. Most arrests are alcohol-related. Once in jail they are far more likely to commit suicide or be beaten by guards than non-Aboriginals. The government will now provide "bail hostels" for those denied bail for lack of a fixed address, increase recruitment of Aboriginals into police forces, and fund anti-alcohol programs.

In a potentially far-reaching case, the High Court ruled that the Miriam Aboriginal people of the Murray Islands off the north coast had retained ownership of their land under common law through traditional land titles. Aboriginals claim ownership to most of the land, but before this case the government had refused to recognize any form of land tenure prior to the British settlement in the late 1770s.

Citizens have complete freedom of religion. Approximately 40 percent of the work force is part of the country's powerful, independent unionized sector. On 10 November, 100,000 people protested in Melbourne against proposals by the Victoria state government to limit strikes to 5 days and cancel state-set minimum wage and working conditions.

Austria

Polity: Federal
parliamentary democracy
Economy: Mixed
capitalist
Population: 7,873,000
PPP: $13,063
Life Expectancy: 74.8
Ethnic Groups: Austro-German majority, a Slovene minority, and Eastern European immigrant and refugee groups

Political Rights: 1
Civil Liberties: 1
Status: Free

Overview:

The election of President Thomas Klestil, legislation against neo-Nazis, and Austria's changing role in Europe were among Austria's major news stories in 1992.

Klestil, a member of the Christian Democratic Austrian People's Party (OVP), replaced fellow conservative Kurt Waldheim. Waldheim's dishonesty about his record in the German army during World War II had embarrassed Austria and crippled his ability to represent the country internationally. In the first round of the presidential election on 26 April 1992, the four contenders were: Klestil (OVP); Rudolph Streicher (Social Democratic Party-SPO); Heide Schmidt of the right-wing populist Austrian Freedom Party; and Robert Jungk (Green Alternative). Neither Streicher (40.7 percent) nor Klestil (37.2 percent) had enough votes to win outright. With the votes of Freedom Party supporters, Klestil beat Streicher in the run-off by a margin of 56.85 percent to 43.15 percent.

The Republic of Austria began in 1918 after the defeat of its predecessor, the Austro-Hungarian Empire, in World War I. Austrian independence ended in 1938 when Nazi Germany annexed its territory. After Germany's defeat in World War II, the Republic of Austria was reborn in 1945, but the Western Allies and the Soviet Union occupied the country until the 1955 signing of the Austrian State Treaty. This agreement guaranteed Austrian neutrality and restored its national sovereignty.

The Austrian system of government features a largely ceremonial president, chosen directly for a six-year term. He appoints the chancellor, the government's chief executive, whose party or coalition commands majority support in the National Council, the 183-member lower house of parliament. Its members are elected directly for four-year terms. The upper house is the 63-member Federal Council, which the provincial assemblies choose by proportional representation. Federal Council members have four- to six-year terms, depending on the term of their respective provincial assemblies. The chancellor is Social Democrat Franz Vranitzky, who took office in 1986. Following inconclusive National Council elections in 1986, the SPO began a grand coalition government with the OVP. In the general election in October 1990, the senior partner in the ruling coalition, the SPO, won 43 percent of the vote and 81 seats in the lower house, a gain of one seat. Its junior partner, the more conservative OVP, garnered only 32 percent and 60 seats, a 17-seat decline. Picking up conservative votes, the right-wing populist Freedom Party took 17 percent and 33 seats, a gain of 15 seats. The environmentalist Greens won 4.5 percent of the vote and 9 seats, a gain of one.

Following the OVP's disappointing performance in the 1990 election, the Socialists announced their willingness to renew the coalition, in order to keep the Freedom Party out of government. Led by Joerg Haider, the Freedom Party made significant gains in local and regional elections in 1991. In the Viennese municipal election, the party more than doubled its portion of the vote and surpassed the OVP to become the second largest party in the city. In late 1992, Haider demanded a total halt on immigration and threatened the government with an anti-immigrant petition campaign.

Realizing that the Waldheim case and the Haider controversy had undermined Austria's liberal democratic image, Chancellor Vranitzky declared in July 1991 that Austria must accept a share of moral responsibility for the sins of the Third Reich. This statement represented a break from the more popular Austrian view that Austrians had been Hitler's first victims and were therefore absolved of guilt.

Alarmed by the activities of neo-Nazis, the Austrian police arrested several right-wing extremists, including would-be Führer Gottfried Küssel, and uncovered a neo-Nazi organization in January 1992. Neo-Nazis had made plans to topple the government, but the threat is not taken seriously. The number of neo-Nazis in Austria is believed to be small, perhaps between 50 and 300 hard-core members and more than a thousand sympathizers. Parliament passed legislation placing new restrictions on their already illegal activities. In October 1992, vandals desecrated Eisenstadt's Jewish cemetery with Nazi slogans.

Since the collapse of communism in Eastern Europe in 1989, Austria has sought to redefine its international role. During the Cold War, the country presented itself as a bridge between the two camps in Europe, but it is now seeking to join the European Community (EC). The EC is positively inclined towards Austrian membership, but is concerned that Austrian neutrality could cause problems if the Community gets involved in defense policy. Austria, however, is no longer rigidly opposed to joining a Western security structure and hopes to join the Community by 1995. The EC has put off a decision until 1993.

Political Rights and Civil Liberties: Austrians have the right to change their government democratically. Voting is compulsory in some provinces. Four parties won seats in the 1990 National Council elections.

Nazi organizations are illegal, and the 1955 State Treaty prohibits Nazis from enjoying freedoms of assembly and association. However, for many years former Nazis found a home in the Freedom Party, which still seems sympathetic to the Nazi period. In 1992, the parliament outlawed the following: belittling the Holocaust and publicly denying, approving, or justifying Nazi crimes against humanity. These limits on expression apply to print, broadcast and other media. The same legislation also lightened jail sentences for Nazi activities, because juries often acquitted people in cases for which they felt the sentences were too harsh. The Austrian police enforce anti-Nazi statutes unevenly, tending to act more when extremist activities get international attention.

Austrian provinces have significant local power and can check federal power by choosing the members of the upper house of parliament. There is a Slovenian minority which has had some disputes with the Austro-Germans over bilingual education.

The media are generally free from government restrictions. There are a few, rarely used restrictions on press freedom which allow the removal of publications from circulation if they violate laws on public morality or security. Broadcast media belong to an autonomous public corporation. There is freedom of religion for faiths judged consistent with public order and morality. Recognized denominations must register with the government.

The judiciary is independent. Refugees had long used Austria as the first point of asylum when they left Eastern Europe and the Soviet Union. Until March 1990, Austria had an open door policy for people fleeing Eastern Europe, but now the country requires that all prospective newcomers apply for a visa. The government now draws a distinction between political and economic refugees.

Business and labor groups play a major role in formulating national economic policy. Most Austrian workers must belong to Chambers of Labor, which represent workers' interests to the government. Trade unions, on the other hand, negotiate for workers with management.

Azerbaijan

Polity: Presidential-parliamentary (transitional)
Economy: Statist transitional
Population: 7,146,000
PPP: na
Life Expectancy: 70.0
Ethnic Groups: Azeris, other Turkic, Russians, Armenians

Political Rights: 5
Civil Liberties: 5
Status: Partly Free

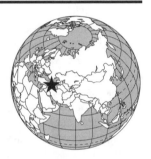

Overview:

Political instability continued to plague Azerbaijan in 1992, leading to the resignation and subsequent attempt to retake power by President Ayaz Mutalibov, and a victory by the nationalist opposition Azerbaijan Popular Front (APF) in the June presidential elections. In addition to renewed fighting in the predominantly Armenian enclave of Nagorno-Karabakh, political unrest flared up in the Nakhichevan Autonomous Republic, a region on the Iranian border separated from the rest of the country by Armenia.

After the collapse of the Soviet Union in 1991, 96 percent of the electorate voted in favor of independence in a 29 December referendum. Three months earlier, Mutalibov, a hardliner who had resigned as first secretary of the Communist party 10 days after the 19 August coup attempt against Soviet President Mikhail Gorbachev, was elected president. The election of Mutalibov followed the withdrawal of Zardusht Ali-Zade of the Azerbaijan Social Democratic Group. The opposition Popular Front led by Ebulfez Elchibey held only 40 of the 350 seats in the Communist-dominated Supreme Soviet, which was elected in a 1990 election marred by irregularities. Amid anti-government rallies in October, the Supreme Soviet created a National Council, a permanent 50-seat legislative body, half of whose members would be picked by the president, half by the opposition.

In early January 1992, President Mutalibov imposed direct rule on Nagorno-Karabakh, further exacerbating tensions in the war-torn region. Christian Armenians make up a majority of the population in Nagorno-Karabakh, but Azerbaijan has controlled the region since 1923. Fighting had intensified a month earlier after Russia announced it would withdraw former Soviet units stationed in the area. In February, mediation efforts by Iran, Russia and other nations failed, as the government resisted calls by Armenia for the introduction of peacekeeping forces under the aegis of the United Nations and the Conference on Security and Cooperation in Europe (CSCE). The government charged that such actions would "internationalize" the conflict.

By March, military gains by Armenian self-defense forces in Nagorno-Karabakh precipitated a political crisis. On 6 March, in the face of rising popular fury over his government's failure to protect the Azeri minority, President Mutalibov resigned during an extraordinary session of parliament. During week-long APF-led demonstrations in several major cities, protestors called for the government to step down, citing, among other things, the massacre of civilians by Armenian forces in the city of Khojaly. Parliament selected Yagub Mahmedov, chairman of the Supreme Soviet, as interim president, and Prime Minister Hasan Hasanov was asked to form a new government. However, Hasanov was ousted in a power struggle on 4 April and replaced by his deputy, Feirus Mustafayev. Presidential elections were scheduled for 7 June.

The political crisis escalated in May when parliament voted overwhelmingly to restore former President Mutalibov to power. Mutalibov's return was facilitated by another Azeri battlefield defeat at Shusha, the last Azeri-controlled stronghold in Nagorno-Karabakh. Mutalibov introduced a two-month state of emergency in the capital city of Baku, banning outdoor meetings and strikes, while restricting the freedom of political parties and the press. He also cancelled presidential elections. On 15 May, thousands of anti-government protesters seized parliament, the presidential palace and the state television building after a brief battle with pro-Mutalibov forces. Joined by renegades from the army, APF supporters took control of Baku's airport and several cities and towns. At least one person was killed and three wounded in the clashes. Arif Gadzhiyev, a member of the National Council formed after Mutalibov had resigned in March, said the APF-dominated council was claiming interim control of the country and called Mutalibov's restoration "an unconstitutional coup." The Front promised June elections would be held as planned. Mutalibov, who disappeared, was later rumored to be hospitalized in Moscow. In a televised address, senior APF leader Isa Gambarov said that toppling Mutalibov paved the way for an Azeri offensive to regain lost territory in Nagorno-Karabakh. On 19 May, parliament voted to dissolve itself and transferred authority to the National Council. Gambarov was subsequently named speaker of parliament and acting president.

Although the National Council promised to follow democratic principles, limits were put on political activities. On 22 May, Boris Kevorkov, first secretary of the Nagorno-Karabakh Communist Party, was arrested without explanation. A week later, the Ministry of Defense issued a decree that, in addition to calling for all members of informal military formations to disband and surrender their weapons, banned public demonstrations and imposed a special visa requirement for those wishing to enter Azerbaijan. The decree further empowered the police to arrest and detain people for up to 30 days, to stop and search vehicles, and to search private homes.

Also in May, clashes between Azeri and Armenian forces spread to Nakhichevan, prompting the region's leader, Gaider Aliyev, to publicly consider seeking assistance from neighboring Turkey, which under a 1921 treaty signed with Soviet Russia was made a guarantor of Nakhichevan's security. Aliyev, former first secretary of the Azerbaijan Communist Party, was once a member of the Soviet Politburo.

On 7 June, APF leader Elchibey was elected president with 59 percent of the vote. He had campaigned on a promise to withdraw Azerbaijan from the Commonwealth of Independent States (CIS) and to keep Nagorno-Karabakh in the country. Nizami Suleimanov of the Democratic Union of the Intelligentsia of Azerbaijan received approximately 34 percent and consequently claimed that the vote had been falsified. Suleimanov intended to launch a campaign of civil disobedience against the new leadership. Turnout among the 3.9 million eligible was reportedly 74 percent. Foreign observers reported that, with the exception of minor irregularities, voting was free and fair.

In July, President Elchibey issued a presidential decree calling for the disarming of all illegal militias in the country. The government acknowledged that retired Turkish military officers were serving as advisors to the Azeri army. On 7 July, Etibar Mahmedov, head of the radical Azerbaijan Independence Party, denounced President Elchibey's consolidation of power as unconstitutional.

In August, as fighting intensified in Nagorno-Karabakh, Interior Minister Iskander Gamodov reported that a coup attempt against the president was squelched on 15 August and that all plotters were arrested. No other details were provided. Meanwhile, the situation in Nagorno-Karabakh continued to deteriorate as Azeri forces launched new offensives to reclaim areas lost to Armenians. Azeri fighter bombers attacked Stepanakert, capital of Karabakh, and other towns along the borders of the two republics. The government declared a state of emergency in regions of Azerbaijan where fighting was heavy. Armenian President Levon Ter-Petrossian appealed for assistance from the CIS under a joint defense pact.

In late September, in a move intended to force Armenian residents to flee, the Azeri military mounted a large-scale offensive in Nagorno-Karabakh from the south and east. Casualties on both sides were reportedly high. Azeri forces claimed to have established artillery control over two stretches of the so-called Lachin Corridor, the sole means to Karabakh from Armenia.

Although Azerbaijan has been slow in adopting market-oriented economic reforms, the government took steps towards privatizing retail and service industries in August. The government also moved to stop barter transactions between Azerbaijan and all foreign and CIS states. Azerbaijan's industrial output, however, declined by approximately 50 percent and it remained one of the poorest of the former Soviet republics. After Azerbaijan introduced its own currency, the *manat*, and freed prices, it was approved for membership in the International Monetary Fund and the World Bank.

In another issue, Kurds demanded self-determination and autonomy over Kurdish territory that was given to Azerbaijan by the former Communist regime. There were reports that the Azeri army had attacked Kurdish settlements.

Political Rights and Civil Liberties: Azeris have the right to change their government democratically. The National Council is functioning as an interim legislative body pending parliamentary elections as yet unscheduled.

Public demonstrations and freedom of assembly have been limited by the new APF-led coalition government. The judiciary is not entirely independent from government interference. A July presidential decree called for the creation of a new security body—the

"Special Administration"—to be empowered to oversee all security and military-related matters and to be under the direct, personal jurisdiction of the president.

After the Azeri Communist Party was driven from power in June, President Elchibey submitted a draft law on the media to the National Council, but the Council demanded substantive revision. The revised version was passed by the National Council in July, but the text was not publicized. The newspapers of the former Azeri Communist Party were taken over by the new leadership. However, the press faced financial problems with the rising costs of paper and publishing. In August, the government granted subsidies enabling newspapers to continue publication, and journalists were granted the right to travel on public transportation without payment. Television and radio are state-owned and -run, but an independent news agency, ASSA-IRADA, began operating in Baku in January 1992. Some information is reportedly censored by the government.

The ministry of justice announced it had registered 8 official political parties, and another 15 submitted applications for recognition. A member of the Azerbaijan Social Democratic Party reported he was forced to leave Baku by actions from the APF against the SDP leadership. He claimed APF leaders had seized all levers of power in the re-public, and would score an "overwhelming victory" in upcoming parliamentary elections.

The ongoing conflict in Nagorno-Karabakh has impinged on religious freedom. Non-Muslims in Azerbaijan face discrimination, while Azeris in Nagorno-Karabakh face problems with the majority Christian Armenians. There have also been reports of persecution of Kurdish minority. The Lezgin national movement leaders in May demanded an end to the compulsory drafting of members of national minorities into the Azerbaijani armed forces. The contingencies of war have infringed on freedom of movement in Nagorno-Karabakh and along its borders. There are relatively few limitations on foreign travel.

Workers are organized in the former Communist-controlled Azerbaijan Council of Trade Unions.

Bahamas

Polity: Parliamentary democracy
Economy: Capitalist-statist
Population: 264,000
PPP: $11,293
Life Expectancy: 71.5
Ethnic Groups: Black (85 percent), white (15 percent)

Political Rights: 1
Civil Liberties: 2
Status: Free

Overview: After 25 years in office, Prime Minister Lynden O. Pindling and the ruling Progressive Liberal Party (PLP) were swept from power in a parliamentary election held on 19 August 1992. Hubert A. Ingraham, leader of the victorious Free National Movement (FNM), became the new prime minister and moved quickly on campaign promises to make government more open and accountable.

The Commonwealth of the Bahamas, a 700-island nation in the Caribbean, is a member of the British Commonwealth. It became internally self-governing in 1967 under the leadership of Pindling and the PLP. Independence was granted in 1973. The British monarchy is represented by a governor-general.

Under the 1973 constitution, there is a bicameral parliament consisting of a 49-member House of Assembly directly elected for 5 years, and a 16-member Senate, with 9 members appointed by the prime minister, 4 by the leader of the parliamentary opposition, and 3 by the governor-general. The prime minister is the leader of the party commanding a majority in the House. Islands other than New Providence and Grand Bahama are administered by centrally appointed commissioners.

In the 1982 and 1987 elections, the PLP fell short of the three-quarters majority it had previously enjoyed, as the Pindling government was dogged by allegations of corruption and high official involvement in narcotics trafficking. In the 1987 elections, the PLP won 31 seats, the FNM 16 and independents 2.

In a by-election in June 1990 marred by charges of fraud by both parties, the FNM retained its Marco City, Grand Bahama, parliamentary seat vacated by the death of FNM leader Cecil Wallace-Whitfield. Mr. Ingraham, a lawyer and former cabinet official expelled by the PLP in 1986 for his outspoken criticism regarding drug and corruption allegations, was selected by the FNM as the new official opposition leader.

The two main issues in the 1992 campaign were corruption and economic recession. The 45-year-old Ingraham vowed to bring honesty, efficiency and accountability to government. Pindling, 62, the Western hemisphere's longest-serving, freely elected head of government, relied on his image as the father of the nation's independence.

But many voters were born since independence and confronted high unemployment as a result of a five-year economic downturn. The PLP and the FNM are both centrist parties, although the FNM is more oriented to free enterprise and a "less government is better" philosophy. The perception that the Pindling government had become ineffectual and unresponsive moved most voters toward the FNM.

On 19 August, approximately 90 percent of the electorate turned out. The FNM won 31 seats in the House of Assembly and the PLP won 17. Prime Minister Ingraham was sworn in two days later. Voting for one seat ended in a virtual tie and was to be decided by an electoral court by the end of the year. Pindling held on to his own seat and became the official opposition leader.

Promising a fresh era of "government in the sunshine," Ingraham said that cabinet papers and details of meetings would be made available to the media for the first time, and that House of Assembly debates would be televised. He also vowed that public funds and jobs would be distributed according to merit, a break with the patronage system under Pindling.

Political Rights and Civil Liberties: Citizens are able to change their government democratically. Unlike the elections during the 1980s, the 1992 vote was relatively free of irregularities and allegations of fraud. In 1992, the use of indelible ink to identify people who had voted was utilized for the first time.

Constitutional guarantees regarding the right to organize political parties, civic organizations and labor unions are generally respected, as is the free exercise of religion. Labor, business and professional organizations are generally free. There is a right to strike, although demonstrations were sometimes broken up by police under the

Pindling government, with demonstrators subject to temporary detention. Nearly 30 percent of the work force is organized and collective bargaining is extensive.

There is an independent Grand Bahama Human Rights Association, as well as at least two other independent rights groups, which frequently criticize the government on police, constitutional and other issues. In recent years, there have been continuing reports of police brutality during the course of arrests and interrogations. Human rights groups have also criticized harsh conditions and overcrowding in the nation's prisons.

A major concern is the condition of the illegal Haitian immigrant population, which is estimated at 50,000, nearly 20 percent of the Bahamian population. The influx has created tension because of the strain on government services during the economic recession. The Pindling government tried to develop programs to better integrate the Haitian population, but human rights groups charge that Haitians are treated inhumanely by the authorities and the public, and in many cases are deported illegally. Following through on a campaign pledge, the Ingraham government began taking a tougher stand on illegal Haitian immigrants in the fall of 1992, repatriating hundreds to Haiti and planning the construction of a detention center.

Full freedom of expression is constrained by strict libel laws which the Pindling government used against the independent press. Under Pindling, radio and television were controlled by the government and often failed to air pluralistic points of view. In one of its first legislative moves, the Ingraham government proposed a bill dismantling the state's monopoly on broadcasting.

The judicial system is headed by a Supreme Court and a Court of Appeal, with the right of appeal under certain circumstances to the Privy Council in London. There are local courts, and on the outer islands the local commissioners have magisterial powers. Despite anti-drug legislation and a formal 1987 agreement with the U.S. to suppress the drug trade, there was lingering evidence that under Pindling drug-related corruption continued to compromise the judicial system and Bahamian Defense Force.

Bahrain

Polity: Traditional monarchy
Economy: Capitalist-statist
Population: 531,000
PPP: $10,804
Life Expectancy: 71.0
Ethnic Groups: Bahraini (63 percent), other Arab (10 percent), Asian (13 percent), immigrant groups, Iranian

Political Rights: 6
Civil Liberties: 5
Status: Partly Free

Overview:

Bahrain's territorial disputes with Qatar continued in 1992 despite efforts by other Gulf Cooperation Council (GCC) members to mediate the conflict. In a controversial move, Bahrain also became the first Gulf country since the Gulf War to urge better relations with Iraq.

The Al Khalifah family has ruled this Persian Gulf nation as a traditional monarchy since 1782. The country is currently ruled by Emir Sheikh 'Isa ibn Salman Al Khalifah, his eldest brother (the prime minister) and his son (the Crown Prince). Bahrain gained independence from Britain in 1971 and established a constitutional monarchy. Approved in June 1973, the constitution made the emir the hereditary ruler and established a National Assembly with thirty popularly elected members. In 1975, however, the emir began to rule by decree, as he was entitled to do under the constitution. One of his decrees was to suspend the constitutional provision for an elected assembly and dissolve the National Assembly, which he found to be dominated by "alien ideas." The emir appoints the 15-member Cabinet and prime minister, as well as the municipal councils in urban areas and the *mukhtars* who govern in rural communities.

The ruling family is Sunni Muslim, while roughly 60 percent of the population is Shi'ite. The regime is increasingly wary of the possibility of fundamentalist upheaval, especially since the Iranian Revolution in 1979. The most threatening underground opposition groups have been the Iran-backed Shi'ite Islamic Front for the Liberation of Bahrain, which launched a coup attempt in 1981, and the Islamic Call Party, which seeks to establish an Islamic state. There are two secular radical groups with apparently limited appeal.

The dispute over territorial waters has disrupted relations between Bahrain and Qatar since Bahrain's independence. The disputed islands include Humar, Fasht al-Dibal and Jaradah Shoals. The territorial dispute with Qatar intensified in 1986 over Fasht al-Dibal. On 16 April 1992, Qatar issued a decree that set territorial waters at 12 nautical miles, and it also defined an "adjacent area" of another 12 nautical miles. In July, Bahrain rejected Qatar's decision to take the case unilaterally to the International Court of Justice (ICJ). The case, Bahrain argued, should have been presented to the Court in a joint request.

Political Rights and Civil Liberties:

Bahrainis do not have the right to change their government democratically. There have been no elections since 1975 when the emir began ruling by decree. In a limited way, citizens participate politically by attending the emir's open-air audiences. Criticism of the regime's legitimacy is not tolerated, political parties are banned, and meetings with any political undertones are banned. In the beginning of 1992, a participant in a seminar for GCC intellectuals in Kuwait, a Bahraini theologian, was arrested upon his return to Bahrain for delivering a lecture in which he argued for elected parliaments, freedom of expression, the rule of law, and curbs on the powers and privileges of the ruling family. He was later released on bail.

Although the press is privately owned, past government censorship policies have been transformed into self-censorship. Radio and television are state-owned. Since the outbreak of the Gulf War, there has been a limited and informal relaxation of restrictions on freedom of speech and assembly. However, telephone calls and correspondence are subject to monitoring through an extensive and effective police informer network.

While the constitution provides for the right of free assembly, public political demonstrations or meetings are prohibited. Political organizations are prohibited, but social and sports clubs serve as a forum for limited and discreet discussions. They are usually closely monitored by the government. Some private professional associations are allowed to function, and public religious events are tolerated, but they too are monitored closely. No unions exist in Bahrain, only government controlled "workers' committees," comprising over 10 percent of the work force. In 1982, the government gave permission to form the joint labor-management consultative committee (JCC). Thirteen JCCs have been established in major industries, representing approximately 70 percent of Bahrain's industrial labor force. There are no collective bargaining agreements and workers do not have the right to strike.

The court procedures do not guarantee fair trials. Defendants are either tried in ordinary civil or criminal courts with procedural guarantees or, if requested by the prosecutor, in the Security Court with no procedural guarantees.

There have been occasional reports and complaints of arbitrary detention, torture and the absence of impartial inspection of prison and detention facilities. Security laws allow for broad arrest powers against suspected political activists.

Jews, Baha'is and expatriate Christians are allowed to practice their faith in their own place of worship, which they are allowed to build. Sunni Muslims enjoy more favored treatment than Shiites. Citizens are free to travel within and outside the country, but the government has denied passports for foreign travel in the past for political reasons.

Women face far fewer cultural and legal restrictions than in other Islamic countries. Many own and inherit property and may also represent their own interest in public and legal matters. However, there have been complaints by women's groups of problems of unequal wages and opportunities in the workplace.

Bangladesh

Polity: Parliamentary democracy
Economy: Capitalist-statist
Population: 111,445,000
PPP: $820
Life Expectancy: 51.8
Ethnic Groups: Bengali (98 percent), Bihari (1 percent), various tribal groups (1 percent)

Political Rights: 2
Civil Liberties: 3
Status: Free

Overview: Bangladesh continued its relatively smooth democratic transition in 1992 under prime minister Khaleda Zia. Key issues facing the government included political unrest, a flood of refugees from Burma, and the continuing investigation of former president H.M. Ershad.

Bangladesh (formerly East Pakistan) won independence in December 1971 during a war between India and Pakistan. In 1981, army rivals assassinated President Ziaur Rahman in an unsuccessful coup attempt. Army chief of staff Gen. H.M. Ershad ousted Rahman's short-lived successor in a March 1982 coup. The country's democratic route began with Ershad's resignation on 6 December 1990, following weeks of intense civilian protests against his authoritarian rule. Former Supreme Court Justice Shahabuddin Ahmed took over as caretaker president and quickly made preparations for competitive elections.

Going into the election, two leading opposition parties stood as favorites to form a new government. They were the Awami League, headed by Sheik Hasina, daughter of the country's first president, and the Bangladesh National Party (BNP), headed by Khaleda Zia, widow of assassinated president Rahman. Although Ershad was under arrest, the Electoral Commission reversed an earlier ban and allowed his National Party to field candidates.

The country's first untainted elections were held on 27 February 1991 for the 300 directly elected seats in the 330-member National Assembly (30 seats are reserved for women). The BNP took 138 seats; the Awami League, 85; Ershad's National Party, 35; the fundamentalist Islamic Assembly, 18; with the remainder split among smaller parties and independents. Re-polling took place in six constituencies, giving the Awami League 4 more seats and the Islamic Assembly and the tiny National Democratic Party each one more. The Islamic Assembly, which abhors the secular, pro-Indian Awami League, threw its support behind the BNP. This allowed Zia's party to name 28 of the 30 women's seats and secure a parliamentary majority. On 5 March acting president Ahmed named Zia as the first female prime minister of this predominantly Muslim country.

In June 1991, the government announced it would scrap the presidential system in favor of a Westminster-style parliamentary democracy. In a 15 September referendum, 84 percent of the citizens approved the plan. On 19 September, parliament swore in Zia as head of government, and six days later it approved the BNP-nominated Abdur Rahman Biswas as president.

In 1992, the government faced a minor crisis over Muslim fundamentalist Golam Azam, who along with the Islamic Assembly supported Pakistan during the 1971 war. Azam fled to Pakistan after the war, was stripped of his Bangladeshi citizenship in 1973 and returned to the country in 1977 with a Pakistani passport. Following the Islamic Assembly's strong showing in the 1991 vote, he was elected party chairman.

Azam's political revival renewed popular anger against him. The opposition Awami League tried to disgrace the government over its tacit coalition with his Islamic Assembly. Under pressure, the government arrested Azam on 23 March for violating the Foreigners Act by heading a political party without being a citizen. The arrest touched off several rounds of rioting between his supporters and opponents seeking his trial and execution. After opposition MPs boycotted the parliamentary budget session in June, the government agreed to formally try Azam and drop charges against 24 people arrested for holding a mock tribunal which hung him in effigy.

During the year, the government also stepped up its investigation into former leader Ershad, who has been stripped of the seat he won in the 1991 elections. In June 1991, he was given ten years in jail on weapons charges, and in January 1992 he received three more years for illegal currency possession. One official noted, "This case is just the appetizer. The main course is coming." The next day, the government charged him with receiving kickbacks in the purchase of three British-built aircraft. On 10 July, prosecutors indicted him and four others for taking $16.4 million in kickbacks in a military contract with an unnamed United States company.

Zia's government also faces rising violence on university campuses, the continuing insurgency in the Chittagong Hill Tracts, and the flood of refugees from neighboring Burma. Following a gun battle on 3 September which killed two activists, the BNP suspended Jatiyabadi Chatra Dal (JCD), its student wing at Dhaka University. At the time 80 students had died during the year in campus strife.

In the southeast, insurgents from various Buddhist tribes including the Chakma are fighting for control of the 5,200 square-mile Chittagong Hill Tract. The government has tacitly encouraged an influx of Muslim Bangladeshis to the region in order to reduce overcrowding in other areas. The Buddhist tribes now make up 60 percent of the population, down from 90 percent four decades ago, and want greater autonomy over the resource-rich area. On 5 November, rebel leaders met with government officials and agreed to find a political solution to the conflict, which over the years has killed 4,000 and forced 30,000 refugees to India.

In the east, some 265,000 refugees from the military regime in Burma refuse to be repatriated until their safety can be assured. The two countries signed a repatriation pact in April, but few refugees have returned to Burma. Another human rights issue involves some 250,000 Bihari Muslims who favored (then) West Pakistan in the 1971 war, and remain in squalid camps awaiting emigration to Pakistan.

The country has complied with numerous International Monetary Fund guidelines for reforming the economy, including introducing a 15 percent value-added tax, gradually reducing protective tariffs, and partially privatizing the state sector. The economy has been devastated by natural disasters such as the April 1991 typhoon which killed 139,000.

Political Rights and Civil Liberties: Citizens changed their government in February 1991 in internationally observed elections that were generally free of violence. By contrast, three people died and 100 were injured in the February 1992 voting for 3,945 village councils. Voting was postponed in at least eight centers after partisans attempted to grab ballot boxes and ballots.

The press has operated with a new vigor since Ershad's fall. The country has 119 daily newspapers, 444 weeklies, and over 300 magazines, most of them launched after the 1991 elections. However, journalists are wary of proposed legislation which would empower the Bangladesh Press Council to cancel journalist licenses for alleged biased or sensationalized reporting. In addition, the government is considering distributing advertising to magazines and newspapers based on its determination of how objective their reporting is rather than their circulation figures. Most publications heavily depend on advertising revenues from the government or state-owned enterprises. A July report by the Bangladesh Human Rights Commission said that in the first half of 1992, one journalist had been killed, five others arrested and 83 were "victims of police atrocities." It also said that the state-controlled media had censored coverage on the trial of former president Golam Azam. Opposition groups accuse the government of reneging on a pre-election promise to privatize the electronic media.

The Special Powers Act (SPA) of 1974 allows police to detain suspects for an interim period of 30 days to prevent "any prejudicial act." If formally charged, they can be held while being investigated, subject to a judicial review after six months. The government has used the SPA against both criminal and political suspects. The judiciary is independent of the government, although the system is characterized by massive backlogs and corruption. Detainees and accused criminals are frequently tortured or mistreated. Freedom of association is respected in practice.

In 1988, Islam was declared the state religion, but the government respects the rights of Buddhist, Hindu and Christian minorities. Civil servants and workers in the Chittagong Export Processing Zone are barred from unionizing, and all unions face restrictions on who can hold office. The 1958 Essential Services Ordinance allows the government to bar strikes for three months in any sector it considers essential. Strikes are often accompanied by violence.

Barbados

Polity: Parliamentary democracy
Economy: Capitalist
Population: 258,000
PPP: $8,351
Life Expectancy: 75.1
Ethnic Groups: Black (80 percent), white (4 percent), mixed (16 percent)

Political Rights: 1
Civil Liberties: 1
Status: Free

Overview: In 1992, Prime Minister Erskine Sandiford and the governing Democratic Labour Party (DLP) appeared to have turned the economy around after a precipitous two-year slump. By the fall, the pressure from political opponents, business, and labor against the government's economic austerity program seemed to be diminishing.

Barbados, a member of the British Commonwealth, became internally self-governing in 1961 and achieved independence in 1966. The British monarchy is represented by a governor-general.

The system of government is a parliamentary democracy. The bicameral parliament consists of a 28-member House of Assembly (the twenty-eighth seat was added in 1991) elected for five years by direct popular vote, and a 21-member Senate, with 12 senators appointed by the prime minister, 2 by the leader of the parliamentary opposition, and 7 by various civic interests. Executive authority is invested in the prime minister, who is the leader of the political party commanding a majority in the House.

Since independence, power has alternated between two centrist parties, the DLP under Errol Barrow until 1976, and the Barbados Labour Party (BLP) under Tom Adams from 1976 until Adams' death in 1985. Adams was succeeded by his deputy, Bernard St. John, but the BLP was soundly defeated in the 1986 elections. The DLP took 24 seats to the BLP's 3 and Barrow returned as prime minister. Barrow died suddenly in June 1987 and was succeeded by Erskine Sandiford.

The DLP's majority was reduced in February 1989 when four House members, led by former finance minister Richie Haynes, broke away from the DLP to form the National Democratic Party (NDP). Haynes became the leader of the opposition on the strength of the NDP's four-to-three seat advantage over the BLP. The ruling DLP retained 20 seats.

Economic issues dominated the campaign for the 1991 election. The gross domestic product declined in 1990 for the first time in seven years, primarily because of decreased revenues from tourism, manufacturing and the sugar industry. Higher oil prices, a result of the Persian Gulf crisis, cut into already dwindling hard currency reserves. The opposition parties pressed their cases on unemployment, which the government estimated to be 17-18 percent, and increasing drug abuse and crime, particularly among youth.

Nonetheless, the DLP was able to win an eighteen-seat majority in the January 1991 election. The BLP, led by former foreign minister Henry Forde, bounced back from its dismal 1986 showing to take ten seats. The NDP failed to break the two-party system, winning no seats. Voter participation dipped to 62 percent, down from 76 percent in 1986.

Amid the continuing economic slide, the Sandiford government pushed austerity legislation, including a public sector pay cut passed in the House by only one vote. Near the end of 1991, the country was crippled by a two-day general labor strike backed by the BLP and mass demonstrations, a level of turbulence not seen in Barbados in over twenty years.

In early 1992, Sandiford ignored threats of a no-confidence motion in parliament and pressed forward with the IMF-prescribed stabilization program and a revision of the tax system. The IMF rewarded the government with a $65 million loan in the spring. By September, the economy was showing signs of recovery and the BLP and other critics of Sandiford's economic policy were keeping a lower profile.

Political Rights and Civil Liberties:

Citizens are able to change their government through free and fair elections. Constitutional guarantees regarding freedom of religion and the right to organize political parties, labor unions and civic organization are respected. Apart from the parties holding parliamentary seats and the NDP, there are other political organizations, including the small left-wing Workers' Party of Barbados. Human rights organizations operate freely. There are two major labor unions and various smaller ones, which are politically active and free to strike.

Freedom of expression is fully respected. Public opinion expressed through the news media, which is free of censorship and government control, has a powerful influence on policy. Newspapers are privately owned, and there are two major dailies. There are both private and government radio stations. The single television station, operated by the government-owned Caribbean Broadcasting Corporation (CBC), presents a wide range of political viewpoints.

The judicial system is independent and includes a Supreme Court that encompasses a High Court and a Court of Appeal. Lower court officials are appointed on the advice of the Judicial and Legal Service Commission. The government provides free legal aid to the indigent.

In 1992, human rights concerns continued to center on the rising crime rate and the justice ministry's decision in 1991 to return to the practice of flogging as punishment for armed robbery. Judicial whipping had not been used for several decades, but its use was never abolished by law. Human rights groups protested that flogging violated a constitutional ban on torture or inhuman and degrading punishment. In September 1992, the Court of Appeal formally outlawed the practice.

Belarus (Byelorussia)

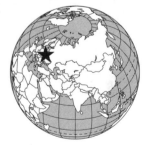

Polity: Presidential-parliamentary
Economy: Statist transitional
Population: 10,263,000
PPP: na
Life Expectancy: 72.0
Ethnic Groups: Belarussians, Russian, Ukrainians

Political Rights: 4
Civil Liberties: 3
Status: Partly Free

Overview:

In 1992, Belarus (formerly the Byelorussian Soviet Socialist Republic) marked its first full year as an independent state. Major political issues included attempts by opposition groups to hold a referendum on early parliamentary elections, disagreements over the pace and direction of economic reforms, and the evolution of Belarus's relationship to other members of the Commonwealth of Independent States (CIS).

In the period of *glasnost* and *perestroika*, the Byelorussian Soviet Socialist Republic remained under the strong influence of the local Communist party *nomenklatura*. The republic's leaders opposed the reform policies of Soviet President Mikhail Gorbachev and remained loyal to the central Communist apparatus in Moscow. Political opposition to central rule was sparked by Moscow's indifference in the wake of the 1986 Chernobyl nuclear disaster. About 20 percent of the population, or 2 million people, lived on land contaminated by the radioactive fallout.

In the first multi-candidate elections to the Belarusian Supreme Soviet (parliament) in the spring of 1990, the democratic opposition, galvanized by the Belarusian Popular Front (BPF), gained 37 of 360 seats. Along with the bloc of reform-minded Communists, the BPF was able to exercise considerable influence on the government. In 1990, the Supreme Soviet voted to make Belarusian the official language, and declared the republic's sovereignty within the Soviet Union. Nevertheless, the Communist party was able to retain its power and privileges, and the democratic opposition remained relatively weak.

During the 19 August 1991 coup attempt against Gorbachev, the government and parliamentary presidium remained cautious and noncommittal. After the collapse of the coup, the parliament voted to declare the republic's independence and change its name to the Republic of Belarus. Later that year, the parliament elected Stanislau Shushkevich, a national-minded moderate democrat, to be its chairman. On 8 December, Shushkevich, along with the presidents of Russia and Ukraine, signed a declaration on the establishment of the Commonwealth of Independent States. A loose successor to the Soviet Union, the CIS's coordinating headquarters are in Minsk, the capital of Belarus. It is not by accident that the CIS was born in the Belarusian capital; the republic has often acted as a buffer or mediator between its two more powerful neighbors, Russia and Ukraine.

The Popular Front and other opposition groups criticized Shushkevich over the formation of the CIS, and accused him and the government headed by Prime Minister Vyachislav Kebich (most of whose cabinet were former Communist officials) of too closely following Russia's lead. On 29 December 1991, the Popular Front decided to call for a referendum to dissolve parliament.

On 4 January 1992, representatives of five political parties and trade unions met with Popular Front deputies to discuss the organization of the referendum, accusing the government and parliament of failing to initiate reforms. To punish opposition deputies, Shushkevich withheld their quarterly bonus payment, saying that they had not fulfilled their duties.

On 2 February, a new political movement—New Belarus—was formed, uniting several left-of-center groups. Its platform supported the referendum petition drive, multi-party elections for a smaller parliament of full-time deputies, and division of legislative and executive powers. Two days later, the prime minister said his government would not resign.

On 13 February, in a surprise move, the Central Electoral Commission gave official permission for the petition drive and the referendum. To be valid, the petition needed the signatures of 350,000 citizens. On 4 March, the Supreme Soviet presidium and government issued a statement accusing the opposition of increasing social tensions by collecting signatures. In a speech to the Supreme Soviet, Shushkevich warned that the situation was becoming critical, calling on parliament to approve a law on democratic elections to local governments while accusing the local bureaucrats of impeding reforms.

On 13 April, the referendum petition drive was completed, and 446,000 signatures were presented to the Central Electoral Commission. The Commission validated 383,000 signatures, more than the minimum required. Rather than hold the referendum, parliament voted on 29 October to hold early elections in March 1994, one year before its current term expires.

On 18 May, the Belarusian Supreme Court overruled the Justice Ministry's decision to refuse the registration to the Party of Communists of Belarus (PCB). The ministry had ruled that the PCB was a direct successor of the suspended Communist Party of Byelorussia (CPB) and, as such, its activities were illegal. With 15,000 members, the PCB claimed to be a new party and the largest political organization in Belarus.

On 3 June, the Belarusian National-Democratic Party held a three-day conference on "Building a Democratic State," which was attended by participants from other post-Communist countries. On 10 August, a number of pro-Communist and pro-Russian organizations, including the Party of Communists, the Fund for Protection of Servicemen, and the White Russia Slavonic Assembly, established a coordinating group to promote what they called political and social stability and serve as an electoral bloc.

In foreign and defense policies, Belarus aimed at securing its independence, but remained cautious and worked for strong ties with Russia and other CIS states. On 11 January, the Supreme Soviet voted to create a ministry of defense, and for subordination of former Soviet troops on its territory, except the strategic forces, to Belarusian jurisdiction. On 14 February, at a summit of CIS leaders, the Belarusian delegation stated Belarus's intention to have its own armed forces at the end of a two-year period. With the start of the year, Belarus's nuclear weapons began to be transferred to Russia for dismantling.

On 18 March, parliament adopted six laws related to establishing its own defense forces. On 20 July, Belarus and Russia signed the Treaty on Cooperation in the Defense Sphere. The treaty sought to coordinate the military activities and regulate the strategic forces under CIS command. On 6 August, an extraordinary session of the Presidium of the Supreme Soviet criticized the agreement between Russia and Ukraine on the division of the Black Sea Fleet. In its statement, the presidium accused Russia and Ukraine of violating previously adopted CIS agreements on strategic forces.

One embarrassing incident occurred in February, when Foreign Minister Piotra Krauchanka, in a meeting with a European Community delegation, stated that Belarus laid claim on Lithuanian border areas, including its capital, Vilnius. Krauchanka later recanted, stating it was only his private view.

Belarus's economic policy was characterized by a cautious approach towards establishing a market-oriented economy. The Popular Front and other opposition groups accused the government of delaying reforms and trying to preserve the old centralized system. On 21 February, the government decided to nationalize all former USSR property on its territory. On 25 March, the Supreme Soviet adopted a law on land ownership, specifying its three forms: private, state and collective. In May, the National Bank of Belarus began issuing multiple-use coupons to cover the shortage of money in circulation. On 10 July, Belarus became a member of the IMF and the World Bank.

Political Rights and Civil Liberties: The last parliamentary elections of 1990 did not truly provide the citizens and political groups with an equal chance to elect or be elected to the republic's parliament. Independent organizations were able to put their candidates on the ballot, and the democratic Popular Front gained 37 seats, but the former Communist party dominated the media and harassed the opposition. Since independence, the political situation has not changed significantly.

Parliament adopted the first draft of the constitution on 22 May, and the opposition was able to collect enough signatures for the holding of a referendum on early elections. In April, the parliament adopted a plan for legal reform based on the rule-of-law. Several political parties and organizations of various orientations were registered, although their recognition among the public was rather limited. There are some independent trade unions, but the heirs of the old, government-controlled unions dominate the scene. Freedom of religion is respected, although there were tensions between the government and the Catholic Church over the latter's strong connections to the Catholic Church in Poland.

Freedom of the press is restricted because mass media are either government-owned or -subsidized. A new law on entry and exit is being prepared to replace the old-style Soviet law. Meanwhile, there were several cases of "secrecy refuseniks"—people who had worked in military-related areas and were denied exit permits.

Belgium

Polity: Parliamentary democracy
Economy: Capitalist
Population: 10,041,000
PPP: $13,313
Life Expectancy: 75.2
Ethnic Groups: Fleming (55 percent), Walloon (33 percent), mixed and others (12 percent), including Moroccan, Turkish and other immigrant groups

Political Rights: 1
Civil Liberties: 1
Status: Free

Overview: After forming a governing coalition of four Socialist and Christian Democratic parties, Jean-Luc Dehaene became Belgium's new premier in February 1992. Dehaene, a Flemish Christian Democrat, formed the four-party coalition after two other politicians had failed to do so following the inconclusive general election of November 1991.

Modern Belgium dates from 1830, when the territory broke away from the Netherlands. A constitutional monarchy, Belgium has a largely ceremonial king who symbolizes the unity of this ethnically divided state.

The Dutch-speaking Flemings comprise about 55 percent of the population and the Francophone Walloons make up about 33 percent. The rest of the population is of bilingual, mixed or other background, including a small German minority near the German border. Belgium is divided into separate linguistic zones for the Flemings, Walloons, Germans and multi-cultural Brussels, the headquarters of the European

Commission. There have been frequent disputes between the two dominant language groups. For much of Belgian history, the Walloons dominated culture and the economy, while the Flemings had no legal status. To inspire Flemish enlistment in World War I, King Albert promised "equality in right and in fact."

Due to ethnic divisions, Belgian political parties are split along linguistic lines. Both Walloons and Flemings have parties ranging across the political spectrum. Governments come and go rapidly. There have been more than 30 cabinets since World War II. However, many of the same politicians and political parties reappear frequently in coalition governments. The bicameral parliament has a Senate, which combines directly and indirectly elected members, and a Chamber of Representatives, which the people elect directly on the basis of proportional representation. Each house has a term of up to four years. The heir to the throne (King Baudouin's nephew) has the right to a Senate seat. The current Senate has 183 members, while the Chamber of Representatives has 212.

A center-left coalition under Christian Democratic Prime Minister Wilfried Martens governed from 1987 to late 1991. That coalition consisted of both Socialist parties, both Christian Democratic parties, and Volksunie, the moderate Flemish nationalist party. Martens's coalition split in October 1991 when Flemish and Walloon parties squabbled over arms sales and government contracts that each side believed would have aided the other linguistic group.

The general election of November 1991 produced losses for the Christian Democrats, Socialists, Francophone Liberals, and Volksunie. The right-wing Flemish Vlams Blok, the Greens, Flemish right-wing Liberals, Flemish Libertarians, and the Francophone National Front made gains. The small Francophone Federalists held their ground. Because the voters increased the standing of environmentalist and anti-immigrant parties, the government is under pressure to address their concerns.

The Dehaene government has a deficit-reduction program aimed at meeting the standards for European currency union. The measures include stricter welfare policies, higher social security taxes, and closing tax loopholes.

Eager to settle cultural and linguistic disputes, Dehaene announced a major constitutional deal in September 1992. Flemings and Walloons will have enhanced autonomy in their respective regions. They will be able to deny elected office to members of the other group who live in their region. This may solve the issue of elected politicians refusing to take competency tests in the regionally dominant language. There is growing talk of Flemish independence.

Political Rights and Civil Liberties: Belgians have the right to change their government democratically. Nonvoters are subject to fines. Political parties organize freely, usually along ethnic lines. Each language group has autonomy within its own region. Voters elect regional councils, but the national government appoints the provincial governors.

In general, there is freedom of speech and of the press. However, Belgium law prohibits some forms of pornography and incitements to violence. Libel laws may have some minor restraining effects on the press and restrictions on civil servants' criticism of the government may constitute a small reduction of freedom of speech. Autonomous public boards govern the state television and radio networks, and ensure that public broadcasting is linguistically pluralistic. The state has permitted and licensed private radio stations since 1985. There is freedom of association. Most workers belong to trade union federations. The largest labor group is Catholic and another major federation is social democratic.

Freedom of religion is respected. The state recognizes and subsidizes Christian, Jewish and Muslim institutions. Other faiths are unrestricted. The monarch and his consort have a religious role. According to Belgian tradition, the seventh son or seventh daughter born to any Belgian family has the king or queen as godparent.

The judiciary is independent. The government appoints judges for life tenure. Belgium has a generally good record on the rights of the accused, but there have been some problems with extended pretrial detentions. Since 1985, the municipalities around Brussels have had the right to refuse to register new residents from countries outside the European Community. In 1988 the central government set up a commission to handle political asylum cases.

Belize

Polity: Parliamentary democracy
Economy: Capitalist
Population: 229,000
PPP: $2,662
Life Expectancy: 69.5
Ethnic Groups: Majority of mixed ancestry, including black, Carib, Creole and mestizo

Political Rights: 1
Civil Liberties: 1
Status: Free

Overview: Belize is a member of the British Commonwealth. The British monarchy is represented by a governor-general. Formerly British Honduras, the name was changed to Belize in 1973. Internal self-government was granted in 1964 and independence in 1981. Because neighboring Guatemala refused to recognize the new state, Britain agreed to provide for Belize's defense.

In 1991, Guatemala officially recognized Belize and diplomatic relations were established in September of that year. In 1992, negotiations continued between the two countries to reach a final accord on Guatemala's 134-year-old claim to an undefined part of Belizean land. Belize and Britain agreed that the 1,600-member British military force would remain in Belize pending resolution of the dispute.

Belize is a parliamentary democracy with a bicameral National Assembly. The 28-seat House of Representatives is elected for a five-year term. Members of the Senate are appointed; five appointed by the governor-general on the advice of the prime minister, two by the leader of the parliamentary opposition, and one by the Belize Advisory Council.

In the first post-independence election in 1984, the center-right United Democratic Party (UDP) won 21 seats in the House, overturning 30 years of rule by George Price's center-left People's United Party (PUP), which took the remaining 7 seats. The UDP's Manuel A. Esquivel replaced Price as prime minister.

In the most recent national elections held in 1989, Price returned as prime minister as the PUP won 15 seats in the House to the UPD's 13. The Belize Popular Party (BPP) failed to win a seat.

In 1989, the PUP won the Belize City Council elections, taking all nine council seats and ending twelve years of UDP control of local government in the nation's capital, where nearly 30 percent of the population resides. In March 1991 municipal elections, the PUP won majorities in five out of country's seven Town Boards.

In January 1992, the UDP split over proposed government legislation allowing Guatemala access to the Atlantic Ocean. The legislation was designed to move forward territorial negotiations with Guatemala. A number of key UDP figures were expelled from the party for opposing the bill, which was passed with the backing of the UDP leadership. Other UDP members resigned in protest. In February, the out-group formed a new party, the National Alliance for Belizean Rights (NABR), led by former UDP elder statesman Philip Goldson. The NABR occupied two seats in the House, those of Mr. Goldson and Hubert Erlington, thereby reducing the UDP representation from 13 to 11. The next national elections are due in 1994.

Political Rights and Civil Liberties:

Citizens are able to change their government through free and fair elections. While the UDP and the PUP dominate the political scene, there are no restrictions on the right to organize political parties. Civic society is well established, with a large number of nongovernmental organizations working in the social, economic and environmental areas. Labor unions are independent and free to strike. There are nearly a dozen active trade unions, and close to a third of the work force is unionized. Disputes are adjudicated by official boards of inquiry, and businesses are penalized for failing to abide by the labor code. There is freedom of religion.

The judiciary is independent and nondiscriminatory and the rule of law is guaranteed. The formation of a Security Intelligence Service (SIS) by the UPD government in 1988 to combat drug traffickers was criticized by the PUP, and led to the creation of the Belize Human Rights Commission to address charges of physical and verbal abuse and wrongful arrests by security forces. The PUP dissolved the SIS after returning to office in 1989.

In recent years, human rights concerns have focused on the plight of migrant workers and refugees from neighboring Central American countries—primarily El Salvador and Guatemala—and charges of labor abuses by Belizean employers. Among an estimated 30,000 aliens in Belize (nearly 15 percent of total population), more than 6,000 registered under an amnesty program implemented in cooperation with the United Nations High Commissioner for Refugees. After a peace accord was reached in El Salvador in December 1991, the UNCHR began a repatriation process for Salvadoran refugees in Belize.

There also has been concern about the increase in violent crime, much of it related to drug trafficking and gang conflict. Because most of the 600-member police force goes unarmed, in 1992 the government instituted a policy of joint patrols between the police and the 600-member Belize Defense Force. The government claimed criminal activity subsequently diminished, but the human rights commission warned of the potential for increased rights abuses.

There are five independent newspapers representing various political viewpoints. Belize has a literacy rate of over 90 percent. Radio and television, however, have have played an increasingly prominent role in recent years. There are fourteen privately owned television stations including four cable systems. At the end of 1990, the PUP reduced government involvement in the broadcast media by creating an independent board to oversee operations of government-owned outlets.

Benin

Polity: Presidential-parliamentary democracy
Economy: Statist-transitional
Population: 4,995,000
PPP: $1,030
Life Expectancy: 47.0
Ethnic Groups: Aja, Barriba, Fon, Yoruba

Political Rights: 2
Civil Liberties: 3
Status: Free

Overview:

In 1992, the government of President Nicephore Soglo continued to face Benin's chronic economic problems. The government also brought corrupt officials of the prior regime to trial and fended off a brief military uprising at mid-year.

The Republic of Dahomey achieved its independence from France on 1 August 1960. General Ahmed Kérékou seized power in a 1972 coup. He renamed the country "Benin" in 1975 and established a Marxist-Leninist state under the banner of his Benin People's Revolutionary Party (PRPB). The regime's militant Youth League advanced and safeguarded political orthodoxy, while suspected political enemies suffered arbitrary arrest, imprisonment, torture and extrajudicial execution. By 1988, Benin was effectively bankrupt, bled by official corruption and incompetence, and besieged by widespread work stoppages and student-led strikes. In December 1989, after a series of moves to consolidate its hold on power, the regime entered into negotiations with the exiled political opposition in an effort to fend off economic and political disaster. The resulting Paris agreement laid the foundations for the country's transition to multi-party democracy.

A national conference assumed sovereign control over the country in early 1990, appointing an interim government to prepare for democracy. Stripping Kérékou of his effective power as president, though not his formal position as head of state, the conference selected an interim prime minister, Nicephore Soglo, to lead the country through a year-long transition to competitive elections. Local multi-party elections in late 1990 were followed by legislative and presidential elections during the first quarter of 1991. In addition, a new democratic constitution was ratified by popular referendum. In March 1991, two rounds of balloting for president resulted in a conclusive victory for Prime Minister Soglo over Kérékou.

Although Kérékou himself has been given immunity, some of his associates now face prosecution for corruption. Mohamed Amadou Cissé, former Minister of State in

Charge of Security for the Kérékou regime, was sentenced in September 1992 to 10 years in prison. Cissé, Kérékou's personal soothsayer, stood accused of having transferred the equivalent of $8.5 million in public funds to private accounts overseas and abusing the authority of his office.

A suspected coup attempt in May led to the detention and questioning of six military officers. One, a former deputy chief in Kérékou's now-dissolved presidential guard, escaped custody and fled to an army garrison in the north of the country. Confronted at the garrison by loyalist paratroopers in July, Captain Pascal Tawes took flight with armed followers.

The Soglo administration continued to address the country's acute economic problems by implementing an unpopular austerity program. Benin has been hard hit by budget cuts made under IMF restructuring guidelines. Soglo, formerly associated with the World Bank, has been able to use his connections to increase multilateral lending to the country. One of the government's first economic measures has been to prune back a public sector swollen with the country's university graduates. In the past, over-staffing of government ministries has been a response to an underdeveloped private sector incapable of employing most Beninois with higher degrees. As civil servants lose their jobs, tensions among the nation's educated elite are growing.

Political Rights and Civil Liberties: Benin's citizens can change their government democratically. Twenty-five parties are represented in the National Assembly. The national media reflect a wide range of political views, and private broadcasting is permitted. However, the content of reporting in the official media is increasingly controlled by the new regime; journalists in the state radio and television services are reportedly pressured to favor the government's point of view. Private journalists have been threatened with legal action for displeasing the authorities. François Comlan, publisher of the *L'Observateur*, was fined the equivalent of $3700 and sentenced to six months in jail for criminal libel due to the title of one article—"Soglo, with Cissé on his arm"—and the contents of an issue printed but never distributed.

Other newspapers such as the *Tam-Tam Express* and *le Soleil* have come under fire for what the president has characterized as "irresponsible journalism." The periodicals have criticized the alleged inordinate influence of the president's wife in national politics.

The Soglo government has made a special effort to professionalize law enforcement personnel in order to eliminate arbitrary behavior such as the levying of on-the-spot "fines" on innocent passers-bye. There are no major restrictions on religion, and both domestic and international travel are unrestricted. Freedom of assembly is generally respected, but authorities can ban gatherings if there is a risk of "serious disturbance." The right to strike is constitutionally protected. Civil servants have gone on strike demanding retraining programs and wage hikes. Among other rights violations, women continue to be subjected to female circumcision and arranged marriages with little or no say in the matter. The independent Benin Commission on Human Rights exists to guard against recurrence of the widespread human rights violations.

Bhutan

Polity: Traditional
monarchy
Economy: Pre-industrial
Population: 683,000
PPP: $750
Life Expectancy: 48.9
Ethnic Groups: Bhotia (60 percent), Nepalese
(25 percent), indigenous (15 percent), Tibetan refugees

Political Rights: 7
Civil Liberties: 6
Status: Not Free

Overview: In 1992, Bhutan continued depopulating its southern areas of ethnic Nepalese, some of who trace their roots in the country for generations. The King claims that an influx of Nepalese in the past several decades has diluted the indigenous Bhuddist culture.

The British began guiding the foreign affairs of this isolated Himalayan kingdom in 1865. India took over this role in 1949, agreeing not to interfere in domestic matters. In 1972, 19-year-old Jigme Singye Wangchuk succeeded his father to the throne. The King governs the country with the assistance of a Council of Ministers and a Royal Advisory Council. A 150-member National Assembly meets briefly twice a year to do little more than pass the King's legislation. Every three years 105 National Assembly members are elected by village headmen in Buddhist areas and family heads in Hindu regions. Twelve Assembly seats go to religious groups and 33 are appointed by the King. Political parties are heavily discouraged and none exist.

The country's sixth five-year plan (1987-92) introduced a program of *Driglam Namzha* (national customs and etiquette) to reinvigorate Buddhist culture. The government banned the teaching of the Nepalese language in schools, and required citizens to adopt the national dress of the ruling Drukpa class. Candidates for the civil service were required to speak Dzongkha, which is known only to about one-fifth of the population.

The program took on a new dimension after the 1988 census showed Nepalese Ghurkas to be in the majority in five southern districts. In 1989, the King said the population was actually roughly half the size the census indicated, and declared that all but 28,000 of some 600,000 Nepalese in the country were illegal immigrants under a 1985 citizenship act. This act required them to show evidence that they or their families had lived in the country prior to 1958, which proved impossible for most in a society which is highly illiterate and lacks basic administrative systems. The vast majority of ethnic Nepalese in Bhutan, who claim their ancestors have lived in the country for generations, were thus rendered stateless.

Several parties were formed in 1989 and 1990 by Nepalese to protest the measures and the impending expulsion of ethnic Nepalese. Among them was the Bhutan People's Party (BPP), which organized several protests in the south in September 1990 to push for political and social reforms. Security forces violently dispersed the demonstrators. The BPP claimed over 300 were killed, although other reports suggest far fewer. In September 1991, India agreed to crack down on anti-Bhutan activity by ethnic Nepalese living in the Indian states of West Bengal and

Assam in return for an end to cross-border raids by the Bhutanese army. The now-outlawed BPP and other groups receive assistance from Nepal's Congress Party and other leftist groups.

In March and April 1992, the Nepalese government protested to King Wangchuk over the expulsion of Nepalese. By early September, some 100,000 ethnic Nepalese had reportedly either been expelled or had fled since the beginning of the year. Refugees claimed that entire villages in the south had been emptied by the government. Bhutan claimed that less than 8,000 people had been expelled, and regional experts admitted the true figure was difficult to determine since Nepalese have been crossing back and forth over Bhutan's borders for years. Bhutan also claimed that many of those expelled had been illegal migrant workers from India and Nepal.

The King has taken bold measures to modernize a near-primitive, agrarian economy. The country is attempting to boost exports of fruit, cement and coal while diversifying its trading partners to reduce dependence on India. English is taught in schools and professional training is emphasized. In recent years, the country has joined international lending organizations and has increased its diplomatic ties.

Political Rights and Civil Liberties: Bhutanese cannot change their government democratically. Decision-making is highly centralized around the King and a small staff of Bhuddist aristocratic elites. Political parties are legal but discouraged, and none exist. The Bhutan People's Party, which operates out of Nepal, and the People's Forum for Human Rights are both outlawed. Both the government and dissidents accuse each other of human rights abuses, although lack of foreign access to the Kingdom makes such charges difficult to confirm. The U.S. State Department says that similarities in the stories of ethnic Nepalese refugees indicate credible evidence of physical abuse by police and army forces. Police reportedly conduct house searches against dissidents. Amnesty International reports that on 4 February the King released 313 political prisoners, bringing to 1,348 the number released since early 1990.

Judges are appointed by the King and handle all aspects of each case. The accused lack a legal right to an attorney, and few are defended due to the country's lack of lawyers. By tradition, citizens have the right of final appeal to the King. Because of the country's low 12 percent literacy rate, the written media plays a minor role in politics and society. The state-run weekly *Kuensel* is the country's only regular publication, although Indian and other foreign papers circulate freely. The country has no television stations, and in 1989 the government ordered all television antennas dismantled to prevent citizens from viewing foreign broadcasts. However, a Japanese-developed television system is in the works. Criticism of the monarchy is prohibited in the media. The government must approve all assemblies and associations, and there are no civil sector institutions such as communal, economic or professional groups. The Druk Kargue sect of Mahayana Buddhism is the official state religion, and some 6,000 Buddhist lamas (priests) wield fairly strong political influence. Hindus and others freely worship although proselytizing is illegal. Citizens can travel freely internally and abroad, although only 3,000 visitors are allowed into the kingdom each year. Trade unions and collective bargaining are not permitted.

Bolivia

Polity: Presidential-legislative democracy
Economy: Capitalist-statist
Population: 7,802,000
PPP: $1,531
Life Expectancy: 54.5

Political Rights: 2
Civil Liberties: 3
Status: Free

Ethnic Groups: Mixed (25-30 percent), Quechua Indian (30 percent), Aymara Indian (25 percent), European (10-15 percent)

Overview:
Stunning gains by populist newcomers in the December 1991 municipal elections underscored the mounting cynicism about traditional politics. With citizens incensed by years of economic austerity and government corruption scandals, Max Fernandez, multi-millionaire brewer and self-styled presidential candidate, loomed large with the approach of the May 1993 election.

Since achieving independence from Spain in 1825, the Republic of Bolivia has endured recurrent instability and extended periods of military rule. The armed forces, responsible for over 180 coups in 157 years, returned to the barracks in 1982, and the 1967 constitution was restored with the election of President Hernan Siles Suazo. The July 1985 election of President Victor Paz Estenssoro of the Nationalist Revolutionary Movement (MNR) marked the first peaceful transfer of power between two democratically elected presidents in 25 years.

The constitution provides for the election every four years of a president and a Congress consisting of a 130-member House of Representatives and a 27-member Senate. If no presidential candidate receives an absolute majority of the votes, Congress makes the selection from among the three leading contenders. Municipal elections are held every two years.

The MNR candidate in the May 1989 presidential election was Gonzalo Sanchez de Lozada, former planning minister under Paz Estenssoro and architect of a market-oriented austerity program that had ended hyperinflation. The main challengers were retired general Hugo Banzer, leader of the conservative National Democratic Action (ADN) and a former military dictator (1971-78), and Jaime Paz Zamora of the social democratic Movement of the Revolutionary Left (MIR).

Sanchez de Lozada obtained a slim plurality over Banzer in second and Paz Zamora in third. The tight finish led to fierce horse-trading in the new Congress, where the MNR took 49 seats, the ADN 46 and the MIR 41. Banzer opted to back Paz Zamora for president in exchange for the ADN receiving over half the cabinet positions. Paz Zamora was elected president by Congress in August 1989.

In 1990, a dispute between the MIR-ADN ruling coalition and the MNR over control of the Supreme Court and the electoral courts turned into a constitutional crisis. When the Supreme Court sided with the MNR, the government used its parliamentary majority to impeach eight of the twelve justices. The Court then threatened to annul election results from 1989 in three regions, which would have left the government without legal standing.

The crisis was resolved in mid-1991 when the eight justices were reinstated and both sides agreed to depoliticize the judicial and electoral systems. A new electoral court consisting of five politically independent magistrates was created, and a new voter registration was carried out.

Despite the promise of reform, the results of the December 1991 municipal elections indicated that corruption and factionalism in the main political parties had taken their toll. Big victories were scored by the Civic and Solidarity Union led by beer magnate Max Fernandez, and the Conscience of the Fatherland Party led by former talk show host Carlos Palenque, which won in the capital of La Paz. Both tapped into widespread discontent by striking a nationalist, anti-establishment stance.

President Paz's efforts to privatize money-losing state enterprises and open Bolivia, the poorest country in South America, to foreign investment have resulted in a series of often violent labor strikes led by the Bolivian Workers Central (COB). In early 1992, La Paz was practically paralyzed for ten weeks by violent student and worker protests.

Unrest spread to the military, where four factions of the Army and Navy issued anonymous communiqués that railed against government corruption and cuts in defense spending, while identifying with officers in Venezuela that had attempted to overthrow the government there in February 1992. The emergence of two indigenous guerrilla movements, with possible connections to drug traffickers and the Maoist Shining Path guerrillas in neighboring Peru, added to the instability.

A rallying point for government opponents has been the agreement to cooperate with the U.S. in an anti-drug program involving the Bolivian military. Bolivia is now the world's second largest producer of cocaine. The U.S.-sponsored program has drawn sustained political fire from peasant unions representing Bolivia's 50,000 coca farmers; the COB, the nation's largest labor confederation; nationalist sectors of the military; and all opposition parties.

As the 1993 election approached amid mutual allegations of drug-related corruption between the traditional parties and a wave of U.S.-bashing, the MNR's Sanchez de Losada was running neck-and-neck with Max Fernandez. Banzer, the MIR-ADN candidate, trailed badly in the polls. Fernandez, who also was alleged to be involved in drugs, had not yet defined a political program. But his humble origins and the fact that he is a mestizo appeared to give him the edge among an electorate wanting an end to politics-as-usual.

Political Rights and Civil Liberties: Citizens are able to change their government democratically, but are disenchanted with a system in which the president is ultimately chosen by the Congress. Opinion polls show overwhelming support for directly electing the president by a simple majority.

Constitutional guarantees regarding free expression, freedom of religion, and the right to organize political parties, civic groups and labor unions are generally respected. But political expression is restricted by recurring violence associated with labor strife and the billion-dollar-per-year cocaine trade. Also, the emergence of small indigenous guerrilla groups has caused an overreaction by security forces against legitimate government opponents. The languages of the indigenous population are officially recognized, but the 40 percent Spanish-speaking minority still dominates the political process.

The political landscape features political parties ranging from fascist to radical left.

There are also a number of indigenous peasant movements, some demanding full autonomy for the various Indian "nations."

There is strong evidence that drug money has penetrated the political process through the corruption of government officials and the military, and through electoral campaign financing. The drug trade also has spawned private security forces that operate with relative impunity in the coca-growing regions.

Unions are permitted to strike and have done so repeatedly against the government's economic restructuring program, which has left more than a quarter of the work force idle. Strikes, however, are usually broken up by force, frequently with the use of the military.

The judicial system, headed by a Supreme Court, has been marginally more effective since the return to civilian rule. But it remains over-politicized and subject to the compromising power of drug traffickers. A judicial reform commission was named in 1991, but with few concrete results. There are nine District Courts, and local courts to try minor offensives.

Human rights organizations are both government-sponsored and independent. Allegations of police brutality, torture during confinement and harsh prison conditions have been on the increase since 1991, and there has been intimidation against independent rights activists.

The press, radio and television are privately owned and free of censorship. There are a number of daily newspapers including one sponsored by the influential Catholic church. Opinion polling is a growth industry. Five years ago there was no television, but there are now more than 60 channels. The impact has been most evident in the media-based campaigns of the prominent political parties. In 1991, the media protested a new law passed by the Congress which limits paid political messages. Journalists covering corruption stories have been subject to verbal intimidation by the government and occasional violent attacks.

Bosnia-Herzegovina

Polity: Presidential-parliamentary democracy (mostly foreign-occupied)
Economy: Mixed-statist (severely war-damaged)
Population: 4,213,000
PPP: na
Life Expectancy: 70.0
Ethnic Groups: Slavic Muslim (44 percent), Serb, (33 percent); Croat, (17 percent)

Political Rights: 6
Civil Liberties: 6
Status: Not Free

Overview: In 1992, this former Yugoslav republic bordering Serbia, Croatia and Montenegro, was embroiled in a horrific war, as local Serb militias, backed by the remnants of the former Yugoslav People's Army (YPA), waged a bloody campaign of so-called "ethnic cleansing" in the formerly Muslim and Croatian territories within the republic. By year's end, Serbs controlled over 75 percent of the country, with Muslims isolated in several towns and cities, including the capital, Sarajevo, whose 380,000 citizens (including 60,000 Serbs) endured a near year-long siege that left them without electricity, food and medical supplies. The war claimed an estimated 100,000 mostly civilian lives and left 1.6 million Bosnians homeless. All sides committed terrible atrocities, but Serbs were the most egregious offenders as international observers confirmed the existence of dozens of death camps, where prisoners were routinely executed, tortured or starved. In women's detention centers, over 50,000 women, mostly Muslim, were systematically abused and raped. By the end of the year, steps were being taken at the urging of the U.S. and others to convene war-crimes tribunals to ferret out and punish those responsible.

Bosnia-Herzegovina became one of six constituent republics of Yugoslavia in November 1945. During World War II, the region was the scene of brutal internecine conflict that killed 700,000 people, mostly Serbs. As Yugoslavia's federal system began to unravel, the republic's first multi-party elections were held in late 1990, with the three nationalist parties representing indigenous Muslim, Serb and Croatian constituents winning a majority in the restructured 240-member bicameral Assembly. Muslim Alija Izetbegovic was named president; Croat Jure Pelivan, prime minister; and Serb Moncilo Krajisnik speaker (president) of the Assembly.

After Croatia and Slovenia declared independence from Yugoslavia in June 1991, fighting quickly spread to Bosnia-Herzegovina with incursions by the YPA and attacks by well-armed Serb militiamen. By September, Serbs had declared an "autonomous province" on the Montenegrin border, and a number of other "autonomous regions" were announced by Serb militants. President Izetbegovic had earlier called for an international effort to disarm the Yugoslav army and pension off its mainly Serbian officers, but he was ignored.

In a 29 February referendum on independence, 99 percent of voters favored secession from Yugoslavia. The Serbs boycotted the vote. At the end of February, the three main national groups, meeting in European Community-brokered talks in Lisbon, agreed to recognize the existing borders of Bosnia. The meeting included Radovan Karadzic, leader of the Bosnian Serbs, and Mate Boban, head of the Croatian Democratic Union, who would later head the self-styled Croatian republic within Bosnia. President Izetbegovic, leader of the Party of Democratic Action, issued a declaration of independence on 3 March. Two weeks later, Muslim, Croat and Serbian leaders agreed in Sarajevo to divide the country into three autonomous units based on the "national absolute or relative majority" in each area. However, the agreement was never enforced.

The United States recognized the new state on 7 April. As fighting intensified, it became clear that the out-gunned Muslims and their Croat supporters, the Croatian Defense Council (CDC), were overmatched by the estimated 100,000 Serbs, who were supplied by the neo-Communist government of Slobodan Milosevic in Serbia. Moreover, nearly 70 percent of the former Yugoslavia's military storage and manufacturing facilities were in Bosnia, making access to arms easy despite an international boycott. Throughout the year, it became apparent that Croatia and Serbia, if allowed, would likely carve up Bosnia, leaving the mainly urban-dwelling Muslims without territory. In several battles, CDC forces abandoned the Muslims, as in Bosanski Brod in October, and there were persistent reports that Serbs and Croats actually fought together against Muslims.

At the end of March, the government appealed to the U.N. for the deployment of peacekeeping forces, and in mid-April a small group of observers was sent to the western part of the country. In April, Serbs announced the formation of a rump-Yugoslavia made up of Serbia and Montenegro. Meanwhile, Serbian forces continued to make military headway, and by May Sarajevo was under siege. At the same time, Muslims and Croats in captured areas were either killed, shipped off to camps, or forced to flee. Towns and villages were depopulated and razed. An estimated 700,000 Bosnian and Croat refugees were living in Croatia by the end of the year. Others had fled to Germany, Hungary and elsewhere.

In June, as ceasefires continued to break down, the U.N. Security Council considered forms of intervention to end the bloodshed and provide humanitarian aid to Sarajevo. French President François Mitterand made a bold visit to the besieged capital to assess the situation. On 29 June, Sarajevo airport was briefly in the hands of U.N. peacekeepers, mainly 850 Canadians, whose mission was to secure relief. Several weeks later, the Security Council voted to send an extra 500 troops for Sarajevo.

On 17 July, Lord Carrington, the European Community's peace negotiator for Yugoslavia, announced that the warring parties had agreed to hand over heavy weapons in Bosnia to the U.N., a promise that was never kept. By August, talks, U.N. resolutions, trade and arms embargoes, and numerous ceasefires did not stop the slaughter. Pressed by the U.S., Britain and France agreed in early August to support a Security Council resolution authorizing the use of "all necessary means," including force, to ensure that food and medicines got through to the Bosnians. But on the ground, the situation continued to deteriorate. In the northwestern city of Bihac, 300,000 Muslims were surrounded by Serbs. The other main Muslim enclave, the area around Sarajevo, was under siege, as was Mostar, held by Bosnian Croats.

A London conference on the conflict ended on 27 August without substantive progress. Six working groups were established to start an ongoing negotiating process in Geneva. Serbs did agree to allow convoys of aid to travel from Mostar to Sarajevo, but local commanders sporadically ignored the agreement. On 2 September, Serb militiamen hit the Sarajevo headquarters of the U.N. Protection Force in Bosnia, and the U.N. was prevented by local commanders from inspecting artillery batteries, a violation of earlier agreements. Former Polish Prime Minister Tadeusz Mazowiecki, leader of a visiting U.N. human-rights team, recommended that U.N. forces in Bosnia intervene to prevent serious human-rights violations; although the U.N. balked at such a move.

On 22 September, the U.N. General Assembly voted to deny Yugoslavia's seat to the rump-Yugoslavia. Meanwhile, Croat and Muslim forces did make some headway against Serb troops in the east, along the Drina River, whose bridges formed Bosnia's road-link to Serbia. In the southwest, the CDC retook some positions lost in Herzegovina. Muslim forces broke the five-month encirclement of Goradze. The northern corridor linking Serbs in Krajina (in Croatia and under U.N. control) with those in Bosnia and Serbia was briefly cut by Muslim forces.

Also in September, former U.S. Secretary of State Cyrus Vance, the U.N. mediator, and David Owen, the EC's negotiator, met the three Bosnian factions in Geneva, although there was little movement on Bosnia's constitutional future or a ceasefire. Meanwhile, another 6,000 soldiers were sent to Bosnia to protect relief convoys.

Despite Serb denials, "ethnic cleansing" continued into the fall. In early October, hundreds of Muslim refugees poured into Sarajevo from the suburbs after being evicted by Serb militia. They recounted incidents of massacres, rape and abuse. Serbian leaders released some prisoners from detention camps. But artillery and aircraft continued to pound Sarajevo and Gradacac, the northernmost Muslim stronghold in Bosnia, and Serb forces captured Bosanski Brod, giving them a tentative corridor across northern Bosnia and Croatia. On 6 October, the U.N. voted unanimously to set up a commission of experts to take evidence of "grave breaches of international humanitarian law." The Security Council began deliberations on an air-exclusion zone over Bosnia. On 14 October, it was announced that Lord Owen and Serb leader Karadzic had reached an agreement for Bosnian Serb warplanes to be switched to airfields in Serbia or Montenegro and put under U.N. inspection.

On 19 October, President Izetbegovic met in Geneva with President Dobrica Cosic of the truncated Yugoslavia in their first face-to-face meeting since the start of the crisis and urged all parties to speed delivery of relief supplies to Sarajevo. Meanwhile, tensions continued between Muslims and Croats, who controlled almost one-third of the country and had established a Croatian state within Bosnia. Croatian forces had seized control of a broad chunk of Bosnia west and south of Sarajevo. Bosnian officials claimed that Serb and Croat forces had agreed not to interfere with each other on several fronts, and there was renewed speculation that Croatia and Serbia planned to partition Bosnia. Croatian President Franjo Tudjman broke several pledges of support to President Izetbegovic, and government-controlled newspapers in Croatia were calling the Bosnian government a "hotbed of Islamic fundamentalists."

On 21 October, President Izetbegovic offered a concession in Geneva by agreeing to send a senior military officer to take part in talks on ending the hostilities around Sarajevo. The announcement came after two days of meetings with Presidents Tudjman and Cosic and mediators Vance and Owen. Two days later, commanders of the three main forces met in Sarajevo to begin talks on a relief operation, but no agreement was reached. The next day, CDC and Serb forces attacked Muslim positions in several key towns in northern and central Bosnia.

At the end of the month, Lord Owen said that Serbs had flown no combat aircraft but were infringing on other parts of the U.N. no-fly zone resolution. Mediators in Geneva also announced that they had drawn up a plan for a new-style state in Bosnia with a central government including all ethnic groups under the plan, up to ten regional administrations would have authority over language education and law enforcement. But continued fighting, including the seizure of the Muslim town of Jajce, dimmed prospects that the proposed constitution could be implemented. Serb leader Karadzic was openly scornful of the Vance-Owen constitution; on 9 November he called for the division of Bosnia into three nationally defined units, with Serbs getting the largest. He also said that Sarajevo should be divided into separate ethnic areas.

By the end of November, over 22,000 U.N. personnel were in Bosnia in the largest U.N. peacekeeping and aid operation since the Congo in 1960. French soldiers and Serbs exchanged gunfire as U.N. forces continued to encounter difficulties in delivering food and medicine to needy civilians. On 15 November, Gen. Ratko Mladic, military leader of Bosnia's Serbs, told the U.N. that if the Muslims in Sarajevo continued to hold out in enclaves, he would starve them out.

By year's end, the U.N. said that there had been more than 100 violations of the no-fly zone. The U.S. met with other countries to try to stiffen enforcement of the ban, but no consensus was reached. Meanwhile, the fraud-marred election on 20 December of hardline nationalist Slobodan Milosevic to the Serbian presidency, and the subsequent no-confidence vote against moderate Prime Minister Milan Panic of Yugoslavia, dashed hopes for a quick negotiated settlement. On 30 December, there were reports that 10,000 Muslim fighters had amassed near Sarajevo in an effort to break the siege.

Political Rights and Civil Liberties: War and the creation of self-proclaimed Serbian and Croat "republics" within Bosnia-Herzegovina seriously undermined the political and democratic rights of Bosnian citizens. Human rights violations were rampant, as civilians faced deportation, execution, sexual abuse, torture, kidnapping, hostage-taking and unlawful imprisonment. Nearly 10,000 children were killed or had vanished. Tens of thousands of women, mostly Muslims, were systematically raped. Over one million people were displaced and left homeless. International organizations found egregious violations of the Geneva Convention and the Genocide Convention. The federal government and parliament essentially stopped functioning, as many officials fled the war zone and the country. The rule of law had completely broken down in most of the country in 1992.

Most newspapers stopped printing, but the daily *Oslobodjenje* in Sarajevo continued to publish despite the siege. By October, six staff members had been killed and 10 wounded by Serbian fire. Radio transmission was sporadic throughout the year. The war made domestic and international travel difficult, if not impossible. Refugees and evacuees often came under sniper fire throughout the country, resulting in the deaths of civilians, including children. Freedoms of association and assembly were circumscribed by the realities of war. Muslims, Catholic Croats and Orthodox Serbs practiced their religion in territories they controlled, but religious minorities in all regions faced persecution or death. The issue of trade unions was made moot by economic upheaval caused by the war and massive social dislocation.

Botswana

Polity: Parliamentary democracy and traditional chiefs
Economy: Capitalist
Population: 1,360,000
PPP: $3,180
Life Expectancy: 59.8
Ethnic Groups: Tswana (95 percent), Baswara, Kalanga and Kgalagadi (4 percent), European (1 percent)

Political Rights: 1
Civil Liberties: 2
Status: Free

Overview: This land-locked, thinly populated southern African country is one of the few working democracies on the continent. Major news stories in 1992 included a government scandal, the completion of a large military airbase, and a border dispute with Namibia.

Formerly a British colony, Botswana became independent in 1966. The chief of state is Dr. Quett K.J. Masire, leader of the Botswana Democratic Party (BDP), which has held power since independence. Opposition parties, including the Botswana National Front, the Botswana People's Party and the Botswana People's Union, formed a coalition in 1991. Charging that elections have been rigged, the coalition has demanded that an all-party commission oversee future balloting.

Three top government officials implicated in a land scandal were dismissed from their posts and suspended from their prominent BDP party positions in March 1992. The scandal was exposed by the press. The officials included Vice President Peter Mwusi, Agriculture Minister and BDP Secretary-General Daniel Kwelagobe, and Assistant Minister of Local Government and Lands Michael Tshipinare. The officials were accused of illegally using public properties.

In 1992, Botswana reportedly completed the largest military airfield in sub-Saharan Africa; the project reportedly cost over 20 percent of the country's annual Gross Domestic Product. The independent Botswanan press speculated that the airfield would be leased by the United States Air Force, but the American Government has dismissed the rumors as "fanciful."

Neighboring Namibia pursued its territorial dispute with Botswana over the Chobe River island of Sedudu. The land at issue is a potentially lucrative location for tourism. During 1992, the countries exchanged warnings and engaged in symbolic flag-raising on the island. The two countries formed a technical committee to determine the boundary.

Although Botswana was one of the poorest countries in the world at independence, large-scale mining of its principal resource, diamonds, has led to 13 percent economic growth and a foreign exchange reserve among the highest in the Third World. Despite Botswana's increasing wealth, only 5,000 people are employed in its three diamond mines and 60 percent of the population earns less than $100 a year. Although most citizens engage in subsistence farming, much of the country's land is either marsh or desert. Botswana suffers from rising unemployment in the non-agricultural sector, now at a rate of over 25 percent. The government's inability to solve the problem of unemployment has meant continued dependence by many Botswanans on low-paying jobs in the informal sector.

Political Rights and Civil Liberties: Botswanans can change their government democratically, but the same party has controlled the country since independence. The judiciary is independent. There are no restrictions on religion, travel or association. The right to assemble is usually respected, but permits for gatherings may be denied if there is a risk of violence. Discrimination and exploitation of the San (Bushmen) are persistent problems largely ignored by the government.

The press is free and presents opposition viewpoints. Although the Botswana Press Agency is part of the Department of Information and Broadcasting, it operates with a large measure of autonomy and can be critical of the government. A freelance journalist was detained in January 1992 for two days after he disclosed the contents of a sensitive government document in an article about a public workers strike. The National Security Act allows prison terms of up to 30 years for those who have transmitted such "secrets" to what the government considers its enemies. Foreign reporters have been deported for displeasing authorities.

Unions are well organized and have a formal right to strike, but strikers may be dismissed if they do not first submit to mandatory arbitration. Approximately 15,000 illegally striking government workers were fired in November 1991. There is only one major labor confederation, the Botswana Federation of Trade Unions.

Brazil

Polity: Federal presiden-
tial-legislative democracy
Economy: Capitalist-
statist
Population: 150,794,000
PPP: $4,951
Life Expectancy: 65.6
Ethnic Groups: Caucasian (54 percent), mixed (39 percent),
black (6 percent), pure Indian (less than 1 percent)

Political Rights: 2
Civil Liberties: 3
Status: Free

Overview:
Fernando Collor de Mello, after being exposed at the center of a huge graft and influence-peddling scheme, became the first Latin American president to be removed from office by constitutional means. Amid political uncertainty and a seemingly intractable economic crisis, he was formally replaced by Itamar Franco, the vice president, after an impeachment trial in the Senate.

Brazil retained a monarchical system after gaining independence from Portugal in 1822, but became a republic in 1889. Democratic rule has been interrupted by long periods of authoritarian rule, most recently under military governments from 1964 to 1985.

The return to civilian rule in 1985, the result of a controlled transition transacted by the military with opposition political parties, culminated in the 1985 electoral college balloting won by Tancredo Neves. Neves died soon after and Jose Sarney, his vice-presidential running mate, became the first civilian president in 21 years. Direct elections for a bicameral Congress were held in 1986. The Senate and the Chamber of Deputies formed a constituent assembly that produced a new constitution.

The 1988 constitution provided for a president to be directly elected on 15 November 1989 for a five-year term. The Congress was retained, with a 72-member Senate directly elected for eight years and a 503-member Chamber of Deputies directly elected for four years. Brazil is divided into 26 states and the Federal District of Brasilia. State governors and legislatures are elected, as are municipal governments. The constitution provides for a plebiscite in 1993 to decide whether to keep the presidential system, change to a parliamentary system, or reestablish a monarchy.

The top contenders among 22 candidates for president in 1989 were Collor, a political newcomer from the center-right National Reconstruction Party (PRN); Luis "Lula" da Silva of the leftist Workers' Party (PT); and Leonel Brizola of the social democratic Democratic Labor Party (PDT). The main issues were Brazil's massive foreign debt, uncontrolled inflation, corruption, crime and the deteriorating condition of the nation's poor, who make up nearly two-thirds of the population.

Collor obtained 28 percent of the vote in the first round. Silva edged out Brizola for second. Collor won the runoff a month later, taking 53 percent of the vote, and became the first directly elected president in nearly three decades.

The 42-year-old Collor vowed to clean out government corruption and modernize the economy. But two economic shock programs failed to control inflation and left the economy in deep recession. Collor's plan to overhaul the statist economy was undermined in 1991 by a hostile Congress wielding the 1988 constitution, a populist document that mandates spending on behalf of a vast array of special interests and makes structural reform nearly impossible.

Corruption scandals dogged the Collor government from the outset, but in May 1992 Collor was directly implicated in a $55-million graft and influence-peddling scheme. In the ensuing months the media exposed the money trail and verified the charges, sparking a wave of popular protest and demands that Collor resign. When Collor refused, the Congress—a diverse and generally feckless group of 19 parties tied to labor, big business and regional interests—came under pressure to impeach him.

Under Brazilian law Collor needed only a third of the votes in the Chamber of Deputies to block impeachment. In August, it looked like he might buy his way out of trouble by siphoning millions of dollars into pork-barrel projects of swing-vote legislators. But in late September, with massive demonstrations filling the streets of Brazil's major cities and the media covering each legislator's every move, the Chamber voted for impeachment by a margin of 441-38. He was subsequently tried for illicit enrichment and perjury in the Senate and impeached in December.

Itamar Franco, the vice president, assumed the powers of the presidency on 2 October. Franco stitched together a cabinet with representatives from seven different parties. By November, he was drawing criticism for failing to give the new government any direction. The municipal elections held throughout the country in October and November indicated a considerable shift to the left as the PT, which declined to participate in the Franco government, made significant gains. At the same time, the nation was gearing for the 21 April 1993 plebiscite in which Brazilians would choose between a presidential, a parliamentary or a monarchial system. Polls indicated a preference for a parliamentary system. The next presidential elections are scheduled for October 1994.

Hurt by defense budget cuts and Collor's exposure and cancelation of a secret atomic-bomb project, the military had been restive since 1991. As the Congress moved closer to impeaching Collor, there were fears the armed forces would take control of the government. But the military kept its distance throughout the process, stating that it would continue to support constitutional rule.

Political Rights and Civil Liberties:

Citizens are able to change their government democratically. Constitutional guarantees regarding free expression, freedom of religion and the right to organize political parties and civic organizations are generally respected. Over two dozen political parties span the spectrum from left to right. However, mounting levels of criminal violence and police corruption, fueled by economic recession and the burgeoning drug trade, have created a climate of generalized insecurity.

Numerous independent human rights organizations are active. Despite the constitutional guarantees against torture and inhuman treatment during confinement, rights groups continue to report extensive and systematic abuses in police detention centers and in the overflowing, violence-plagued prisons. In October 1992 over 100 inmates were summarily executed by military police during a riot at a Sao Paulo prison.

Vigilante "death squads" linked to the police and financed by local merchants, are responsible for hundreds, possibly thousands, of extra-judicial killings a year. Violence, including disappearances and forced prostitution, against the 35 million children living in poverty, is systematic, with hundreds of "street kids" murdered annually. Various government initiatives have done little to curtail these practices.

The judicial system is headed by an 11-member Supreme Court whose members must be approved by the Senate. It was granted substantial administrative and financial autonomy by the 1988 constitution, but remains bureaucratic, overloaded and, reflecting the political system as a whole, chronically corrupt. However, during the 1992 impeachment proceedings the Court displayed remarkable independence in fending off Collor's attempts to manipulate the process. There are federal courts in the state capitals and states have their own judicial systems. There are also special labor and electoral courts. In 1991, the Supreme Court ruled that a man can no longer kill his wife and win acquittal on the ground of "legitimate defense of honor," but in subsequent cases juries have ignored the ruling, as they are entitled to do.

At the local level, courts are under-financed, poorly staffed, intimidated by monied interests, and overwhelmed by the national crime wave. As a result, there is little public confidence in the judicial system. Poorer citizens, beset by inflation and unemployment, have resorted to lynchings, with hundreds of mob executions reported since 1991. The middle class, already shrinking and unable to afford costly private security measures, is targeted by kidnappers who often operate in league with underpaid, corrupt police.

Violence associated with land disputes continues unabated. It is estimated that 2 percent of Brazil's landowners control nearly 60 percent of arable land, while the poorest 30 percent share less than 2 percent. In recent years, hundreds of activists, Catholic church workers and rural unionists have been killed by paramilitary groups hired by large landowners, with only a handful of cases brought to court. There are also persistent reports of forced prostitution and slave labor camps maintained by ranchers and police in the Amazon region. Rubber tappers, Indian tribes and environmentalists continue to be targets of violence, including assassination, associated with the huge Amazon basin development projects initiated under military rule. The constitution gives Brazil's quarter million Indians legal sanction. In 1991 the government created Indian reserves, but in 1992 it appeared unable to guarantee the security of these lands.

Industrial labor unions are well organized and politically influential. The right to strike is permitted by the 1988 constitution. Although unions have protested that subsequent legislation is vague and restrictive, hundreds of strikes were carried out during Collor's time in office.

The press is privately owned, vigorous, competitive and uncensored. There are daily newspapers in most major cities and many other publications throughout the country. Radio is mostly commercial. Although overseen by a government agency, television is independent and a powerful political instrument. Roughly two-thirds of the population is illiterate, while 85 percent of households have television sets. The huge TV Globo dominates, but there are three other networks, plus educational channels. The media, featuring a new breed of investigative journalists, played a central role in exposing corruption within the Collor government and in maintaining the momentum for a constitutional resolution of the crisis. Congressional hearings and the vote of each legislator were broadcast on national television during Collor's impeachment.

Brunei

Polity: Traditional monarchy
Economy: Capitalist-statist
Population: 275,000
PPP: $14,590
Life Expectancy: 73.5
Ethnic Groups: Malay (65 percent), Chinese (20 percent), other (15 percent)

Political Rights: 7
Civil Liberties: 6
Status: Not Free

Overview:

During 1992, Brunei carried out restrictive domestic policies under the concept of the Malay Muslim Monarchy. This concept calls for a social order imbued by traditional Malay-Bruneian and Islamic values. Among other restrictions, this strict policy discourages singing and dancing in public.

Proclaimed an independent sultanate in January 1984, this tiny, oil-rich monarchy on the northern border of Borneo is ruled by Sultan Hasanal Bolkiah. The constitution permits the sultan, whose family has ruled the area for over 500 years, to override decisions of the legislative and executive bodies. In 1962, a party opposed to the sultan won a large majority in legislative elections. In December of that year, an armed uprising was put down with the aid of British troops. The sultan then assumed emergency powers, which he has held ever since.

Brunei carried out an active regional foreign policy in 1992. The sultanate signed the Asian Free Trade Area Accord. The treaty outlines a free trade zone and reduces tariffs over a fifteen-year period. The country also entered the regional dispute over the Spratly Islands, a potentially oil- and mineral-rich territory in the South China Sea. China, Malaysia, the Philippines, Taiwan and Vietnam have also staked claims to the area. Unlike other contenders, such as the Chinese, Brunei has not set up a military outpost on the Spratlys.

Political opposition is practically non-existent in Brunei. In 1985 some activists established the Brunei National Democratic Party. The government forbade party membership to its employees (53 percent of the labor force). In 1988, the government imprisoned the party leaders for two years. The state banned the party after the leaders' release in 1990. In 1986, the government approved the formation of the Brunei National Solidarity Party. It remains ineffectual and has only several dozen members.

Political Rights and Civil Liberties:

The people of Brunei cannot change their government democratically. There is no national electoral process and almost no partisan activity. Citizens may seek to influence the government through village headmen and district officers who meet regularly with residents.

The constitution does not protect freedoms of speech, the press, privacy, association or assembly. The one independent newspaper practices self-censorship. The government requires registration of all organizations.

Women have lower status in civil and commercial affairs and do not receive equal pay or benefits. Muslim women must wear the *tudong*, a traditional head covering. Non-Muslims are not required to comply, and few do. The constitution provides limited protection for non-Muslims. The government hinders replacement of non-Muslim clergy. In 1991, the government closed Buddhist temples and shrines, claiming lack of government registration. However, minorities engage freely in business and do prosper. Most Chinese are stateless non-citizens who may not own land. The 20-year residency requirement and difficult Malay language test render citizenship almost impossible to attain.

The judiciary is independent. Hong Kong provides judges for the High Court and the Court of Appeals, under a treaty of friendship with the UK. The Internal Security Act permits detention without trial for two-year renewable periods and is invoked against those accused of sedition. In 1988, flogging (under the supervision of a physician) became the punishment for 42 crimes.

Trade unions are legal. Collective bargaining has no explicit legal protection, but some takes place anyway. About 5 percent of the workforce belongs to unions, all of which are in the petroleum industry. The right to strike has an uncertain legal position, and no strikes occur.

Bulgaria

Polity: Parliamentary democracy
Economy: Statist-transitional
Population: 8,866,000
PPP: $5,064
Life Expectancy: 72.6
Ethnic Groups: Bulgarian (85 percent), Turkish (9 percent), Gypsy (3 percent), Macedonian (3 percent)

Political Rights: 2
Civil Liberties: 3
Status: Free

Overview: In 1992, incumbent President Zhelyu Zhelyev won Bulgaria's first direct presidential elections. Other major issues included the resignation of Prime Minister Filip Dimitrov's cabinet, an economic crisis caused by the collapse of trade with members of the Commonwealth of Independent States (CIS), and the convictions of former Communist leaders.

In December, parliament approved the new government of Prime Minister Lyuben Berov (an economic adviser to President Zhelyev), who was backed by the Turkish-based Movement for Rights and Freedoms (MRF) and the (formerly Communist) Bulgarian Socialist Party (BSP).

The Union of Democratic Forces (UDF) won the October 1991 parliamentary elections by a narrow margin, gaining 110 of 240 seats in the unicameral legislature. The BSP won 106 seats, and the MRF won 24 seats. Following the elections, the UDF formed a coalition government with the MRF and Filip Dimitrov became prime minister.

On 12 January 1992, 22 candidates participated in the first round of presidential elections. UDF candidates Zhelyu Zhelyev and Blaga Dimitrova, running for president and vice-president, failed to win a majority, getting 44.6 percent of the vote. Velko Valkanov and Rumen Vodenicharov, nationalist candidates supported by the BSP, came in second with 30.5 percent of the vote. Zhelyev and Dimitrova won the second round on 19 January with 52.8 percent of the vote.

Tensions between the UDF and the BSP increased following the elections. On 22 February, a UDF rally called for banning the BSP. UDF leaders accused the BSP of preparing a coup to overthrow the government. On 3 March, President Zhelyev attempted to assuage the conflict between the two major parties by calling for national unity during the transition to democracy. At the same time, conflict arose between the presidential and parliamentary factions of the ruling UDF. On 9 April, the confrontation between the UDF and the BSP sharpened after participants in a BSP-led demonstration mobbed a UDF deputy who was later assaulted by a Socialist deputy on the floor of parliament.

Representatives from twenty member groups attended the UDF congress on 11-12 April and called for structural and personal changes in the government. On 20 May, Prime Minister Dimitrov responded by replacing seven key cabinet members, including the controversial defense minister accused of allowing arms shipment to Syria, Libya and Iran.

In July, the governor of National Bank resigned, citing a "smear campaign" against him in the press, following an article linking him with former Communists. The resignation was seen as a serious blow to Bulgaria's policy of monetary stabilization and efforts to reduce its $12 billion external debt.

On 24 July, the government survived a no-confidence motion introduced by the Socialists, who accused the government of lacking a clear economic program and opting for a "policy of confrontation."

Political turmoil between the parliamentary faction of the UDF and President Zhelyev continued in the fall over division of power and the pace of economic reforms. On 24 September, parliamentary Chairman Stefan Savov resigned and, supported by the BSP and MRF, led a renewed no-confidence motion. The MRF linked the continuation of its support for the government to a slower approach to economic reform and personnel changes in the economic, defense and security ministries.

The rift between the government and president deepened in October when Prime Minister Dimitrov accused Zhelyev of defamation aimed at destabilizing the government. In an attempt to test his strength, Dimitrov called for a vote of confidence on 28 October; the vote was 120-111 against the government, forcing the cabinet to resign. On 12 November, following negotiations between the UDF and MRF, President Zhelyev asked Dimitrov to form a new cabinet.

Despite the passage of a republican constitution in July 1991, calls for the restoration of constitutional monarchy in Bulgaria persisted in 1992. Simeon II, the exiled son of Tsar Boris III, issued appeals for his installment as head of state. In January a royal press center was opened in Sofia. In March, after a meeting with Simeon in Spain, MRF leader Ahmed Dogan called for a referendum on restitution of royal prerogatives contained in the pre-1944 constitution. In September, Simeon asked that a Grand National Assembly restore him as a king without a referendum. President Zhelyev rejected these appeals.

The removal of former Communists from most top positions following parliamentary and presidential elections paved the way for a vigorous campaign to investigate crimes committed under the Communist regime. President Zhelyev called for clearing Bulgaria's tarnished reputation in connection with its involvement in the 1978 "umbrella murder" of dissident Georgi Markov in London, and the 1981 attempted assassination of Pope John Paul II in Rome. In June, General Vlado Todorov was sentenced to 14 months in prison for his role in the destruction of secret files in the Markov case. In February, parliament established a committee to investigate the anti-Turkish and anti-Gypsy campaigns during the Communist era.

Former Prime Ministers Andrei Lukanov and Grisha Filipov were arrested in July for misappropriation of state funds. On 4 September, following an 18-month trial, the former Communist party chairman and state leader Todor Zhivkov was found guilty of embezzling $24 million in state funds and sentenced to seven years in prison.

Since its victory in the 1991 parliamentary elections, the pro-market UDF has taken steps toward transforming Bulgaria's command economy into a market-based system. In December 1991, Bulgaria's first stock exchange began operation, but, in an attempt to combat inflation, the government froze consumer prices under its control during January 1992. On 20 March, parliament approved a law on return of land confiscated by the Communists. On 23 April a law on privatization of state and municipal property was passed.

In September, Bulgaria resumed payments on its $12 billion foreign debt, reversing a 1990 decision to suspend all principal and interest payments. After the collapse of trade with the CIS countries following the switch to hard currency trading, unemployment reached 500,000, or 13 percent of the labor force.

Political Rights and Civil Liberties: A multi-party system was enshrined in Bulgaria's new constitution of 1991 and, in January 1992, Bulgaria held its first direct presidential elections.

Bulgarian law provides for public trials in criminal cases. A number of former top Communist officials were arrested and convicted for misappropriation of state funds and inciting inter-ethnic tensions during the Communist era.

Citizens freely express their views and freedoms of association and assembly are generally respected. The law on association provides for legal registration of independent groups. In April 1992, the Constitutional Court rejected an appeal, supported by 93 BSP deputies, to declare the MRF an unconstitutional party because of its ethnic base.

There was a lessening of inter-ethnic tensions in 1992, although there were sporadic outbursts of discontent against national minorities, especially the Turks who make up 10 percent of the population. The teaching of Turkish in heavily populated Turkish areas was made optional in 1991; Bulgarian nationalists responded to the decision by calling for a boycott of classes in the city of Kardzhali.

A large number of diverse newspapers and periodicals are published. With few exceptions, radio and television are government-owned, and there were allegations made by trade unions and opposition parties of pro-government bias in the official media. Private radio and television stations are permitted, but face stringent licensing requirements.

Freedom of worship is respected, although the government regulates churches and religious institutions through the Directorate on Religious Beliefs.

There are few restrictions on international and domestic travel, and special residence permits are no longer required for major urban areas. There are several trade and agricultural unions, and strikes are permitted in most industries and sectors. In March 1992, the Podkrepa trade union broke with the UDF over economic policy, especially the closing of unprofitable mines, and called on the government to resign. In April the government responded to a miners' strike by dismissing the industry minister and agreeing to spend more money on modernization in the mining industry.

Burkina Faso

Polity: Dominant party
(military-dominated)
Economy: Mixed statist
Population: 9,567,000
PPP: $617
Life Expectancy: 48.2
Ethnic Groups: Bobo, Mossi, Samo, other

Political Rights: 5
Civil Liberties: 5
Status: Partly Free

Overview:

In 1992, political tension eased in Burkina Faso as the government seemed more inclined to accept political pluralism and key opposition leaders accepted both the dominance of the ruling party and ministerial positions in the new cabinet.

This land-locked, arid, and extremely poor central-west African country (known as Upper Volta until 1984) has been ruled since October 1987 by President Blaise Compaoré. In the 32 years since it gained independence from France, Burkina Faso has never changed its head of state through direct multi-party elections. Compaoré himself seized control of the state by overthrowing the charismatic populist Captain Thomas Sankara. Sankara had come to power in 1983 during a military coup in which Compaoré was an important conspirator. The Compaoré regime refers to the '83 coup as a "revolution."

In 1991 President Compaoré abandoned his original opposition to multi-partyism and allowed several independent parties of diverse political orientation to join the ruling Organization for Popular Democracy/Labor Movement (ODP-MT) and its allies as legal entities. In a June 1991 referendum, 93 percent of voters supported a constitution adopted by the ODP-MT-dominated parliament. That year a growing coalition of opposition parties formed the Coordination of Democratic Forces (CDF), which attempted to resist the regime's unilateral decisions on the direction of political change. But access to decision-making power eluded the opposition, as the president rejected its demands that he convene a sovereign national conference of all Burkinabé political forces to take interim control of the state until the holding of free and fair elections. Repeated government-opposition meetings in 1991 broke down after stalemate.

Burkina Faso's transition to multi-party democracy completely stalled during the December 1991 presidential election. All five candidates challenging incumbent President Compaoré withdrew from the race in a gesture of protest. They did so after the regime refused to meet an opposition deadline to set the date for a national conference, which would appoint an all-party transitional administration to impartially conduct any future elections. The regime and its supporters—gathered together within the Alliance for the Respect and Defense of the Constitution—asserted that a sovereign conference would unconstitutionally call into question the legitimacy of the head of state and his regime. On 1 December 1991, Compaoré was re-elected by default by a quarter of those registered. The low turn-out was declared a moral victory by opposition spokesmen, who charged that the election was a sham intended to give a veneer of legitimacy to an undemocratic, military-dominated regime.

The election of Compaoré was preceded by anonymous threats against opposition figures and arson attacks against their party offices. Approximately 130 people were arrested after violent opposition to the regime and the election that included looting of commercial businesses and burning of vehicles by street rioters. Some protestors burned ballot boxes and disrupted polling places. Security forces in the cities of Ouahigouya and Bobo-Dioulasso responded with arrests and flogging of demonstrators. One of the withdrawn presidential candidates was assassinated and another shot by parties unknown in mid-December. The government condemned the attacks, indefinitely postponing legislative elections scheduled for 9 January, but opposition party spokesmen accused the regime of having had prior knowledge. Nevertheless, opposition leaders did not rule out resumption of political dialogue with the government.

A few days after the attacks, President Compaoré announced that he would convene a "national reconciliation forum" before the end of January. The CFD agreed to participate if their physical safety was ensured, inquiry into the assassination attempts was seriously pursued, and protestors arrested in Bobo-Dioulasso were released. The government agreed to release all those not caught in the act of pillage. The forum begun on 11 February, but was soon suspended by the president when the opposition insisted upon live media coverage of the proceedings.

The CFD had already lost a key member, the Alliance for Democracy and Federation (ADF), before the forum was cancelled. After a cabinet reshuffle, that party's leader assumed a portfolio in the new administration as a minister of state. After the defection of the ADF, a number of major opposition parties decided to contest rather than boycott the re-scheduled legislative election. In an atmosphere of relative calm, 27 of 65 legalized political parties participated in the 24 May election. Thirty-five percent of the electorate voted. The ODP-MT took 78 out of 107 seats, with eight allied and opposition parties sharing the rest. In June, the centrist National Convention of Progressive Patriots/Social Democratic Party (CNPP/PDS), which won eight seats in the new legislature, joined ex-CFD members ADF and the African Democratic Rally to form a new and expanded cabinet of 29 government ministers. Altogether seven parties were represented, including the ODP-MT and three small allies, and Compaoré appointed Youssouf Ouedraogo to serve as the new prime minister.

During 1992, the president of The Gambia accused Compaoré of harboring armed Gambians involved in an abortive plan to overthrow their government. Meanwhile, charges continued that the Burkinabé regime was providing material support to the forces of the rebel Charles Taylor of the National Patriotic Front of Liberia. Compaoré denied both accusations.

Political Rights and Civil Liberties:

Burkinabés now have limited means to change their government democratically. Although the December 1991 presidential elections took place amid violence and intimidation, the legislative elections in May 1992 were declared reasonably free and fair by international monitors.

The Burkinabé Movement for Human Rights has declared that a formal state of law is being achieved in Burkina Faso. Criminal and civil cases are generally adjudicated fairly by the regular court system. However, arbitrary abuse of authority by members of the armed forces remains a problem: a July attack on civilians by rioting soldiers in the town of Fada-Ngourma left 83 injured. And freedom of assembly was suspended during the political upheavals of late 1991.

Bowing to opposition pressure, more than 4,000 people punished for political or trade union activity since the 1983 coup were ordered rehabilitated in January 1992 by Compaoré. By late 1992, there were reportedly no political prisoners in Burkina Faso.

The government has pledged its acceptance of the principle of a free press through operation of a new information code. Apart from state-owned sources of information, Burkina Faso has both independent print and broadcast media. There are no significant restrictions on freedom of religion. Foreign travel is usually unrestricted. Nonpolitical business, social, cultural and religious organizations are generally free to function. Although trade unions have the right to strike and enjoy relative independence, explicitly anti-government activities have not been permitted in the past.

Burma (Myanmar)

Polity: Military
Economy: Mixed statist
Population: 42,502,000
PPP: $595
Life Expectancy: 61.3
Ethnic Groups: Burman (68 percent), Karen (7 percent), Shan (6 percent), Rakhine (4 percent), Chin, Kachin, Mon and Arkanese totaling 1 million

Political Rights: 7
Civil Liberties: 7
Status: Not Free

Overview:
Burma's ruling military junta met with opposition groups in June 1992 to plan a constitutional convention and outline an eventual transfer to civilian rule. During the year, the army released political prisoners, re-opened universities and lifted martial law. However, the regime continues to disregard basic rights, and the new constitution will grant the military a leading role in state affairs.

Occupied by the Japanese during World War II, Burma achieved independence from the British in 1948. Prime Minister U Nu led a parliamentary democracy for a decade before resigning when his Anti-Fascist People's Freedom League (AFPFL) split along factional lines. A caretaker government under army commander General Ne Win organized elections in 1960 which brought U Nu briefly back to power. The army overthrew the civilian government in 1962 amidst an economic crisis, political turmoil and threats from ethnic rebel groups.

During the next 26 years, Ne Win's Burmese Socialist Program Party (BSPP) turned one of the region's richest countries into an impoverished backwater. In September 1988 approximately 3,000 people were killed when the army cracked down on massive, peaceful pro-democracy demonstrations. Army leaders General Saw Maung and Brigadier General Khin Nyunt placed the country under the military rule of a new State Law and Order Restoration Council (SLORC). The junta said it planned to hold elections and transfer power to a civilian government.

The first competitive elections in three decades were held on 27 May 1990. The National League for Democracy (NLD) attracted widespread support, mostly due to its dynamic secretary general, Aung San Suu Kyi, who the SLORC had placed under house arrest in July 1989 for her pro-democracy activities. The party won 392 of the 485 seats contested, while the SLORC-sponsored National Unity Party, the successor to the BSPP, won just 10.

The SLORC refused to recognize the results, and jailed hundreds of NLD members, including several elected MPs. In December 1990, a core of NLD MPs set up a government-in-exile in rebel-held territory near the Thai border, but no country has recognized it.

The junta consolidated its power in 1991 on several fronts. Numerous political parties, including the AFPFL, were banned. The army launched fresh offensives against the Karen National Union (KNU), a rebel group fighting for an independent state or increased autonomy for the Karen people. Other ethnic rebel groups were co-opted through arrangements allowing them a share of the lucrative opium trade in exchange for peace. The only significant dissent during the year came in December following a ceremony in London granting Suu Kyi the Nobel Peace Prize in absentia. Several hundred student demonstrators were arrested at Rangoon University, and all schools were immediately closed.

The modest but unexpected reforms initiated in the spring of 1992 were likely orchestrated by the mercurial Ne Win, who is reportedly concerned with the country's growing international isolation. At 81, the former leader holds no official title but remains the the country's ultimate arbiter. The first sign of change came on 23 April when the SLORC replaced hardline prime minister and junta leader Saw Maung with General Than Shwe. The next day, the junta surprisingly announced it would meet with elected MPs to set the framework for a constitutional convention, and would release all political prisoners not considered security threats. A dozen were initially released, including aging former prime minister U Nu. The government also said it would allow Aung San Suu Kyi's family to visit her.

On 23 June, the SLORC opened the first of three rounds of talks with 28 representatives of seven parties, including the NLD. The junta said it would hold a constitutional convention in early 1993, which would then yield to a constituent assembly, composed of elected MPs, which would approve a draft constitution. The constitutional referendum would presumably be followed by a national referendum and new general elections. At the last meeting, on 10 July, the SLORC announced that delegates to the constitutional convention would be drawn from elected MPs, ethnic groups, workers and professionals.

The government reopened the country's universities on 24 August. In September, the SLORC lifted the overnight curfew and removed two martial law decrees that had allowed military judges to try civilians in Mandalay and Yangon. Imposed three years earlier, the military tribunals were notorious for snap trials and harsh sentences.

The SLORC also halted offensives in the spring against two large minority groups. After heavy fighting early in the year, the government announced in April a unilateral ceasefire with the KNU, the best-armed of the numerous ethnic rebel armies. The government avoided a conflict with Bangladesh by agreeing on 28 April to repatriate nearly 300,000 Muslims, known as Rohingyas, which the army began systematically pushing across the border in 1989. The refugees have accused the army of murder, rape, forced evictions and torture. By year's end, however, the two countries had failed to settle the details of the repatriation. The government also ceased attacks on elements of the Kachin Independence Army, as well as on Naga tribesmen and the insurgent National Socialist Council of Nagaland in the north. On 10 July the government invited rebel groups to join in the drafting of the new constitution in return for a cease-fire, but skirmishes with the KNU were reported in July and August.

By the end of the year, the limited extent of the reforms was apparent. On 2 October the junta announced an 18-member commission that will ensure a leading role for the military in politics. In addition, according to the *Far Eastern Economic Review*, many of the 585 "political prisoners" released by the regime were actually common criminals. The magazine reported earlier that political prisoners who were released were warned by the Directorate of Defense Services Intelligence that they will be re-arrested unless they inform on opposition groups. Despite a new pledge on 5 October to halt offensives against the rebel groups, attacks continued in the fall.

In addition, numerous military decrees remain in place, such as Order 288 which bans meetings of more than five people. An expanded 29-member government announced on 26 September includes cabinet posts for the navy and air force heads and three regional army commanders. Although many analysts said the appointments suggested a consolidation of the junta's power, others said powerful intelligence chief Khin Nyunt had in effect demoted the officers to cabinet posts in order to consolidate his own control of the army. Military spending rose 18 percent in the new fiscal year, giving the armed services one-third of the country's budget. The military is well-armed and recently purchased over $1 billion of Chinese weapons.

Political Rights and Civil Liberties:

Burmese citizens cannot change their government democratically. The military-controlled State Law and Order Restoration Council (SLORC) has promised to hold a national convention in early 1993 to develop guidelines for drafting a new constitution, although the army will retain a central role in politics and society.

The junta denies its citizens fundamental human rights. Freedoms of speech, press and association are nonexistent. The U.S. State Department estimated at the beginning of the year that the government holds 2,000 political prisoners. Suspects can be legally detained for up to five years without trial, and detainees and political prisoners are frequently tortured. The Directorate of Defense Services Intelligence maintains an elaborate network of spies and informants, routinely searches homes, intercepts mail and monitors telephones. In September 1992, the SLORC lifted the last of the martial law decrees allowing military tribunals to try civilians, but the judiciary is still firmly controlled by the regime.

The army forces villagers to act as human minesweepers ahead of troops, and frequently uses civilians as porters, often until they die of exhaustion and hunger. Young teenagers have been pressed into battle against rebel groups, often stiffened with shots of liquor. The nation's universities, which had been closed since December 1991, re-opened in August after teachers were sent to indoctrination camps. Religious practice has been brutally suppressed. Hundreds of monks were arrested and several killed in an October 1990 raid on monasteries suspected of supporting pro-democracy activities. The government continues to forcibly relocate poor urban residents to squalid "new towns" in rural areas. There are no independent trade unions, and workers have no bargaining rights.

Burundi

Polity: Dominant party (military-dominated)
Economy: Mixed capitalist
Population: 5,821,000
PPP: $611
Life Expectancy: 48.5
Ethnic Groups: Hutu (85 percent), Tutsi (14 percent), Twa pygmy (1 percent)

Political Rights: 6
Civil Liberties: 5
Status: Partly Free

Overview:

In 1992, Burundi was plagued by armed rebel attacks against the government, reprisals on unarmed civilians by government troops, and an attempted *coup d'état* by ex-officials opposed to political reform. Despite these setbacks, multi-party elections remained scheduled for April 1993.

Burundi is a small and densely populated former Belgian colony in Central Africa. Its ethnic Tutsi minority has dominated an ethnic Hutu population six times as large for hundreds of years. Since independence in 1962, over 100,000 people, mostly Hutus, have died in outbreaks of inter-ethnic violence. Despite the potential for violent Hutu rebellion and Tutsi reaction, President Pierre Buyoya cautiously began broadening his exclusively Tutsi regime when he appointed Hutu Adrien Sibomana as prime minister in October 1988. Before 1991, Major Buyoya, who seized control of the state from another Tutsi military regime in a September 1987 coup, rejected abandoning the one-party system. He argued that "democracy within a single party" would foster national unity.

While it was still the country's only legal political party, the Unity for National Progress (Uprona) approved a draft National Unity Charter at an extraordinary party congress in December 1990. The Charter was intended to formally abolish ethnic discrimination and to permit the creation of a new constitution to further democratization. In March 1991, the president established a commission charged with drafting the new constitution. When the commission released the draft document in early 1992, its language permitted multiple legal political parties as long as they were not regionally, ethnically or religiously based. In a March 1992 referendum, 90 percent of voters approved the proposed constitution. Later in the month Buyoya resigned his leadership of Uprona to make the office of the president non-partisan.

On 15 April, President Buyoya promulgated a law that legalized opposition parties. As the number of legal political parties grew, many began to call for an all-party transitional government that would prepare for the planned multi-party elections. The regime declined to share power with the new parties during the run-up to elections, stating that the president would instead consult with them on a regular basis. On 17 November, Buyoya appointed a 33-member National Electoral Preparatory Commission to prepare a new electoral code and come up with a framework for conducting the elections. Less than a week later, the president created another commission to allow the parties to make proposals to the government on topics such as access of the opposition to the public media, public financing of parties, and an electoral code.

Several Hutu political movements of varying militancy oppose Tutsi dominance of society and the government. Most prominent is the clandestine Party for the Liberation of the Hutu People (Palipehutu). In its French-language communications Palipehutu denies it is either subversive or anti-Tutsi. However, its tracts and broadcasts in indigenous Kirundi preach hatred of the Tutsi and call for violent political change. It launched repeated offensives in 1991 and 1992, mainly on the countryside of northwestern Burundi. Government troops have been able to blunt the attacks, but at a cost of up to 3,000 casualties. Refugees state that authorities do not limit their attacks to insurgents, but target innocent civilians for summary execution. Other Hutus have been severely beaten and tortured after being detained for suspected association with Palipehutu.

Among the dozen or so opposition parties that have sought legal status under the new constitution, one of the most important is the non-violent Burundi Front for Democracy (Frodebu). Formerly a predominantly Hutu political association, Frodebu was forced to recruit Tutsi into its leadership to avoid being proscribed as an ethnically based party. Before the constitutional referendum, Frodebu publicly criticized the government for not including the political opposition in the constitutional commission. It has also condemned the violence of both Palipehutu and Burundian authorities. Palipehutu has dismissed Frodebu as an organization willing to compromise the Hutu right to rule.

Meanwhile, powerful Tutsi chauvinists, both civilians and soldiers, have pressed the regime for an end to all political concessions to the Hutu majority. They have condemned any release of civilians imprisoned on suspicion of collaboration with Palipehutu. On 4 March, as many as 200 Tutsi soldiers at an army camp unsuccessfully tried to muster support for Buyoya's overthrow. A month later three former government ministers, a few other retired senior officials, and some military officers were arrested on suspicion of having participated in or known of the uprising before it was attempted. All were linked to exiled former President Jean-Baptiste Bagaza, Tutsi leader of the prior regime and a reputed hardline opponent of power-sharing with the Hutu.

Relations between the Burundian government and the regime in neighboring Rwanda continue to be sensitive. Rwanda, in ethnic composition almost a mirror-image of Burundi, is ruled by a Hutu-dominated military junta under assault by a Tutsi-dominated insurgent movement. Palipehutu has repeatedly been given media access in Rwanda, and its anti-Uprona tirades are a source of continuing concern to Burundian authorities. The Buyoya regime has charged that some Rwandan officials are patrons of Palipehutu, providing logistical support for insurgent activity. Burundi claims that Palipehutu uses refugee camps within Rwanda that hold Burundian Hutus as bases from which to launch attacks against Burundian territory. Burundian officials have pressured Rwanda to better police its side of the border against Palipehutu penetration. The two countries signed a security pact in 1992.

Political Rights and Civil Liberties: Burundians do not yet have the right to change their government democratically. The new multi-party constitution, approved by referendum in March 1992, has strong guarantees of minority rights to protect the country's Tutsi minority.

The Tutsi elite has long dominated national political life. The judiciary is not independent of the government. Separate courts deal with military and civil cases. The police and state security agents still make arrests without warrants. Hutu political activists continue to be arrested and held in indefinite detention as prisoners of conscience. Hutus arrested on unsubstantiated suspicion of complicity with Palipehutu have been subjected to torture, beatings and forced starvation under interrogation. Others have "disappeared" while in custody. The regime's Special Investigation Brigade Police and army paratroopers are alleged to have murdered over a thousand civilians from late November 1991 into 1992, essentially in reprisal for Palipehutu attacks. As was the case after soldiers murdered thousands of Hutus in 1988, the government has largely failed to investigate and prosecute human rights abuses during 1991-92.

On 4 February, the legislature passed a new press law that guarantees freedom of speech and permits the creation of privately owned periodicals and broadcasting facilities. Under the new law, opposition parties are to be granted access to state-owned radio and television for campaigning purposes. The government has allowed the opposition to hold public rallies.

Despite rights guarantees in the new constitution, the majority Hutu tribe still faces *de facto* discrimination. The Burundian League of Human Rights attempts to spotlight abuses. The Buyoya regime has abandoned the repressive anti-religious policies of its predecessor. There are restrictions on domestic travel, but emigration and foreign travel are generally unrestricted. The government dissolved the former Uprona-controlled National Trade Union Confederation at the end of 1991, and there have been moves to cut labor free of direct government control.

Cambodia

Polity: Transitional
Economy: Statist
Population: 9,054,000
PPP: $1,025
Life Expectancy: 49.7
Ethnic Groups: Khmer (93 percent), Vietnamese (4 percent), Chinese (3 percent)

Political Rights: 6
Civil Liberties: 6
Status: Not Free

Overview: An ambitious peace process in Cambodia threatened to unravel in 1992 as the Khmer Rouge rebel group refused to disarm and launched several land-grabbing military attacks. At year's end, 16,000 U.N. troops worked to demobilize 450,000 soldiers and restore order in a country that has been battered by decades of civil war.

Cambodia achieved independence from France in 1953 under Prince Norodom Sihanouk. In 1970, army general and prime minister Lon Nol overthrew the Prince in a bloodless coup amidst economic stagnation, unrest over the government's violent suppression of a 1967 peasant revolt and the use of Cambodian territory by rival Vietnamese forces. After years of fighting, Lon Nol's right-wing regime fell in April 1975 to the Communist Khmer Rouge. Led by Pol Pot (Brother Number One), the Khmer Rouge ruthlessly emptied and destroyed cities in a genocidal attempt at creating a classless agricultural society. During the reign of the Khmer Rouge, approximately one to three million Cambodians died of torture or starvation. Vietnam invaded Cambodia in December 1978 and installed the Communist Kampuchean People's Revolutionary Party under Khmer Rouge defector Heng Samrin.

In 1982, three anti-Vietnamese groups joined in an uneasy coalition to fight the government and the Vietnamese occupying army. Led by Prince Sihanouk, the three groups were: the Chinese-backed Khmer Rouge, the Prince's Sihanouk National Army, and the Khmer People's National Liberation Army, led by a former prime minister, Son Sann. As the Khmer Rouge was by far the most powerful of the rebel armies, the fighting essentially became a proxy war between Vietnam and China. In mid-1988, Vietnam removed 50,000 of the estimated 140,000 troops it had in Cambodia, and announced a complete withdrawal in September 1989. The three resistance armies seized more territory in border areas but were unable to overthrow the government. In 1990, the five permanent members of the U.N. Security Council drafted a peace plan calling for a U.N.-run transitional administration that would demobilize the armies and supervise elections.

Fighting continued in early 1991 as all sides tried to increase their territory to gain negotiating leverage. Following a shaky cease-fire in May, several rounds of internationally supervised talks were held over several months. The Khmer Rouge repeatedly stalled the negotiations, but were kept in line by China, which backed peace process. For its part, the ruling Khmer People's Revolutionary Party officially dropped its Marxist-Leninist ideology, came out in favor of a multi-party system and market economy, and changed its name to the Cambodian People's Party (CPP). Prince Sihanouk, Sonn San, nominal Khmer Rouge leader Khieu Samphan, Prime Minister Hun Sen and the representatives of eighteen countries finally signed a peace accord in Paris on 23 October 1991. The accord called for the U.N. Transitional Authority in Cambodia (UNTAC) to run five key ministries—Defense, Finance, Foreign Affairs, Information, and Public Security. It placed Prince Sihanouk at the head of a largely symbolic Supreme National Council (SNC), composed of the leaders of the four factions. The accord also authorized UNTAC to place troops in temporary cantonments and to demobilize and return 70 percent of the soldiers to civilian life.

UNTAC will also organize and supervise Cambodia's first free elections. All sides compromised in agreeing to the electoral formula. The government wanted a single-seat, first-past-the-post system that would allow it to take full advantage of its administrative network throughout the country. The opposition favored a nationwide proportional representation system to ensure its groups of winning some seats. The parties accepted a proportional system using the country's twenty provinces as constituencies, allowing each faction to do well in its stronghold. Anyone who can claim a Cambodian parent will be allowed to vote, regardless of place of birth.

In November 1991, Sihanouk and his followers entered into a coalition with the government to alienate the Khmer Rouge. A raging mob bloodied and nearly lynched Khieu Samphan upon his return to the capital, as citizens vowed revenge on the guerrilla group for the deaths of their friends and relatives. Sihanouk abandoned the coalition in December in order to keep the peace process together. The SNC finally met in the capital on 30 December and called for a rapid deployment of U.N. troops.

In 1992, the Khmer Rouge refused to comply with the peace process, apparently biding time to gain more land and increase its support base. In the spring, it refused to mark off land mine areas and allow U.N. officials access to its territory. New Khmer Rouge offensives in Kompong Thom and Siem Riep Provinces threatened to re-ignite the civil war. In January, Khmer Rouge mortar attacks left entire villages in flames and sent 10,000 people fleeing. In March, the government launched its own offensive, and fighting flared along Highway 12, which the Khmer Rouge wanted to cut off to protect its northern stronghold in Preah Vihear province.

On 13 June, the government's army, the KPNLF and Sihanouk's army began compliance with Phase Two of the peace process—cantonment and disarmament. The Khmer Rouge refused to begin demobilizing, claiming that Vietnamese soldiers and advisors remained in the country. The faction also called for the SNC to hold greater authority and for the government to be dissolved. This would contravene the Paris accords, which allow the former Communist government to remain largely intact until free elections are held. The group seized four more villages in Preah Vihear in fresh fighting in July.

At a 24 August SNC meeting, the Khmer Rouge introduced yet another condition for disarming—redrawing the border with Vietnam to recover territory the Hun Sen regime had ceded in fraternal agreements. On 2 September, a frustrated Sihanouk told reporters that the peace process should continue with or without the Khmer Rouge, particularly because the other three groups controlled most of the country. The Khmer Rouge's continuing intransigence finally forced the U.N. to take punitive measures. On 30 November, the Security Council imposed trade sanctions on areas of the country under Khmer Rouge control, and said free elections would be held in mid-1993 with or without the rebel group. The effectiveness of the sanctions depends largely on neighboring Thailand's willingness to disrupt the profitable illicit border trade in timber and gems. The same day, the Khmer Rouge announced it had formed a political wing, the National Unity of Cambodia Party, which would participate in the elections if all of the group's demands are met. In December, the Khmer Rouge's participation in the election seemed even less likely after the group made a mockery of the peace process by briefly holding U.N. peacekeeping troops hostage on several occasions.

Before elections are held, UNTAC must repatriate and register approximately 370,000 refugees, mostly from camps in Thailand. The process began on 30 March, and by 28 August, 100,000 people had returned to their homeland. They receive food for at least 200 days, as well as a choice between a cash grant, a housing plot, or farm land. Although the Paris Accords give the U.N. sole responsibility in this area, the four factions have attempted to persuade refugees to resettle in their areas to build support bases for the elections. Millions of land mines scattered across the country have hampered the repatriation process, and given Cambodia the highest proportion of physically disabled people in the world.

The end of the civil war has led to a surge of economic activity, particularly in Phnom Penh. The U.S. lifted a 17-year-old trade embargo against the country, and on 22 June, 33 countries and 12 non-governmental organizations pledged $880 million in aid to rebuild the country's infrastructure and resettle refugees.

Political Rights and Civil Liberties:

The elections planned for mid-1993 will be the first free vote in Cambodian history. Currently, the country is run by a figurehead Supreme National Council, composed of representatives of four factions that signed a peace accord in October 1991. Day-to-day affairs are administered by the U.N. Transitional Authority in Cambodia, and by the former Communist government. In January, the SNC issued a joint communiqué giving citizens new political freedoms, including freedom of expression and of association. UNTAC's human rights office has been investigating charges of political harassment and illegal land seizure. Western magazines, along with several new English-language newspapers, are available, and UNTAC has its own broadcasting station.

During this transitional period, most of the country's institutions are in flux. The government has released political prisoners and opened its prisons to foreign inspection.

In 1992, there were numerous incidents of political violence, including several grenade attacks on party offices of followers of Prince Sihanouk and Son Sann. Several political figures have been targeted. In January, unknown gunmen shot former transportation minister Oung Phan, who had recently formed a political party to contest the elections. Tea Bun Long, an outspoken critic of government corruption, was killed in a separate shooting incident.

Banditry, murder and rape by disaffected soldiers are rampant, and crime and random violence are on the rise. Age-old animosity has led to increasing attacks on Vietnamese villagers. Approximately 200,000 Vietnamese live in the country, many of whom trace their roots in Cambodia for several generations. On 10 October 1992, 398 Vietnamese anti-Communist guerrillas and their families surrendered their weapons and prepared to resettle in the West. The guerrillas had been part of the United Front for the Liberation of Oppressed Races, an umbrella of minority hill tribes who had fought the Vietnamese government in the 1970s before fleeing to Cambodia.

Cameroon

Polity: Dominant party (military-dominated)
Economy: Capitalist
Population: 12,658,000
PPP: $1,699
Life Expectancy: 53.7
Ethnic Groups: Adamawa, Bamiléké, Beti, Dzem, Fulani, Mandari, Shouwa, other—over 100 tribes and 24 languages

Political Rights: 6
Civil Liberties: 5
Status: Not Free

Overview:

In 1992, the government of Cameroon perpetuated its rule through a rigged presidential election and military repression. At the end of the year, the opposition threatened to wage civil war.

The Republic of Cameroon, located on the Gulf of Guinea in west-central Africa, was formed in 1961 with the merger of former British and French colonial possessions. This dual Anglo-French colonial heritage is still reflected in the often sharp divisions between the 20 percent anglophone minority and the 80 percent francophone majority. Additional racial, ethnic, religious and political divisions initially led to a loose federal structure emphasizing regional government. By 1965, however, a shift to a centralized unitary regime had begun, culminating in the political dominance of President Ahmadou Ahidjo in 1972. In 1982, Ahidjo resigned and elevated Prime Minister Paul Biya to the presidency. Soon thereafter, the unicameral 150-member National Assembly eliminated the office of prime minister, thereby vesting all executive power in Biya. The present system calls for a strong president directly elected by universal suffrage. The president has the power to appoint and dismiss local leaders, members of the legislature, and cabinet ministers.

Competitive elections of a sort were held for the first time in 1988, but all the candidates were approved by the leadership of the single-party Cameroon People's Democratic Rally (CPDR). In the face of strong public discontent, President Biya announced his commitment to multi-partyism in June 1990. Nevertheless, Biya conceded none of his power and, in 1991, the opposition demanded such measures as a national conference, the dissolution of the CPDM-monopolized legislature, and an end to the government's public-broadcasting monopoly. Biya rejected these demands, but the opposition followed with public protests and strikes. Following a meeting with opposition leaders, the government announced a compromise agreement on 13 November 1991. Disruptive demonstrations lessened and the regime permitted public meetings. The government also abolished provincial martial law regimes.

The first multi-party legislative elections in over 25 years were held 1 March 1992. Only 32 of 60 opposition parties participated. The main opposition participants included the largely Muslim and northern-oriented National Union for Democracy and Progress (UNDP), which descends from ex-President Ahidjo's party, and the Democratic Movement for Defense of the Republic (MDDR). Fearing electoral fraud, two groups boycotted the election: a faction of the Union of Cameroonian Peoples (UPC), which is strongest in the city of Douala and the Littoral Province, and the Social Democratic Front (SDF), which is strongest in the anglophone-dominated west. The ruling CPDM won 88 of 180 seats, allowing it to form a majority with the MDDR, which won 6 seats. The UNDP won the largest number of opposition seats, 68. The UPC won 18. Although some of the opposition parties alleged electoral fraud, international observers found the election marred more by poor administration than deliberate rigging. Fifteen percent of the eligible population voted.

Following the election, prominent figures from the opposition continued to call for a sovereign national conference create a transitional government. At the same time, opposition parties attempted to agree on a joint candidate to oppose Biya in the upcoming presidential election, supposedly slated for early 1993. But the government moved the election date forward to October 1992, rejecting demands that the polling be administered by an independent electoral commission. The regime also refused to re-open voting registration, disenfranchising opposition supporters who had boycotted the March legislative elections.

By the time the election was held on 11 October, Biya's major competitors were the SDP's Fru Ndi and Bello Bouba Maïgari, leader of the UNDP. Before the national electoral commission released the official results, the minister of communications and the state-controlled media projected a victory for President Biya. The opposition petitioned to have the election annulled in the face of evidence of massive fraud, but its petitions were rejected. The commission suspiciously delayed for two weeks before confirming Biya's victory. According to the official results, the top two finishers were Biya, with 39 percent, and Fru Ndi, with 35 percent. Maïgari, who came in third, asserted that Fru Ndi had won. International observers concluded that the election was not fair. But having promulgated a law in September that limited the election to one round, Biya declared victory.

Even as tensions rose throughout the country after the election, the president sent security forces and the police to the streets to maintain order. Hundreds of protesters in the country's anglophone northwest were imprisoned after the regime declared a state of emergency. In late November, Amnesty International reported evidence of systematic torture of the detainess by security police. The regime asserted that those detained were only common criminals and not political prisoners, but newspapers reporting details of the crackdown were confiscated by authorities. A court in the northwest ordered the release of the detainess by December, but the regime responded by transferring them to the central prison in the capital of Yaounde.

Fru Ndi declared after the election that it was he who had won, and in late October publicly detailed his first steps as president even while troops menacingly surrounded his home. But Biya was inaugurated on 3 November and appointed Simon Achidi Achu as prime minister on 25 November. The U.S. responded to the fraudulent election and subsequent repression by suspending further foreign aid.

Political Rights and Civil Liberties: The Cameroonian people do not have the right to change their government democratically. According to international observers, the October 1992 presidential election was marred by fraud. Despite charges of pervasive judicial corruption, courts are generally not subject to government interference when dealing with nonpolitical matters.

Out-spoken independent periodicals continue to be alternately banned and unbanned by the government on political grounds. By law, publications must be presented for review by state censors before distribution. Most nongovernment newspapers and magazines suspended publication for one week in mid-1992 to protest press restrictions.

Torture is common for those incarcerated. Amnesty International charged in 1992 that approximately 70 inmates of a prison camp had recently died of starvation and disease through neglect by the authorities. In early January 1992, members of the banned human-rights group CAP *Liberté* were arrested, severely beaten, and denied medical attention. In 1992, security forces repeatedly assaulted peaceful demonstrators and attendees at opposition meetings. The government bans strikes and closely controls trade unions.

Canada

Polity: Federal parliamentary democracy
Economy: Capitalist
Population: 27,352,000
PPP: $18,635
Life Expectancy: 77.0
Ethnic Groups: British, French, other European, Asian, Caribbean black, aboriginal or native (Indian and Inuit), others

Political Rights: 1
Civil Liberties: 1
Status: Free

Overview: In a vote with far-reaching implications, Canadians rejected a major constitutional reform package in a referendum on 26 October 1992. Known as the Charlottetown agreement, the package would have recognized the largely Francophone Quebec province as a distinct society, created an elected Senate with equal provincial representation, increased provincial powers at the expense of the federal government, and granted self-government to aboriginal groups. Disturbed by some elements of the agreement and angry at the economic recession, 56 percent of the voters defeated the deal. Charlottetown's demise could trigger Quebec's withdrawal from Canada. Officially, the referendum was non-binding, but it was politically decisive.

When federal, provincial and aboriginal leaders negotiated the agreement at Charlottetown, Prince Edward Island, in August 1992, they attempted to hold together a country that has deep-rooted divisions. The French and British colonized different parts of Canada in the seventeenth and eighteenth centuries. Following the Treaty of Paris in 1763, Britain governed both the Francophone and Anglophone areas until it granted home rule with the British North America Act (now called the Constitution Act) in 1867. The British monarch remains the titular head of state, acting through the largely ceremonial Canadian Governor-General. Britain retained a theoretical right to overrule the Canadian Parliament until 1982, when Canadians established complete control over their own constitution.

The Canadian Parliament is bicameral. The House of Commons has 295 members elected from single-member districts (ridings). The Senate has more than 100 members, whom the government appoints to represent the country's provinces and territories. The provinces have some significant local powers.

Traditionally, Canadians have held that theirs is basically a major-party-dominated system, but at the federal and provincial levels, there is an increasingly fractious multi-party system. The governing party is Prime Minister Brian Mulroney's Progressive Conservatives (Tories), who support business-oriented economic policies and the North American Free Trade Agreement (NAFTA) with the U.S. and Mexico. If adopted in 1993, NAFTA would roll back trade barriers among the three North American countries during the 1990s. The chief opposition Liberal Party, headed by Jean Chretien, an anti-separatist Quebecker, supports activist government economic policies and opposes North American free trade. The second opposition party is the social democratic New Democratic Party (NDP), led by Audrey McLaughlin. The NDP is pro-trade union and anti-NAFTA. New Democrats control three provinces including Ontario, Canada's largest. Bloc Quebecois, headed by ex-Conservative Lucien Bouchard, advocates Quebec's sovereignty. Since April 1991, the Bloc has been the federal affiliate of Parti Quebecois, the provincial independence party headed by Jacques Parizeau. The provincial Equality Party backs Anglophone rights in Quebec. The fast-growing, anti-bilingual Reform Party, led by Preston Manning, surpassed the Conservatives in many Western areas during 1991-92, and threatened to undercut the Tories in the West at the 1993 general election. Another anti-bilingual party, the Confederation of the Regions Party (CoR), has been the chief opposition in New Brunswick, the only officially bilingual province, since 1991. In the West, the Social Credit Party has controlled some provincial governments. Founded as a movement to control the economy through currency manipulation, the "Socreds" are a populist conservative party, supported in western agricultural areas.

In 1982, Canada's constitution added a charter of rights and freedoms, which common law had covered previously. Limiting the binding nature of the rights and freedoms, one constitutional clause, known as the "notwithstanding clause," permits provincial governments to exempt themselves from applying the charter within their jurisdictions. After holding out against the new constitution, Quebec agreed to accept it in 1987 in return for a recognition by the federal government and the other provinces that Quebec constitutes a "distinct society" within Canada. This was the heart of the Meech Lake accord, named after the place where the constitutional negotiations took place. Quebec invoked the "notwithstanding clause" to keep its provincial language law which restricts the use of English in signs. Many English-speaking municipalities reacted by declaring themselves official English zones. There was a widespread feeling among Anglophone Canadians that recognizing Quebec as a distinct society in the constitution could give it extraordinary powers to limit the rights of non-French Canadians. Generally, Anglophone Canadians did not dispute Quebec's distinctive nature, but questioned whether its distinct status justified curtailing the Charter of Rights and Freedoms and whether Quebec deserved to have constitutionally implied powers which other provinces would not get.

Under the terms of the Meech Lake deal, all provinces had to ratify the new constitution in 1990 in order to make the pact effective. After months of national debate, two provinces, Newfoundland and Manitoba, failed to ratify Meech Lake.

The defeat of Meech Lake was a sharp political setback for Prime Minister Mulroney. His Progressive Conservatives had won the 1988 federal parliamentary election with strong support in Quebec. A bilingual Quebecker, Mulroney had sought to keep his province within Canada through the adoption of Meech Lake. The pact's failure angered Quebec's Francophone majority and increased support for Quebec sovereignty.

With the death of Meech Lake, the Quebec government investigated provincial constitutional options, and decided to hold a referendum on sovereignty by 26 October 1992. Quebec's Liberal Premier Robert Bourassa demanded that Canada approve radically decentralized government or face such a plebiscite. (Ultimately, Quebec put off the sovereignty issue, and voted on the same constitutional reforms as the rest of Canada.) Bourassa's plan called for exclusive provincial control over 22 fields of government. Mulroney attacked Bourassa's plan for a weaker central government, saying he would not accept a "part-time Canada." Mulroney shuffled his cabinet in April 1991 and appointed former Prime Minister Joe Clark to the new post of Minister for Constitutional Affairs. Mulroney and Clark hoped to keep Canada intact with constitutional reforms acceptable to both Quebec and the other provinces.

Attempting to prevent Quebec's secession from Canada and to buy time, Mulroney appointed a panel chaired by Keith Spicer to solicit the views of the Canadian public on the constitution and the political system. The Spicer Commission reported in 1991 that the country was out of sync with itself, disgusted with its leadership, opposed to provincial privilege (except in Quebec) and desirous of radical change. The commissioners proposed protecting Canadian national symbols and instituting significant government reforms. In September 1991, the Mulroney government followed up Spicer with a proposed constitutional overhaul. The provincial government of Ontario countered with a proposal for adding social rights to the constitution. The Spicer Commission and the Mulroney reform package led to months of negotiations which culminated in the Charlottetown agreement.

The three major national parties and many native groups campaigned for the Charlottetown provisions, but some major party provincial leaders (especially in the West) backed the "No" campaign. The largest groups on the "No" side were the

Reform Party, Parti Quebecois, the feminist National Action Committee on the Status of Women, and some native organizations. With the defeat of the "Yes" forces, the major parties focused on the faltering economy and NAFTA, but Parti Quebecois looked ahead to a possible vote on Quebec independence within two years.

The possible break-up of Canada has many serious implications. For example, a sovereign Quebec would have to negotiate its economic relationship with Canada and new trading arrangements with other countries, especially the U.S. Other possible costs of independence include severe economic stress and loss of territory for Quebec, especially if Indians were to attempt secession. In 1992, Ovide Mercredi, national chief of the Assembly of First Nations, a native federation, said that if Quebec were to secede, the natives in Quebec must have the right to self-government. The province's departure from Canada would leave Francophones in other Canadian provinces without Quebec's political and cultural protection.

Political Rights and Civil Liberties:

Canadians have the right to change their government democratically. Due to government canvassing, Canada has nearly 100 percent effective voter registration. The Federal Court of Appeal ruled in 1992 that prisoners have the right to vote in federal elections.

The provinces, especially Quebec, have significant powers. In recent years, Canada and the provinces have given more autonomy to the aboriginals. As power devolves to native groups, questions arise about the constitutionally guaranteed equal rights of native women under the traditionally patriarchal tribal governments. Following native demands, federal and provincial leaders included Indian and Inuit rights in the Charlottetown agreement. The accord's defeat leaves the fate of their political demands and land claims unclear. However, in 1992 the Canadian government negotiated with the Inuit to create Nunavut, a largely Inuit homeland, out of the Northwest Territories. Once operational, the new jurisdiction would have one-fifth of Canada's territory.

In general, civil liberties are very strong and protected by the Charter of Rights and Freedoms. However, the "notwithstanding clause" allows liberties to be curtailed. Rights may also be limited to some extent by unevenly enforced laws which prohibit some forms of pornography and hate literature and by measures which allow some censorship by provincial film boards. In February 1992, the Supreme Court ruled that "undue exploitation of sex" or depictions of sex involving violence, degradation, dehumanization and children are illegal and represent justifiable limitations on freedom of expression.

Quebec placed limits on free expression during the 1992 referendum campaign. Due to campaign finance regulations, groups and individuals had to join unified "Yes" and "No" campaign committees. The provincial government's policy had chilling effects on anything else it defined as campaigning. For example, the Royal Bank of Canada decided to self-censor a report it had had prepared on the economic effects of Quebec independence. Quebec used prior restraint on *The Globe and Mail*'s publication of a taped car-phone conversation between two Quebec officials. The officials discussed Premier Bourassa's alleged cave-in at the Charlottetown talks. Other provinces allowed the newspaper to run the story.

The media are generally free, but there are some restrictions. There is an autonomous government broadcasting system, the CBC, which has both English and

French channels. There are also private broadcasters, magazines and newspapers. In 1991 the Canadian Radio Television and Telecommunications Commission relaxed regulations dictating the precise mixtures of music radio stations could play, but there are still rules defining and encouraging "Canadian musical content."

The Supreme Court expanded free expression in 1992 when it struck down a section of the criminal code that had prohibited spreading "false news." The case involved Ernst Zundel, a pro-Nazi publisher, who had propagated the idea that the Holocaust had never taken place.

A generous welfare system supplements a largely open, competitive economy. Property rights for current occupants are generally strong, but increasing Indian land claims have led to several rounds of litigation and negotiation.

Trade unions and business associations are free and well-organized. Religious expression is free and diverse. However, there are some special rules about religious education. Since the founding of the Canadian government in 1867, in various provinces there have been state-supported religious (or "separate") school systems, but not all denominations have government-backed systems. Complying with an appeals court ruling in 1990, the province of Ontario ordered its public schools to avoid education in a particular religion, but it also specified that the schools may provide education about religions in general. In 1991-92, Jewish and Protestant groups in Ontario challenged the provincial policy of giving financial aid to Catholic schools. They charged that the subsidies violated the freedom of religion and equality sections in the Charter of Rights and Freedoms.

The judiciary is independent and the courts often overturn government policy. In 1992, the Supreme Court ruled that thirteen or fourteen month delays in trials are reasonable. This case clarified a 1990 decision suggesting that eight months was the limit. The earlier ruling had triggered the dismissal of thousands of cases. In 1992, black and native leaders charged that the police and the justice system discriminated against them. Police shootings of blacks in Ontario and Quebec and the acquittal of Los Angeles police in the Rodney King beating in the U.S. led to black protests and a rampage in Toronto on 4 May 1992. The Canadian Human Rights Commission criticized the government in 1992 for cancelling the Court Challenges Program, which had given the poor legal aid money to secure their rights under the Charter of Rights and Freedoms.

Homosexuals won the right to serve in the armed forces in 1992 when the Supreme Court applied the equal rights provisions in the Charter to them.

Quebec's language laws limit the cultural and educational rights of non-French Canadians. For example, immigrants may not send their children to Anglophone schools in Quebec, although Anglo-Canadians may do so under some circumstances. Anglophone children may attend English schools in Quebec if at least one parent is an Anglophone Canadian and if that parent had an English-language education for the last three years of secondary school. Quebec bans English on outdoor commercial signs in the province.

In 1992, Canada accepted an Argentinian homosexual's application for asylum. By validating his argument that his sexual orientation had been the cause of his persecution, Canada set an international precedent for asylum cases. The Canadian government also introduced legislation to limit immigration, preventing refugees from seeking asylum in more than one country.

Cape Verde

Polity: Presidential-par-
liamentary democracy
Economy: Mixed statist
Population: 403,000
PPP: $1,717
Life Expectancy: 67.0
Ethnic Groups: Overall ethnic unity among all racial groups,
Mestiço/Mulatto, Black African, European

Political Rights: 1
Civil Liberties: 2
Status: Free

Overview: A cluster of islands off the coast of west-central Africa, Cape
Verde began its post-colonial existence politically linked to
Guinea-Bissau, another former Portuguese dependency. The
leadership of Cape Verde severed this connection in 1979 after the government in Guinea-
Bissau was overthrown in a coup. The 1980 Cape Verdian constitution established a single-
party state under the tutelage of the leftist African Party for the Independence of Cape Verde
(PAICV). Legislative authority was vested in a unicameral National People's Assembly.

Cape Verde's move toward multi-partyism began officially at a PAICV party
congress in February 1990. The leadership advocated constitutional amendments to
pave the way for competitive elections and eliminate reference to the guiding role of
the PAICV in society. The national legislature later voted to permit alternative party
slates in parliamentary polling and direct elections for president. Carlos Veiga, a
former activist in the PAICV, led the eight-month-old opposition party Movement for
Democracy (MPD) to a convincing victory in the January 1991 parliamentary election.
In presidential elections held the following February, MPD-supported independent
candidate and former Supreme Court Justice Antonio Mascarenhas Monteiro beat
incumbent President Aristides Pereira. For fifteen years, Pereira had ruled Cape Verde
as leader of the PAICV. The MPD continued to consolidate its political gains in the
December 1991 local elections, winning ten of fourteen local councils.

Cape Verde's per capita income is among the highest in West Africa. Many
citizens survive on remittances sent by expatriates working abroad or from Social
Security checks sent to retirees who have spent their working lives in the U.S.
Agricultural opportunities are limited on the arid islands and the fishing industry is
still underdeveloped. The new government hopes to boost the economy by encouraging foreign investment and developing the tourism industry. Key to the MPD election
strategy in 1991 was its charge that the authoritarian PAICV regime had deliberately
kept Cape Verde underdeveloped by discouraging tourism on ideological grounds.

Political Rights   Citizens are able to change their government through free and fair
and Civil Liberties: elections. Criminal and civil cases are generally adjudicated fairly
and expeditiously; there are no known political prisoners.

Public criticism of the government is now tolerated, but the regime warned the press
to avoid sensationalism in April 1992. The MPD government has begun drafting a new
constitution to replace the quasi-Marxist one inherited from the previous regime. Under
the new document, significant power will be shifted from the executive branch to the

legislative. The president retains the right to dissolve the National Assembly and call new elections. Freedoms of religion, association and assembly are respected. Unions no longer need belong to the PAICV-affiliated labor federation, the *Central Sindical.*

Central African Republic

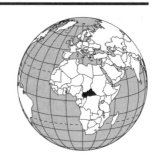

Polity: Dominant party (military dominated)
Economy: Capitalist-statist
Population: 3,154,000
PPP: $770
Life Expectancy: 49.5
Ethnic Groups: Baya (34 percent), Banda (27 percent), Mandja (21 percent), Sara (10 percent)

Political Rights: 6
Civil Liberties: 5
Status: Partly Free

Overview:
Following pro-democracy protests in 1991, the Central African Republic's government announced its commitment to multi-party democracy. By the end of 1992, however, the regime was still resisting substantive political reforms.

This former French colony has been under the leadership of General André Kolingba since 1981, when he overthrew the regime of self-styled Emperor Jean-Bedel Bokassa. General Kolingba immediately established the Rally for Central African Democracy (RDC) as the country's sole legal political party.

During an extraordinary party congress in 1990, the RDC declared that it would try to eradicate government corruption and meet the salary demands of striking teachers. The party leadership also announced a commitment to greater freedom of the press. However, the party categorically rejected the adoption of a multi-party system. The opposition responded with demands for a sovereign national conference, composed of representatives of the country's major interest groups, to establish a transitional government leading to multi-party elections.

On 2 July 1991, following a series of national strikes and demonstrations, the Parliament reversed a 31-year ban on opposition parties and approved a bill to introduce multi-party democracy. Despite this concession, protests continued. Protesters tied their demand for a national conference to demands for public employee wage increases and payment of student scholarship arrears. Toward the end of 1991, a mediator appointed by the government offered 19 February 1992 as the date for convening a major gathering on the country's political future. In November, the regime held preliminary negotiations with the opposition, which demanded that the national conference be held before the end of the year. In December, President Kolingba again rejected demands that the national conference be granted sovereign power as an attempted "civilian coup d'etat." He affirmed that a "broad national debate" would eventually be held and a new electoral code promulgated.

Negotiations reconvened in January 1992, but suddenly ended when the opposition walked out, alleging that the regime was attempting to control the agenda and pack the talks with its own supporters. After talks again resumed in February, negotiators agreed to set up a committee to prepare for a conference of some sort. But Kolingba continued to express hostility to a sovereign national conference; he asserted that the public had clearly told him of their opposition to the idea. He again proposed a non-sovereign national debate, which would have no power to reorganize the government. With no middle ground possible on the issue of sovereignty, the negotiations collapsed in May. Frustrated with its inability to force a sovereign conference on Kolingba, the opposition 14-party United Forces Coalition (CFD) has accused France of bolstering the president's position.

Soon after, Joseph Bendounga of the opposition Democratic Movement for the Renaissance and Evolution of Centrafrica wrote an open letter to the president condemning his "demagoguery and hypocrisy." In the letter, Bendounga rejected any claim of sovereignty for the president's "minority regime." The opposition leader also dismissed the broad national debate as the president's "family lobby," a forum for yes-men. Bendounga was sentenced to six months imprisonment for insulting the head of state.

Undeterred by the stalemate in discussions with the CFD, the president proceeded with arrangements for his national debate. On 1 August, as the president's national debate opened, police charged into a non-violent opposition demonstration and beat CFD leader Jean Claude Conjugo to death. Unrepentant, the regime termed the presence of the U.S. Ambassador at Conjugo's funeral an undiplomatic "provocation."

On 7 September, Kolingba announced legislative and presidential elections would be held on 25 October and 8 November. The CFD selected Abel Goumba of the Patriotic Front for Progress as its presidential candidate. David Dacko, former Centrafrican president, returned from a ten-year exile and stated that he too would be a candidate for the office. In all, five presidential aspirants were joined by hundreds of legislative candidates contesting 84 seats in the national assembly.

The government suspended the first round of elections on 25 October in the capital of Bangui and the city of Berberati after violent clashes and multiple charges of polling irregularity. Both the regime and the opposition tried to fix blame on the other with allegations of ballot box tampering and intimidation by polling place observers. The Supreme Court annulled all election results on 28 October. President Kolingba's term of office expired on 28 November, but he extended it until after new elections were held.

On 4 December, President Kolingba appointed General Thimotee Malendoma, leader of the Civic Forum party, as prime minister. Civic Forum was suspended from the CFD in early August for participating in the president's grand national debate in spite of the opposition alliance's collective decision to boycott it. Less than a month after his appointment, Malendoma accused presidential aides of trying to undercut his authority and "sabotage" elections that had been re-scheduled by the regime for February 1993.

Political Rights and Civil Liberties:

Citizens of the Central African Republic cannot change their government democratically. The country permitted opposition parties to form in 1991, but remains a *de facto* one-party state totally dominated by the president's ruling RDC.

Although the RDC-controlled parliament occasionally criticizes the government, it remains subservient to the president. Political expression construed as "insulting the head of state" is a criminal offense. The constitution guarantees equal rights for all citizens, but the Bamingua pygmies are frequently discriminated against. Despite the RDC's calls for greater freedom of expression, the government-controlled media reflect official policy and citizens still cannot openly criticize the government. Government troops frequently disperse peaceful demonstrations with force. Except for select political cases, the government does not interfere in the judicial process, which appears relatively fair. However, inadequate staff, occasional corruption, and loose interpretation of evidence (sometimes involving witchcraft and sorcery) often compromise judicial proceedings.

Freedom of religion is generally respected. Most workers are members of unions affiliated with the independent Syndical Union of Central African Workers labor federation (USTC). While unions are generally free from government interference in non-political matters, labor strikes were banned in the latter half of 1991. At the time, labor leaders were imprisoned and USTC headquarters occupied by the army.

Chad

Polity: Military
Economy: Capitalist
Population: 5,239,000
PPP: $582
Life Expectancy: 46.5
Ethnic Groups: Arab, Bagirmi, Sara,Wadai, Zaghawa, other

Political Rights: 6
Civil Liberties: 6
Status: Not Free

Overview:

Located in north-central Africa, Chad gained independence from France in 1960. Upon the withdrawal of French troops in 1965, domestic factions began to struggle for control, presaging an on-again, off-again civil war that continues to the present. Hissein Habré's Armed Forces of the North (FAN), with French assistance, overthrew the Goukouni Oueddei regime in 1983. Habré managed to hold on as president until he was overthrown by Deby at the end of 1990.

Deby, a former army commander, had fled Chad for Sudan in April 1989 after a coup attempt he reportedly led against Habré failed. In exile, Deby formed the Patriotic Salvation Movement (MPS) and began to plan Habré's ouster. In November 1990, Chadian rebels under Deby's command rolled out of their bases in Sudan's Darfur region and attacked army garrisons in eastern Chad. Routing government forces, the largely Zaghawa-ethnic insurgents sped across the country and captured the capital of N'Djamena by 2 December. President Habré had already fled the city for Cameroon. Deby became president.

Declaring that the MPS would institute multi-party democracy and guarantee civil liberties, Deby dissolved the National Assembly and suspended Habré's new constitution within days of taking power. He later formally assumed the presidency as head of a provisional administration, which was eventually replaced by a more conventionally-organized government with a prime minister. In February 1991 a "committee of experts" drew up a national charter, to remain in effect for 30 months. At the end of this interim period, there is to be a national referendum to vote on whether to accept another constitution.

The regime came out with a draft law for the legalization of parties in October 1991, and announced that a sovereign national conference would be convened in May or June of 1992. The president named a commission in December 1991 to prepare for the conference, but it was repeatedly postponed and not held by the end of 1992.

On 16 March 1992, the government approved the first two opposition parties. Several other parties were subsequently recognized, and although ethnically and religiously based parties are illegal, almost every party formed during the year drew its support from an ethnically different region of the country. To broaden support for the provisional regime, new Prime Minister Joseph Yudeman appointed several members of legalized opposition parties to his cabinet. However, there is still no firm date yet for national elections.

Throughout the year the security situation in the country remained tense, due to sporadic cross–border incursions by rebels loyal to the ousted Habre, as well as violence in the capital. In late December 1991 forces loyal to Habre, called the Movement for Democracy and Development (MDD), had begun a raid centered on the town of Bol in the Lake Chad area. Initial rebel successes were reversed by MPS troops by the first week in January, and the MDD forces retreated back over the border into Niger and Nigeria. France briefly put warplanes on alert and reinforced by a third its 1,000-member troop strength in the country, garrisoned there by agreement with the Chadian government. In late January, and again in May and June, there was renewed fighting in the Lake Chad region. Although peace agreements were signed in June and in early October, fighting resumed again in October.

Meanwhile, the situation remained tense in the capital of N'Djamena throughout the year. At the same time the army was attempting mopping-up operations against the initial MDD incursion in January, armed security forces were unleashed on those in the capital area suspected of failing to support the MPS. As homes were assaulted, at least ten people were summarily killed for protesting their arrests. Most of the 60 people detained were former officials of the Habré regime and members of a legal opposition political party. A few weeks later, after considerable criticism from abroad, authorities announced the release of all political prisoners.

On 21 February, the government claimed it had stopped a coup attempt "by armed men in military uniform." However, opposition and human rights leaders claimed that the government manufactured the incident in the midst of public anger over violence by soldiers against civilians. The next day thousands of people marched in the capital to demand Deby's resignation. On 18 June, the government announced another coup attempt, this by the National Council for Recovery (CNR), an anti–Deby group led by former health minister Abbas Koti. The attempt was the third claimed by the government since October 1991. After the conspiracy was uncovered, rebel troops of the CNR initiated clashes with government forces in northern Chad.

Political Rights and Civil Liberties:

Chadians do not have the right to change their government democratically. Upon taking power in December 1990, President Idris Deby suspended Hissein Habré's 1989 constitution. The suspended document included provisions that formally guaranteed freedoms of association and expression, the right to a fair trial and freedom from arbitrary arrest. According to the president, the proposed replacement constitution will have many of the same rights among its provisions.

President Deby abolished the Habré political police force, but he has maintained the National Security Force. According to Amnesty International, hundreds of civilians have suffered detention, torture, disappearances and extrajudicial execution at the hands of Deby's Republican Guard and the security police. Prolonged incommunicado detention without charge is common. Ordinary courts have been partially superseded by the Military Court and Special Court of Justice. In these reactivated tribunals of exceptional jurisdiction, the charges are usually politically motivated, defendants are presumed guilty, and judgments are commonly subject to manipulation by the regime.

The Deby government has warned journalists of using "freedom of the press to discredit the institutions of the Republic." The official media serves the interests of the regime. Independent journalists are harassed and assaulted by the authorities. A national union of journalists exists, and called a strike in August to protest censorship.

A new labor federation, the Union of Chadian Trade Unions, was formed to replace a predecessor too closely associated with the Habré regime. In 1992, it led a general strike in support of its demands for payment of salary arrears and the end to economic austerity measures that would discharge civil servants. The Chadian Human Rights League was set up in 1991, and publicly protested abuses by the Deby government. Off-duty soldiers killed the vice president of the Chadian Human Rights League in February 1992.

Chile

Polity: Presidential-legislative democracy
Economy: Capitalist
Population: 13,600,000
PPP: $4,987
Life Expectancy: 71.8
Ethnic Groups: Mestizo, Spanish, other European, Indian

Political Rights: 2
Civil Liberties: 2
Status: Free

Overview: After a decisive victory in the first municipal elections in two decades, the ruling coalition of President Patricio Aylwin looked toward general elections in December 1993. The right-wing opposition continued to block reforms that would subordinate the armed forces to civilian authority, and the coalition hoped to secure in 1993 the two-thirds legislative majority necessary to revise the constitution that dates back to military rule.

The Republic of Chile was founded after independence from Spain in 1818. Democratic governance predominated in this century until the overthrow of the socialist government of Salvador Allende in 1973. General Augusto Pinochet became head of state, dissolved Congress, and banned independent political activity.

The 1980 constitution established a permanent tutelary role for the military in a transition to a "protected" democracy. It also provided for a plebiscite in which voters could reject another presidential term for a government candidate. In October 1988, 55 percent of Chilean voters said "no" to a second term for Pinochet, which meant the government had to hold competitive presidential and legislative elections.

The 1988 campaign of the 16-party "Command for the No" was based on reforming the constitution. After the plebiscite, Pinochet's supporters urged him to negotiate with the Command, leading to an agreement on 54 constitutional changes. Revisions included increasing the number of elected senators in the Congress from 26 to 38 (nine would still be appointees of the Pinochet government); the end of the ban on Marxist parties; and the reduction of the presidential term from eight to four years. The center-left Coalition for Democracy (formerly the Command for the No) nominated Christian Democrat Patricio Aylwin for president. Right-wing parties backed either Hernan Buchi, Pinochet's former finance minister, or businessman Francisco Errazuriz. Because Aylwin vowed not to make major changes in the free-market, free-trade thrust of the economy, civil-military relations were the main issue. The 1980 constitution allows Pinochet to remain commander of the army, the strongest branch of the 57,000-man armed forces, until 1997.

In December 1989, Aylwin won the presidency with 55.2 percent of the vote. The Coalition won a 72-48 majority in the 120-member Chamber of Deputies, and 22 of 38 elected Senate seats. But with nine senators appointed by the outgoing government, the Coalition fell short of a majority in the 47-seat Senate.

The Aylwin government has whittled away at the military's autonomy. In 1990, a Truth and Reconciliation Commission was formed to investigate human rights violations committed under military rule. Pinochet indulged in some saber-rattling, but with a number of his own officers apparently in favor of an apolitical role for military, he eventually backed down.

The Commission's report implicated the military and the secret police at the highest levels in the death or disappearance of 2,279 people between September 1973 and March 1990. However, in 1978 the Pinochet regime issued an amnesty for all political crimes, and the Supreme Court, packed by Pinochet before leaving office, has blocked the government's efforts to lift it.

The Court, however, after persistent coaxing by Aylwin, made a dramatic turnaround on a related issue—the 1976 murder in Washington of former Chilean ambassador to the U.S., Orlando Letelier, and his assistant, Ronni Moffit. In late 1991, the Court ruled that the alleged authors of the crime—retired General Juan Manuel Contreras and Colonel Pedro Espinosa—be tried in civilian courts. They were formally indicted in November 1992.

In 1992, the government prepared a package of constitutional revisions that included returning to the executive the power to appoint and replace the commanders of the three armed forces and the police, and doing away with the nine appointed senators. Opinion polls showed 60-70 percent backing for these reforms. But amending the constitution requires a two-thirds majority in both houses, and the right-wing opposition in the Senate effectively blocked the reforms.

In the 28 June 1992 municipal elections, the Coalition won 53.4 percent of the vote, with three right-wing parties splitting 37 percent. In the aftermath, Coalition parties began jockeying for the presidential nomination, with Eduardo Frei of the Christian Democrats and Ricardo Lagos of the Party for Democracy the main contenders. The Coalition vowed to unite behind a single candidate.

In fall 1992, a scandal involving allegations of military spying on politicians sparked demonstrations and renewed calls for the subordination of the military to civilian authority. Pinochet put the army on alert, accused the media of an anti-military campaign, and initiated procedures to bring sedition charges against the state television station and a newspaper. As in prior instances of civil-military tension, the Aylwin government patiently waited for Pinochet to finish blowing off steam. The chances of a military takeover appeared slim, but rather than risk provoking Pinochet, the Coalition appeared willing to wait until it secured the two-thirds legislative majority necessary to change the constitution.

Political Rights and Civil Liberties: Citizens are able to change their government through free and fair elections. After a constitutional amendment in 1991, the first municipal elections in two decades were held in June 1992. Most of the laws limiting political expression were eliminated by the 1989 constitutional reforms, and the political spectrum runs from Marxist to fascist. Religious expression is unrestricted, although in 1992 a tiny Nazi group claimed credit for profaning Jewish gravesites.

The Aylwin government restored nearly complete media freedom. There are scores of publications representing all points of view. Radio is both private and public. The national television network is operated by the state, but open to all political voices. There are three noncommercial television stations run by universities.

A number of restrictive laws remain on the books, including one that grants power to military courts to convict journalists for sedition or libeling members of the armed forces. Also, the media is occasionally the target of left-wing terrorist attacks. In September 1991, the general manager of *El Mercurio*, the nation's largest newspaper, was abducted and released after a substantial ransom payment five months later.

Negotiations between the Aylwin government, labor unions and the private sector resulted in significant reform of the draconian labor code inherited from the Pinochet regime. Strikes are legal and collective bargaining has been expanded beyond the level of the firm. However, a number of provisions that violate international labor standards remain on the books.

Under Pinochet, the power of military courts was greatly expanded at the expense of the civil court system. He also packed the Supreme Court with lifetime appointees before leaving office. In 1992, a judicial reform package remained in limbo because of right-wing opposition in the Senate.

Although a successful prosecution of the Letelier case (described above) would not establish accountability for all the crimes investigated by the Truth and Reconciliation Commission, it would breach the wall of impunity around the military and renew the possibility of lifting the 1978 amnesty. The prosecution was being led in 1992 by the only Supreme Court judge the Aylwin government has had the opportunity to appoint. Meanwhile, advances have been made in a number of cases not covered by the 1978 amnesty, as several civilian judges have shown determination despite legal and political pressures on their jurisdiction.

There were over 400 political prisoners when the Aylwin government took office. By fall 1992, all but about forty had been pardoned. The remaining prisoners, convicted of violent actions by military courts, were to have their cases retried in civil courts, pending the necessary judicial reforms.

There continues to be sporadic terrorist actions by remnants of the Manuel Rodriguez Patriotic Front (FPMR), the former armed wing of the Communist party, and the bizarre anarcho-hedonist Lautero Front. Human rights groups have expressed concern about new anti-terrorist legislation which broadened police powers. There are frequent reports of abuses including torture, although there is no evidence of a systematic policy.

In 1990, Chile ratified the Inter-American Convention on Human Rights and formally recognized the jurisdiction of the Inter-American Human Rights Court for the interpretation and enforcement of the provisions contained in the convention.

China

Polity: Communist
one-party
Economy: Statist
Population: 1,162,771,000
PPP: $2,656
Life Expectancy: 70.1
Ethnic Groups: Han Chinese (93 percent), Azhuang, Hui,
Uygur, Yi, Miao, Manchu, Tibetan, Mongolian, others

Political Rights: 7
Civil Liberties: 7
Status: Not Free

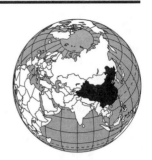

Overview:
The Chinese Communist Party (CCP) held its 14th congress in October 1992, promoting several economic reform advocates, rural cadres and military representatives to top Party posts, while calling for the creation of a "socialist market economy" and firmly ruling out even modest political reforms. The moves reflected the continuing influence of 88-year-old paramount leader Deng Xiaoping.

CCP Chairman Mao proclaimed the People's Republic of China on 1 October 1949 following the Communist victory over the Nationalist Kuomintang. In an attempt to regain power of a fractious CCP, Mao launched the Cultural Revolution in 1966. The national campaign terrorized intellectuals and anyone remotely suspected of bourgeois or foreign influences. By its end in 1976, up to a million had died, and millions more had been disgraced, including Party Secretary Deng Xiaoping. Following Mao's death in September 1976, Deng assumed several top-level posts.

By the mid-1980s, calls for democracy began to increase. In December 1986, students protested in several cities demanding political liberalization and improved living standards. In 1987, hardliners in the CCP engineered the sacking of party General Secretary Hu Yaobang, blaming him for allowing the protests, and replaced him with Zhao Ziyang.

In April 1989, several thousand students gathered in Tiananmen Square to mourn Hu's death, later boycotting classes to demand democratic reforms. By mid-May, the protests had spread to other cities, and several thousand students had begun hunger strikes. The Beijing demonstrations ended in a bloody army assault in Tiananmen Square beginning on 4 June, in which hundreds, perhaps thousands, were killed. The hardliners seized the opportunity to suppress liberal officials and student leaders. Jiang Zemin replaced Zhao Ziyang as party chief.

Despite the image of Party unity, the leadership remains split over the pace and extent of economic reform. The hardliners, or "leftists," are led by 87-year-old Chen Yun and Premier Li Peng and favor continued central economic planning and rigid Marxist-Leninist political orthodoxy. Their "rightist" opponents, led by Deng, are trying to improve living standards through free-market reforms in order to keep the people content with the CCP's hegemony.

In January 1992, Deng, who no longer holds any official post and is in failing health, made a surprise visit to the Shenzen and Zhuhai Special Economic Zones in southern Guangdong province, his first public appearance since February 1991. Granted a high degree of autonomy, the two zones are the among the world's fastest growing economies. An enthusiastic Deng called on the Pearl River Delta area to become Asia's "fifth dragon" in world trade. His calls for speedy economic reform were echoed in the widely circulated Central Committee Document # 2, which also warned against political liberalism.

On 24 February a front-page essay in *People's Daily* declared "economically underdeveloped countries...can only grow and prosper by making correct use of capitalism," including increasing foreign trade, attracting foreign investment, and using "methods from contemporary bourgeois economic theories." The article called for "adequately developing the capitalist economy inside China as a useful supplement to the socialist economy." This radical admission in a paper normally considered a mouthpiece for the hardliners epitomizes the struggle for control of the media, which is currently run largely by reform-oriented Li Ruihuan and hardliner Deng Liqun.

In March, the Politburo called upon the government to "firmly hold to the Party's basic line (on economic reform) for 100 years without wavering," according to the *People's Daily*. The servile National People's Congress, meeting from 20 March to 3 April, predictably approved and backed "rightism" while criticizing Li Peng for not pushing for greater economic growth. It also approved the mammoth Three Gorges Dam project on the Yangtze River, which will displace over one million people and will be the largest construction project in the country's history.

In June, the hardliners received a serious setback with the death of one of the eight "revolutionary elders" who, Deng among them, effectively set policy for the country. Eighty-three-year-old Li Xiannian, an unreconstructed orthodox Marxist, had joined the CCP in 1927. According to the *Far Eastern Economic Review*, two other conservatives, Wang Zhen, 84, and former Beijing mayor Peng Zhen, 90, are reportedly close to death.

The much-awaited CCP 14th Party Congress—the first congress since the Tiananmen Square massacre—set out the party's basic line for the next five years. On 12 October, General Secretary Jiang opened the congress by calling for a "funda-mental restructuring of the economy" and imploring the government to "strengthen the people's democratic dictatorship." Later in the week, the nearly 2,000 delegates unanimously accepted Jiang's report calling for a "socialist market economy."

The party announced a new Central Committee on 18 October, consisting of 189 full members and 130 alternates, nearly half of them new members. Two of the three new members named to the Politburo's seven-man standing committee, the country's highest formal power structure, were notable for what they represent. They are: deputy premier Zhu Rongji, a top economic reformer; 76-year-old General Liu Huaqing, the first military man appointed to the standing committee since the mid-70s; and Hu Jintao, a moderate.

Two big losers were President Yang Shankun, who lost his Politburo seat, and his half-brother Yang Baibang, who lost on the Secretariat and the Central Military Commission while being "promoted" to the Politburo. Along with Liu's standing com-mittee appointment, several central committee positions went to military officers, most likely in an attempt to secure the army's loyalty in case the CCP's power is threatened. A larger than expected share of central committee seats also went to rural cadres.

The idea of a "socialist market economy" leaves much room for latitude, although in its basic form it includes state enterprises, small-scale private businesses, and the "township and village enterprises" that are owned by villagers and use surplus agricultural labor. In early September, the government lifted price controls on 593 goods, leaving just 89 items under artificially set prices. In November, the government announced it would end grain coupons throughout the country in 1 to 3 years. Increasingly, the highest echelons of the state, including top cadres, the Ministry of Public Security, and the army leadership, have set up money-making enterprises.

The government's admission that it is "a glorious thing to be rich" has provided cover for an often frenetic drive to make money. Notably, the most serious public disturbances since 1989 occurred for economic rather than political reasons. On 10 August, police fired tear gas to disperse over a million people who had lined up to buy applications for a lottery for the right to buy stocks on the Shenzhen exchange. The crowd, which had been waiting impatiently for several days, began rioting when the brokerages ran out of applications, leading many to suspect that officials were hoarding forms for friends and relatives. The Shenzhen and Shanghai markets are among the few opportunities for investment in the country, and the value of their stocks has risen dramatically, albeit due to their scarcity rather than quality. Many Chinese, lacking market experience, misinterpret this and assume that stocks will only rise.

In another key issue, the government ended its investigations of former Party chief Zhao and two close associates, Bao Tong and Wu Jiaxing, accused of sympathizing with the 1989 democracy movement. In July, Bao Tong received a seven-year sentence for leaking state secrets and spreading counterrevolutionary propaganda. Bao had been a member of the central committee and was the highest figure to be brought to trial in a decade. In September, a court sentenced Wu Jiaxiang to a relatively lenient three-year term. The court released Wu, the last person known to be waiting for a trial stemming from the 1989 protests, because he had already spent three years in prison. On 9 October, the CCP's central committee ended its three-year investigation into Zhao's activities, neither clearing his name nor punishing him further.

Abroad, China's image is still marred by the June 1989 Tiananmen Square massacre and by the country's human rights record. The United States in particular has been concerned by reports of exports being made by prison labor, and by Chinese nuclear technology sales to developing countries.

Political Rights and Civil Liberties:

Chinese citizens cannot change their government democratically. The Chinese Communist Party (CCP) holds ultimate authority in this one-party state. A handful of aging revolutionary veterans makes the top decisions. Eight smaller parties are allowed to function under the CCP's umbrella.

The government has one of the world's most dismal human rights records, with torture and abusive punishment widespread. Foreign human rights observers are frequently rebuffed: in January 1992 three Canadian MPs planning to investigate human rights abuses and place a wreath at Tiananmen Square were briefly detained, and in April two U.S. Senators attempting to travel to Tibet were denied Chinese visas. In May, seven European labor activists, including MPs from three countries, were detained and expelled for opening a banner in Tiananmen Square that said "Long Live Free Trade Unions."

The government controls most aspects of its citizens' daily lives. Workers are dependent on their work units for their jobs, housing, food coupons, and permission for family decisions such as marriage. The country's one-child population control policy rewards complying couples with preferential health care and educational benefits, while punishing others through fines and demotions. As male children are considered more economically valuable due to their labor and ability to care for aging parents, the policy has reportedly encouraged female infanticide.

Freedoms of speech and of press are sharply curtailed. The government, which controls all media, shut down several non-state newspapers that supported the 1989 democracy movement, including the Shanghai-based *World Economic Herald*. The radio signals for BBC and the Voice of America are frequently jammed, and the government has attacked United States plans for a "Radio Free Asia" broadcasting service.

In 1992, foreign journalists came under increased harassment. In two notable cases in May, officials interrogated a BBC correspondent for several hours, and State Security officers confiscated materials from the office of the *Washington Post* and interrogated bureau chief Lena Sun for two hours. In June, several foreign journalists covering the anniversary of the 1989 Tiananmen Square massacre were detained. Several were roughed up, and police brutally beat a Japanese cameraman.

Academic and cultural freedoms are essentially nonexistent. Freedom of assembly is restricted by rigid guidelines for permits. The government bars any demonstration or gathering considered inimical to the interests of the state or society. Since 1990, all organizations must be approved by the government. However, in June, a former student leader who defected to the U.S. claimed that a human rights network called the All-China People's Autonomous Federation secretly operates on the mainland. On 1 September, the government detained 24-year-old Shen Tong, who had returned to China from exile in the United States to attempt to register a human rights group. Police deported Shen in late October, although two others who were arrested, Qi Dafeng and Qian Liyun, have not been released.

The judiciary is subservient to the CCP, and due process rights are often flouted. The accused are not presumed innocent and over 99 percent are convicted. Defense lawyers lack adequate time to prepare cases and generally do not proclaim their clients' innocence; instead they merely appeal for leniency. Writing in the 16 June 1992 issue of *Yunnan Legal News*, a court official claimed that police ignorance of the law leads to frequent torture to extract confessions. Ordinary workers generally receive harsher sentences than students or intellectuals. Vagrants and the unemployed are frequently detained without cause. Articles 90-104 of the Criminal Law code list counterrevolutionary crimes, which supersede constitutionally guaranteed rights. The government can legally sentence citizens to reeducation camps without judicial proceedings. In September, the human rights group Asia Watch released a report detailing the harsh conditions for political prisoners at the Lingyuan prison in northeastern Liaoning Province.

Organized religion, which had been heavily suppressed during the Cultural Revolution, has been allowed to develop to some extent through government-approved religious organizations. Unofficial Catholic and Protestant churches are sometimes tolerated if they maintain a low profile, although many have been raided and closed. Several clergy members are reportedly detained. Citizens lack the freedom to change residence or jobs without permission from the government and work unit, and the right to emigrate is restricted. Independent trade unions do not exist.

Colombia

Polity: Presidential-
legislative democracy
Economy: Capitalist-
statist
Population: 34,252,000
PPP: $4,068
Life Expectancy: 68.8
Ethnic Groups: Mestizo (58 percent), Caucasian (20 percent),
Mulatto (14 percent), Black, (4 percent), Indian (1 percent)

Political Rights: 2
Civil Liberties: 4
Status: Partly Free

Overview: **P**resident Cesar Gaviria began 1992 with an approval rating
of nearly 70 percent. Ten months later, his administration had
been battered by an energy crisis, labor strikes, corruption
scandals, escalating guerrilla and drug-related violence, and the jailbreak by
Colombia's top drug kingpin. By the fall, Gaviria's ratings had plummeted to less
than 20 percent and his ambitious plan to strengthen democracy had run aground.

Colombia won independence from Spain in 1819. The Republic of Colombia was
established under the 1886 constitution. The Liberal and Conservative parties have
traditionally dominated Colombian politics. In 1957 the two parties formed the National
Front in which they ruled together. After 1974, the parties competed in direct presidential and congressional elections. Municipal elections were held for the first time in 1988.

Gaviria, the Liberal candidate, initiated a process of political reform after winning
the May 1990 presidential elections. In December 1990, voters elected a 74-member
constituent assembly that included politicians from left to right, former left-wing
guerrillas and labor, religious and native Indian leaders.

The new constitution was promulgated on 5 July 1991. It provided for the
dissolution of the Congress elected in 1990 and new elections for an expanded
bicameral Congress and 27 departmental governors. The constitution was designed to
break the traditional oligarchical grip on government and curtail institutionalized
corruption. It abolished the system of discretionary funds that allowed members of
Congress to pay for patronage and re-election campaigns at public expense. The new
constitution also restricts government-funded travel abroad, prohibits legislators from
holding second jobs and bars relatives from running for office.

The constitution also removed the president's authority to appoint departmental
governors, created the elective office of vice-president, limited presidents to single four-
year terms, gave Congress veto powers over the Cabinet and restricted state-of-
emergency powers to 90 days. However, because it also regulates so many areas of the
nation's political, social and economic life, it increased the likelihood of judicial gridlock.

The October 1991 congressional elections indicated that Colombian society would only
slowly absorb the political reforms. Despite a new voter system that gives all parties equal
billing on the ballots and the participation of more than a dozen highly diverse political
groups, only three of every ten eligible voters turned out. The 70 percent abstention rate, high
even by Colombian standards, was repeated during the March 1992 municipal elections.

Voters stayed away because political violence escalates during electoral campaigns and due to a widespread belief that politics is too corrupt for elections to matter. In the 1990 campaign, hundreds of people—including three presidential candidates—were killed by drug traffickers, left-wing guerrillas, and the military. During the 1991 and 1992 campaigns, party offices were bombed and hundreds of people were killed, including at least a dozen candidates. Prior to the 1992 municipal vote, one in every five of the 1,024 outgoing mayors faced investigation on corruption charges.

The Liberal and Conservative machines, with the capability to get supporters to the polls, continued to dominate the political system. In 1991, the Liberals won 56 of 102 seats in the Senate and 86 of the 161 seats in the Chamber of Representatives. Three Conservatives factions took 24 seats in the Senate and 44 in the Chamber. The Democratic Alliance M-19, a former guerrilla group, won 10 percent of the vote.

Gaviria hoped the new constitution would entice still active guerrilla groups to join the political system. In 1991, the government initiated talks with the Revolutionary Armed Forces of Colombia (FARC) and the National Liberation Army (ELN), the country's two oldest insurgent groups, but the talks broke down in mid-1992. The guerrillas, increasingly involved in criminal activities like kidnapping and drug trafficking, unleashed a major offensive in the fall. The government declared a state of emergency as hopes faded for an end to three decades of insurgency.

Gaviria also sought to reduce drug-related violence and corruption, which have seriously weakened the authority of the state. In 1991, he offered traffickers lenient court treatment in exchange for turning themselves in. Medellin cartel leaders, including kingpin Pablo Escobar, held out until it was clear the new constitution would ban extradition. According to the weekly *Semana*, the cartel bribed over half the members of the constituent assembly to ensure passage of the non-extradition clause.

Escobar and his entourage surrendered in June 1991 and took up residence in a cushy compound complete with high-tech communications facilities. On 22 July 1992, he and nine lieutenants bribed their way to freedom during a botched attempt to transfer them to a real prison. Two months later, a judge who was about to convict Escobar for the 1986 killing of a newspaper publisher was murdered amid a wave of cartel attacks that left dozens of police agents dead in Medellin. Meanwhile, the Cali cartel ignored the government's enticements and expanded into the heroin trade.

Gaviria's woes were compounded by a severe energy shortage, renewed guerrilla attacks on power lines and oil installations, and poor management of hydro-electrical facilities. Daily rationing of electricity, coupled with labor strikes and falling commodity prices, damaged the economy and made the normally energetic business community jittery. By November 1992, Gaviria's approval ratings had dropped to less than 20 percent.

Political Rights and Civil Liberties: Citizens are able to change their government through elections. The 1991 constitution provides for much broader participation in the political system, including two reserved seats in the Congress for the country's small Indian minority. It also expands religious freedom by ending the privileges of the Catholic church, which has long enjoyed the advantages of an official religion.

However, constitutional rights regarding free expression and the freedom to organize political parties, civic groups and labor unions are severely restricted by political and drug-related violence and the government's inability to guarantee the security of citizens, institutions and the media. Violence during electoral campaigns is a primary cause of high voter abstention.

Political violence in Colombia continues to take more lives than in any other country in the hemisphere, with an average of more than ten killings, disappearances or kidnappings per day. Those responsible include the military and security forces, drug-traffickers, left-wing guerrilla groups, right-wing paramilitary groups, and possibly thousands of assassins-for-hire. Another category of killings is the "social clean-up"— the elimination of drug addicts, street children and other marginal citizens by "popular militias" often linked with the police. In the first eight months of 1992, there were more than 850 kidnappings, over half by left-wing guerrillas. All perpetrators of political violence continue to operate with nearly total impunity.

There are a number of independent human rights organizations, but rights activists, as well as labor, peasant and student organizations, are consistently the targets of violence and intimidation. One activist was slain in January 1992 after a colleague had published an Op-Ed article in the *New York Times* denouncing rights violations by the Colombian military. Between January 1990 and March 1992, nearly 200 trade union members were killed according to the International Confederation of Free Trade Unions, making Colombia the most dangerous country in the world for organized labor.

In the last decade, the entire judicial system has been severely weakened by the onslaught of the drug cartels and generalized political violence. Much of the system has been compromised through corruption and extortion. In the last seven years, more than 300 judges and court personnel, as well as a justice minister and an attorney general, have been killed.

Under the new constitution, the judiciary, headed by a Supreme Court, was revamped. A U.S.-like adversarial system was adopted and government prosecutors are able to use government security services to investigate crimes. Previously, judges investigated crimes without the help of major law enforcement agencies.

The new measures have brought some success in dealing with common crime, but the judiciary remains vulnerable and ill-equipped for handling high-profile drug cases. To protect the judiciary from drug traffickers, President Gaviria instituted a system of 84 "faceless judges." But by 1992 it was evident the traffickers had penetrated the veil of anonymity after one judge was murdered and two others fled the country. Nearly half the nation's other 4,500 judges receive constant death threats and are unprotected. By the end of 1992, Colombia had yet to successfully prosecute a major trafficker.

Upon enactment of the 1991 constitution, the government lifted a state of siege imposed in 1984 in response to drug-related violence. Observers hoped that removing the measures would diminish the sense of impunity within the army and security forces. The military, however, was untouched by constitutional reform. No demands were made on spending accountability and mandatory military service was left intact. Moreover, the new constitution guarantees that cases involving police and military personnel accused of human rights violations will be tried in military rather than civilian courts. Human rights groups expressed concern that a state of emergency declared in response to a guerrilla offensive in the fall of 1992 further lessened civilian control of the armed forces.

Radio is both public and private. Television is a government monopoly, but public anger over slanted news programs sparked a movement in 1992 to privatize the industry. The press, including numerous daily newspapers and weekly magazines, is privately owned and uncensored. Although no sector of Colombian society has been left untouched, the press and broadcast media have been hit especially hard by the drug-related and political violence. Dozens of journalists have been murdered in the last decade, and journalists were killed at a rate of nearly one per month in 1991-92.

Numerous others have been kidnapped and nearly every newspaper, radio station and broadcast news program is under constant threat. A number of newspapers have been forced to close their regional offices and a few radio stations have been forced off the air. In late 1992, the government banned the publication or broadcast of communiqués from guerrilla and criminal organizations.

Comoros

Polity: Dominant party
Economy: Capitalist
Population: 494,000
PPP: $732
Life Expectancy: 55.0
Ethnic Groups: Arab, Comoran, East Indian

Political Rights: 4
Civil Liberties: 2
Status: Partly Free

Overview: The Comoros, a tiny state consisting of three islands in the Indian Ocean off Madagascar, declared its independence from France in 1975. The first head of state in the independent country, Ahmed Abdallah Abderrahman, served only briefly before being ousted in a coup. Abdallah resumed leadership of the country in 1978 after seizing power with the assistance of a group of mercenaries under the command of Colonel Bob Denard. Abdallah stood for election unopposed in 1978 and 1984, consolidating the power of his one-party regime. Abdallah successfully fought a succession of coup attempts over the next five years; but in late 1989, he was assassinated, reportedly on orders of Colonel Denard. Supreme Court Justice Djohar was installed as interim president while Denard and 21 other mercenaries left the country under pressure from the French government.

In March 1990, the Comoros held its first multi-party presidential elections since independence. In the second round, Djohar of the Comoran Union for Progress (Udizma) defeated former Federal Assembly President Mohamed Taki of the National Union for Democracy in the Comoros by a margin of 55 to 45 percent. The election, however, was marred by irregularities and allegations of fraud. Despite a challenge by Taki, winner of the first round, the Supreme Court validated the results.

Following the elections, Taki partisans staged anti-Djohar demonstrations and, in August 1990, the government asserted it had foiled a coup attempt. Taki, who had fled to France, was charged in February 1991 with criminal complicity in the alleged coup. However, the Djohar regime reached an agreement in Paris with Taki to form a coalition "national union government" in November 1991. Taki announced that he and President Djohar had agreed to convene a national reconciliation conference, which labor, political and religious leaders would attend. Taki said that he and other opposition figures would immediately return to Moroni, the Comoran capital, to participate in the new administration. Dissatisfied with Djohar's concessions to Taki, the pro-government Udizma went into opposition. On 31 December, all Comoran political parties signed a pact acknowledging Djohar as the legitimate president and calling for an end to political violence and electoral fraud.

The national reconciliation conference formed what turned out to be only the first of three "interim" coalition cabinets on 6 January, with the goal of drafting a new constitution and leading the country to legislative elections within four months. Taki was named prime minister. A constitutional referendum was scheduled for 24 May and the elections for June. The national reconciliation conference did not adjourn until early April, but the first government of national unity lasted only a month longer, dissolving after a financial scandal was uncovered. The successor administration had a reshuffled cabinet, but Taki remained as prime minister. In July, Taki was sacked when it was discovered that he had secretly appointed a former French mercenary as special advisor on foreign investment. The mercenary, Patrick Cline, allegedly participated in the attempted coup attempt against Djohar in 1990.

On 19 September 1992 thousands of opposition supporters demonstrated against the Djohar administration in the capital of Moroni, blockading the streets and clashing with security forces. A week later a few hundred army mutineers led by two sons of former President Abdallah seized the national radio station and announced a takeover. Arrested by loyalist troops, the rebels were imprisoned in an army barracks. Fellow soldiers from the same military unit made unsuccessful attempts to free the mutineers on 13 and 19 October before retreating to a remote corner of the island of Grand Comore. The regime accused former prime minister Mohamed Taki of a significant role in the attempted coup.

Two rounds of voting for a national legislature on 22 and 29 November in most of the Comoros led to a tentative majority in the federal assembly for pro-presidential candidates. After disturbances and evidence of irregularities in the balloting during the first round, the National Electoral Council cancelled results in Moroni and the town of Mbeni, and rescheduled all voting there for December. Some opposition parties called for a boycott of the elections. Notable among those urging abstention were Udzima and Taki's National Union for Democracy on Comoros.

Political Rights and Civil Liberties:

Citizens of the Comoros voted in the country's first multi-party elections in 1990. The election, however, was marred by irregularities and allegations of fraud.

The judicial system is based on both Islamic law and the French legal code. In civil and criminal cases, the judiciary is independent. The Supreme Court justices imprisoned for attempting a civilian coup d'etat against President Djohar in 1991 were released in 1992. Public criticism of the government is tolerated and there are many discussion groups and political groupings, including 22 political parties. Although Islam is the state religion, adherents of other faiths are permitted to worship freely. There are no serious restrictions on freedom to travel. Trade unions and strikes are permitted; health workers, teachers and other public employees walked off their jobs in early 1992 to protest government cost-cutting measures, including substantial civil servant lay-offs.

Congo

Polity: Presidential-
parliamentary democracy
Economy: Mixed statist
Population: 2,337,000
PPP: $2,382
Life Expectancy: 53.7
Ethnic Groups: Bakongo, Matéké, M'bochi, VIli, pygmy, other

Political Rights: 3
Civil Liberties: 3
Status: Partly Free

Overview: In 1992, Pascal Lissouba of the Pan-African Union for Social
Democracy (UPADS) was elected president in the Congo's
first free presidential elections. But military assertiveness—
including attacks on civilians in January and November—overshadowed the democratic transition.

Ten years after winning independence in 1960, this former French colony in
central-west Africa became the African People's Republic of the Congo, a one-party,
Marxist-Leninist state run by the Congolese Workers' Party (PCT). After seizing
control in a 1979 coup, General Denis Sassou-Nguesso ruled as both PCT chairman
and president of the country until early 1991, when a sovereign national conference
limited the president's functions to signing international treaties and representing the
country at formal ceremonies.

The one-party system began to change in mid-1990, when the PCT Central
Committee issued a communiqué stating that the Party would drop Marxism-
Leninism as its official ideology and guarantee basic rights, including freedoms of
assembly, expression and association. The communiqué also said that the country
would likely move away from one-party rule in 1991. The Central Committee
recommended that a national convention be held to debate the specifics of a
transformation and set a timetable for multi-party elections. It followed this
pronouncement a few months later by legalizing the formation of new political
parties. On 10 December 1990, the PCT officially abandoned Marxism-Leninism
and adopted a social democratic platform.

In March 1992, the national conference convened, and delegates disbanded the
PCT's rubber-stamp legislature and directed that a new pluralist constitution be
drafted. A 153-member legislative High Council of the Republic (CSR) was created to
implement the national conference's decisions during a one-year period of transition.
New municipal, legislative and presidential elections were slated for 1992, and Andre
Milongo, a former World Bank official, was elected transitional prime minister by the
conference.

After the conference adjourned in June 1991, a coalition of 40 political
parties and associations calling itself the National Alliance for Democracy rallied
to the side of President Sassou-Nguesso and the PCT. With the freer atmosphere
prevailing within the country, prominent Congolese political exiles returned to the
country to form new political parties, many of which joined the anti-PCT
Coordinated Forces for Change. In December 1991, the transitional government
adopted a new constitution.

In January 1992, mutinous paratroopers demanding that Prime Minister Milongo retract his dismissal of several high-ranking army officers occupied the national radio station and international airport. While some in the military called for Milongo's dismissal, tens of thousands of civilian Milongo supporters took to the streets and erected barricades, fearing that the mutiny would turn into a coup d'etat. The army tried to disperse the crowds with tear gas, and five civilian protesters were killed by gunfire. Milongo briefly went into hiding. In the end, the prime minister canceled his attempted replacement of officers and fired deputy defense minister Michel Gangguo, who the military disliked. At the same time, the top military brass asserted that they had no interest in overthrowing the civilian administration.

After repeated postponements, the election schedule got underway, beginning on 15 March with the constitutional referendum. The new constitution was approved by 96.32 percent of the electorate.

In municipal elections on 3 May, Pascal Lissouba's UPADS and Bernard Kolelas' MCDDI emerged as two of the strongest new political parties. UPADS took 449 local seats, the MCDDI 297, with 193 going to the PCT and 86 to the Assembly for Democracy and Social Progress (RDPS). Six mayors and nine regional prefects were forced to resign amid charges of local electoral fraud.

Elections for the 125-seat National Assembly in June and July showed the same pattern of MCDDI and UPADS dominance. The UPADS won 39 seats, the MCDDI 29, and the PCT 19; two smaller parties split the rest. As the presidential elections approached, Milongo's chances to dominate the post-transition political scene dwindled as many faulted his transitional administration for political incompetence and harsh economic austerity policies. In the 2 August first round of the presidential election, he was eliminated, coming in after third-place finisher Sassou-Nguesso. Pascal Lissouba won 61 percent of the vote in the 16 August presidential run-off against Bernard Kolelas, who garnered 39 percent.

In the fall, the UPADS plurality position in the Assembly made it vulnerable to attacks by the opposition. Most notably, the opposition charged that Lissouba had struck a deal before the second round of the presidential election with Sassou-Nguesso, winning his endorsement in return for an agreement to grant the former leader immunity from prosecution on corruption charges. In early October, the National Assembly appointed the PCT's Andre Mouele as its new president, beating out a candidate of UPADS. On 13 November, Prime Minister Stephane Maurice Bongho-Nouara of UPADS resigned following a recent no-confidence vote in the National Assembly.

The motion was filed by a new coalition between the PCT and the seven-party Union of Democratic Renewal (UDR). With a parliamentary majority of 66 out of 125 seats, the PCT-UDR bloc demanded that President Lissouba choose a new prime minister from among its ranks. Instead, Lissouba reappointed Bongho-Nouara, dissolved the Assembly, and announced that new elections would be held on 30 December.

While PCT-UDR leaders denounced the president's action as unconstitutional, their supporters took to the streets in protest. After police fired on demonstrators, killing at least three, representatives of the PCT-UDR and those supporting the president hammered out an accord that cancelled plans for December legislative elections and directed Lissouba to appoint a new prime minister. Claude Antoine da

Costa was selected on 7 December to head a government consisting of 60 percent PCT-UDR ministers and 40 percent ministers from the pro-Lissouba National Alliance for Democracy. Elections were rescheduled for March and the Assembly was dissolved.

Political Rights and Civil Liberties: Citizens of Congo have the right to change their government democratically.

Freedom of expression and association are guaranteed in a new constitution approved in a November 1991 referendum, but the November 1992 attack on demonstrators casts doubt on their guarantees in practice. The judiciary has created a professional group to defend its members against manipulation by other branches of government.

There are no restrictions on freedom to travel, nor on religious practice. The umbrella Congolese Trade Union Confederation (CSC), formerly controlled by the PCT, is now independent. Unions are allowed to form without affiliating with the CSC.

Costa Rica

Polity: Presidential-legislative democracy
Economy: Capitalist-statist
Population: 3,187,000
PPP: $4,413
Life Expectancy: 74.9
Ethnic Groups: Spanish with mestizo minority

Political Rights: 1
Civil Liberties: 1
Status: Free

Overview: After relaxing a harsh economic adjustment program, President Rafael A. Calderon Jr. regained some ground after a sharp fall in popularity in 1991. Meanwhile, presidential contenders from both major parties were maneuvering for the primary elections in 1993.

The Republic of Costa Rica achieved independence from Spain in 1821 and declared itself a republic in 1848. Democratic constitutional government was instituted in 1899 and briefly interrupted in 1917 and 1948. The 1949 constitution, which bans the formation of a national army, has been the framework for democratic governance ever since.

The constitution provides for three independent branches of government. The president and the 57-member Legislative Assembly are elected for four years and are prohibited from succeeding themselves. The Assembly has co-equal power, including the ability to override presidential vetoes. Members of the judicial branch are elected by the Assembly.

Fierce primary campaigns preceded the February 1990 election. The social democratic National Liberation Party (PLN) elected Carlos Manuel Castillo as its presidential nominee, and the conservative Social Christian Unity Party (PUSC) elected Calderon. Seventeen political parties were eventually registered by the independent electoral tribunal. For the tenth time in forty years, the executive branch turned control of the police over to electoral authorities during the election period.

Calderon led in the polls as the PLN tried to overcome widespread publicity surrounding charges of drug trade connections among high party officials. A number of PLN leaders were forced to resign party positions in the wake of reports of involvement issued by a special Assembly commission.

The campaign was marked by mutual accusations of corruption and illegal campaign funding by both major parties. Polls showed the electorate was more interested in economic issues. To diminish the impact of the "poll wars" characteristic of Costa Rican campaigns, the electoral tribunal prohibited the publication of opinion surveys during the month before the vote.

Nearly 80 percent of the electorate voted on 4 February 1990. Calderon defeated Castillo by 51.4 percent to 47.3 percent. Exit polls showed many voters had turned away from the PLN because they feared an excessive concentration of power in one party. The PLN had held the presidency for two straight terms, and 16 out of the previous 20 years.

In the Assembly the PUSC rose to a majority position with 29 members (up from 25), while the PLN dropped to 25 (down from 29). The three remaining seats were won by the left-wing Pueblo Unido party, the Cartagines Agricultural Union, and the Generalena Union. The PUSC won a majority of the 81 municipal district races.

The Calderon administration implemented an austerity and privatization program to reduce a widening public sector deficit and a mounting foreign debt. The program received high marks from international creditors and private economists, but provoked a widespread backlash, including a series of public-sector labor strikes, from a population accustomed to the some of the best social services in Latin America.

As Calderon's ratings plummeted in 1991, six presidential aspirants began contending for the PLN nomination. In 1992 the PLN frontrunner appeared to be Jose Maria Figueres, son of three-time former President Jose "Pepe" Figueres. Another contender was Margerita Penon, wife of former President Oscar Arias. The chief contender for the PUSC nomination was legislator Miguel Angel Rodriguez, who trailed behind most PLN candidates in the polls.

Key issues in recent years include drug-related corruption—Costa Rica has become a major transshipment point for South American cocaine traffickers—and violent land disputes between peasant organizations and large-scale farmers. Both problems underscore Costa Rica's tenuous status as the only demilitarized state in the region.

Costa Rica has been an easy target for drug-traffickers because it has no army, navy or air force. But calls for strengthening the national police force have been countered by alarm over the proliferation of paramilitary groups in the hire of rural landowners.

Coupled with the difficult economic situation, security problems and drug-related corruption will continue to test the institutions of Latin America's strongest democracy. In 1992, polls showed that citizens were increasingly dissatisfied with the way their political system was functioning.

Political Rights and Civil Liberties: Citizens are able to change their government through free and fair elections. Constitutional guarantees regarding freedom of expression, freedom of religion and the right to organize political parties, civic organizations and labor unions are respected.

Numerous allegations implicating both major parties in drug-tainted campaign contributions were made during the 1990 election. In mid-1992, a bipartisan congressional commission proposed new laws prohibiting campaign contributions from foreigners and limiting the size of contributions from Costa Ricans.

Labor unions are active and permitted to strike. Since 1990, labor federations have staged a series of stoppages to protest the increased cost of living and the government's privatization program. There also has been continued confrontation between independent labor unions and the so-called Solidarismo movement. The unions, with support from the International Confederation of Free Trade Unions (ICFTU), charge that Solidarismo is a private sector instrument for co-opting workers and denying collective-bargaining rights guaranteed by the constitution. In 1992, the Calderon government agreed to amend the labor code to prevent Solidarismo groups from impeding union activities.

Press, radio and television are free of censorship. There are a number of independent dailies and weeklies serving a society that is 90 percent literate. Television and radio stations are commercial, with at least six private television stations providing an influential forum for public debate. Freedom of expression, however, is marred by a 21-year-old licensing requirement for journalists. A 1985 Inter-American Human Rights Court ruling determined that licensing of journalists is incompatible with the American Convention on Human Rights.

Members of the independent judicial branch are elected for eight-year terms by the legislature. There is a Supreme Court with power to rule on the constitutionality of legislation, as well as four courts of appeal and a network of district courts. The members of the Supreme Electoral Tribunal are elected by the Supreme Court.

In recent years, the judiciary has been called upon to investigate unprecedented charges of human rights violations made by the independent Costa Rican Human Rights Commission and other rights activists. A number of cases, including allegations of arbitrary arrests and accusations of brutality and torture committed in secret jails, have been made against special police units since 1989, leading to the formation of a special legislative commission to investigate rights violations.

The murder of two suspected drug traffickers by police in February 1992 added to an ongoing controversy over the military training the nation's various police branches have received in the last decade. Costa Rica eliminated its army in 1949, but anxiety over the volatile situation in neighboring Nicaragua in the 1980s caused the country's leaders to accept training from the United States and other countries. In mid-1992, a legislative commission called for a reorganization of the police under one ministry, with minimum standards for hiring police within a civil service structure that allows for "eminently civilian training."

The judicial system also has been marked by delays in the hearing of cases, creating a volatile situation in overcrowded prisons and increased inmate violence. The root of the problem appears to be the nation's economic slump, which has led to a rise in violent crime at a time of budgetary cutbacks affecting the judicial branch.

Croatia

Polity: Presidential-par-
liamentary democracy
(partly foreign occupied)
Economy: Mixed-
statist
Population: 4,550,000
PPP: na
Life Expectancy: 70,0

Political Rights: 4
Civil Liberties: 4
Status: Partly Free

Ethnic Groups: Croats (77 percent), Serbs (12.2 percent),
Muslims (1 percent), Hungarians, Slovenes, Czechs, Albanians,
Montenegrins, Ukrainians, others

Overview:

In 1992, Croatia marked the first anniversary of independence
from Yugoslavia plagued by the terrible costs of civil war.

Fighting killed approximately 10,000 people and displaced
another 700,000. War damage and lost revenue cost the economy over $40 billion.
Meanwhile, the war in neighboring Bosnia-Herzegovina, where Croats make up 18
percent of the population, forced hundreds of thousands to seek refuge in Croatia.

Following the collapse of the Austro-Hungarian empire after World War I, Croatia
joined the new state of Yugoslavia in 1918. During World War II, the Axis powers set
up a short-lived puppet fascist state in Croatia. When the war ended, Croatia again
became part of Yugoslavia, this time under Communist dictator Marshal Josip Broz
(Tito). Croatian nationalism, although suppressed by the Serb-dominated federal
government, occasionally surfaced, including separatist movements that brought numerous
arrests and a change of leadership in the Croatian republic in January 1972.

Age-old animosities between Orthodox Serbs and Catholic Croats resurfaced in
1991, as the Yugoslav confederation began to unravel. The rotating collective
presidency implemented after Tito's death became ineffectual with the collapse of the
League of Communists of Yugoslavia (LCY) and the arrival of hardline nationalist
leaders, particularly Slobodan Milosevic in Serbia. Milosevic's machinations to
undermine the central Yugoslav government under Prime Minister Ante Markovic led
to conflicts with Croatia, which had advocated a looser confederation. Negotiations
between republic leaders failed because of irreconcilable differences on how loosely or
tightly Yugoslavia's ethnic-based components should be knit, as well as the political
role of the Serbian-dominated Yugoslav People's Army (YPA). Growing Serbia nationalism, fueled by Milosevic's fiery oratory, further spurred Croatia's Serbian minority,
concentrated mainly in east Croatia, to expand armed militias and demand autonomy.

On 25 June 1991, Slovenia and Croatia declared independence. Within a month,
YPA units had turned on Croatia, joining armed Serb militias. A series of subsequent
cease-fires brokered by the European Community (EC) collapsed, fighting intensified,
and out-gunned Croatian forces lost ground to Serbian militias and YPA units.
Dubrovnik and Vukovar came under intense bombardment. Both sides committed
atrocities, including civilian massacres. By year's end, Serbs controlled about one-third
of Croatia and declared an autonomous region, the Krajina Serbian Republic (RSK).

In December, all sides agreed to the deployment of 10,000 U.N. troops (later increased to 14,400) in three regions with predominantly Serbian populations. The plan called for complete withdrawal of pro-Serbian Yugoslav Army units and disarming local Serb militias.

In January 1992, the European Community, prompted by Germany, recognized Slovenia and Croatia (the United States followed on 7 April). In February, fighting subsided after the U.N. Security Council voted to send a peacekeeping force. On 23 February, Milan Babic, president of the RSK Assembly, bowed to public pressure in Krajina and from the Serbian government in Belgrade and agreed to cooperate with U.N. troops and monitors, which were deployed in mid-March. The so-called "protected zones" covered a broad strip along the Croatian borders with Serbia and Bosnia-Herzegovina. Despite the U.N. presence, Serb militiamen continued a policy of "ethnic cleansing," forcibly expelling Croats and other non-Serbs from Serb-dominated areas in Croatia.

In May, the YPA halted its withdrawal form eastern Croatia, prompting fears that war could erupt anew. On 29 May, Dubrovnik came under artillery attack from Serb and YPA forces hours after negotiations with U.N. and Croatian authorities on the continuing YPA withdrawal from around the city. Another serious challenge to the truce occurred in June when Croatian forces launched an assault on Serb-held areas, including the city of Knin, the RSK capital. Croatia halted its advance after the U.N. Security Council threatened to impose sanctions.

On 9 July, RSK President Goran Hadzic agreed to return Serb-dominated regions outside the protected zones to Croatian control. On 21 July, RSK leaders agreed to negotiate their republic's status at EC-sponsored talks with Croatia. Serbs dropped demands that Croatia first formally recognize the RSK's independence.

In September, tensions and reports of abuses by Serbian irregulars rose sharply in eastern Croatia; friction mounted between U.N. peacekeepers and Serbian leaders, who refused to disband as many as 16,000 paramilitary forces. Consequently, Croatia refused to withdraw its forces, scuttling U.N. demilitarization plans. The U.N. also reported that expulsions of non-Serbs were continuing and that there had been 400 "acts of terrorism," including dozens of killings and beatings of non-Serbs, since April. In some areas, Serbs had moved into homes of expelled Croats; in the Baranja region, the Serbian population jumped from 25 percent before the war to 70 percent. Similar situations arose in Croat-controlled areas. By October, approximately 300,000 Serbs had fled to Serbia and Serb-controlled Bosnia, and in some areas Serb leaders instituted a pass system to prevent refugees from leaving. In the RSK, residents faced increased lawlessness and economic isolation. In September, the RSK administration decided to call elections following squabbles in the top leadership, although a date was not fixed.

Wars in Croatia and Bosnia had an impact on the political climate and the government of President Franjo Tudjman, whose center-right Croatian Democratic Union (HDZ) coalition won 206 of 356 seats in the bicameral parliament in 1990. Many Croatians were critical of overly nationalistic HDZ tendencies, while others, particularly those in war zones, felt Zagreb had abandoned them. The first group tended to support the more liberal political parties; the latter looked toward more militant, right-wing political forces. Partly because of the war and partly to squelch dissent, the government—made up of many former Communists—began to show authoritarian tendencies. Mid- and high-level officials not loyal to the HDZ were purged from the federal and many local governments. Pressure was put on media considered too critical of the regime.

Croatia's constitution, promulgated in 1990, accorded the president significant powers. Once in office, Tudjman relied on the government institutions he had appointed, notably the Supreme State Council, the Council for Development and Transformation, and the War Council, rather than on the legislature, where his HDZ had a majority. During the post-independence war in 1991, there was broad acceptance of the necessity of strong central leadership and national unity. In 1992, with the war all but over, Tudjman's political support was somewhat eroded.

In the midst of the turmoil, the government scheduled national elections for president and parliament for 2 August. The opposition argued against holding an election during wartime, since many people, both Croats and Serbs, were displaced. During the 37-day campaign, President Tudjman maintained that Croatia should observe the U.N. agreement and seek through negotiation the return of territory lost to Serbia. His opponents expressed disappointment with the U.N.'s progress. A top priority of all parties was the return of displaced persons, a rapid post-war reconstruction, and other social issues. All opposition parties pledged to decrease the constitutional power of the presidency.

President Tudjman received 56.73 percent of the vote, followed by Drazen Budisa of the Croatian Social-Liberal Party (HSLS), 21.87 percent; and Savka Dabcevic-Kucar of the Croatian People's Party (HNS), 6.02 percent. The two runners-up had past Communist connections, and none of the three top finishers had genuine democratic credentials. Finishing fourth with 5.4 percent of the vote was Dobroslav Paraga of the neo-fascist Croatian Party of Rights. Its name came from the far-right party that produced the Ustase, the Hitler- and Mussolini-backed group that established the Croatian Nazi protectorate in 1941.

Candidates running for seats in the Chamber of Deputies were elected by a combined system of proportional representation and direct ballot. Participating political parties drew up state lists (ballots on which a voter must vote for a particular party rather than for individual candidates) for 17 seats. Only six parties and one regional coalition received the necessary 3 percent of the vote entitling them to seats. No party won a real majority; the HDZ received 43 percent of ballots cast (for a total of 85 seats) and HSLS won 14 seats. Four deputies, all independents, were elected by ethnic minorities that make up less than 8 percent of the population. The new Chamber of Deputies had at least 136 deputies representing eight parties and five independent candidates.

The first session of the new parliament convened on 7 September. Stipe Mesic, former member of the Yugoslav collective presidency, was elected president of the body. President Tudjman named his former chief of staff, Hrvoje Sarinic, prime minister.

In domestic affairs, the government faced the challenge of postwar reconstruction and an economy marked by hyperinflation and massive debt. Monthly inflation stood at 26.5 percent by May. Unemployment was high (24 percent) and the national income was about 30 percent lower than in May 1990. Despite a 1991 privatization law, approximately 80 percent of Croatia's assets remained state property. From June 1990 to March 1992, only 35 privatization projects were approved, involving mostly medium-sized firms and enterprises bought out by employees.

The war in Bosnia was Croatia's most immediate foreign policy concern in 1992. In May, there were reports that Serb and Croat officials, meeting secretly in Austria, had agreed to partition the newly independent country, thus leaving Muslims without a homeland. On 17 June, however, Bosnia announced plans for a formal military alliance with Croatia. But Croatian troops in Bosnia, which had held onto Croat-dominated areas, moved into the Muslim interior and around Sarajevo, the Bosnian capital. President Tudjman also encouraged Bosnian Croats to proclaim their own "independent" republic, opening the way for the possible incorporation of Bosnian territory into Croatia. In June, Mate Boban, leader of the Croatian Defense Council in Bosnia, declared a quasi-independent state on the one-third of Bosnia not already seized by the Serbs. It was disclosed in July that as part of an agreement on "wider military cooperation," Croatia had demanded that the 700,000 Croats in Bosnia be considered dual citizens of Croatia and Bosnia.

Also in July, Croatia announced it had absorbed nearly 580,000 refugees from fighting in Bosnia and parts of Croatia and would not accept any more, shipping new arrivals directly to the borders of its northern neighbors, Slovenia and Hungary. In August, Croatian police reportedly rounded up male Bosnian refugees, most of them Muslims, and shipped them back to Bosnia for forced induction into militia units fighting the Serbs. Vice President Mate Ganic acknowledged the sweeps violated the rights of those involved, but said they were necessary to head off a social explosion in Croatia.

On 24 September, Croatia moved to further consolidate its grip over southwestern Bosnia-Herzegovina by signing a military alliance negotiated in June with the Bosnian government. The alliance coincided with fresh moves by President Tudjman to end the U.N. mandate in Croatia so that the country could regain control over its territory.

In related issues, ongoing negotiations between Croatia and the Yugoslav federal government under Prime Minister Milan Panic were undermined in October when Serbian President Milosevic withdrew from the talks. Held in Zagreb, the negotiations focused on the re-establishment of economic relations and the return of Croatian refugees to the U.N.-protected zones in Serb-held areas of Croatia. On 20 October, President Tudjman and President Dobrica Cosic of the truncated Yugoslavia signed an agreement committing both sides to work for peace, mutual recognition and an end to "ethnic cleansing."

Political Rights and Civil Liberties: The presence of U.N. forces, the vast displacement of citizens by war, and Serb control of one-third of the country seriously limited the ability of Croatians to change their government democratically.

Although the 2 August presidential and parliamentary elections were judged generally free and fair by international observers, a vote for the smaller Chamber of Provinces could not be scheduled because many areas were outside Zagreb's control. Moreover, many in the U.N.-protected war zones did not vote. The vote was boycotted by the Serbian population, which opposes remaining part of Croatia. According to monitors from the Commission on Security and Cooperation in Europe, "The greatest problems with the elections was the lack of real openness in explaining decisions, providing information and seeking opposition input."

While political parties are free to organize and participate in the electoral process

(29 parties fielded candidates in the election), the government announced in October that four parliamentary leaders of the HSP, the pro-fascist organization whose leader finished a distant fourth in the August vote, were being investigated on suspicion of terrorist activities and inciting violence. Parliament initiated procedures to lift the suspects' parliamentary immunity; the HSP countered that the procedures pointed to the "logically undemocratic conduct" against the party. In the spring, Zagreb police prevented a group of well-known leftist politicians from holding a convention to found a new party.

The judiciary is not wholly independent from the executive. Vladimir Seks, a right-wing leader of the HDZ, was named the country's chief prosecutor. Laws that restrict speech are still on the books, and Seks supported investigations against politicians and journalists charged under those statutes. A leading Serb politician in Croatia, Milorad Pupovac, was investigated under Article 197 ("spreading of false information") after he said that children in Croatia raised in the Serbian Orthodox Church were being forcibly converted to Catholicism.

Although Croatia has a varied and lively independent press, there were persistent charges that President Tudjman's tight reign on the government-controlled press, as well as television and radio, limited access and exposure to opposition groups, particularly during the election campaign. The principal complaint against Croatian Television (HTV) was that it focused unfairly on the HDZ. Croatian Youth Television (OTV) was reportedly more open to opposition coverage. Affiliates of Croatian Radio throughout the country were allegedly under the close control of the main office in Zagreb. The weekly magazine *Novi Danas* was victimized by government authorities, who expelled the publication from its Zagreb offices.

During most of the war, government law and regulation limited coverage of the fighting. Other laws and regulations make the establishment of an independent television station in Croatia effectively impossible. In 1992, journalists and media organizations critical of government policies or officials faced legal actions, dismissals from employment, harassing phone calls and physical abuse. Several journalists—including Viktor Ivancic, editor of a satirical weekly, and Tanja Torbarina, a satirist for *Globus*—were charged under Article 197, which carries a five-year jail term.

Croatians can organize business associations and civic organizations, although there are some restrictions. Freedom of movement, particularly within the country, is restricted by the realities of war. While freedom of religion is nominally assured, Roman Catholic Croats were persecuted or expelled from Serb-controlled areas, while Orthodox Serbs suffered at the hands of Croats. In January, local militiamen and Yugoslav Army pathologists collected hard evidence of a mass killing by Croat extremists of Serb civilians from the town of Gospic on the Adriatic coast. As of January, at least 5,000 people were still missing in Croatia. Serb insurgents and the YPA executed and tortured countless Croat civilians during the seven-month war. Incidents of massacres, atrocities and expulsions continued throughout 1992.

Independent trade unions are allowed to organize, but there are limitations on the right to strike.

Cuba

Polity: Communist one-party

Economy: Statist

Population: 10,846,000

PPP: $2,500

Life Expectancy: 75.4

Ethnic Groups: Relatively homogeneous admixture of Caucasian and black

Political Rights: 7

Civil Liberties: 7

Status: Not Free

Overview: The icy treatment received by Fidel Castro during a Latin American summit held in Madrid in July 1992 underscored Cuba's isolation. With the economy collapsing and the U.S. tightening a 30-year trade embargo, the defiant Castro proceeded to place Cuba under a virtual state of siege. In September, he declared that "we revolutionaries prefer death a thousand times" to giving up Cuba's socialist system.

Cuba achieved independence from Spain in 1898 as a result of the Spanish-American War. The Republic of Cuba was established in 1902, remaining subject to U.S. tutelage under the Platt Amendment until 1934. On 1 January 1959, Castro's guerrillas overthrew the dictatorship of Fulgencio Batista, who had ruled for 18 of the preceding 25 years.

Since 1959, Castro has dominated the Cuban political system, transforming it into a one-party, Marxist-Leninist state. Communist structures were institutionalized by the 1975 constitution approved at the first congress of the Cuban Communist Party (PCC).

The constitution provides for a National Assembly which, in theory, designates a Council of State which, in turn, appoints a Council of Ministers in consultation with its president who serves as head of state. In reality, Castro is responsible for every appointment. As president of the Council of Ministers, chairman of the Council of State, commander-in-chief of the Revolutionary Armed Forces (FAR) and the first secretary of the PCC, Castro controls every lever of power in Cuba. The PCC is the only authorized political party and it controls all governmental entities from the national to the municipal level. All political activity outside the PCC is outlawed.

After the collapse of the Eastern bloc, Castro reaffirmed Cuba's adherence to Marxism-Leninism and made "Socialism or death" the official battle-cry. In 1990 he announced that Cuba was entering a "special period in peacetime," a euphemism for a drastic austerity program involving severe cutbacks in energy consumption and tighter rationing of food and consumer items.

The failed coup in Moscow in 1991 and the subsequent dissolution of the Soviet Union ended Castro's last hope that he would not be cast adrift. In deals with former Soviet republics, Cuba has been able to reconstitute only about one quarter of its lost trade with the Soviet Union and its national income has shrunk by more than half since 1989. International credits have dried up because of Cuba's inability to service its $6 billion debt with Western lenders.

The fourth congress of the PPC, held in 1991, doused any expectations that

Castro might change his hard-line position. Before the congress every human rights organization on the island made public statements urging free elections, a general amnesty of political prisoners and respect for human rights. The government responded with attacks by "rapid action brigades" orchestrated by state security and the jailing of eight rights activists.

At the congress Castro rejected pluralist democracy as "complete rubbish" and one-party Marxist-Leninist rule was reconfirmed. The PCC Politburo was expanded to include younger members, but the result was a further concentration of people loyal to Castro. The congress gave priority to wooing foreign investment and development of the tourist trade.

In 1992, Castro oversaw a series of constitutional revisions. The establishment, in principle, of direct elections to the National Assembly was designed in large part to convince Spain and Latin America that Cuba was open to political reform and therefore deserving of greater economic cooperation. But in July, Castro was cold-shouldered at the Ibero-American summit held in Madrid and mocked in the Spanish media.

After the summit, Castro evidently gave up the idea of trying to placate Latin and European governments that had been pressing for democratization in Cuba. In the fall of 1992 Carlos Aldana, the No. 3 man in Cuba after Castro and his brother Raul, was ousted from the government and the PCC. Aldana had seemed to offer a more moderate side of the regime, at least in international circles.

But in the wake of the Madrid fiasco, and with high-level defections on the increase, Castro adopted a bunker mentality, his main priority to preserve total personal control of the regime. The revised constitution makes the president the head of a newly created National Defense Council, whose mission is to "direct the nation in conditions of a state of war, during the war, or general mobilization or a state of emergency." That freed Castro from having to make time-consuming explanations to the PCC apparatus and gave him greater ability to foil any possible concentration of discontented officers in the military.

At the same time, tolerance for criticism in Cuban society all but disappeared. Prior to Madrid, a number of political prisoners were released, a transparent attempt to buy some political breathing room. Afterward, dissidents were swept up in a crackdown and given prison sentences of seven to fifteen years on charges of distributing propaganda against the government.

By fall 1992, economic conditions in Cuba had deteriorated to unprecedented levels. Aiming to step up pressure, the U.S. passed a law barring foreign subsidiaries of U.S. companies from trading with Cuba. Food accounted for nearly 90 percent of Cuban imports from U.S. subsidiaries and the two-way trade amounted to more than $700 million in 1991. The law also banned ships that trade with the island from U.S. ports for six months. The island appeared to be approaching what Castro called the "Zero Option," in effect the devolution into a pre-industrial society cut off from the rest of the world.

Castro used the new U.S. law as a rationale for tightening the nationwide security net. Beating the drum for greater national defense and patriotic duty, he installed the so-called Single Vigilance and Protection System. It coordinates the military, the police and the Committees for the Defense of the Revolution, the PCC neighborhood watchdog network, to defend against internal and external threats.

By the end of 1992, it was difficult to determine how long the Cuban people would tolerate the increasing deprivation and repression. But Castro appeared bent on making the last chapter of the Cuban Revolution, whenever it is written, a violent episode.

Political Rights and Civil Liberties: Cubans are unable to change their government democratically. All political and civic organization outside the PCC is illegal. Political dissent, spoken or written, is a punishable offense. With the possible exception of South Africa, Indonesia and China, Cuba under Castro has had more political prisoners per capita for longer periods than any other country. The educational system, the judicial system, labor unions, professional organizations, cultural groups and all media are tightly controlled by the state. Outside of the Catholic church, whose scope remains limited by the government, there is no semblance of independent civil society.

Since 1989, Cuba's small community of human rights activists and political dissenters has been subject to regular and severe crackdowns. Hundreds of human rights activists and dissenters have been jailed or placed under house arrest. Others have been assaulted in the streets and in their homes by plainclothes police and the "rapid action brigades," mobs organized by state security either through the Committees for the Defense of the Revolution (CDRs) or separately.

There are continued allegations of torture in the prisons and in psychiatric institutions, where a number of the dissidents arrested in recent years have been incarcerated. Since 1990, the International Committee of the Red Cross has been denied access to prisoners. According to Cuban rights activists, more than one hundred prisons and prison camps hold between 60,000 to 100,000 prisoners of all categories. According to international human rights organizations, there are between 200 and 300 political prisoners. In November 1992, domestic rights groups indicated that more than 300 rights activists were in prison. In 1991 and 1992 the United Nations voted to assign a Special Representative on human rights in Cuba, but the Cuban government categorically refused to cooperate.

Freedom of movement and freedom to choose one's residence, education or job are restricted. Attempting to leave the island secretly is a punishable offense. In 1991, however, enforcement was relaxed as Castro turned to a traditional safety valve for ridding the island of dissenters. He also lowered the age to twenty for people wanting to travel abroad, provided that the host nation gave them a visa. Nonetheless, some well-known dissidents who have received visas were denied exits permits. In 1992, there was evidence that a sharp increase in refugees arriving in the U.S. was the result of a smuggling network operating with the connivance of cash-strapped Cuban authorities.

Official discrimination against religious believers was lifted by constitutional revision in mid-1992. The measure was welcomed by the Catholic church, which has seen an increase in membership in recent years. However, by the end of the year, there was little evidence that discrimination had ended in practice. Moreover, there were at least two incidents in which suspected dissidents were dragged out of church services by state security agents, one during a mass presided over by the archbishop of Havana.

As was evident during the 1989 show trials of officers charged with drug-trafficking, and during the trials of human rights activists and other dissidents, due process is alien to the Cuban judicial system. The job of defense attorneys accepted by the courts is to guide defendants in their confessions.

The government has continued restricting the ability of foreign media to operate in Cuba. Journalist visas are required and reporters whom the government considers hostile are not allowed entry. Foreign journalists interviewing dissidents risk being detained and expelled, and in a few cases reporters have been beaten up. A Mexican television news service closed its office in Cuba in 1992, claiming it was being denied the freedom to operate effectively.

Cyprus (Greek)

Polity: Presidential-legislative democracy

Political Rights: 1
Civil Liberties: 1
Status: Free

Economy: Capitalist
Population: Entire island: 717,000, Greeks: 574,000
PPP: $9,368 (sector not specified)
Life Expectancy: 76.2
Ethnic Groups: Greek majority, Turkish minority, and small Maronite, Armenian, and Latin communities

Overview:

In 1992, the leaders of the Greek and Turkish Cypriot communities held intense negotiations and the first face-to-face meeting regarding the reunification of Cyprus. However, the U.N.-sponsored talks were unable to break deadlock over the constitutional and territorial questions. Cyprus remained divided into two sections, separated by a buffer zone manned by U.N. peacekeeping forces.

Cyprus gained independence from British colonial rule in 1960. Since independence, the country has been plagued by tensions and sporadic violence between the Turks and Greeks living on the island. The U.N. established a 2,000-member peacekeeping force in 1964. Following an unsuccessful coup attempt aimed at unifying the island with Greece in 1974, Turkey invaded and occupied the northern Cyprus. Following the invasion, Turkey installed 35,000 troops. As a consequence, approximately 200,000 Greek Cypriots were forced to flee their homes and settle in the south of the island. In 1983, the Turkish Cypriots declared an independent "Turkish Republic of Northern Cyprus" (TRNC), which is recognized only by Turkey. (*See separate report on Turkish-occupied Cyprus under Related Territories.*)

There was renewed international interest in resolving the conflict following the liberation of Kuwait in 1991. In August 1991, President George Bush announced that he would reconvene an international conference in Washington based on the format of "two plus two," in which Greece, Turkey, and the two Cypriot communities would participate. The Greek and Greek Cypriot sides rejected the proposal as giving legitimacy to the existence of the TRNC and the Turkish occupation.

The prime ministers of Greece and Turkey met in January 1992; they announced their intention to normalize bilateral relations and sign a friendship pact. Greek Cypriots feared that the Greeks would reach an accommodation with Turkey over their heads. However, Greek Prime Minister Constantine Mitsotakis assured Cypriot President George Vassilliou that normalization with Turkey would be impossible without solving the Cyprus problem.

On 4 March, more than 20,000 Greek Cypriot women formed a human chain along the U.N.-patrolled 112-mile buffer zone separating the two sides; the demonstrators demanded the withdrawal of Turkish troops, reunification of the island, and return of refugees to their homes.

On 10 April, the U.N. Security Council adopted a resolution urging both parties to cooperate in reaching a solution. The resolution warned that U.N. peacekeeping forces could not stay on the island indefinitely.

In June, TRNC president Rauf Denktash met with the U.N. secretary general to discuss the details of the U.N. proposal. On 17 July, Vassilliou met with Denktash for the first time; both leaders expressed a cautious optimism about the prospects for reunification.

On 14 August, following a three-week period of intense talks, the negotiations adjourned because Denktash objected to discussion about the reduction of Turkish Cypriot territory in a future federative state.

A two-week round of talks ended inconclusively on 11 November. Subsequently, the U.N. secretary general blamed Denktash for obstructing the talks by introducing issues outside of the U.N.-proposed framework.

Political Rights and Civil Liberties:

Greek Cypriots can change their government democratically. Suffrage is universal, and elections are free and fair. The republic has multi-party politics and a presidential-legislative system of government. The president is elected for a five-year term and appoints his own cabinet. The House of Representatives has legislative authority. The House includes empty seats for the Turkish community and observer members from the Maronite, Armenian and Latin communities.

The judicial system is independent. Greek Cypriots have freedoms of assembly and association. Workers have the right to strike, and most of the labor force is unionized. Trade unions are independent and function freely.

Freedom of religion is respected, although the Greek Orthodox Church enjoys special status as a state institution. Freedom of the press is respected. There are private radio stations, and a new law allows for the establishment of private television stations. As a result of the 1974 invasion, 1,619 Greek Cypriots are still missing. The rights of Greek Cypriot refugees to their property in the Turkish-occupied area remain unsettled.

Czecho-Slovakia (Note: Through 31 December 1992)

Polity: Federal-
presidential
parliamentary democracy
Economy: Statist
transitional
Population: 15,724,000
PPP: $7,420
Life Expectancy: 71.8
Ethnic Groups: Czech (65 percent), Slovak (30 percent),
Magyars, Ukrainians

Political Rights: 2
Civil Liberties: 2
Status: Free

Overview:
In 1992, three years after the 1989 "velvet revolution" ended 41 years of Communist rule, Czech and Slovak leaders took concrete steps to dissolve the 74-year-old Czecho-Slovakian federation. The results of June national elections underscored irreconcilable political differences between the governments of the Czech lands (the western and central regions of Bohemia and Moravia) and Slovakia, the largely Catholic, industrialized eastern republic. After the elections, occasionally bitter negotiations focused on bringing a peaceful end to the country by 1 January 1993. Opinion polls, however, consistently showed that most Czechs and Slovaks opposed a complete split.

One noted casualty of the impasse was federal President Václav Havel, the noted playwright and former political prisoner, who led the umbrella Civic Forum coalition to victory in the 1990 national elections. Havel resigned in late July as Slovak parliamentarians overwhelmingly approved a declaration of sovereignty for the Slovak republic. Earlier in the month, nationalist Slovak deputies had blocked Havel's re-election as federal president, and though he could have stayed on until October, he decided to step down rather than oversee the break-up of the country.

The country's disintegration had gained momentum in 1991, as parliamentary leaders from the two republics failed to agree on how to share power. In an 88-point treaty that would have served as a basis for a federal constitution, Czech and Slovak leaders agreed on only 22 points. Key disagreements centered on Slovakia's economic hardship and the country's rapid push toward a market economy. Unemployment in Slovakia reached over 10 percent, while it remained around 5 percent in Czech lands. Burdened with large, inefficient factories geared for Soviet-bloc markets, Slovakia's economy spiraled downwards. The defense industry, of which 80 percent was located in Slovakia, stopped production following a unilateral decision by the federal govern-ment in Prague. Slovak leaders complained that out of 3,000 joint ventures with Western companies, only 600 landed in Slovakia.

Growing support for a new federal-Slovak relationship led to the foundation of new parties and a split in the umbrella Public Against Violence (PAV), Civic Forum's counterpart in Slovakia. In March 1991, then-Slovakian Prime Minister Vladimir Meciar was ousted after he left the coalition government to form his own party, the Movement for a Democratic Slovakia (MDS). Meciar, a reconstituted old-line

Communist and ardent nationalist, became the most popular politician in Slovakia, supported by workers, trade unionists and inhabitants of poor rural regions of central Slovakia.

After six months of wrangling over the federation's fate, the June 1992 elections for the federal and republic parliaments were essentially a referendum on the country's future. The federal chamber is composed of two houses: the 150-member (75 from each republic) House of Nations, directly elected for a five-year term; and the House of the People, which has 150 members elected on the basis of population for five-year terms. Each republic also has a National Council (parliament).

The two clear winners were the pro-market federal Finance Minister Václav Klaus, whose Civic Democratic Party (ODS) won 37 seats in the upper House and 48 seats in the House of the People; and Meciar, whose Movement for a Democratic Slovakia won 33 and 24 seats, respectively. Given the fundamental ideological differences between them, there was scant room for compromise on the issue of unity, particularly since any draft law must be approved by the majority in the House of the People, as well as by both the Czech and Slovak parliaments. Constitutional laws need a three-fifths majority in each chamber; the same is true of the election of the federal president.

Several popular figures from the immediate post-Communist elite fared poorly in the elections. The Civic Democratic Movement (OH), which included Foreign Affairs Minister Jiri Dienstbier, was effectively wiped out. The Civic Democratic Alliance, whose supporters included federal Economics Minister Vladimir Dlouhy, narrowly made it to the Czech National Council but failed to win the 5 percent necessary for representation in the Federal Assembly. The Slovak Social Democratic Party, led by Alexander Dubcek, the former leader who oversaw the liberalizing Prague Spring ultimately crushed by Soviet tanks in 1968, won only five seats in the House of Nations and none in the House of the People or the Slovak National Council. Slovakian Prime Minister Jan Carnogursky's Christian Democratic Union won only six seats in the House of the People and eight in the House of Nations. In the House of Nations, the right-of center parties won an absolute majority in the Czech chamber; Slovak nationalists and leftists, both opposed to rapid economic reforms, totally dominated the Slovak chamber. The party breakdown virtually assured gridlock on the federal level.

Trends were similar in the republican National Councils. Ten of the 19 members of the Czech government lost their seats in the Czech National Council, including Prime Minister Petr Pithart (OH). Twelve off 22 members of the Slovak government failed to win seats in the Slovak parliament. A total of eight parties and coalitions won seats on the Czech National Council, including the ODS-Christian Democratic Party with 76 seats (out of a total of 200); the Left Bloc, with 35 seats; the Social Democrats with 16; the Christian Democratic Union-People's Party with 15; the Republican Party with 14; the Civic Democratic Alliance, with 14; and the Movement for Self-Administrative Democracy Association for Moravia and Silesia with 14. No one party or group won enough seats for a solid basis required for crucial policy decisions.

Five parties were represented in the Slovak parliament: Meciar's Movement for a Democratic Slovakia, which won 74 of the 150 seats; the Democratic Left; the Hungarian Coexistence; Carnogursky's Christian Democratic Movement; and the

Slovak National Party. Only two votes shy of an absolute majority, Meciar's party faced a weak and fragmented opposition.

Prospects for saving the federation dimmed almost immediately after the elections when the first meeting between republic prime ministers Klaus and Meciar broke up after just six hours. While Czechs seemed to accept as inevitable Meciar's three-point program for the new Slovak parliament—passing a declaration of sovereignty, drafting a Slovak Constitution and electing a Slovak president—it became evident that the Slovak leader envisioned a loose confederation under a vaguely defined economic and defense umbrella. Slovak leaders also demanded their own, currency-issuing central bank and their own right to borrow to finance an economic policy that included restoring state subsidies to industry, slowing privatization and increasing social benefits—policies directly opposed to those of Klaus. Slovaks also wanted their own army. Klaus rejected the demands for a looser confederal structure. At the end of June, Czech and Slovak leaders meeting in Bratislava, Slovakia's capital, announced that they had agreed to prepare a peaceful split. President Havel's call for a referendum on the issue was ignored.

In July, the new federal government was sworn in. It was a coalition of members of the ODS, the MDS, and the Christian Democratic Union-People's Party. The federal cabinet was reduced from 16 to 10. Because Klaus and Havel had already agreed to limit the jurisdiction of the federal cabinet, leading Czech and Slovak politicians had no desire to be part of a new, interim federal government. Jan Strasky of the ODS, a deputy prime minister responsible for economic reform, was named prime minister of a caretaker government.

On 3 July, the Federal Assembly voted not to re-elect Havel, who failed to receive the necessary three-fifths of the votes in the House of the People and in the Slovak chamber of the House of Nations. Most of the opposition came from the MDS and the Slovak National Party. Havel's defeat, and subsequent resignation, accelerated the disintegration of Czechoslovakia.

In mid-July, the new government of the Czech republic announced it was laying the groundwork for an independent Czech state. "The Czech government must take all necessary steps to make the Czech republic able to exist as an independent state, in case of the failure of future negotiations with Slovakia, the paralysis of the federal organs, or a Slovak secession," Prime Minister Klaus told the republic's parliament. Meanwhile, Meciar, apparently surprised by his counterpart's endorsement of a quick "divorce," seemed to back away from his previous stance, suggesting that Slovakia was not ready for outright independence.

On 23 July, Czech and Slovak leaders agreed to the formal abolition of the federation and pledged to begin drafting a law on separation that would include several alternatives for deciding the country's break-up, among them an agreement between the two republics' parliaments, a declaration by the federal Assembly and a referendum. The most contested point was in the economic sphere, where no consensus could be reached on a common currency.

By August, it was clear that many citizens, both Czech and Slovak, resented the high-handed way Klaus and Meciar were pushing for a break-up, and there were increased calls for a referendum. Referendum supporters contended that the federal constitution specifies that the only way to dissolve the common state is by referendum. To dissolve the state without a referendum, parliament would have to muster a three-fifths majority to amend the constitution. On 25 August, Meciar said during a break with meetings with Prime Minister Klaus that the federation would cease to exist on 1 January 1993. Three days later, after the sixth round of constitutional talks, the two men announced that the country would be divided into two separate states linked by a customs and currency union.

On 1 September, the Slovak parliament approved Slovakia's first post-war constitution, marking another step toward the breakup of the federation. The Hungarian coalition, representing the estimated 600,000-strong Hungarian minority, cast the only votes against the document. On 24 September, the federal parliament voted to debate legislation allowing it to dissolve the federation, overriding opposition demands that the country's future be put to a referendum. The legislation included a draft law on the divisions of power between the two successor states and a bill dividing federal assets between Czechs and Slovaks. The package was strongly opposed by leftist deputies who favored a national plebiscite. Parliament also failed to elect a president to replace Havel. However, on 1 October, parliament rejected a government bill allowing dissolution of the federation without a referendum, as polls continued to show fewer than 40 percent of Czechs and Slovaks approved a split. The Assembly resolved to set up a commission for Czechoslovakia's transformation into a Czech-Slovak union.

On 8 October, the federal Assembly approved legislation that amended the constitutional law on the Czechoslovak federation. The law transferred power to the republics and abolished a large part of federal bodies. Two days later, both sides said that agreements had been achieved in principle on such issues as citizenship, ownership rights to safeguard investors, and the division of mutual quotas for exports of individual products. On 14 October, the federal government abolished several government agencies. A bill was also introduced on the abolition of Czechoslovak Radio, Czechoslovak television and the CSTK, the national press agency. The following day, Prime Minister Klaus announced that Havel would be the ODS candidate for Czech president after the break-up.

On 26 October, the Czech and Slovak governments meeting in Javorina, north Slovakia, approved a draft agreement on forming a customs union between the two republics after they become independent. The process of dividing the armed forces also proceeded in October.

The Czech and Slovak governments met in Zidlochovice on 9 November and in Bratislava on 23 November, to discuss new draft agreements that were to govern Czech-Slovak relations after the dissolution. Eight agreements, mainly governing economic relations, were concluded in Zidlochovice, and five more in Bratislava.

On 25 November, the federal Assembly voted to dissolve the federation, and thus itself and other federal institutions, on 1 January 1991.

On 2 December, parliament approved the dissolution of Czechoslovak Television, Czechoslovak Radio and the CSTK.

Political Rights and Civil Liberties:

Citizens have the right to change their government democratically, but the results of free and fair elections held in June hastened actions to dissolve the Czecho-Slovak federation by 1 January 1993.

In 1992, the failure to resolve the Czech-Slovak conflict resulted in a constitutional stalemate that undermined the functioning of the federation. In both Czech lands and Slovakia, however, political parties are free to organize and participate in the political process.

A 12-member Constitutional Court, which began to function in early 1992, marked an important step in building a system of checks and balances between the executive, the legislature and the judiciary. An independent judiciary was established by law in 1991. In 1991, the government adopted the so-called *lustrace* law that banned from public offices and jobs anyone suspected of having collaborated with the Communist government. In March 1992, more than 90 deputies opposed to the law petitioned the Constitutional Court to examine the law's constitutionality.

While independent newspapers flourish in both republics, the Slovak government allegedly restricted press freedom in Slovakia. Slovak Prime Minister Meciar began holding press conferences by invitation only, and Slovak editors and television leaders complained of government efforts to intimidate them. As a result, the opposition press has all but disappeared, and pro-Meciar journalists set up an association called "For the True Picture of Slovakia." In September, Meciar demanded the "ethical self-regulation" of reporting about Slovakia. Meciar also called for the abolition of federal television, claiming it was biased against Slovakia. In July, the Slovak government cancelled the sale of a large printing company to a private investor with foreign capital backing. It justified its actions by arguing that "a state monopoly is better than a private monopoly." In September, the Slovak National Council, dominated by Meciar's party, took over the supervision of Slovak television.

The rights of freedom of assembly and association are generally respected. In terms of minority rights, Slovakia's substantial ethnic Hungarian population has expressed concern about Meciar's support for strengthening an already restrictive language law.

In March 1992, 61 deputies issued a new draft law on the restitution of church property. On 15 April, parliament rejected the law, with opponents arguing that if property were returned to the churches, collective agricultural farms would lose much of their land. On 11 May, the Czechoslovak Bishops' Conference published a statement saying that "the rejection of the law...seriously damaged the constructive process of developing cooperative relations between the state and the Church."

There are no restrictions on domestic or foreign travel. Over 90 percent of workers belong to independent labor organizations, including the Czech and Slovak Confederation of Trade Unions (CSKOS) and the Confederation of Slovak Trade Unions (KOS SR).

Denmark

Polity: Parliamentary
democracy
Economy: Mixed
capitalist
Population: 5,168,000
PPP: $13,751
Life Expectancy: 75.8
Ethnic Groups: Overwhelmingly Danish, a small German
minority, various small immigrant groups

Political Rights: 1
Civil Liberties: 1
Status: Free

Overview: In 1992, Denmark shocked the European Community by
rejecting the Maastricht treaty on European union.

Denmark is the oldest monarchy in Europe and the only
Scandinavian country presently a member of the European Community. Today the
role of royalty in state functions is largely ceremonial. Since 1972, Denmark's
ceremonial head of state has been Queen Margrethe II. Real political power rests with
the parliament, the *Folketing*, a unicameral chamber consisting of 179 members. Of
the 179 legislators in the Folketing, 135 are elected in seventeen districts. As autonomous regions, Greenland and the Faroe Islands send two representatives each to the
Folketing. The remaining 40 Danish seats are allocated on a proportional basis to
representatives chosen from parties that receive more than two percent of the popular
vote.

Because of the large number of parties and the 2 percent hurdle needed to enter
the Folketing, Danish parliamentary politics are marked by shifting and collapsing
coalitions. The most recent shift in Danish politics occurred in parliamentary elections
in December 1990, when the Radical Liberal Party left the ruling coalition with the
Conservatives. However, Poul Schlueter and his Conservative Party were able to
maintain a minority government in coalition with the Liberal Party. Schlueter has been
prime minister, maintaining various coalitions in Denmark since 1982. The Conservative-Liberal coalition held 59 seats after the vote in 1990. The Social Democrats
remained strong with 69 seats. The government maintains its margin over the
opposition with the support of small centrist and conservative parties.

The European Community has been a perennial topic in Danish politics for
decades. Until recently, most political parties opposed working within a united Europe.
The Social Democratic Party, the largest opposition party, remains critical of the
Community's machinery, but has taken a more pro-Europe stance since 1990.

On 2 June 1992, Danes voted against the Maastricht treaty on European integration by a margin of 50.7 percent to 49.3 percent. Polls showed that voters did not
want to be overwhelmed by larger European countries, especially Germany. The
government had known that anti-German sentiment could be an obstacle to the treaty,
so it negotiated for a treaty protocol giving the country the right to prohibit Germans
from purchasing summer homes in Denmark. In May, parliament had voted in favor
of the European treaty by a margin of 130 to 25, with one abstention and 23 absent.

The Conservative, Liberal, and Social Democratic parliamentarians backed Maastricht, while the Socialist People's Party and the right-wing populist Progress Party opposed it. The Christian People's Party was split in the issue. The Social Democrats' leadership was not united on the Maastricht treaty, and party supporters voted against the treaty in the referendum.

In September 1992, Prime Minister Poul Schlueter announced that there would be a new referendum in mid-1993, and that Denmark wished to opt out of the planned single European currency. He hoped that Danish voters would back Maastricht if their country could negotiate some exceptions to the deal for an integrated Europe. Foreign Minister Uffe Ellemann Jensen announced that the treaty would be presented to the voters with proposals to make EC decisions more democratically.

Political Rights and Civil Liberties:

Danes have the right to change their government democratically. There is a wide range of political parties, including various Communist parties, a radical right-wing party, a green party and a party advocating the philosophy of a nineteenth century economist, Henry George.

Freedoms of assembly and association are respected. There is free press, which reflects a variety of political opinions. The state finances radio and television broadcasting, but the state-owned television companies have editorial boards that operate independently. The state permits independent radio stations, but regulates them tightly.

The government subsidizes the Lutheran Church, which is the established church of Denmark. Over 90 percent of the Danish populace is affiliated with the state church. Although there is an established church, freedom of religion is respected.

Discrimination against people based on race, gender and language is illegal in Denmark. However, there have been reports of attacks by civilians on recent non-Nordic immigrants. The state has not made any major attempts to combat the rise of racism, but Denmark has pioneered equality for homosexuals. In 1989, it became the first country ever officially to sanction marriages between people of the same gender.

Workers have the right to organize and strike. However, in 1991 the Queen's staff filed a complaint in the European Court of Human Rights about their lack of a labor contract. They have been trying to obtain one since 1973. The royal employees received no response from the Danish labor court when they brought up their case in 1989. Approximately 90 percent of the wage earners in Denmark are affiliated with free trade unions. The umbrella organization in the labor movement is the Danish Federation of Trade Unions, which is linked with the Social Democratic Party. Labor organizations not affiliated with the Danish Federation of Trade Unions have often met fierce resistance from the more established unions.

Djibouti

Polity: Dominant party
Economy: Capitalist
Population: 433,000
PPP: $730
Life Expectancy: 48.0
Ethnic Groups: Isas, Afars, Arabs

Political Rights: 6
Civil Liberties: 6
Status: Not Free

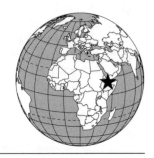

Overview:

In 1992, the standoff continued between the government of President Hassan Gouled Aptidon and the insurgent Revolutionary Front for Unity and Democracy (FRUD), which controls approximately two-thirds of Djibouti.

President Gouled and his Popular Rally for Progress (RPP) have ruled this northwestern African republic since independence was granted by France in 1977. A member of the Somali-speaking Isa, arguably the largest ethnic group in the country, the president was indirectly elected by the Chamber of Deputies at independence and has since been directly re-elected twice in one-party elections. Although President Gouled has consistently named a member of the rival Afar ethnic group as prime minister, Isas effectively control the ruling party, the army and the bureaucracy.

In 1981, disturbed that Gouled ran unopposed, Afars formed the Djibouti Peoples' Party (PPD). Shortly after, the government arrested PPD leaders and formally established a one-party system. Since then, all candidates have been RPP members. In light of the continent-wide move toward multi-partyism, the RPP re-assessed one-party rule in March 1991. But the party ultimately concluded that political pluralism outside of the single-party framework was unnecessary in Djibouti.

As a result of the civil war that broke out the following November in Afar-populated northern Djibouti, Gouled immediately reversed course and said that a referendum on multi-partyism would be held within six months of the ouster of the "foreign armed bands" from the country. One-party elections originally scheduled for April 1992 were canceled and multi-party elections were called for 20 November. In January 1992, the regime began to draft a new constitution without allowing for opposition participation. Completed three months later, the finished document provided for a strong-president system with a minimum of checks and balances, and a limit of four legal political parties.

In November 1991, guerrillas of the FRUD attacked several Djiboutian army garrisons in the far northern part of the country. The RPP government claimed that a substantial number of the attackers were demobilized Ethiopian soldiers attempting to create a unified ethnic Afar state out of adjacent pieces of Djibouti, Eritrea and Ethiopia. FRUD claimed that its movement was multi-ethnic, native Djiboutian, and pro-democratic. The rebels charged that the many of those fighting on behalf of the regime were Isa mercenaries from Ethiopia and Somalia.

Claiming that it was a victim of external aggression, the Gouled regime attempted to invoke a military treaty with France that would have committed French troops to its defense. Reading the conflict as internal to Djibouti, France merely moved to deploy forces garrisoned in Djibouti to the border with Ethiopia and attempted to mediate between FRUD and the regime. Angered by France's refusal to come to the aid of his regime and dismissing any thought of negotiating with FRUD, Gouled ignored a series of cease-fires unilaterally called by the insurgents and sent his military on futile attempts to dislodge the rebels from the northern two-thirds of the country they had seized. Rebels in the field were offered amnesty if they disarmed, but unarmed opponents, including a FRUD spokesman, spent much of their time in prison. At the same time, the government used para-military National Security Forces (FNS) and police to root out suspected FRUD sympathizers in the Djiboutian civilian population. In December 1991, authorities opened fire during a raid on an Afar district of the capital, killing as many as 40 civilians and wounding 90.

A truce called by the FRUD in late February 1992 was suspended a month later when the regime did not respond to French attempts to get negotiations started. Serious incidents of fighting did not resume until July, however. In the interim, the rebels called for resignation of the government and formation of a transition government to prepare for a sovereign national conference. At the same time, nine illegal opposition parties, including the FRUD, met in Paris and formed a united front. In late June, President Gouled announced a September referendum on the draft constitution. The opposition called for a boycott of the referendum. In June, 14 members of FRUD were released from prison, and in July the president granted pardons to a handful of prominent political exiles. Opposition parties were legally permitted as of 20 September.

The draft constitution was approved on 4 September by a reported 96.8 percent margin, with a reported turnout of 75 percent of registered voters. The government immediately called for FRUD to disarm and release all of its prisoners as preconditions for negotiations. Although rebels released 25 soldiers, they refused to release any more until former President Ali Aref Bourhane and a dozen other recently sentenced political prisoners were released. The government rejected FRUD's terms and peace talks were postponed indefinitely in late November.

The ruling RPP won all legislative seats in 18 December elections. Only two other parties—the Democratic National Party (PND) of Adan Robleh Awaleh and the Party for Reviving Democracy (PRD)—met the strict requirements for legalization, which included no associated military wing or regional affiliation. FRUD was constitutionally unqualified to field candidates and the PND boycotted the balloting. Only PRD candidates challenged RPP in the election. Presidential elections are scheduled for April 1993.

Political Rights and Civil Liberties:

Citizens of Djibouti do not have the means to change their government democratically. However, the government announced the legalization of opposition parties and held legislative elections in 1992.

In political cases, the State Security Court is not independent of the government, defendants are not entitled to the legal counsel of their choice, and the tribunal's decision may not be appealed. Political dissidents are often detained without charge for extended periods of time. As many as 300 detainees were allegedly tortured in 1991; some prisoners have been extrajudicially executed after their arrest by officials, and people have been attacked in their homes by security police. On 11 July 1992, opposition leader Ali Aref Bourhane, an Afar and leader of colonial Djibouti from 1967 to 1977, was sentenced to ten years imprisonment along with eight others for allegedly plotting against state security.

All media are government-controlled, and criticism of the regime, the RPP, or government policies is not allowed. Journalists are considered public servants. Freedom of speech and association is severely constrained. Public demonstrations require prior authorization. In July 1992, paramilitary police fired on demonstrators marching in support of Ali Aref Bourhane as his trial got underway; thirteen were injured.

Tribalism and clan division are exacerbated by the government's favoritism toward the president's own Mamassan clan within the Somali-speaking Isa tribe. Djibouti is predominantly Sunni Muslim, but Islam is not the official religion. There is no official pressure to abide by Muslim diet and dress regulations. Expatriates worship freely. Freedom of travel inside and outside the country is generally respected. The country has a large refugee population, but the authorities have usually not recognized the refugee status of those fleeing civil war in neighboring countries. With the reported exception of Isas who have fled Somalia, refugees have at times been forcibly repatriated. There is an Association for the Defense of Human Rights. All unions must belong to a government-controlled labor federation, and 10 percent of every worker's salary is automatically deducted for the "righteous defense of the state."

Dominica

Polity: Parliamentary democracy
Economy: Capitalist
Population: 87,000
PPP: $3,399
Life Expectancy: 76.0
Ethnic Groups: Black and mulatto with a minority Carib enclave

Political Rights: 2
Civil Liberties: 1
Status: Free

Overview:

The Commonwealth of Dominica has been an independent republic within the British Commonwealth since 1978.

Internally self-governing since 1967, Dominica is a parliamentary democracy headed by a prime minister and a House of Assembly with 21 members elected to five-year terms. Nine senators are usually appointed, five by the prime minister and four by the opposition leader in the House.

Prime Minister Eugenia Charles, the first woman to head a government in the English-speaking Caribbean, narrowly won a third term in general elections held on 28 May 1990. Although opinion polls had pointed to an easy victory, the ruling Dominica Freedom Party (DFP) won in just eleven of the twenty-one constituencies. The two-year-old centrist United Workers Party (UWP) led by Eddison James, former head of the Banana Growers Association, took second with six seats and replaced the leftist Dominica Labor Party (DLP), which came third with four seats, as the official opposition.

In April 1991, the two opposition parties tried to take advantage of a lagging economy by uniting behind a no-confidence motion against the government. But the motion was defeated when all eleven DFP members in parliament voted against it.

The death of DLP leader Michael Douglas led to a by-election in the northern constituency of Portsmouth in July 1992. The election was won by Douglas's brother, Rosie, who handily defeated the ruling DFP candidate.

Political Rights and Civil Liberties: Citizens have the right to change their government democratically. There are no legal restrictions on political, labor or civic organizations. In September 1992, primary school teachers boycotted the first day of classes to protest the government's refusal to recognize the Dominica Association of Teachers as their bargaining agent. The government contended that the right to conduct salary negotiations belongs, by law, solely to the civil service union.

Since the last elections, the small population of Carib Indians (approximately 3,000), many of whom live on a 3,700-acre reserve northeast of the capital, have been represented in the House of Assembly by Carib parliamentarian Worrel Sanford.

Freedom of religion is generally respected. However, the small Rastafarian community charges that their religious rights are violated by a policy of cutting off the "dread locks" of those who are imprisoned. The Rastafarians also charge that non-Dominican Rastafarians are illegally banned from entering the country.

The press is generally free, varied and critical. Television and radio, both public and private, are open to views from across the political spectrum. Opposition parties have charged that the board appointed to oversee state-run media is manipulated by the government. Nonetheless, in 1990, television was used for the first time as an effective campaign tool by all parties. In May 1992, the ruling DFP used its parliamentary majority to ban the UWP's *Voice of the People* from covering parliamentary proceedings for the remainder of the year after an article appeared in the paper accusing the parliamentary speaker of bias.

There is an independent judiciary and the effectiveness of the rule of law is enhanced by the court system's embrace of the inter-island Eastern Caribbean Supreme Court. The government has criticized the attendance of citizens at conferences in Cuba and Libya, but does not restrict travel to those countries.

The Dominica Defense Force (DDF) was disbanded in 1981 following attempts to overthrow the government by supporters of former Prime Minister Patrick John with the assistance of the DDF. John was convicted in 1986 for his involvement in conspiracy and given a twelve-year prison sentence. He was released by executive order in May 1990 and now heads the National Workers Union.

Dominican Republic

Polity: Presidential-legislative democracy
Economy: Capitalist-statist
Population: 7,471,000
PPP: $2,537
Life Expectancy: 66.7
Ethnic Groups: Complex, mestizo and mulatto (70 percent), Caucasian (15 percent), and black (15 percent)

Political Rights: 2
Civil Liberties: 3
Status: Free

Overview: Few Dominicans believed President Joaquin Balaguer when he stated in 1992 that he would not run for a seventh term in the May 1994 elections. But after the death of his sister, his closest confidant, and the popular rejection of a garish Columbus Day celebration in October, it appeared the blind, 86-year-old leader might be prepared to bow out.

Since achieving independence from Spain in 1821 and Haiti in 1844, the Dominican Republic has endured recurrent domestic conflict. The assassination of General Rafael Trujillo in 1961 ended 30 years of dictatorial rule but led to renewed turmoil. The military overthrow of the elected government of Marxist Juan Bosch in 1963 led to civil war and U.S. military intervention in 1965. In 1966, under a new constitution, civilian rule was restored with the election of Balaguer of the right-wing Social Christian Reformist Party (PRSC).

The constitution provides for a president directly elected for four years, a Congress consisting of a 120-member Chamber of Deputies and a 30-member Senate also directly elected for four years. The governors of the 26 provinces are appointed by the president. Municipalities are governed by elected mayors and municipal councils.

Balaguer was re-elected in 1970 and 1974 but defeated in 1978 by Silvestre Antonio Guzman of the social democratic Dominican Revolutionary Party (PRD). Guzman's inauguration marked the first time in the country's history that a democratically elected president had transferred power to an elected successor. The PRD stayed in power in 1982 with the election of President Salvador Jorge Blanco, but Balaguer was elected again in 1986.

The main candidates in the 16 May 1990 election were Balaguer and fellow octogenarian Juan Bosch of the leftist Dominican Liberation Party (PLD). The other contenders were the PRD's Jose Peña Gomez, and Jacobo Majluta, who had split from the PRD to form the Institutional Revolutionary Party (PRI).

Campaign issues included the country's strapped economy, poverty and unemployment, and government corruption. Although marred by sporadic violence resulting in a number of deaths and injuries, the campaign was one of the most wide-open in the nation's history. In addition to daily rallies, voters were inundated by political advertisements, radio and television talk show discussions, and relentless campaign coverage by nearly a dozen daily newspapers.

Monitored by former U.S. President Jimmy Carter and other international observers, voters cast ballots for president, and legislative and municipal candidates. The abstention rate of 40 percent was the highest since the establishment of democratic rule. The initial count gave Balaguer the edge over Bosch, with Peña Gomez coming in a strong third. Both leaders claimed victory, with Bosch crying fraud and threatening to send his followers into the streets. Carter intervened and the frontrunners agreed to a recount by the Central Electoral Council.

The recount gave Balaguer 35.1 percent of the vote against 33.8 percent for Bosch, but the PRSC lost its legislative majority. In the Chamber of Deputies, Bosch's PLD took 44 seats, the PRSC took 42, the PRD 32, and the PRI 2. In the Senate, the PRSC won 16 seats, the PLD 12, and the PRD 2.

In 1991 the government was plagued by labor strikes and street protests demanding that Balaguer resign, but in early 1992, the Balanguer administration seemed to recover. Economic indicators had improved and the PLD, which had refused to recognize the legitimacy of the 1990 election, was stricken by internal disputes.

In September, however, the official celebration of the 500th anniversary of Columbus's arrival in the New World prompted widespread protests, often ending in violent crackdowns by police. Many people, especially blacks, expressed outrage at Balaguer's six-year spending spree, including the construction of the colossal "Columbus Lighthouse" costing an estimated $70 million. The Dominican Republic is the fourth poorest country in the Western hemisphere. Because of the controversy, Latin American leaders declined invitations to the celebration and Pope John Paul II distanced himself from the Columbus observances during a five-day visit. For Balaguer, the flop was made worse by the death of his sister, his only confidant, whose funeral kept him from presiding over the inauguration of the lighthouse.

In the aftermath, Balaguer appeared dejected and many Dominican observers predicted he would not run in 1994. Opinion polls indicated that Peña Gomez stood the best chance of succeeding him. Bosch, who turned 83, saw his fortunes decline as the PLD split, with the left-wing of the party breaking off to form the Alliance for Democracy (APD).

Political Rights and Civil Liberties:

Citizens are able to change their government through regularly scheduled elections, but an increase in electoral fraud in recent years threatens the integrity of the system. An opinion poll in 1992 showed that 68 percent of Dominicans believe Balaguer rigged the 1990 election, and a similar percentage felt that despite a new electoral code things would not be different in 1994.

Constitutional guarantees regarding free expression, freedom of religion and the right to organize political parties and civic groups are generally respected. There are over a dozen political parties that occupy a wide spectrum and regularly run candidates in elections. But political expression is often restricted by the climate of violence associated with political campaigns and government-labor clashes, and by the repressive measures taken by security forces and the military.

Human rights groups are independent and active. In 1992, these groups reported on poor prison conditions and continuing allegations of police brutality, including torture, and arbitrary arrests by the security forces. During the September 1992 demonstrations against the Columbus celebration, human rights activist Rafael Efrain Ortiz and another protester were shot to death by police. A number of other activists, including two union leaders, were beaten.

Labor and peasant unions are well organized. While legally permitted to strike, they are often subject to government crackdowns. General strikes in 1991 were repressed by the military, resulting in dozens of deaths and hundreds of injuries. A new labor code was instituted in June 1992, establishing standards for workplace conditions and strengthening the right to organize unions and bargain collectively. However, companies in the 27 industrial free zones, employing almost 10 percent of the nation's workforce, appeared unwilling to comply. Unions reported that more than 200 free-zone workers were fired during the summer for union organizing.

The government has been criticized for the slave-like conditions of Haitians, including children, forcibly recruited to work on state-run sugar plantations. In 1991, the government responded by repatriating tens of thousands of the estimated 500,000 Haitians living illegally in the Dominican Republic. Domestic and international rights groups reported that a large but undetermined number of black Dominicans were also expelled. The repatriations were discontinued after the September 1991 coup in Haiti, and the new labor code recognizes the right of sugar workers to organize. But reports of abuses continued in 1992, and the situation was exacerbated by the influx of refugees fleeing the violent repression in Haiti.

The press, radio and television are mostly privately owned. Newspapers are independent and diverse but occasionally subject to government pressure through denial of advertising revenues. There are dozens of radio stations and at least six commercial television stations, but broadcasts are subject to government review. In February 1992, the government banned Creole radio broadcasts to Haiti. In September, two radio station newscasts were banned during the Columbus celebration protests.

Supreme Court judges are elected by the Senate. The Court appoints lower court judges and is also empowered to participate in the legislative process by introducing bills in the Congress. However, the judicial system, over-politicized and prone to corruption, remains weak and offers little recourse to average citizens.

Ecuador

Polity: Presidential-legislative democracy
Economy: Capitalist-statist
Population: 9,996,000
PPP: $3,012
Life Expectancy: 66.0

Political Rights: 2
Civil Liberties: 3
Status: Free

Ethnic Groups: Complex, Indian (approximately 30 percent), mestizo (50 percent), Caucasian (10 percent), and black (10 percent)

Overview:
On 5 July 1992 71-year-old Sixto Duran Ballen handily defeated Jaime Nebot Saadi in a presidential run-off election between two right-wing candidates. In his first months in office President Duran weathered a wave of protest against his economic restructuring package. But with only minority support in the legislature, and with the nation's political institutions losing credibility, Duran looked to be in for a stormy term.

The Republic of Ecuador was established in 1830 after achieving independence from Spain in 1822. The nation's history has been marked by interrupted presidencies and periods of military rule. The most recent military government paved the way for a return to civilian rule with a new democratic constitution approved by referendum in 1978.

The 1978 constitution provides for a president elected for a four-year term by universal adult suffrage, with a second round of voting between the two front-runners if no candidate wins a majority in the first round. There is a 77-member unicameral National Chamber of Deputies with 65 members elected on a provincial basis every two years, and 12 elected on a national basis every four years. Municipal governments are elected.

In the January 1988 election, Duran of the ruling right-wing Social Christian Party (PSC) ran a poor third to Rodrigo Borja of the social democratic Democratic Left (ID), and Abdala Bucaram of the populist Ecuadorian Roldosist Party (PRE). Borja defeated the fiery Bucaram in the May 1988 run-off and succeeded President Leon Febres Cordero of the PSC.

Borja's presidency was undermined by institutional confrontations between the executive and the legislature as opposition parties ganged up to block government initiatives by using a narrow parliamentary majority to impeach six cabinet ministers.

Impeachment of government officials, allowed by the constitution, has been a staple of the country's fragmented politics since the return to elected government in 1979.

Borja's term was also marked by labor strikes, Indian groups demanding autonomy and land, an inability to reduce an entrenched 50 percent inflation rate, and a failure to alleviate the more than 60 percent poverty rate in what is one of South America's poorer countries.

By early 1992 more than a dozen political parties had registered candidates for the upcoming election. The leader in the opinion polls was Duran, who had split from the PSC to form the Republican Union party (PUR), followed by Jaime Nebot of the PSC and Abdala Bucaram. Raul Baca, the candidate of the ruling ID, trailed badly.

On 17 May 1992 Duran came first with 31.9 percent of the vote. Nebot, with 25 percent, edged out Bucaram, 21.5 percent, to make it into the second round.

With both Duran and Nebot advocating market-oriented economic policies, the run-off campaign was a clash of personalities. Duran, an architect with considerable experience in public office, offered the patrician style associated with the political elite of Quito, the nation's highland capital where Duran was once mayor. The 45-year-old Nebot, a lawyer and businessman, displayed the fiery demeanor characteristic of the teeming coastal city of Guayaquil, the nation's largest city and business hub.

On 5 July 1992 Duran won a decisive victory with 57 percent of the vote. But he took office with a weak hand. In the May election, his PUR had won only 13 of 77 legislative seats. The PSC had won 21, Bucaram's PRE 13, with the remaining 26 divided among ten other parties. Prospects for an alliance with the PSC diminished as Nebot opted to stake out opposition turf, underlining the fact that personal rivalries count more than ideology in Ecuadoran politics. In the fall, opposition parties were already initiating impeachment proceedings against one of Duran's cabinet ministers, raising the specter of the legislative gridlock which had plagued former administrations.

Duran had promised a program of gradual economic reform during his campaign. But when he unveiled a series of shock measures after taking office, the response was a series of labor strikes and civil disturbances which prompted him to mobilize the military. Protests leveled off by November, but leaders of the United Workers Front (FUT), representing close to a quarter of the work force, threatened renewed actions against Duran's privatization program.

Also on a protest footing was the National Confederation of Indigenous Nationalities of Ecuador (Conaie). Conaie stunned Ecuador's establishment in June 1990 by mobilizing more than a million people across the country in what is referred to as "the uprising." Among Conaie's demands are land grants and special sovereignty for the indigenous population, including oil and mineral rights, and the disbanding of paramilitary units established in the countryside by large landowners. Although Conaie backed off its threat to boycott the 1992 election, it mobilized impressive demonstrations in October against celebrations of Columbus's discovery of America.

The Duran administration also had to contend with an increase in political and criminal violence, much of it associated with a surge in drug-trafficking, as well as the emergence of a small guerrilla group claiming allegiance to the Maoist Shining Path in neighboring Peru.

Political Rights and Civil Liberties:

Citizens are able to change their government democratically. Constitutional guarantees regarding freedom of expression, religion, and the right to organize political parties, labor unions and civic organizations are generally respected. There are more than a dozen political parties ranging from right to left. Competition is fierce and election campaigns are marked by sporadic violence.

Opinion polls and an increase in voter abstention in recent years show that the credibility of political institutions is declining. There is also increasing evidence that drug traffickers have penetrated the political system through campaign funding, and sectors of the military through bribery. Ecuador has become a major transshipment point for cocaine passing from neighboring Colombia to the U.S.

Labor unions are well organized and permitted to strike. A number of national and local work stoppages have taken place in recent years in response to government efforts to restructure the economy. In late 1991, unions protested amendments to the 60-year-old labor code which reduced statutory severance pay and put limits on public sector strikes.

Newspapers, including at least six dailies, are privately owned or sponsored by political parties. They are free of censorship and generally outspoken. Radio and television stations are privately owned, although the government controls radio frequencies. Broadcast media are supervised by two independent associations. There are nearly a dozen television stations, mostly commercial, that play a major role during political campaigns. The rise in drug-related violence has put reporters in jeopardy. In March 1992, a journalist campaigning against the drug trade was murdered by unknown assailants.

The judiciary is headed by a Supreme Court appointed by the legislature. The Court supervises the superior courts which, in turn, supervise the lower court system. However, the Court is frequently caught in political tugs-of-war between the executive and the legislature and its impartiality is usually in doubt. The judiciary in general is undermined by the corruption that permeates the political system.

Independent human rights organizations operate freely and there are frequent allegations of police brutality and torture by security forces, particularly during rural land disputes. In 1991, the government dissolved a police investigative unit implicated in many abuses and announced a human-rights training program for police. But rights activists charged in 1992 that abuses were still committed with impunity because police personnel are tried in police rather than civil courts.

Egypt

Polity: Dominant party (military-dominated)
Economy: Mixed statist
Population: 55,680,000
PPP: $1,934
Life Expectancy: 60.3
Ethnic Groups: Eastern Hamitic (90 percent), Greek, Syro-Lebanese, other

Political Rights: 5
Civil Liberties: 6
Status: Partly Free

Overview:

In 1992, Muslim fundamentalists seeking to overthrow the government launched numerous terrorist attacks in southern Egypt against Coptic Christians and tourists, killing nearly 80 people. Meanwhile, as part of a strategy to undermine the government, the fundamentalists continued to provide social services in destitute areas, including relief after a deadly earthquake hit Cairo in October. Security forces rounded up several hundred suspected militants in a series of sweeps during the year, although implementation of a harsh new anti-terrorist law ran into legal difficulties.

A military coup overthrew the Egyptian monarchy in July 1952. Military leaders established a republic in 1953. Despite the outward trappings of a multi-party system, politics are dominated by President Hosni Mubarak and the ruling National Democratic Party (NDP). Under the 1971 constitution, executive power is vested in the president, who is nominated by the People's Assembly and elected for a six-year term by a national referendum. The president names the cabinet, and appoints military leaders, provincial governors and other officials. Most policies are implemented through presidential decrees, which have the power of law, and the 454-member Assembly primarily approves policy rather than initiates it. The NDP maintains its influence through its control of radio and television, as well as patronage given out through the large state sector.

In the November 1990 elections, held after the Supreme Court ruled the April 1987 vote unconstitutional because of restrictions on the opposition, the NDP took 348 seats, against 6 seats for the leftist opposition National Progressive Unionist Party; independents won 85 seats. Ten seats were set aside for presidential appointees, and seven seats were left vacant. Four opposition groups boycotted the election because the government refused to allow an independent group to oversee the vote. The government also refused to lift the emergency regulations that have been in effect since President Anwar al-Sadat's assassination by Muslim fundamentalists in October 1981.

Since succeeding Sadat, President Hosni Mubarak, who won a second term in July 1987, has eased speech and press restrictions, eliminated chronic food shortages and reduced still-persistent official corruption. However, reform of the heavily centralized economy still faces strong opposition from fundamentalists and entrenched state workers, making it difficult for the government to cope with a rapidly expanding population.

Mubarak has also pursued a two-tiered strategy for countering fundamentalism. 1) the government promotes itself as a staunch supporter of Islam to co-opt orthodox Muslims, who might otherwise side with the extremists or the non-violent Muslim Brotherhood, and 2) it cracks down hard on extremist groups that call for the violent overthrow of the government and the immediate implementation of Islamic law. To bolster its pro-Islam credentials, the government promotes religion through the media, and frequently bans or censors anti-Islam publications. The government claims that 90 percent of the laws adhere to Islamic codes, but the Islamic criminal code has not been adopted.

Many of the extremist groups have recently begun operating in the countryside, which is beset by high unemployment. In many areas in the south the militants have seized control of small villages and towns, where they hand out brutal punishments in line with Islamic law. Often with the cooperation of the police, they demand protection money and "taxes" from Coptic Christians, and forbid public weddings and funerals. Street battles between Muslim militants and Christians are common, and militants frequently raze and burn Christian houses and businesses.

This routine violence escalated sharply in 1992. Most notably, in the worst single episode of sectarian violence since 1981, on 4 May, Muslim militants killed 13 Copts in a raid on the southern village of Manshiet Nasser. On 9 June, Farag Foda, an outspoken anti–fundamentalist university professor, died a day after being shot in Cairo. The captured gunmen claimed that their fundamentalist group, Holy War, had compiled a hit-list of journalists, teachers and other prominent anti–fundamentalists.

The government responded to increasing attacks with a crackdown in late June that resulted in the arrest of several hundred militants in the south. Among those arrested were more than 100 men who had fought alongside the *mujahideen* in Afghanistan. In July, Parliament passed a tough anti-terrorist law which includes the death sentence for such activity.

On 12 October, a major earthquake hit Cairo, killing more than 500 people and wrecking more than 8,000 structures. The quake provided fundamentalist groups with a unique opportunity to undermine the government. While official emergency services were slow to provide help to the poorer areas, the groups rushed to provide relief centers and funds for homeless people, particularly in hard-hit slums. On 19 October, riot police were deployed in the capital after a night of protests by homeless people angry with the government's slow response to their plight.

The quake and its aftermath coincided with a fresh wave of fundamentalist attacks on tourists and tourist sites, including the 21 October killing of a British tourist. Despite the violence and quake destruction, the government held municipal elections on 3 November, although most opposition groups again boycotted. The NDP won 95 percent of the seats after the government disqualified so many challengers that the ruling party's candidates ran unopposed in more than two-thirds of the seats.

By year's end, the government crackdown continued, but implementation of the new anti-terrorist law proved difficult. In early December, security forces arrested 650 more suspected radicals during an eight-day sweep in a Cairo neighborhood where the *al-Gamaa al-Islamiya* (Islamic Group), the strongest fundamentalist group, had essentially been the local government. However, in the first test of the new law, on 8 December a civilian court invalidated 8 death sentences and 31 prison terms handed down earlier by a military court, and ordered a new trial. The government, meanwhile, continued to accuse Iran of arming the fundamentalists, and Sudan of providing training camps.

Political Rights and Civil Liberties: The ruling National Democratic Party controls the People's Assembly, radio and television, the large public sector, labor unions, and licensing power over newspapers and political parties. As a result, Egyptians do not have the right to change their government democratically.

In May 1991, parliament voted to extend the state of emergency, in effect since the 1981 assassination of President Anwar al-Sadat, until June 1994. Under the Emergency Law, suspects can be detained without charge for 90 days, and for an additional six months with a court order. The Law also allows for extrajudicial searches of people or property. Political activists are routinely kept under surveillance. The Ministry of the Interior's General Directorate for State Security, which enforces the state of emergency and conducts investigations of opposition figures, has been accused of torture and abuse of detainees and prisoners.

The judiciary is generally considered independent of the government. In a notable example, the Supreme Constitutional Court in 1990 struck down the electoral law for discriminating against the opposition and ordered the People's Assembly dissolved, leading to new elections. The court system includes ordinary criminal courts, a Court of Ethics for charges such as "endangering the public safety," and State Security Courts, which try cases such as armed insurrection. When a suspect is indicted under the Emergency Law, the Court is designated an Emergency State Security Court, from which the only appeal is to the president. The president can also order a defendant retried, and a detainee can be rearrested without charge even if freed by a court order.

Egyptian citizens and private publications freely criticize the government, although the prosecutor general occasionally imposes temporary media bans on sensitive topics, such as corruption cases. In June 1992, the government shut down the daily *Misr al-Fatah* for criticizing what it called undo Saudi financial influence in the Egyptian media. Although the Press Law provides for fines or imprisonment for criticizing the president, opposition journalists do so without retribution. Major national dailies are government-owned and largely uncritical of the government. The government frequently censors books it considers anti-Islamic. On 12 January, a court sentenced writer Alla Hamed to eight years in prison, declaring his book *The Distance in a Man's Mind* to be blasphemous to Islam. Books and art works can be banned without a court order. Street demonstrations are banned, except on campuses. The government can revoke the permit of an NGO involved in prohibited political activities, and can merge two or more associations, which has been done to shut down undesirable groups.

Islam is the state religion, but minority groups generally worship freely. On 11 November, in response to rising militant fundamentalism, the government placed all mosques under the control of the Ministry of Religious Affairs. Conversions from Islam to another religion are heavily discouraged. Minority groups must obtain a presidential decree to build or repair houses of worship; Copts complain their applications are frequently denied. Citizens can travel freely internally, but restrictions on travel abroad apply to men who have not completed compulsory military service, and to women, who must obtain permission from their fathers if unmarried and under 21, or from their husbands if married. Workers are free to unionize, but all trade unions must belong to the government-affiliated Egyptian Trade Union Federation. Strikes are illegal, and violators face strict penalties.

El Salvador

Polity: Presidential-leg-
islative democracy
(military influenced)
Economy: Capitalist-statist
Population: 5,574,000
PPP: $1,897
Life Expectancy: 64.4
Ethnic Groups: Mestizo (89 percent), with small Indian and
Caucasian minorities

Political Rights: 3
Civil Liberties: 3
Status: Partly Free

Overview: The government of President Alfredo Cristiani and the
guerrillas of the Farabundo Marti National Liberation Front
(FMLN) signed a peace accord in January 1992 and a cease-

fire in the twelve-year civil war was reached in February. After numerous delays by both sides in complying with the complex terms of the accord, United Nations mediators brokered an extension of the pact beyond the October deadline. But a definitive end to El Salvador's civil war still seemed months away.

El Salvador declared independence from the Captaincy General of Guatemala in 1841 and the Republic of El Salvador was established in 1859. More than a century of civil strife and military rule followed. The 1979 coup by reformist officers was the first breach in the historical alliance between the military and the landed oligarchy. But the new junta's attempt to institute a democratic opening was undermined by the outbreak of civil war as the FMLN squared off against the military and right-wing forces.

Despite the conflict, in 1982 Salvadorans elected a constituent assembly which drafted a new constitution in 1983. Jose Napoleon Duarte was elected president in 1984. The constitution provides for a president and vice-president elected for a five-year term, and a unicameral National Assembly elected for a three-year term. Municipal elections are held every three years.

Duarte's Christian Democratic Party (PDC) defeated the right-wing National Republican Alliance (ARENA) in the 1985 legislative and municipal elections. ARENA was founded in 1981 by Roberto d'Aubuisson, a cashiered army officer linked to right-wing death squads that lost to Duarte in the 1984 election.

After being marginalized by three democratic elections in four years, the FMLN turned to bombings, civilian assassinations and attacks on the country's economic infrastructure. In 1987, however, exiled political leaders allied with the FMLN accepted Duarte's invitation to return to El Salvador and formed the Democratic Convergence (CD). At the same time, ARENA took a moderate turn as businessman Alfredo Cristiani replaced d'Aubuisson as ARENA's president and led the party to victories in the 1988 legislative and municipal elections.

The main contenders in the 19 March 1989 presidential election were Cristiani, the PDC's Fidel Chavez Mena, and the CD's Guillermo Ungo. Cristiani won a first-round victory with 54 percent of the vote.

In November 1989, the FMLN mounted its largest offensive in nine years. The offensive showed that the FMLN remained a potent military force, but lacked the popular support to overthrow the government. It also proved that the government could not defeat the FMLN militarily. In April 1990, both sides agreed to U.N.-mediated negotiations.

Twenty months of talks finally resulted in the signing of a complicated peace pact on 16 January 1992. The 94-page document called for a cease-fire on 1 February and the separation of forces into designated areas. The FMLN agreed to disarm in five stages by 31 October and the government agreed to reduce the 60,000-member military by half and eliminate counterinsurgency battalions. A U.N. peacekeeping force would monitor the ceasefire and assist in the formation of a new, civilian-led national police force that would include former guerrillas and replace the old security forces.

The accord also called for the creation of commissions on human rights (including one to "purify" the armed forces of rights abusers), a program to provide land for former FMLN combatants and peasant sympathizers, reorganization of the judicial and electoral systems, and FMLN participation in economic reconstruction programs.

The implementation of the accord moved forward unevenly and was punctuated by mutual accusations of noncompliance. By the fall, the accord appeared in danger of breaking down. The key issue was the purge of military officers recommended by the Ad Hoc Commission comprised of three prominent Salvadorans. The secret list of officers included the powerful defense minister, General Rene Emilio Ponce, and his deputy. The military appeared ready to scuttle the pact.

Amid coup rumors and threats from right-wing death squads, U.N. officials intervened in November and brokered an agreement to extend the deadline. The FMLN agreed to demobilize fully by 15 December and Cristiani, under heavy pressure from the U.N. and Washington, agreed to purge or transfer about 100 officers accused of rights violations and corruption by early 1993. The question was whether the military would accept the purges or whether another crisis would break out.

Meanwhile, the FMLN transformed itself into a political party. Approval of its application for formal recognition by the national electoral commission was pending the demobilization of its guerrilla fighters. The next presidential, legislative and municipal elections are scheduled for March 1994. Opinion polls taken in late 1992 showed the FMLN running neck-and-neck with the PDC behind the frontrunner, ARENA.

Political Rights and Civil Liberties:

Citizens are able to change their government democratically. The constitution guarantees free expression, freedom of religion and the right to organize political parties, civic groups and labor unions. Although the 1992 peace accord led to a significant reduction in human rights violations, political expression and other civil liberties continued to be restricted by right-wing death squads and government forces that still acted with impunity.

Political rights have widened significantly in recent years. The return of left-wing political exiles in 1987 presented voters with the widest choice and most open campaigns in the country's history. There are now a dozen or more active political parties ranging from right to left, six of which won seats in the 84-member National Assembly in 1991. The FMLN was expected to be formally recognized as a political party after completing the demobilization of its guerrilla units. In March 1992, a new five-member national electoral commission was formed, and for the first time included a representative from the left. The commission began work on a new electoral code.

Political killings committed by the military and right-wing death squads in 1992 were down compared with 1991, but 21 killings took place in August. There were also continuing reports of death threats and torture of detainees in the custody of security forces. A U.N. observer mission to monitor human rights has been in place since mid-1991 and issues regular reports. Under the peace accord, a Human Rights Ombudsman office was established in 1992. An attorney for the office was attacked and wounded by two gunman in July. Both the office and the U.N. mission received death threats, as did the independent human rights groups that have operated since the 1980s.

Underlying all rights abuses is the absence of an effective system of justice. The judicial system traditionally has been understaffed and poorly funded, riddled with corruption, and intimidated by the military and security forces. The September 1991 conviction of two officers in the 1989 murder of six Jesuit priests is the only time military officers have been held accountable for human rights violations, despite overwhelming evidence of military involvement in the deaths of thousands of civilians.

The 1992 peace accord called for an overhaul of the judiciary to increase its independence from the executive and decrease the Supreme Court's control over the lower courts. It also called for the nine Supreme Court judges to be nominated by an independent judicial council and elected by a two-thirds vote of the National Assembly. However, political disputes in 1992 led to delays in implementing the reforms and many judges refused to cooperate with the U.N. mission monitoring human rights and judicial reform.

The accord also called for a new National Civilian Police incorporating former FMLN guerrillas. A training academy was set up and the new force was established by late 1992. However, the government delayed the disbanding the military-run National Guard and Treasury Police, forces notorious for abusing human rights.

In January 1992, the FMLN and the government agreed to an amnesty law that covered rights violations by both sides during the war. But there were important exceptions. Anyone already convicted by a civilian tribunal would remain in jail. Moreover, under the peace accord, the U.N. established a Truth Commission made up of three prominent international figures mandated to investigate the most serious human rights violations since 1980. The commission was given the power to recommend suspects for prosecutions, and was to deliver its report in January 1993. The case of the army massacre of nearly 800 civilians in the town of El Mozote in 1981 was expected to be given prominence.

The recent political liberalization is reflected in the press, radio and television. Most media are in private hands, but the limited, right-wing perspective has opened considerably. Election campaigns feature televised interviews with all candidates and debates between left- and right-wing politicians. In 1992, the FMLN's formerly clandestine Radio Venceremos was newly installed in San Salvador and began competing with nearly 70 other stations. Opinion polls are a thriving industry and given wide coverage in publications that span the political spectrum from right to left.

The media remain targeted by political violence. Several journalists have been killed and a number of outlets bombed in the last two years. The office of SALPRESS, a private news agency, was firebombed in July 1992 and the agency's director was targeted by death threats. In early 1992, there were a number of cases of intimidation against foreign journalists.

Labor, peasant and university organizations reestablished themselves after being decimated in 1980-82. Strikes, as well as marches and other forms of assembly, are permitted and occur frequently. However, labor unions remain subject to violent intimidation and crackdowns by right-wing death squads and the military. Nearly two dozen trade unionists were killed by death squads in the first eight months of 1992, while dozens more were detained and abused by security forces. Unions have also been denied the right to organize in newly created economic zones and other enterprises. A number of union leaders have been denied permission to leave the country.

Equatorial Guinea

Polity: Military
Economy: Capitalist-statist
Population: 367,000
PPP: $706
Life Expectancy: 47.0
Ethnic Groups: Bubi, Fang, Puku, Seke

Political Rights: 7
Civil Liberties: 6
Status: Not Free

Overview: A former Spanish colony in west-central Africa, Equitorial Guinea became an independent republic in 1968. After independence, Macias (later Macie) Nguema Biyogo of the Popular Ideal of Equatorial Guinea was elected president. In 1969, amid inter-ethnic and political turmoil, President Macie seized emergency powers and unleashed a decade-long reign of terror. Declaring himself president for life in 1972, he crushed virtually every segment of society: suppressing the Catholic Church; shutting down the school system; expelling Nigerian contract workers essential to the economy; sinking the fishing fleet to prevent people from escaping; forcing the exodus of most remaining Spaniards and educated citizens; and murdering and publicly crucifying opponents.

On 3 August 1979, President Macie was overthrown by his nephew Teodoro Obiang Nguema Mbasogo in a military coup. Macie was hunted down and executed for crimes that included treason and genocide. On assuming power, Colonel Obiang formally banned political parties and oversaw the adoption of a new constitution, which formalized his own monopoly on power. In 1987, the self-proclaimed President Obiang launched the Democratic Party of Equatorial Guinea (PDGE), the only legal party. On 25 June 1989, running unopposed, Obiang was elected in the first presidential election since the coup. A clique from Mongomo, Obiang's hometown in the Fang ethnic area, wields disproportionate political power over national affairs. President Obiang's birthday is a national holiday.

Until 1991, President Obiang rejected multi-partyism as a foreign ideology. But, fearing a loss of foreign aid, the government began to change its rhetoric, if not its actions, by mid-1991. In May, the PDGE Central Committee publicly recommended the adoption of a multi-party system. A PDGE national congress the following August formally directed the president to conduct a transition to multi-partyism. However, responding to calls for the legalization of exiled opposition groups and the convening of a sovereign national conference, President Obiang warned against "premature and disorderly democratic changes."

The move toward multi-partyism accelerated in late 1991, when Spanish Prime Minister Felipe Gonzalez threatened to end Spanish economic assistance unless the government implemented political reform. On 17 November 1991, a new constitution allowing for a "transitional" government was ratified by referendum in a straight up-or-down vote. The document effectively excludes the regime's exiled political opponents from the next presidential election by requiring all candidates to be residents of the country for at least ten years; the next presidential election is scheduled for 1996. The constitution also grants a president legal immunity for acts committed before, during and after his term of office.

A month later, the government legalized political parties, but the law also required party founders to make a $160,000 security deposit into a bank account. Parties would also have to be approved by the president's hand-picked council of ministers. Those who have suffered a loss of rights due to their opposition are not permitted to form a party. Parties formed on a tribal, regional, or provincial basis are prohibited.

President Obiang inaugurated his "era of pluralism" in late January 1992 by convening a transitional government whose new council of ministers included some members not formerly associated with the regime. In response, the opposition in exile in Spain and France has organized itself into the "Civic Negotiating Committee for Equatorial Guinea" and called for both the convening of a sovereign national conference and the formation of a transitional government leading to internationally supervised elections. The president replied by inviting those in exile to accept the offer of amnesty and return to their country in order to participate in the transition already put in place by his regime.

Despite the president's formal guarantees of multi-partyism, opposition activists operate in barely tolerated illegality or remain in exile. Faced with the costly security deposit required to register new parties, and the fact that political prisoners continue to languish in prison, the opposition decided to push for better terms before agreeing to openly participate in politics. Amnesty International received reports that some of those who did accept amnesty and end their exile were imprisoned soon after their return. In early September, 24 members of one illegal party were beaten, arrested, and tortured in detention by authorities for their non-violent political organizing.

Political Rights and Civil Liberties:

Citizens of Equatorial Guinea cannot change their government democratically. Despite the government's professed commitment to multi-party democracy, human rights abuses continued in 1992.

The judiciary is controlled by the regime. Although the new constitution allows for freedoms of expression and press, five members of an opposition group were arrested and beaten in February after one tried to hand a copy of the opposition periodical *La Verdad* to someone departing the country on a foreign flight. Charged with "insulting the head of state," they were pardoned by the president on the occasion of his birthday in June. A general amnesty law was promulgated on 8 January 1992, but when exiled opposition leaders returned, they were reportedly detained and tortured. Opposition activist Feliciano Moto was beaten to death by presidential guards in April, and two of his associates were arrested on political grounds.

Estonia

Polity: Presidential-
parliamentary democracy
(ethnic limits)
Economy: Statist
transitional
Population: 1,581,000
PPP: na
Life Expectancy: 71.0
Ethnic Groups: Estonian (61 percent), Russian, Ukrainian,
German, other (36 percent)

Political Rights: 3
Civil Liberties: 3
Status: Partly Free

Overview: In 1992, top news stories in Estonia included the
resignation of Prime Minister Edgar Savisaar's government, national elections, and the passing of a new
constitution and citizenship law.

Dominated by Sweden in the 16th and 17th centuries and annexed by Russia in
1704, Estonia became independent with the collapse of the Russian empire in 1918.
Two decades of independence ended when Soviet troops occupied Estonia during
World War II. The 1939 Hitler-Stalin Pact forcibly incorporated Estonia, Latvia and
Lithuania into the USSR. Under Soviet rule, over 100,000 Estonians either were
deported or died in labor camps. Government-sponsored Russian immigration
substantially changed the ethnic composition of Estonia's population during the Soviet
period; ethnic Estonians constituted 88 percent of the population before Soviet
occupation and only 61.5 percent in 1989.

Estonia's road to independence from the USSR started in November 1988, when
the Estonian Supreme Soviet (later Supreme Council) proclaimed that its laws
superseded those of the Soviet Union. In 1989, Estonian was restored as the official
language. On 18 March 1990, the pro-independence Popular Front won the republic's
first free elections since 1940. Before the elections, a vote was held for an alternative,
499-member "Congress of Estonia," composed of independence groups who viewed
the Supreme Council elections as a legitimization of Soviet occupation.

On 3 March 1991, 78 percent of voters approved a plebiscite on independence.
At the end of the month, the 105-member Supreme Council declared the beginning of
a two-year transition to independence. One day after the attempted coup against Soviet
President Gorbachev in August 1991, the Supreme Council declared Estonia's
independence. Shortly thereafter, Estonia was recognized by most countries, including
the crumbling USSR.

Nineteen-ninety-two opened with a severe economic crisis, due to the loss of
trade with the former Soviet Union. To address the economic crisis, on 16 January,
the Supreme Council voted to grant special emergency powers to the government led
by Prime Minister Savisaar. The emergency powers were granted thanks largely to the
25 Russian deputies on the Council. On 20 January, however, the Council refused to
establish a commission to implement the emergency measures, thus undermining the
effectiveness of its previous vote.

Faced with the inability to rule effectively, the Savisaar government resigned on 23 January. A week later, the Supreme Council approved a new transitional government under former Minister of Transportation Tiit Vahi. A non-party candidate, Vahi formed a cabinet of specialists rather than professional politicians, and called for cooperation among all political groups. He also called for holding new elections, and decided not to implement the economic emergency measures, which were revoked after a parliamentary vote on 11 February.

In March, the shadow Congress of Estonia, essentially a nationalist lobby with no legislative power, announced it opposed granting voting rights to persons who emigrated during the Soviet occupation, branding them "illegal immigrants." It also pressed for a constitutional referendum by 3 May and for conducting a referendum on whether to ban former high-ranking Communist officials from holding top-level civil service posts.

On 6 April, the Supreme Council passed an electoral law regarding members of a new 101-member State Assembly (Riigikogu) that was scheduled to succeed the Council by the end of the year. It specified that all candidates must speak Estonian and be Estonian citizens residing permanently in Estonia.

The drafting and approval of the new constitution were crucial prerequisites to holding new elections. A draft was prepared by a 60-member Constituent Assembly, which had been named by the Supreme Council in September 1991 to prepare a new constitution. Half the members of the Assembly were chosen by the Supreme Council itself, and half by the nationalist Congress of Estonia. The main issue confronting the Assembly was whether to adopt a parliamentary system or one favoring a strong presidency. The presidential option was favored by Supreme Council Chairman and head-of-state Arnold Ruutel, some Popular Front stalwarts, and the Communists. In the end, however, the parliamentary option was supported by the Estonian National Independence Party (the country's largest political party) and other center-right groups. It specified a unicameral, 101-member State Assembly and a largely ceremonial presidency.

On 28 June, 91 percent of voters approved the draft constitution, which took effect on 3 July. On 9 July, the Supreme Council voted to hold parliamentary and presidential elections on 20 September. By 6 August, when the state election commission stopped accepting applications for presidential candidates, four coalitions were able to collect the 10,000 signatures necessary for putting their nominees on the ballot. By 13 August, 633 candidates for parliament were registered. In the presidential campaign, the moderate Safe Home coalition backed Supreme Council Chairman Ruutel, while the Popular Front supported Rein Taagepera, an Estonian-born California professor. The center-right Fatherland (Pro Patria) coalition backed former Foreign Minister Lennart Meri, and the Estonian National Independence Party nominated Lagle Parek, a former political prisoner.

During the elections on 20 September, Ruutel won the largest plurality of votes, 42.5 percent; Meri received 28.8 percent, and Taagepera and Paerek 23.7 and 3.9 percent of the votes, respectively. On 5 October, parliament—by a vote of 59-to-31—chose Meri over Ruutel, a former Communist party official who was president before the 20 September elections. Many deputies said that Ruutel was unacceptable because of his Communist past and ties with industrial managers. Meri, a cultural historian, had to overcome allegations that his father—a prominent pre-World War II Estonian diplomat—had been an informer for the KGB.

One of the most emotionally charged issues in 1992 involved establishing the legal definition of an Estonian citizen. On 26 February, the Supreme Council voted to re-establish the Citizenship Law of 1938 retroactive to 6 November 1991. According to the 1938 law, amended by the vote, all persons who moved to Estonia after 1940, and their descendants, must apply for citizenship. Prerequisites for obtaining citizenship included: a two-year residence period beginning 30 March 1990, a one-year waiting period from the day of application, and basic proficiency in Estonian. The law's adoption disenfranchised a large majority of the 600,000 Russians living in Estonia, preventing them from voting in the constitutional referendum and national elections. On 28 June, the second question on the referendum was whether to allow those who applied for citizenship by 5 June 1992 to vote in the elections. The question, affecting approximately 5,000 persons, was rejected by the voters. Proponents of the citizenship law claimed that up to 50,000 Russians were eligible for automatic citizenship but never bothered to apply for it.

In foreign policy, the most important issues facing Estonia pertained to the stationing of ex-Soviet troops on its territory. On 27 December 1991, the Russian parliament ratified the interstate treaty with Estonia, concluded in January 1991. However, the adoption of the restrictive citizenship law caused the Russian parliament on 17 July 1992 to call for suspension of the treaty and sanctions against Estonia. On 22 September, shortly after Estonia's elections, Moscow warned it would defend the rights of the Russian-speaking population by whatever means necessary.

At the beginning of the year, the Supreme Council declared all Soviet military installations to be Estonian property. Talks on troop withdrawal proved difficult, however. The Russian government initially favored removing the estimated 25,000 troops by the year 2000, demanding that Estonia pay for their upkeep and transfer. Estonia demanded a much earlier deadline. In July and August, there were several exchanges of gunfire between the fledgling Estonian Defense Union and Russian troops, with each side accusing the other of starting the shooting. In June, a preliminary agreement on the troop withdrawal was reached, but without a definite timetable.

Despite economic woes in 1992, Estonia was considered the most advanced former Soviet republic in its transition to the market system. By early 1992, there were some 1,200 foreign-owned companies, which generated 4 percent of the GDP. Estonia was the first ex-Soviet republic to leave the ruble zone, introducing its own convertible currency, the kroon, on 20 June 1992.

Political Rights and Civil Liberties:

On 3 July, Estonia adopted a new constitution guaranteeing political and civil rights to its citizens. However, the adoption of a strict citizenship law excluded many people from participating in the national elections. The constitution does include a provision on the rights and responsibilities of noncitizens.

A new judicial system was established, guaranteeing the independence of the courts. Freedom of association and assembly is generally respected, although in February the registration of the Russian Democratic Movement of Estonia, whose members included many hardline Communists, was rejected on the ground that its program was incompatible with the aims of an independent Estonia.

Freedom of speech is respected, and there is a lively independent press, both in Estonian and Russian. An independent commercial television station started operations in June. Freedom of religion is guaranteed. There are no restrictions on domestic or international travel. Independent unions and labor organizations exist.

Ethiopia

Polity: Transitional   **Political Rights:** 6
Economy: Statist   **Civil Liberties:** 4
Population: 50,420,700   **Status:** Partly Free
PPP: $392
Life Expectancy: 45.5
Ethnic Groups: Afar, Amhara, Harari, Oromo, Somali, Tigrean, others

Overview:

One year after the downfall of Mengistu Haile Mariam's Marxist-military dictatorship, hope for a rapid and orderly democratization in Ethiopia faltered in 1992. The first in a projected series of multi-party elections was held in June, but according to neutral observers, intimidation and fraud plagued the vote for local and regional assemblies. The self-proclaimed "transitional" government led by President Meles Zenawi of the Ethiopian People's Revolutionary Democratic Front (EPRDF) also faced a sporadic rebellion by ethnic Oromos unhappy with the dominant role played by ethnic Tigreans in the new national order, as well as ethnic-based secessionist movements in Afar and in Somali-dominant regions in the south.

The dominant movement within the EPRDF coalition, the Tigrean People's Liberation Front (TPLF) of the northern Tigre province, began in 1975 as a student-led Marxist-Leninist movement opposed to President Mengistu. Within the multi-member EPRDF coalition, the TPLF, which characterized itself as "revolutionary democratic," launched other ethnically based movements committed to its political program, including the Oromo People's Democratic Organization (OPDO) and the northern Amhara-based Ethiopian People's Democratic Movement (EPDM).

Two months after its May 1991 military victory over Mengistu, the EPRDF convened a conference of 26 Ethiopian political groups that had opposed Mengistu's rule. TPLF/EPRDF leader Zenawi was formally elected president of a newly formed Transitional Government of Ethiopia (TGE), which was projected to serve for two years. The conference adopted a charter empowering a multi-party, 87-member Council of Representatives to act as a legislature until national elections to be held before 1994. The EPRDF held 32 seats, including 10 held by the TPLF, and 26 seats were allocated to five Oromo groups. The Council replaced the former 835-member National Assembly, which collapsed with the fall of Mengistu. The conference also called for the creation of an independent judiciary and the protection of civil liberties.

By recognizing the right of ethnic groups to self-determination, the charter provided the initial framework for establishing "ethnic federalism." As conceived, each of the country's ethnic groups would be democratically represented in one of fourteen new provinces. In late 1991, the regime established new ethnically based provinces. Local and regional elections scheduled for early 1992 were to fill representative assemblies in these provinces.

In 1992, the TGE, heavily influenced by the EPRDF, continued its attempt to consolidate control over all of Ethiopia except for the autonomous province of Eritrea (*See Report under Related Territories*). EPRDF forces, which were designated the national army during the transitional period, tried to maintain internal security, but several ethnic-based armed movements from the fractious southern two-thirds of the country continued to resist the TGE's authority. The most important of these, the secession-oriented Oromo Liberation Front (OLF), initially subscribed to the charter and joined the TGE as the second-largest party on the council. However, the OLF eventually attacked EPRDF troops to eject them from its territorial homeland. Violating the charter, the OLF enlarged its army and recruited demobilized members of Mengistu's army. Other ethnic secessionist groups included: the Afar Liberation Front (ALF), whose principle objective was an Afar state within the Ethiopian Federation; the Somali Abo Liberation Front (SALF), a source of Somali opposition to the Ethiopian government in the southern region of the country; and the Ogaden National Liberation Front (ONLF) on the Somali border.

In 1992, ethnic militants blew up bridges and blockaded or mined highways, often cutting off emergency food supplies to famine-stricken areas. An important railroad line to Djibouti was repeatedly blocked, and EPRDF garrisons were targeted. The EPRDF struck back, sometimes with deadly force. Militias of the OLF, OPDO and other groups also fought each other for territory, resulting in several thousand casualties.

Violence threatened to derail the elections, particularly fighting between the EPRDF and OLF. In April, both sides agreed to stop fighting and allow elections. But shortly before the June election, the truce collapsed, the OLF withdrew its ministers and representatives from the TGE, and fighting broke out with EPRDF troops. The EPRDF soon blunted the OLF offensive, however, and both sides re-entered mediated talks.

During the run-up to the 21 June vote, the EPRDF and its allied parties expected an easy victory, partly due to the makeup of the electoral committees. Positions on electoral committees at the regional, zonal and district levels were filled with representatives of all significant political parties in their regions. But while these committees were relatively independent of EPRDF control, they were usually powerless to act on complaints of fraud or intimidation. On the other hand, neighborhood (*kebelle*) electoral committees were neither locally representative nor independent of the EPRDF. Their membership was either hand-picked by EPRDF administrators or chosen in "snap elections" in April and May; the latter were poorly publicized to preclude participation by opposition supporters. Contrary to the election rules, these powerful *kebelle* electoral committees rarely included members of independent political parties

According to numerous reports, *kebelle* committees commonly refused to register partisans of opposition parties to vote, sometimes arresting and imprisoning those who persisted in demanding the right to register. Unable to garner enough valid signatures from registered supporters, would-be opposition candidates in the local and regional elections had their candidacy petitions rejected by election officials. EPRDF soldiers and armed militants often forcibly closed down offices of independent political movements. Authorities repeatedly detained opposition party organizers and potential candidates without charge or expelled them from population centers. In suppressing local opposition organizing, the officials often said they were "controlling common crime." At the same time, the OLF, the most powerful of the opposition groups, succeeded in some localities in totally blocking registration or the formation of electoral committees, as well as any non-OLF or even non-Oromo political activity. For its part, the regime made little effort to register voters in areas that its forces did not securely dominate.

The elections, monitored by approximately 265 international observers, were held in a tense atmosphere outside the EPRDF's popular support base in northern Ethiopia. In the south, despite apparently minimal popular support and sometimes no knowledge of the local language, EPRDF-affiliated candidates took all but a handful of seats. Due to violence and administrative difficulties, balloting was postponed in the secessionist Afar and Somali regions as well as the eastern city of Harar. Parties not affiliated with the EPRDF, such as the OLF and the All Amhara People's Organization, either withdrew days before the balloting in protest, or were almost completely shut out when the votes were tallied. The EPRDF and its affiliates gained over 95 percent of the seats. This effectively ensured that the regional and district governments would be neither secession-minded nor resistant to the difficult economic adjustment measures ahead.

Although President Meles had earlier pledged to repeat the elections if found to be "lacking in democratic content," he rejected the findings of international observers that irregularities had compromised the integrity of the vote. Although the TGE set up a electoral review commission on 16 July to scrutinize complaints of fraud and intimidation, the regime announced on 24 August that the elected councils had been inaugurated.

Political Rights and Civil Liberties:

Ethiopians are not able to choose their government in free and fair democratic elections. International observers concluded that the 1992 elections, though flawed, showed that the TGE had "begun to open up the political system." National executive and legislative elections are proposed for sometime before 1994.

In contrast to the Mengistu regime, the TGE generally does not systematically deny the rights to a fair trial before an impartial court, but political activists have been imprisoned without charge under security acts and there have been numerous cases of police abuses of due process. Freedom of movement has been limited by ongoing guerrilla warfare and ethnic violence in several regions. Criticism of the regime is only sporadically tolerated; the independent Ethiopian Human Rights Council is particularly active in exposing abuses. During the period before the June elections, however, freedom of expression was compromised as opposition political activity was sharply restricted and individuals were imprisoned for such offenses as "speaking against the National Charter." On paper, freedom of religion and both ethnic and linguistic self-determination are guaranteed. The regime appointed a commission on 6 August to draft a democratic constitution that is to be submitted to a constituent assembly for review. The final document is to be in place before national elections in 1993.

The sudden demobilization of a half million soldiers of the Mengistu regime has led to widespread destitution and banditry by many who retained their arms. Since the dismissal of corrupt Mengistu-appointed police, the TGE has relied on EPRDF soldiers and a system of neighborhood-based Peace and Stability Committees (PSCs) to maintain order and apprehend law-breakers. Common criminals and alleged human rights violators from the former regime are the main targets. The EPRDF soldiers and PSCs have been accused of frequently imposing punishment without due process, and human rights groups have expressed concern about the lack of clear guidelines to constrain such abuses. Police officers are slowly being trained to take over law enforcement, but there is still no local police force in many places.

In addition, EPRDF troops, the OLF, and other armed movements have been accused of harassing and murdering unarmed civilians in southern Ethiopia. For example, populations of Amhara settlers suffered repeated deadly attacks, particularly by Oromo militants seeking an "ethnic cleansing" of territory claimed for an independent Oromia.

Over a thousand high-level officials of the prior regime have been held without charge since May 1991. The transitional government has promised them fair trials, and a special prosecutor was appointed in September. Judges are being appointed for what the TGE promises will be an independent judiciary.

A press law promising freedom of expression took effect in 1992. Independent publishing has been possible since 1991, but television and radio remain in the hands of the government. A labor code promulgated in 1991 allows workers to organize independent trade unions.

Fiji

Polity: Parliamentary democracy and native chieftains (ethnic limits)
Economy: Capitalist
Population: 750,000
PPP: $4,192
Life Expectancy: 64.8
Ethnic Groups: Indians (49 percent), Fijian (46 percent), other Pacific islanders, Chinese (6 percent)

Political Rights: 4
Civil Liberties: 3
Status: Partly Free

Overview: Fiji held elections in May 1992 under a racially biased constitution which ensures ethnic Fijians a perpetual majority in parliament. New prime minister Sitiveni Rabuka, the former army officer who led the overthrow of an Indian-dominated government in 1987, received broad support for his coalition government in return for an agreement to review the constitution.

Fiji's paramount chiefs ceded sovereignty over these South Pacific islands to the British in 1874 to end frequent territorial conquests among rival kingdoms. The current population is roughly evenly split between ethnic Fijians and the descendants of Indian agricultural workers who migrated to the islands in the early 1900s. After the April 1987 elections this balance allowed the Indian-backed National Federation Party (NFP) to form a government with the trade-union supported Fijian Labor Party (FLP), breaking the 17-year rule of the predominantly ethnic-Fijian Alliance Party.

Alarmed by the emerging political influence of the Indian community, (then) Lieutenant Colonel Sitiveni Rabuka led a pair of bloodless coups in 1987 which overthrew Bavadra and a subsequent provisional government. With 85 percent of the land held in perpetuity by ethnic Fijians, the coups were supported by many who feared the Indians would confiscate their property. Ratu Sir Kamisese Mara, who had led the now-defunct Alliance Party since independence in 1970, took over as prime minister of an interim government.

In January 1990, the country returned to full civilian rule. The interim government promulgated a new constitution granting ethnic Fijians a perpetual majority in parliament. It sets aside for them 37 of the 70 seats in the House and 24 of the 34 seats in the unelected Senate. The Indians received 27 of the remaining House seats, with 5 going to the "other races," mostly Chinese and European, and one to the island of Rotuma. The unelected Great Council of Chiefs, a group of traditional rulers, secured the right to select the president and appoint the ethnic Fijian Senate seats.

In 1991, the Chiefs backed the formation of the Fijian Political Party (FPP) to unite ethnic Fijians in the coming elections. However, rifts among ethnic Fijians made a bloc vote unlikely. Many oppose the Chiefs' emphasis on traditional customs and resent their influence in politics. Melanesian western Fijians in particular feel they are underrepresented by the FPP and the mainly Polynesian, eastern-based Chiefs. A fragmented ethnic Fijian vote could allow an Indian party to form a governing coalition despite the constitutionally-installed bias. In March 1992, Rabuka warned that if his FPP failed to win a majority, ethnic Fijians might "rise in protest" again.

The first post-coup elections were held over eight days in May 1992, with 171 candidates running in 52 constituencies. In the ethnic Fijian balloting, the FPP took 30 seats, the extremist Fijian Nationalist United Front (FNUF), which called for the expulsion of all Indians, 5, and independents 2. The Indian seats were split between the NFP with 14 and the FLP with 13. The General Voters Party (GVP) took the 5 seats reserved for "other groups."

With the FPP six seats short of an outright majority, party rivals Rabuka and Finance Minster Josevata Kamikamica both maneuvered to craft a workable coalition. On 2 June President Sir Penaia Ganilau announced that Rabuka would be prime minister in a government consisting of the FPP, the GVP the FNUF and several independents. Both the NFP and the FLP agreed to support the government outside the coalition after Rabuka agreed to review the 1990 the constitution.

Political Rights and Civil Liberties: Fijians changed their government in May 1992 under a constitution which ensures ethnic Fijians a majority in parliament. The constitution was promulgated in 1990 by an unelected government and without a referendum, casting serious doubt on its legitimacy. In addition to dispensing with the "one-man, one-vote," system, it allows parliament to abrogate constitutionally-protected civil liberties in emergency situations, theoretically allowing ethnic Fijians to do so unilaterally through their guaranteed majority. To perpetuate politics along traditional lines, the ethnic Fijian seats in parliament are heavily weighted in favor of the rural areas, where voters tend to support ethnic Fijian parties and traditional leaders in greater numbers. The government further discriminates against Indians by giving at least half of all civil service jobs to ethnic Fijians. Although Indians formed a slight majority of the population before the 1987 coups, a minor exodus left the population at 49 percent ethnic Fijian and 46 percent Indian by the end of 1991.

The judiciary is based on the British system and is independent of the government. Detainees occasionally suffer from police abuse, but the accused generally receive due process rights. The Fiji Intelligence Service, created in 1990, can conduct house searches, intercept mail and tap telephones. Freedom of speech is unrestricted, but the press operates under restrictions which often lead to self-censorship. Under the Press Correction Act, the minister of information can require a paper to publish a "correcting statement" to an article under threat of sanction, and the government can arrest editors for publishing "malicious" statements. Because of this, the media generally refrains from sharp criticism of the government. Public assemblies can be restricted for security reasons. This has led to controversy, most notably in December 1991 when the Fiji Mine Worker's Union claimed the government denied its application for a march for political rather than the stated security reasons.

All religions worship freely, although the Indian community resents the partial ban on commercial activities on Sundays; the ban is supported by the Christian ethnic Fijians. Citizens can travel freely at home and abroad. In an effort to boost exports, the government has placed restrictions on the country's unionized sector. In 1991, several draconian anti-labor laws were dropped, including one authorizing 14-year jail terms for disrupting vital industries such as sugar cane harvesting and processing. However, new regulations limit the grounds for strikes, while another law preventing individuals from holding more than one industrial position was apparently aimed at powerful Fijian Trade Union Congress leader Mahenrda Chaudry.

Finland

Polity: Presidential-parliamentary democracy
Economy: Mixed capitalist
Population: 5,028,000
PPP: $14,598
Life Expectancy: 75.5
Ethnic Groups: Finns, Swedes, Lapps

Political Rights: 1
Civil Liberties: 1
Status: Free

Overview: The collapse of the Soviet Union in late 1991 had major economic, political, and military consequences for Finland in 1992. In early 1992, post-Soviet Russia and Finland agreed to treat each other as equal sovereign states, reversing decades of Soviet domination of the smaller country. Finns are concerned about the instability just over the Russian border, and about the safety of nearby Russian nuclear power plants.

The USSR's disintegration eliminated previously guaranteed export earnings for

Finland's companies. As a result, the Finnish economy worsened in 1992, when unemployment climbed over 16 percent. Prime Minister Esko Aho's center-right government applied for membership in the European Community in March 1992, hoping to re-orient the economy to the West. The country belongs to the European Economic Area (EEA). EEA countries have worked out a trading arrangement under which EC farm products will compete in Finland in 1993.

The Conservatives and Social Democrats are pro-EC, but the agricultural Center Party is divided on the issue. On the one hand, the Center's supporters worry about European farm policy. On the other hand, the party's conservative voters may not want to break the coalition government over Europe, thereby risking the left's return to power. Some Finns fear that joining the EC would endanger Finnish neutrality, but the end of the Cold War has made this concern less meaningful. As a sign of the new era in 1992, Finnish defense forces purchased combat jets from the U.S.-based McDonnell Douglas aerospace firm.

As investor confidence in Finland declined in April 1992, currency dealers sparked a huge outflow of money from Finland. Aho responded with cuts in unemployment benefits, pensions, government jobs, foreign aid, and defense spending. Workers protested the cutbacks by staging short, selective strikes in industry, transportation and public services. The Finnish mark endured pressure on world currency markets in September. The government let the mark's value float. Voters punished the center-right coalition, putting the Social Democrats first in October's local elections. The government avoided a general strike in November by agreeing with the unions to raise taxes instead of cutting unemployment benefits.

Aho's coalition took office after the March 1991 general election. The previous government had been a coalition dominated by the Social Democrats and Conservatives. Due to declining economic conditions, the Social Democrats and Conservatives lost ground in the 1991 election. Aho's Center Party increased its representation in the parliament and formed a coalition with the Conservatives, the Swedish People's Party, and the Finnish Christian Union. The Social Democrats, the Left Alliance, the Greens, the Rural Party, and the Liberals are in the opposition. Women hold about 40 percent of the parliamentary seats, and a new intake of young MPs reduced the body's average age below forty.

The present constitution of Finland dates from 1919. It provides for a 200-seat parliament elected by universal suffrage based upon proportional representation. The head of state is the president, who serves a six-year term, and has some significant powers. If a candidate for the presidency receives a majority of the popular vote, he or she becomes president. However, if there is no majority of the popular vote in favor of any one candidate, an electoral college selects the president. The president appoints the prime minister from the party or coalition which commands the majority of the parliament. The president can initiate and veto legislation, is directly responsible for foreign affairs and has the responsibility for some domestic affairs. In addition, the president may dissolve the parliament at any time and call for elections. The current president of Finland is Mauno Koivisto, a Social Democrat.

Political Rights and Civil Liberties: Finns have the right to change their government democratically. Freedom of assembly and association are respected. Groups whose membership is more than one-third foreign, must obtain permission from the government to operate in Finland. There is a wide selection of publications available to the Finnish public. Newspapers are private. Traditionally, many parties have owned or controlled newspapers, but several partisan dailies folded in 1991. For years the press restrained itself in dealing with issues sensitive to the Soviet Union, but this self-censorship died with the Soviet Union, if not before. The Finnish Broadcasting Company controls most of the radio and television programming in Finland. There are programs for both Finnish and Swedish speakers. An independent commercial television station transmits on a limited basis.

There are two established churches in Finland, one Lutheran and the other Orthodox. The state finances both of the established churches. Approximately 88 percent of the Finnish population is Lutheran. There is freedom to worship for other faiths.

It is illegal to discriminate on the basis of race, religion, gender, language or social status in Finland. There have been reported attacks perpetrated by civilians on non-Nordic immigrants. The Finnish government has condemned these acts of violence and has taken action to fight racism. In addition, the Finnish state investigates cases of gender-based discrimination.

Workers have the right to organize and strike. An overwhelming majority of Finns are organized in free unions. The Central Organization of Finnish Trade Unions (SAK) dominates the labor movement in Finland.

France

Polity: Presidential-par-
liamentary democracy
Economy: Mixed
capitalist
Population: 56,876,000
PPP: $14,164
Life Expectancy: 76.4

Political Rights: 1
Civil Liberties: 2
Status: Free

Ethnic Groups: French, regional minorities (Corsican, Alsatian, Basque, Breton), and various Arab and African immigrant groups

Overview: On 20 September 1992, French voters approved a referendum on the Maastricht Treaty for a stronger European Community by a margin of 51.04 percent to 48.95 percent. Internationally, the referendum's result appeared to revive the chances for the Maastricht Treaty, which had run into trouble across the continent. Domestically, exit polls showed the high "No" vote represented many voters' dissatisfaction with the ruling Socialists and President François Mitterrand's policies.

The referendum followed bitter debates and divisions in parliament and the country. At an extraordinary joint session of the Senate and National Assembly on 23 June, members approved the constitutional amendments necessary for the treaty.

Provisions included free movement for European Community nationals, use of a single European currency, and local voting rights for citizens of other European Community countries resident in France. Although the parliamentarians backed the measures overwhelmingly, the Rally for the Republic (RPR), the Gaullist opposition party, staged a walkout. The RPR was split over the Maastricht question. Party leader Jacques Chirac and the Gaullist elite generally backed the treaty, but most party supporters opposed it. The Union for French Democracy (UDF), the center-right opposition grouping under former President Valery Giscard D'Estaing, supported Maastricht, but a significant minority of UDF voters did not. Although parliamentary approval sufficed legally to express French support for the treaty, Mitterrand called for a referendum after Denmark rejected Maastricht in June. He believed that a popular vote for the treaty would strengthen the European cause.

RPR politicians Philippe Seguin and Charles Pasqua led the anti-Maastricht campaign. They appealed to voters' concerns that France would lose sovereignty to an overly centralized European government. The Communist party and the far-right, anti-immigrant National Front also campaigned for a "No" vote. During the week before the vote, international currency markets were in chaos and Mitterrand revealed he had prostate cancer. On referendum day, the question passed with the support of most elites, urbanites, overseas electors, and voters living near the German border. Farmers, laborers and southerners were major groups voting "No."

Aside from the referendum and his illness, Mitterrand faced major difficulties in 1992, his eleventh year in office. His Socialist Party suffered a serious defeat in regional elections, carrying only 18 percent of the vote. Jean-Marie Le Pen's National Front, the Greens, and Generation Ecology made significant gains. As a result of the Socialist defeat, Mitterrand replaced his outspoken, left-wing prime minister, Edith Cresson, with the more moderate Pierre Bergevoy. The Socialists faced the possibility of losing the next National Assembly elections in 1993 as voters blamed them for mounting unemployment, labor unrest, AIDS-tainted blood, a tough agricultural trade deal, and violent racial tensions between the French and immigrant populations. The public perception grew that the Socialists' fund-raising techniques were corrupt, especially after the indictment of Socialist politician Henri Emanuelli for his alleged role in gaining campaign contributions.

Political Rights and Civil Liberties: The French have the right to change their government democratically. The current system of government, the Fifth Republic, dates from 1958. As designed by Charles De Gaulle, the presidency is the dominant institution in this mixed presidential-parliamentary system. The people elect the president directly through a two-round system. In the first round, candidates of all parties appear on the ballot. If no candidate reaches a majority, then a run-off takes place between the two top finishers of round one. The parliamentary bodies are the 577-member National Assembly, which the people elect directly in two rounds, and the 318-member Senate, which is chosen by an electoral college of local elected officials. However, the foregoing constitutional arrangements could change by 1993. President François Mitterrand has discussed reducing presidential terms from seven to five years, electing legislators by proportional representation, and strengthening parliamentary power and judicial authority.

The government may place up to five years of restrictions on the political rights of anyone convicted of committing racist, anti-Semitic or xenophobic acts. Under the Fifth Republic constitution, the president has significant emergency powers and the right to rule by decree under certain circumstances. These represent potential threats to democracy.

The press is largely free, but there are some restrictions on expression, and the government is involved in subsidizing journalism and registering journalists. The state is secretive, and limits criticism of the president. For example, the government charged two journalists with "breach of confidence" following their use of a classified police document in researching a book on terrorism. They were acquitted. The broadcast media became increasingly free and competitive in the 1980s. There is no government monopoly; private radio stations are growing. National Front members assualted journalists at a rally in November 1992. The media retaliated by boycotting a Le Pen speech. One television network threatened to ban him from the air.

Several local authorities restricted freedom of assembly by banning National Front rallies or forbidding the Front to use public facilities. A court overturned such a ban in the city of Strasbourg. Police broke up farmers' demonstrations in June 1992, but the protesters had formed blockades that stopped traffic.

France's anti-terrorist policy includes the expulsion of suspected Basque terrorists, a procedure that is also applied to foreigners believed to be assisting Middle Eastern terrorist organizations. The laws contain "urgency" procedures that allow the government to expel foreigners without any possibility to appeal the decision. Faoud Ali Saleh, an Islamic fundamentalist who terrorized France in the 1980s, stood on trial in 1992, rejecting his lawyer for not being "Islamic enough," but the justice system appointed new defense attorneys on his behalf. French law allowed the government to try Saleh's colleagues in absentia. In November 1992, Corsican separatists led a bombing campaign in France and Corsica. Atef Bseiso, the PLO's security chief, was killed by mysterious assassins in Paris in June 1992. In 1992 the International Federation of Human Rights responded to race riots and ethnic violence in France, accusing French police of "endemic racism." The human rights group recommended the abolition of two police practices: identification checks and detention without charge.

In 1991, the government legalized the widespread security agency practice of compiling dossiers on thousands of French citizens. Previously, intelligence agents had no legal authorization to do this. The Interior Ministry announced that individuals would be able to review the files concerning them.

In 1992, the French government proposed detaining asylum seekers at airports for 30 days without access to a lawyer. The Constitutional Council ruled this anti-asylum measure unconstitutional because Article VIII of the constitution guarantees the availability of legal counsel to anyone requesting it.

Religious freedom is respected. Religious schools receive financial assistance from the national government. Business, agricultural and labor groups have freedom of association. The labor movement has competing Communist and non-Communist federations.

In 1992, France ended a ban on industrial night work for women. The International Labor Organization had asked for a relaxation of the ban in 1990, and the European Court of Justice had ruled in 1991 that the ban was incompatible with sexual equality.

Gabon

Polity: Dominant party
Economy: Capitalist
Population: 1,106,000
PPP: $4,735
Life Expectancy: 52.5
Ethnic Groups: Duma, Fang, Mpongwe, Shogo, other

Political Rights: 4
Civil Liberties: 4
Status: Partly Free

Overview: In 1992, Gabon continued its transition to multi-party democracy. The first competitive presidential elections are scheduled for 1993.

Situated on the west coast of Central Africa, Gabon gained independence from France in 1960. Its first president, Leon M'Ba, created a one-party state under his Gabon Democratic Bloc (BDG). M'Ba died in 1967 and was succeeded by his vice president, Albert-Bernard Bongo (later known as Omar Bongo). Bongo outlawed all opposition groups and maintained the one-party rule of a renamed BDG, now the Democratic Party of Gabon (PDG). He was last elected president in 1986 to a seven-year term, running unopposed as the sole PDG candidate.

Widespread political unrest prompted Bongo to take steps toward multi-partyism in 1990. Competitive legislative elections were held in October 1990. Although the elections were judged to be relatively fair by impartial observers, eight seats were re-contested due to charges of irregularity at the polls. By spring 1991, the PDG was left with only 63 seats in the 120-seat National Assembly. The largest opposition groups are the National Rally of Lumberjacks (RNB), with 18 seats, the Gabonese Progress Party (PGP) with 17, and the newly formed African Forum for Reconstruction (FAR) with 7 seats. The FAR was formed on 1 February 1992 by the merger of three smaller opposition parties. Nine parties have organized a opposition bloc called the Democratic Opposition Coalition. By the beginning of 1992, the ruling PDG had increased its presence in the National Assembly to 66 seats.

In December 1991, the government of Prime Minister Casimir Oye-Mba survived a no-confidence vote. PDG deputies united in opposition to the measure. Another motion was rejected by a slightly greater margin six months later, in June 1992. Opposition parties continued to pressure Oye-Mba's administration for political concessions throughout 1992. Their demands included state financing of campaigns for the upcoming 1993 presidential election; opposition participation on any national electoral commission; equal access by the opposition to state media; local elections before the 1993 presidential race; a re-drawing of electoral district boundaries; and an accurate census of the Gabonese population.

To reinforce their legislative activity, the opposition staged strikes and demonstrations. The opposition RNB called a general strike for early February. Despite localized clashes between police and protesting RNB supporters in the capital of Libreville, the effort at major disruption was initially unsuccessful. But RNB actions were soon bolstered when COD leaders called for a two-day shut-down of activity in the economic center of Port Gentil for 24-25 February. The government announced an indefinite government ban on all rallies, but protesters ignored the order.

The national press reported sporadic violence in the city between security forces and demonstrators during the political strike. Simultaneously, national oil workers rallied in support of a labor strike for higher wages and greater employment of Gabonese nationals in their industry. When strike action had temporarily subsided by the end of February, the ban on public protest was lifted.

Most opposition demands were formally met after negotiations between the regime and opposition in early March. But political confrontation re-ignited when the body of a teacher killed by a rubber bullet was discovered at the site of a clash between striking teachers and police in Libreville. The COD called for a protest march and a general strike until after her funeral. President Bongo eased tensions when he met with teacher representatives and agreed to a number of their labor demands after expressing regret for the death.

President Bongo will face serious competition from opposition candidates if he decides to seek re-election in 1993, when his latest seven-year term of office ends.

Although Gabon has one of the highest per-capita incomes in Africa, it has significant economic problems. A substantial portion of the government's budget is earmarked for foreign debt servicing, and the national wealth is sapped by high inflation and corruption in the public sector.

Political Rights and Civil Liberties:

Under a new constitution, citizens of Gabon can change their government democratically. The first multi-party legislative elections were held in 1990, and presidential elections are scheduled for 1993.

Proceedings in criminal cases are generally fair, but prisoners in security cases can be held without charge. Prison conditions are harsh, and beating is standard during interrogations.

An increasing number of independent publications print investigative reports and vigorously take views at variance with those of the government. The government announced plans in May 1992 to further expand regular access to the state-owned broadcast media for opposition spokesmen. The new National Communications Council has vowed to defend reporters from official harassment.

Freedom of religion is respected in this 60 percent Christian nation, and there are no significant restraints on domestic or foreign travel. Restrictions on association and assembly have been loosened in the past year. Political rallies and meetings are generally not interfered with unless there is potential for violence. Rally organizers must give the government three days notice prior to a public gathering. In early 1992, university students went on strike for immediate payment of scholarships arrears. After the auditorium at Omar Bongo University was burned down on 3 February 1992 and students of a technical university set up barricades on and off campus, the government closed both schools and forbade gatherings on their premises. Within a week, authorities dispersed two rallies because organizers failed to receive the necessary authorization. Despite laws limiting the right of workers to organize and to strike, work stoppages and protests were common in 1992.

The Gambia

Polity: Presidential-legislative democracy
Economy: Capitalist
Population: 909,000
PPP: $886
Life Expectancy: 44.0

Political Rights: 1
Civil Liberties: 2
Status: Free

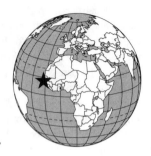

Ethnic Groups: Mandingo (40 percent), Fulani (19 percent), Wolof (15 percent), Jola (10 percent), Serahuli (8 percent)

Overview:

Located in West Africa, The Republic of The Gambia is a narrow country bordered on three sides by Senegal. President Sir Dawda Jawara and his People's Progressive Party (PPP) have led the country since independence in 1965. Jawara has been directly elected under a multi-party system since 1982. Although the PPP has been in power for 27 years, opposition parties operate freely and have contested every election.

In December 1991, President Jawara surprised his supporters by announcing that he would not run for re-election in 1992. Within two weeks, however, leading members of the PPP convinced Jawara to change his mind and seek re-election. On 29 April 1992, Jawara won re-election with 58.4 percent of the vote. His main political rival, Sherif Mustapha Dibba, leader of the National Convention Party (NCP), received 22 percent. Candidates of three other minor parties divided the rest.

The unicameral, directly elected House of Representatives has 51 members who serve for five-year terms. In the 1992 legislative election, also held 29 April, 36 seats were contested. The PPP won 25 seats, a loss of six. Apart from the NCP, other legal political parties include the Gambian People's Party, the United Party, the leftist People's Democratic Organization for Independence and Socialism, and the right-of-center People's Democratic Party. On 11 May, Jawara announced a new government, designating Saihou Sabally as vice-president.

In an incident that disturbed the country's relatively placid political atmosphere, on 3 February 1992, a group of 30 Gambian soldiers left their barracks without permission to march in protest against the government's alleged failure to pay them for military service in Liberia. More seriously, in late March officials in the capital of Banjul asserted that a guerrilla force of several hundred Gambian rebels was poised to invade the country and oust the government. Allegedly trained in Libya and grouped in Burkina Faso before the invasion, the rebel force apparently abandoned its plans when they were prematurely exposed. The rebels were said to be headed by Kokoi Samba Sanyang, who had escaped capture in 1981 after leading an abortive coup in which at least 600 died. The Gambian press reported that he had most recently served as a lieutenant in Charles Taylor's insurgent National Patriotic Front of Liberia. Apart from the Gambian collaborator who had defected to Nigeria and disclosed the conspiracy, seven suspected conspirators were arrested by Gambian authorities.

The Gambia's top foreign affairs issue in 1992 involved fallout from the domestic conflict in Senegal. Thousands of people were forced to flee for the Gambia from southern Senegal.

Political Rights and Civil Liberties: Despite the 27-year dominance of the PPP, Gambians have the right to change their government democratically.

The judiciary is independent of government interference, and the judicial system is based on the English model. Islamic *shari'a* law governs marriage, divorce and inheritance for Muslims, and tribal customary law covers these areas for non-Muslims. In May 1992, President Jawara declared an amnesty for all but the leadership of the Movement for Justice in Africa, which were involved in a coup attempt against him in 1981.

Gambians can exercise free speech. Political party newspapers and various weekly publications can and do criticize the government vigorously. Opposition parties were given equal air time on the state-owned radio station during the 1992 election campaign. There are generally no restrictions on association and assembly. Religious freedom is respected. Gambians are free to emigrate and travel is generally unrestricted. There are two main labor federations, and workers have the right to strike.

Georgia

Polity: Parliamentary democracy (insurgencies)
Economy: Statist transitional
Population: 5,476,000
PPP: na
Life Expectancy: 72.0
Ethnic Groups: Georgians (70 percent), Russians, Armenians, Azeris, Ossetians, others (30 percent)

Political Rights: 4
Civil Liberties: 5
Status: Partly Free

Overview: In 1992, violent struggles between supporters and opponents of deposed President Zviad Gamsakhurdia plagued Georgia. Violence also flared in two separatist regions that attempted to secede in 1992. In October, former Soviet Foreign Minister Eduard Shevardnadze was elected speaker of parliament and head of state.

Georgia declared independence from the Soviet Union on 9 April 1991. In May, the fiercely nationalistic Gamsakhurdia was elected president by a large majority. However, opposition to Gamsakhurdia grew after his ambiguous reaction to the unsuccessful attempt by hardline Communists to overthrow Soviet President Mikhail Gorbachev in August 1991. Following the dissolution of the Soviet Union in December, Georgia did not join the new Commonwealth of Independent States (CIS), as the struggle between Gamsakhurdia and his opponents intensified into all-out war. On 22 December, Gamsakhurdia took refuge in the parliament building surrounded by the opposition forces.

On 2 January 1992, opposition parties declared the formation of a Military Council, which imposed a state of emergency and a curfew in the capital, Tbilisi, and named Tengiz Sigua, who had broken with Gamsakhurdia in August, as the prime minister. On 6 January, Gamsakhurdia escaped the parliament building and went into exile. Less than two weeks later, he returned from exile and, in a speech in his home region of western Georgia, declared a "civil war" against the Military Council. The Council's forces dispersed a group of 6,000 demonstrators in Tbilisi, killing several people. In late January, Gamsakhurdia loyalists clashed with Military Council forces, which ultimately gained control of Gamsakhurdia-held territory in western Georgia.

On 5 February, the Council issued a decree forbidding rallies and demonstrations in the capital. During an 18 February press conference with the president of the Chechen Autonomous Republic, Gamsakhurdia refused to resign as president. On 24 February, the Council issued an invitation for Eduard Shevardnadze, a native Georgian living in Moscow, to return to the country. On 10 March, the Military and Consultative Councils ceded power to a State Council, which served as a temporary legislative and executive body. The State Council named Shevardnadze as the head of the new government.

On 12 March, Gamsakhurdia and 70 deputies of the dissolved parliament convened in Groznyi, the Chechen capital. They condemned the State Council and called for a campaign of disobedience. The next day, troops loyal to Gamsakhurdia took hostage a group of senior defense officials and National Guardsmen. On 17 March, an agreement between the State Council and the rebels resulted in the release of hostages, but on 29 March, fighting resumed as the State Council ordered a mobilization of National Guard reservists following the occupation of several western Georgian towns by Gamsakhurdia supporters. On 26 May, Shevardnadze met with his old friend, U.S. Secretary of State James Baker, who arrived specifically to boost Shevardnadze's support among the population.

Political violence continued to resurface when, on 13 June, a car bomb exploded in front of the house of the State Council deputy chairman, killing seven civilians. Two weeks later, some 300 Gamsakhurdia rebels took over a television center and transmitting tower in Tbilisi, declaring that "legitimate government" had been restored. After a six-hour siege, the rebels surrendered and were arrested. On 6 July, another group of Gamsakhurdia supporters blew up two strategic railway bridges in western Georgia, and surrounded a school building in which the paramilitary group Mkhedroni (The Knights of Georgia) was located. Six people were killed when the government units forced the insurgents to retreat.

On 9 July, rebels in western Georgia kidnapped a deputy prime minister. In early August a group of top security officials, including the interior minister, suffered the same predicament when they met with the rebel leaders to negotiate his release. The government dispatched 3,000 soldiers to free the hostages; by early September, the rebels released the last of the hostages.

On 4 August, the State Council announced the end of the state of emergency and a partial amnesty to Gamsakhurdia supporters as part of a policy of reconciliation before legislative elections. On 24 August, Shevardnadze announced his intention to run for the elective office of the Speaker of Parliament on the ticket of the Mshvidoba (Peace) bloc, whose largest constituent was the renamed Communist party. However, due to criticism from other parties of an unfair advantage, he decided on 31 August to run without the endorsement of any party.

On 11 October, 86 percent of eligible voters participated in the elections. Shevardnadze won the post of Speaker with 96 percent of the vote. Due to continued fighting, the election did not take place in 4 of the 88 electoral districts. Of the 150 seats reserved for political parties, the moderate Mshvidobo bloc gained the most with 29. The conservative "11 October" bloc won 18 seats. A large number of smaller parties and blocs garnered the rest. Eighty-four seats were contested in single-member districts. On 6 November, the newly elected parliament nominated Shevardnadze to the position of titular head of state.

Disputes surrounding separatist regions and ethnic minorities caused further contention and bloodshed in 1992. On 19 January, the majority of the population of the South Ossetian Autonomous Region voted in a referendum to join North Ossetia, an autonomous region of Russia. The conflict in South Ossetia began in 1989 amidst allegations of Moscow's intent to remove the region from Georgia's control. In the subsequent nationalist backlash, approximately 100,000 Ossetians were driven out of their homes, fleeing mostly to North Ossetia.

On 7 January, the new Military Council released the Ossetian leader Torez Kolumbegov from his year-long confinement in jail. But tensions and skirmishes continued. On 2 May, both sides agreed to a draft peace settlement that called for the return of refugees and lifting of transportation blockades against South Ossetia. Shortly thereafter, renewed fighting broke out; 40 people were killed. On 20 May, unknown gunmen killed 36 Ossetian refugees fleeing the region. Shevardnadze condemned the attack and pledged "no mercy" for the perpetrators. The North Ossetian parliament demanded a full investigation and extradition of the gunmen. In early June, the fighting resumed as Georgian forces shelled the South Ossetian capital, Tskhinvali. On 14 July, a peacekeeping force of 600 Russian, North Ossetian, and Georgian soldiers was deployed in a four-mile wide security zone separating the two sides. The move followed an agreement reached by the leaders from Georgia, Russia and North and South Ossetia to work out a peaceful solution. But fighting continued and an estimated 700 people were killed in the conflict during the months of July and August.

Another trouble spot was the western region of Abkhazia, which declared independence on 23 July. Abkhazia has had an uneasy relationship with the Georgian government since 1930, when the region was downgraded from a Soviet Socialist republic to an autonomous region within Georgia. Although Abkhazians constituted only 18 percent of the region's 550,000 people, half of the seats in the regional legislature were reserved for them. In August 1990, following a dispute with the Georgian parliament, the non-Georgian deputies to the Abkhazian parliament declared the region a full Soviet republic. The Georgian parliament declared the vote invalid.

On 25 July, the State Council annulled Abkhazia's latest declaration of independence and sent large reinforcements of Georgian troops to take control of the region. At the same time, Russia dispatched units of paratroopers to protect army units stationed there and facilitate the evacuation of Russian civilians. On 18 August, Georgian troops entered the region's capital, Sukhumi. On 19 August, the self-proclaimed Confederation of Mountain Peoples, consisting of members from Russia's Muslim North Caucasus region issued an ultimatum for Georgian forces to withdraw, threatening to dispatch volunteers to fight on the side of Abkhazians. Despite the September signing of a peace accord that provided for the deployment of CIS peacekeeping forces, sporadic fighting continued into December.

Political Rights and Civil Liberties:

Georgians have the right to change their government democratically. Forty-six parties and blocs participated in October 1992 parliamentary elections. International and local election monitors reported no major irregularities.

Violence between the Military Council and deposed president Gamsakhurdia supporters permeated the public life in the first months of 1992. Council forces dispersed pro-Gamsakhurdia demonstrations with bullets and dogs, killing at least four people. Violent struggles in the autonomous regions continued throughout the year, claiming more than 1,100 lives.

On 4 August, the State Council announced an amnesty for supporters of Gamsakhurdia. It was not clear how many people would benefit from the amnesty; 250 people were reportedly arrested since January for their political affiliation. In November, Amnesty International reported several executions of people found guilty of treason in military courts.

There were reports about harassment and arbitrary arrest of independent journalists, and instances of closures of independent newspapers throughout the year. In October, the Defense Ministry forbade the media to publish reports relating to the armed forces. Other violations of civil liberties included the accusations of police detaining family members of suspects who could not be found. And while freedom of association is generally respected, a restrictive Soviet-era law is still in place.

According to Vsmaron (Brotherhood), the only Ossetian organization registered in Tbilisi, Ossetians are repeatedly harassed, discriminated against and arrested under false pretenses. The chairman of Vsmaron was kidnapped in March; at the end of the year, his whereabouts was still unknown.

Freedom of religion is respected in this largely Christian country. There is no established state church, although attempts were being made to assign that role to the Georgian Orthodox Church. There are some restrictions on domestic and foreign travel and violence in some areas makes travel hazardous.

Germany

Polity: Federal par-
liamentary democracy
Economy: Mixed
capitalist
Population: 80,556,000
PPP: $14,507
Life Expectancy: 75.2
Ethnic Groups: German and numerous immigrant groups

Political Rights: 1
Civil Liberties: 2
Status: Free

Overview:

In 1992, Germany faced the myriad economic, social and political ramifications caused by the absorption of the former German Democratic Republic (GDR) in 1990. Key issues included the economic recession in western Germany and the virtual economic collapse in the newly reconstituted Laender (states) of former East Germany; the large influx of asylum-seekers from Eastern Europe and the Third World and the ensuing right-wing violence directed against them; and increased popular support for far-right parties.

April elections to the state legislatures of Schleswig-Holstein and Baden-

Wuertemberg showed growing support for nationalist right-wing parties. In the prosperous southern state of Baden-Wuertemberg, a stronghold of the Christian Democratic Union (CDU) of Chancellor Helmut Kohl, the right-wing Republican Party won 10.9 percent of the vote, up from 1 percent in 1988. The Christian Democrats remained the strongest party, but were forced into a "grand coalition" with the Social Democrats (SPD). In the more rural and recession-ridden northern state of Schleswig-Holstein the extreme German People's Union (DVU), running under the slogan "Germany for the Germans," won 6.6 percent of the vote. The DVU had earlier won seats in another state legislature, the Bremem parliament.

Another rebuff of mainstream parties occurred on 24 May in the first Berlin city-wide elections since 1946. The CDU and SPD received slightly more than 60 percent of the vote combined. The leftist-environmental Coalition 90 received 13 percent, and the ex-Communist Party of Democratic Socialism (PDS) received 11 percent, (and 30 percent in the former East Berlin). The right-wing Republicans received 8.1 percent of the vote.

Germans also had to face coming to terms with the recent past in former East Germany. The opening of the secret police (Stasi) files revealed that many prominent eastern German politicians had once collaborated with Communist authorities. Lothar de Maiziere, the first non-Communist East German prime minister prior to unification, and a close associate of Chancellor Kohl, was forced to withdraw from politics in 1991. In April 1992, one of the most popular Eastern politicians, Brandenburg Prime Minister Manfred Stolpe, was accused of collaborating with the Stasi while working as a Lutheran lay official.

In March, parliament found a commission to investigate 40 years of Communist rule, chaired by Rainer Eppelmann, a former prominent opposition figure in East Germany. There was renewed discussion, reminiscent of the post-Nazi era, over the question of individual responsibility after the courts sentenced several of the former border guards accused of killing people attempting to flee East Germany.

On 3 June, Berlin prosecutors indicted Erich Honecker, former East German Communist Party chief, for issuing shoot-to-kill orders resulting in 49 deaths. Honecker was returned to Germany in July after spending more than a year hiding in the Chilean embassy in Moscow.

Faced with high unemployment and what many eastern Germans view as second-class status in a united Germany, a Committee for Fairness was formed in June to protect the interests of people in the eastern part of the country. The Committee was led by former GDR Communist chief Gregor Gysi, head of the PDS, and Michael Diestel, a CDU politician.

Throughout the year, right-wing groups, mostly in eastern Germany, launched violent attacks against foreigners. Refugees submitted more than 400,000 applications for political asylum, almost double the number from the previous year. The number of anti-foreigner attacks exceeded 1,600 and resulted in 11 deaths. The worst violence occurred in the Baltic city of Rostock in August, when 1,000 right-wing radicals attacked Gypsy refugees from Romania and Vietnamese "guest workers." Following the riots, some 400 participants were arrested, and foreigners were evacuated from the city. On 18 September, the German and Romanian governments concluded an agreement on deporting asylum-seekers who failed to qualify for political asylum.

The growing number of people seeking asylum, and the rise in right-wing violence and xenophobia, heightened discussion about limiting Germany's generous asylum laws enshrined in its constitution. The conservative-liberal coalition agreed on constitutional changes, and won over the Social Democrats to achieve the two-thirds majority required to change the constitution.

On 8 November, an anti-violence demonstration called by the political leaders from major parties, and attended by more than 300,000 people, ended in violence when leftist radicals prevented President Richard von Weizsaecker and Chancellor Kohl from speaking by hurling eggs and paint bombs.

With a sluggish economy, the country was overburdened with the high cost of financial transfers to the new eastern states, which surpassed $100 billion a year. The popularity of Chancellor Kohl hit a low point, with only about one-third of the voters polled willing to support his party. In September, Kohl admitted that his predictions of a less painful union proved too optimistic, and called for a "solidarity pact," in which employers, unions, and wealthy individuals would sacrifice equally in financing reunification.

The slumping economy led to the largest wave of labor unrest since World War II. On 25 April, public service employees began an 11-day strike, disrupting transportation, postal services, and garbage collection. Faced with a 4.8 percent annual inflation rate, unions demanded a 9.5 percent wage increase, while the government was unwilling to offer more than 4.7 percent. On 7 May the strike ended when both parties accepted a 5.4 percent across the board increase. Although the compromise was rejected by rank-and-file members, union leadership overrode the rejection using a union by-law option.

One of the passionate social issues in 1992 involved abortion. In the unification agreement of 1990, the East and West German lawmakers were unable to decide which of the two abortion laws should prevail in the united Germany. Instead, a compromise was reached maintaining the existing laws until an all-German parliament would decide the issue by 1993. The West German law set strict restrictions on abortion, while the East German law allowed abortion on demand in the first trimester. On 26 June, the Bundestag (lower house) voted for a compromise between the two laws, allowing for abortion in the first trimester in case of distress, and requiring counseling before abortion. The law was adopted by the Bundesrat (upper house) and signed by President Richard von Weizsaecker. However, the government of Bavaria and 247 CDU/CSU deputies submitted a petition to the Federal Constitutional Court asking the judges to declare the law unconstitutional. In response the Court issued a temporary injunction allowing for the application of the two former laws until the issue of constitutionality was decided.

In foreign policy Germany focused on pushing ahead with ratification of the Maastricht Treaty on a stronger European Community. In July the government began the ratification process, and in September Chancellor Kohl asked parliament for introduction of a "European clause" to the constitution.

On 23 September, the Foreign Minister Klaus Kinkel told the U.N. General Assembly that Germany would be willing to become a permanent member of the U.N. Security Council, and promised to revise the constitution to allow for German military involvement in peacekeeping and peacemaking activities under the U.N. auspices. In March, a scandal involving German arms shipments to Turkey caused the resignation of Defense Minister Gerhard Stoltenberg and his top aides. In July, the opposition Social Democrats failed to bloc a government decision to send a destroyer and reconnaissance aircraft to monitor arms embargo against Serbia.

Several well-known political figures left the stage during the year. In April, Foreign Minister Hans-Dietrich Genscher resigned after serving 18 years. Willy Brandt, the most respected and influential politician in post-World War II German history, died on 8 October. Shortly thereafter, Petra Kelly, co-founder of the Green Party, died in a suicide pact.

Political Rights and Civil Liberties: Germans have the right to change their government democratically. The federal system allows for considerable amount of self-government among the 16 constitutive states. The judiciary is independent; accused have free access to counsel.

As a consequence of the Nazi era, German Basic Law (constitution) requires all political parties to be democratic. The Communist, and the neo-Nazi Socialist Reich, parties were outlawed in the 1950s. However, there are various leftist and rightist parties. The far-right Republican Party and the German People's Union, and the ex-Communist Party of Democratic Socialism, gained popularity in 1992. The government banned some neo-Nazi groups in 1992.

The large number of foreign asylum-seekers, and the economic difficulties caused by the reunification, led to increased violence against foreigners. In October, human rights groups criticized the government for failing to adequately protect foreigners, and giving light sentences to perpetrators of right-wing violence.

Germans enjoy freedom of religion and expression, although the use of Nazi symbols is illegal. The press and broadcast media are free and independent, and offer pluralistic points of view. Business, labor and farming groups are free, highly organized, and politically influential. Under Germany's co-determination law, management and labor have equal representation on the boards of major companies.

Ghana

Polity: Dominant party
Economy: Capitalist-statist
Population: 16,009,000
PPP: $1,005
Life Expectancy: 55.0
Ethnic Groups: Some fifty in number, the majority being Akan (including the Fanti), followed by the Ashanti, Ga, Ewe, and the Mossi-Dagomba

Political Rights: 5
Civil Liberties: 5
Status: Partly Free

Overview: Ghana held its first multi-party elections in eleven years on 3 November 1992. The balloting resulted in a disputed victory for President Jerry Rawlings and his National Democratic Congress (NDC) party.

Rawlings led the 1981 military coup that toppled the two-year-old elected government of Dr. Hilla Limann. As chairman of the Provisional National Defense Council (PNDC), Rawlings immediately suspended the constitution, dissolved the National Assembly, and outlawed political parties. Voting took place in 1988 for District Assemblies, which implement regime policies on a local level. The regime nominated those standing for election; independents and political dissidents were not eligible. The PNDC indicated at the time it would eventually extend this no-party electoral process to the national level.

Grudgingly responding to long-standing calls for civilian constitutional rule, in May 1991 Rawlings stated his intention to set up a national Consultative Assembly (CA) to draft a new constitution. The clear outlines of Rawlings' plan for "true democracy" in Ghana soon became apparent. The PNDC unilaterally framed the national debate on democratization by strictly limiting participation in the CA. Opposition groups were not legally recognized until May 1992 and were barred from any role in drafting the constitution. A few independent organizations unaffiliated with the regime, such as the Ghana Bar Association, refused to send representatives to the CA. The opposition Movement for Freedom and Justice, headed by Professor Adu Boahen, pointed out that the CA had received no electoral mandate from Ghanaians to draft or propose a constitution.

The proposed draft constitution, originally intended to be ready by the end of 1991, was not finished until 27 March 1992. One day before the CA officially adopted the final text, three "transitional provisions" were suddenly incorporated into the constitution without discussion. The provisions granted the PNDC indemnity for all acts it committed during its rule. The opposition vainly protested; on 28 April, the government held a referendum on the constitution. Forty-eight percent of registered voters participated in the referendum, and 92.6 approved the new constitution. In the straight up or down vote, the choice before the electorate was limited: a new constitution or continuing rule by the military junta.

On 18 May, the PNDC promulgated Law 280, which permitted the creation of new political parties. The new law, operating in tandem with a constitution not technically operative until 1993, blocked any non-registered voter from founding a party or running for office. The regime refused to re-open registration despite evidence that registration rolls were packed with the names of citizens deceased since 1988. Furthermore, the names of many who did register—and were still alive—were apparently no longer recorded. The Interim Electoral Commission (INEC) asserted that updating the register of voters would cost too much and delay the return to constitutional rule.

In August, seven of ten legalized opposition parties met in an effort to field a single candidate to oppose Rawlings' likely bid for re-election. This Alliance of Democratic Forces called for a transition government, new voter registration rolls, opposition representatives on the INEC, and equal access for all political parties to the state media. But it could not agree on a single presidential candidate. The government rejected the Alliance's demands. Despite strong objections to the way in which the regime was running the transition, the opposition decided not to boycott the presidential election.

The PNDC's political opposition represented two different Ghanaian political traditions. The first tradition was politically and economically populist, derived from the example of the country's first president, Dr. Kwame Nkrumah. The second tradition has long supported democratic liberalism and free market capitalism in line with the philosophy of the early political activist J.B. Danquah and former President Kofi Busia. The Danquah/Busiaists united in one party, the New Patriotic Party (NPP), and behind one presidential candidate, Adu Boahen. The Nkrumahists were unable to agree on a single presidential candidate in 1992, so three factions backed different candidates and a fourth faction attached itself to what eventually became the Rawlings re-election effort.

PNDC Chairman Rawlings resigned his air force commission on 14 September in accord with the constitutional prohibition on active members of the military running for office. He made his candidacy official three days later as standard-bearer for the NDC, a party formed in June. Although the PNDC had formally permitted multi-partyism in May, most opposition candidates for president were unable to start legally campaigning until August. While opposition candidates were waiting to receive certificates of legalization from the government, Rawlings and other PNDC stalwarts had already long been campaigning at state expense.

Jerry Rawlings won the 3 November presidential election with 58 percent of the vote. The NPP's Boahen came in second with 30 percent of the vote. Protests immediately broke out in centers of NPP support, but they were soon contained. The opposition denounced Rawlings' victory as the product of wide-spread electoral fraud despite qualified declarations by international observers that the election was free and fair. The NPP and other parties declared a boycott of the legislative election, originally scheduled for 8 December, until the voter register was impartially revamped and the INEC reconstituted to allow for opposition membership. The balloting was postponed twice as the regime amended the electoral law in an attempt to entice opposition party candidates to ignore the boycott and run as independents. The legislative election was finally held on 29 December, but almost all opposition candidates boycotted the vote, leaving Rawlings' supporters with a commanding victory.

Political Rights and Civil Liberties:

Despite multi-party elections held at the end of 1992, substantial obstacles to free and fair participation meant Ghanaians still did not have the means to change their government democratically.

While most ordinary criminal cases are handled by courts based on the British system, in 1992 political offenders were subject to trial by "public tribunals" answerable to the PNDC. According to Africa Watch, defendants were often convicted to imprisonment or death without due process of law. Two other repressive laws were also in effect until 30 September 1992: the Preventative Custody Law, which provided for indefinite detentions without trial for cases involving a "threat to national security"; and the Habeus Corpus Amendment Law, which prohibited courts from reviewing the grounds for such indefinite detention. These detention laws were replaced with the Public Order Law, which allows fourteen days detention without charge.

One of the three "transitional clauses" incorporated into the new constitution by the military regime bars the courts from ever reversing any penalties imposed by the PNDC during its years in power. Another provision essentially prohibits investigations into charges of malfeasance by regime functionaries. The third grants members of the regime and their agents blanket immunity from prosecution for any official acts committed during the life of the PNDC.

The Newspaper Licensing Law was used to muzzle the press until March 1992. It was replaced in May by the National Media Commission Law. Under the earlier law, a number of independent periodicals were banned, and publicly aired allegations of official corruption brought quick arrest and detention for the offending journalist. The state-owned media never seriously criticized the government during the life of the PNDC. In mid-1992, the Ghana Journalists Association called for greater press freedom and an end to taxes on newsprint. During the period leading up to the presidential election, the private press began to express views critical of the regime.

Because Ghana had no constitution in effect until January 1993, such rights as freedoms of expression, assembly and association were only granted at the discretion of the ruling junta. The Religious Bodies Registration Law restricted freedom of religion; Mormons and Jehovah's Witnesses merited a special PNDC directive that prohibited full practice of their faiths. The ban on Jehovah's Witnesses was lifted in late 1991, but members are still subject to prosecution for refusing to salute the national flag. The right of opposition figures to travel abroad may be suspended by the regime. The independent Trade Union Congress (TUC) is well organized and active. Civil servants staged several strikes to demand wage hikes in the last half of 1992.

Greece

Polity: Parliamentary democracy
Economy: Mixed capitalist
Population: 10,304,000
PPP: $6,764
Life Expectancy: 76.1
Ethnic Groups: Overwhelmingly Greek with Macedonian and Turkish minorities

Political Rights: 1
Civil Liberties: 2
Status: Free

Overview:

In 1992 Greece struggled to adjust its economic performance to suit European Community (EC) standards. Greece also successfully insisted that EC member states refrain from recognizing the former Yugoslav Republic of Macedonia, because that breakaway country bears the name of a Greek province.

Located on the southern tip of the Balkan peninsula, Greece fought for independence from the Ottoman Empire in the 1820s and 1830s. After its victory, the country became a monarchy in 1835. In a series of wars in the early twentieth century, Greece increased its territory in Europe. After Axis occupation during World War II, civil war broke out between the Communist and royalist forces. With Western aid, the constitutional monarchy prevailed. In 1967, a military junta took control and held power until 1974, when the country turned to parliamentary democracy.

The Greek parliament has 300 members who serve for a maximum term of four years. There are both single-member and multi-member parliamentary districts. The political party (or coalition) that wins a majority of seats names the prime minister, who then forms the government. The parliament elects the president, who is a largely ceremonial figure. The conservative New Democratic Party controlled the government from 1974 to 1981, when the Pan-Hellenic Socialist Movement (PASOK) took over. Under Prime Minister Andreas Papandreou, PASOK renewed agreements for U.S. bases in Greece and reversed its anti-NATO and anti-EC positions.

The New Democracy Party won the last parliamentary elections of April 1990 and Constantine Mitsotakis became prime minister. Subsequently, Papandreou faced bribery charges. Following the most publicized political trial in modern Greek history, the judges acquitted Papandreou but convicted two other Socialist politicians in January 1992. PASOK recovered some ground with a by-election victory for the seat vacated by one of the convicts. In a clear protest against conservative policies, the victor increased the Socialist vote by more than 30 percent above the last general election showing.

The unproductive economy is the government's main domestic problem— including high inflation, large deficits, and falling per capita gross domestic product. Greek officials blame the present crisis on the years of Socialist rule, the sprawling public sector and the overstaffed state bureaucracy. Tax collectors are often corrupt, and as much as 40 percent of the economy goes untaxed. Under the Socialists, the state controlled two-thirds of the economy and employed one out of every five workers. In 1990, Mitsotakis's New Democracy Party won election with a mandate to restructure and privatize the economy, drastically reduce the number of state employees, and cut inflation and the budget deficit. In 1991, the EC approved a $3 billion credit for Greece on the condition that the government would reduce its $15 billion budget deficit, confront tax evasion, start taxing farmers (one-third of the work force), bring inflation below 10 percent, cut the number of state employees by one tenth, and adopt other austerity measures, all by 1993.

In 1992, the Greek government carried out the EC credit deal with privatization and pension reform programs that led to job losses, strikes, New Democracy intra-party tensions and a cabinet reshuffle in December. State pension payments had reached nearly 40 percent of government spending. Some pensions had given retirees 90 percent of their old incomes. Married women had the right to retire after only fifteen years' service. Under the new policy, the government is raising the retirement age, cutting benefits, and raising the required employee contributions. Workers in public power plants, transport, the postal service, and state banks reacted to the austerity plan by striking. However, the government believed it had to proceed with severe policies, to qualify Greece for the single European currency area.

In July 1992, the Greek parliament passed the Maastricht Treaty on European union by a vote of 286-9. Only Communists and Ecologists voted against the deal.

Also in 1992, Greece exerted pressure on the EC and the U.S. to withhold recognition of Macedonia. Foreign Minister Antonis Samaras pushed Greece's hardline approach on this issue until Mitsotakis dismissed him in April 1992. Mitsotakis had been quiet publicly about Macedonia until the dismissal. He then adopted Samaras's policy on recognition and acted as his own foreign minister for several months.

Political Rights and Civil Liberties:

The citizens of Greece have the right to change their government democratically. The media are generally free, but there are some restrictions on expression in the libel laws. For instance, publications that are deemed to be offensive to the president or to religious beliefs may be seized by order of the public prosecutor. Greece also has a controversial law on the press and terrorism; the law bans "unwarranted" publicity for terrorists, including the publication of terrorists' proclamations after explosions. The government owns and operates the television stations, but time is allocated to all the major political parties.

There is freedom of association and all workers, except the military and the police, have the right to form or join unions. Unions are linked to political parties, but are not controlled by them or by the government in their day-to-day operations. Strikes against the government are permitted.

Greek Orthodoxy is the state religion and approximately 98 percent of the population belongs to the Church. The constitution prohibits proselytism by all religious groups. Greece offers noncombatant military service but does not provide a nonmilitary alternative to the universal conscription of men for national service. Jehovah's Witnesses and other conscientious objectors can be tried and sentenced to three to five year terms in military prisons. In 1992, the Greek government levied a one-time tax on property owners, including the Mount Athos monastic settlement. After the monks threatened to shut down operations, the government gave them a religious exemption from the tax.

The Turkish Muslim minority, whose religious rights were guaranteed under the 1923 Treaty of Lausanne, objects to the Greek government's choosing the *mufti*, the leader of the Muslim community. The state prevents the Muslims from controlling their own charities. Human Rights Watch reported in 1992 that the Turkish minority had gained improvements in property rights, but that problems still remained with expropriation, deprivation of citizenship, and cultural and linguistic rights.

In 1992 Amnesty International charged Greece with torture in its prison system and with a failure to punish the perpetrators. The Greek government denied the charge, and said that an outside investigation would be "a grave insult" to the nation.

Grenada

Polity: Parliamentary democracy
Economy: Capitalist-statist
Population: 84,000
PPP: $3,673
Life Expectancy: 71.5
Ethnic Groups: Mostly black

Political Rights: 1
Civil Liberties: 2
Status: Free

Overview:

Prime Minister Nicholas Braithwaite came under increasing pressure in 1992 due to a stubborn economic slump and increasing popular dissatisfaction. Only half way through its five-year term, the government had to fend off mounting calls for its resignation.

Grenada, a member of the British Commonwealth, is a parliamentary democracy. The British monarchy is represented by a governor-general. Grenada became self-governing in 1958 and gained independence in 1974. The state also includes the islands of Carriacou and Petit Martinique.

Prime Minister Eric Gairy was overthrown in a 1979 coup d'etat by Maurice Bishop's Marxist New Jewel Movement. Amid a factional fight in October 1983, New Jewel hard-liners murdered Prime Minister Bishop. Bernard Coard and General Hudson Austin took control of the country and declared martial law. Sir Paul Scoon, the governor-general and only duly constituted executive authority in the country, formally asked for international assistance. A joint U.S.-Caribbean military intervention removed Coard and Austin, and Scoon formed an advisory council to act as an interim administration.

In elections held in late 1984, the New National Party (NNP) of Herbert Blaize defeated Gairy's rightist Grenada United Labour Party (GULP). The NNP, a coalition of three parties, took fourteen of fifteen seats in the House of Representatives. The bicameral parliament also consists of an appointed Senate, with ten members appointed by the prime minister and three by the leader of the parliamentary opposition.

In 1989, the NNP coalition unraveled, leaving Prime Minister Blaize with the support of only six representatives in the House. Blaize formed The National Party (TNP) from among his six remaining supporters, but he died in December 1989 after a prolonged illness. He was replaced by his deputy, Ben Jones, and elections were called.

The five main contenders in the 1990 campaign were: the TNP headed by Jones; the centrist National Democratic Congress (NDC) led by Nicholas Braithwaite, former head of the 1983-84 interim government; the New National Party (NNP) headed by Keith Mitchell; the leftist Maurice Bishop Patriotic Movement (MBPM) led by Terry Marryshow; and the GULP.

On 13 March 1990, the NDC won seven seats, the GULP four, and the NNP and TNP two each. After the GULP, NNP and TNP failed to form a coalition government, the governor-general appointed Braithwaite prime minister. On 19 March, one of the GULP's victorious candidates defected to the NDC, giving the new government a one-seat majority. Then, Jones and the other TNP candidate accepted cabinet positions, giving the NDC a 10-5 majority.

Gairy failed to win in his own constituency and the GULP's Winnifred Strachan was named official opposition leader. Two GULP parliamentarians then left the party, one in 1990 and another in 1991. One joined the NDC, restoring its 10-5 majority following the 1991 resignation of the TNP's Jones from the cabinet. A year later, Gairy expelled the last two GULP parliamentarians from the party, leaving the GULP without a voice in the House.

In 1992, the government's economic austerity and privatization program came increasingly under attack. In June, a poll conducted by the University of the West Indies indicated that 75 percent of the population was dissatisfied with the government, while half felt it should resign and that a general election be held. According to the poll, Keith Mitchell was the most popular choice for a new prime minister with 29 percent, followed by Ben Jones with 17 percent. The next general election is not constitutionally due until 1995.

Political Rights and Civil Liberties: Citizens are able to change their government democratically. Constitutional guarantees regarding the right to organize political, labor or civic groups are generally respected. There are numerous independent labor unions and the right to strike is recognized.

The MBPM, founded by former members of the New Jewel Movement after the return to democratic governance, has complained that its representatives have been detained for questioning after returning from conferences in Libya. However, the MBPM was able to participate freely in the 1990 general elections, as it had in 1984, and saw its share of the vote fall from 5 to 2.4 percent.

The exercise of religion and the right of free expression are also generally respected. Newspapers, many of which are weekly political party organs, are independent. Radio is operated by the government but open to independent voices. There have been some complaints that the government has impeded the establishment of independently operated radio. Television is independently operated.

In 1992, the home of the publisher of the weekly *Grenada Voice* was the target of an arson attack, possibly by one of an increasing number of drug-dealing gangs. Also in 1992, the editor of the *Grenada Voice* was denied accreditation to cover parliament by the House speaker after publishing an editorial criticizing the speaker.

There is an independent, nondiscriminatory judiciary whose authority is generally respected by the police. In 1991, Grenada rejoined the Organization of Eastern Caribbean States court system, with right of appeal to the Privy Council in London. In 1990, the Braithwaite government set up a five-member committee, including independent public figures, to monitor prison conditions. There are no political prisoners.

After a two-year trial, thirteen men and one woman, including Bernard Coard and General Hudson Austin, were found guilty in 1986 of the 1983 murder of Maurice Bishop and sentenced to death. The proceedings continued into 1991 as the defendants appealed their sentences. In July 1991, the Grenada Court of Appeals turned aside the last of the appeals, and reports circulated that Coard and four others would be hanged. However, the government decided to commute the death sentences to life imprisonment for all fourteen defendants after a series of appeals by international human rights organizations.

Guatemala

Polity: Presidential-legislative democracy (military dominated)
Economy: Capitalist-statist
Population: 9,710,000
PPP: $2,531
Life Expectancy: 63.4
Ethnic Groups: Ethnically complex, with more than 60 percent Mayan and other Indian

Political Rights: 4
Civil Liberties: 5
Status: Partly Free

Overview: During President Jorge Serrano's second year in office, negotiations to end the decades-long guerrilla war remained stalemated amid a climate of terror fueled by armed civilian patrols controlled by the army, military-linked death squads, burgeoning drug traffic and rampant street crime.

The Republic of Guatemala was established in 1839, eighteen years after independence from Spain and following the breakup of the United Provinces of Central America (1824-1838). The nation has endured a history of dictatorship, coups d'etat, and guerrilla insurgency, with only intermittent democratic government. After a 30-year stretch of repressive military rule, Guatemala returned to civilian government in 1985 with the promulgation of a new constitution and the election of President Vinicio Cerezo of the Christian Democratic Party (PDC).

The constitution provides for a five-year presidential term and prohibits re-election. A 116-member unicameral National Congress is also directly elected for five years. The governors of 22 departments and the capital, Guatemala City, are appointed by the president. Municipal governments are elected.

Among the candidates in the 1990 election were Alfonso Cabrera of the PDC, Rene de Leon Schlotter for the Social Democratic party, and newspaper publisher Jorge Carpio Nicolle of the centrist National Center Union (UCN). The frontrunner in the opinion polls was former dictator General Efrain Rios Montt (1982-83), whose law-and-order rhetoric struck a chord amid a mounting wave of political and criminal violence. But the Supreme Court ruled Rios Montt ineligible because the constitution bars former dictators from returning to power.

Serrano, a right-wing businessman and former head of the rubber-stamp legislature during Rios Montt's short, brutal reign, inherited the general's following. In the 11 November 1990 election, Serrano, with 24 percent of the vote, came second to Carpio with 26 percent. For the 6 January 1991 runoff Serrano, who like Rios Montt is an evangelical Christian, portrayed himself as an anti-politician and won by a 2-to-1 margin in a vote marked by a 55 percent abstention rate.

Upon taking office, Serrano blasted critics of Guatemala's human rights record, including the U.S. government, and promised to negotiate peace with the left-wing guerrillas of the Guatemalan National Revolutionary Unity (URNG).

Starting in April 1991, a series of U.N.-monitored talks with the guerrillas were held in Mexico City. By fall 1992, the negotiations remained deadlocked over human rights issues, and the U.N. observer had bowed out at the request of the government, which viewed him as sympathetic to the URNG. Democratization and human rights are only the first of 11 points on the agenda the two sides drew up in 1991.

The military high command, which initially appeared to support negotiations, took a hard line in 1992, making it clear it would not reduce its 40,000-member armed forces, or dismantle the 500,000-member Self-Defense Patrols, a vast paramilitary apparatus through which it controls the countryside. Under pressure from hardline factions in the officer corps that called the talks "treasonous," military leaders appeared to be holding out for a complete surrender by the thousand or so URNG fighters.

Two coup attempts by nationalist junior officers failed during the Cerezo administration. In the first half of 1992, a wave of anonymous bomb attacks was read by some observers as a destabilization campaign by hardline officers, backed by wealthy families and vested interests, to pave the way for a possible third coup attempt. Other analysts suggested that cocaine traffickers, possibly linked to corrupt elements in the military, were responsible.

With peace talks gridlocked and political and criminal violence unabating, Serrano's poll ratings declined steadily, and he turned increasingly to the army for support. In October 1992, he came under added pressure when Rigoberta Menchu, an exiled Guatemalan Indian leader and rights activist, won the Nobel Peace Prize. The award angered the military and its right-wing civilian backers who consider Menchu an agent of the URNG. Caught in the spotlight, Serrano was forced to offer lukewarm congratulations, but he denied Menchu's request to be included in the peace talks.

Political Rights and Civil Liberties: Citizens are able to change their government through elections, but the powers granted to civilian administrations by the constitution are greatly restricted by the armed forces. In August 1991, the nation's vice president publicly acknowledged that the military remains the dominant institution in the country.

The constitution guarantees religious freedom and the right to organize political parties, civic organizations and labor unions. There are nineteen legally registered political parties from social-democratic left to radical right, most representing small interest groups. Total party membership is less than 10 percent of the electorate.

Political expression is severely restricted by a climate of terror reminiscent of the early 1980s. In the last three years, there has been a dramatic increase in political and criminal violence including murder, disappearances, bombings and death threats. Political parties, student organizations, street children, peasant groups, labor unions, Indian organizations, human rights groups, and the media are all systematically targeted.

In the early 1980s, 200 or more people a month were slain. Under civilian government, dissent and political organizing are no longer tantamount to suicide. But in 1990-91 the level of violence and the rate of political killings were the highest since the return to civilian government in 1986. During the 1990 election campaign, over a dozen political party figures were killed, and more than half the presidential and legislative candidates received death threats. According to Guatemalan rights activists, disappearances and political killings occurred at the rate of over two a day in 1991. The numbers appeared to diminish somewhat in 1992, but only as a result of more selective repression and psychological terror.

The principal human rights offenders are the military (particularly the G-2 intelligence unit), the police and security forces, and a network of death squads-for-hire linked to the armed forces and right-wing political groups. The rural network of paramilitary Self-Defense Patrols controlled by the army is also responsible for rights violations.

The civilian government's failure to address human rights violations is most evident in the dysfunctional judicial system and the corruption-plagued police force. The security forces retain a monopoly over criminal investigations, civil courts are politicized and intimidated by the military, and military personnel are tried in military courts, all of which makes the system a black hole for any legal or human rights complaints.

In August 1992, the official human rights ombudsman elected by the Congress described "a civil government without the power to stop impunity." The only change has been the initiation of prosecution in cases that get international attention. But even then, cases go nowhere as judges and witnesses are intimidated. Or, if the trial is held in a military court, a few soldiers may be scapegoated while officers are routinely acquitted.

There are a number of independent human rights organizations, the Mutual Support Group (GAM) among the most prominent. But rights groups regularly receive threats and their offices are frequently raided and bombed. Over two dozen activists have been slain or disappeared since the return to civilian government in 1986, more than in any other country in the Western hemisphere. In October 1992, less than a week after activist Rigoberta Menchu received the Nobel Peace Prize, two of her associates were assaulted and left naked on the street in Guatemala City by unknown attackers.

The Runejel Junam Council of Ethnic Communities (CERJ) works on behalf of the country's Indians, a majority of the population and probably the most segregated and oppressed indigenous community in the Western hemisphere. Although mass killings of Indians during army anti-guerrilla sweeps have diminished since 1985, they have not stopped. CERJ also reports on the military's systematic violation of the constitutional article that states no individual can be forced to join any type of civil-defense organization against his will. Since CERJ was founded in 1988, over 100 members have received death threats, over two dozen have been killed or disappeared, and numerous others have been driven into exile. In May 1992, the home of CERJ leader Amilcar Mendez was bombed.

Labor unions have re-established themselves since the return to elected government and often exercise their right to strike. But they are frequently denied the right to organize and subjected to mass firings. Moreover, dozens of unionists have been killed and labor activists are targets of black-listing, physical attacks and death threats, particularly in rural areas. Since 1991, over two dozen trade unionists have fled into exile. Between January 1990 and mid-1992, unionists were killed at a rate of nearly 2 per month, making Guatemala one of the most dangerous countries in the world for trade unionists.

The press and a large portion of the broadcast media are privately owned. There are several independent newspapers offering pluralistic points of view. There are dozens of radio stations, most of them commercial. Five of the six television stations are commercially operated.

Since 1989, journalists increasingly have been subject to arbitrary detention, torture, bombing attacks and death threats. Nearly two dozen journalists, including the vice-president of the national journalists association, have been driven into exile, and much of the media has been cowed into self-censorship. A number of radio stations and publications have closed because of threats. Since 1991, attacks on the media have increased, with one journalist arrested and tortured after criticizing President Serrano. In 1992, Serrano himself lent credence to allegations of a systematic official campaign to stifle the media by hurling broadsides against outlets critical of the government.

Guinea

Polity: Military
(transitional)
Economy: Capitalist
Population: 7,784,000
PPP: $602
Life Expectancy: 43.5
Ethnic Groups: Fulani (35 percent), Malinke (25 percent),
Susu (15 percent), others

Political Rights: 6
Civil Liberties: 5
Status: Partly Free

Overview: Under the leadership of Ahmed Sekou Touré, Guinea declared independence from France in 1958. Touré's dictatorial Democratic Party of Guinea (PDG) ruled the country until his death in 1984. Three days after Touré died, the army overthrew the PDG and has since ruled the country through the Military Committee of National Redressing (CMRN), under the leadership of General Lasana Conté.

During the first years of his reign, Conté opened the country to foreign investment but kept it closed to political pluralism. In October 1989, he promised to bring multi-party democracy to Guinea, a promise that is yet to be fulfilled. In December 1990, Guineans approved a new constitution, which calls for a presidential system and a unicameral legislature to be set up within five years. In January 1991, in accordance with the new constitution, the CMRN was dissolved and replaced by the Transitory Committee of National Recovery (CTRN). The 36-member transitional legislature was composed of both civilians and military personnel, all of whom were presidential appointees. Conté served as its head. Although the CTRN promised to legalize opposition parties and guarantee an independent judiciary, it made little progress toward political liberalization in 1991.

In response to protests by the National Democratic Forum (FDN) coalition of opposition groups, Conté gave up the CTRN presidency on 9 January 1992. On 6 February he reshuffled his cabinet, replacing nine senior military officers with civilians. Opposition parties were legalized on 3 April, when the new constitution went into effect. Legislative elections were scheduled for 27 December 1992, but were later delayed.

Pressure on the regime from its domestic opponents, always suspicious of Conté's commitment to political reform, continued in 1992. On 14 February, the presidential motorcade suddenly came up against a roadblock set up by protesting students. A Molotov cocktail was thrown at Conté's car, and he narrowly escaped death. There was another assassination attempt on 14 October, when unknown gunmen shot at Conté's car.

Regime opponent Alpha Condé returned to Guinea on 31 May. Although Condé joined other opposition figures in calling for a sovereign national conference to take control of the democratic transition, Condé refused to associate himself with the FDN position that Conté must immediately resign. Condé's party, the left-leaning Rally of the Guinean People (RPG), refused to unite with most other opposition parties under the banner of the FDN coalition.

Most of the 40 Guinean political parties are ethnically based. Of the three largest parties, members of the pro-Conté Party of Unity and Progress (PUP) are largely Susu, those of the Union for the New Republic (UNR) are predominately Fulani, and members of the RPG are almost entirely Malinké. In 1992 there were repeated violent clashes between supporters of the various parties. In early July, the Guinean Human Rights Organization denounced PUP and its supporters for instigating most of the partisan conflict. Most notable was the July "Kamsar incident," a fight between members of PUP and UNR during which three people died and 40 were injured. Opposition critics also accused the Conté regime of fueling the inter-ethnic violence by discriminating against non-Susu ethnic groups. The government banned political demonstrations in late July.

Alleging that the election census conducted by the regime was irregular, several opposition groups formed a united front in October called the Front for Struggle and Government (FLG). Because the regime ignored their demand for a neutral electoral commission to conduct a population census and voter registration, the FLG pushed for postponement of legislative elections scheduled for December 1992. The government announced on 19 December that elections would be postponed until 1993. No date was given for the rescheduled balloting.

In 1992, the Conté regime continued to call on multilateral lenders and Western governments for greater economic assistance. Recent cut-backs at state enterprises and government ministries have cost 50,000 public sector jobs. User fees are now demanded for health, education, and basic utility services that many cannot afford. More vigorous collection of taxes and customs duties have led to crackdowns on suspected petty smugglers, and violence occasionally results. Guinea hosts some 200,000 Sierra Leoneans and 400,000 Liberians, all refugees from conflicts in their own countries.

Political Rights and Civil Liberties:

Despite the legalization of political parties in 1992, Guineans still do not have the right to change their government democratically.

The judicial system is erratic, due to inefficiencies and corruption. Some accused felons have had to remain in jail for up to three years awaiting a trial. Village chiefs still handle much of the local justice system in the traditional manner. The State Security Court handles political crimes. Administrative detention is permitted, but most detainees stay in jail for only a few days. Amnesty International charged that political opponents of the Conté regime continued to be beaten, detained and tortured in 1992. Some opposition figures claimed that the regime had set up death squads to assassinate them. On 27 October 1992, Amadou Oury Bah, leader of a small opposition party, was arrested by presidential guards. Released the next day, he stated that his arrest was in connection with that month's attempt on the life of President Conté.

Government authorization is required for public gatherings and the police often use violent means to break up protests. On 27 August, a march by women supporters of the opposition was violently dispersed by security police; approximately 100 arrests were made.

Although 85 percent of the Guinean population is Muslim, there is no official state religion and the government does not interfere in sectarian affairs.

Almost all journalists are state employees. The state-owned weekly, *Horoya*, once under tight control of Touré's party, is now independent. In 1991, an association of newspaper publishers, the Guinean Association of Independent Press Publishers, was established to defend press freedom. There are independent newspapers, but the lack of paper makes printing difficult. The government controls radio and television, which concentrates on development issues instead of potentially controversial news.

Guinea-Bissau

Polity: One party (military-dominated) transitional
Economy: Mixed statist transitional
Population: 1,003,000
PPP: $820
Life Expectancy: 42.5
Ethnic Groups: Balanta, Fulani, Malinke, Mandjague as well as mulatto, Moorish, Lebanese and Portugese minorities

Political Rights: 6
Civil Liberties: 5
Status: Partly Free

Overview: In 1992, Guinea-Bissau prepared for the first multi-party election in the country's independent history. Originally scheduled for the last two months of the year, both presidential and parliamentary balloting was postponed until March 1993.

After over a decade of armed struggle, Guinea-Bissau won independence from Portugal in 1973. The current president, Brigadier General João Bernardo Vieira, came to power in 1980 after a coup overthrew the first leader of the independent country, Luis de Almeida Cabral. The 1984 constitution codified the supremacy of the long-ruling PAIGC (African Party for the Independence of Guinea-Bissau and Cape Verde). In indirect elections held in June 1989, Vieira, the only candidate, was elected to another five-year term.

At a party congress in January 1991, the PAIGC formally declared it no longer considered itself the sole legal political force in the country. The leadership concluded that it needed to accept pluralism to receive the Western investment needed for its economic liberalization program. The congress voted to propose both a new electoral law and a thorough constitutional revision. In December 1991, the legislature created the office of prime minister, which Vieira had abolished seven years earlier.

In May 1991, the National Assembly passed a law legalizing political parties. The legalized parties included: the RGB/MB (Guinea-Bissau Resistance/Bafata Movement), FLING (Front for the Struggle of Guinea-Bissau Independence), the United Social Democratic Party, and the Democratic Front. There were early indications that election rules proposed by the PAIGC would have blocked the legalization of regionally or tribally based parties. This would have barred both RGB/MB and the FLING from fielding candidates. The RGB/MB was alleged to represent only the Balanta peoples, and FLING was said to represent primarily the Mandjague ethnic group. In the end, both parties were legalized.

At first, the regime proposed a three-year transition to multi-partyism, with elections coming at the end of 1993. In March 1992, the timetable was moved forward; presidential elections were slated for 15 November and legislative elections for 13 December. The opposition's demand for June 1992 elections were ignored.

The PAIGC continued to maintain sole control over the nature and timing of the transition, denying any role for the opposition. In February 1992, four opposition parties formed a democratic forum to coordinate activities. They called for a public demonstration to protest the government's refusal to consult with them. Although the government banned political rallies during the Carnival season at the end of February, opposition activists continued to publicize plans for a 29 February march. On 25 and 26 February, government security agents detained and beat some members of the opposition who were publicizing the upcoming march. On 7 March, the opposition held a demonstration in the capital of Bissau that attracted approximately 30,000 people. Speakers denounced official corruption, malfeasance and human rights abuses. They demanded that a national conference representing all social sectors and political movements be immediately convened to chart the country's future. The regime ignored the opposition's demands.

In May, PAIGC dissidents from the so-called "121 group" broke away from the party and formed the Party of Renovation and Development (PRD). In 1991, the group had called for a quicker pace of internal party democratization and national political liberalization. The PRD leadership joined other opposition parties in calling for the creation of a transitional administration to govern until elections.

The opposition's goal of a sovereign national conference was no closer to realization by mid-1992 than it had been at the beginning of the year. In June, the Democratic Forum coalition threatened to take to the streets unless the regime acceded to its demand that a neutral, all-party electoral commission be created to conduct the elections. In July, the opposition warned that it would form a shadow cabinet unless the neutral commission was immediately formed. Although the president had repeatedly rejected this demand, he suddenly reversed course and set up the all-party electoral commission on 18 August. A month before presidential elections scheduled for November 1992, President Vieira postponed all elections until March 1993 at the earliest.

Supporters of six opposition parties demonstrated in the capital on 30 November after the government indicated that elections might be further postponed until mid-1993.

In mid-December 1992 Senegalese planes mistakenly bombed a border town within Guinea-Bissau while attempting to attack separatist rebels from Senegal's adjacent Casamance region. Two people were killed and several were injured. Senegalese authorities apologized for the raid and Guinea-Bissau's president recognized the incursion as an accident.

Political Rights and Civil Liberties: Although multi-party elections are scheduled for 1993, the citizens of Guinea-Bissau have not been able to change their government democratically. In 1992, the state remained dominated by its military and the ruling PAIGC.

The judiciary remained a part of the executive branch. The regime retained the power to arbitrarily detain individuals suspected of anti-state activities. Although the PAIGC leadership claimed that it had no political prisoners, it has detained some political activists who attempted to distribute anti-government literature. Government approval is not formally required for peaceful, nonpolitical assemblies. Christians, Muslims and animists can worship freely. The are two independent periodicals and a state-owned newspaper in circulation. The regime controls the broadcast media. The only union, the National Union of Guinea-Bissau (UNTG), was effectively controlled by the Party until recently. The constitution does not guarantee the right to organize or bargain collectively.

Guyana

Polity: Parliamentary democracy
Economy: Mixed statist
Population: 805,000
PPP: $1,453
Life Expectancy: 64.2
Ethnic Groups: Complex, East Indian (52 percent), black (36 percent), mixed (5 percent), Amerindian (4 percent), and the remainder European

Political Rights: 3
Civil Liberties: 3
Status: Partly Free

Overview: The victory by Cheddi Jagan of the People's Progressive Party (PPP) over President Desmond Hoyte in the 5 October 1992 election brought an end to 28 years of authoritarian rule by the People's National Congress (PNC). But with the military, police and civil service still under PNC influence, and with the anti-democratic constitution imposed by the PNC in 1980, the election was only a first step toward establishing democratic rule.

A member of the British Commonwealth, Guyana had been ruled by the black-based PNC since independence in 1966. Under President Forbes Burnham, Guyana was re-designated a socialist "cooperative republic" in 1970, and the PNC retained power through fraudulent elections and repression. In 1980, Burnham installed a new constitution which formalized the "paramountcy" of the PNC in all government spheres. It provides for a president with virtually unlimited powers and a 65-seat National Assembly elected every five years. Twelve seats are occupied by locally elected officials.

Hoyte became president after Burnham died in 1985 and was re-elected to a full term in an election that was fraudulent in every respect. With the statist economy in shambles, Hoyte began seeking Western assistance and implementing an economic liberalization program.

In 1990, U.S legislators and international human rights organizations convinced Washington to tie economic assistance to political reform. As the Guyanese opposition stepped up demands for free elections, Canada and Great Britain also applied pressure.

Jagan's East Indian-based, Marxist PPP, the social democratic Working People's Alliance (WPA), and three smaller parties joined in the Patriotic Coalition for Democracy (PCD). A civic movement, the Guyanese Action for Reform and Democracy (GUARD), was formed, backed by the Anglican and Catholic churches, the Guyanese Human Rights Association (GHRA), independent labor unions, and business and professional groups.

Hoyte gave ground in 1990 when he asked the Council of Freely Elected Heads of Government headed by former U.S. President Jimmy Carter to help with electoral reform. Carter brokered three major changes demanded by the opposition—a new voter registration list, a preliminary vote count at the polling stations, and a revamped election commission. Hoyte also agreed to have the election monitored by Carter's group and a Commonwealth team.

The reforms caused the election to be pushed far beyond May 1991, when it was called for by the constitution. After two postponements, two special extensions to the life of the parliament, two election commissions, and two failed efforts to create a valid voter registration list, the vote was finally scheduled for 5 October 1992.

During the campaign, Hoyte touted recent economic growth and promised improved living conditions. But the social costs of the PNC's austerity program in what was already one of the poorest countries in the Western hemisphere had been severe.

For his part, Jagan decided the PPP could win on its own and the PCD unraveled. Jagan had moderated his Marxist rhetoric since the collapse of communism and now presented himself as a democrat and the only candidate capable of ending PNC rule.

The election came down to race. Since the first elections under internal self-rule in the 1950s, the PNC and the PPP leaned on *apan jhaat*, a Hindi expression meaning "vote your race." With Indo-Guyanese outnumbering Afro-Guyanese by nearly 20 percent, the PPP won every election until 1964, when Burnham won with the assistance of London and Washington.

The WPA, the only mixed-race party in the country, campaigned on a platform of multi-racial cooperation. It was also the only party other than the PPP and PNC that ran a full slate of candidates.

As expected, the Indo-Guyanese majority turned out for Jagan. When it became evident he was winning, the PNC orchestrated violent disturbances, apparently trying to establish a pretext for annulling the vote. But with Carter and the Commonwealth observers pressing Hoyte to call off the PNC cadres and urging the election commission to proceed with the count, the process was completed.

Jagan was elected president with 53.5 percent of the vote, and Hoyte took 42.3 percent; the percentages mirrored the country's racial composition. The WPA message was lost amid the racial polarization as its candidate, economist Clive Thomas, won less than two percent of the vote.

In the legislature, the PPP took 36 of 65 seats, with the PNC taking 26, the WPA 2, and the centrist United Force (UF) 1. By November both the WPA and the UF had decided to support the new government. Hoyte became the official opposition leader.

Jagan was inaugurated amid continuing tension and uncertainty. The 6,000-member military said it would respect the new government, but it remained, like the police, a PNC-dominated institution. Similarly, the government bureaucracy was occupied mostly by PNC people.

Jagan promised that the PPP would not seek revenge against the former rulers, and that his government would strengthen democracy by representing all Guyanese. But given the deeply rooted racial animosity in Guyanese society, it appeared he would be hard pressed to keep his commitment. Municipal elections were expected in 1993.

Political Rights and Civil Liberties:

Despite racial violence, serious registration foul-ups and delays in the voting process, the Guyanese people were able to express their political will in the 1992 election. However, the 1980 constitution gives the president of the country inordinate powers and provides a framework for virtual one-party rule. Whether the new PPP government would seek constitutional reform, and how it would cope with a military and police still under PNC influence, were key questions as President Jagan began his first year in office.

The constitution grants the right of free expression, freedom of religion and the right to organize political parties, civic organizations and labor unions. In the last year of the Hoyte government and during the 1992 electoral campaign, these rights were generally respected. However, political rights and civil liberties rested heavily on government tolerance rather than institutional protection.

The judicial system, while nominally independent, is understaffed and was easily influenced by the former Hoyte government. Prisons are overcrowded, with deplorable conditions leading to numerous deaths by starvation and AIDS.

The Hoyte government took some steps to professionalize the police, but opposition supporters and independent labor were still subject to harassment and violent intimidation, and the right of habeas corpus was not consistently respected. The police also were lax in providing security, and in some cases were complicitous, when PNC supporters ignited violent, anti-East Indian disturbances during the 1992 election. Under Hoyte, the government also used the police to curb organizational efforts by the 40,000 Amerindians residing in the interior of the country.

The Guyana Human Rights Association (GHRA) is independent, effective and backed by independent civic and religious groups. The Hoyte government tried to impede its work through a series of libel actions, but attempts at outright intimidation had diminished by 1992.

Labor unions are well organized; most public sector unions are allied with the PNC and agricultural unions with the PPP. There are a number of independent unions. Strikes are legal, but under PNC rule often led to violence during clashes with the police and the arbitrary dismissal of public sector workers.

In 1986, a new independent newspaper, the *Stabroek News,* was permitted to join a number of political party publications and the *Catholic Standard*, an outspoken church weekly. The former PNC government made excessive use of libel suits and controlled access to hard currency to curb the independent press. Public radio was primarily a PNC instrument when it was in power. There are a number television stations which rely mostly on foreign programming via satellite. Under the PNC, local content was heavily influenced by the government.

Haiti

Polity: Military
Economy: Capitalist-
statist
Population: 6,432,000
PPP: $962
Life Expectancy: 55.7
Ethnic Groups: Black (majority) and mulatto

Political Rights: 7
Civil Liberties: 7
Status: Not Free

Overview: More than a year after the overthrow of President Jean-Bertrand Aristide, Haiti's military rulers continued to resist international pressure for restoring democracy. Meanwhile, the Haitian people struggled to survive amid systematic repression, lawlessness and economic deprivation not seen since the Duvalier dictatorship.

Since gaining independence following a slave revolt in 1804, the Republic of Haiti has endured a history of poverty, violence, instability and dictatorship. A February 1986 military coup ended 29 years of rule by the Duvalier family. The army ruled directly or indirectly for the next five years, often in collusion with remnants of the *Tontons Macoute*, the sinister paramilitary organization of the Duvaliers.

Under international pressure, the military allowed for the election of a constituent assembly that drafted Haiti's twenty-third constitution. It was approved in a March 1987 referendum, but a campaign of terror by the military and the Tontons Macoute culminated in a bloodbath that aborted national elections eight months later.

In March 1990, General Prosper Avril left the country during a nationwide protest, handing power over to General Herard Abraham. Abraham yielded to a coalition of political parties and civic groups and accepted Supreme Court justice Ertha Pascal-Trouillot as interim president. The provisional government reinstated the constitution and prepared for a new election.

The 1987 constitution provides for a president directly elected for five years, a directly elected parliament composed of a 27-member Senate and an 83-member House of Representatives, and a prime minister appointed by the president.

The two main contenders in the internationally monitored 16 December 1990 election were Marc Bazin, a former World Bank official, and Rev. Jean-Bertrand Aristide, a popular radical priest whose outspoken opposition to dictatorship had made him the target of numerous assassination attempts.

Aristide was elected in a landslide, taking nearly 70 percent of the vote. He praised the military for defending democracy and appointed a new chief, General Raoul Cedras, who had received high marks as head of the military commission in charge of electoral security.

President Aristide's record during his brief tenure was mixed. Article 295 of the constitution gives the president authorization for six months to "carry out any reforms deemed necessary in the Government administration and the judiciary." Aristide, opting for the broadest interpretation of this article, formed a government from among his most trusted if politically inexperienced associates, and initiated a program to strengthen the judicial system, establish civilian authority over the military and end official corruption. The result was a dramatic reduction in political violence and greater respect for political rights and civil liberties than at any other time in the nation's history.

Haiti's mostly mulatto elites were furious over Aristide's bid to end their control over the economy—0.5 percent of the population absorbs nearly half the country's income, much of it illicit. Their representatives in parliament attempted a no-confidence vote, which was also supported by many formerly pro-Aristide deputies who had been left out of his government. Aristide, like many charismatic leaders before him, succumbed to the temptation to exceed his constitutional authority by inciting his legions of supporters to violence.

At the same time, Aristide's effort to set up a new police force, trained by Swiss experts and under the control of the justice ministry as required by the constitution, rankled the military, which was accustomed to enriching itself through graft, contraband activities, and drug-trafficking. Amid rumors of a coup, Aristide responded with an incendiary speech, attacking the military and the wealthy and calling upon his supporters to take action. He concluded with a transparent reference to lynching with a burning tire around the neck.

Aristide was overthrown on 30 September 1991 and barely escaped the country. General Cedras, either an instigator or a willing participant, condoned the coup carried out by units under the command of Major Michel Francois, who was later promoted to colonel. The military installed a puppet government headed by President Joseph Nerette, an aging Supreme Court judge, and Prime Minister Jean-Jacques Honorat, a lawyer and former director of tourism under Jean-Claude Duvalier.

The Organization of American States (OAS) imposed an economic embargo on Haiti to press for the restoration of the Aristide government. In February 1992, the OAS appeared to have brokered an agreement in which Aristide would be recognized as president, while Rene Theodore, a political opponent, would become prime minister and form a government that would work out a timetable for Aristide's return. The agreement broke down after Aristide refused to endorse amnesty for the military, and after soldiers commanded by Colonel Francois invaded the parliament as it was about to vote on the accord.

In June, the military removed Nerrete and Honorat and installed Bazin as prime minister, leaving the presidency vacant. Bazin was directed to use his international contacts to help end Haiti's economic and political isolation. But he was given little leeway to negotiate and remained essentially powerless as the military retained control over all governmental institutions.

Five months later, the OAS asked former Jamaican Prime Minister Michael Manley to take on the role of "facilitator." Manley wanted some indication a negotiated solution was possible before accepting. But the porous economic embargo was having little effect on the military and its allies among the elites, while causing astonishing suffering among the general population. The military was demanding at minimum a total amnesty—a condition Aristide refused to accept. Moreover, hard-line officers like Colonel Francois made it clear Aristide would never be allowed to return, suggesting that any agreement brokered by Manley might provoke a second coup. Manley urged U.N. involvement to break the apparent stalemate.

Political Rights and Civil Liberties: Although the 1987 constitution and the parliament were not formerly suspended after the September 1991 coup, political rights and civil liberties are virtually nonexistent under military rule. The repressive structures of the Duvalier dictatorship have been re-established, returning the country to the absolute lawlessness of the past. The chiefs of Haiti's 515 rural sections, disbanded by Aristide, are back in place with their private armies which overlap with the paramilitary *Tontons Macoutes* who have returned as well. In the capital of Port-au-Prince, the police are headed by Colonel Michel Francois, the hard-line military officer who led the coup and controls the city through terror. The judiciary was purged of Aristide appointees after the coup and functions as an arm of the military, if at all.

In mid-1992, international human rights groups estimated there had been at least 1,000 extrajudicial executions since the coup. Local monitors, which operate underground at great risk, put the figure higher, charging that the military disposes of bodies itself in order to mask the toll.

Tens of thousands of Aristide supporters have gone underground to escape persecution, and over 40,000 people have tried to flee Haiti by boat since the coup. The entire population remains in a permanent state of fear; arrests are arbitrary and extortion by the police and section chiefs is systematic. Conditions in detention centers are wretched and it appears the only way to avoid torture is to pay off the authorities. Reports of prisoners being beaten to death were frequent in 1992. According to doctors, victims of attacks that are able to escape detention are often tracked down in hospitals and hauled away.

Since the coup, the independent media have been either physically destroyed, repressed or intimidated into operating under a high degree of self-censorship. Most of the Creole radio broadcasts, the main source of news for the predominantly non-French-speaking population, were shut down. Numerous station managers and journalists have been imprisoned, tortured or driven underground or into exile. At least four were killed. Foreign journalists are frequently threatened by section chiefs in rural areas.

The civil society that had been emerging under Aristide—labor unions, peasant groups, community organizations—has been decimated. Moreover, the network of religious and humanitarian organizations, which traditionally have provided the only assistance to Haiti's poor, was virtually crushed by the end of 1992. These organizations were the only conduit for foreign aid, particularly in rural areas where two-thirds of the population live. Their demise, coupled with the effects of the economic embargo, raised the specter of mass starvation. Haiti is the poorest nation in the Western hemisphere.

The grassroots organizations connected to the Catholic church have been subject to repression, and a number of pro-Aristide priests have been forced underground. Most of the Catholic bishops, however, have adopted a neutral position, which the military portrays as approval of its regime. Willy Romelus, the only bishop to speak out, has been the target of military intimidation. The Vatican representative was the only prominent diplomat to attend the installation of Marc Bazin as prime minister.

After being installed as prime minister in June 1992, Bazin announced that political protests would be allowed and that local elected officials could resume their posts in the countryside. But the few officials who came out of hiding were attacked, and when university students attempted to hold a brief demonstration a few weeks later, police and armed Tontons Macoutes in civilian dress opened fired, wounding dozens.

After the OAS attempted to restart negotiations with the government toward the end of the summer, the level of repression increased. Three people who were caught putting up posters welcoming an OAS mission in August were killed by police. The arrival of a small OAS monitoring team two months later appeared to have no effect other than to provoke hard-line factions of the military seeking to ensure that Aristide never returns.

Honduras

Polity: Presidential-leg-
islative democracy
(military influenced)
Economy: Capitalist-statist
Population: 5,462,000
PPP: $1,504
Life Expectancy: 64.9
Ethnic Groups: Mostly mestizo, some Caucasian, approximately
7 percent Indian

Political Rights: 2
Civil Liberties: 3
Status: Free

Overview:
Prospects for limiting the military's autonomy dimmed in 1992 as the Honduran Congress shied away from a proposed bill that would have placed the armed forces under the control of the elected civilian government. The persistence of human rights abuses underscored the weakness of the country's governmental institutions.

After achieving independence from Spain in 1821, and after the breakup of the United Provinces of Central America (1824-1838), the Republic of Honduras was established in 1839. Its history has been marked by military rule and intermittent democratic government. A democratic trend began with the election of a constituent assembly in 1980, the election of President Roberto Suazo of the Liberal Party (PL) in 1981, and the promulgation of a democratic constitution in January 1982.

The constitution provides for a president and a 130-member, unicameral Congress elected for four years. In the 1981 and 1985 presidential races, parties could nominate more than one candidate. The winner was the leading candidate of the party with the most votes overall. Thus, Jose Azcona, one of three PL candidates, was elected to succeed President Suazo in the November 1985 election with only 27 percent of the vote, less than the 43 percent received by Rafael Callejas of the National Party (PN), the other major political party.

In 1988, the electoral tribunal instructed parties to hold primary elections. Roberto Flores won a four-way race to become the PL candidate; the PN nominated Callejas. The key campaign issues were government corruption and the declining economy. Honduras is one of the hemisphere's poorest nations.

In the November 1989 election, Callejas defeated Flores, taking a little over 50 percent of the vote. The PN took a majority of seats in Congress and won control of over two-thirds of the country's 283 municipal governments. The governors of the country's eighteen regional departments are appointed by the executive. The inauguration of President Callejas in January 1990 marked the first ballot-box transfer of power to an out-party in 57 years. The next election is scheduled for November 1993.

President Callejas has implemented a sweeping economic restructuring program. But massive layoffs, government spending cuts and an overhaul of the land reform program have alienated the labor and peasant sectors, which have staged a number of crippling strikes since 1990.

Since the return to civilian rule, the 24,000-member military has retained influence over civilian governments on security issues. It controls its own budget and has used its clout to become one of the main players in the corruption-plagued economy. The constellation of military-owned businesses makes the armed forces one of the largest corporations in the country.

After a series of grisly, military-linked slayings in 1991, the armed forces came under increased domestic and international pressure—including a 50 percent cut in U.S. military aid—to be held accountable for corrupt activities and rights violations. In an unprecedented concession, the military allowed civilian courts to try two officers implicated in the murder of a student. Commander-in-chief General Luis Alonso Disqua then agreed to consider a bill submitted to the Congress by a small social democratic party that would subordinate the military to civilian authorities by eliminating the position of commander-in-chief in favor of a civilian-appointed defense minister.

In 1992, however, Disqua and the 52-member Superior Council of the Armed Forces pressured legislators to shelve the bill and to allow Disqua to extend his mandate as military chief. By law, the Congress elects the chief of the armed forces, who commands for a three-year period, from a list of nominees provided by the military. In reality, the military's first choice is routinely approved. Disqua's term was to run out in January 1993, but in September 1992, the Congress voted to repeal the three-year term limit. Most of the votes came from the ruling NP, whose executive committee is headed by General Disqua's brother.

The vote was criticized by some PL leaders and the media, and by the business, labor and peasant sectors. The most noted protest came from mid-level military officers who, in an anonymous communiqué, condemned Disqua and the high command for corruption and connivance with dishonest politicians. The communiqué echoed an earlier manifesto issued in February that demanded the high command make way for "true soldiers of the Fatherland," and included positive references to army officers who had attempted to overthrow the Venezuelan government that same month.

Political Rights and Civil Liberties:

Citizens are able to change their governments through elections, but there is little civilian authority over the military. Constitutional guarantees regarding free expression, freedom of religion and the right to form political parties, labor unions and civic organizations are generally respected.

There are a half dozen legal political parties ranging from left to right. At least one small guerrilla group remains active. But since a 1990 government amnesty implemented with the cooperation of the United Nations, most radical leftist groups have disarmed and resurfaced as political organizations.

Political expression has been restricted by an increase in political violence in recent years. Sporadic left-wing violence was accompanied in 1992 by several political killings carried out by right-wing extremists, particularly against unionists, students, and peasant groups. The military is responsible for most rights violations, including extra-judicial killings, arbitrary arrests and torture during confinement. Independent rights activists also have been targeted; at least one was killed in 1991.

The government human rights office has acknowledged a pattern of abuses by the armed forces, and the Callejas administration said it was committed to bringing violators to justice. By 1992, however, the military had permitted only one case to be heard in a civilian court. The armed forces have yet to be held accountable for more than 100 disappearances dating back to the early 1980s.

The judicial system, headed by a Supreme Court, remains weak and undermined by corruption. A few civilian judges have tried to assert themselves in cases involving rights violations, but most judges are ambitious political appointees with no desire to confront the military. Most cases against the armed forces, including criminal charges, remain in the purview of military courts, away from the public eye, and usually result in dismissal of charges.

Labor unions are well organized, have the legal right to strike, and have been able to reach collective bargaining agreements in some of the industrial free zones. The government occasionally resorts to mobilizing the military and hiring scab workers to break strikes in the key banana and mining industries. Labor leaders, religious groups and indigenous-based peasant unions pressing for land reform have been subject to official repression and violent attacks.

The press and broadcast media are largely private. There are several daily newspapers representing various political points of view, but the practice of journalism is restricted by a licensing law. In recent years the government has threatened several of the approximately 100 radio stations and a number of print journalists with suspension for interviewing human rights monitors and labor activists. Nonetheless, the media has become more emboldened in covering human rights issues and criticizing the military.

Hungary

Polity: Parliamentary democracy
Economy: Mixed statist transitional
Population: 10,331,000
PPP: $6,245
Life Expectancy: 70.9
Ethnic Groups: Hungarians (95 percent), Slovak, German, Romanian minorities

Political Rights: 2
Civil Liberties: 2
Status: Free

Overview: Deepening economic recession, the legal accountability of former Communists for past crimes, and the growing militancy of the nationalist wing of the ruling Hungarian

Democratic Forum (MDF) were among key issues facing Prime Minister Jozef Antall as Hungary entered its third year of post-Communist democracy. Another key concern was the escalating war in the former Yugoslavia, particularly the influx of approximately 50,000 refugees and the fate of the 400,000-strong Hungarian minority in Serbian-controlled Vojvodina.

Hungary has a unicameral 386-member parliament. After free elections in May 1990, the MDF held 165 seats; the liberal Alliance of Free Democrats, 92; the Independent Smallholders, 43; the Christian Democrats, 21; the Hungarian Socialist Party (formerly the ruling Communist Hungarian Socialist Workers Party), 33; and FIDESZ, a former student group, 21. The ruling coalition includes the MDF, the Smallholders and the Christian Democrats.

In early 1992, Hungarians debated a law passed in November 1991 that would have extended the expired statute of limitations for crimes committed during 45 years of Communist rule. President Arpad Goncz, a member of the Free Democrats, referred the statute, sponsored by the MDF, to the Constitutional Court. Opponents of the law feared that its adoption would spur an indiscriminate witch hunt for former Communists. On 3 March, the Constitutional Court ruled unanimously that the law violated the legal guarantees of the new constitution.

In 1992, a sluggish economy, a rise in the number of illegal immigrants and refugees and fallout from the war in Yugoslavia contributed to growing discontent among nationalist politicians and a strain on the ruling coalition. In March, there was a partial split between the MDF and the Smallholders led by Jozsef Torgyan. Although 35 of 45 Smallholder deputies continued to support the government, Torgyan left the coalition, and on 25 March he and an estimated 20,000 supporters rallied in Budapest to demand that the government resign and be replaced by a cabinet of "experts."

In a May parliamentary by-election in Bekescsaba, the MDF-endorsed candidate finished third behind the Free Democrats and the second-place Hungarian Socialists Party. But voter apathy continued to be a problem. The first round of the vote was invalid because less than 50 percent of eligible voters participated; in the second round, which required 25 percent participation, 34 percent of voters turned out. Apathy and a strong showing by the HSP could present serious problems to the MDF in general elections scheduled for 1994, particularly if the economy deteriorates.

The MDF also faced dissension from the right. In the fall, an article by MDF Vice President Istvan Csurka blamed Hungary's problems on a conspiracy by Jews, communists, liberals, the International Monetary Fund and bankers to destroy the government and smother Hungary's national revival. Csurka even called into question the Trianon peace treaty, the territorial settlement after World War I which cost Hungary 60 percent of its land area and left 3.5 million ethnic Hungarians living in neighboring states. Significantly, the moderate prime minister was reluctant to condemn the author, although he did describe the essay as "politically mistaken and harmful."

Although thousands rallied in Budapest to protest the essay, it seemed to articulate the frustration of many Hungarians with the government's apparent inability or reluctance to purge those who made their money or influence under the former Communist regime. Their indignation has grown as the economic depression has deepened.

Another issue was Prime Minister Antall's health. Since 1990, he has been undergoing chemotherapy for lymphoma. Although the government assured that the prime minister's illness did not impede his ability to govern, rumors persisted that he was gravely ill. To complicate matters, the law of succession is vague. In the event of a temporary illness, the internal affairs minister, Peter Boross—an independent—would assume the prime minister's duties.

As the year drew to a close, the Hungarian recession proved far deeper than originally anticipated. Gross Domestic Product (GDP) fell 5 percent, a drastic revision of an original forecast of zero growth. Unemployment was expected to rise from 11 percent to at least 17 percent in 1993. Economic output, which fell 10.2 percent in 1991, continued to drop. Inflation stood at approximately 35 percent, and the budget deficit soared.

In other areas, privatization continued to transform the economy, and exports in the first quarter of 1992 rose 12 percent over the unprecedented 31 percent growth in 1991. In May, Hungary eased the sale of state companies, giving consultants free rein to sell medium-sized state enterprises. Under a "simplified privatization plan," the state devolved to private consulting firms responsibility for 278 of the country's 2,000 state companies. The focus of the plan was to give preference to domestic over foreign investors in the face of mounting social opposition to foreign ownership.

Approximately $1.7 billion in foreign capital flowed into Hungry in 1991. Attempts to restore rural land to private ownership were less successful. The collapse of the Soviet market left Hungary producing one-third more food than the domestic market could consume, and 7 percent of arable land was taken out of production while livestock was reduced by 15 to 30 percent.

In foreign policy, Hungary focused on its goal of "reintegration" into Europe. The country was admitted to the Council of Europe and signed an association agreement with the European Community. Hungary maintained good relations with all the former Yugoslav states except Serbia. Serbian forces and Yugoslav federal aircraft violated Hungary's border several dozen times as the war in Bosnia escalated.

In 1992, 50,000 illegal aliens flocked to Hungary from Asia, Africa and Eastern Europe. In addition, over 50,000 refugees from Croatia and Bosnia escaped into Hungary. The presence of so many foreigners taxed services and accommodations and led to several incidents of attacks on immigrants.

Political Rights and Civil Liberties: Hungarians can democratically change their government. The constitution and new laws guarantee an independent, impartial judiciary. A shortage of skilled jurists and legal professionals continues to be a problem. Minister of Justice Istvan Balsai was criticized for selecting judges who had received the votes of only a minority of their peers, but legal experts agreed that he had not broken the law in his appointments. The Ministry of Justice was also preparing a draft law that would transfer the Prosecutor's Office from the parliament's jurisdiction and place it directly under the ministry's control. The main justification for the measure was that prosecutors should be placed under the branch of government responsible for executing law, as is the case in many Western countries with continental legal systems. The opposition expressed fears that putting the prosecutor's office under the executive would result in greater government influence over that office.

In March, the Constitutional Court overturned a law that would have allowed the government to try former Communists who committed crimes during four decades of Communist rule. Citizen are free to express their views, and there is a broad spectrum of independent newspapers and other publications. Freedom of assembly and association are guaranteed and respected. In 1992, there were between 10,000 and 20,000 civic associations concerned with cultural, religious, social and political issues.

Freedom of conscience and religion is viewed as a fundamental liberty not granted by the state or any other authority. There are no serious restrictions on domestic or foreign travel.

In May, the government was accused of inhumane and illegal treatment of aliens in a detention camp in Kerepestrarcsa outside Budapest, a former Communist prison holding 7,000 alien deportees, mostly economic migrants from Asia, Africa and Romania. Members of the opposition Free Democrats as well as Amnesty International criticized what they called arbitrary detention and abuses in the camps.

Workers are organized in the independent Confederation of Hungarian Trade Unions (MSzOSz) and the Democratic League of Independent Trade Unions. There are several non-affiliated unions. Most workers have the right to strike, excluding judicial and military personnel and police.

Iceland

Polity: Parliamentary democracy
Economy: Capitalist
Population: 260,000
PPP: $14,210
Life Expectancy: 77.8
Ethnic Groups: Icelander

Political Rights: 1
Civil Liberties: 1
Status: Free

Overview: Iceland took a strong stand on environmental policy in 1992. The North Atlantic country took part in the Earth Summit at Rio de Janeiro in June, and urged other states to stop oceanic and atmospheric pollution.

In the 1991 parliamentary elections, the conservative, pro-Europe Independence Party obtained 26 seats in the legislature to become the strongest party. It formed a new coalition government with the Social Democrats, who hold 10 seats. The prime minister is David Oddsson of the Independence Party. With 13 seats, the Progressive Party went into opposition after nearly 20 years in government. The left-wing People's Alliance and the Women's List hold the remaining 14 opposition seats.

Iceland's parliament, the *Althing*, is a bicameral legislature composed of 63 members elected to four-year terms. Forty-nine members of the parliament are selected on the basis of proportional representation from eight districts; the remaining are chosen based on each party's percentage of the national vote. The parliament divides itself into two houses after elections, an upper house composed of 21 members and a lower chamber with 42 members. Every four years, voters elect a president, the ceremonial head of state, who chooses the prime minister from the party or coalition able to command a parliamentary majority.

Iceland has a parliamentary tradition dating from the tenth century. After disaffected Norsemen settled Iceland in the tenth century, Iceland flourished as an independent republic until the thirteenth century, when it came under Norwegian rule. In the fourteenth century, Iceland came under Danish control and remained under rigid colonial control until 1874, when it received limited autonomy within the Kingdom of Denmark. In 1944, when British and American forces occupied Denmark, Iceland achieved full independence. A major issue in Icelandic politics is the country's relationship with the European Community (EC). A major obstacle to Iceland's entrance into the EC concerns Iceland's fishing industry. Iceland fears competition with heavily subsidized European fishing industries and therefore seeks a restriction of European fishing subsidies before entering the EC.

Political Rights and Civil Liberties: Icelanders have the right to change their government democratically. Freedoms of association, assembly, and expression are generally respected. There are both independent and party-affiliated newspapers. There is a public broadcasting service, which is run by an autonomous board. The U.S. Navy also broadcasts from its NATO base in Iceland. The constitution forbids censorship.

Over 95 percent of the population belongs at least nominally to the state-supported Lutheran Church. There is freedom of worship for non-established churches.

It is illegal to discriminate on the basis of language, race, gender and social status in Iceland. However, the Women's List alleges that there are cases of unequal pay for women. Workers have the right to organize and to strike.

India

Polity: Parliamentary democracy
Economy: Capitalist-statist
Population: 882,575,000
PPP: $910
Life Expectancy: 59.1
Ethnic Groups: Indo-Aryan (72 percent), Dravidian (25 percent), other

Political Rights: 3
Civil Liberties: 4
Status: Partly Free

Overview: In December 1992, Hindu fundamentalists leveled a 16th century mosque built on a holy Hindu site in the Indian town of Ayodhya, bringing a long-simmering religious dispute to a climax in which at least 1,300 people were killed and 5,000 wounded in the worst sectarian carnage since independence. In the aftermath, Prime Minister P.V. Narasimha Rao dismissed four opposition–led state governments, outlawed several religious organizations and arrested approximately 2,500 activists.

India achieved independence from Britain in February 1947. Faced with escalating political and religious tension, the country was partitioned into largely Hindu India, under prime minister Jawaharlal Nehru, and Muslim Pakistan. Nehru's daughter, Indira Gandhi, led the country from 1966-1977 and from 1980 to 1984. Her son Rajiv Gandhi became prime minister following her assassination in October 1984.

In the November 1989 elections, V.P. Singh of the Janata Dal Party led the centrist National Front coalition to victory, forcing Gandhi's Congress Party into opposition for the second time since independence. Singh's short-lived government failed to achieve any noticeable reforms and provoked communal violence. An August 1990, suggestion that 27 percent of government and public sector company jobs be set aside for members of "backward classes," which, on top of the existing quota for "untouchables," would bring 49.5 percent of all public sector posts under quota, led to widespread rioting across northern India. In September, the Hindu nationalist Bharatiya Janata Party (BJP) withdrew its support of the government after police arrested its leader for participating in a march to the town of Ayodhya, where a radical Hindu group planned to build a temple on the site of a 16th century mosque. In the fall of that year nearly 1,000 were killed in Hindu–Moslem violence related to the temple issue.

In November 1990, Singh's government lost a no-confidence vote. After new elections, Rajiv Gandhi threw the support of the Congress Party behind a breakaway group of the Janata Dal Party, called the Janata Dal (Socialist), headed by new prime minister Chandra Shekar.

Shekar resigned in March 1991 due to the weak position of his minority government. On 21 May, with balloting under way for a new parliament, Tamil separatists assassinated Ghandi in Madras, throwing the country into chaos. The election was concluded on 15 June, although voting was cancelled in Jammu and Kashmir due to separatist activity, and postponed in Punjab, where 20 candidates were assassinated and a record 5,800 people were killed by year's end. Of the 511 contested seats, the Congress Party (223 seats) and its smaller allies won 239, the National Front 128, and the BJP and its allies, 123. Veteran Congress Party politician P.V. Narashima Rao became prime minister of a minority government.

In 1992, Rao's political fortunes rose early in the year but ultimately slumped over the mosque controversy. In January, the government announced elections would be held in February in Punjab, ending the Presidential (federal) Rule declared there in May 1987. The state has been in turmoil since Indira Gandhi ordered an attack on the sacred Sikh Golden Temple in 1984. On 17 January, the four factions of the major Sikh separatist party, the Akali Dal, said they would boycott the elections rather than implicitly accept Indian rule by participating. Prior to the vote, militant Sikhs demanding a theocratic state stepped up their campaign of bombings and shootings, frequently targeting teachers, who serve as polling officers.

On 13 February approximately 250,000 soldiers, state police and paramilitary troops braced for election-day violence. Although Sikh extremists had threatened to kill the first five people who entered each polling station, no major incidents were reported, and, remarkably, only two people were killed and 30 injured. The Congress Party won 12 of the 13 federal seats, and 87 of 117 state seats. Beant Singh headed a state administration sworn in on 25 February.

Sikh extremists managed to score a victory of sorts by keeping the turnout low (estimated between 22 and 28 percent). Those who did vote were mostly Hindus—in some Sikh villages, not a single person voted. Opposition groups charged that the Congress Party held the elections solely to pick up seats in the federal parliament.

Following the Punjab election, the government easily survived a no-confidence vote on 9 March. Almost immediately afterwards new details began emerging in a kickback scandal implicating government officials involved with a lucrative 1986 arms deal with the Swedish firm Bofors. On 31 March, Foreign Minister Madhavsinh Solanki resigned, allegedly after urging Swiss authorities to delay an investigation into the use of Swiss bank accounts to launder the kickbacks. On 1 April, the prime minister promised a full investigation.

In mid-April the Congress Party held a watershed congress—for the first time in six decades, no member of the Ghandi family was present, and elections for top positions were held for the first time in twenty years. The delegates all but rejected Nehru's big-state sector socialist model in favor of a more open economy.

Rao emerged from the Congress with increased support for his government, but the temple issue soon threatened to undermine his position. On 19 July, new Muslim-Hindu clashes broke out in Ayodhya. Three days later, the Supreme Court ordered the state government of Uttar Pradesh to prevent construction of a Hindu temple on the site, which would destroy the mosque in the process. On 25 July, Hindu fundamentalists agreed to stop work on the temple after Rao personally appealed for calm.

However, on 1 December Hindu fundamentalists led by the BJP said they would ignore a court injunction issued two days earlier and proceed to build the temple. On 6 December, a Hindu mob destroyed the mosque, touching off a week of violence between Hindus and Muslims. In response, Prime Minister Rao shut down four BJP-led state governments and had several BJP members arrested for inciting the violence. But Rao also came under intense pressure to resign over the government's failure to protect the mosque and quell the ensuing riots.

Throughout the year, the government also faced unrest in several other states. Riots in the southern state of Karnataka began in December 1991, after a court order to divert water resources to neighboring Tamil Nadu. A strike early in 1992 protesting the order led to violence against Tamils living in the city of Bangalore, and riots caused approximately 15,000 Tamils to flee the state. One cabinet minister noted, "It has nothing to do with water or jobs anymore. It's just blind hate." In Tamil Nadu, police arrested 2,400 opposition party members in mid-September who went on a rampage after top leaders of their party were arrested for supporting separatists in Sri Lanka.

In the state of Bihar, Maoist rebels killed 37 people in a five-hour rampage through the village of Patna on 13 February. In this highly undeveloped state, the Maoist Communist Center often targets rich landlords, who protect their interests with private armies. On 15 September tribesman in southern Bihar began an economic blockade to demand a separate state called Jharkand. Residents of the area, which includes parts of three other states, are mainly of lower castes and live in what the *Economist* describes as "fourth-world conditions."

The prime minister's most notable achievement has been in the area of economic reform. When Rao took office, India was on the verge of defaulting on its $71 billion foreign debt for the first time in its history. Since then, the government has devalued the Indian currency, the *rupee*, cut subsidies on food and other goods, and mothballed some loss-making state enterprises. Most strikingly, this deeply nationalistic country has been catering to foreign businesses by reducing licensing requirements and allowing foreign firms to take minority control of domestic businesses.

Finance Minister Manmohan Singh introduced a budget on 29 February calling for tight fiscal policy and less state intervention. More reform is necessary—tariffs have been reduced, but still remain at 150 percent on some goods; and 90 of the 244 largest state-enterprises are bankrupt. Dismantling them will leave hundreds of thousands out of work, as will laying off some of the country's 19 million bureaucrats.

The economic changes are all the more important with the breakup of the Soviet Union, formerly India's biggest patron. Rao has broken new ground by taking a more conciliatory stance towards the United States, and by establishing full diplomatic relations with Israel. In August, inconclusive talks were held with Pakistan over Kashmir (*A separate report on Kashmir is included in the Related Territories section*) and nuclear proliferation.

Political Rights and Civil Liberties:

Indian citizens can democratically change their government, but elections, and daily life, are marked by ethnic, caste-based and separatist strife. During the 1991 elections, at least 150 people nationwide died in related violence, and armed thugs disrupted balloting in many areas, particularly in Bihar, Andhra Pradesh and Uttar Pradesh. The government postponed voting in 2,594 stations out of 600,000 nationwide because of ballot stuffing or other irregularities. State politics are increasingly dominated by criminal gangs, particularly in Bihar. Security forces are regularly accused of human rights violations.

The police and security forces have broad powers against suspects. The National Security Act allows suspected security risks to be detained for one year (two in Punjab) without a trial. The Terrorist and Disruptive Activities Act (TADA) allows courts to use voluntary confessions to police; in practice, eyewitnesses say police use brutality to extract confessions under the cover of the law. "Disruptive" acts under the TADA include speech or actions that challenge the sovereignty of the country, most often applied to Sikh separatism. Under the Terrorist Affected Areas Act, people accused of "waging war" against the government are presumed guilty and must prove their innocence. Other acts allow the government to tap telephones and seize mail.

The judiciary is considered independent of the government, and defendants generally receive due process rights. However, the system is massively backlogged and justice is almost always delayed. Abuse of detainees and prisoners, especially those from lower castes who are unaware of their rights, occurs frequently. Common criminals, women, and mentally disturbed people are frequently jailed together. Three classes of jails exist, based on status in society, with the lowly Class "C" cells reserved for people with low educational levels who cannot prove they pay taxes. Prisoners in the "C" cells suffer the most abuse.

An independent press vigorously criticizes the government, although critics express concern over the government's control of newsprint and public sector advertising. Of greater concern is the Official Secrets Act, which allows the government to censor sensitive security articles. In addition, the Press Council of India, an independent board of journalists under a government–appointed director, can criticize journalists for articles which might incite violence. Although the Council's findings are not binding, journalists say the threat of rebuke from their peers often leads to self-censorship. State-run television and radio are often accused of pro-government slants. Freedoms of assembly and association are generally respected.

All religious groups are allowed to worship freely in this secular state. Citizens can travel freely in the country, except in border areas where security permits are needed.

Workers are free to join unions of their choice, and although many unions are nominally related to political parties, most operate independently. Public sector unions must give two weeks notice before striking, and the Essential Service Act allows the government to bar strikes in specified industries. The International Labor Organization estimates the country has 44 million child laborers, many of whom work in slave–like conditions after being "sold" by their families.

Indonesia

Polity: Dominant party (military-dominated)
Economy: Capitalist-statist
Political Rights: 6
Civil Liberties: 5
Status: Partly Free
Population: 184,475,000
PPP: $2,034
Life Expectancy: 61.5
Ethnic Groups: A multi-ethnic state—Javanese (45 percent), Sundanese (14 percent), Madurese (7.5 percent), Coastal Malays (7.5 percent), other (26 percent)

Overview: Indonesia's ruling Golkar party won 67.5 percent of the vote in the June 1992 parliamentary elections, down slightly from its 1987 share. Soon after this so-called "feast of democracy," 71-year-old President Suharto, already the longest serving head of state in Asia outside of North Korea, announced he would seek a sixth term in 1993. In another major issue, a December earthquake on Flores and two other islands killed more than 2,500 people.

The fourth most populous country in the world, Indonesia consists of over 13,000 islands of the Malay archipelago. The country proclaimed independence from Dutch colonialism and the occupying Japanese in August 1945 under the fiercely nationalistic President Sukarno. In October 1965, the Army Strategic Reserve, led by General Suharto, thwarted a coup attempt by the Indonesian Communist Party (PKI). In the ensuing months, the army killed several hundred thousand PKI members and suspected members. The legislature removed Sukarno from power in March 1967, and elected Suharto president one year later.

Suharto's "New Order" administration has stressed economic development and political stability. The guiding state philosophy, *Pancasila*, consists of five principles—monotheism, justice for all citizens, political unity, democracy through consensus, and social justice. In practice, the government cites Pancasila to limit discussion of political change or religious and ethnic matters.

Suharto's political organization, Golkar, is a coalition of social and advocacy groups rather than a true political party. Besides Golkar, two significant parties exist, but neither considers itself an opposition party in the traditional sense. The Indonesian Democratic Party (PDI) is a coalition of Christian and nationalist groups that appeals to urban blue-collar workers and younger voters. It favors a more open political system, a greater focus on individual rights, and a more equitable distribution of income. The United Development Party (PPP) is a coalition of Islamic groups that were forced together by Suharto. In the 1987 elections, Golkar won 73 percent of the vote, the PPP 16 percent, and the PDI 11 percent.

Suharto has been elected by the People's Consultative Assembly for five five-year terms since 1968. He has never faced any opposition, and these "elections" simply confirm his decision to hold another term. The Assembly consists of 500 members chosen by the president and provincial governors, as well as members of the PDI and the PPP in proportion to their representation in parliament. The Assembly also includes the entire 500-member parliament, which has 400 members elected via proportional representation and 100 seats set aside for the military. The parliament has never initiated nor blocked a single piece of legislation during Suharto's tenure. Members of Abri (the armed forces) are not allowed to vote for fear of compromising the military's neutrality in its constitutionally established role as the stabilizing force behind the country's development.

During the spring campaign for the June 1992 parliamentary elections, Golkar repeatedly restricted the activities of the PDI and PPP. Two PPP speakers were barred from addressing crowds, one for telling voters to cast ballots along religious lines, and another for allegedly "discrediting the government." On 30 April, the government banned seminars on politics and political debates from private television and radio during the campaign. Meetings of the Forum for Democracy, a group of pro-democracy intellectuals who called on citizens to boycott the vote, were banned in February and April on the grounds that they had not properly applied for a permit. However, on 30 April, 37 Muslim organizations were allowed to hold a prayer rally in support a sixth term for Suharto. Although the campaign, and the election itself, was relatively free of violence, on 27 May, scores of youths were injured in a clash between PDI and Golkar supporters. The PDI closed its campaign with a spectacular rally on 31 May that drew more than 2 million people.

Approximately 90 percent of the electorate turned out for the 9 June vote. Golkar's share of the vote fell to 67.5 percent, which still gave it a commanding 282 of the 400 contested seats. The PPP took 17.5 percent and the PDI 15 percent. The government claimed that its solid, yet reduced, majority showed both that it still had strong support and that the vote was fair.

Suharto ended months of speculation on 20 October, when he accepted Abri and Golkar's nomination for the presidency. In a country with rising incomes and education, many citizens believe that his authoritarian rule is anachronistic. The president has also been criticized over the monopoly interests granted to his children. Although the PDI successfully parlayed these issues into a greater share of the parliamentary vote, Suharto will likely run unopposed, and his re-election is virtually assured.

In 1992, Indonesia continued to face criticism over the November 1991 massacre in the disputed province of East Timor (*A separate report on East Timor is included in the Related Territories section*). In March, the government announced that it would no longer accept development aid from the Netherlands because of the Dutch insistence on linking aid and human rights. In April, the government banned non-governmental organizations (NGO) from accepting Dutch assistance. Groups such as the Legal Aid Institute and the Institute for Defense of Human Rights, which often are the only true opposition to the government's policies, receive over four-fifths of their funding from Dutch NGOs.

The economy, which had been dependent on oil exports, has been diversified since the early 1980s. Foreign investors can now own large businesses. However, the country still has a $70 billion foreign debt, a poor infrastructure, and a highly regulated agricultural sector.

Political Rights and Civil Liberties:

Institutional barriers and President Suharto's political dominance effectively prevent Indonesians from being able to change their government. The June 1992 parliamentary elections were noticeably free of violence and irregularities. However, Golkar used both the power of incumbency and a variety of measures to ensure itself an overwhelming majority.

Political parties must embrace the consensus-oriented *pancasila* philosophy, limiting their ability to advocate substantial change. Parties are not allowed to campaign on potentially divisive issues such as religion or the dominant role of the Chinese in business. All civil servants and employees of state-run firms must work and vote for Golkar. Candidates were allowed 15 minutes per day on state radio and television, but speeches were reviewed beforehand, and debates were prohibited from private radio and television. Opposition parties were barred from organizing at the village level, where the majority of the population lives.

Human rights abuses continue in Aceh, located at the northern tip of Sumatra, where Indonesian forces are accused of torture and extrajudicial detention and execution against suspected members of the secessionist Aceh-Sumatra Liberation Front.

Under the government's controversial "transmigration" policy, approximately 2,500,000 people have been voluntarily relocated since 1969 from the densely packed islands of Java to other areas such as Sumatra and Kalimantan. Critics say the policy is environmentally destructive, and infringes upon those already living in the outlying areas.

Freedom of speech and of press are restricted by the conformist pancasila philosophy. Private radio and television stations are required to use government-produced news programs. The government has banned or revoked the licenses of papers for publishing articles considered controversial. In June, the government banned four publications: a Legal Aid Foundation report on the trials of 15 Acehnese accused of separatist activities, an Australian publication which contained reports considered potentially embarrassing to the country's leaders, and two books, *Chinese, Javanese and Maduranese* and *A Hymn on Indonesian Culture*, the latter for its pro-Communist orientation.

Freedom of assembly is not generally restricted, although organizations must get permission to hold regional or national meetings. The judiciary is not fully independent; the executive branch appoints and can dismiss judges. Rights granted to criminals under the Indonesia Criminal Procedures Code (KUHAP) are often flouted, and suspects are commonly tortured and abused to extract confessions. Police can detain people suspected of subversive activities for one year without filing charges. A shadowy Agency for Coordination of Assistance for the Consolidation of National Security (BAKORSTANAS) is exempt from KUHAP and has wide latitude in dealing with suspects considered threats to national security.

Although 90 percent of the population is Muslim, other faiths generally practice freely. Advocating a Muslim state is illegal. Chinese are forbidden to operate all-Chinese schools, cultural groups and trade associations, or publicly display Chinese characters. A March 1992 immigration law allows the government to bar citizens from either leaving the country or returning from abroad for up to 30 months if they are considered threats to national stability or or religious unity. Under this law, approximately 17,000 Indonesians cannot leave the country.

All workers have the legal right to bargain collectively and strike, but most potential strikes are avoided through negotiation or police intimidation.

Iran

Polity: Presidential-parliamentary (clergy-dominated)
Economy: Capitalist-statist
Population: 59,651,000
PPP: $3,120
Life Expectancy: 66.2
Ethnic Groups: Persian, Turkic, Arab, other

Political Rights: 6
Civil Liberties: 6
Status: Not Free

Overview:

In April and May 1992, Iranians elected a new parliament filled with supporters of President Ali Akbar Hashemi Rafsanjani, who had previously been attacked by hardliners for his efforts to open up the economy and end the country's international isolation. However, after the election, many of Rafsanjani's supporters in the new parliament blamed his modest liberalizations for a surge in violence in major cities. This criticism led the president to cancel plans for widespread economic reforms.

Since the 1979 revolution that toppled the regime of Shah Mohammad Reza Pahlavi, Iran has been governed as an Islamic republic. Power is held by the President and the 12–member Council of Guardians, which must approve all bills passed by the 270–member *majlis* (parliament) as being in accordance with Islamic law. The country is still recovering from the devastating effects of the eight-year war with Iraq, which began in 1980 over a longstanding dispute regarding the Shatt al–Arab waterway.

In recent years, much of the middle class has become increasingly impoverished, while a handful of merchants and well-connected officials have grown rich. Monthly inflation runs at 20 percent, three-hour daily blackouts are the norm, and many people have been forced to take two or three jobs to survive. The situation has led to widespread discontent with the Islamic revolution.

Since being elected in July 1989 with 95 percent of the vote, President

Rafsanjani has initiated limited economic reforms within the confines of Islamic law. Many of his efforts were initially blocked by the majlis, which had been dominated by staunch anti–Western, radical supporters of the late religious leader Ayatollah Ruhollah Khomeini. These hardliners interpret Islamic law to mean that all large industries should be state–controlled, and medium–sized ones run by Islamic cooperatives. They also favor government subsidies, price controls and economic self–sufficiency.

In the process of seeking support for his policies, Rafsanjani has transformed the once largely ceremonial presidency into a key position. Prior to December 1990 elections for the 82-member Assembly of Experts, a body of Islamic scholars who decide the succession of the nation's spiritual leaders, Rafsanjani successfully got the Council of Guardians to change the eligibility for Assembly membership. Many leading radicals were purged, and Rafsanjani's influence over the body increased.

More importantly, Rafsanjani got an opportunity to purge the hardliners from the majlis in the 1992 elections. The Council of Guardians, which must approve all candidates, eliminated 1,100 of the staunchest hardliners from the list, including 40 sitting MPs, leaving 2,030 candidates in the race. All candidates had to meet strict religious and political criteria, namely that they must "be Iranian, with practical belief in and commitment to Islam and the Islamic Republic of Iran, and loyal to the constitution."

After the first round on 10 April, 133 candidates received the necessary 30 percent to win a seat and avoid going to the second round, held 8 May. Pro–Rafsanjani candidates, many of whom are Western–educated technocrats, scored a rout in the Teheran area and polled strongly in the countryside, winning roughly three-quarters of the seats overall in the majlis. With control of the majlis, the Assembly of Scholars, and the backing of the Council of Guardians, and no obvious threat of renewed war with Iraq, the president had a mandate for cautious economic reform and a possible rapprochement with the West.

However, violence in several major cities soon derailed any chances for even moderate reforms. Since August 1991, unskilled laborers have been fighting to save their squatter settlements from destruction by municipalities seeking to end an influx of villagers. The cities, already strained to provide adequate local services, say they are unable to accommodate the tens of thousands of people living in makeshift homes. The violence surged in May, presenting the first serious challenge to the government since the 1979 revolution.

On 1 June state radio reported that tens of thousands of shantytown residents in Mashhad had rampaged and looted for four days after the local government tried to raze squatter dwellings. At least nine people were executed in June in Mashhad and Shiraz, and others faced jail terms and floggings. More rioting broke out in Bowkan in June.

In a strong rebuff to Rafsanjani, many of the President's supporters blamed the unrest on his economic reforms, and called for a return to revolutionary values. Facing heavy pressure, on 24 August Rafsanjani said the government would avoid introducing widespread reforms, and would allow only limited foreign investment. The President claimed economic conditions were improving, and said the country would instead seek what he variously called a "mixed economy" and a "pure Islamic economy." He also pledged to improve and expand services in health care and transportation.

A dispute over three islands in the Persian Gulf pushed Iranian–Arab relations to their lowest point since the war with Iraq. Since 1971 the islands, which control shipping lanes through which 20 percent of the world's oil passes, have been administered by both Iran and the United Arab Emirates. In April, Iranian officials on one of the islands told residents, many of whom were citizens of the Emirates, to obtain Iranian documents or leave. Negotiations on the issue fell through in the fall after Iran refused to discuss what amounted to its annexation of the islands.

The government has been steadily rebuilding its military since the end of the war with Iraq, including efforts to acquire nuclear weapons and technology. Western governments say the country has been expanding relations with the Central Asian republics of the former Soviet Union to obtain nuclear weapons.

Political Rights and Civil Liberties:

Iranians cannot change their government democratically. Although there are elections for president, the parliament, and the Assembly of Experts, all candidates must be "pro–revolution" and approved by the Council of Guardians. State control is maintained through an extensive security apparatus under the Ministry of Intelligence and Security, and enforced through arrests, summary trials, and executions. Authorities can legally enter homes, confiscate mail, and install wiretaps. A U.N. report released in February said that in 1991 there were approximately 884 executions, up from 500 in 1990, and called the use of the death penalty "manifestly excessive." The report also said there are persistent reports of torture, including amputations and floggings.

Religion dominates all government affairs in this Islamic republic. The president and most top officials, as well as many MPs, are clergymen. The small Christian, Jewish and Zoroastrian groups are recognized by the constitution, and have seats reserved in parliament. They are also permitted to practice their religion and maintain schools, but are frequently harassed. Citizens cannot question the legitimacy of the religious government.

The two-tiered judiciary consists of civil courts for political offenses, and revolutionary courts for political, religious, and drug offenses. In the civil courts, the accused often have the right to a public trial and counsel. However, the judges, as with any government positions, must meet political and religious qualifications, and can often be bribed. Lawyers have been punished for zealously pursuing cases. In the revolutionary courts, there are no procedural safeguards, and trials have lasted for less than five minutes. Many defendants are not permitted access to a lawyer, cannot appeal, and cannot call witnesses on their behalf. Revolutionary courts can overturn the decisions of civil courts.

The constitution allows for freedom of expression only when it is not contrary to "Islamic principles." Most publications are controlled by the government, and independent newspaper and magazine publishers run the risk of arrest if they are overly critical of the government. The Ministry of Islamic Guidance must approve all books before they are published. Newspapers are often associated with government factions, and often criticize government policies. However, they are forbidden to criticize the establishment of the Islamic Republic, or to promote ethnic minority rights.

The government allows only state-sponsored marches or demonstrations. There are few truly independent organizations or associations. Citizens are free to travel internally, but males of draft age are restricted from travelling abroad, and political suspects are prohibited from leaving the country. The government–controlled national House of Labor, formed in 1982, is the only authorized national labor organization. Smaller labor councils and guild unions are closely allied to the government.

Iraq

Polity: One-party
Economy: Statist
Population: 18,223,000
PPP: $3,510
Life Expectancy: 65.0
Ethnic Groups: Arabs (75 percent), Kurds (15 percent), Turks and others

Political Rights: 7
Civil Liberties: 7
Status: Not Free

Overview:

Iraq played a dangerous game of brinkmanship in 1992, repeatedly flouting U.N. orders to destroy its weapons of mass destruction and end its attacks on the Shiites and Kurds, only to back down when the threat of a multi-national armed response appeared likely. By year's end, Saddam Hussein's country had been partitioned, with protective zones established for the Kurds in the north and the Shiites in the south.

Iraq won independence from the British in 1932. A pan-Arab revolution in 1958 overthrew the monarchy and established a left-wing republic. Ba'ath extremists took power in 1968 and installed the Arab Ba'ath Socialist Party (ABSP) at the head of government. Saddam Hussein, considered the strongman in the regime since 1973, took power formally in 1979 as president, Chairman of the Revolutionary Command Council, and Secretary General of the Regional Command of the ABSP. Hussein and his ruling elite are Sunni Moslems, but Shiites make up 55 percent of the population.

In September 1980, a dispute with neighboring Iran over the Shatt al-Arab waterway erupted into a fierce war that lasted until August 1988. While still recovering from that war, Iraq triggered an international response when it invaded Kuwait on 2 August 1990, raising fears it would attack other neighbors and spark an oil crisis. The U.N. immediately placed an embargo on the country amidst reports that Iraqi soldiers were pillaging Kuwait. A United States-led coalition began air and missile attacks in January 1991, and liberated Kuwait in February. An estimated 100,000 Iraqis were killed or wounded.

Following its defeat, the government faced revolts from the Kurds in the north and Shiites in the south. (*A separate report on Kurdistan appears in the Related Territories section*). The army ruthlessly crushed the Shiite uprising, causing approximately 200,000 to flee to the southern marshlands to escape ground and tank assaults. By the end of March, the government captured the northern city of Kirkuk, causing hundreds of thousands of Kurds to flee to the mountains. By late April an estimated 4,000 Kurds per day were dying in squalid camps on the Turkish border. The U.S. and other countries set up a military task force in southern Turkey to protect the Kurds if the Iraqi army began a major attack.

Iraq's chemical arms and nuclear facilities were left partially intact after the war. The government admitted that it had conducted research involving weapons-grade uranium, but denied that it was for an arms program. The government obstructed several U.N. inspection teams in 1991, but eventually thousands of documents were seized that indicated a chemical weapons stockpile of 46,000 munitions, including 30 warheads for Scud ballistic missiles.

In 1992, Hussein continued to violate the Gulf War cease-fire agreement by attacking Kurds and the Shiites living in the far south, and by disrupting U.N. inspectors. In mid-February, Shiite rebels came under new armor and air strikes in the marshlands north of Basra. On 12 March, the Security Council warned a defiant Deputy Prime Minister Tariq Aziz that Iraq must fully comply and destroy its chemical and biological weapons and ballistic missiles. Aziz promised more information on his country's weapons capabilities, but rejected calls for more inspections and for the weapons facilities to be destroyed rather than converted. The Council also demanded an end to the blockade against the Kurds in the north and the campaign against the Shiites. Iraq's intransigence raised the possibility that a coalition might again be assembled to destroy the weapons or topple Hussein. Iraq temporarily averted a showdown on 20 March when U.N. officials said they had received new information about the country's Scud missile and chemical stocks.

In April, the government began destroying an atomic facility at al-Atheer believed to be the core of its atomic weapons program. However, tensions rose again after the army moved missiles and troops into the Kurdish region north of the 36th parallel. Allied planes in the region were placed on a state of alert, and on 14 April the U.S., Great Britain and France demanded that Iraq withdraw anti-aircraft missile batteries and cease military flights north of the 36th parallel. During the week, tanks and artillery attacked Shiites in the marshes while the army shelled Kurdish towns in the north. The fighting has pitted the under-armed Kurdish rebels using Kalashnikov rifles, grenade launchers and light anti-aircraft guns against the heavy weapons of the Iraqi army.

In early July, sketchy details emerged about a pair of failed coup attempts. Initial reports on 2 July said that Baghdad defense units had stifled a coup attempt on 29 June by a mechanized brigade of the elite Republican Guards. The brigade never even made it out of its barracks. The U.S. State Department reported factional fighting among elements of the military and security forces from 30 June to 2 July in the northern city of Kirkuk. An American intelligence report released on 9 July said that an assassination plot by four Republican Guards on Hussein's motorcade on 29 June had been foiled. The link between the two reported attempts remains unclear. An estimated 200 officers were eventually purged, with many apparently executed. Unconfirmed reports spoke of widespread arrests in Baghdad.

In July, the government provoked a standoff with U.N. weapons inspectors attempting to get into the Ministry of Agriculture where documents from the country's weapons program were supposedly stored. After waiting 17 days to enter the ministry, the inspectors left on 22 July, fearing for their safety after demonstrators slashed tires and hurled eggs and vegetables. The same day, Shiite rebels reported coming under several days of heavy attacks in the southern marshlands. Republican Guard troops burned the Shiites' flimsy reed houses to flush them out of the area.

On 26 July, Iraq again capitulated and allowed a team of inspectors full access into the Agriculture Ministry. However, hours earlier Hussein announced that the "mother of all battles" he had promised a year earlier was not over yet. Towards the end of the month the standoff continued as Shiite rebels reported new fighting in the southern marshlands, including attacks by fixed-wing aircraft.

The country's economic difficulties increased in late July after the government cracked down on merchants accused of profiteering from food shortages. At least 42 merchants were executed and others were tied to telephone polls and pelted with rotten eggs. Fearful of being accused, many traders simply stopped importing goods, and basic foodstuffs such as rice and sugar were soon in short supply. Merchants were also reluctant to import goods because of a 50 percent drop in the value of the Iraqi currency, the dinar, which allegedly occurred in part because the U.S. and other foreign governments flooded the country with fake bank notes. On 12 August, Hussein promised major efforts to improve the economy; he appointed Deputy Prime Minister Tariq Aziz as head of a special commission to investigate the bribery and black market dealings that had sprang up because of the embargo. Many prices have risen upwards of 400 percent since the war. Unconfirmed reports from Iran said demonstrations were held in Baghdad on 19 August to protest the execution of Walid al-Adami, a popular businessman, poet and preacher who was convicted of profiteering.

By late August, the U.S., Britain and France agreed a stronger response was needed to end the attacks on the Shiites, who were reportedly coming under napalm attacks and by some accounts faced up to 100,000 Iraq troops. The three nations established a no-fly zone south of the 32nd parallel on 27 August and gave their jets orders to shoot down any Iraqi military aircraft flying there. Although Hussein initially said he would go to war if his planes were downed, by the end of the summer no Iraqi planes ventured into the zone, and the ground battles with the rebels dwindled into skirmishes. However, on 27 December, a U.S. fighter shot down an Iraqi fighter which had penetraded the zone.

In September, 60 members of the Iraqi opposition held an unprecedented meeting on Iraqi soil in the Kurdish-controlled northern town of Shaqlawa. The gathering of Shiite clerics, Kurds, nationalist Arabs and others declared their unity and pledged to establish a federal government if Hussein is overthrown.

The government is protesting an April U.N. decision giving the southern port of Umm Qasr to Kuwait. The Gulf War cease-fire had directed the U.N. to redraw the boundary according to a 1963 agreement that favored Kuwait.

Political Rights and Civil Liberties:

Iraqi citizens cannot change their government democratically. Saddam Hussein wields absolute authority as the head of one of the most repressive regimes in the world. His inner circle is composed mostly of relatives and friends from his birthplace, Tikrit. They include his 24-year-old son, Qusai, who heads the Special Security Apparatus that controls the three main security departments. One half-brother is in charge of the national police, while another heads the security directorate. The rubber-stamp National Assembly holds no power.

The army has indiscriminately attacked population centers in the north and south as part of its campaign against Kurdish and Shiites rebels. Summary executions and torture are frequently used as punishment and to instill fear in the populace. Security forces routinely enter homes without warrants under the pretext of investigating "security offenses." According to U.N. inspector Max van der Stoel, hundreds of thousands of Shiites, Kurds and political prisoners are in danger of torture, execution and detention. "Scarcely a day passes without executions or hangings," he said in February.

The judiciary consists of special courts for security trials and regular courts for all others. Ordinary cases generally proceed with basic safeguards such as the right to counsel. Security cases are normally closed, suspects lack due process rights and are frequently tortured to extract confessions. Freedoms of speech, press and association are nonexistent. All media are state-owned and act as propaganda outlets. The government monitors religious activity through the Ministry of Endowments and Religious Affairs, which has authority over the appointments of clergy, the content of religious literature and religious gatherings. Many Shiite cultural institutions have been destroyed, and its leaders have been detained. The small Christian and Jewish communities generally are allowed to practice freely within their places of worship, but Christians are not allowed to hold religious meetings outside their churches, and Jews are restricted in traveling abroad.

Numerous areas in the country are off-limits to for citizens for security reasons, and travelers face frequent checkpoints along highways. Free trade unions do not exist and strikes do not occur.

Ireland

Polity: Parliamentary democracy
Economy: Capitalist
Population: 3,532,000
PPP: $7,481
Life Expectancy: 74.6
Ethnic Groups: Irish (Celtic), English, and small immigrant communities of others

Political Rights: 1
Civil Liberties: 1
Status: Free

Overview:
In 1992, a series of business and government scandals triggered the resignation of Prime Minister (*Taoiseach*) Charles Haughey, the premiership of Albert Reynolds, and a watershed general election. Taking advantage of the scandals and rising unemployment, the historically third-place Irish Labour Party made dramatic gains in the general election on 26 November. Having slashed the strength of Fianna Fail and Fine Gael, the historically leading center-right parties, Labour played the pivotal role in forming a new coalition government. By year's end, Fianna Fail and Labour were prepared to form their first coalition government with each other. The issues of abortion, Northern Ireland, and the European Community also played major roles in the country's political debates during the year.

Following centuries of British domination and occupation, 26 of Ireland's 32 counties won home rule within the British Commonwealth in 1921. The six counties of Northern Ireland have remained part of the United Kingdom. In 1948, Ireland proclaimed itself a republic outside the Commonwealth. The Irish constitution claims Northern Ireland, but the republic has only a consultative role in the North under the Anglo-Irish Accord of 1985. The Unionist parties, which represent the Protestant majority in the North, oppose the Anglo-Irish Accord, because they fear that the mostly Catholic republic's involvement in the six counties could cause Irish unification. In 1992, the Irish and British governments and the constitutional parties from the North attempted to negotiate a new political arrangement for the six counties. Unionist leaders insisted that any deal had to involve a removal of the Irish constitutional claim to the North. Ultimately, the talks changed nothing.

The Republic of Ireland has a bicameral legislature, consisting of a Senate and a more powerful lower house, the Dail. The comparatively powerless upper house has 60 members and can delay legislation. Its term lasts as long as that of the Dail, a maximum of five years. The prime minister, universities, and occupational panels name or elect senators. The Dail has 166 members elected by the single transferable vote method of proportional representation. The head of government is Albert Reynolds (Fianna Fail). As leader of Fianna Fail, Charles Haughey failed to secure a majority in the Dail in the 1989 general election. Consequently, Haughey formed a coalition with the small, center-right Progressive Democrats Party, led by Des O'Malley. Following months of business and government scandals, Haughey resigned effective 10 February 1992. Reynolds replaced him after a vote by the Fianna Fail parliamentarians.

Controversy over a scandal cut Reynolds' term short. During 1992, a special tribunal investigated allegations of corruption in the beef industries owned by Larry Goodman, a close Haughey associate. Des O'Malley testified that, as a cabinet member, Albert Reynolds had extended too much export insurance to Goodman. In turn, Reynolds accused O'Malley of dishonesty, thereby breaking up the coalition government and necessitating November's general election. In that contest, Fianna Fail had its worst showing since the 1920s, 39.1 percent of the vote and 68 seats. Fine Gael received 24.5 percent of the vote and 45 seats, its worst showing since the 1940s. Labour won 19.3 percent of the vote and 33 seats, doubling its representation from the previous Dail. The Progressive Democrats captured 4.7 percent of the vote and 10 seats, a slight gain. Democratic Left, a new left-wing party that split off from the formerly Soviet-backed Worker's Party, took 2.8 percent and four seats. The environmentalist Greens garnered 1.4 percent and one seat. Independents took five seats.

Mary Robinson, the largely ceremonial, popularly elected President of the Republic is head of state and appoints the *Taoiseach* from the party or coalition able to command a majority in the Dail. Robinson, a former Labour Party senator, supports women's rights and liberal social legislation, and has tried to expand her office's symbolic and rhetorical powers. Her election and liberal views have encouraged major politicians to advocate changes in laws on such lifestyle and morality issues as divorce, birth control, homosexuality, and abortion.

An abortion case dominated Irish politics during the first half of 1992. A fourteen-year old girl, who had become pregnant by a friend's father in an alleged rape, sought an abortion in England. After the girl's parents notified the Irish police of their plans, the Attorney General issued a ruling prohibiting the girl from leaving the country for the operation, on the grounds that abortion is unconstitutional in Ireland. This ruling re-ignited controversy over the 1983 amendment to the Irish constitution that outlaws abortion, but "with due regard" for the mother's life. Since the government had sought and won protection for Ireland's abortion policy within the European Community, the abortion case became entangled in the campaign for Irish ratification of the Maastricht treaty on European unification. The government promised that it would present measures to assure the rights to abortion information and travel for abortions once voters passed the Maastricht referendum in June 1992. Both pro-and anti-abortion groups were suspicious of the government's European policies, but the electorate voted for Maastricht 69.1 percent to 30.9 percent. Most Irish voters decided that the economic benefits of European unity outweighed all other concerns, especially with unemployment running over 20 percent. After the Maastricht vote, the government introduced three referenda on abortion. At the general election in November, Irish voters backed the right to obtain information on abortion and the right to travel to have an abortion in another country. The electorate rejected the third proposal that would have allowed abortion to save the life of the mother, except in the case of threatened suicide. Both pro- and anti-abortion groups had campaigned against the third proposal, the former believing it too narrow, the latter holding it too broad.

Political Rights and Civil Liberties:

Irish voters can change their government democratically. Citizens register to vote through a government-sponsored household survey. However, only diplomatic families and security forces abroad have the right to absentee ballots overseas.

The press is comparatively free, but there is censorship on moral grounds, such as the ban on Madonna's book, *Sex.* Before the November 1992 referendum, newspaper distributors suppressed issues of foreign journals that included abortion advertisements. Harsh libel laws provided Reynolds a tool for attacking critics in 1992. He sued various media and Senator John Murphy for libel. *The Sunday Independent* complained that the libel suits could "stifle robust public debate" over the Maastricht treaty.

Terrorist organizations, such as the Provisional IRA, are illegal, but Sinn Fein, the IRA's political wing, is legal. The Irish government allows Sinn Fein the right to organize and campaign for elections, but uses the anti-terrorism laws to exclude Sinn Fein representatives and members of paramilitary and "subversive" groups from the broadcast media. However, broadcast journalists may report Sinn Fein's views and quote from its publications. A High Court judge ruled in July 1992 that broadcasters had exceeded the law in banning an interview with a striking workers' leader who happened to be a Sinn Fein member. An autonomous public corporation, RTE, operates television and radio outlets. The government considered privatizing RTE TV2. Many homes receive British and other international broadcasts through cable television.

Due to occasional spillovers from the violence in Northern Ireland, the police have special powers to detain and question suspected terrorists. The Irish Republic and the United Kingdom have an extradition agreement that allows accused terrorists to be tried in Britain for crimes allegedly committed in the U.K. Irish law allows the courts to prevent extraditions for crimes that have political motivations. After a case in which an IRA man escaped extradition through this political exception in 1991, the Irish government tightened the law.

The judiciary is independent, but some judges came under fire in 1992. The government removed a high court justice from the presidency of the Law Reform Commission after he made statements on abortion policy and the European Community. A great public outcry followed a Dublin judge's decision to let a rapist go free for a year. Politicians reacted with proposed legislation to allow the government to appeal such decisions.

The voters rejected divorce in a 1986 referendum, but the government introduced a divorce proposal in 1992. The government restricts artificial methods of birth control, but is liberalizing condom sales. The European Court of Human Rights ruled in 1990 that Irish laws proscribing homosexual acts were a denial of human rights. In 1992, the government made its most recent unfulfilled promise to reform these laws.

The Roman Catholic Church remains strong, but other faiths have religious freedom. There have been Protestant presidents and a Jewish mayor of Dublin. The Irish-speaking minority forms the only significant indigenous, minority cultural group. Irish-speakers are concentrated in a small collection of areas called the *Gaeltacht*, located chiefly along the West coast. The government protects their linguistic tradition through various subsidies and other program. Business is generally free, and free trade unions and farming groups are influential.

Israel

Polity: Parliamentary democracy
Economy: Mixed capitalist
Population: 5,233,000
PPP: $10,448
Life Expectancy: 75.9
Ethnic Groups: Jewish majority, Arab minority

Political Rights: 2
Civil Liberties: 2
Status: Free

Overview:

In the June 1992 elections, former Israeli war hero Yitzhak Rabin carried the Labor Party to its first victory in 15 years. Rabin promised a less dogmatic approach to Jewish housing settlements in the West Bank and Gaza Strip and greater flexibility in the peace negotiations with the Arabs. He also assured Israelis that he would not compromise the country's security interests.

Israel was formed in 1948 out of less than one-fifth of the original British Palestine Mandate. Much of its short history has been marred by war with its Arab neighbors, who rejected a United Nations partition plan which would have also created a new Arab state. Several Arab nations attacked the new country on independence day in May 1948. Israel also fought Egypt in 1956, and, in June 1967, routed several Arab armies in six days after Egypt closed the Gulf of Aqaba to its ships, taking the Gaza Strip, the West Bank, the Golan Heights (which it annexed in 1981) and East Jerusalem. (*See report on Occupied Territories under related territories.*) Israel kept these territories following the October 1973 war, and signed a peace treaty with Egypt in 1979, leading to the return of the Sinai in 1982. The same year, Israel invaded southern Lebanon to neutralize Palestinian Liberation Organization (PLO) guerrillas operating there; currently its troops maintain a "security zone" in southern Lebanon.

The conservative Likud party formed a governing coalition under Prime Minister Menachem Begin after the 1977 elections, ending 29 years of center-left rule. At the 1984 elections, Likud failed to attract enough smaller parties to form a "blocking majority" in the Knesset (parliament), and entered into an uneasy coalition with the Labor Party. After another close Likud victory in 1988, the two major parties again entered a "national unity" government, but Labor withdrew in March 1990.

In January 1992, two right-wing parties (Tehiya and Moledet) quit the governing coalition over reports that Prime Minister Yitzhak Shamir would introduce a plan for limited Palestinian self-rule in the West Bank and Gaza Strip. Without these two parties, the Likud coalition lost its majority, forcing the Knesset on 4 February to call early elections for June.

On 19 February, the Labor Party held the country's first-ever primary vote, allowing its rank-and-file to select the top name on its party list, who is the potential prime minister. Yitzhak Rabin, the victorious military commander in the 1967 war who became the country's first native–born prime minister in 1974, unseated another former prime minister, Shimon Peres. The voters considered Rabin more likely to attract moderate Likud voters, due to his combination of pragmatism towards the peace negotiations with the Arabs and credibility in protecting Israel's security interests. In contrast to Labor's open vote, on 20 February the 2,800-member Likud central committee picked Prime Minister Shamir to remain in his post as party chairman over Foreign Affairs Minister David Levy.

While Peres cemented Labor's unity by gracefully conceding defeat, Likud faced a revolt by moderates seeking progress in the ongoing Arab-Israeli peace talks, and by Sephardic (Middle-Eastern and North African-born) voters, who harbor a long-standing distrust of the party's European-descended leadership, personified by the 77–year–old, Polish–born Shamir. Tensions rose after a second round of central committee voting for the next 50 spots on the party list. Two hardliners, Housing Minister Ariel Sharon and Defense Minister Moshe Arens, pooled their supporters to outmaneuver the Moroccan–born Levy for the second and third positions on the party list.

On 30 March, Levy quit Likud, claiming that Shamir and others were condescending towards the Sephardim, and had dangerously jeopardized relations with the U.S. by continuing to build settlements in the West Bank. Levy rejoined only after Shamir promised his backers a quota of government appointments. The party's image was further tattered by an April report by the state comptroller that accused the government of waste, mismanagement and corruption, particularly in Sharon's Housing Ministry.

Opinion polls in the run-up to the election showed a close race, foreshadowing another "national unity" government. However, in the 23 June vote, Labor took a commanding 44 seats versus 32 for Likud, with other seats going to the Meretz coalition, with 12; Tzomet, with 8; the Sephardic Torah Guardians (Shas), with 6; the National Religious Party (NRP) with 6; United Torah Jewry with 4; the Arab-Communist Democratic Front with 3; Moledet, with 3; and the Arab Democratic Party, with 2.

Many voters ultimately blamed Likud for the slow pace of the peace talks, and were angry at what they considered to be disproportionate funding for Jewish settlers in the occupied territories. In addition, shortages of jobs and housing for the over 400,000 Jews who have arrived from the former Soviet Union since 1989, combined with an already slow economy, boosted the unemployment rate to 11.6 percent at the time of the election.

In contrast to recent years in which small religious groups held the balance of power in fragile coalitions, the surprising success of the dovish Meretz and the hardline Tsomet offered Rabin the possibility of forming a fully secular majority coalition. In an attempt to reconcile the two parties' differences on the pace of Jewish housing settlement in the occupied territories, Rabin distinguished between critical "security settlements" which should be continued in frontline areas, and expendable "political settlements" in areas which did not enhance the country's safety. This new flexibility convinced the U.S. in July to extend $10 billion in loan guarantees needed to resettle the new immigrants.

Rabin's assurances were ultimately not enough for Tsomet, and on 9 July, after giving Meretz head Shulamit Aloni the education cabinet post, the prime minister formed a 62-seat coalition with Meretz and the left-wing, religious Shas. Five Arab legislators agreed to support the government from outside the coalition.

Religious groups immediately protested the appointment of a secular liberal to the Education Ministry, which has been at the center of a debate over how much funding the government should give to religious schools and organizations. By September, Shas threatened to pull out of the coalition to protest Aloni's remarks disparaging religious influence in society. On 2 November, Shas helped the government survive four no–confidence votes after receiving an apology from Aloni and an agreement that religious groups would get more influence in the public schools. However, on 1 December, the Meretz bloc hinted it would withdraw if the Labor party shelved a new bill guaranteeing human rights. Religious parties urged Rabin to oppose the bill because it is grounded in secular principles.

The Labor victory, and the Knesset's vote in March to hold direct elections for the prime minister beginning in 1996, convinced Likud to enact party reforms. On 15 November, in what one pundit called "a burial of the old politics," the Likud central committee agreed to hold primaries in March 1993 to name a party leader, who will be its candidate for prime minister. The clear Likud front-runner is 43–year–old Benjamin Netanyahu, the former U.N. ambassador who excels at the communications skills needed to run an American–style campaign.

Labor's victory raised perhaps unrealistic expectations for a fast, successful conclusion to the Arab-Israeli peace talks which began in October 1991. Although during its negotiations with Syria the government had raised the possibility of withdrawing from the Golan Heights, on 25 October Rabin said in the interest of security any withdrawal would be partial. On 1 November, Israel and Jordan agreed in writing that they would ultimately seek a formal peace treaty.

Throughout 1992, tensions were high along the Lebanese border. On 16 February, Israeli special forces killed the leader of the fundamentalist, pro–Iranian Party of God, Sheik Abbas Musawi, in southern Lebanon. The attack led to several days of gun battles. In December, Israel drew international rebuke for deporting from the West Bank and Gaza to Southern Lebanon, more than 400 Muslim extremists accused of having terrorist links.

Political Rights and Civil Liberties: Israelis can change their government democratically. Parties representing Arabs and far-right Jewish groups hold seats in parliament, although the extremist Kach party of the late Rabbi Meir Kahane, and an offshoot, the Kahane Lives party, are banned under a 1988 law outlawing racist parties.The declaration of independence describes Israel as a Jewish state that respects the rights of minorities.

The judiciary is independent from the government. Security cases can be tried by a military court and closed to the public, and the Shin Bet security force is accused of practicing psychological and physical torture against Arabs and Arab sympathizers.

The diverse press features over 600 privately-owned publications in several languages, many of which are critical of the government. However, articles considered to be dealing with security matters must be cleared by a military censor. On 1 December, the government revoked the press credentials of two foreign journalists and reprimanded four others for failing to submit articles about a November military training accident to a military censor. Television and radio are state-owned, but have independent editorial boards.

The Labor–led government, which has ignored violations of the law prohibiting contact with the PLO, asked parliament on 2 December to repeal the ban. Earlier in the year Abie Nathan was freed after spending almost six months in prison for meeting with PLO leader Yasser Arafat. It is also illegal to display Palestinian flags or express open support for the Palestinian Liberation Organization (PLO).

All faiths are permitted to practice freely, and each religious community has authority over marriage and conversion. Citizens are permitted to travel freely abroad and internally, except in areas that may be under emergency regulations. Arabs claim discrimination in receiving municipal funds as well as education and housing outlays, and as they are not subject to the draft, are at a disadvantage in obtaining various subsidies linked to military service. Prime Minister Rabin has promised that the government would try to close the "substantial gap between the Jewish and Arab communities in a number of spheres." Workers are free to strike and organize in unions of their choice. Some 80 percent of the workforce are members of unions linked to Histadrut (General Federation of Labor).

Italy

Polity: Parliamentary democracy
Economy: Capitalist-statist
Population: 58,026,000
PPP: $13,608
Life Expectancy: 76.0
Ethnic Groups: Italian (Latin), various immigrant groups, and a small Austro-German minority

Political Rights: 1
Civil Liberties: 2
Status: Free

Overview: An inconclusive general election, the poor economy, and rising Mafia violence were the major developments in 1992. Modern Italian history dates from the nineteenth century movement for national unification. Most of Italy had merged into one kingdom by 1870. Italy began World War I on the side of Germany and Austria-Hungary, but switched to the Allied side. As a consequence, Italy won territory that had belonged to Austria. The country lived under the fascist dictatorship of Benito Mussolini from 1922 to 1943. A referendum in 1946 ended the monarchy and brought in a republican form of government.

Since the abolition of the monarchy, the head of state has been a largely ceremonial president, who is elected for a seven-year term by an assembly of members of Parliament and delegates from the Regional Councils. The president chooses the prime minister, who is often, but not always, a member of the largest party in the Chamber of Deputies, the lower house of Parliament. Members of the 630-member Chamber are elected directly by proportional representation for a term of up to five years. There are 315 Senators elected regionally for five-year terms. The President can appoint five Senators for life and becomes one himself upon leaving office.

Italians used the national elections in April 1992 to cast protest votes against mounting political corruption. For example, a major scandal emerged in Milan implicating many associates of former Prime Minister Bettino Craxi, leader of the Socialist Party. The Milan scandal involved construction companies' giving bribes to public officials in return for contracts. Milan's mayor resigned, and 76 other politicians came under investigation. By December, Craxi himself was in trouble for allegedly taking illegal contributions for party funds.

The collapse of communism since the previous general election also affected the vote. The Christian Democrats, long Italy's dominant party, found their traditional, anti-Communist theme had become irrelevant. Until 1990, the Communists had been the largest opposition group. At a party congress that year, reform Communist leader Achille Occhetto proposed that the party adopt a new name, symbol, and philosophy. In 1991, the party became the Party of the Democratic Left and adopted a tree symbol. Hardliners left the party and started the Communist Refoundation Party.

The party system has been fragmenting along regional lines in recent years. In the North in 1991, five regionalist parties formed a bloc under the leadership of the Lombardy League, which is hostile to the economically backward South. Playing on regional animosities, the Lombardy League won 9 percent of the national vote in 1992, hurting the Christian Democrats, who garnered less than 30 percent of the vote for the first time since 1946. The Socialists also lost ground as a result of the Milan bribery scandal. Other votes went to the Green Party, to La Rete (The Network), a southern, anti-Mafia party, and to 54 different parties and splinter groups backing causes ranging from sex parks to fast lane highways.

A clear sign of voter displeasure was the low voter turnout; only 67 percent, of the electorate voted, down from 81 percent in 1987.

The center-left, four-party coalition (the Christian Democrats, the Socialists, the Liberals, and the Social Democrats) won a majority of seats in the Chamber of Deputies, but the slender 16-seat margin over all other parties made it difficult to pursue significant political or economic reform.

Following the election, Prime Minister Giulio Andreotti and President Francesco Cossiga, both Christian Democrats, resigned, throwing Italy's government into chaos.

According to the Italian constitution, the parliament had 15 days to elect a new president, who would name a new prime minister.

Parliament voted sixteen times before it elected President Oscar Luigi Scalfaro, a Christian Democrat. During the voting, officials had to reform ballot procedures after they discovered that members had cast extra ballots. At one point during the voting, deputies traded blows on the floor of the chamber and threw water balloons at each other. After his election, President Scalfaro appointed Prime Minister Giuliano Amato, a Deputy Leader of the Socialist Party. He reassembled the four-party coalition.

Amato had to deal with severe economic problems that could exclude Italy from European economic integration. The country's deficit is more than double that of other European Community members. By 1992, the country's total debt reached 103 percent of gross domestic product, 40 percent above the maximum allowed by the Maastricht Treaty on European union. Italy has only two years to address the crisis under the treaty. Amato proposed an austerity budget in 1992, consisting of $70 billion in higher taxes and lower social spending. However, waves of sometimes violent strikes and demonstrations in the summer and autumn caused the government to draft a softer plan. Workers and shopkeepers balked at the idea of more expensive health care and less generous pensions. There is also significant political resistance to proposals to privatize some of Italy's nationalized corporations, because the parties fear losing these sources of patronage.

Mafia violence and other crime also plagued Italy in 1992. Before the general election, Mafia gunmen killed Salvo Lima, a major Christian Democrat, in Palermo. The Italian government had designated Giovanni Falcone to head a special anti-Mafia agency, but on 23 May a car bomb killed Falcone, his wife, and three bodyguards. The assassination set off protests and strikes across the country. After Falcone's death, the government proposed new legislation including more protection for mobsters who give evidence against organized crime, tougher requirements for grants of house arrest, and lengthening the time allowed for investigation before requiring the case be dropped or charges brought.

On 19 July, an explosive killed Paolo Borsellino, the chief prosecutor who was in line to succeed Falcone. "Democracy does not reign in this city," said Palermo's Mayor Aldo Rizzo. The government responded to Borsellino's death by moving 55 Mafiosi from Palermo prisons to an island off the Tuscany coast. On 25 July, the government deployed 7,000 troops to Sicily. Two days later, gunmen killed Giovanni Lizzio, a top anti-Mafia investigator. Lizzio had pursued criminals in Catania, Sicily's second largest city.

The Mafia is responsible for an estimated one-third of the annual homicides in Italy. In November and December, authorities arrested and indicted hundreds of people in anti-Mafia sweeps.

Political Rights and Civil Liberties:

Italians have the right to change their government democratically. However, Italy often gets a new cabinet between elections as a result of the shifting pattern of political deals rather than as a consequence of changing public opinion. There is freedom of political organization, but Mussolini's Fascist movement was outlawed. Elections at the national, regional, and local levels are competitive. There is some friction between the Italians and the Austro-German minority in the northern area of Alto Adige, which was part of the Austro-Hungarian Empire until World War I. The media are generally free and independent, but there are some minor restrictions on the press in the areas of obscenity and defamation. There are both public and private broadcasting companies.

The Italian court system is notoriously slow for criminal cases, divorces, and everything else. The government instituted trial reform in 1989 with the hope of getting speedier justice.

Italians have freedom of association. There are competing labor federations with differing ideological orientations. In 1991, the left-wing General Confederation of Italian Labor (CGIL) broke its ties with the former Communists. Since several episodes of friction between Italians and foreign workers in 1989, pressure has grown to control immigration. A new edict in 1992 allows authorities to expel foreigners accused of serious crime. Human rights groups complained that the edict created a separate and summary justice for foreigners. In 1992, Italy had prepared for an influx of more than 60,000 refugees from the former Yugoslavia, but considerably fewer arrived. During 1992, right-wing extremists vandalized Jewish propery and cemeteries. In November, they clashed with Jewish youth on Roman streets.

There is freedom of religion. Although the Catholic Church is still the dominant one, it is no longer the state church. Italians who do not evade the income tax can designate contributions to churches on their tax forms.

Ivory Coast

Polity: Dominant party
Economy: Capitalist
Population: 12,951,000
PPP: $1,381
Life Expectancy: 53.4
Ethnic Groups: Baule (23 percent), Bete (18 percent), Senufo (15 percent), Malinke (11 percent), over 60 tribes

Political Rights: 6
Civil Liberties: 4
Status: Partly Free

Overview:
Two years after holding muti-party presidential and legislative elections that were widely believed to have been rigged, President Félix Houphouët-Boigny continued to crack down on opposition protesters.

A former French colony, Ivory Coast achieved independence in 1959. Houphouët-Boigny has ruled since independence under the banner of the Democratic Party of the Ivory Coast (PDCI).

In response to large anti-government demonstrations in early 1990, the president authorized the creation of other political parties. He also had the National Assembly create the post of prime minister, to which he appointed former Central Bank head Alassane Dramane Ouattara. Ouattara immediately reduced the number of government ministries and replaced several aging presidential loyalists with technocrats. He also began implementing austerity measures as part of a structural adjustment program. However, the government has refused International Monetary Fund calls to cut in civil-servant salaries and end of price supports for the country's major export crops of cacao and coffee.

One of the first of more than 25 new parties to register in 1990 was the Ivorian Popular Front (FPI), led by Laurent Gbagbo, one of Houphouët-Boigny's most persistent and outspoken critics. In October 1990, Gbagbo ran against Houphouët-Boigny in the first multi-party election since independence. Gbagbo officially received only 20 percent of votes cast, but the balloting was marred by electoral fraud on behalf of the PDCI. In the face of opposition charges of rigging, the regime admitted that the elections were "poorly organized." Elections for the 175-member National Assembly in November were similarly marred by charges of vote-rigging. The PDCI won 163 seats, the FPI 9 and the Ivorian Workers' Party one, along with 2 independents.

In the midst of anti–government student demonstrations in May and June 1991, government troops brutally disrupted a student assembly held in a stadium. The troops turned out the lights, stormed the structure, beat many students, and raped at least three of the women present. In response to strong public outcry, the president appointed a commission of inquiry.

Reporting back to him on 29 January 1992, the commission recommended that the rapists and the army commander who ordered the attack be punished. However, Houphouët-Boigny ignored the commission's recommendation, stating that the army commander was "doing his job" and that his actions were "best for the country." The president's response precipitated days of protest and arson by angry students. Security police arrested student leaders and attempted to disperse the demonstrators with grenades, tear gas, and billy clubs.

During an officially authorized protest march organized by the opposition on 18 February, a group of rioters split off from the marchers and attacked cars, shops, and the main courthouse. Scores of people were injured as the police struck back against the violent protesters, but the arrested included many peaceful demonstrators and even some who had not participated in the march. Laurent Gbagbo of the FPI, the president of the Ivorian League of Human Rights, a prominent student leader and a number of others were detained. Most were prosecuted on the basis of a law hurriedly promulgated and backdated to the day before the march, which held protest organizers criminally liable for the violent acts of others during a demonstration. Gbagbo and the others were fined and sentenced to one to three years in prison.

Houphouët–Boigny and Prime Minister Ouattara dismissed the international outcry that greeted the judgments. When it appeared that the appeals court judge might reverse the convictions of Gbagbo and other appellants, the justice minister dismissed a jurist from the case. By avoiding an acquittal, the stage was set for Houphouët–Boigny to demonstrate magnanimous treatment of his law–breaking political opposition. On 30 July the PDCI-dominated National Assembly passed a bill both granting amnesty to the imprisoned opponents of the regime and giving immunity to soldiers accused of human rights abuses. Gbagbo and other political prisoners were released within a few days.

After the 1990 election, Gbagbo had called for a power-sharing agreement with the PDCI. More recently, the FPI has called for the resignation of Ouattara and the formation of a transition government to draw up a new constitution and fix a date for new election. Ouattara rejected the proposals in August 1992. In late December 1992, fifteen opposition political parties united in the Union of Democratic forces alliance.

Political Rights and Civil Liberties: Ivorians cannot change their government democratically. In 1990 Ivory Coast held its first multi–party presidential and legislative elections, but they were widely believed to be rigged by the Houphouët–Boigny regime, which has ruled since 1960.

The nominally independent judicial system is generally fair in ordinary criminal cases, but it usually follows the lead of the government in cases involving "national security." In 1992, political prisoners were held in police custody without charge beyond the lawful 96-hour limit. Whatever the evidence of an offense may be, the president has the right to determine whether or not to charge someone with a crime. In rural areas, justice is still administered at the village level through the traditional forum of debate.

Radio and television are state–controlled, and criticism of the regime in the official media is rare. Private newspapers were allowed to circulate after the authorization of opposition parties in 1990. In late 1991, the president appointed a commission "for the transparency and the pluralism of the press," a group with the power to make unannounced visits to press enterprises and impose random fines. In January 1992, all copies of two opposition newspapers were seized, and their publishers were prosecuted and sentenced to 18 months imprisonment, for "offending the head of state." They were pardoned along with two other imprisoned journalists in July.

Although freedom of assembly is guaranteed in the constitution, the right can be suspended at will by the authorities. In 1992, peaceful demonstrations were broken up by security police. During the first week in October, rallies by the unemployed and opposition partisans were dispersed by security police soon after the regime banned all public demonstrations. In July 1992, an "anti-vandalism" law was adopted that provides for 5 to 20 years imprisonment and a fine of $40,000 for those convicted of instigating political violence.

Freedom of movement is generally respected, although there are still reports of citizens being harassed at roadblocks. Freedom of religion is respected. With rare exception, women do not enjoy equal rights in practice.

Workers have the right to organize, but almost all union activity takes place within the government–sponsored General Union of Ivory Coast Workers (UGTCI). The university teachers' union is one of the only independent groups. Although the constitution guarantees the right to strike, the UGTCI rarely gives permission to do so.

Jamaica

Polity: Parliamentary democracy
Economy: Capitalist
Population: 2,507,000
PPP: $2,787
Life Expectancy: 73.1
Ethnic Groups: Black majority; mixed race, European and Asian minorities

Political Rights: 2
Civil Liberties: 2
Status: Free

Overview:

Prime Minister Michael Manley, plagued for years by deteriorating health, resigned from politics on 28 March 1992. Following a tempestuous campaign, delegates of the ruling People's National Party (PNP) elected former deputy prime minister P.J. Patterson as his successor.

Jamaica, a member of the British Commonwealth, achieved independence in 1962. It is a parliamentary democracy, with the British monarchy represented by a governor-general. The bicameral parliament consists of a 60-member House of Representatives elected for five years, and a 21-member Senate, with 13 senators appointed by the prime minister and the other 8 by the leader of the parliamentary opposition. Executive authority is invested in the prime minister, who is the leader of the political party commanding a majority in the House.

Since independence, power has alternated between the social democratic PNP and the conservative Jamaica Labour Party (JLP). Manley was prime minister from 1972 to 1980. JLP leader Edward Seaga held the post from 1980 until February 1989 when the JLP was defeated in general elections by the PNP.

The 1989 campaign was marked by a significant reduction in political violence, owing in large part to an Agreement and Declaration on Political Conduct signed by Seaga and Manley, and supported by civic and religious organizations. More than 750 people died in election-related violence in 1980; 13 died in 1989. With 57 percent of the popular vote, the PNP won 44 seats in the House; the JLP took the remaining 16.

In the March 1990 local elections, the PNP won all but one of the twelve disputed municipal councils. Only half of the electorate turned out. Local governments have become increasingly ineffectual over the last decade. The JLP's defeat led to a rift between Seaga and five top JLP officials.

Manley adhered to the program begun by the JLP—deregulation, spending cuts, tax reform, tariff reduction and privatization of state enterprises. But falling income, high inflation, and continuing unemployment problems led to a decline in PNP popularity; its approval rating dropped to less than 25 percent by the time of Manley's resignation.

The battle to succeed Manley was bitterly fought. Polls showed that the leading candidate among party followers was Portia Simpson, the labor minister and an outspoken populist. But the internal election was limited to 3,200 party delegates, who by a 3 to 1 ratio chose Patterson, a low-key moderate who had resigned as deputy prime minister three months earlier because of his involvement in a conflict-of-interest controversy.

Patterson maintained Manley's economic program and by the end of 1992 there were some signs of recovery. Also, the divisions within the PNP appeared to be mending.

The JLP continued to be plagued by internal disputes dating back to 1990. One JLP parliamentarian whom Seaga had expelled from the party crossed the floor to join the PNP in March 1992. In July, the JLP convention was marred by violent incidents and charges of intimidation of delegates.

By the end of 1992, the PNP had rebounded in the opinion polls. But the largest percentage of those polled chose neither party, reflecting increasing disillusion with the performance of both parties. The next general election is due by March 1994.

Political Rights and Civil Liberties: Citizens are able to change their government democratically. Constitutional guarantees regarding the right to free expression, freedom of religion and the right to organize political parties, civic organizations, and labor unions are generally respected. While the JLP and PNP dominate the political scene, there are a number of small parties ranging from left to right. Labor unions are politically influential and have the right to strike.

Newspapers are independent and free of censorship and government control. Journalists occasionally are the targets of intimidation during election campaigns and political gatherings. Broadcast media are largely public but open to pluralistic points of view. For over a decade, public opinion polls have been an integral part of the political process. There is one television station, which is state-owned. However the government has announced it would grant two new broadcast licenses—one for a commercially operated television station and another for an island-wide radio station.

An independent judiciary system is headed by a Supreme Court and includes several magistrate's courts and a Court of Appeal, with final recourse to the Judicial Committee of the Privy Council in London. However, the legal system is slow and inefficient in responding to charges of police brutality and severe prison conditions.

There is a mounting backlog of cases in the judicial system due to a steep increase in violent crime over the last two years (there were over 500 deaths due to violence in the first ten months of 1992), a shortage of court staff at all levels of the system, and a general lack of resources. The Jamaica Council for Human Rights, the country's main human rights organization, reports that allegations of police brutality, including apparent cases of extra-judicial executions, have been on the increase since 1989. Some cases have been successfully prosecuted, with victims receiving court-ordered, monetary reparations, but officers guilty of abuses usually go without punishment and many cases remained unresolved.

In response to the resurgence of gang violence—mostly drug-related but with strong political overtones—the Manley government re-introduced the controversial Suppression of Crime Act in August 1990. The act, first introduced in 1974 but phased out in 1989, gives the security forces sweeping powers of search and arrest. The reinstatement of the anti-crime act was criticized by the Human Rights Council and legal groups who claim it is unconstitutional. In August 1992, Prime Minister Patterson announced that the act was again to be phased out.

Japan

Polity: Parliamentary democracy
Economy: Capitalist
Population: 124,366,000
PPP: $14,311
Life Expectancy: 78.6
Ethnic Groups: Japanese, Korean, and small immigrant groups

Political Rights: 1
Civil Liberties: 2
Status: Free

Overview:

In 1992, the fallout from a major scandal forced Japanese political godfather Shin Kanemaru to resign in disgrace from parliament. The scandal also created a split in the ruling Liberal Democratic Party's (LDP) largest and most influential faction, and prevented the government from taking action on critical issues, including responding to foreign pressure to open up the country's rice market. Most damaging were charges that gangsters had played a role in elevating Noboru Takeshita to the premiership in 1987.

Following its defeat in World War II, Japan adopted an American–drafted constitution, which invested law-making authority in the Diet (parliament) and ended the emperor's divine status. The center-right LDP has controlled the lower house of the Diet and dominated post-war politics since its formation in 1955. The party is split into several factions, which are driven more by influence and patronage than ideology. Top political posts are often rotated among factional leaders. The LDP's main opposition comes from the Social Democratic Party of Japan (SDPJ), which has shed much of its overtly Marxist agenda but has yet to convince voters that it has much of a platform beyond radical pacifism. Smaller centrist parties lack the resources to challenge the LDP.

In the late 1980s, a stock scandal, fallout over an unpopular consumption tax, and the resignation of Prime Minister Sosuke Uno over a sex scandal rocked the government. A vengeful electorate ended the party's majority in the upper House of Councillors for the first time at the 1989 elections, leaving it with only 109 of the 252 seats. (Half of the upper house seats come up for election every three years.) LDP bosses named the obscure Toshiki Kaifu of the party's tiny, unscathed Komoto faction, prime minister in August 1989. The LDP recovered with a solid showing in the February 1990 House of Representatives elections, where it won 275 seats, the SDJP 136, the Komeito party 45, the Communist Party 16, and the Democratic Socialist Party (DSP) 14. However, the party's earlier upper house losses forced it to rely on the Komeito and the DSP to pass legislation.

Kiichi Miyazawa replaced Kaifu in October 1991 after the latter angered party bosses by trying to pass an electoral reform package. Kaifu had wanted to eliminate multiple–seat districts because the high cost of contesting them fosters corruption, but this would have downsized the Diet and caused LDP members to lose seats. Another proposal would have redrawn the districts. The Supreme Court considers the current system "unconstitutional but valid" since some rural seats represent just one-sixth the population as urban ones. The LDP, which draws its core constituency from the countryside, favors the current flawed system.

Miyazawa largely dropped the issue of electoral reform, and instead concentrated on a controversial bill that would allow up to 2,000 Japanese troops to participate in U.N. peacekeeping activities. The SDJP argued this would violate Article Nine of the 1947 constitution, which prohibits the country from developing military forces for anything but a purely defensive role. After several months of parliamentary maneuvering, the bill finally passed in June 1992.

The 26 July upper house elections were centered in the recent peacekeeping vote and economic problems, including tight bank credit, falling land values and stock market prices well off their December 1989 peak. Paradoxically, a weak economy favors the LDP, because no other party has the credibility or experience to be trusted in a downturn. Although the low 50.8 percent turnout indicated some discontent with the LDP, the party won an impressive 69 seats. The SDPJ and the Japan Communist Party both suffered a net loss in seats, winning only 22 and 6 respectively. Notably, the recently formed New Japan Party, an anti-corruption, centrist opposition group featuring media personality Yuriko Koike, won four seats.

New revelations about long-rumored links between top politicians and a parcel delivery company linked to the *yakuza* (mafia) dominated politics for the remainder of the year. Earlier in the year, Hiroyasu Watanabe, former president of the Sagawa Kyubin delivery company, had told police he had paid $17.2 million to a dozen politicians between 1988 and 1991. On 27 August, MP Shin Kanemaru, who had used his influence to virtually dictate the rise and fall of four prime ministers, admitted he received $4 million in cash from the company in 1990. The 78-year-old Kanemaru quit as LDP vice–chairman and as head of the party's dominant Takeshita faction.

At Watanabe's bribery trial, which began on 22 September, prosecutors charged that Sagawa Kyubin had donated vast sums of money to politicians to secure business favors. They also detailed what had been previously been vague allegations about mafia links, charging that Watanabe had approached gangster head Susumu Ishii in 1987 to silence the right–wing Kominto (Emperor's Subjects) group, which had been protesting Noboru Takeshita's impending election as prime minister. Many speculated that the Kominto had damaging evidence about Takeshita's role in a bank scandal that it threatened to release, and that Kanemaru had been the one who had approached Watanabe on behalf of Takeshita.

On 25 September, Kanemaru mailed prosecutors a formal guilty plea on the charge of having illegally accepted money. Under the deal, he did not have to answer questions about possible mob links and paid only a minor fine.

The public and the media, largely passive spectators to past corruption scandals, reacted with unusual hostility when the mafia links and the prosecutor's deferential treatment of Kanemaru became evident. On 14 October, Kanemaru finally resigned from parliament, leaving the party without a dominant figure and throwing the Takeshita faction into chaos. A series of rancorous meetings were held to name a new faction head, with many members strongly opposed to Kanemaru's protégé Ichiro Ozawa, who is widely disliked for his strongarm tactics. After the faction formally named Keizo Obuchi to the post on 28 October, Finance Minister Tsutomu Hata, a key Ozawa supporter, responded by forming a breakaway "policy study group."

On 11 December, after further revelations, the Takeshita faction formally split into two rival groups. Hours later, Prime Minister Miyazawa named a new cabinet in an apparent effort to deflect attention from the scandal. By year's end, the events had prevented the government from addressing economic problems.

Abroad, new revelations about Japanese atrocities during World War II made closer ties to South Korea and other Asian countries unlikely in the near future. In January, the government admitted that the army had kidnapped and forced tens of thousands of Korean, Chinese and other Asian women to work as "comfort girls" during World War II. Previously, it had maintained that private interests had run the brothels. Relations with Russia deteriorated after President Boris Yeltsin canceled a trip to Japan in September. Yeltsin was to have discussed returning the Kurile Islands, but backed down after facing strong pressure at home from Russian nationalists.

Political Rights and Civil Liberties:

Japanese citizens can change their government democratically. The ruling LDP has stayed in power through its skillful handling of the economy, the lack of a viable opposition, and an electoral system weighted towards rural areas. Of particular concern is the flow of money and patronage that allows top powerbrokers in the party to wield influence over appointments. In addition, the LDP has been accused of paying off opposition members for crucial votes.

The judiciary is independent of the government, and strong procedural safeguards exist for the accused. Freedom of speech and press are respected. The right of association is not infringed. There is complete freedom of religion; Buddhism and Shintoism have the most adherents. Citizens can travel freely domestically and abroad.

The main human rights issue is the discriminatory treatment of minority groups. Members of the 680,000-strong Korean community are not automatically granted citizenship at birth, and must submit to an official background check and adopt Japanese names in order to become citizens. They generally are denied top corporate jobs. Both Koreans and the Burakumin community, who are members of a feudal-era untouchable class, face discrimination in housing and employment.

Women hold a traditionally subservient status, but continue to make inroads in politics and business. In April, in the first successful sexual harassment charge in Japan, a court ruled that a company had violated a woman's rights after lewd remarks by a male employee drove her to quit. Workers, with the exception of police and firefighters, can join independent trade unions. The Japanese Trade Union Confederation (Rengo) represents 8 million workers and is an active force in politics. In October, day-laborers rioted in Osaka to demand emergency relief money. These non-unionized workers have been hardest hit by the business slump.

Jordan

Polity: Monarchy and elected parliament
Economy: Capitalist
Population: 3,400,000
PPP: $2,415
Life Expectancy: 66.9

Political Rights: 3
Civil Liberties: 3
Status: Partly Free

Ethnic Groups: Palestinian and Bedouin Arabs, small minorities of Circassians, Armenians, and Kurds

Overview:

In 1992, Jordan's King Hussein, who marked his fortieth year on the throne, continued a modest liberalization process that began in 1989 with the country's first parliamentary elections in 22 years. During the year, the King abolished the last remnants of martial law and legalized political parties. However further political openings could be stalled by fears of Islamic fundamentalists taking power through the democratic process.

Under the 1952 constitution, the King can dissolve parliament, form and dismiss governments, and make major policy decisions. The parliament consists of a Senate appointed by the King, and an 80-member lower house last elected in 1989. That election gave Muslim fundamentalists 32 seats, conservative and tribal clan groups 17, and leftists and Arab nationalists 11, with 20 others representing designated minority groups.

In April 1992, the King abolished the last remnants of martial law, in effect since 1967. On 5 July, the parliament, with the King's approval, formally legalized political parties after a 36-year ban. The parties will be allowed to take part in parliamentary elections scheduled for 1993. The King is depending on the development of secular parties to counter the influence of religious groups such as the Muslim Brotherhood.

In the summer, the parliament showed its new influence by handling a pair of corruption cases for the first time in its 66-year history. On 4 August, the Lower House indicted a former minister, and fell only a few votes short of sending ex-prime minister Zaid Rifai to trial. The debates in the Lower House were open to the press, and state-run television aired parts of the meeting.

On 11 August, the King celebrated his fortieth anniversary on the throne. Later in the month the 57-year-old Hussein underwent surgery, causing anxiety among citizens. Doctors removed both his kidney and ureter after tests showed malignant cancer cells.

Soon after the King's surgery, the government arrested a number of armed Muslim fundamentalists reportedly belonging to *Shabab al-Nafir al-Islami* (Vanguard of Muslim Youth). Remarkably, they included two Parliamentary deputies, Yaqoob Qarrash and Leith Shubeliat, who were accused of possessing explosives and attempting to topple Hussein. The first sedition case against lawmakers in the country's history began on 8 September. Two merchants also on trial testified that they received arms and explosives from Qarrash, whom they called the leader of the organization. Both Qarrash and Shubeliat were sentenced to 20 years in prison.

The country is still facing significant economic and diplomatic problems stemming from the Gulf War. After Iraq invaded Kuwait in August 1990, King Hussein tried to maintain a position of neutrality by both condemning the invasion and assailing the Western military presence in Saudi Arabia. Attempting to retain his long-time influence with the United States, King Hussein agreed to abide by the international embargo against Iraq, but he maintained ties with Iraqi President Saddam Hussein and allowed some goods to flow to Iraq through Jordan.

Since the war ended, the country has repeatedly denied charges that it has violated the U.N. sanctions, but it admitted that smuggling took place despite its precautions. The economy, which is already saddled with debts of $8 billion, has clearly been hurt by the loss of most of its trade with Iraq.

In 1992, Jordan attempted to appease the United States by being the first Arab country to accept the American invitation to a new round of peace talks with Israel in Washington. The government, defying opposition from the Muslim Brotherhood and other domestic opponents of the talks, remains determined to continue participating in the process with the hope of making gains on water rights, refugees, the environment and disarmament.

The Gulf War severely intensified an already acute economic crisis. During the war, some 275,000 Palestinians holding Jordanian passports were deported to Jordan from Iraq and Kuwait, along with thousands of other nationals who fled as refugees. This influx has boosted the unemployment rate to 83 percent among refugees, and approximately 25 percent among the entire population, and increased rental costs nationwide by 50 percent. A deteriorating standard of living has left about one million Jordanians living below the poverty line, with upwards of 150,000 unable to meet basic needs.

Political Rights and Civil Liberties: Although parliamentary elections were held in 1989, ultimate power remains in the hands of King Hussein. The King can essentially block any constitutional change, because he appoints the Senate, which along with the elected lower house must approve constitutional amendments with a two-thirds majority. The June 1991 National Charter outlined a commitment to democratic rights and freedoms, but also underscored the ultimate power of the monarchy. Political parties are now free to organize as long as they do not receive funding from abroad. Approximately 50 parties have already formed.

The country has one of the better human rights records among Arab countries, but minor abuses continue to occur. Physical abuse of detainees and prisoners has been drastically reduced during the past several years. The practice of detention without charge has decreased since 1989. The court system is in the process of change—martial law courts are scheduled to be phased out for civilian matters, and most other cases have been assigned to the civilian courts.

The government has stopped direct censorship of the media, and opposition journals and foreign newspapers circulate freely. However, *Al-Ribat*, a weekly publication of the Muslim Brotherhood published outside Jordan, has not yet received official recognition inside the country, and the government banned the February issue because it reportedly "slandered some Arab leaders." The government still owns over 50 percent of each of the four main newspapers, which offer mostly government views.

Citizens now freely criticize the government. The government has also allowed banned writers to resume their work. Public demonstrations require permits, which have been routinely granted since 1989. Islam is the state religion and 90 percent of Jordanians are Muslims. The government adheres to the constitutional guarantee of freedom of worship and most religions experience no restrictions on their practice. Religious sects must be registered and recognized by the government in order to manage property and administer schools. The only sect that is not recognized is the Bahai sect.

There are no restrictions on movement except in military areas. Married women must have written approval of their husbands to travel. The government has ended the practice of withholding passports for political reasons and has returned all confiscated passports to political dissidents. All Palestinians who came to the country after 1948 have full citizenship, and enjoy unrestricted rights to work and own property. Trade unions are independent of the government, and all workers, except foreigners, have the right to join. Strikes are legal only after arbitration efforts fail.

Kazakhstan

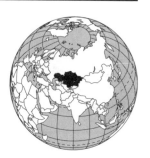

Polity: Dominant party
Economy: Statist
transitional
Population: 16,947,000
PPP: na
Life Expectancy: 70.0
Ethnic Groups: Russian (40 percent), Kazakh (36 percent), Ukrainian (6 percent), others (17 percent)

Political Rights: 5
Civil Liberties: 5
Status: Partly Free

Overview: Economic reform, maintaining social peace in a multi-ethnic country, drafting a new constitution, and the status of strategic nuclear missiles were among major issues facing President Nursultan Nazarbaev in 1992.

Kazakhstan is the second-largest former Soviet republic, stretching from the Caspian Sea east to the Chinese border.

President Nazarbaev, a former member of the Soviet Politburo and former first secretary of the Kazakhstan Communist Party, became Kazakhstan's first directly elected president on 1 December 1991, getting a reported 99 percent of the vote. Later in the month, with the demise of the Soviet Union, Kazakhstan declared its independence. It subsequently joined the Commonwealth of Independent States (CIS), a loose confederation of former Soviet republics. The unicameral, 358-member Supreme Council (legislature) was elected in April 1990, with 338 deputies belonging to Nazarbaev's Communist (subsequently Socialist) Party. The Azat (Freedom) Party is the largest non-Communist party.

Ethnic Kazakhs, descendants of a Turkic-speaking nomad people, constitute only 40 percent of the population, and there are substantial Russian and

Ukrainian minorities. In October 1991, a Popular Congress of Kazakhstan was established in Alma-Ata to unite various independent groups. Its aim was to act as a coalition bloc of differing ethnic and political groups, united in their aim to work for the establishment of a tolerant society, and offering a counterbalance to the Socialist Party. Among those represented were Nevada-Semipalatinsk, a popular environmental group; Azat; the Russian Edinstvo (Unity) group; and the Kazakh Language League.

In 1992, under Nazarbaev's leadership, Kazakhstan managed to remain an oasis of relative tolerance and stability in a troubled region, where conflicts had flared up in the Caucuses, Tajikistan and Uzbekistan. Legislation was adopted granting citizenship to all residents and stressing the importance of treating all ethnic groups equally.

Several Kazakh nationalist parties enjoyed a limited popular support. In October, three nationalist parties, including Alash and Jeltoqsan, combined to form a Republican Party, calling for a "complete decolonization of the republic." In November, the Supreme Court refused to re-register Edinstvo, which had been demanding that Russian be given the status of an official language. In July, Kazakh had been declared the only official language, but Russian was recognized as the language of "international communication."

In 1992, the revival of Islam, which had begun in the late 1980s after social constraints were loosened by Soviet President Mikhail Gorbachev's policy of glasnost, continued. The number of religious communities and worshippers attending services increased considerably. Support for Muslim fundamentalism was limited, however. In February, President Nazarbaev stated that Kazakhstan and Russia should do anything to prevent the rise of Iranian-style fundamentalism in Central Asia. The following month, members of the radical Islamic Alash Party were put on trial for assaulting Mufti Ratbek Nysambaev, whom they accused of being a KGB agent.

In political issues, a key concern in 1992 was the adoption of a constitution. On 2 June, a draft of a new document was adopted by the Supreme Council. In subsequent months, approximately three million people participated in public constitutional discussions organized by the government, and some 18,000 proposals were introduced to the Constitutional Commission headed by President Nazarbaev. In November, a national conference on the constitution was held in Alma-Ata, reviewing the proposals. In December, the parliament began the final debate on ratification, which had not been completed by year's end.

On the economic front, Kazakhstan made some progress in privatizing small businesses and housing in 1992. The breakdown of the central command system, and high levels of inflation triggered a large decline in economic output. Large reserves of petroleum in the Caspian oil basin attracted several foreign oil companies, which signed contracts to invest $40 billion over the next forty years. The U.S.-based Chevron Oil Company signed a contract on 18 May. There were no plans to privatize land, which the president claimed would inevitably trigger "disagreements."

Kazakhstan is one of four former Soviet republics where nuclear missiles were deployed. Following the dissolution of the Soviet Union, 104 of those missiles still remained in place. In December 1991, the leaders of the four—Ukraine, Russia, Belarus and Kazakhstan—renounced the use of nuclear weapons and agreed to a single command structure. In February 1992, a schedule for the dismantling of nuclear weapons in Kazakhstan was agreed upon, a process that was to be completed by 1999. In March, there was international concern over reports that nuclear missiles from Kazakhstan had been smuggled to Iran, an allegation angrily denied by Kazakh officials. On 15 May, a collective security agreement among the four ex-republics was signed, specifying Russian security guarantees for Kazakhstan and the other republics in case of aggression.

Political Rights and Civil Liberties: During 1990 legislative elections to the republic's Supreme Council (parliament), the opposition had limited means to put their candidates on the ballot. Most of the parliament's members were former Communists who became members of the newly established Socialist Party, or decided not to have any party affiliation. Outside of parliament, there are more than 120 smaller parties. Religious parties are disallowed, although two nationalist Kazakh parties that stress Islamic values are tolerated outside the legal framework. New parliamentary elections are scheduled for 1993, following the adoption of new constitution. In the presidential elections of December 1991, the law stipulated that prospective candidates needed to collect 100,000 signatures in a short pre-election period, thus allowing Nazarbaev to run unopposed.

There were no serious inter-ethnic tensions in 1992. Newly passed laws forbid discrimination based on ethnicity, religion, or language.

Press freedom is largely unrestricted, with some 450 publications published in Kazakh, Russian and other languages offering divergent points of view. Besides the government-controlled radio and television, two private television stations existed in the capital.

Freedom of association is generally respected, although organizations opposed to independence or inciting interethnic tensions are refused registration, as was the case with the Russian Edinstvo. There are no serious restrictions on freedom of religion. Domestic and international travel are also largely unrestricted.

There are several trade unions, including the Independent Trade Union Center (ITUC) with twelve member unions, one of which is the powerful coal miners' union of Karaganda, which staged several small strikes in 1991. Unions lobby the government and educate the public on labor issues.

Kenya

Polity: Dominant-party
Economy: Capitalist
Population: 26,164,000
PPP: $1,023
Life Expectancy: 59.7
Ethnic Groups: Kikuyu (21 percent), Luhya (14 percent), Luo
(13 percent), Kalenjin (11 percent), Somali (2 percent), other

Political Rights: 4
Civil Liberties: 5
Status: Partly Free

Overview:
Kenya held its first multi-party elections in 26 years on
29 December 1992. President Daniel arap Moi, who
ended the ruling Kenya African National Union's
(KANU) one-party monopoly the year before, won the presidential election, while
KANU took a majority of the parliamentary seats. International observers said the
vote was marred by fraud.

Kenya is a multi-ethnic country bordering on the Indian Ocean and Lake Victoria
in East Africa. In 1978, President Daniel Teroitich arap Moi took office after the
death of the country's first president, Jomo Kenyatta. Arap Moi heads KANU, formed
in 1969 and established by constitutional amendment in 1982 as the only legal party.
The unicameral National Assembly, whose 200 representatives have been KANU
members, re-appointed arap Moi to successive five-year terms in 1983 and 1988.
Arap Moi's political power is based on alliances with various provincial barons and
an inner circle that consists primarily of his own minority Kalenjin ethnic group.

Until December 1991, the regime firmly rejected calls for multi-party democracy.
Officials warned citizens who called for political change against "straying into politics,"
which a government minister asserted ought to be left to those who have received a
"mandate from the public" in the one-party elections. The regime often went beyond
issuing warnings to clamping down on dissenters through repeated arrest and detention.

Following more than 20 years of one-party rule, on 2 December 1991 President
arap Moi announced the end of the KANU's legal monopoly on power. The move
came days after Western governments, in an unprecedented move in Paris, decided to
condition any additional aid to clear evidence of political reform. The U.S. announced
it had planned to give Kenya $47 million in economic and social assistance in 1992,
but would instead only grant $9 million to non-government humanitarian agencies.

The multi-party constitution became effective on 20 December 1991. The
president refused to indicate when he would schedule elections, calling the element of
surprise his "secret weapon." The President also marshalled the support of the
country's civil servants, ordering them to serve KANU's interests in the coming
electoral campaign. During the following months, the opposition repeatedly complained
that public officials refused permits to hold opposition rallies, closed down opposition
campaign offices, only registered KANU supporters to vote, and denied the opposition
access to the state-owned broadcast media. The opposition also condemned the
president's hand-picked electoral commission as biased. During the campaign period,
unknown attackers assaulted opposition officials and ransacked their offices.

During the year several factors threatened to delay the vote. In early January, rumors spread that arap Moi intended to foment inter-communal conflict as an excuse to use the military to pacify the country. In this way, a suspension of the constitution would mean that the president would not have to face electors. Authorities briefly detained four prominent opposition figures for allegedly fanning the rumor. On 18 January, Nairobi was the scene of an opposition rally attended by 150,000 people, reputedly the largest crowd since independence in 1963.

In March 1992, ethnic clashes in the Rift Valley of western Kenya erupted; gangs of Kalenjin attacked ethnic Luo and Kikuyu residents. Kalenjins were attacked in Nairobi in sporadic reprisals. Before opposition parties were legalized, the regime had asserted that anything but a one-party system would cause social fragmentation along ethnic lines, threatening Kenyan national stability. Thousands of people fled their homes and hundreds were killed during the following months as the skirmishes continued. The opposition charged KANU officials were orchestrating the inter-ethnic violence. The regime responded by variously blaming "Communists," foreign governments, the opposition, and tribal land disputes for the trouble.

Despite these difficulties, on 28 October arap Moi dissolved Parliament in preparation for elections. The election was first scheduled for 7 December, but it was later postponed until 29 December when the High Court granted the opposition more time to prepare. The Court charged that arap Moi's attorney-general had illegally tried to shorten the campaign period to favor the better-organized KANU.

The main opposition parties contesting the vote were the small Democratic Party and the two parties that arose from the larger but fractured Forum for the Restoration of Democracy (FORD). An intra-party struggle in August and September for control of FORD party offices precipitated the party's split. Oginga Odinga, an early Kenyan nationalist leader and an ethnic Luo, led one faction; Kenneth Matiba, a former member of Parliament, recent political prisoner, and an ethnic Kikuyu, led the other. The division of FORD into Odinga's FORD-Kenya and Matiba's FORD-Asili became final in mid October.

The 29 December elections were marked by widespread irregularities. Arap Moi won with 36.7 percent of the vote, while Kenneth Matiba obtained 28 percent, Oginga Odinga 17 percent, and Mwai Kibaki 16 percent. KANU won 95 of 188 parliamentary seats, with arap Moi allowed by law to appoint 12 more seats. Though the opposition claimed fraud and intimidation, both domestic and international monitoring groups did not endorse new elections.

A regional drought struck Kenya in 1992. Hundreds of thousands of refugees fleeing war and famine in Somalia, Sudan, and Ethiopia inundated the country.

Political Rights and Civil Liberties: Despite President Daniel arap Moi's December 1991 decision to legalize opposition parties, Kenyans cannot change their government democratically. A constitutional amendment allows the president to form a cabinet from his party even if that party won less than a majority of seats in the Kenyan parliament.

Even dissident members of the ruling party have frequently been subject to suspension and imprisonment; arap Moi has stated that the concept of a "constructive opposition" is foreign to Africa. Freedom of assembly for political purposes remains constrained by use of the Public Order Act. The president banned political meetings for two weeks in late March 1992, using growing inter-ethnic conflict as his pretext. Those attending unauthorized meetings are subject to beatings and arrest by the police.

In early March 1992 baton-wielding riot troops forcibly drove 20 women from a Nairobi park to break up their public hunger-strike in sympathy with political prisoners.

The independence of the judiciary is now theoretically greater because the president surrendered power to appoint and fire judges to a special panel in 1991. However, the panel consists of members answerable to the president. Kenyan courts have regularly rejected affidavits filed on behalf of jailed dissidents alleging torture and other ill-treatment by the Directorate of State Security Intelligence. The Preservation of Public Security Act allows for the unlimited detention of suspects in political cases.

The law forbids expression that tends to "excite disaffection against the Government of Kenya." In 1992, the government continued its campaign of harassment against *Society, Financial Review,* and other anti-KANU periodicals, pressuring private printers to refuse to print the periodicals, confiscating issues deemed objectionable, and charging editors with sedition. The government controls television and radio, which reflect official positions and policy. The regime has pressured the media not to cover opposition party activities. Journalists have been beaten at the scene of a number of news events.

Religious denominations need government approval to operate in the country. Authorities have frequently harassed and restricted the activities of Protestant churches and implicitly threatened the lives of ecclesiastics active in opposition politics. The leadership of the Central Organization of Trade Unions (COTU), the only legally recognized federation, has close ties with the arap Moi regime. At the end of December 1991, sixteen unions split off from COTU and announced the formation of the independent National Congress of Trade Unions.

Kiribati

Polity: Parliamentary democracy
Economy: Capitalist-statist
Population: 75,000
PPP: na
Life Expectancy: 54.0
Ethnic Groups: Kiribatian (Micronesian, 84 percent), Polynesian (14 percent), other (2 percent)

Political Rights: 1
Civil Liberties: 2
Status: Free

Overview: Formerly the Gilbert Islands, the Republic of Kirabati consists of 33 islands with a total land area smaller than New York City, scattered over 2 million square miles of the Pacific Ocean. It has been an independent member of the British Commonwealth since it gained independence in July 1979.

The unicameral parliament is composed of 35 members elected directly from 23 constituencies, along with a representative nominated from the Banaba Island community by the Banaban Rabi Council of Leaders. Parliamentary elections are held every four years. The President, a member of parliament, is directly elected from a list of three to four candidates nominated by the parliament. Local Island Councils are established on all inhabited islands. Politics are generally conducted on a personal rather than political level, although three parties exist—the ruling National Progressive Party, the Christian Democratic Party, and the United Kirabati Party. The president is limited to three terms, so Iremia Tabai, who had been president since independence, stepped down in 1991 and was succeeded by Teato Teannaki, who won the July 1991 presidential election.

The economy is supported through fishing, copra production, and farming. Several countries, most notably Britain and Japan, have recently attempted to modernize and develop the fishing industry, which is critical to the country's economic future. License fees from countries that fish in its waters provide a major source of revenue. In October 1992 Kirabati joined several island nations in signing an agreement controlling outside access to regional fishing zones. The government has pledged to help the 400 residents of Banaba Island—whose economic development came to a standstill after phosphate mining ended there in 1979—to modernize their agricultural and fishing methods.

Political Rights and Civil Liberties: The citizens of Kirabati can change their government democratically. Political parties play a relatively minor role, and generally coalesce around timely issues. Fundamental rights such as freedom of assembly, press and speech are enumerated in the constitution and respected by the government. The radio station and newspaper are government-run but offer pluralistic viewpoints. The independent judiciary system is modeled on English common law. Freedom of religion is guaranteed by the constitution, and people of all faiths can practice freely. A minor dispute arose a week before the 1991 parliamentary election when the Catholic magazine *Te Itoi Ni Kirabati* ran an editorial asking Catholics to vote for candidates of their own religion, but this had no apparent effect on the election. The constitution does not prohibit discrimination on the basis of sex in Kirabati's traditionally male-dominated society, but women are gaining equal rights in education and entering the workforce in increasing numbers. Workers are free to organize into unions. The Kirabati Trade Union Congress is composed of seven trade unions and has approximately 2,500 members.

Korea, North

Polity: Communist
one-party
Economy: Statist
Population: 22,227,000
PPP: $2,172
Life Expectancy: 70.4
Ethnic Groups: Ethnically homogeneous—Korean

Political Rights: 7
Civil Liberties: 7
Status: Not Free

Overview: In 1992, the trickle of foreign visitors now being allowed
into North Korea reported seeing desperate people in the
countryside foraging for acorns and grass to survive. Even in
the cities, the government now encourages people to live on two meals a day for
"health" reasons. Stalinist leader Marshall Kim Il Sung has grudgingly begun opening
his nuclear facilities to international inspection, a prerequisite to receiving needed
foreign aid.

The Democratic People's Republic of Korea was formally established in September 1948, three years after the partition of the Korean peninsula. Its sole ruler has
been Marshal Kim, the longest-serving head of state in the world, who has created a
cult based largely on his supposed leading role in fighting the Japanese in the 1930s.
Kim's all-encompassing "ideology," *juche* (I myself), stresses national self-reliance and
independence from the vagaries of the market system, and is used to justify the
country's virtual isolation from the rest of world.

The government nurtures a slavish devotion to the Kim family by indoctrination
through the media, the workplace, the military, schools, mass spectacles, cultural
events, and some 35,000 Kim statues and ubiquitous portraits. Despite the dismal
standard of living in this one-party Communist dictatorship, the government repeatedly
tells its citizens, "We have nothing to envy." Eerily, because they know little about
the world beyond the country's borders, many citizens agree.

Juche calls for the "Great Leader" to be succeeded by his son, "Dear Leader"
Kim Jong Il. In December 1991, the ruling Worker's Party elected the younger Kim
to replace his father as Supreme Commander of the military. This breached the
constitutional requirement that the president be the head of the military, and appeared
to be the first stage of the anticipated power transfer.

In a rare interview with the *Washington Times* in April, Kim announced that his
son had assumed day-to-day control of the country. Diplomats say the younger Kim
is unstable, if not a psychotic megalomaniac, and warn of the dangers of his eventually being in charge of a million-man army possibly equipped with nuclear weapons.
However, Kim Jong Il is reportedly unpopular with the military leadership, and could
be sacked soon after his father's death. Despite the country's impoverishment, massive
celebration's were held for Kim Il Sung's 80th birthday on 14 April 1992. To
celebrate, Kim gave himself the additional title of Generalissimo.

During the year, the country came under continued pressure to allow access to its
nuclear facilities. Due to a lack of hard evidence, expert estimates of the country's
nuclear arms capability range from "a few months away" to several years.

This issue is tied to a series of moves between the two Koreas, which have never formally ended their 1950–53 war, towards eventual reunification. On 13 December 1991, the countries agreed to a non-aggression pact, and on 31 December, representatives met at the border compound of Panmunjom in the Demilitarized Zone to sign a pledge to ban nuclear weapons from the peninsula. The two countries also agreed to form a Joint Nuclear Control Commission to inspect potential weapons facilities. The December accords were formally ratified on 19 February 1992, and the countries inaugurated the Joint Commission one month later.

On 9 April, after a six-year delay, the government ratified an agreement allowing inspectors from the IAEA access to the nuclear facilities, including a controversial complex at Yongbyon, which the United States says may be a reprocessing plant capable of producing weapons-grade plutonium. On 15 April, North Korea released a videotape of the Yongbyon plant and, on 4 May, it released a 100-page description of the facility, which it termed a "radiochemical laboratory" for nuclear waste research. It also admitted that it possessed a small amount of plutonium, although not enough for an atomic weapon. In mid-May, the government allowed IAEA director Hans Blix to make a preliminary on-site visit to Yongbyon. Blix later said he found no evidence that the country currently has enough material for a nuclear weapon.

On 7 September, the two Koreas reached an accord on limited cross-border economic exchanges. Their nuclear talks, which are separate from those with the IAEA, remained stalled, largely over the South's demand that either side be able to conduct spontaneous "challenge" inspections. In mid-October, frustrated by a lack of progress in the talks, the U.S. and South Korea agreed to resume planning for their annual military exercises, which had been suspended in January to encourage the negotiations. The North responded by pulling out of the talks, which remained stalled at year's end.

Although foreign access to the country is limited, by most accounts the economic situation is desperate. The government is urging people to eat two meals per day due to a food shortage, and according to various sources, people in the poorest areas survive on acorns, grass and leaves. Electricity shortages are frequent, factories run at 40–50 percent of capacity, and agricultural plowing is often done manually. The U.S., Japan and South Korea say they will continue to withhold investment until the nuclear issue is solved. The South's new diplomatic ties with China only increased the North's isolation.

The government is slowly acknowledging the economic crisis. On 8 April, Finance Minister Yun Ki Jong said that spending would increase in the coming year to "more satisfactorily solve the problems of food, clothing and housing." Although she claimed that military spending accounts for only 11.6 percent of the budget, analysts from the South say that in reality nearly half the budget goes to defense and related industries. To boost output, farmers have been quietly permitted to sell limited amounts of produce at market prices. However, on 29 December, China, North Korea's largest trading partner, announced that all trade would have to be on a cash basis, rather than barter.

Political Rights and Civil Liberties: North Koreans cannot change their government democratically. The Supreme People's Assembly consists of state-approved candidates from the Korean Worker's Party, and has no independent power. Opposition parties are illegal. The country's one-party system is built around the cult of Kim Il Sung, and its citizens are perhaps the most isolated in the world. The slightest effrontery to the Kim family is considered a political offense. The judiciary is completely subserviant to the goverment, and by various estimates some 150,000 or more political prisoners are held in prison camps. Defectors say some political prisoners are "re-educated" and released, while others languish in brutal conditions. Prisoners are reportedly routinely tortured, and the Penal Code provides for capital punishment for a broad spectrum of "crimes against the revolution." Surveillence of the population is routine, apartments are inspected monthly, and citizens, particularly children, are encouraged to be informers.

Freedoms of speech, press and association do not exist. All media are controlled by the government, radios and televisions are pre-tuned to government stations, and foreign media are blocked out to the extent possible. Religion is suppressed; where it exists it is closely controlled by the government. Permission to travel outside one's village is generally denied. Citizens cannot emmigrate and rarely are allowed to leave the country. Free trade unions do not exist, and strikes are prohibited.

Korea, South

Polity: Presidential-parliamentary democracy
Economy: Capitalist-statist
Population: 44,284,000
PPP: $6,117
Life Expectancy: 70.1
Ethnic Groups: Ethnically homogeneous—Korean

Political Rights: 2
Civil Liberties: 3
Status: Free

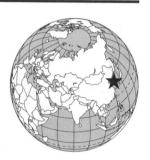

Overview:

Kim Young Sam of the ruling Democratic Liberal Party (DLP) beat opposition leader and longtime rival Kim Dae Jung to win South Korea's December 1992 presidential election. However, the DLP lost its majority at the March parliamentary elections, and throughout the year came under relentless attack from a billionaire businessman who ran for president as a third-party candidate.

The Republic of Korea was formed in August 1948. Under the authoritarian rule of General Park Chung Hee, who took power in a May 1961 coup, the country began a period of intense industrialization. Following Park's assassination in 1979, Chun Doo Hwan led another military-backed government. In June 1987, violent protests rocked the country after Chun picked another army general, Roh Tae Woo, as his successor. On 29 June 1987, Roh announced sweeping reforms, including direct presidential elections and a restoration of civil liberties.

The country's best-known opposition leaders, Kim Young Sam and Kim Dae Jung, both ran in the December 1987 presidential election, allowing Roh to win with just 35.9 percent of the vote. The election left many South Koreans with a lingering anger at "The Two Kims" for squandering the opportunity to end military-backed rule. A revised constitution went into effect in February 1988. The document guaranteed basic rights, and limited the president to a single five-year term and took away his power to dissolve parliament.

In January 1990, Kim Young Sam and another opposition leader, Kim Jong Pil, startled their supporters by merging their parties with the governing Democratic Justice Party. Renamed the DLP, the governing party now controlled 220 of the 299 Assembly seats. The move left Kim Dae Jung as the country's sole opposition leader, and branded Kim Young Sam, who allegedly received assurances that he would be the DLP's presidential candidate in the 1992 elections, as an opportunistic turncoat.

In April 1991, following a weak performance in the first round of the country's first local elections in 30 years, Kim Dae Jung merged his Party for Peace and Democracy with a minor opposition party to form the New Democratic Union. This new party fared poorly in the second round, and Kim merged it with Lee Ki Teak's small Democratic Party, creating a new center-left opposition Democratic Party.

Three separate elections were slated for 1992—for the National Assembly, for mayors and provincial governors, and for the presidency. In January, Chung Ju Yung, the billionaire founder of Hyundai, formed the Unification National Party (UNP). Running a pro-business campaign which threatened to siphon off DLP votes from the right, the 76-year-old Chung claimed the country to be "in a total crisis," citing a 10 percent inflation rate, a growing external debt, as well as widespread corruption.

In calling for the government to stop meddling with the *chaebol* (large industrial conglomerates such as Hyundai), Chung challenged the traditional government–business relationship in which the government controls credit access and often forces restructuring and other measures without compensation. Almost paradoxically, Chung also favored breaking up the chaebol to promote competition. Chung also attacked the not-so-secret corporate practice of funneling money to government election campaigns in return for preferential treatment. In January, he created an uproar by describing the $34 million in "donations" he himself had given to Roh's government for political favors. Following this embarrassing disclosure, the government harrassed Hyundai through tax audits and arrested six top executives.

The 24 March Assembly elections attracted a relatively light 71.9 percent of the electorate, and were marred by allegations of fraud and vote-buying. Several days before the election, four agents of the Agency for National Security Planning were arrested for stuffing mailboxes with anti-opposition literature, and on 22 March an army officer claimed the military may have rigged up to 560,000 absentee ballots. Officers allegedly pressured conscripts into voting for the ruling party, and may have cast some ballots without the soldiers' knowledge.

A total of 1,047 candidates contested the Assembly's 237 directly-elected and 62 proportionately distributed seats. Weakened by Chung's attacks and a slow economy, and facing a unified opposition on the left, the DLP lost its majority, winning 38.5 percent of the vote and taking 149 seats. The Democratic Party won a strong 97 seats, while the surprising UNP took 31, the tiny Party for New Political reform took 1, along with 21 mostly pro-government independents.

In late March, Kim Young Sam and veteran MP Lee Jong Chan formally entered the DLP's presidential primary. As part of his democratic reforms, Roh had earlier decided to throw the nomination open to the party's 6,886 delegates even though he supported Kim. Lee dropped out on 17 May after claiming delegates had been coerced into voting for Kim, who won the party vote two days later running unopposed. Almost immediately, thousands of students hit the streets in Seoul and 20 other cities, calling Kim a traitor for the 1990 merger and claiming the nomination amounted to a continuation of military-backed rule.

In June, the two main opposition parties began boycotting parliament to protest Roh's decision to delay the local elections until at least June 1995, rather than hold them by the end of the month as planned. The president expressed concern over the high cost of holding the elections and worried that political rallies would draw people away from factories and farms. The opposition, pointing to evidence that appointed bureaucrats in these local offices had tampered with presidential elections in the past, said that elected local officals were necessary to keep the December presidential balloting honest. On 12 August, leaders of the three main parties formed a committee to resolve the election dispute and combat electoral fraud.

The corruption issue peaked on 31 August, when a provincial official said DLP officials gave him $109,000 to buy votes prior to the March elections. In an effort to project a clean image and protect his lead in the polls, Kim Young Sam asked Roh to remove the prime minister and name a neutral cabinet to oversee the December presidential vote. These demands angered many DLP MPs, who accuse Kim of arrogance and say he wields too much influence in the party.

On 18 September, President Roh agreed to appoint a neutral cabinet, but in a move which effectively ended his political alliance with Kim, also said he would resign from the DLP to show his neutrality. On 7 October, Roh picked university president Hyun Soong-Jong as prime minister, replaced three other ministers, and asked the rest of the 25-member cabinet to resign from the party. On 10 October, DLP majority-faction head Park Tae Joon quit the party, prompting the defection of several other MPs.

The 18 December presidential vote, the cleanest in the country's history, was the first in three decades in which none of the candidates had a military background. Kim Young Sam received 42 percent, Kim Dae Jung 34 percent, and Chung 15 percent.

In 1992, the government continued to pressure North Korea to allow inspection of its nuclear facilities. In February, the two governments formally signed a non-aggression pact and a pledge to ban nuclear weapons from the Korean peninsula, both of which had been agreed to in December 1991. However, by year's end the nuclear talks were deadlocked over the South's insistence that either side be permitted to make surprise inspections. South Korea established diplomatic relations with China on 24 August.

Political Rights and Civil Liberties: South Koreans can change their government democratically. Despite charges of tampering, there was no evidence of systematic fraud in the March 1992 National Assembly elections.

Personal freedoms have expanded greatly since the 1987 pro-democracy demonstrations, but a number of repressive security measures remain in force. The National Security Law (NSL), which allows the government to detain people who support or cooperate with "antistate" organizations (i.e., North Korea), was amended in 1991 to cover only actions that could knowingly harm society. Thousands of former detainees remain under surveillance. Sixty-two people were arrested under the NSL in September 1992 for setting up an underground Communist party.

Freedoms of speech and of press are generally respected, but the NSL prohibits the reading and discussion of pro-North Korean topics and materials. The Law on Assembly and Demonstrations has been used to prohibit student rallies considered a threat to public order.

Common criminals are frequently abused to extract confessions. The court system is growing increasingly independent of the government, but can still be influenced in political cases. In response to demands for an independent judiciary, the government established a new Constitutional Court in 1988. Although the Court has declared legislation unconstitutional in twenty cases since 1989, it has been slow in rejecting the so-called "evil laws" from the previous authoritarian regime; in April 1990, it ruled the NSL anachronistic but constitutional.

There is complete freedom of religion in the country. Domestic travel is unrestricted, but travel to North Korea is heavily limited despite recent agreements allowing for greater exchanges. Organized labor faces significant restrictions: all unions must be affiliated with either the Federation of Korean Trade Unions or the independent Korean Federation of Clerical and Financial Workers, and teachers and most government workers cannot unionize. Strikes are prohibited in government agencies, state-owned enterprises and defense industries, and are restricted through mandated cooling-off periods in all industries, as well as through government-imposed arbitration in key sectors such as transportation, utilities, and banking.

Kuwait

Polity: Traditional monarchy and limited legislature
Economy: Mixed capitalist-statist
Population: 1,379,000
PPP: $15,984
Life Expectancy: 73.4
Ethnic Groups: Kuwaitis and other Arabs, and various foreign workers

Political Rights: 5
Civil Liberties: 5
Status: Partly Free

Overview:

Opposition candidates won 31 of the 50 seats in Kuwait's October 1992 National Assembly elections, the first vote since the Emir, Sheik Jaber al-Sabah, shut down the parliament in 1986. Strict eligibility requirements for men, and a complete ban on female participation, left only 15 percent of the population eligible to vote.

The al-Sabah dynasty has ruled Kuwait since 1759. Britain handled the emirate's foreign affairs and defense from 1899 until 1961. Under the 1962 constitution, executive power is vested in an emir from the al-Sabah family, who rules through an appointed prime minister and Council of Ministers. The National Assembly, which has only limited powers to initiate and veto legislation, has been a forum for diverse viewpoints over the years. The Emir suspended the Assembly from 1976 to 1981, and again in 1986, after MPs criticized his selection of ministers and called for public inspection of the country's financial records. In response to growing calls for the Assembly's revival, elections were held in June 1990 for 50 seats of a 75-member interim National Council, which was to serve until a new Assembly was elected in 1994.

Calls for greater democracy increased after the August 1990 Iraqi invasion, which many blamed on the government's failure to recognize the threat and prepare for it adequately. In October, while in exile in Saudi Arabia, the Emir agreed to hold elections in 1992 in exchange for support from the opposition. In June 1991, several months after the country's liberation, the Emir reconvened the National Council in advance of elections for a new National Assembly.

In February 1992, voter registration for the October elections took place. Only 92,000 "first-class" males, who were over 21 and could prove their ancestors lived in Kuwait before 1920, were eligible to vote. The Emir broke an earlier pledge that women would be allowed to vote.

The 26 May elections for the Chamber of Commerce and Industry—not normally considered a political affair—foreshadowed the government's disapointing showing at the National Assembly elections. After the al-Sabah family politicized the election by putting its supporters up as candidates, over 11,000 turned out to vote, far more than the approximately 1,500 who had participated in past Chamber elections. Many citizens felt the family wanted to gain control of the Chamber specifically to limit the influence of Board Chairman Abdul Aziz al-Saqr, who favors democratic reforms. Ultimately al-Saqr and his supporters won 23 of the 24 seats.

In the run-up to the National Assembly election, opposition candidates took advantage of the *diwaniyas* (traditional family gatherings held in homes) to campaign. Major issues discussed at the diwaniyas included calls for the restoration of the constitution, controversy over the $24 billion bank bailout plan passed by parliament on 31 March, and continuing fallout over the government's actions regarding the Iraqi threat and subsequent invasion.

Although the 1986 ban on political parties remained in effect, seven informal opposition groups emerged in their place. Six of them favored continuing the emirate in some capacity, but called for the government to be more accountable and politics open to wider participation. Only one group, the radical Islamic Popular Grouping, openly challenged the ruling family's constitutional status as a hereditary emirate.

Roughly 85 percent of the "first-class" males turned out for the 5 October elections, which were contested by 278 candidates running for 50 seats in 25 districts. The opposition took a surprising 31-seat majority, split between 19 candidates linked to Islamic groups and 12 others with generally left-wing views. Most of the candidates who had been on the interim National Council were rejected. However, the new government named by the royal family minimized the opposition's gains. On 13 October, the Emir reappointed his heir, Crown Prince Sheik Saad as prime minister, despite opposition calls for the two offices to be split. On 17 October, Sheik Saad announced a new cabinet with six ministries going to elected MPs, more than ever before; but the Sabah family held on to the key foreign affairs, defense, interior and information posts.

Political Rights and Civil Liberties:

Kuwaiti citizens cannot democratically change their government. The hereditary emirate holds executive powers, and only about 15 percent of the population was eligible to vote in the October 1992 National Assembly elections. Although opposition candidates won

31 of the 50 seats, the emir can suspend the body at any time. The constitution remains suspended, and political parties not allowed.

During the election campaign, opposition groups defied a ban on public rallies and criticized the government despite censorship restrictions. Campaigning was limited, difficult, and costly for the candidates, who were not allowed to use radio or television. Several dozen women marched outside various polling places during the election to protest not being able to vote. In May, the government barred seven opposition groups from holding a "popular conference" on the country's future. The government also ordered the pro-democratic Kuwait Graduate Society to cancel a workshop on democratic participation co-sponsored by the Washington-based International Republican Institute. The group had held a similiar workshop in February.

A major human rights issue has been the treatment of Palestinians, 400,000 of whom have been expelled since the war ended for allegedly supporting Iraq. Several hundred have been put to trial or continue to be detained on collaboration charges. In the first round of trials in 1991, which international groups widely condemned for their harshness, 29 were sentenced to death and 72 were jailed. The death sentences were later changed to life imprisonment. In April 1992, the collaboration trials resumed against 40 more Palestinians. Also facing discrimination are the approximately 200,000 Bidouns, who lack Kuwaiti citizenship. Many were born in Kuwait or have lived in the country for years, but cannot own houses, travel abroad or work for private companies. In addition, Asian women in menial jobs continue to suffer physical abuse from employers, forcing several hundred to take refuge in their embassies.

The judiciary is independent and suspects generally receive fair trials, except in the State Security Courts, which do not provide adequate due process rights. Judges are appointed by the Emir for lifetime tenure and the Justice Ministry rarely exercises its power to remove judges.

Citizens are prohibited from criticizing the Emir, the ruling family, or Islam. The government officially lifted prior censorship on 12 January 1992, and the press has generally been free to express opposition to the government. Radio and television are government-owned and controlled. The Ministry of the Interior must approve any public meeting of more than five people.

Islam is the official religion, but the tiny Arab Christian minority is permitted to practice freely. However, foreign nationals adhering to Eastern religions such as Hinduism cannot build prayer houses.

Citizens can travel freely within the country, but husbands can prevent their wives from leaving the country, and representatives of associations wishing to travel abroad to participate in international meetings must receive permission from the government. Workers have the right to form unions, which are largely independent even though they receive 90 percent of their budgets from government subsidies and are subject to financial oversight by the government. The government can also dissolve unions. The Labor Law requires that before striking workers must submit their grievances to compulsory negotiation.

Kyrgyzstan

Polity: Presidential-par-
liamentary (transitional)
Economy: Statist
transitional
Population: 4,506,000
PPP: na
Life Expectancy: 68.0
Ethnic Groups: Kirgiz (52.3 percent), Russian (21.5 percent),
Uzbek (12.9 percent), Germans, others

Political Rights: 4
Civil Liberties: 2
Status: Partly Free

Overview:
In 1992, this former Soviet republic continued to consolidate democratic gains launched two years earlier under the so-called "silk revolution." President Askar Akaev, a physicist, faced growing economic difficulties, public discontent regarding governmental reorganization, and increased pressure from nationalist parties and Communists, many of whom continued to sit in parliament. Nevertheless, Kyrgyzstan was widely considered the closest to a Western-style democracy in Central Asia.

Like other Soviet republics, Kyrgyzstan (known then as Kirgizia), which borders China and Uzbekistan, declared full independence shortly after the failed coup against Soviet President Mikhail Gorbachev in August 1991. In late 1990, faced with mounting socio-economic and political problems, as well as Kirgiz-Uzbek violence in the Osh region, the republic's Supreme Soviet created the post of president and named Akaev, a liberal reformer, to the office. The same year, several informal associations emerged, the most important being the Kirgiz Democratic Movement, an umbrella group consisting of several opposition organizations.

On 31 August 1991, 12 days after the abortive coup in Moscow, the republic's Supreme Soviet declared Kyrgyzstan's independence from the USSR. On October, President Akaev ran unopposed and was elected president. After the vote, he said he was dismayed that no one was willing to run against him. A spokesman for the Kirgiz Democratic Movement, however, complained the opposition did not have enough time to gather 25,000 signatures needed to register.

In the first half of 1992, President Akaev moved to restructure the government and introduce a draft constitution that called for the appointment of a prime minister by the president. During the first week of January, students had marched in the capital, Bishkek (formerly Frunze), demanding the resignation of ministers and leaders with connections to the former Communist party. Several political parties also called for holding a nationwide referendum on the dissolution of parliament and the holding of new elections of people's deputies. In early February, Erkin Kyrgyzstan, a republican party, began a petition drive aimed at forcing a referendum. The party suggested reducing parliament from the current 350 members to about 120. The referendum was also supported by the newly formed Asaba Party, which backed President Akaev but opposed the presence of old-Party *nomenklatura* in parliament, 90 percent of whose members were former Communist functionaries. By 1 April, however, the campaign was cancelled because it was far short of the required 300,000 signatures.

In February, President Akaev made himself the head of government and halved the number of ministries and departments. Parliament subsequently approved the appointment of Felix Kulov as vice president, whose duties included coordinating the work of law-enforcement bodies and the organization of the national guard and other defense matters. On 2 March, parliament endorsed the new government structure and the new government, which included President Akaev's hand-picked prime minister, Tusunbek Chyngyshev. Two days later, parliament discussed a draft law dividing the power of local administrations. Vice President Kulov said that the country would get stronger executive bodies at the regional, municipal and district levels, and that chief local administrators would be appointed by the president. The presidiums of local soviets (councils) would be dissolved. The soviets would be preserved in villages, cities, districts and regions as representative government bodies authorized to deal with budget formation and taxation, and have the right to vote a measure of no-confidence in chief local administrators by a two-thirds majority.

On 30 June, President Akaev introduced to parliament a draft constitution prepared by the Constitutional Commission. The document stressed national sovereignty, civil liberties and property rights. On the division of powers, the constitution concentrated state power in the executive and "de-Sovietized" the legal system and local administration.

Shortly thereafter, Erkin Kyrgyzstan presented two alternative drafts that called for a parliamentary rather than a presidential republic. The Democratic Movement said the alternative drafts would prevent presidential authority from degenerating into authoritarian rule. During the 24 July Supreme Soviet debate on the constitution, the president came under fierce attack from nationalists and Dzhumgalbek Amanbayev, former leader of the republic's Communist party. With a fragmented democratic opposition, former Communists became more active, leading Kazal Akmatov of the Democratic Movement to warn that "the offended old Party nomenklatura is preparing to put up real opposition to the president and economic reforms." Despite intense lobbying by President Akaev, by year's end, a final constitution had yet to be adopted.

In other issues, the government sought to ameliorate the concerns of ethnic Russians, Germans and other minorities who feared discrimination, particularly in land distribution, in the face of rising Kirgiz nationalism. In early February, President Akaev signed a degree establishing German national districts in the Chu Valley and other areas densely populated by Germans. In March, the government formally legalized formation of two German districts. Problems continued to surface in Osh, site of Kirgiz-Uzbek violence in 1990. In May, leaflets distributed in the predominantly Uzbek region called for holding a referendum linking the territory to Uzbekistan. On 29 May, President Akaev held a roundtable meeting with representatives of various ethnic groups, and expressed concern at the ethnic hostility promulgated in the nationalist press and the growing emigration of Germans and Russians.

In July, the Kyrgyzstan National Renewal Party proposed in the Supreme Soviet that privatization be halted in the state sector because most shares would go to mainly urban, non-Kirgiz citizens. Asaba also demanded that land allotted as private property be given only to ethnic Kirgizians. At an October meeting of the Coordinating Council of the Democratic Movement, a government spokesmen reprimanded nationalists: "You have embarked on a path of counteraction against not only national minorities and the government of Kyrgyzstan, but also the entire people."

As in all former Soviet republics, the principal and most difficult issue in

Kyrgyzstan was balancing economic restructuring and the implementation of free-market reforms with social needs in order to avert popular unrest. In January, following Russia's lead, the government liberalized prices, thus raising the cost of most goods. The move led to student protests demanding grant increases to offset higher costs. In April, the president signed a decree that instructed the government to help enterprises and individuals carry on free trade and ensure the unrestricted traffic of goods. A decree dealing with agrarian reform pledged state support to agriculture to stimulate the production and purchase of the most important categories of agricultural products. The long-term measure envisaged the privatization of state and collective farms as well as other agricultural enterprises, although parliament resisted direct selling of land.

On 4 July, parliament adopted a "shock therapy" program proposed by President Akaev and developed in conjunction with the International Monetary Fund (IMF). The measures, which included strict control of state finances, banking and manufacturing, aimed to stabilize the economy by year's end. The plan included the closing of 200 unprofitable enterprises, privatization of almost half of state-owned property by 1993, and the deregulation on all goods by January 1993 (except bread, flour, gas, electric power and some strategic minerals). In October, President Akaev met with IMF representatives in Bishkek, who approved the economic plan and announced that the country would need at least an annual $300 million over the next 10 years to develop its farming sector, mining and coal industries, as well as oil exploration and production.

In other issues, President Akaev in June announced that Kyrgyzstan would be entitled to all troops and their headquarters stationed on its territory. The forces would report directly to the country's State Defense Committee. The government also sought international assistance in fighting a growing narcotics trade in the country.

Political Rights and Civil Liberties: Citizens have the right to democratically change their government. Political parties are flourishing; several were created in 1992. Citizens are free to express their views. Although a final draft of the constitution has yet to be approved, all envision an independent judiciary with adequate safeguards for defendants. A draft citizenship law, based on a European model of civil society and the rule of law, would grant citizenship to people irrespective of their nationality, race or religion. Freedom of assembly and association are respected in practice.

Rapidly worsening economic conditions have affected the media. The Russian-language daily, *Slovo Kyrgyzstana*, which offered varied commentary both supportive of critical of the president's policies, was forced to reduce distribution. A new press law passed by parliament in August contained several prohibitions. The press was prohibited from inciting violence and ethnic friction, revealing commercial and state secrets, insulting religious feelings, and using offensive language. There were also restrictions on publishing information on ongoing judicial investigations without first obtaining written permission from the state prosecutor's office. In a June meeting with local press, radio and television officials, President Akaev criticized overly nationalistic commentary.

Conscious of the rise of Islamic fundamentalism in the region, President Akaev has repeatedly asserted that he intends to assure a secular state modeled after Turkey. Religious rights are respected for Muslims, Christians, Buddhists and other faiths. There are no significant restrictions on domestic and international travel. Workers are organized in the Kyrgyz Trade Unions Federation.

Laos

Polity: Communist one-party
Economy: Mixed-statist
Population: 4,440,000
PPP: na
Life Expectancy: 49.7
Ethnic Groups: Multi-ethnic—Lao (50 percent), Thai (20 percent), Phoutheung, Miao (Hmong), Tao and others

Political Rights: 7
Civil Liberties: 6
Status: Not Free

Overview: Laotian president Kaysone Phomvihane, a veteran Marxist revolutionary who led the country since the Communist takeover in 1975, died on 21 November 1992. The death of Kaysone, the undisputed head of the Laotian Communist movement since the mid-1950s, creates a serious leadership gap as the ruling Lao People's Revolutionary Party (LPRP) slowly introduces capitalism and continues to suppress any political opposition. Nouhak Phoumsavan succeeded Kaysone as president.

This landlocked, southeast Asian country became a French protectorate in 1893. Following the Japanese occupation during World War II, the Communist Pathet Lao (Land of Lao) fought the returning French, winning complete sovereignty on 23 October 1953. Neutralist, communist and conservative factions formed a coalition government in 1962, but began fighting each other in 1964. In the late 1960s and early 1970s, the United States bombed heavily North Vietnamese and Pathet Lao forces who were fighting the neutralist government led by Souvanna Phouma. In May 1975, the Pathet Lao overran the capital of Vientiane, and established the one-party Lao People's Democratic Republic seven months later.

The LPRP introduced the New Economic Mechanism (NEM) in 1986 to revive an economy decimated by a decade of central planning. Under the NEM, farms have been fully privatized, over 100 out of some 600 state enterprises have been leased or sold, and more than 300 joint ventures have been signed. Despite a severe drought in 1991 that reduced rice output, overall GDP continues to rise. Inflation has dropped sharply since the government reduced credit to unprofitable state enterprises, tightened the money supply and offered higher interest rates for private savings. Although a government ban on logging has reduced foreign earnings, garment manufacturing has provided a growing source of revenue. State Bank governor Pany Yathotou expects inflation to be a modest 7 percent in 1992, and predicts 7 percent GDP growth in 1993. The country is also negotiating new credit from the International Monetary Fund.

Political changes, however, have been minimal. In August 1991, the rubber-stamp National Assembly approved the country's first constitution, which ambiguously mixes socialist rhetoric and economic reality. It formally makes the LPRP the "leading organ" of the political system and places the government under the Leninist doctrine of "democratic centralism." At the same time, it requires the state to protect private ownership "by domestic capitalists and foreigners who make investments" in the country. Notably, opposition parties are not expressly banned, leaving open the possibility that the government will allow rival parties to form in the future.

After approving the document, the Assembly elected premier and party leader Kaysone Phomvihane to a new, expanded presidency. Veteran Marxist revolutionary General Khamtay Siphandon succeeded him as premier. The president is the head of the armed forces, can remove the premier, and can ratify and abolish foreign treaties.

The 20 December 1992 National Assembly elections were an exercise in party conformity. Election guidelines announced in October all but excluded the possibility of any true opposition candidates running. A 20 October radio broadcast said that all National Assembly members must "be consistently loyal to the cause of the party" and be able to "understand and implement the line, plans, and policies of the party." Although Article 2 of the October election law says that "all Lao citizens... are eligible to run as candidates," Article 8 gives the Lao Front for National Construction responsibility for "proposing and endorsing" candidates, each of whom must submit reference documents that include the date of "joining the revolution."

The government signed a treaty in February 1992 ending a 17-year rift with Thailand. This should give the country improved access to Thai ports. The Thai government pledged to reduce tariffs on Lao wood products and help its poorer neighbor develop its tourism industry. Some four-fifths of consumer goods are imported from Thailand.

Political Rights and Civil Liberties: Laotians cannot change their government democratically. The Lao People's Revolutionary Party (LPRP) is the only existing political party. Current election laws allow only party-approved members to run for National Assembly seats, although the August 1991 constitution does not explicitly prohibit other political parties.

The legal system is subservient to the government, although several foreign lawyers have been assisting the government in implementing limited safeguards, such as public trials. Torture and mistreatment of detainees and prisoners occurs infrequently. The government has released nearly all of the tens of thousands of people who were sent to "re-education camps" following the communist victory in 1975. However, it continues to hold eight officials of the former government on the pretext that they committed crimes while in detention and are now common criminals. Also detained are three high-level ministers, who denounced the one-party system in late 1990. Surveillance of citizens, carried out by the LPRP and the Ministry of the Interior, has been significantly relaxed.

Freedoms of speech and press are nonexistent. Newspapers and electronic media are controlled by the government and reflect its views. All associations are controlled by the LPRP, and anti-government demonstrations are illegal. Freedom of religion is generally respected, and the government is supportive of Buddhist organizations and activities. Citizens can generally travel freely, and the government is wooing back exiles and refugees who fled the 1975 Communist takeover. The government is dominated by ethnic Lao, although it is attempting to integrate minority groups. All labor unions are controlled by the government-affiliated Federation of Lao Trade Unions, and strikes are not permitted.

Latvia

Polity: Presidential-
parliamentary democracy
(ethnic limits)
Economy: Statist
transitional
Population: 2,702,000
PPP: na
Life Expectancy: 71.0
Ethnic Groups: Latvians (52 percent), Russians (34 percent), Ukrainians, Poles, Byelorussians, Lithuanians, Jews

Political Rights: 3
Civil Liberties: 3
Status: Partly Free

Overview:

The most important problems facing Latvia in 1992, its first full year of independence after a 51-year Soviet occupation, included securing its sovereignty, passing a new citizenship law, and reforming the economy.

Latvia was an independent republic from 1918 to 1940, when it was annexed by the Soviet Union as a result of the Hitler-Stalin Pact. More than 50 years of Soviet domination caused a massive influx of Russians; the proportion of ethnic Latvians in the population fell from 77 percent in 1940 to 52 percent by 1991. Despite this massive "Russification," Latvian nationalism was galvanized by the liberalizing policies of *glasnost* introduced by Soviet President Mikhail Gorbachev in the late 1980s.

In July 1989, the Latvian Supreme Council (legislature) adopted a "declaration of sovereignty" and amended the Latvian constitution to assert the supremacy of its laws over those of the Soviet Union. In spring 1990, the first free elections to the Supreme Council resulted in the Popular Front of Latvia (PFL), an umbrella organization of pro-independence groups, winning the majority of seats.

In January 1991, several people were killed and many more wounded when Soviet Internal Ministry troops clashed with unarmed civilians. In a March 1991 referendum on independence, 73 percent voted "yes" to the question, "Are you for a democratic and independent Latvian republic?" The August coup attempt against President Gorbachev greatly accelerated the independence process, and Latvia declared independence on 23 August. Shortly thereafter, it was recognized by most countries, including the Soviet Union. The Supreme Council symbolically reinstated the 1922 constitution, and formed a commission to draft a revision that reflected current political circumstances.

In January 1992, Minister of State Janis Dinevics disclosed the names of members of the Communist party and the parliamentary faction Ravnopravie (Equality), who had appealed in January 1991 to institute Soviet presidential rule in the republic. Several Russian-speaking deputies were subsequently ousted from parliament.

On 20 February new charges were brought against former Communist Party leader Alfred Rubiks, accusing him of attempting to overthrow the government in January 1991. The next month, the Supreme Council appointed a special commission to investigate crimes against humanity in the Nazi and Communist era.

In an address to the Supreme Council on 12 May, Prime Minister Ivars

Godmanis asked for special powers to deal effectively with economic restructuring and privatization. Controversy arose around the Citizenship and Naturalization Department and its director Maris Plavnieks, who was accused of overstepping his authority. The prime minister responded by firing Plavnieks, replacing him with Australian-born Viestus Kamups. The department itself was transferred from the oversight of the ministry of justice to that of the ministry of state.

On 9 July the Supreme Council voted to oust 15 deputies, most of whom belonged to the pro-Communist and pro-Russian Ravnopravie faction. The vote followed the recommendations of a special parliamentary committee investigating the activities of anti-independence groups in the period May 1990 to August 1991. Members of the Ravnopravie accused the Supreme Council of political reprisals against their group, and vowed to appeal to international courts and human rights organizations.

On 30 September, the Supreme Council voted to amend the pre-war legislation on parliamentary elections by lowering the voting age requirements from 21 to 18 years, and instituting a 4 percent hurdle for parties to be granted seats in the new *Saeima* (parliament).

The question of citizenship remained an unresolved and divisive issue. In October 1991, the Supreme Council adopted a series of guidelines for defining who qualified for Latvian citizenship. Only those who were citizens in 1940 and their descendants were automatically granted citizenship. For others, stringent requirements were set. They included: a conversational knowledge of Latvian; knowledge of Latvian legal structures; 16 years of residence; and renunciation of citizenship from another state. The guidelines were criticized by various human rights groups as too restrictive, and by some nationalist groups, who wanted most Russians to leave the country, as not going far enough. In February, an organization of pro-Latvian Russians was established to protect their interests within the framework of an independent Latvia.

In March, Supreme Council Chairman Anatolijs Gorbunovs criticized the parliament about its indecision on the final law on citizenship, stating that inaction hampered other badly needed reforms. Gorbunovs called for a popular referendum on the issue, restricted to persons entitled for automatic citizenship, and stated that he favored a 10-year residence requirement.

In foreign policy the most pressing problem was the presence of approximately 80,000 Soviet troops in Latvia, the largest such concentration in the three Baltic states. In November 1991, the Supreme Soviet had passed a resolution claiming all property occupied by Soviet forces. The Soviet military, however, refused to abide by the resolution, insisting the property belonged to Russia. In January 1992, parliament announced that Latvia did not recognize the annexation by the Russian Federation after World War II of six counties in eastern Latvia. On 25 March 1992, Latvian Foreign Minister Janis Jurkans, along with his counterparts from Lithuania and Estonia, asked the Conference on Security and Cooperation in Europe (CSCE) to help them in the troop withdrawal.

During bilateral Latvian-Russian talks on 28 May, the Latvian delegation rejected the Russian proposal to withdraw the troops from its territory by 1999. On the same day, following the decision of the regional board of Dobele to station patrol units on the roads leading to Russian military bases in order to bar entry of new conscripts, the Russian military dispatched armed columns to prevent the Latvians from carrying out their action. But on 6 August, the three Baltic states and Russia agreed to work out a withdrawal timetable acceptable to all parties.

In March, the Supreme Council adopted a series of laws dealing with privatization of state enterprises. The government also introduced a transitional currency, the rublis, to become legal tender alongside the Russian ruble. The move was made to alleviate the drastic shortage of currency caused by high inflation. On 20 July, the rublis became Latvia's sole legal tender, and the Russian ruble was withdrawn from circulation. A convertible currency, the lats, is to be introduced sometime in the future. In August, Latvia became a member of the World Bank, and in September, it became the first former Soviet republic to be granted a full-fledged loan from the IMF.

Political Rights and Civil Liberties:

Citizens of Latvia can change their government democratically. However, according to the guidelines of the new citizenship law, a large portion of those who immigrated to Latvia after the 1940 Soviet takeover and their descendants might be excluded from citizenship and voting rights. By the end of 1992, however, the new citizenship law had not yet been adopted, and the election date to *Saeima* (legislature) had not been set.

Freedom of association and assembly are generally respected, and there are several well-organized political parties. On 8 April, the government lifted travel restrictions on residents wishing to travel abroad.

There is an independent press in both Latvian and Russian languages. However, the government has occasionally hampered the Russian-language press. The government stopped publication of an issue of the Russian-language *Baltiyskoye Vremya* that was already being printed, closed the paper's bank account, and seized its property without formally charging the paper with any criminal offense. The independent press also faces major economic difficulties. To draw public and government attention to the unavailability of newsprint, newspaper editors and publishers organized a protest action and did not publish from 17 to 24 February. The government agreed to help alleviate the problem by finding alternate sources of newsprint.

A new law on radio and television was passed on 6 May. It specified the creation of separate administrative bodies for radio and television. At the same time, it guaranteed their independence from political interference, and provided for the creation of a Radio and Television Council to assign channels and frequencies to private stations.

Freedom of religion is respected in this largely Lutheran country. Since independence, a free trade union confederation has been established.

Lebanon

Polity: Presidential-
parliamentary
(military and
foreign-influenced)
Economy: Mixed statist
Population: 3,439,000
PPP: $2,250
Life Expectancy: 66.1

Political Rights: 5
Civil Liberties: 4
Status: Partly Free

Ethnic Groups: Eastern Hamitic (90 percent), Greek, Syro-Lebonese

Overview:

In 1992, Lebanon held its first parliamentary elections in two decades. Amidst the presence of 40,000 Syrian troops which were brought in to maintain order under a 1989 accord, voters elected mostly pro-Syrian candidates, although anti-government Muslim fundamentalists made surprising gains. Christian parties and most Christian voters staged a boycott, claiming the presence of the Syrian troops made a fair election impossible.

The first step towards ending the country's civil war, which began in 1975 between Muslim, Christian and Druse militias took place at Taif, Saudi Arabia in November 1989. An Arab-League-sponsored accord drafted there provided for a new constitution that would distribute some power from the traditionally favored Christians to the Muslims. The accord continued the tradition of a Christian presidency, but transferred many of the executive powers to the cabinet, which would be headed by a Sunni Muslim prime minister as before. Future parliaments would be split evenly among Muslims and Christians, ending the 6:5 ratio favoring Christians which had been codified in the 1943 constitution. The accord also pledged to end the traditional practice of distributing government positions along religious lines, and allowed Syria to maintain up to 40,000 troops in Beirut and other cities until September 1992.

In October 1990, Lebanese and Syrian troops defeated Christian troops loyal to General Michel Aoun, who opposed the accord and refused to relinquish power to the central government. Aoun's defeat finally ended a civil war that had killed more than 150,000 people. In December 1990, President Elias Hrawi named a 30-member, half-Christian, half-Muslim cabinet that included the leaders of several warring militias. In May 1991, the government signed treaty linking its economic and security policies with Syria, which effectively gave control of the country to its more powerful neighbor.

As the government prepared to hold elections in mid-1992, the country experienced its worse economic crisis since independence. Prices of essential goods soared to their highest levels, unemployment hit 30 percent, and a decision by the Central Bank in February to suspend support for the pound caused a sharp devaluation in the currency. A series of strikes in mid-April organized by the General Federation of Labor Unions virtually shut down Beirut and other major cities. Many citizens blamed the difficulties on widespread corruption and the government's inflation-producing policies, which included increasing the salaries of civil servants by 120 percent earlier in the year.

On 5 May, reports that the pound, once one of the strongest currencies in the region, had plummeted to a record low touched off two days of riots. Demonstrators attacked the prime minister's residence and burned shops and banks. On 6 May, Prime Minister Omar Karami resigned, and one week later President Hrawi asked former Prime Minister Rashid Sohl to form a new government. The decision to name Sohl, as with other key moves, reportedly came directly from Syrian president Hafez al-Assad.

Sohl announced a new 24-member cabinet on 16 May, again split evenly among Christians and Muslims. On 16 July, the parliament, which had been renewing its mandate every two years while the civil war prevented elections, passed a law clearing the way for the country's first vote in 20 years. The new parliament would have 128 seats, distributed equally among Christians and Muslims. Immediately, hardline Christians protested holding the elections before the Syrian army, which controls approximately 70 percent of the country, withdrew from the major cities. Although the Taif Accord specifically allows Syrian troops to remain in the cities until the elections, the hardliners claimed this military presence would intimidate voters and could lead to a rubber-stamp, pro-Syrian parliament.

On 24 July, the government announced the elections would be held as planned in three stages—23 August in the eastern Bekka Valley and the northern province, 30 August in Beirut and the Christian and Druse surrounding areas, and 6 September in the south. However, in August, the Phalange Party, the largest Christian group, joined four other major Christian parties in announcing an election boycott and in urging Christian voters to stay away from the polls.

All three rounds of voting were held under labor strikes called by the Christian parties, and few Christians—in some districts less than 2 percent—turned out to vote. The government expected to sweep the first round, but received a shock when unofficial results showed big gains by the Iranian-backed Hezbollah fundamentalists, who opposed the Taif Accord and were contesting elections for the first time ever. For the election, Hezbollah had joined with the mainstream Syrian-backed Amal movement in an uneasy alliance to prevent the election of moderate Shiites. The two rival Shiite groups had turned on each other toward the end of the civil war.

Before the official results were out, parliament speaker Hussein Husseini demanded the first round be voided, accusing the opposition of "forging the elections and proceeding with the forgery even during the poll counting." Prime Minster Sohl rejected the demand and said that the remaining rounds would proceed as planned. Three ministers, including Phalange head George Saddah, quit the government in protest.

The final two rounds were held on schedule, and results released on 8 September showed that of the 64 Muslim seats, Amal took 18, Hezbollah 12, along with 15 supporters of former prime minister Selim al-Hoss, 11 supporters of Karami, and 8 supporters of Defense Minister Michel al-Murr. The 64 Christian seats were won by independents or by candidates who ran on Muslim tickets and who were elected with Muslim votes. (Five seats allocated to Christians in Kesrouan province remained vacant due to an initial absence of candidates, and were filled in a special by-election on 11 October.) Although Hezbollah and other fundamentalists controlled the largest single bloc, by some counts up to 20 seats, they figured to wield little influence because three-fourths of the seats were won by nominally pro-Syrian candidates.

On 22 October, President Hrawi named Sunni businessman Rafik al-Hariri prime minister. Even with the new government in place, Syria said on 22 November it will not withdraw until all the political changes are completed, including abolishing the 49-year-old system of distributing government posts along religious lines.

Fighting in the south between Hezbollah and Israeli troops holding a 6-mile deep "security zone" escalated during the year. An Israeli helicopter raid on 16 February killed Hezbollah leader Sheikh Abbas Musawi, leading to several days of intense artillery barrages and rocket attacks across the border. On 17 June, government intervention secured the release of the last two Western hostages held by fundamentalist groups in the area, ending a decade of hostage ordeals. Israel says it will not quit its security zone until all factions threatening its northern areas are disarmed.

Political Rights and Civil Liberties: Lebanon held parliamentary elections in 1992 for the first time since 1972, although the vote was marred by a Christian voters' boycott, as well as charges of fraud and irregularities. The government redrew the country's six electoral districts to favor pro-Syrian candidates, including Druze warlord Walid Jumblatt and Amal leader Nabih Berri. Due to the gerrymandering, the number of votes needed for a seat ranged from 5,000 to up to 100,000 in some districts. Independent candidates reported being harassed and intimidated. Scattered violence resulted in several deaths, ballot boxes were looted in some areas and an election official in one village was kidnapped for several hours. The Israeli-backed South Lebanese Army prevented people living in the Israeli security zone in the south from voting by blocking roads and warning that anyone leaving to vote would not be allowed to return.

The judiciary is considered independent, but the court system faces backlogs. Freedom of press is respected and dozens of newspapers exist, although many are heavily influenced by their domestic and foreign supporters. The Syrian-Lebanese pact of May 1991 gives the government a monopoly over radio and television until the year 2012. In January 1992, the government moved to curtail 40 television and 150 radio stations operated by private militias, political parties and other groups. It announced that licenses would only be granted to "commercial" television stations that do not show news broadcasts, effectively limiting news broadcasts to the official Tele Liban station. Freedom of association is generally respected. There is no official religion, and the numerous Christian denominations, Muslims, and Druze worship freely. Citizens can travel freely, except in the Israeli-held zone. Workers, except government employees, are free to unionize and strike.

Lesotho

Polity: Military
transitional
Economy: Capitalist
Population: 1,880,000
PPP: $1,646
Life Expectancy: 57.3
Ethnic Groups: Sotho (99 percent)

Political Rights: 6
Civil Liberties: 4
Status: Partly Free

Overview:

A constitutional monarchy within the British Commonwealth since 1966, Lesotho is a small, mountainous country entirely surrounded by South Africa. The present head of state is King Letsie III, but the head of the nation's military council, currently Pitsoana Ramaema, holds substantial power. Major General Justin Lekhanya took over the country as the head of the Council in 1986, when he overthrew the civilian dictatorship of Prime Minister Chief Leabua Jonathan of the Basotho National Party (BNP). In 1991, Ramaema overthrew Lekhanya and took over as head of the military council.

After seizing power in 1986, Lekhanya dissolved the parliament and banned all political activity. Shortly before he was ousted, however, he set up a National Constituent Assembly (NCA) to rewrite the nation's constitution and provide for a system of multiple political parties. A civilian-run democracy was promised by 1992. After the 1991 coup, the NCA submitted the finished constitution to Colonel Ramaema and the military council for approval. The new junta promised a return to civilian rule, and in May 1991, Ramaema lifted the five-year-old ban against political parties. In January 1992, parties were permitted to register for the parliamentary election scheduled for June.

In May, the regime postponed the election, citing difficulties in registering voters and drafting the necessary legislation. Elections were rescheduled for 28 November but subsequently postponed again for the same reasons. Although a number of parties have formed to contest the elections, either the former ruling BNP or its long-time rival the Basotholand Congress Party (BCP) are deemed the contenders most likely to form a democratically elected government if and when balloting occurs.

In August 1992, King Moshoeshoe II (King Letsie III's father) returned to Lesotho from exile in London. Lekhanya had stripped Moshoeshoe of his powers in 1990 for continuing to challenge the will of the major general. After Moshoeshoe fled to Britain, Lekhanya offered the throne to Letsie. Moshoeshoe had planned to return to Lesotho in May 1992, but delayed his departure after the British government warned him that the Lesothan regime feared the exiled king's return would provoke anti-Military Council turmoil. Throughout 1992 the ruling Military Council warned Moshoeshoe and his supporters that Letsie would continue as king whether or not his father returned to Lesotho. The Council said that Moshoeshoe would return as a chief, if he returned at all. The council also emphasized that the position of Lesothan king had been reduced by recent practice to a figurehead. Moshoeshoe's opponents suspected that he sought to regain a portion of the power that the king once enjoyed as head of state.

Lesotho's economy is heavily dependent on the Republic of South Africa for employment and energy. A major source of foreign exchange is remittances from migrant gold and diamond miners working in South Africa. Some Lesothans support the incorporation of Lesotho into South Africa after the transition to a government elected on a "one man, one vote" basis.

Political Rights and Civil Liberties: At the end of 1992, Lesothans could not change their government democratically. The judiciary is relatively independent. The 1984 Internal Security Act allows the government to detain individuals without charge. The regime announced in March 1992 that political parties could hold rallies without obtaining government permission. In May, it proclaimed that the pre-electoral activities of registered political parties would be fairly covered by state broadcasting. The private press is able to criticize the government. Non-political associations are free to organize. Domestic and foreign travel is generally unrestricted. Workers formally have the right to organize and strike, but restrictive labor codes make it difficult.

Liberia

Polity: Transitional (military- and foreign-influenced)
Economy: Capitalist
Population: 2,777,000
PPP: $937
Life Expectancy: 54.2
Ethnic Groups: Sixteen major tribes, including the Krahn, Mandingo, Gio and Mano (95 percent), Americo-Liberians (5 percent)

Political Rights: 7
Civil Liberties: 6
Status: Not Free

Overview: Liberia's continuing civil war has left at least 50,000 people dead, destroyed most of the nation's infrastructure, and sent hundreds of thousands of refugees fleeing to neighboring countries.

Liberia was founded in 1847 by freed American slaves, whose descendants are known as Americo-Liberians. The present conflict has its origins in the ten-year brutal reign of General Samuel Doe, who overthrew the elected government of William Tolbert in 1980. An Americo-Liberian elite dominated the Tolbert administration, as it has the country's politics since 1878. A member of the Krahn, one of the most deprived of Liberian ethnic groups, Doe became the first indigenous African to rule the country. He consolidated his power by giving top regime positions to other Krahn (who make up 4 percent of Liberia's population). The Doe regime was responsible for a pattern of human rights abuse against non-Krahns.

In December 1989, the rebel National Patriotic Front of Liberia (NPFL) began to attack government troops from neighboring Ivory Coast. Led by Charles Taylor, an Americo-Liberian and former Doe cabinet member, most soldiers in the NPFL are of the Gio and Mano ethnic groups. By mid-1990, the capital, Monrovia, became a city under siege, with shortages of food, water and medicine. An off-shoot of the NPFL captured Doe and tortured him to death.

Fearing the effect the war could have on their own countries, members of the Economic Organization of West African States (ECOWAS) sent an armed monitoring group (ECOMOG) to defend Monrovia in August 1990. Within months, ECOMOG troops from Nigeria, Ghana, Guinea, the Gambia, and Sierra Leone had pushed the NPFL away from the capital, although the rebel group controlled the rest of the country. An ECOWAS-sponsored Interim Government of National Unity (IGNU), with Liberian Amos Sawyer as President, was set up in November 1990. The NPFL formed its own government, the National Patriotic Reconstruction Assembly, in the interior town of Gbarnga. The contending sides declared a ceasefire at the end of 1990, which held throughout 1991.

A possible break in the political stalemate occurred at an October 1991 conference in Yamoussoukro, Ivory Coast. Sponsored by ECOWAS, it saw the NPFL sign an agreement—the so-called Yamoussoukro IV—to disarm and encamp its troops under ECOMOG supervision. Taylor agreed to lift NPFL roadblocks restricting travel and to begin disarmament 60 days from the signing of the accord. Elections were to follow in six months. By the end of 1991, however, the 8,000 ECOMOG troops were still bottled up in Monrovia awaiting Taylor's permission to deploy. The NPFL had not yet begun to disarm. Taylor continued to demand that border posts employed to control the inflow of weapons into Liberia be jointly manned by ECOMOG and the NPFL, a condition refused by ECOWAS.

Frustrated with Taylor's failure to honor the terms of Yamoussoukro IV, the IGNU officially imposed a trade embargo on the 95 percent of the country controlled by his army. The embargo went into effect days before the 15 January disarmament deadline. A week earlier the interim government had issued new bank notes to deprive the NPFL of the use of old currency looted during the 1989-90 civil war. Taylor responded by making it illegal even to possess the new bills in NPFL territory.

Taylor continued to assert throughout 1992 that he was the president of the lawful Liberian government and prevented from occupying the seat of government by a Nigerian-led occupation force. On 7 April, he signed another peace accord in Geneva meant to reaffirm commitments to disarm and encamp, but he repudiated it as the product of undue pressure once he was back in Africa. During 1991 and 1992, he signed a half dozen joint communiques and agreements and then ignored them. In November 1992, the Associated Press reported that the NPFL had secretly prepared for war by training troops in Burkina Faso and Libya. Taylor has sponsored armed Sierra Leonean and Gambian rebel movements attempting to overthrow their governments.

Hostilities between the NPFL and the Sierra Leone-based United Liberation Movement for Democracy (ULIMO) continued from September 1991 through 1992. ULIMO is composed of armed anti-Taylor Liberian refugees—mainly Krahns and Mandingos—and former soldiers of the Doe regime. The NPFL leader has used the anti-Taylor ULIMO as justification for not disarming his own troops. ULIMO spokesmen asserted that only force could resolve problems with the NPFL. Yamoussoukro IV required ECOMOG to establish a buffer zone on the Liberia-Sierra

Leone border to separate the adversaries, but the NPFL stymied deployment of peacekeeping troops until 30 April 1992. By late 1992, ECOWAS members Senegal and Mali had also sent members of their military to reinforce ECOMOG forces. The NPFL tortured and executed six Senegalese soldiers after seizing them near the border only one month after deployment began. Taylor's rebels also ambushed other peacekeeping contingents, and ECOMOG decided to withdraw most of its forces back to Monrovia.

In early August, ECOWAS gave Taylor until the end of the month to comply with the terms of all the agreements he had signed. But major fighting soon renewed. After fighting off earlier NPFL attacks into Sierra Leone, ULIMO firmly seized the initiative in mid-August. By October, ULIMO reached the outskirts of Monrovia after having driven the NPFL out of two Liberian counties. In the interim, ECOMOG initiated a blockade, seizing ships suspected of ferrying arms to the NPFL.

On 17 October, Taylor officially broke a two-year ceasefire with ECOMOG, mounting his largest offensive since the civil war ended in 1990. He began with artillery attacks on Monrovia to soften up the city's defenses. The NPFL then sent guerrillas into the capital in an attempt to deal with ECOMOG "interference" once and for all. Two hundred thousand refugees fled to the safety of IGNU territory in Monrovia. The NPFL shut down water and communications facilities serving the capital, tightening the siege.

ECOMOG responded by shelling NPFL positions surrounding the capital, and launched bombing runs on Gbargna, the port of Buchanan and other Taylor strongholds. By late November, infantry forces of the 7-nation coalition had driven most rebel holdouts from the swamps around Monrovia. At the same time, the U.N. voted to give ECOWAS additional authority for its blockade. Long-time Taylor-sympathizer President Félix Houphouët-Boigny of the Ivory Coast reinforced the U.N. measure by sending troops to seal his side of the Liberian border to arms transshipments.

Political Rights and Civil Liberties:

Liberians do not have the right to choose their government democratically. A five-member interim election commission was sworn in on 13 January 1992, with both NPFL and IGNU members, but it was unable to organize free and fair multi-party elections.

The rule of law has broken down in most of the country. Pursuant to the Yamassoukro IV accord, an *ad hoc* supreme court was formed in March 1992; three of its judges are appointed by the NPFL and two by the IGNU. Its actual authority, however, remains almost nil. Human rights abuse is common in both NPFL and ULIMO occupied Liberia. Undisciplined and violence-prone troops of the rebel armies habitually mistreat civilians and steal their possessions. In October 1992, five American nuns and a number of Liberian novices were slain behind NPFL lines as Taylor's forces attacked Monrovia.

Political dissent is not tolerated in NPFL territory. Monrovia enjoys freer speech. While the print media in the capital is free to report without fear of repression in matters unrelated to internal security, NPFL or ULIMO authorities strictly regulate all information in the rest of the country. The stridently partisan NPFL newspaper, *The Patriot,* is the only newspaper Taylor's forces allow to circulate freely in its territory. Both the interim government and the NPFL control their own radio stations.

The NPFL restricts freedom of movement, especially between Monrovia and the other counties. Refugees from armed fighting must evade NPFL checkpoints on most roads to escape. A half million people are internally displaced within Liberia, and another million have sought sanctuary in neighboring countries.

Although the NPFL does not interfere with Christian worship, it prevented the politically suspect Muslims of the Mandingo ethnic group from worshipping in their mosques until February 1991. Charles Taylor has accused the Mandingos of siding with the Krahns. Even after he lifted the ban, Africa Watch still reported Muslims singled out for harassment or extrajudicial execution.

Libya

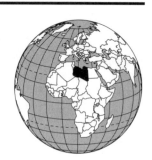

Polity: Military
Economy: Mixed statist
Population: 4,485,000
PPP: $7, 250
Life Expectancy: 61.8
Ethnic Groups: Arab , Berber, Tuareg

Political Rights: 7
Civil Liberties: 7
Status: Not Free

Overview: In 1992, Libya's strongman, Colonel Mu'ammar al-Qadhafi, ignored a U.N. Security Council resolution demanding the extradition of the two Libyan suspects wanted by three countries for the bombing of Pan Am Flight 103, which blew up over Lockerbie, Scotland, in December 1988, killing 270 people. The resolution also called on Libya to cooperate with an investigation into the 1989 destruction of a French airliner over West Africa that claimed 177 lives. Despite Libya's plea at the International Court of Justice in The Hague, U.N. sanctions went into effect on 15 April. As a result, the Libyan economy has deteriorated considerably and domestic political pressure is increasing against the regime.

In 1992, tensions reportedly grew between Qadhafi and his second-in-command, Major Abdul Salam Jalloud, who has been making concessions to Libya's Islamic fundamentalists. As a force with a potent ideology, Islamic fundamentalists pose a threat to the regime. There were also several reports of the population's displeasure with the current system's incompetence, corruption and oppression.

Qadhafi redesigned his regime in 1992, holding local elections in October. This device aimed at giving the appearance of popular control over 13 ministries by creating 13 separate 1,500 member bodies, consisting of one representative from each community. However, ultimate power and authority remain in Qadhafi's hands.

International pressure had more effect on Libya than domestic structural tinkering. On 21 January 1992, the U.N. Security Council unanimously adopted Resolution 731, which insisted on Libya's complete cooperation in bringing the bombing suspects to justice. The resolution also demanded the extradition of four Libyans, including Qadhafi's brother-in-law, accused by France of bombing a French UTA airliner over Niger in 1989.

Libya claimed that the accusations against the two suspects were based on "false premises and assumptions." The country refused to hand over the suspects, allegedly because Britain, France and the United States refused to share the results of their investigations with Libya. Qadhafi's regime asserted that it would investigate and try the officials in Libya. In February 1992, journalists witnessed the court examination of the two suspects. The pair made a two-minute court appearance before being taken away. The judge later read from a prepared text stating that the Libyan government lacked sufficient evidence to build a case, and that they would be willing to allow the case to be handled by the International Court of Justice, the U.N., or the Arab League.

On 26 March 1992, a French judge ordered the extradition from Libya of a Palestinian official of the terrorist Abu Nidal organization, Samir Mohammed Ahmed Khaidir, accused of planning a July 1988 attack that killed nine people on a cruise ship off the coast of Greece. Three of the victims were French citizens. Libya appealed to the International Court of Justice for an emergency injunction to ban any economic or military measures by the United States and Britain to gain custody of the suspects. On 15 April 1992, the Court rejected Libya's appeal.

On 31 March 1992, the U.N. Security Council adopted Resolution 748 imposing an air and arms embargo against Libya and urging the expulsion of Libyan diplomats. The resolution requires Libya to renounce terrorism.

In March 1992, Britain reported that the Libyan government was denying exit visas to foreigners. Libyan U.N. Ambassador Ali Elhouderi denied the charge.

After international sanctions took effect on 15 April, Qadhafi began expelling diplomats of countries that supported the U.N. measures. The one million foreigners living in Libya feared possible repercussions from the sanctions. Russia began pulling out 3,000 military advisers, technicians and their families. Libyan travelers and foreign workers flooded into Egypt and Tunisia in search of planes to foreign destinations.

In May 1992, Libya claimed that it was renouncing terrorism but it still refused to hand over the two suspects to the United States and Britain. It vowed to expel any person who "proved to be involved in acts of terrorism." In June 1992, Libya reiterated its decision to allow the trial of the two suspects under Arab League or U.N. auspices.

Discontent among the Libyan population and some government officials has been growing. During June 1992, the official Libyan press attacked Qadhafi's policies and urged a more pragmatic foreign policy, including cooperation with the United States. Despite the move by the General People's Congress in July 1992 approving the release of the suspects, Libya continued to delay the extradition. In September 1992, on the twenty-third anniversary of the military coup that brought him to power, Qadhafi admitted that his country was facing economic problems and that it could not afford to pay its employees.

The widespread security apparatus in Libya has not been able to prevent the population's complaints against the regime. Libyan citizens have complained of government mismanagement, lack of funds for health services, housing and schools. Discontent even surfaced in Libya's congress, usually a rubber stamp for Qadhafi's policies, when one woman deputy complained that her region was "economically deprived." However, the Secretary General of the congress silenced her. Qadhafi's costly political and economic projects, such as the drive to produce an army of one-fourth of the population, have consumed billions of dollars in revenues. Many grandiose projects, including an effort to build a $25 billion artificial river, have failed. Many Libyans lack such basic services as water and sewer systems. Hospitals and schools lack equipment and qualified staff.

In August 1992, Libya's foreign minister announced that the sanctions cost Libya $4.6 billion in lost trade and increased social costs. The economy will be hit harder if the embargo extends to include Libyan oil, which accounts for almost all of Libya's export earnings. Germany and Italy have strongly opposed such sanctions since they import Libyan oil in large quantities.

Political Rights and Civil Liberties:

Libyans do not have the right to change their government democratically. Qadhafi rules Libya with the help of his Revolutionary Committees. There is no constitution. Governing principles come from Qadhafi's "Green Book." Qadhafi, his aides, and committees acting in his name make major government decisions. He appoints officials ranging from military figures to junior level personnel.

Qadhafi rules through a series of Revolutionary Committees and intelligence agencies under his personal control. Nominal power lies with the general secretary of the General People's Congress, which is elected by municipal groups called People's Committees. The Revolutionary Committees oversee the People's Committees and screen all candidates.

The system prohibits political parties or any other types of associations. Participation in elections is mandatory and Revolutionary Committees must approve all candidates.

Freedom of expression is severely limited. People's Committee meetings and the General People's Congress tolerate some difference of opinion. Citizens generally refrain from criticizing the regime out of fear of the extensive surveillance network inside the country. The state owns and controls the Libyan media. Revolutionary Committees run a daily newspaper and several other smaller newspapers. The government also censors available foreign publications. Libyans can receive foreign broadcasts. Publishing opinions contrary to government policy is prohibited. During 1992, the Libyan press criticized Qadhafi's call for Arab unity, proposed reconciliation with the West, and advocated the extradition of the two bombing suspects to the United States and Britain. Whether the government orchestrated this criticism or not is unclear. In June 1992, Libyan officials roughed up an Egyptian Associated Press reporter covering the General People's Congress and forcibly took her press credentials. Officials later apologized for the incident.

There is no freedom of assembly or association. Only government-sponsored demonstrations are allowed. The right of association is granted only to those affiliated with the regime. Any party activity that opposes the basic principles of the "Revolution" is punishable by death.

Libya maintains an extensive security apparatus. Local Revolutionary Committees and People's Committees also have security functions. The government does not respect the right to privacy. An extensive informer network monitors the population. Prisoners in Libya are reportedly tortured during interrogations. Approximately 100 political prisoners are reportedly held in secret detention centers. Libya's arbitrary judicial system does not provide for fair trials. Detainees are often sentenced without trial, and death sentences are applied for many offenses.

Discrimination exists based on ethnic status, specifically against Berbers and Tuaregs in the south. In an attempt to eliminate Berber identity, Qadhafi has tried unsuccessfully to force Berbers to marry only non-Berbers. Cultural norms make women second-class citizens, but Qadhafi has tried to expand their access to higher education and employment opportunities. Women receive basic military training and are subject to military draft. A husband's permission is required for women to travel abroad. Female circumcision is reportedly still practiced among some tribal groups in the south.

Libya is predominantly Muslim. The regime banned the Sanusiyya Islamic religious sect. The government allows the small Christian population to practice and conduct services. There are two churches in Libya. The regime oppresses Islamic fundamentalists and monitors mosques for political activity.

Libyans are free to travel within the country, except in certain security areas. Exit permits are required to travel abroad. Libyan students studying abroad are subject to interrogation upon returning home and are usually placed under surveillance.

Trade unions are under strict government control, and Libyan workers do not have the right to join unions of their own choice. There is no collective bargaining, and no right to strike. Labor laws do not apply to the 1.5 million foreign workers in Libya. Despite past efforts at privatization, the Libyan economy remains essentially state-controlled.

Liechtenstein

Polity: Prince and parliamentary democracy
Economy: Capitalist-statist
Population: 30,000
PPP: na
Life Expectancy: 69.5
Ethnic Groups: Alemannic German, Italian, other European

Political Rights: 1
Civil Liberties: 1
Status: Free

Overview: **A** national referendum favoring membership in the European Economic Area (EEA), a common market linked with the European Community (EC), was the most significant development in 1992.

Prince Hans Adam II, the head of state, argued with parliament about the timing of referenda on joining the EEA and on the advisability of acting separately from Switzerland on European integration. The issue arose, because Liechtenstein and Switzerland have a currency and customs union. The Prince threatened to dismiss the government and dissolve parliament after they refused to accept his proposed schedule for voting. Ultimately, in late October, Hans Adam accepted parliament's schedule of voting on 11 and 13 December, following the Swiss vote on the EEA on 6 December. The parliament promised the Prince that the Swiss result would not necessarily bind Liechtenstein's decision on Europe. The political leadership promised to "explore the possibility of joining the EC jointly with Switzerland, so as not to move into isolation." In their referendum, the Swiss voted "No."

In October 1992, Swiss troops on military exercises crossed the unmarked border into Liechtenstein. They claimed later that they thought their planned destination was a Swiss town when in reality it lay in Liechtenstein. The small country protested against what the Swiss called a mistake.

The Principality of Liechtenstein was created in its current form in 1719. Most Liechtensteiners are descended from the Germanic Alemanni tribe. Prince Hans Adam's Austrian ancestors purchased the country's land. The royal family lived primarily in Moravia (once a part of the Austro-Hungarian Empire, now a Czech land) until 1938, when the spread of Nazism forced them to Liechtenstein. Between Czecho-Slovakia's independence in 1918 and the Communist takeover in 1948, that country confiscated Liechtenstein's royal estates without compensation. Since the fall of Communism in 1989, Hans Adam has attempted to reclaim the family's Czech properties, but the Prague government has refused to give him either land or compensation. The disputed land consists of 1600 square kilometers, about ten times the size of Liechtenstein. Prague refuses to recognize Liechtenstein's independence, but the principality has ways of fighting back. For example, Hans Adam has used his country's veto power in the European Free Trade Association to block better trading terms for the former Communist state.

The prince appoints a prime minister from the majority party or coalition in the fifteen-member Landtag (Parliament), whose members serve for four-year terms. Called "hallowed and sacrosanct" by the constitution, the monarch has the right to veto legislation. Hans Adam's father vetoed only one bill, a proposed hunting law. Parties with at least eight percent of the vote receive proportional representation in the Landtag. The leading parties are the moderately liberal Fatherland's Union, the conservative Progressive Citizens' Party, the Christian Social Party, and the liberal, Green-oriented Free Voters' List. The major issue in the March 1989 elections was museum construction. Major local concerns include overdevelopment and the large number of foreigners in the labor force. The Swiss handle Liechtenstein's defense (which apparently includes accidental invasions) and foreign affairs, but the principality joined the United Nations in 1990.

Political Rights and Civil Liberties: Liechtensteiners can change their government democratically. Control shifts between parties. Voters may decide issues directly through referenda. Women have had voting rights nationally since 1984. Major parties publish newspapers five times each week. Residents receive radio and television freely from other countries. Liechtenstein has no broadcast media. The country is too small to have numerous organizations, but association is free. The prosperous economy includes private and state enterprises.

Lithuania

Polity: Presidential-
parliamentary democracy
Economy: Statist
transitional
Population: 3,736,000
PPP: na
Life Expectancy: 72.0
Ethnic Groups: Lithuanian (80 percent), Russian, Ukrainian,
Byelorussian, others (20 percent)

Political Rights: 2
Civil Liberties: 3
Status: Free

Overview:
In 1992, Lithuanian voters angered by continued economic difficulties, repudiated the Sajudis popular movement that had paved the way to independence in 1991. Voters elected the Democratic Labor Party, made up mostly of ex-Communists, to 79 of 141 seats in the new parliament. Election results marked a serious setback to reformist President Vytautas Landsbergis, who earlier had lost a referendum on expanding presidential powers when not enough voters participated in the vote.

Lithuania regained its independence after the failed coup attempt against Soviet President Mikhail Gorbachev in August 1991. The republic, an independent state from 1918 to 1940, was forcibly incorporated into the Soviet Union under the Hitler-Stalin Pact. With the advent of *glasnost* and *perestroika* in the mid-1980s under Gorbachev, Lithuanians began to assert their drive to leave the Soviet Union. Free elections to the Supreme Council (parliament) in February 1990 gave a clear victory to the pro-independence forces united in Sajudis, and the government declared independence in March. But it wasn't until after the failed August coup in 1991 that Lithuania's independence was assured and recognized by major countries of the world, including the Soviet Union.

Lithuania's political problems stemmed directly from economic difficulties caused by the collapse of the Soviet trading bloc and the transition to a market economy. Of particular significance was the virtual cut-off of energy supplies from Russia, leading to shortages of gasoline and home-heating fuel. Some members of Sajudis accused the Russians of using fuel as a weapon to undermine President Landsbergis and the Sajudis government led by Prime Minister Gediminas Vagnorius. In addition, Sajudis had split into several factions, with some supporting a strong presidency and others, such as the Sajudis Central, warning that such a move could undermine democracy and lead to authoritarian rule.

By February 1992, over 360,000 signatures had been collected calling for a referendum on the presidency. On 12 March, parliament set the referendum date for 13 May. The referendum failed because less than 50 percent of all registered voters approved the measure. After the vote, Deputy Supreme Council Chairman Kazimieras Motieka and 34 other deputies accused Landsbergis of polarizing public opinion by conducting the referendum.

The government came under intense pressure in the spring. On 14 April, the Center Faction accused the prime minister of pursuing misdirected social and economic policies. Less than a week later, a deputy prime minister and several cabinet ministers resigned because of the prime minister's proposal to replace from 30 to 50 percent of all public administration employees. On 12 May, parliament rejected the prime minister's dismissal of several officials he had accused of sabotaging economic reforms. Four days later Prime Minister Vagnorius submitted his resignation, but President Landsbergis asked him to remain in office. However, on 14 July, Prime Minister Vagnorius was removed after a non-confidence vote in parliament. He was quickly replaced by Aleksander Abisala, who retained most of the cabinet ministers from the previous government.

In July, the Supreme Council adopted a new law on elections for parliament, allotting 71 seats single-member districts and 70 multi-member ones. A minimum of 4 percent of the vote was required for parties and social groups to win representation in parliament.

On 13 October, a draft of a new constitution was approved and put on the ballot as a referendum during the parliamentary elections. The draft called for a presidential-parliamentary system of government. On 25 October, voters approved the constitution and, in a surprise move, gave the ex-Communist Democratic Labor Party (DLP) 44.9 percent of the vote. Sajudis, which had spear-headed independence, won 19.9 percent, and its ally—the Christian Democratic Party—won 11.4 percent. DLP leader Algirdas Brazauskas promised to improve relations with Russia, and suggested that market reforms would continue but at a slower pace. Sajudis Chairman and state President Landsbergis accused Moscow of "actively participating" in the election by blocking deliveries of fuel and raw materials. On 25 November, Brazauskas was overwhelmingly elected chairman of the parliament, a post that made him acting president of Lithuania. His only challenger, Social Democratic Party leader Alouzas Sakalas, received seven votes. Brazauskas will retain the post until presidential elections slated for before 31 March 1993.

Major foreign policy issues in 1992 included the withdrawal of Soviet troops from Lithuania and a border dispute with Belarus. In September 1991, Lithuania signed an agreement with the Soviet Union that called for troop withdrawal to begin that December. However, following the dissolution of the USSR, it was not implemented. On 9 January 1992, the Lithuanian government issued an official protest against Russian military exercises conducted on its territory and banned new conscripts from entering Lithuania.

In April, there was an avalanche of threats against the government from the Russian Vice President Aleksandr Rutskoi and Russian officers stationed in Lithuania in connection with the arrest of a Navy commander accused of participating in the August coup. On 15 May, the Lithuanian National Defense opened fire on a column of military vehicles traveling without permits. On 14 June, 91 percent of voters in a special referendum favored an immediate withdrawal of Soviet troops to be completed by year's end, and financial compensation for damages resulting from Soviet occupation. The following month, the last Russian military units left the capital, Vilnius, and on 8 August, Lithuania reached an agreement with Russia specifying that all Russian troops would be withdrawn by 31 August 1993.

On 29 October, however, Russian President Yeltsin issued a decree suspending the withdrawal from all three Baltic states. Yeltsin cited lack of housing in Russia and the need to protect Russian-speaking minorities from discrimination. On 25 November, the U.N. General Assembly unanimously urged Russia to swiftly withdraw former Soviet forces from all three Baltic states.

In a 24 February meeting with a European Community delegation, the Belarus foreign minister stated that Belarus laid claim to the border areas of eastern Lithuania, including its capital, Vilnius. The issue was defused when he recanted, stating that it was only his private opinion. Subsequent meetings between the parliamentary chairmen of both countries indicated the willingness of both countries to develop good relations.

In economic matters, on 29 Aprils Lithuania became the first ex-Soviet republic to become a member of the International Monetary Fund and the World Bank. In April, the government issued coupons to complement Russian rubles as a first step towards introducing a Lithuanian currency, the litas.

Political Rights and Civil Liberties: Lithuanians have the right to change their government democratically. The first democratic elections in its post-World War II history occurred in 1990. Freedoms of association and assembly are respected. Freedom of the press is generally respected, although a Press Monitoring Administration is responsible to the Justice Ministry. In June, the Attorney General instituted criminal proceedings against the editor of *Jura Krantas*, a Klaipeda monthly, following its publication of offensive anti-Russian statements. There are several independent radio stations, but they broadcast out of state facilities. Lithuanian television had only one channel until 1 January 1992, when a second channel was established.

There is no established state religion, and freedom of religion is respected in this overwhelmingly Roman Catholic Church country. The rights of ethnic minorities are respected, although the Polish-speaking population accused the government of discrimination in connection with the postponement of local elections in predominantly Polish-speaking areas. Freedom of domestic and international travel is guaranteed. On 21 February, members of various independent trade unions formed the Lithuanian Trade Union Association.

Luxembourg

Polity: Parliamentary democracy
Economy: Capitalist
Population: 388,000
PPP: $16,537
Life Expectancy: 74.9
Ethnic Groups: Mostly Luxembourger, 28 percent foreign (mostly Italian and Portuguese)

Political Rights: 1
Civil Liberties: 1
Status: Free

Overview: The Luxembourger parliament's approval of the Maastricht Treaty on European union was the top news development in 1992.

The second country to approve the treaty, Luxembourg had a national debate about the treaty's granting local voting rights to other European Community (EC) nationals. Since outsiders constitute one-third of the resident population, Luxembourg's politicians worked out a deal with the EC to exempt the country from the voting rights provision. With that exemption approved, the parliament approved the treaty by a margin of 51 to 6 on 2 July.

The Grand Duchy of Luxembourg received international recognition as an independent neutral country in 1867. However, Germany occupied the country during both world wars. Since World War II, Luxembourg has been a major advocate of European unity, and belongs to both the European Community and NATO.

Grand Duke Jean is head of state. He appoints the prime minister from the party or coalition able to command a majority in the 60-member Chamber of Deputies. Voters elect deputies by proportional representation for a maximum term of five years. There is also an appointive Council of State, whose 21 members have life terms. The Chamber can overturn the Council's decisions. In the general election held 18 June 1989, the center-right Christian Social Party won 22 seats, the Socialist Workers' Party 18, and the liberal Democratic Party 11. The growing Green Alternative won four seats, and the Communists captured one. Winning four seats, a new single-issue force, the Five-Sixths Party, advocates pensions worth five-sixths of the final salary for all workers, and not just for the civil service. The prime minister, Jacques Santer, heads a Christian Social-Socialist coalition government.

Political Rights and Civil Liberties: Luxembourgers have the right to change their government democratically. Non-Luxembourgers have no right to vote in national or local elections, but they are free otherwise. There is freedom of speech and of the press. Print journalism is private and uncensored, except for restrictions on pornography. Broadcast media are state-chartered and free. The country has freedom of association. The steel industry, the agricultural interests, and small businesses all have lobbying groups. Affiliated with the Socialist and Christian Social parties, two competing labor federations organize workers. The population is mostly Catholic; there is religious freedom and no state church. The productive economy is largely private.

Macedonia

Polity: Presidential-parliamentary democracy
Economy: Mixed statist
Population: 1,949,000
PPP: na
Life Expectancy: 70.0
Ethnic Groups: Macedonians (64.6 percent), Albanians (21 percent), Turks (4.8 percent), Romanies (2.7 percent), Serbs (2.2 percent), Macedonian Muslims (2.5 percent)

Political Rights: 3
Civil Liberties: 4
Status: Partly Free

Overview: In its first full year of independence, the former Yugoslav republic of Macedonia faced several critical problems, among them ongoing ethnic tensions inside its borders, the reluctance of the international community to recognize its sovereignty, and serious economic conditions brought on by the dissolution of Yugoslavia, a subsequent economic embargo by Greece and the war in Bosnia.

Macedonia is a multi-ethnic Balkan state bordering Serbia, Greece and Albania. Historically a region of contention, Macedonia was ruled by the Ottoman Turks for 500 years prior to the Second Balkan War in 1913, after which its territory was divided among Greece, Serbia and Bulgaria. Several of its neighbors have contended that there is no distinct Macedonian ethnic identity.

Macedonia voted to separate from Yugoslavia on 8 September 1991, as the Yugoslav federation was unravelling after the secession of Croatia and Slovenia earlier that year. Three-quarters of the republic's registered voters, with ethnic Albanians abstaining, participated in a referendum that endorsed independence by a large margin. The unicameral, 120-seat Macedonian Assembly (parliament) was elected in a three-stage process that concluded on 9 December 1990. The Internal Macedonian Revolutionary Organization-Democratic Party for Macedonian National Unity (VMRO), won 37 seats, and the Social-Democratic League of Macedonia (formerly the League of Communists of Macedonia) won 31 seats. The predominantly Albanian Party of Democratic Prosperity (PDP), carried 25 seats. Former Yugoslav Prime Minister Ante Markovic's Party of Reform Forces won 18 seats; the Socialist Party of Macedonia, 4; the Party of Yugoslavs, 1; and independents, 3. Following the vote, Kiro Gligorov of the Social-Democratic League was named president of the country, and Nikola Kljusev was named prime minister.

Shortly after the republic had declared its independence, Greece said that it would never recognize Macedonia until the republic removed the word "Macedonia" (also a region in northern Greece) from its official name. Greece, which then imposed an economic embargo on Macedonia, persuaded the European Community (EC) and the United States to withhold formal recognition. The first country to recognize Macedonian independence was Bulgaria, followed by Turkey, Greece's historic rival.

Nineteen-ninety-two began with the Assembly's adoption of EC-requested constitutional changes on 6 January. The government also declared that a planned referendum on political and territorial autonomy by ethnic Albanians was illegitimate. Nevertheless, on 11 and 12 January, 92 percent of registered Albanians voted in favor of autonomy. The same day, as a reaction to the referendum, in the sole Macedonian village in the Struga area, surrounded by mainly Albanian settlements, some 2,000 residents voted in favor of their own republic (the Macedonian Republic of Vevcani), with the right to join a Macedonian federation.

Tensions with neighboring Greece and Serbia also increased during the year. In February and March, Macedonian airspace was violated twice by Greek aircraft. According to Macedonian authorities, there are some 43,000 Serbs in Macedonia, although the Montenegrin newspaper *Pobjeda* said there are really about 300,000. In February, 10,000 Serbian residents of Kumanovo gathered for a peaceful protest against the decision of Macedonia not to participate in the Yugoslav community. They were led by leaders of the League of Communists-Movement for Yugoslavia. Special units of the Macedonian militia also occupied border areas with Greece and Albania in an attempt to stop transportation of military equipment to Serbia.

Ethnic tensions continued, and on 14 February, 50 members of the ultra-nationalist Serbian Radical Party (SRS) and the Serbian Chetnik Movement (SCP) blocked the entrance to the Yugoslav People's Army (YPA) headquarters of Uranje, demanding that the YPA protect Serbs living in the Skopje area and Kumanovo. On 18 March, after months of delay, Macedonia's ministry of home affairs registered the Skopje-seated Democratic Party of Serbs (DPS), the first political party of Serbs in Macedonia, in an effort to assuage tensions. The same month, the fourth Albanian party in Macedonia was founded, the Albanian Democratic Union-Liberal Party. After negotiations, the YPA withdrew its forces on 27 March.

On 3 April, at a rally of Albanians on the city square of Struga, a so-called Republic of Albanians in Yugoslavia—known as Ilirid—was proclaimed publicly for the first time. In response, on 9 April the Interior Ministry issued a statement that it would ban or disperse all unscheduled rallies in the republic and prosecute organizers. Pristina television in Albania reported that the Macedonian Internal Ministry closed all border crossings with Kosovo, the Albanian enclave within Serbia.

In June, Macedonia approved the U.N. Security Council resolution on sanctions against Serbia, the country's leading trading partner, which would ultimately cost the Macedonian economy about $1.3 billion. In addition, Macedonia had to deal with approximately 40,000 refugees from Bosnia-Herzegovina living in private homes or refugee camps.

At the Lisbon conference the same month, Greece continued to block Macedonia's recognition, and gained the support of the 12-member EC and the United States. It was decided to extend recognition to the republic only "under a name which does not include Macedonia." Denko Maleski, Macedonia's foreign minister, resigned in protest against the Lisbon decision. Parliament passed by 92 to 2 a vote of no confidence in the Kljusev government for its failure to obtain international recognition of Macedonia. The Lisbon decision prompted protests by more than 100,000 Macedonians in Skopje, the capital.

After a two-month process, a new government was formed in September headed by Branko Grvenkovski of the Social Democratic Union (SDZ). The new government included five Albanians from the Party for Democratic Prosperity, a Turk from the Democratic Union of Turks (minister of culture), and representatives from the centrist Reform Forces Liberal Party (RS-LP), the Socialist Party (SDSM, former Communists), and the Party for Emancipation of Roma (representing the Gypsy minority).

Ethnic tensions rose on 6 November, when four Albanians were killed and a dozen injured in a clash with Macedonian police. Several policemen had beaten up a 14-year-old Albanian boy, who was illegally selling cigarettes at the market. Approximately 2,000 Albanians turned out to protest and gunfire was exchanged between the Albanians and the special Macedonian police unit.

The Macedonian economy remained in crisis throughout the year. Inflation during the year was running at about 200 percent per month, unemployment had risen above 20 percent, and industrial production had fallen by 18 percent by the end of January. Although Macedonian exports increased in 1991, the impact of the economic blockade maintained by Greece and Serbia weakened the economy.

Political Rights and Civil Liberties: Macedonians can change their government democratically. A fully independent judiciary and rule of law have yet to be completely established. In accordance with parliament's decision, the Macedonian News Agency (MIA) was founded in February. In March, the government decided to allocate 190 million denars from the budget for press subsidies. On June 3, a team from the Macedonian Information Ministry tried forcibly to seize the premises and property owned by Tanjung (Yugoslavian Information Agency) for the last 17 years. There are two major dailies in Skopje, *Vecer* and *Nova Makedonija*. Government-owned radio and television broadcast programs in Macedonian, Turkish and Albanian.

Freedoms of expression, association and assembly are *de facto* limited for Albanians and other minority groups. The government threatened to ban or disperse what it considered illegal assemblages. The new law on citizenship requires 15 years of residence before citizenship is granted.

Freedom of religion is respected. The majority of the population is Orthodox Christian, with Islamic minorities. Citizens can travel freely domestically and internationally. Trade unions are allowed to organize, and strikes are permitted in all industries and sectors.

Madagascar

Polity: Transitional
Economy: Mixed statist
Population: 11,942,000
PPP: $690
Life Expectancy: 54.5
Ethnic Groups: Merina (26 percent), and seventeen smaller groups, all various Malayo-Polynesian and Negroid admixture

Political Rights: 4
Civil Liberties: 4
Status: Partly Free

Overview: In 1992, Madagascar voters approved a new democratic constitution, but clashes between the opposition and supporters of President Didier Ratsiraka threatened to derail the democratic transition. On 25 November 1992, the first round of presidential elections was won by Albert Zafy, president of the transitional State Higher Authority (HAE).

Madagascar, a large island and five small isles located off the south-eastern coast of Africa, won independence from France in 1960. President Ratsiraka has ruled Madagascar since 1974. In March 1990, a High Constitutional Court decree permitted independent political parties; since then, a number of ideologically diverse parties have been legalized.

In June 1991, partisans of the "Active Forces" opposition coalition launched a series of major protests in the capital and other major cities. The opposition demanded a new constitution, the convening of a sovereign national conference, and the resignation of Ratsiraka. People rallied by the hundreds of thousands in non-violent demonstrations. The authorities usually avoided the use of force while policing the gatherings. On 8 August, Ratsiraka appointed Guy Razanamasay as prime minister. However, a new cabinet announced later in the month included no opposition figures.

Following continued unrest, on 29 October Ratsiraka and Razanamasay agreed to form a new unity government that would include representatives of the opposition. They also agreed to dissolve both the National Assembly and the Supreme Revolutionary Council, establishing instead a transitional High State Authority. In addition, a new constitution would be drafted and submitted before a national referendum by the end of 1992. On 23 November, Zafy was named president of the High State Authority.

A new cabinet announced on 19 December divided ministerial portfolios almost equally between Ratsiraka supporters and opposition figures. At the time, there was an agreement to hold a national conference to draw up the new constitution, with presidential and legislative elections to follow the constitutional referendum.

The major issues in 1992 were the drafting of the constitution and the presidential election. The promised "National Forum" was convened in February to draft a new constitution and electoral law. In March, the forum was disrupted by several incidents of violence, including two grenade attacks launched outside the hall where the Forum was meeting. After the second disruption, the proceedings were relocated to a military facility. On 31 March, security forces killed eight Ratsiraka supporters and injured 40 other protesters in a pro-federalist crowd of 500, which unsuccessfully attempted to storm the facility. The Forum's 1,400 participants, drawn predominantly from the Active Forces movement, were only then completing their work.

The completed constitution was submitted to the electorate for ratification on 19 August after repeated postponements. The proposed document, which provided for a unitary state by reducing local autonomy and shifted power to the national legislature from the president, was approved by 73 percent in a turnout of approximately 65 percent of registered voters. Ratsiraka, with an eye to the upcoming presidential race, decided to step back from the more intransigent elements among his supporters and participate in the referendum. The constitution went into effect on 14 September.

During the year, the anti-Ratsiraka opposition moved to strengthen its position. In mid-February, the High State Authority announced the planned suspension and replacement of the "Decentralized Communities"—local authorities owing their position to the Ratsiraka regime. But some of the local Ratsiraka loyalists in charge in coastal Madagascar immediately responded by stating that they would resist any attempts to replace them.

In March and October, there was heightened tension in the port of Antsiranana as supporters of Ratsiraka and the Active Forces clashed. In August, during the run-up to the constitutional referendum, pro-federalist civilians reinforced by some members of the presidential guard called for a boycott of the election and burned ballot boxes, ballots, and booths. They declared some coastal regions to be "self-governing" and temporarily seized some provincial radio stations and airports in northern and eastern coastal towns to bolster their defiance of the transitional government. In October, armed federalists in coastal areas forced the shut-down of oil pipelines and seized government buildings. Some observers warned that the country was on the verge of civil war.

Meanwhile, Ratsiraka geared himself for the presidential race. The president's support came mainly from coastal Malagasys, which he courted during campaign forays outside his closely-guarded presidential palace during the summer and fall. Ratsiraka's supporters championed a new-found faith in "federalism," but the Active Forces viewed it as a smokescreen to perpetuate the president's long-centralized control. Despite the opposition's desire to see him forced to leave public life permanently at the earliest possible moment, Ratsiraka announced in June that he would run for another term of office.

Although according to his own original timetable Ratsiraka would not have had to face voters again until 1996, he joined seven other candidates in presidential elections held on 25 November. His chief rival was Zafy, who had narrowly escaped injury in late March when a truck bomb aimed at his house failed to hit its target before exploding.

The three leading candidates in the vote count were Zafy, with 46 percent, Ratsiraka, with 28.6 percent, and former Maoist Manandafy Rakotonirina, with 10 percent. The second round was scheduled for late January 1993.

Political Rights and Civil Liberties: A multi-party system was formally introduced in Madagascar in 1990, but a government/opposition stand-off has delayed the realization of democracy. An independent judiciary functions without government interference. There is a vibrant private press, and censorship of the print media was officially abolished in 1990. When the government attempted to re-impose censorship under the state of emergency called in 1991, the private press refused to cooperate. Television is government-controlled, though there are now independent private radio stations. There are a number of national labor organizations, most affiliated with political associations. Workers have the right to join unions and strike.

Malawi

Polity: One-party
Economy: Capitalist
Population: 8,709,000
PPP: $620
Life Expectancy: 48.1
Ethnic Groups: Chewa, Nyanja, Tumbuku, other

Political Rights: 6
Civil Liberties: 7
Status: Not Free

Overview: In 1992, several of Malawi's foreign lenders announced a suspension of non-humanitarian aid until the regime of President Hastings Kamuzu Banda improved its human rights record. While the government attempted to appease lenders with paper reforms, it continued to stifle dissent.

A densely populated, land-locked country in southeast Africa, the Republic of Malawi has been ruled since independence in 1964 by Banda, head of the ruling Malawi Congress Party (MCP). The 91-year-old ruler, designated president-for-life in 1971, holds absolute power. The unicameral National Assembly is largely elected, but all candidates are MCP-approved. The president appoints certain "nominated" members of parliament who are not required to seek election.

In 1991, at both the MCP party conference and later before the National Assembly,

Banda publicly called for open debate on adopting a multi-party system. Both bodies solidly voted for continuing "one-party democracy," which opposition critics suggest was the result demanded by Banda. On 31 December, the president dissolved his cabinet. One week later, Banda formed a new cabinet, with John Tembo as Minister of State in the President's office. Increasingly, responsibility for day-to-day governing is shifting to the powerful Tembo, a member of the MCP Executive Committee. Banda and Tembo are assisted by Mama C. Tamanda Kadzamira, Tembo's niece and the country's Official Hostess.

On 8 March, a pastoral letter criticizing the regime's human rights record was read in Catholic churches throughout Malawi. After the regime publicly denounced the letter as seditious, the one archbishop and six bishops were promptly taken into custody. Angry cabinet ministers reportedly decided that the churchmen would die for their statement. The bishops' lives may have been saved, however, when an international outcry led to the president's assurance that they would not be killed. However, one Irish-born bishop was expelled from the country on short notice.

The first in a series of public protests took place on 16 March, when students of the University of Malawi demonstrated in support of the bishops. They were fired upon by security forces, and reportedly a number were wounded. A phenomenon unseen in Malawi for many years, that demonstration was followed in early May by others in which striking workers demanding wage hikes and political change were joined by other anti-regime protesters. As many as 40 people may have died and hundreds were wounded when authorities opened fire as they battled with demonstrators in a number of cities.

In an 18 October radio address, Banda unexpectedly announced a referendum, without giving a date, in which citizens would decide whether to keep the current system, or adopt a multi-party system. Only three weeks earlier, at the ruling party's convention, Banda had claimed that citizens were satisfied with his one-party rule.

President Banda's announcement of a referendum was followed within days by formation of another group supporting multi-party democracy, the United Democratic Front (UDF). Following the lead of other opposition movements, it called for a new voters' role to replace the current registrar for one-party elections. In late October, the regime began arresting and detaining hundreds of opposition activists for possessing newly issued membership cards, asserting that cards were seditious documents. Political rallies and meetings were broken up despite opposition complaints of intimidation. The government cautioned that the referendum campaign did not mean that opposition parties could operate freely.

Several illegal internal and exiled opposition groups have emerged to challenge the government. The internal organizations include the clandestine United Democratic Party, founded in March, and the Alliance for Democracy (AFORD), launched in September. Among the exile groups, most prominent is the Zambia-based United Front for Multi-party Democracy, begun in mid-1991. Opposition demands include the release of political prisoners, a general amnesty, suspension of the authoritarian constitution and drafting of a replacement by a constituent assembly, and creation of a government of national unity to manage the transition to multi-party elections.

Throughout 1992, the regime continued to crack down on dissent. On 6 April Chakufwa Chihana, secretary general of the Southern Africa Trade Union Coordination Council, was arrested at the national airport. He was returning from a meeting of the Malawian opposition in exile in Zambia, where he was given the task of organizing a conference in Malawi that would promote political pluralism. He was charged with sedition and briefly released in July before being re-arrested within days after giving an interview to the BBC. Chihana was eventually released on bail on 8 September. On 14 December, Chakufwa Chihana was sentenced to two years imprisonment at hard labor for sedition. The sentencing judge stated the evidence showed that Chihana had intended to incite disaffection and dissatisfaction against Life President Banda.

In mid-July, Aleki Banda (no relation to the president) was released after almost twelve years in detention without charge or trial. A former secretary-general of the MCP, he was allegedly imprisoned for having threatened to go public with evidence of high-level corruption. However, the dissident Orton Chirwa, said to be the longest incarcerated political prisoner in Africa, died in a Malawian prison in late October. He served some twelve years of a life sentence for treason after he and his wife were kidnapped in Zambia in 1980 by Malawian security police. She was still in prison as 1992 drew to a close.

The continued presence of nearly one million refugees from Mozambique put a strain on Malawi's economy, one of the poorest in Africa. Refugees now make up nearly 10 percent of the population. Although the Paris Club of international donors suspended development aid to Malawi in May 1992, the World Bank agreed in June to loan the country over one hundred million dollars.

Political Rights and Civil Liberties:

The Republic of Malawi is ruled by of the most repressive regimes in Africa. Authoritarian power is constitutionally vested in President Hastings Kamuzu Banda and the Malawi Congress Party. All political activity outside of the MCP is deemed criminal, and every Malawian is supposed to be a dues-paying member of the ruling party. Malawian government agents have assassinated or kidnapped dissidents residing in exile.

The judiciary rarely displays independence, although in 1992 a judge ordered the regime to justify its continued detention of opposition leader Chakufwa Chihana. Until that year, criticism of the president and ruling party could lead to decades of incommunicado detention without charge, under the 1965 Public Security Regulations. Those tried in the "traditional courts" for political and other crimes had no procedural rights. Reforms enacted in August permit defendants to choose their own attorneys, hear the charges against them, and be arraigned. Despite the changes, political defendants still face pre-ordained conviction. The government maintains the right to revoke the property rights of those suspected of "economic crimes."

The security apparatus is pervasive and intrusive, and severe abuse of detainees occurs as a matter of course. The police and Banda's Malawi Young Pioneers share the task of repressing dissent. Hundreds were reported to have been arrested and beaten for publicly showing their support for multi-party politics in 1992. Some long-term political prisoners have been released due to pressure exerted by foreign aid donors.

To prevent alternative sources of public information, there are severe restrictions on the unauthorized dissemination of news. A 1992 revision of a law enacted in 1973 makes sending "false information" out of the country, formerly punishable by life imprisonment, a crime now punishable by five years imprisonment. Malawi's tight visa restrictions for foreign journalists have made it one of Africa's most under-reported countries.

Religious groups must register with the government. Jehovah's Witnesses have suffered brutal persecution. Members of the Tumbuku ethnic group and those of South Asian origin also suffer government-sanctioned discrimination. Government employees and civil servants must obtain written permission to travel abroad. The independent Trade Union Congress of Malawi is small, and unions are weak.

Malaysia

Polity: Dominant party
Economy: Capitalist
Population: 18,742,000
PPP: $5,649
Life Expectancy: 70.1
Ethnic Groups: Multi-ethnic state—Malays, Chinese, non-Malay indigenous, Indians and others

Political Rights: 5
Civil Liberties: 4
Status: Partly Free

Overview:
In 1992, Malaysia continued to experience what opposition leader Lim Kit Siang guardedly called an "anti-democratic trend," which includes his own suspension from parliament, a sharp cutback in development funds to opposition-controlled states, and parliamentary procedures that stifle debate. In addition, one of the opposition states may introduce Islamic law.

Malaysia was established in 1963 through the merger of the Federation of Malaya, the British colonies of Sarawak and Sabah and Singapore, which withdrew two years later. The ceremonial head of state in this constitutional monarchy, currently the Sultan of Perak, is chosen for a five-year term by and from among the nine hereditary rulers of the Malay states, and has the power to delay federal legislation. Executive power is vested in the prime minister and the cabinet. The parliament consists of a Senate, with 32 members appointed by the monarch and 26 elected by state legislatures, and a 180-member, popularly-elected House of Representatives. Each state has its own parliament and constitution, and shares legislative powers with the federal government.

The economic success of the country's ethnic Chinese triggered race riots in 1969. In response, the government introduced the New Economic Policy in 1971, which discriminates in favor of Malays through racial quotas in business affairs. Although this has helped transfer some of the wealth into Malay hands, the urban elite has prospered much more than the rural Bumiputras (sons of the soil). A new National Development Policy adopted in 1991 has the same goals, but less rigid target quotas.

The ruling National Front coalition, which currently includes ten parties, has captured at least a two-thirds majority in the lower house in all eight general elections since 1957. At its core is the United Malays National Organization (UMNO), which champions secular Malay interests. However, its claim to represent all Malays through consensual decision-making was challenged in April 1987, when top UMNO figures tried to oust Prime Minister Mahathir Mohamad as party president for alleged government mismanagement and corruption. The dispute led to a party split, with Razaleigh Hamzah subsequently forming a "new" UMNO (UMNO-Baru).

In late 1988, disgruntled UMNO members led by Razaleigh formed Semangat '46 (Spirit of '46, the year UMNO was formed in Malaya). In May 1989, Semangat '46 joined with the Muslim fundamentalist Pan-Malaysian Islamic Party (Pas) and two smaller parties in a Malay-based opposition called the Muslim Unity Movement (APU). In the October 1990 elections, the National Front won 127 seats (UMNO-Baru 71, the Malaysian Chinese Association 18, the Malaysian Indian Congress 6, the social democratic Malaysian People's Movement 5, the United Sabah National Organization 6, along with 21 affilated candidates). The opposition won 53 seats (up from 25 in 1986), led by the left-of-center, Chinese-based Democratic Action Party (DAP) with 20, the United Sabah Party (PBS) with 14, Semangat '46 with 8, and Pas with 7, along with 4 independents.

Critics such as opposition leader Lim Kit Siang have grown increasingly concerned by the reduced debate in parliament, and by the government's cutbacks in development funds to the two opposition-controlled states. Following a series of rancorous parliamentary sessions in the spring of 1992, the speaker ordered a review of the body's standing orders, which may lead to more restrictive parliamentary procedures. Already, the opposition has been hampered by limits on the number of questions an MP can ask on a topic, reduced speaking time on the floor, and by fewer appearances before parliament by ministers. On 14 May, the parliament suspended Lim for the rest of the year after he refused the speaker's request to exit the floor.

Opposition governments in Sabah and Kelantan say the government holds back on the funds to pressure them into joining the National Front. In Sabah, chief minister and PBS head Joseph Pairin Kitingan went on trial in January on corruption charges, and his brother and several others have been detained for allegedly plotting to "take Sabah out of the federation." The multiracial PBS won control of the state in June 1990, and Kitingan pulled the party out of the National Front just days before the October 1990 national elections. Since 1991, UMNO has been registered in the state in an attempt to woo Malays and undermine the broad support for the PBS.

In the heavily-Muslim state of Kelantan, the opposition, Malay-based Pas came into power at the 1990 elections. In April 1992, chief minister Nik Abdul Aziz Nik Mat announced plans to implement *Hudud* (Islamic law) in the state for both Muslims and non-Muslims, which would require an amendment to the federal constitution. On 18 April, Mahathir said the government would support the necessary changes in the constitution, but accused Pas of undermining the federal government's commitment to Islam for political purposes.

Another divisive issue is the role of the sultans in society. After a meeting with UMNO leaders in July, six of the nine sultans agreed to a document reaffirming the constitutional ban on their involvement in partisan politics. In December, Mahathir announced that a special session of parliament in January 1993 would craft an amendment ending the sultan's legal immunity.

Political Rights and Civil Liberties: The ability of Malaysians to change their government democratically is limited by ethnic Malay and United Malay National Organization dominance. A Commonwealth election team rated the 1990 elections free but not entirely fair, largely due to inadequate media access for the opposition and irregularities in voting rolls.

Official policy limits access for non-Malays in education, the civil service, and business licenses and ownership. Despite these advantages, most Malays remain poorer than their non-Malay counterparts.

The government continues to detain former Communists, religious extremists and others without formal charges under the 1960 Internal Security Act and the 1969 Emergency Ordinance. Amendments to the ISA in 1988 and 1989 limited judicial review of detentions. The judiciary is independent in civil and criminal cases, and has shown a high degree of independence in political cases. The Malaysian Bar Council has been at odds with the government since 1988, when the government sacked the Supreme Court Lord President (who heads the judiciary) after UMNO was deregistered. In March 1992, the Bar Council continued the standoff by refusing to recognize the current Lord President.

Freedom of speech is restricted by the 1970 Sedition Act amendments, which prohibit discussion of issues such as the special position of Malays in society. A 1987 amendment makes the publication of "malicious" news an offense and expanded the government's censorship powers. All the major media outlets are owned by the government or by companies owned by National Front parties, and coverage of opposition parties is limited. The 1967 Police Act requires permits for all public assemblies. Following the 1969 riots, political rallies were banned; only indoor "discussion sessions" are permitted. The Societies Act requires any association of more than six members to register with the government; a similiar law applies to student groups, which are barred from political activity.

Islam is the official religion in this secular country, but minority groups worship freely. Malaysians are free to travel within the country, and citizens can travel anywhere in the world except to Israel.

The government must approve and can dissolve all unions, and each labor group can cover only one particular trade or occupation. Strikes are legal but restricted. Unions must provide advance notice in several "essential services." The Ministry of Human Resources can refer a dispute to the Industrial Court for arbitration, during which time a strike is prohibited. In response to pressure to pressure from multina-tional corporations, the government has barred electronics workers from forming a national union. Foreigners working illegally in the country were given a six-month amnesty to register in the first half of 1992; 320,000 workers did so, but up to 100,000 are at large.

Maldives

Polity: Non-party presi-
dential-legislative
(elite clan-dominated)
Economy: Capitalist
Population: 222,000
PPP: $1,118
Life Expectancy: 62.5
Ethnic Groups: Mixed Sinhalese, Dravidian, Arab, and black

Political Rights: 6
Civil Liberties: 5
Status: Not Free

Overview: Environmental disaster shaped new government policies in 1992. Due to the breakdown of coral reefs and sea-wall barriers, the government introduced stringent controls on methods of fishing and banned coral excavation for building materials around inhabited islands. Since most of the population works in fishing and small-scale agriculture, the economic impact of the restrictions is significant. With foreign assistance, the government built new breakwaters and sea-walls to prevent recent changes in the water level from causing floods.

The poor, Islamic, Republic of the Maldives is a string of 1,190 mostly uninhabited coral reef islands in the Indian Ocean. A small, hereditary Sunni elite controls the state. Three-term President Maumoon Adbul Gayoom's governing philosophy alternates between openness and crackdowns on any attempts at democracy. After 815 years of ad-Din Sultanate rule ended in 1968, the country suffered a series of coups until 1988. This spate ended after the Maldives called in Indian troops to quash supposed Sri Lankan Tamil separatist mercenaries, hired by a Maldivan businessman. To reduce the threat of future coups and instability, the government became increasingly autocratic, enlarging the National Security Service and packing the government with Gayoom family members.

The new members elected in the February 1990 elections for the unicameral *Majlis* (Citizens Assembly), sought to enact the first significant reforms since independence. Gayoom spoke of power-sharing with the Parliament and enacted considerable freedom of the press. By April, the government tired of protests against its nepotism and corruption and banned all independent media. In November 1990, the government instituted a retroactive Anti-Terrorism Act that imprisoned members of the press and critics of the government. Businessmen censuring authoritarianism suffered mysterious arson attacks on their property. Again in 1992, the government loosened restrictions on the media. However, Gayoom, fearing loss of power through democratic expression, imprisoned journalists again. Some remain in solitary confinement or internal exile.

Tourism is a major foreign exchange earner. Gayoom is attempting to increase economic integration and development through the South Asian Association for Cooperation.

Political Rights and Civil Liberties:

Maldivians cannot change their government democratically. The president and his cabinet maintain most of the political control. The government owns and operates the only television and radio stations. Law prohibits actions which would "arouse people against the government." The government bans publications with regularity.

The state does not forbid political parties, but does not permit them in practice. Candidates for the Majlis run as individuals. Forty seats are popularly elected; eight are appointed by the president. Every five years, the Majlis selects a single nominee for president, whom the electorate ratifies by referendum. In theory, the Majlis and Cabinet (appointed by the president) advise the president on policy questions. The citizens may criticize the government through direct oral or written complaints.

President Gayoom can appoint and remove all judges. The legal system is based on Islamic law. Criminal punishments include flogging and banishment to remote islands.

The state religion is Islam, and the constitution defines all citizens as Sunni Muslims. The president has the role of protector of Islam. The government does not permit non-Muslim houses of worship, but permits private religious practice. Proselytization and conversion are illegal, under penalty of loss of citizenship. Local Islamic practice circumscribes women's roles. According to the Constitution, women may not become president. However, two women are Majlis members. The state does not prohibit trade unions, but none exist. The government does not recognize the right to bargain collectively or strike.

Mali

Polity: Presidential-par-
liamentary democracy
Economy: Mixed statist
Population: 8,538,000
PPP: $576
Life Expectancy: 45.0
Ethnic Groups: Arab Bedouin, Bambara, Berabish Berber,
Dogon, Fulani, Malinke (50 percent), Songhai, Tuareg, other

Political Rights: 2
Civil Liberties: 3
Status: Free

Overview:

After twelve years of one-party rule and one year of
transitional government, in 1992 the Republic of Mali held
free and fair multi-party elections. Alpha Konare of the
Alliance for Democracy in Mali (ADEMA) was elected president with 69 percent of
the vote in a run-off. However, violence among ethnic Tuaregs in the north continued
to plague the country.

The April 1992 presidential election was the culmination of a process that began
when the country's ruler of 23 years, General Moussa Traoré, was deposed by a
military coup on 26 March 1991. The coup capped two months of often-violent
public demonstrations against Traoré's regime. His overthrow was followed by the
abolition of his Mali People's Democratic Union (UDPM). Traoré himself had ousted
Modibo Keita in a bloodless military coup in 1968.

Public demonstrations in support of a multi-party system began in 1990. Traoré
responded by arresting opposition activists. A number of those detained, beaten and
deprived of food included children as young as eleven. The repeated anti-regime
rallies, well-organized and peaceful at first, sometimes deteriorated into destructive
sprees directed against symbols of the regime. Refusing all dialogue with the opposition, Traoré sent security forces to break up public protests with tear gas, clubs, and
even machine-gun fire. Numerous people were injured and an estimated 160 were
killed. Finally, military officials moved against the president to end the spiral of street
violence.

The leader of the insurgent, all-military "National Reconciliation Council,"
Amadou Toumani Toure, pledged soon after the coup that the junta's role would be
limited to ensuring free elections, and that the soldiers would return to the barracks by
20 January 1992. The Council dissolved itself within the week, ceding power to a 25-
member Transitional Committee for National Salvation (CTSP), which had a mixed
civilian-military membership. A civilian, Soumana Sacko, was named interim Prime
Minister. Traoré and leading members of his regime were jailed in anticipation of
trials for murder and corruption. The first trial opened on 26 November 1992.

A critical task of the CTSP was the organization of a national conference of all
newly constituted political parties to draw up plans for a new electoral code and
multi-party constitution. The two-week conference, which opened in July 1991,
adopted a draft constitution that guaranteed judicial independence and civil liberties.
The constitution was overwhelmingly approved in a national referendum on 12
January 1992. After municipal elections were held 19 January, charges of vote-buying

and irregular procedure in some precincts led to postponement of the legislative balloting scheduled to follow. A number of parties scoring poorly in municipal elections boycotted the subsequent legislative and presidential races. Despite accusations of fraud, international observers judged the series of elections to be essentially fair. ADEMA garnered the most votes in all elections, followed by the long-dormant Sudanese Union-African Democratic Rally, and the National Committee for Democratic Initiative. Participation by registered voters dropped throughout the series of votes, from 43 percent in the referendum to 21 percent in the last round of balloting for president.

Newly elected President Konare declared his first task to be renegotiation of Mali's structural adjustment program. Emphasizing Mali's need to develop the private sector and rely less on civil service employment, on inauguration day Konare told his countrymen not to expect miracles from his administration. Within two weeks of his election, the independent National Union of Malian Workers was threatening to call an indefinite general strike in demand of salary arrears and substantial wage hikes. An agreement with the new government averted the labor action.

Konare appointed economist Yonoussi Touré as prime minister, and two parties joined ADEMA in the new government by assuming ministerial portfolios. In early May, thirteen political parties formed an opposition Front for the Safeguard of Democracy in Mali headed by Konare's competitor in the presidential run-off race, Tieoule Konate.

A continuing problem that successive Malian governments have had to address has been the sporadic unrest among the Tuareg and Arab ethnic minorities in the northern part of the country. After continued hit-and-run attacks by armed bands of Tuaregs on police posts and isolated villages, the military responded with raids on Tuareg encampments that degenerated into massacres of the male inhabitants. Attempting to end the spiral of violence, the transitional government tried to schedule conferences with the four armed Tuareg liberation movements in Timbuktu and Mopti in December 1991. Representatives of the Tuareg and the government agreed to a truce and the release of prisoners at a conference in Algiers in late January 1992. In April, they signed a peace pact. According to its terms, fighting was to stop and Tuareg rebels are to be integrated into the Malian army, an expensive proposition that requires French financing. Despite the pact, sporadic attacks and reprisals continued, and the Tuareg continued to press the government to withdraw its armed forces from northern Mali. There are some 35,000 Tuareg and Arab refugees in Mauritania.

Political Rights and Civil Liberties:

Malians can change their government democratically. Twenty-three political parties competed for municipal, legislative, and presidential elections in 1992. ADEMA controls 76 out of 116 seats in the national legislature.

A number of independent newspapers have sprung up since General Moussa Traoré's fall in 1991. The press has participated freely in national debates about the transition to democracy, prosecution of members of the Traoré regime for corruption and human rights abuse, and the continuing unrest in the north of the country. The national radio and television stations reported the activities of the various political parties fairly during the run-up to elections. The new constitution guarantees freedom of the press, and legislation in 1992 gave private broadcasters the right to operate their own facilities.

International human rights organizations have expressed concern over the Malian army's torture and extrajudicial execution of innocent Tuaregs and Arabs in retaliation for armed attacks by rebels in the north of the country. The new regime announced that those responsible for abuses have and will be punished. The constitution now promises trade union independence. The National Union of Malian Workers was an important force in popular opposition to Traoré during 1991, and now seriously champions workers' interests.

Malta

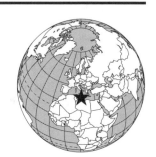

Polity: Parliamentary democracy
Economy: Mixed capitalist-statist
Population: 361,000
PPP: $8,231
Life Expectancy: 73.4
Ethnic Groups: Maltese (mixed Arab, Sicilian, Norman, Spanish, Italian, and English)

Political Rights: 1
Civil Liberties: 1
Status: Free

Overview:

The top news story of 1992 was the ruling Nationalist Party's re-election victory on 22 February. Helped by a prosperous economy, Prime Minister Edward Fenech Adami led the conservative Nationalists to a victory over the socialist Labor opposition by 51.8 to 46.5 percent. The environmentalist Democratic Alternative received 1.7 percent of the vote, but won no seats. Fenech emphasized his support for future full membership in the European Community (EC) while Labor backed cooperation with the EC short of complete integration. Malta has a membership application on file with the EC, and is awaiting a response.

Located in the central Mediterranean, Malta was under foreign rule for most of its history. The British occupied the island in 1800, and it later became a British colony. Malta gained independence from Britain in 1964. The Labor Party won power in 1971, and held office until 1987. In government, Labor followed left-of-center economic policies and a neutral foreign policy. It also ordered some confiscations of church property and restricted private financing for Catholic schools. Labor turned to Libya for aid and support in the early 1980s. The socialists lost control to the Nationalist Party in the 1987 general elections. The Nationalists are attempting to reverse Labor's restrictions on the Roman Catholic Church. On a visit to Malta in 1990, the Pope asked the government to do more to make the Church "free from undue pressures, obstacles, and manipulation." The Nationalists are carrying out a gradual privatization of the state sector.

The parliament, called the House of Representatives, has 65 seats and a maximum term of five years. Voters choose the representatives by proportional representation. Elected by parliament, the largely ceremonial president serves for five years, and appoints the prime minister from the parliamentary majority party. Under a constitutional amendment adopted in 1987, a party getting a majority of the popular vote gets a majority of the seats in parliament. In the previous elections, it was possible for a party to receive a majority of votes while winning only a minority of seats. As a result of the 1992 election, the Nationalists hold 34 seats and Labor holds 31.

Reacting to its recent electoral defeats, Labor has moderated its program. The party has dropped its opposition to private hospitals and free trade, and has improved its relations with the Catholic clergy. After Labor's loss in 1992, its leader, former Prime Minister Karmenu Mifsud Bonnici, announced his intention to step down.

Maltese businesses caused international resentment in 1992 when they skirted the U.N.'s restrictions on trade with Libya. Malta became the chief transit point for Libya early in the year after the world community punished the latter country's involvement in terrorist acts against airline passengers.

Political Rights and Civil Liberties:

The Maltese have the right to change their government democratically, and power alternates between the two major parties.

The government licensed several new private radio stations in 1991, and allocated one each to the major political parties and the Roman Catholic Church. The rest of the stations went to businessmen, journalists, recording studios, and a trade union. The privatization of the major media should increase the variety of broadcast political opinion. Malta's constitution guarantees freedoms of speech and press. The only exception is a law passed in 1987 which forbids foreign involvement in Maltese election campaigns. The press is free, and many newspapers are politically affiliated.

Religion is free for both the Catholic majority and for religious minorities. There are tiny Protestant and Muslim communities. All groups have freedom of association. Many trade unions belong to the General Union of Workers, but others are independent. The Labor Party and the General Workers Union decided to sever their official links to each other in 1992, in order to pursue more independent policies. A constitutional amendment banning sex discrimination takes effect in July 1993.

Marshall Islands

Polity: Parliamentary democracy
Economy: Capitalist-statist
Population: 50,000
PPP: na
Life Expectancy: 72.5
Ethnic Groups: Marshallese (Micronesian)

Political Rights: 1
Civil Liberties: 1
Status: Free

Overview:

The Marshall Islands and Australia were entangled in a passport-buying scandal in 1992. In April, Marshallese Attorney General Dennis McPhillips charged that Gregory

Symons, an Australian businessman, had entered the country in 1991 with the intent of obtaining Marshallese passports for Hong Kong and Taiwanese businessmen. Symons, a friend and alleged partner of Australian Labor politician Graham Richardson, had reportedly assured the entrepreneurs incorrectly that Marshallese passports would guarantee the men immediate entree into the United States. Symons had attempted to trade a major education and technology project to the Marshallese for the passports when the authorities caught him. After the media learned that Richardson, an Australian cabinet minister, had lobbied the Marshallese government on Symons' behalf, the ensuing publicity forced the politician to resign.

Located in the Pacific Ocean, the Marshall Islands were independent until the late 1800s, when the Germans established a protectorate. After World War II Japan governed under a League of Nations mandate until the U.S. Navy occupied the region in 1945. The U.S. administered the islands under a United Nations trusteeship after 1947. The Americans recognized a distinct Marshallese constitution in 1979, thereby causing a *de facto* change in the Marshalls' legal status. However, the Soviets and others waged an international legal dispute for several years over the islands' trusteeship. In 1986, the U.S. notified the U.N. formally that the trusteeship was over, and that the Marshalls had implemented a Compact of Free Association with the U.S. Under the Compact, the Marshalls have self-government, but still depend on American defense. Following changes in Soviet policy and the international political climate, the U.N. recognized the dissolution of the trusteeship in December 1990. In 1991, the Marshall Islands sought and received diplomatic recognition as an independent country and full U.N. membership.

The Marshalls have a parliamentary system. Voters choose the 33 member parliament (*Nitijela*) from 24 election districts. The legislators elect a president and cabinet who are responsible to them. The members serve four-year terms. There is also an advisory body of Micronesian chiefs. The most recent legislative election took place in November 1991. In January 1992, the parliament re-elected President Amata Kabua.

The economy depends heavily on U.S. and other foreign assistance. The U.S. carried out extensive nuclear testing in the Marshall Islands from 1946-58. America has faced numerous lawsuits from residents who cited the nuclear activity as the cause of their illnesses and other problems. In 1990, a panel of judges ruled that plaintiffs could receive $45 million in compensation from the U.S. The Marshallese and other Pacific island delegations expressed their concern at the Earth Summit in Rio de Janeiro in 1992 that the "greenhouse effect" of air pollution could cause water levels to rise and submerge their homes. The Marshallese delegation proposed instituting a center on climate change in their country.

Political Rights and Civil Liberties: The Marshallese have the right to change their government democratically. Elections are competitive, but involve individuals, tendencies, and factions, not formal parties.

There is a bill of rights, which protects most civil liberties. There are some minor restrictions on freedom of movement, due to defense installations and nuclear contamination. The cabinet can deport aliens who take part in Marshallese politics, but it has never done so. Although there is freedom of the press, the government cancelled its printing contract with a critical newspaper company in 1991. Ultimately, the government reversed the cancellation. The islands have private and public broadcast media and a private newspaper. The government respects freedom of association, but there are no trade unions. Marshallese women have formed several associations and an umbrella organization, Women United Together for the Marshall Islands.

Mauritania

Polity: Dominant party (military-dominated)
Economy: Capitalist-statist
Population: 2,103,000
PPP: $1,092
Life Expectancy: 47.0
Ethnic Groups: White and Black Moors, various black sub-Saharan African ethnic groups (Tuculor, Hal-Pulaar, Soninke, Wolof)

Political Rights: 7
Civil Liberties: 6
Status: Not Free

Overview: Mauritania's first multi-party presidential and legislative elections took place in 1992. According to international observers, however, the presidential balloting, won by the incumbent Maaouiya Ould Sid'Ahmed Taya, was marred by significant irregularities, most of them intentional on the part of the government. Following the elections, the government violently oppressed opposition protests, killing several people.

A former French colony, Mauritania has been under military rule since 1978, when military officers ousted President Ould Daddah and established the Committee for National Recovery, later renamed the Military Committee for National Salvation (CMSN). The country has long been beset by animosity between its black, Bantu-speaking ethnic groups, located largely along the country's southern border, and Arabic-speaking Moors of the north and center. The Moors, both white and black, make up about three—ourths of the population. If the disadvantaged black Moors and the non-Moor population are counted together, however, they form 55-60 percent of all Mauritanians. Despite its minority status, the white Moorish elite, including current President Taya, has traditionally dominated the country's politics and economy.

After repeated demonstrations by the opposition, President Taya announced in April 1991 that there would be a constitutional referendum by the end of the year. This was to be followed by multi-party presidential and legislative elections in 1992. The constitution was approved in July 1991.

Initially, the main opposition party Union of Democratic Forces (UFD) announced it would boycott the 24 January 1992 presidential election, alleging the balloting would be rigged in favor of the ruling Social and Democratic Republican Party. However, in early January, the party decided to endorse the independent candidacy of the recently returned expatriate Ahmed Ould Daddah, brother of ex-president Moktar Ould Daddah. Daddah received the backing of several political movements, including the black civil rights group *El Hor*, Muslim fundamentalists, liberals, and Nasserites. Two other minor candidates also challenged President Taya.

The opposition accused the regime of making little effort to register anyone but its supporters. Offices of the registrar were alleged to have remained closed for much of each day as the extended deadline of 14 January for voter registration approached. In the capital of Nouakchott, a bastion of opposition support, those still lined up at registration offices by midnight of the final deadline were dispersed with tear gas.

On election day, the UFD asserted that the authorities had prevented opposition representatives from either officially observing voting stations or accompanying ballot boxes to places where ballots were to be counted. The opposition also alleged vote-buying, intimidation, and the falsification of voter registration cards and lists. Although international observers stated that both sides in the electoral contest had attempted to cheat, they asserted that the government's efforts were more widespread and successful.

On 25 January, the government announced that a second round of voting was unnecessary because Taya had won 63 percent of the vote, with Daddah taking 33 percent. Security police raided Daddah's headquarters in Nouakchott, dispersing his supporters with tear gas, rubber bullets, and truncheons, injuring 22 people. The following day in the port of Nouadhibou, the police attacked the UPD office and broke up a demonstration protesting the earlier deadly attack and the election. As many as 5 people were killed and 160 were arrested. The government claimed that protesters had tried to attack the police with knives and rocks. Dusk-to-dawn curfews were imposed and public rallies were banned. Detainees were later released, while curfews and the ban on gatherings were lifted within two weeks.

Despite opposition charges of fraud, the Supreme Court soon upheld the official presidential election results. In late February, after the government ignored opposition demands for electoral reforms, the opposition decided to boycott the legislative elections scheduled for 6 March and 3 April. Apart from the ruling PRDS, only "independents" and a few minor parties supporting Taya participated. As expected, almost all the winning candidates were of the PRDS. After the elections, the CMSN was formally dissolved, and Sidi Mohamed Ould Boubaker was appointed prime minister in April.

Three hundred thousand anti-government protesters gathered on 3 March to call for an end to racial discrimination; and tens of thousands reportedly protested the day after Taya's inauguration to a new term of office on 18 April. The UFD called for the immediate formation of a transition government, leading to new, credible elections.

Since May 1989, the government has forcibly expelled approximately 60,000 of its own non-Moorish citizens into Senegal. Others have fled the country in the face of property confiscation, torture and extrajudicial killing. In 1992, the expulsions and flight continued at a reduced intensity.

Some members of Mauritania's indigenous non-Moorish ethnic groups have joined guerrilla movements in response to persecution. The African Liberation Forces of Mauritania (FLAM), one of the three guerrilla movements, suspended its armed struggle against the Taya government in July 1991 in response to the regime's preliminary moves toward democracy. However, it announced the resumption of its struggle after the results of the presidential contest were made public.

In April 1992, there was formal rapprochement between the Mauritanian and

Senegalese governments; three years ago they had severed relations in the midst of inter-ethnic strife in both countries. Land borders were reopened and postal and air links were re-established. In the recent past, Mauritania has accused its southern neighbor of turning a blind eye to forays by so-called "Senegalese" (i.e., returning Mauritanian expellees) who have attacked military posts and attempted to reclaim their property in Mauritania.

Political Rights and Civil Liberties:

Multi-party legislative elections held in 1992 were marred by substantial irregularities and allegations of fraud. The opposition charged that the regime prevented black Mauritanians from registering to vote. Mauritanians are allowed to form political parties, but onerous registration requirements prevent them from freely choosing national-level representatives.

The 1991 constitution provides for a strong-president system and formally guarantees freedom of expression, association, and the equality of all citizens. However, the exercise of all rights is limited by the regime's vaguely-defined "national security" concerns. For example, several opposition rallies were violently broken up by securing forces in 1992.

Islamic courts apply *shari'a*, Muslim law, as national law, but enforcement varies. Almost all Mauritanians are Muslim. No court is independent of regime manipulation. Extrajudicial execution and the use of torture against political detainees is frequent. Authorities also reportedly hold prisoners without charge for prolonged periods, often with inadequate food, water, and medical attention. Some dissident military officers remain in internal exile, without formal charge. Other opposition figures have been expelled from the country.

As part of its project of extending Moorish hegemony throughout society, French has been replaced with Arabic as the official language despite the protest of the non-Moorish population. Slavery was formally abolished in 1980, but the United Nations Human Rights Commission estimates there are still some 100,000 enslaved Mauritanians.

A law on freedom of the press was adopted in 1991; however, it is illegal to promote "national disharmony." Material construed by officials as "insulting the President" can also be punished by fine and imprisonment. Four privately owned publications exist, and are subject to varying degrees of censorship. The non-print media is state-controlled.

All unions must belong to the government-controlled general labor confederation, the Mauritanian Workers' Union. The government restricts the right to strike and strongly discourages political involvement by labor.

Mauritius

Polity: Parliamentary democracy
Economy: Capitalist
Population: 1,094,000
PPP: $5,375
Life Expectancy: 69.6

Political Rights: 2
Civil Liberties: 2
Status: Free

Ethnic Groups: Indo-Mauritians (68 percent), Creole (27 percent), Sino-Mauritian (3 percent), and Franco-Mauritian (2 percent)

Overview:
This crowded, multi-ethnic island nation east of Madagascar gained independence from Britain in 1968. Mauritius has one of the longest operating multi-party systems in post-colonial Africa. The transfer of power to a victorious political opposition after a free election, a rare phenomenon in Africa until 1991, was a democratic milestone passed a decade ago in Mauritius. In 1992, Mauritius became a republic within the British Commonwealth.

Parliamentary elections in September 1991 were preceded by shifting political alliances, a persistent feature of Mauritian politics. The Mauritian Militant Movement joined Prime Minister Jugnauth's Mauritian Socialist Movement, a revival of an old partnership. Meanwhile, the Labor Party moved into political opposition and entered the elections in alliance with three smaller parties. The 82 percent voter turn-out gave the opposition only three out of 62 elected seats in the new parliament. Fearing election fraud, the opposition had called for strict international supervision of voting. Following their defeat, the opposition presented considerable evidence of electoral irregularities to the Supreme Court. The Court, however, refused to invalidate election.

Mauritius became a republic in 1992, with a president as titular head of state rather than governor-general representing the British crown. Sir Veerasamy Ringadoo simultaneously became the last governor-general and the first president when he was sworn in on 12 March. The ceremony was boycotted by leaders of two opposition parties, who protested the government's failure to take the issue of republican status to Mauritians in a referendum. As planned, Ringadoo was succeeded within a few months as president by Cassam Uteem.

The country has continued to prosper in the 1990s, with real GDP growth estimated at 6.5 percent a year, unemployment at 2.1 percent, and inflation at 5 percent. Over the past decade the economy, long-dependent on sugar, has benefited from the creation of an export processing zone for diversification into labor-intensive textiles. The country has also built world-class tourist facilities. The government is now encouraging expansion into financial services. Mauritius is creating a welfare system with rising levels of social spending on public health, education, and other services.

Political Rights and Civil Liberties:
Citizens have the right to choose their government democratically in a competitive multi-party system. Mauritian ethnic and religious minorities are assured legislative representation

through a so-called "best loser" system. This requires that seats always be set aside for minorities, regardless of election returns. The judiciary, modelled after the British system, is independent. Although Mauritius became a republic in 1992, its citizens retain the right to appeal Mauritian Supreme Court decisions to Great Britain's Privy Council in some cases. Privately owned newspapers are free to print diverse viewpoints. Freedom of assembly and association is guaranteed, and there are no restrictions on religious freedom. There are nine labor federations encompassing 300 unions, and workers have the right to strike.

Mexico

Polity: Dominant party
Economy: Capitalist-statist
Population: 87,715,000
PPP: $5,691
Life Expectancy: 69.7
Ethnic Groups: Mestizo (60 percent), Indian (30 percent), Caucasian (9 percent), other (1 percent)

Political Rights: 4
Civil Liberties: 3
Status: Partly Free

Overview: Although President Carlos Salinas de Gortari has opened the Mexican economy, Mexico remains the most authoritarian state in Latin America outside of Cuba and Peru. Salinas's hands-on management of key state elections in 1992 and the ruling party's continued domination of the state apparatus indicated that the basis of rule in Mexico is still power, not law.

Mexico achieved independence from Spain in 1810, and established a republic in 1822. Seven years after the Revolution of 1910 a new constitution was promulgated, under which the United Mexican States is a federal republic consisting of 31 states and a Federal District (Mexico City). Each state has its own elected governors and legislatures. The chief executive of the Federal District is appointed by the president. The president is directly elected for a six-year term. A bicameral Congress consists of a 64-member Senate directly elected for six years, and a 500-member Chamber of Deputies elected for three years—300 by direct vote, and 200 through proportional representation. Municipal governments are elected.

The near-total domination of the executive, the Congress and state and local government by the Institutional Revolutionary Party (PRI) since 1929 has been challenged in recent years. Despite systematic electoral fraud, the PRI's presidential vote has declined by nearly half since 1976.

According to official results, Salinas won 50.36 percent of the vote in the July 1988 election, taking only one of every four votes in Mexico City. The main challengers were Manuel Clouthier of the right-wing National Action Party (PAN) with 17 percent, and a coalition of leftist parties and former PRI members led by Cuauhtemoc Cardenas with 31.3 percent. Most Mexicans believed Cardenas actually won the election, and Salinas took office in December 1988 with the weakest mandate of any PRI president.

Under Salinas economic modernization has far outpaced political reform. In 1989, the PRI conceded defeat in a gubernatorial race for the first time ever, to the PAN in Baja California Norte. But the more than two dozen state and municipal elections held between 1988 and 1991 were marked by fraud and crackdowns against opposition protests. Less than 20 percent of Mexico's nearly 2,400 municipalities are governed by opposition parties.

The PRI functions as the electoral arm of the state, and the national election commission, despite opposition representation, is dominated by the PRI and subordinate to the president. In 1991, opposition parties were powerless to prevent the PRI's manipulation of a new voter registration list. The PRI exercises control over most of the nation's media and wields an enormous financial advantage over the opposition. Its use of state resources for political purposes is unbounded and illegal.

In the 1991 mid-term elections, the PRI won a nearly two-thirds majority in the Chamber of Deputies and all but one of the 32 contested Senate seats. The vote was marked by widespread fraud—duplicate voter IDs, repeat voting, ballot-box stuffing and voter intimidation.

Under Salinas the concentration of power in the presidency at the expense of the traditionally rubber-stamp Congress has actually increased. Salinas has implemented more legislation through the executive branch—over 90 percent—than any president since Luis Echeverria (1970-76). At the same time, the military has been given a larger political role and a higher public profile.

In recent years, Cardenas's Democratic Revolutionary Party (PRD) and the PAN have mobilized mass demonstrations to protest outcomes in key state elections. Salinas, concerned by the intensity of the protests and critical coverage by the international media, has removed five governors or governors-elect in order to defuse explosive situations. His actions, however, confirmed the president's final and arbitrary authority in electoral matters.

Gubernatorial elections held in the key states of Michoacan and Chihuahua in July 1992 highlighted Salinas's strategy for preserving one-party domination while ground-shaking economic reforms are increasing the pressure for democratization. In the border state of Chihuahua, Salinas conceded a second governorship to the PAN. The PAN has generally backed Salinas's economic program and its principal component, a North American Free Trade Agreement (NAFTA). Salinas used Chihuahua to counter criticism of Mexico's authoritarian system.

But in the central state of Michoacan, Cardenas's base, Salinas sought to deliver a knock-out blow. The PRD has weakened since 1988 because of internal rifts and an inability to present a coherent alternative to Salinas's economic reforms, but it still represents the main political threat to the PRI.

In Michoacan, the PRI relied more on the use of state resources than traditional forms of fraud. According to official results, PRI candidate Eduardo Villasenor received more votes than his PRD opponent, which may have been true given that the PRI outspent the PRD by an estimated 50-1. But the PRD paralyzed Michoacan for three months with state-wide protests and Salinas, again getting stung in the international media, made Villasenor resign in October.

The PRI's sweep of four state elections in November was marked by renewed

PAN and PRD protests. But Salinas, who had made vague promises of electoral reform in his 1 November state-of-the nation address, refused to bend as he had in Michoacan. Instead the government launched legal action against the protesters, indicating a hardening of policy toward the opposition.

Salinas remained popular on the strength of a $6.5-billion anti-poverty program and the promise of better living through NAFTA. But his political balancing act was proving harder to maintain. The routine of electoral protests and resignations weakened the credibility of the political system and caused dissatisfaction with Salinas within the PRI. That, coupled with an economic downturn in 1992 and uncertainty over the fate of the NAFTA, pointed to a potentially unstable run-up to the 1994 presidential election.

Political Rights and Civil Liberties:

Because of the president's final say in all electoral matters and the ruling party's domination of the state, the electoral system, and the broadcast media, citizens are unable to change their government democratically. Constitutional guarantees regarding political and civic organization are generally respected, and there are over a dozen political parties ranging from right to left. But political expression is often restricted by repressive measures taken by the government during elections, labor strikes, and rural land disputes.

An official human rights commission was created in 1990. But there has been only limited progress in curtailing the systematic violation of human rights—including false arrest, routine torture, disappearances, murder and extortion—by federal security forces and local police. Targets include political and labor figures, journalists, human rights activists, criminal detainees and, with regard to extortion, the general public. Over the last decade nearly 500 people have disappeared. Since 1991, there has been compelling evidence of electronic surveillance by the government of critics, opposition parties, and the official human rights commission itself.

In 1991, the government appointed a new attorney general who declared an "end to the policy of official impunity," and ordered the arrest of a Federal Judicial Police commander implicated in the 1990 murder of human rights activist Norma Corona. The government also enacted new rules of evidence to curb police torture and dismissed dozens of security agents. However, corruption and rights violations remained institutionalized within the judicial police—which routinely makes political arrests under the pretext of drug enforcement—and Mexico's other law enforcement agencies. In 1992, the attorney general ignored a special report by the official human rights commission calling for the arrest of thirteen judicial police officers implicated in a notorious murder-torture case.

The judiciary is headed by a Supreme Court whose members are appointed for life by the president with the approval of the Senate. The Supreme Court is virtually an extension of the executive branch and is prohibited from enforcing political and labor rights, and from reviewing the constitutionality of laws. Overall, the judicial system is weak, politicized and riddled with corruption. Relatively few corrupt government officials ever spend time in jail, and if they do, it is often for minor offenses that serve to cut short investigations of serious crimes. In many rural areas, respect for laws by official agencies is nonexistent. Lower courts and law enforcement in general are undermined by widespread bribery, as is the state bureaucracy. Drug-related corruption is evident in the military, police, security forces, and in a number of state and local governments.

Labor unions are generally corrupt and traditionally allied with the ruling party. Salinas has removed some labor officials, often by force, because they were obstacles to economic reform. The government refuses to recognize unions unaffiliated with the PRI, denying them collective-bargaining rights and the right to strike. Independent unions and peasant organizations are subject to intimidation and violent crackdowns, and dozens of labor and peasant leaders have been killed in ongoing land disputes, particularly in southern states, where indigenous Indian groups comprise over a third of the population.

The press and broadcasting media, while mostly private and nominally independent, are largely controlled by the government through regulatory bodies, dependence on the government for advertising revenue and operating costs, a system of direct payments to journalists, and occasionally by outright intimidation. The PRI's domination of television, by far the country's most influential medium, is evident in the blanket, uncritical coverage the party receives during electoral campaigns. Most newspapers and magazines derive over half of all advertising revenues from official sources, which explains how Mexico City's 30-odd newspapers can survive with an estimated circulation of less than half a million.

More than 25 journalists have been killed or disappeared in the last four years, with most cases still unresolved. Dozens of others have been detained or otherwise threatened. On 13 November 1992, Ignacio Mendoza Castillo, a magazine publisher who two days earlier had filed a complaint with the official human rights commission, was shot and killed in front of his home by an unidentified gunman.

In 1992, the constitution was amended to restore the legal status of the Catholic church and other religious institutions. The rights to own property and conduct religious education, which had long been accorded in practice, were given legal definition for the first time in over a century. Priests and nuns were given the right to vote for the first time in nearly 80 years. In September, the government established diplomatic relations with the Vatican. But Catholic officials protested the continued ban on church ownership of media enterprises.

Micronesia

Polity: Federal parliamentary democracy
Economy: Capitalist
Population: 115,000
PPP: na
Life Expectancy: 70.5
Ethnic Groups: Micronesian

Political Rights: 1
Civil Liberties: 1
Status: Free

Overview:

Micronesia worked on plans to attract private American investment and build economic and political infrastructure in 1992. The country is in the process of moving its capital from Kolonia to Paliker.

Located in the Pacific Ocean, the Federated States of Micronesia was a U.N. trust territory under American administration from 1947 until 1979, when the US recognized the Micronesian constitution. Previously, the islands had been successively under a German protectorate and a Japanese League of Nations mandate. In 1982, the U.S. and Micronesia signed the Compact of Free Association, under which the U.S. retains responsibility for defense. In 1990, the U.N. Security Council voted to recognize the end of American trusteeship. In 1991, Micronesia sought and won international diplomatic recognition and full U.N. membership.

The unicameral legislature consists of one senator at-large from each island state elected for a four-year term, and ten senators elected on the basis of island populations for two-year terms. The senators elect the country's president for a two-year term from among the four at-large senators. Micronesia held legislative elections in 1991. After the voters chose the senators, the legislature voted to replace President John Haglelgam with Bailey Olter. Three of the four island states still have traditional leaders and customs.

Agriculture, tourism, forestry, and fishing are major industries, and public sector employment is substantial. American economic assistance is major, and will continue until 2001.

Political Rights and Civil Liberties: Micronesians have the right to change their government democratically. The people have the freedom to form political parties, but family politics, tendencies, and factions, not Western-style parties, are the vehicles for political activity on the islands.

Micronesia has a bill of rights and provisions for respecting traditional rights. Land is not sold or transferred to non-Micronesians. Otherwise the country respects cultural diversity. Islanders speak eight separate native languages. There is freedom of the press. Governmental authorities operate some media, while private enterprise and religious groups operate others. There is freedom of association, but only a few groups exist. Trade unions are legal, but none exists yet. Legally, there is equality of opportunity, but traditional family status can determine one's chances for advancement.

Moldova (Moldavia)

Polity: Presidential-parliamentary
Economy: Statist transitional
Population: 4,372,000
PPP: na
Life Expectancy: 68.0
Ethnic Groups: Romanian (64 percent), Russian, Ukrainians

Political Rights: 5
Civil Liberties: 5
Status: Partly Free

Overview: In 1992, Moldova continued to re-assert its independence amid armed conflict with the self-proclaimed Trans-Dniester Republic and calls for reunification with neighboring Romania. The ongoing unrest and deteriorating economic conditions led to the resignation in June of Prime Minister Valeriu Muravski, who was replaced by Andrei Sangheli.

Moldova is a predominantly Romanian-speaking former Soviet republic bordering Ukraine and Romania. On 27 August 1991, the republic officially declared independence in the wake of the failed hard-line coup attempt against Soviet President Mikhail Gorbachev. Three days earlier, the government banned all Communist Party activities at workplaces. On 8 December, incumbent President Mircea Snegur, running unopposed and backed by the Moldovan Popular Front (MPF), was re-elected with 93 percent of the vote. By year's end, with the collapse of the Soviet Union, Moldova joined the Commonwealth of Independent States (CIS), a loose confederation of former Soviet republics.

The conflict in the Trans-Dniester region, the eastern sliver of territory on the Dniester River inhabited primarily by Russians and Ukrainians, began in 1990 in response to the increased demands for independence by the Romanian-speaking majority organized in the MPF. In 1940, Soviet Russia had occupied the previously Romanian province of Bessarabia, establishing the Moldavian Soviet Socialist Republic. The Trans-Dniester region was part of the Ukrainian republic until 1940, but after the Soviet annexation, the region was joined with Moldova. In response to secessionist pressure by the MPF, which in February 1990 won 40 percent of the seats in the 218-member parliament, the Gagauz and Slavic minorities proclaimed their own republics: the Gagauz SSR on 19 August, and the Dniester SSR on 2 September. By November, police and Dniester militiamen had fought several pitched battles, and the unrest continued sporadically throughout 1991.

In January 1992, the Moldovan government accused Trans-Dniester leaders and "reactionary circles in Moscow" of continuing armed provocations and attempting to create confrontation between the Romanian and Russian-speaking populations.

In March, a group of villagers attacked a Russian army base around the town of Dubossari, seizing weapons and ammunition. Igor Smirnov, president of the Dniester republic, called for the mobilization of all males between ages 18 and 45. Later that month, President Snegur told parliament that Moldova faced increased difficulties in containing the separatist attacks, and expressed his dismay at Russia's failure to respond to his pleas of finding a peaceful solution to the conflict. On 28 March, Snegur imposed a state of emergency throughout the country, and set a deadline for the separatists to surrender.

On 2 April, Moldovan and Trans-Dniester representatives began preliminary peace talks after reaching an agreement on a ceasefire. The next week, the Trans-Dniester legislature asked for the establishment of CIS peacekeeping forces, as the foreign ministers of Moldova, Russia, Romania and Ukraine opened talks on the conflict.

Following ceasefire violations, President Snegur warned in May that Moldova might be forced to declare war against Russia unless the latter stopped support for the separatists and withdrew units of the 14th Army stationed there. The Russian Army had openly sided with the insurgents by assisting in recapturing the strategic town of Bendery from the Moldovan forces.

In July, the Moldovan and Russian presidents began negotiations on Trans-Dniester, culminating in a 21 July agreement setting principles for a peaceful settlement. The agreement stipulated Moldova's territorial integrity and guarantees for human rights of all residents, including ethnic minorities, and provided for granting of a special status for the Trans-Dniester region. A week later, the joint Russian-Moldovan peacekeeping forces began their deployment. In August, the state of emergency was lifted.

In September, Russia and Moldova began bilateral talks on the withdrawal of the

14th Army, with the Moldovan side demanding that the last units leave by the end of 1994. At the same time, however, the Trans-Dniester parliament voted to establish its own army and air force based on equipment delivered from Russian forces. It also voted to create its own customs and banking systems, and establish a separate citizenship.

Another important political issue related to the dilemma over whether Moldova should remain an independent state, or return to its pre-1940 status as an autonomous region of Romania. President Snegur opposed the idea of reunification, favoring close ties based on equality of the two states. As a disincentive to rejoining Romania, he proposed in January that the Trans-Dniester be allowed to hold a referendum on its future status in case Moldova relinquished its independence.

Snegur's position was criticized by the MPF, which favored merging with Romania. In October, Romania and Moldova agreed to set up a committee to coordinate the activities of their parliaments, and to establish an investment fund to encourage closer economic integration. On 29 November, thousands of Moldovans demonstrated in the capital, Kishniev, demanding reunification with Romania. In December, the two countries signed a military pact in which Romania pledged to help train and arm Moldovan forces.

Political Rights and Civil Liberties: Moldova has a multi-party system, but has not yet had fully democratic elections. During the spring 1990 legislative elections, 80 percent of the deputies elected were Communist party members, many of them endorsed by the MPF. The Communist party was banned in 1991. Other parties include the Social Democratic Party, the National-Christian Party of Moldova, the Union of Peasants and the Organization of Democratic Youth. Ethnicity and political ideology remained a divisive issue, as the Slavic separatists in Trans-Dniester and the Gagauz continued to assert their independence.

In 1990, Moldova passed a language law adopting Romanian as the official language, and prompting the Slavic and Gagauz (Christian Turkish) minorities to complain about discrimination. In 1992, in order to defuse tensions, parliament retracted some of the provisions, allowing for Russian to be used as a language of "inter-ethnic communication," and granting the right to education in native languages in areas with concentrations of ethnic minorities. In February 1992, President Snegur issued a decree granting citizenship to all residents.

The fighting in Trans-Dniester cost more than 500 lives and created almost 100,000 refugees. In the spring, the International Helsinki Federation issued a report criticizing the Trans-Dniester authorities for reconstituting the old Soviet system.

The law on freedom of the press is still pending, and most of the media are government owned. However, censorship is minimal; most newspapers, radio and television provide information critical of government. The government subsidizes ethnic press in several languages (Russian, Ukrainian, Turkish, Yiddish). Freedom of religion is respected, although proselytizing is illegal. Internal freedom of movement is restricted in areas of conflict, and exit visas are required for people wishing to emigrate. The Helsinki Commission reported in July 1992 on several cases of people being denied exit visas, mostly due to administrative negligence.

Trade unions remain holdovers from the Communist past. In August, President Snegur announced the dismantling of the trade union monopoly as part of the program of economic reforms.

Mongolia

Polity: Presidential-par-
liamentary democracy
Economy: Statist
transitional
Population: 2,252,000
PPP: $2,000
Life Expectancy: 65.0
Ethnic Groups: Khalkha Mongols (75 percent), other Mongols
(8 percent), Kazakhs (5 percent)

Political Rights: 3
Civil Liberties: 2
Status: Free

Overview:	The Mongolian People's Revolutionary Party (MPRP) scored
a lopsided triumph in the June 1992 elections, taking 70 out
of 76 seats in the Great Hural. Two years after a peaceful
revolution ended the party's absolute rule, the former Communists benefited from
various institutional advantages and from a backlash against the radical economic
reforms supported by the opposition.

China controlled this vast Central Asian steppe and mountain region for two
centuries until 1911, and again in 1919 until Soviet-backed Marxists revolted in 1921.
The MPRP formed a Communist state in 1924 following three years of nominal rule
by aging Buddhist lamas. For the next 65 years, the country existed as a virtual
republic of the Soviet Union.

The country's one-party system began to crack in December 1989 with the
formation of an opposition association, the Mongolian Democratic Union (MDU),
under dynamic university lecturer Sanjaasurenjiyn Zorig. MDU-organized street protests
and hunger strikes led to the resignation of much of the MPRP leadership in March
1990, and in May the government scrapped the party's legal monopoly. In July 1990,
the country held its first multi-party elections. The MPRP won 357 of 430 seats in
the Great Hural against an unprepared opposition. The MDU's political wing, the
Mongolian Democratic Party (MDP), won just 20 seats, while the remainder went to
minor opposition parties and 21 independents. The MPRP called for a coalition
government, but gave the MDP only token representation in the fourteen-member
cabinet. In September, the Hural named the MPRP's Punsalmaagiyn Orchirbat as
president and the opposition Social Democratic Party's (SDP) Radnaasurenjiyn
Gonchigdorj as vice president.

In February 1991, the MPRP formally abandoned Marxism-Leninism in favor of
"scientific socialism," and named moderate Budragchaagiyn Dash-Yondan as its new
party leader. However, citizens continued to be wary of a core of hardliners in the
party. Thousands rallied in the capital against the MPRP during the August 1991 coup
in the Soviet Union. To allay these fears, the government banned top officials, as well
as police, diplomats, and journalists, from belonging to any political party. Thousands
of people affected, from President Orchirbat on down, left their parties to comply with
the law.

Continuing the democratic transition, the Great Hural passed a new constitution on

15 January 1992. The vote came after two months of acrimonious debate over free market reforms, particularly over land rights. The constitution ultimately provided for private land ownership, renounced socialism, established the country as the State of Mongolia, and removed the yellow Communist star from the flag. It also abolished the two-year-old Little Hural, leaving the Great Hural as a unicameral parliament. The president received powers to name a cabinet and veto all legislation, subject to a two-thirds override.

On 16 January, prime minister Dashiyn Byambasuren announced his resignation, claiming the people no longer supported the government's radical free–market reforms. President Orchirbat and the parliament refused to accept the resignation, and Byambasuren agreed to remain in office until the election. His actions prompted another round of fierce debate in the parliament over the pace of political and economic reforms.

On 28 June, Mongolians voted for a new, smaller Great Hural. Three hundred candidates, many under 30 years old, ran for 76 seats. Over 91 percent of the electorate took part, even though most rural voters had to travel for miles to reach a polling station. The MPRP, split into several factions ranging from orthodox Communists to free-market reformers, took a commanding 70 seats. The reform-oriented Democratic Coalition, headed by 1990 revolution catalyst Zorig and consisting of the MDP and two smaller parties, took only four seats. The European-influenced Social Democratic Party and an MPRP-affiliated independent each took one. The single-seat constituency system, which gave the government its parliamentary landslide, distorted the opposition's credible 43 percent share of the popular vote.

The reasons behind the MPRP's triumph were varied. Several voters told the *New York Times* that they picked the MPRP because they recognized the name or had voted for it in the one-party elections of the past. A pre-election report by the U.S. International Republican Institute detailed the party's other advantages. They included ample funding and control over the media, printing equipment and paper, as well as sufficient stocks of gasoline to campaign in the countryside. The party also received political training and 500,000 tons of newsprint from China. In addition, the representation system in parliament favors rural areas, from where the MPRP draws its bedrock support. The government no doubt also benefited from the confusing array of opposition parties, many of which lacked clear ideological distinctions and the means to campaign effectively.

However, the most important factor may have been the collapse of the economy, which is rebuilding following 70 years of central planning and reliance on Soviet handouts. Voters blamed the current hardship largely on the radical economic reforms associated with the opposition. Industrial output fell 23.7 percent in six months prior to the vote, and families faced difficulties getting enough food and clothes. Oil shipments from Russia were suspended in 1991, causing factories and transportation to shut down. Staples such as flour, rice and sugar are all rationed, and medicine is in short supply. Inflation has risen 1,000 percent since 1990.

The government of new prime minister Puntsagiyn Jasray is expected to continue the reforms, but at a slower pace. On 1 October prices were increased on flour, bread and other goods as the first step towards freeing them entirely. Nearly two-thirds of livestock and 90 percent of the capital of small stores are already privately owned, and foreign donors helped the recovery by pledging $320 million in assistance in

May. All citizens have received $250 in vouchers to invest in the new Mongolian Stock Exchange. Long-range prospects appear bright in a country which contains ample oil and mineral resources, and where livestock outnumber people 25 to 1.

Political Rights and Civil Liberties: Mongolians can change their government through free, although not entirely fair, elections. The Mongolian People's Revolutionary Party had numerous advantages over the opposition in the June 1992 elections, including greater funding and a population-to-seat ratio weighted towards its rural stronghold.

The constitution adopted in 1992 provides for broad protection of fundamental freedoms, which are now generally respected in practice. The judiciary is being reformed in accordance with international standards. The Department of State Security's surveillance apparatus has been greatly reduced, although it can still use wiretaps and other measures. Groups can associate and demonstrate freely.

Although all radio and television stations are government-owned (with the exception of one minor rural radio station), opposition viewpoints are aired. However, the written press faces restrictions because the government controls the distribution of newsprint.

Buddhist practice has revived since 1990, but there is no official religion and Muslims and other small groups can now also worship freely. Workers can organize freely. Most unions are under the umbrella Federation of Mongolian Trade Unions, which broke from the MPRP in 1990 and is now independent.

Morocco

Polity: Monarchy and limited parliament
Economy: Capitalist-statist
Population: 26,200,000
PPP: $2,298
Life Expectancy: 62.0
Ethnic Groups: Arab, Berber, Black African

Political Rights: 6
Civil Liberties: 5
Status: Partly Free

Overview: King Hassan II of Morocco initiated long-awaited economic and political reforms in 1992. On the political side, in September, Moroccan citizens voted for a new constitution which delegated some of the King's powers to the parliament. Economically, the country set out on a course of privatization, decentralization, and currency convertibility. As in the rest of North Africa and the Arab world, the Islamic fundamentalism has gained support among the Moroccan poor, and King Hassan perceives its spread as a threat to the monarchy.

Hassan has ruled the country since 1961. He is commander-in-chief of the armed forces, can dissolve parliament, and appoints provincial governors, judges, and the prime minister. The King has weathered two attempted military revolts in the 1970s and more recent civil disorder in 1981 and 1990 stemming from severe economic conditions.

After demands for long-awaited political reforms by the opposition, led by the nationalist Istiqlal (Independence) Party and the Socialist Union of Popular Forces (USFP), King Hassan allowed a constitutional referendum to take place on 4 September 1992. Moroccans and Western Saharans voted overwhelmingly in favor of a new constitution, under which the King delegates a few of his powers to the government and the parliament. According to official results, voter turnout was 97 percent, and more than 99 percent of the electorate gave their approval to constitutional reforms.

Under the new constitution, the government will be more accountable to the Chamber of Representatives. The Chamber will have the power to approve ministers, the government's program, set up commissions of inquiry, and challenge the government with votes of confidence. The King retains the right to declare a state of emergency, but would not dissolve parliament automatically as in the past. However, King Hassan remains the ultimate authority.

Eight opposition parties and two trade unions boycotted the constitutional referendum. The last elections for the 306-seat parliament took place in 1984. In 1989, a referendum approved King Hassan's proposal to postpone the 1990 elections until 1992, when they did not take place. Opposition parties have charged that the government tampered with past elections. Nonetheless, opposition parties have a substantial minority of parliamentary seats.

On 16 October 1992, elections for municipal and rural councils took place. Opposition parties denounced the results, complaining of fraud and corruption. According to official results, turnout was 75 percent and the parties that form the former ruling coalition in parliament won most of the seats. The three largest opposition parties won approximately 20 percent of the vote. Eight parties and several independents contested the elections, four smaller opposition parties boycotted, complaining of the lack of guarantees that the vote would be free and fair. Opposition parties claimed that large bribes had changed hands, that there had been fraudulent use of polling cards and government officials had put pressure on voters.

In August 1992, Morocco told the U.N. that it would hold general elections in Western Sahara in 1992 whether or not the U.N. executes the self-determination referendum. The U.N. referendum on the future of the territory, originally scheduled for the beginning of 1992, has been delayed by disagreements over who should have the right to vote. Polisario, the Western Saharan independence movement, argues that only those names from the 1974 census should be included, and Morocco wants to add an additional 120,000 people to the electoral list.

In August 1992, a new government headed by businessman Mohamed Karim Lamrani as prime minister was formed, preparing the way for new parliamentary elections.

In October 1992, three French citizens who spent 18 years in the notorious Tazmamart Moroccan prison took King Hassan II to court on defamation charges. This was the first time in history that a foreign head of state was to be tried by an ordinary French court. The event coincided with the holding of municipal elections in Morocco.

After harsh criticism from opposition groups on the economic situation in Morocco, the King made concessions by increasing the minimum wage. The 1992 budget promised more public spending on education, health, housing, and jobs for the 100,000 unemployed Moroccans. The government also released some political prisoners.

Diplomatically, Moroccan relations with Europe and the U.S. were marked with disputes over trade, immigration, and Morocco's internal and external politics. The European Parliament held up approval of a European Community aid package to Morocco worth $483m ECUs ($670m) because of continued Moroccan human rights abuses and delays in implementing the U.N. plan for the Western Sahara.

Morocco executed part of the economic reform plan in spring 1992 by selling several state-owned companies. This was part of a privatization program that called for the disposal of approximately 74 state-owned or controlled enterprises and 37 state-owned hotels. However, Moroccan businessmen questioned whether this would simply be the transfer of title within the ruling elite. With a massive foreign debt, and immense foreign loans, Morocco hopes this program will attract foreign capital and renew domestic growth.

Political Rights and Civil Liberties: Moroccan citizens have limited means to change their government democratically. While the constitution provides for a pluralistic political system and a parliamentary form of government, ultimate power rests with King Hassan II. He has the power to appoint and dismiss ministers, dissolve parliament and rule by decree.

Elected opposition members may attack the government's economic record but not foreign policy, which remains the King's preserve. Past elections, including the 1992 local and municipal elections, reportedly have been rigged. The state suppresses unauthorized groups mostly by political imprisonment, disappearances and torture.

The government limits freedoms of speech and press. Moroccans exercise self-censorship when discussing government policies. Citizens may face reprisals if they discuss any of the three forbidden topics: the monarchy, Morocco's claim to the Western Sahara, and the sanctity of Islam. The government controls the licensing of newspapers and journals. Publications that do not conform to state security requirements may be confiscated. However, during the past two years, there has been a relaxation of censorship in the press. The government subsidizes and controls news media. The government owns the official news agency, an Arabic daily newspaper, the television and one radio station. Foreign publications are available but subject to occasional censorship. Academic freedom is also limited, specifically in scholarly investigations of the monarchy and Islam.

Freedoms of assembly and association are limited. The government may suppress peaceful demonstrations and mass gatherings. The Ministry of Interior approves licensing of associations. Islamists and leftist groups have had difficulty obtaining such approvals.

Torture is widespread. Those who merely criticize the King face imprisonment. In an attempt to change his reputation, the King has been freeing political prisoners and closing down prisons. In January 1992, the King pardoned the last three political prisoners belonging to a group that opposed Moroccan rule over the disputed Western Sahara.

Morocco has a dual legal system. The secular courts are based on the French legal tradition and Islamic courts that handle family and inheritance law for Muslims. The court system is not entirely independent and subject to political intervention and control in certain cases. The government often ignores guarantees of procedural due process.

Islam is the official religion. Approximately 99 percent of Moroccans are Sunni Muslims and King Hassan II holds the title of "Commander of the Faithful." The government permits the small Jewish and Christian communities to practice their faiths. The state considers all other religions heresies and prohibits them strictly. Morocco has far less fundamentalist activity than its neighbors. The government keeps mosques under tight surveillance, and limits or outlaws fundamentalist political activities. Islamic fundamentalists' activities are restricted to education and charitable activities.

Moroccans are free to travel within Morocco proper, but not in Western Sahara, where movement is restricted in militarily sensitive areas. Some Moroccans have been denied passports for political reasons. Women must have permission from their fathers or husbands to obtain a passport.

Although there is no systematic racial discrimination, Moroccan blacks generally occupy the lower social strata. Women have legal equality with men except in areas of marriage and family. Moroccan women have the opportunity for higher education and they have succeeded in areas of law, medicine, education, and government service. They enjoy the right to vote and to run for office, and some women have been elected to municipal councils. Morocco's Berber minority is well represented in the government and the military, and state-owned radio stations broadcast several hours daily in Berber language.

The Moroccan government permits independent trade unions to exist, but selection of union officers is subject to government pressure. There are 16 trade union federations. Workers have the right to organize and bargain collectively and these laws are honored most in the industrial sector of the economy and ignored in the smaller industries.

In 1992, the government initiated a privatization program, but it intends to hold on to key properties, notably transport, communications, and the national phosphate company. Corruption is widespread in the government, and King Hassan and the elite class have a monopoly over many enterprises and businesses.

Mozambique

Polity: Dominant party (transitional)
Economy: Mixed statist
Population: 16,617,000
PPP: $1,060
Life Expectancy: 47.5
Ethnic Groups: Lomwe, Makonde, Makua, Ndau, Shangaan, Thonga, Yao, others

Political Rights: 6
Civil Liberties: 4
Status: Partly Free

Overview: After sixteen years of civil war, Mozambique's Frelimo regime and the rebel movement Mozambique National Resistance (Renamo) signed a peace accord in October 1992.

After more than two decades of fighting Portuguese colonial occupation, the Marxist-Leninist Frelimo established the People's Republic of Mozambique in 1975.

President Samora Machel led the one-party state until he was killed in an airplane crash in 1986. Joaquim Chissano succeeded him as both president and Frelimo party leader. Frelimo banned all political activity in independent Mozambique until 1990, when the party wrote a new constitution that legalized non-violent political opposition. Provincial assemblies elected the unicameral Assembly of the Republic as recently as 1991, but all candidates had to be approved by Frelimo.

Mozambique has been torn by civil war and lawlessness almost since independence. Insurgent since the mid-1970s and presently led by Afonso Dhlakama, Renamo's 30,000-member guerrilla force controls considerable rural territory in central and northern Mozambique. The Frelimo regime's early rural modernization program, which often forced peasants off their traditional lands and into communal villages for convenient organization into production brigades, generated support for the rebellion. The government's forced military recruitment also produced popular resentment. In recent years rampant government corruption has led to further disaffection with Frelimo. However, Renamo has also had a notorious history of human rights abuses against civilians, including the kidnapping of peasants to serve as guerrillas or as forced labor. At least 600,000 people have died since the beginning of the civil war.

The government extended implicit recognition to Renamo as a political force by directly meeting with the insurgents beginning in May 1990. Held in Rome, the talks were mediated by the Italian Government and the Roman Catholic community of San Egidio. Negotiations over a permanent cease-fire and political settlement of the conflict stalled repeatedly in 1991.

Despite the difficulty of reaching a ceasefire agreement, three protocols were signed between October 1991 and March 1992. All were intended to take effect on the signing of a peace accord. Under provisions of the first protocol, Renamo would formally recognize the legitimacy of Frelimo's laws. Renamo had earlier rejected the 1990 constitution and all Frelimo legislation as the product of an illegitimate regime and its non-democratic legislature. Renamo was unable to get the government to agree to a provision that would require the first parliament elected in future multi-party elections to amend the 1990 constitution. The second protocol dealt with political party registration after a ceasefire accord was finally reached. Contrary to a law enacted by Frelimo's national assembly a year earlier, this protocol allowed a party to be legalized without obtaining signatures of registered voters in every region of the country. The third protocol was to guarantee full freedom for establishing and operating private media; the safe return and reintegration of approximately 1.5 million refugees; and procedures for conducting an impartial multi-party election.

By mid-1992 none of the three protocols signed were yet operative because a ceasefire agreement had still not been reached. A break-through was achieved on 4 July, when Renamo's Dhlakama met with the presidents of Botswana and Zimbabwe in the Botswanan capital. Less than three weeks after consultations with Zimbabwe's President Mugabe in Mozambique, President Chissano agreed to his first face-to-face meeting with Dhlakama. In early August, Dhlakama and Chissano met in Rome, paving the way for a joint declaration of intent to sign a cease-fire by 1 October. But the October ceremony was temporarily suspended when Dhlakama raised a new concern at the last moment. He delayed his arrival in Rome, demanding Renamo be allowed to maintain sole administrative authority over all territory that it claims to control—80 percent of the country—until multi-party elections. Frelimo agreed to the stipulation that administrators in areas held by Renamo could include members of Renamo. The treaty was finally signed 4 October, and soon ratified by Mozambique's legislative assembly.

The month that followed the 16 October ceasefire date saw minor jostling between Renamo and government forces for control of territory in some northern areas of the country. But clashes decreased as combatants began to move to designated assembly sites for demobilization in accord with the terms of the Rome agreement. A new unified army of 30,000 is to be drawn in equal measure from the two groups. In addition, Zimbabwean troops guarding major Mozambican transportation corridors are to be sent home, and U.N. observers are to be deployed to verify the ceasefire.

The creation of a unified military will require re-integrating approximately 80,000 armed Mozambican and Renamo combatants into civil society. For years, deserters from both sides have taken to banditry or set themselves up in local fiefdoms independent of outside control. Unless those slated for demobilization can be given solid guarantees of a peaceful livelihood, neither Frelimo nor Renamo fighters are likely to leave the camps without their guns.

The October accord also specified that multi-party elections be held within a year. U.N. officials oppose the holding of elections until demobilization is completed. Renamo's Dhlakama has stated his intention to run for president whenever balloting takes place. Although he predicts that Renamo will win a fair multi-party election, he also promises not to contest a Frelimo victory.

Like much of southern and eastern Africa, Mozambique has been struck hard by a devastating drought. The situation has been exacerbated by the civil war and the internal displacement of many Mozambicans. As many as three million people face the danger of starvation. On 17 July, government and rebel leaders agreed to permit international relief agencies to distribute food in Renamo-held territory for the first time. Throughout Mozambique, however, food assistance has been illegally diverted to soldiers and guerrillas.

Political Rights and Civil Liberties:

Mozambicans cannot change their government democratically. The regime has attempted to distance itself from its Marxist-Leninist history by publicly embracing political pluralism and free markets. A new constitution introduced on 30 November 1990 formally provides for universal suffrage, direct legislative and executive elections, and freedom to form political parties. Fifteen parties have organized. The constitution also guarantees civil liberties and the independence of a depoliticized legal system. The 1990 constitution also concentrates considerable power in the country's chief executive and does not provide restitution for those whose property was nationalized by Frelimo.

Although special revolutionary tribunals hearing national security cases have been abolished, official misconduct during trials of political prisoners reportedly continues. This includes inadequate representation by court-appointed attorneys, placing the burden of proof on the accused, and conviction based on coerced confessions. Members of militia units, soldiers, and military counterintelligence agents continue to violate basic human rights; there are persistent reports of torture, rape, summary execution, and other abuses of those taken into custody. A new security force has replaced the People's National Security Service (Snasp), which was abolished in July 1991 and had a poor human rights record. In response to a surging wave of crime, civilian vigilantism is growing.

Freedom of the press is still somewhat restricted, and foreign journalists are subject to expulsion from the country for reporting the news unfavorably. Government-controlled media reflect official policy, with only occasional criticism of the regime. Religious publications discuss sensitive issues and foreign radio and TV broadcasts from South Africa are received without interference.

All trade unions have had to belong to the Organization of Mozambican Workers. Workers have the right to strike, provided 3 to 4 days advance notice is given.

Namibia

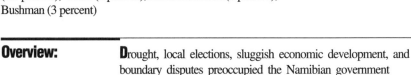

Polity: Presidential-legislative democracy **Political Rights:** 2
Civil Liberties: 2
Economy: Capitalist-statist **Status:** Free
Population: 1,452,000
PPP: $1,500
Life Expectancy: 57.5
Ethnic Groups: Ovambo (50 percent), Kavango (9 percent), Herero (7.5 percent), Damara (7.5 percent), Baster and Colored (6.5 percent), White (6 percent), Nama/Hottentot (5 percent), Bushman (3 percent)

Overview: **D**rought, local elections, sluggish economic development, and boundary disputes preoccupied the Namibian government during 1992.

A former German protectorate, Namibia (formerly South West Africa) was invaded by South Africa during World War I. South Africa administered Namibia under a system of apartheid. Nationalist opposition groups began organizing in the 1950s, and in 1966 the South West Africa People's Organization (SWAPO) launched an armed struggle for independence. In 1978, the U.N. adopted a plan (resolution 435) for Namibian independence, which South Africa did not accept until 1988.

In November 1989, SWAPO candidates won U.N.-supervised pre-independence elections. On 21 March 1990, Namibia officially gained independence, and SWAPO leader Sam Nujoma became the country's first president.

The 1989 elections were contested by ten political groups that vied for the 72 seats in the National Assembly. SWAPO won 41 seats, and the center-right Democratic Turnhalle Alliance (DTA) won 21. On 30 November 1992, SWAPO dominated local and regional elections, winning 38 of the 47 local authority areas contested and 9 out of 13 regional councils. DTA supporters claimed that former SWAPO guerrillas had intimidated and attacked opposition partisans during the campaign.

In 1992, key issues centered around a major cabinet shakeup, the drought and the president's controversial purchase of a luxury jet aircraft. In April, Finance Minister Otto Herrigel resigned, and was replaced by agriculture minister Gert Henekom, a key figure in the government's drought relief program. The move came just one week after the government declared a national emergency due to the drought. Although Nujoma said Herrigel had left the cabinet for "personal reasons," others said he had been forced out because of economic mismanagement.

In the spring, the drought forced Nujoma to appeal to foreign donors for emergency relief aid. In June, in the midst of the crisis, the government angered donors by accepting delivery of a $29 million luxury jet for the president, which it had purchased from France. Although the jet's purchase from a French company was reportedly a condition for receiving development assistance from Paris, Sweden and Norway cited the jet in removing Namibia from the African nations to which they planned to send drought relief. Meanwhile, it was estimated that crop losses approached 90 percent, overwhelmingly impacting on subsistence farmers.

Economic problems continued to plague Namibia in 1992. Namibia runs a deficit due to significant social spending and what some Western donors consider excessive expenditure on prestige items for government officials. Many SWAPO supporters remain frustrated with unrealized hopes that independence and electoral victory would bring quick and substantial material benefits. SWAPO's earlier promises of land, jobs, health care, and improved educational opportunities have borne little fruit so far. In particular, tens of thousands of returned exiles and discharged veterans of SWAPO's guerrilla People's Liberation Army of Namibia have not been able to take advantage of the government's "development brigade" program to provide the unemployed with job training and land. Underdevelopment has been compounded by the additional burden of an estimated 100,000 refugees who have fled from drought, famine and war in neighboring Angola.

Two controversies involving Namibia's international boundary went basically unresolved in 1992. The status of the South African-controlled enclave of Walvis Bay, containing the only deep-water port in the region and physically encircled by Namibian territory, changed somewhat in late 1991 when the two governments agreed to joint administration. Joint administration began in November 1992, but Namibia has indicated that this is an interim measure. It claims Walvis Bay and a number of small uninhabited offshore islands in its constitution. Negotiations on the enclave's ultimate status continued in 1992, but by threatening to "go to the international community," the Namibian government has expressed its impatience with South Africa's reluctance to permit a quick transition to exclusive Namibian control. In the north, both Namibia and neighboring Botswana publicly disputed their respective claims for the Chobe/Kasikili River island in the Strip. Although a technical committee was appointed to determine the boundary, both countries exchanged warnings and engaged in small-scale saber rattling in the meantime.

In early March violence broke out at the scene of a labor action at Namibian Breweries in the capital of Windhoek. The media focused on allegations that peaceful black strikers protesting their 1989 discharge by the company had been severely beaten by white plain-clothes police officers. The officers, from a special tactical squad, were reported to have attacked after the protesters refused to lift their blockade of the brewery entrance. The president and the government criticized the officers for racist behavior, and some senior white commanders were temporarily suspended.

Political Rights and Civil Liberties: Namibians can change their government democratically. An executive president was initially elected by the National Assembly and will later attain office by direct popular vote. The president will be limited to two five-year terms. Constitutional provisions establish regular elections for a bicameral parliament; members of the upper house of the

National Council were chosen through equal regional representation in 1992, and members of the lower Assembly will be selected through proportional representation in 1995. In some cases, the National Council has the power to block legislative initiatives by the National Assembly.

The press freely expresses diverse points of view. The broadcast media are owned by the state, and some sectors of the SWAPO administration have reportedly put pressure on radio journalists to avoid critical reporting of the government. SWAPO's official weekly party newspaper, *New Era*, is state-subsidized, a privilege apparently not extended to periodicals unaffiliated with the Party.

There is a bill of rights, and an independent court system is mandated by the constitution. The right of private property is constitutionally recognized. The National Union of Namibian Workers, with links to the International Confederation of Free Trade Unions, has worked to organize mining, industrial, commercial, and public employee unions since 1986.

Nauru

Polity: Parliamentary democracy
Economy: Mixed capitalist-statist
Population: 9,000
PPP: na
Life Expectancy: 66.0

Political Rights: 1
Civil Liberties: 2
Status: Free

Ethnic Groups: Indigenous Nauruans (mixture of Polynesian, Melanesian, Micronesian (58 percent), other Pacific islanders (26 percent), Chinese (8 percent), European (8 percent)

Overview:

Nauru's parliament re-elected Bernard Dowiyogo as the president of this tiny Pacific island nation in November 1992. The new parliament, itself elected five days earlier, chose Dowiyogo over former cabinet minister Buraro Detudamo.

In 1992, Nauru continued to be locked in a legal dispute with its giant neighbor to the southwest. Australia administered Nauru and sold its phosphate below world market prices before granting it independence in 1968. The ravages of over 80 years of phosphate mining have forced the Nauruans to the fringes of their island, most of which is a scarred wasteland. In November 1991, preliminary hearings before the International Court of Justice opened on the country's claim against Australia for $60 million to rehabilitate the island. Nauruans currently have one of the highest per capita incomes in the world, but that will end in the mid-1990's when the last of the phosphate is mined.

Contrary to Australia's original expectations, the Nauruans have refused to leave their island unless they are given legal sovereignty over another island. The government is looking for new sources of revenue to supplement the phosphate income, much of which has been invested abroad through the Nauru Phosphate Royalties Trust. It is particularly interested in developing a tuna processing industry, which would require training the largely unskilled workforce and· building a desalinization plant; all of the country's water currently must be imported.

Both the eighteen-member parliament and the Nauru Local Government Council (NLGC) are popularly elected. The president is elected by the parliament for a three-year term. The NLGC, representing fourteen districts, provides local government services. While there are no organized political parties, candidates representing a wide variety of viewpoints contest the parliamentary seats.

Political Rights and Civil Liberties: Nauruans can change their government democratically. Voting is compulsory, and individuals run for parliamentary seats according to specific issues or ideas rather than parties. The judiciary is independent of the government, and procedural safeguards protect the rights of the accused. Freedom of speech and of press are respected although, because there is no newspaper, news and ideas are often transferred via word of mouth on the nine-square-mile island. (The country's only publication, the *Government Gazette*, only reports official notices and announcements.) The government-owned radio station broadcasts Radio Australia, the BBC, and local news, and several foreign publications are available. In May 1991, the country's first television station began broadcasting. Freedom of association is respected. There are no restrictions on foreign travel, and any domestic point can be reached by foot. Females may not marry non-Nauruans, and males must get permission from the government to marry foreigners. The government has been slow to address the problem of physical abuse of women, which is generally alcohol-related. Although the constitution allows workers to bargain collectively, the government discourages trade unions and none exist. Any foreign worker who is fired must leave the country within 60 days. Most of the phosphate miners are foreign, many of them from other Pacific countries.

Nepal

Polity: Parliamentary democracy
Economy: Capitalist
Population: 19,851,000
PPP: $896
Life Expectancy: 52.2
Ethnic Groups: Newar, Indian, Tibetan, Gurung, Magar, Tamang, Bhotia, others

Political Rights: 2
Civil Liberties: 3
Status: Free

Overview: In 1992, the Nepalese government contended with mass demonstrations, local elections, a deluge of Bhutanese refugees and a faltering economy.

Nepal has experienced more than two years of sometimes violent transition from traditional monarchy to parliamentary democracy with a constitutional monarch. Bloody political demonstrations in April 1990 forced King Birendra to accept a constitution, which called for a popularly elected parliament and an end to the 29-year ban on political activity. The 1990 constitution created a 205-member House of Representatives, elected from 75 districts, and a 60-member National Council, where seats are determined by party strength in the lower house. The King nominates 10 percent of the members of the upper house after consultation with the prime minister. Following the first election in 1991, the Nepal Congress gained control of the government with 110 seats. With 69 seats, the United Nepal Communist Party became the chief opposition. The rest of the seats were divided among other Communist and anti-monarchist parties and independents. Fearing Communist influence, the Congress Party named anti-Communist Girija Prasad Koirala Prime Minister. The pre-democratic system's bureaucrats chafed at their loss of power and in February 1992 formed the nationalist, pro-monarchy National People's Council (Rashtriya Janata Parishad).

In January 1992, the King threatened to retake power if the democratically elected government proved incompetent. The Communists viewed the King's remarks with contempt and suggested abdication before intervention in the political system. Since then, the King has been a vocal supporter of the system.

In December 1991, the government increased the Council of Ministers from 17 to 24 members, removing several opposition members and adding 13 loyalists. In July 1992, accusations of corruption and fiscal mismanagement forced some ministerial resignations.

On 6 April 1992, on the anniversary of the 1990 anti-government riots, new demonstrations rocked Kathmandu. A coalition of radical Communist parties called a general strike, which led to the riots. In its biggest political challenge since assumption of power, the Congress Party contended with demonstrators who demanded economic reform, controlled inflation, and an end to corruption. Police flooded Kathmandu and opened fired on the protesters. After dozens of deaths, the government put the army on alert, declared a curfew and a moratorium on protests. The Communists accused the government of political intolerance, economic ineptitude, and subservience to India. They demanded the government's immediate resignation. The Congress Party countered that the Communists created the conditions for violence. The Ministry of Education and Culture accused teachers of propagandizing students with leftist politics at the expense of education. Therefore, the ministry banned all teachers from joining parties or campaigning. Concerned with the June local elections, the United Nepal Communist Party distanced itself from the violence and the other more radical Communist parties.

Despite the violence and resulting authoritarian measures, the Congress Party boosted its control in the June local elections. Attempts to steal ballot boxes ended in nine deaths. Second round voting was also marred by violence. The Congress Party came away with more than 65 percent of the vote and gained control of all urban communist bastions in Kathmandu. The radical Communist United People's Front failed to win a single seat, even in their strongholds. The United Nepal Communist Party gained control of five of the 36 municipalities, denied allegations of electoral misconduct, and alleged that radical Communist supporters had hired hoodlums at polling booths to frighten voters.

The massive influx of more than 60,000 Bhutanese refugees of Nepalese descent is crippling Nepal. The 1990 Nepalese democracy movement struck both Nepal and

Bhutan. In contrast to Nepal, King Wangchuk of Bhutan refused any democratization or pluralism for the ethnic Nepalese minority. Bhutan has spurned all Nepalese initiatives to stem the flow of refugees. Nepal appealed to India (which has maintained Bhutan's foreign relations since 1949) for mediation of the crisis but India refused to intervene, insisting it is an internal Bhutanese affair. Koirala's appeals to the South Asian Association for Cooperation were also futile.

In May, the government abolished restrictions on most imports and exports to encourage domestic private industry, reduce massive youth unemployment and correct the massive trade deficit. Four-fifths of Nepal's trade is with India. Businessmen perceived the new regulatory system as entrepreneurial and an attempt at government-business partnership. However, a new political crisis emerged as Koirala attempted to sell hydroelectric power to India in September 1992. It is the only possible customer for Nepalese hydro-electric power. All Communist factions united behind an effort to oust Koirala as anti-India feeling swelled. The sentiment stems from a 1989-1990 trade feud that closed the borders of land-locked Nepal. The opposition feared that dam-building for the hydro-electric plant on the Nepalese-Indian border could flood parts of Nepal. Additionally, despite constitutional requirements, Koirala did not submit the treaty to the parliament for approval. Koirala insisted that the agreement was not a treaty, but an "understanding" and therefore did not require parliamentary approval. An October state visit by Indian Prime Minister Rao failed to assuage the opposition.

Political Rights and Civil Liberties:

Under the 1990 constitution, citizens may change their government democratically. The King retains some residual powers. The government generally respects freedoms of expression, association and the press. However, teachers may not join political parties and the government does not permit Tibetan refugees to protest against China.

Despite its small size and 26 percent literacy rate, Nepal supports more than 400 newspapers. The press is free and offers pluralistic perspectives, including sometimes scathing commentaries on government policy. The state owns and operates the radio and the television stations.

The constitution provides for an independent judiciary. A supreme court, district appellate courts and judicial courts comprise a generally impartial legal system.

The constitution prohibits discrimination, but caste discrimination against "untouchables" (the lowest caste) is widespread. The government permits all types of religious practice, but conversion and proselytizing are illegal. The legal code provides prison terms for any Hindu who converts to another religion and stiffer sentences for anyone trying to proselytize a Hindu. There is a large Buddhist minority and smaller groups of Muslims and Christians.

Due to traditional Hindu practice, women, especially in rural areas, suffer discrimination. Despite legal reforms, women have fewer rights for divorce than men. The constitution requires equal pay for equal work. The constitution specifies that at least 5 percent of each party's candidates must be women. In Nepal's poorer regions, women have been sold into prostitution, frequently to India, and then forced back to Nepal upon contracting HIV infections. The spread of AIDS discouraged the government from active repatriation and rehabilitation.

Slavery is prohibited, but traditional bonded labor is still practiced. The state permits unions and strikes, except in essential services. There are several independent trade unions.

Netherlands

Polity: Parliamentary democracy
Economy: Mixed capitalist
Population: 15,193,000
PPP: $13,351
Life Expectancy: 77.2

Political Rights: 1
Civil Liberties: 1
Status: Free

Ethnic Groups: Dutch (99 percent), Indonesian and others (1 percent)

Overview:

The Netherlands, one of the world's most liberal countries, took steps to become an even more permissive society in 1992. The Dutch parliament legalized the long-tolerated prostitution industry, and major local police departments proposed the free distribution of hard drugs to reduce addict crime and AIDS.

The independence of the Netherlands dates from the late sixteenth century, when the Dutch provinces rebelled against Spanish rule. Located in Western Europe, the country has long-established traditions of representative government and constitutional monarchy. Queen Beatrix is the largely ceremonial head of state.

The Netherlands held its most recent parliamentary election in 1989. Christian Democratic Prime Minister Ruud Lubbers called the election after his right-wing Liberal coalition partners objected to his tough environmental proposals. The top issues in the campaign were the environment, the economy, and the welfare state. The Christian Democrats emerged the leading party in the lower house with 54 seats. They formed the current center-left coalition government with the Labor Party, led by Wim Kok.

The coalition's original governing accord called for limiting defense spending, increasing expenditures on social welfare and the environment, and cutting the value-added tax rate. However, in 1991, inflationary pressures led the government to adopt austerity measures, which included higher rents and fares, and changes in unemployment and disability payment policies. Rebelling against austerity, Dutch rail workers staged both official and wildcat strikes in 1992. The workers sought higher wages and job security.

The Netherlands ceased development aid to Indonesia, its former colony, after the latter announced it could not accept Dutch terms for assistance. Indonesia rejected linking aid and human rights, and wanted no Dutch role in determining Indonesian spending.

Prime Minister Lubbers has announced that he will retire in 1993.

Political Rights and Civil Liberties:

The people have the right to change their government democratically. Power shifts back and forth between center-left and center-right coalitions with the Christian Democrats playing the pivotal role. The bicameral parliament, the States General, is divided into a 75-member First Chamber, which the eleven provincial councils elect indirectly for four-year terms, and a more powerful 150-member Second Chamber, which the voters elect by proportional representation for a maximum term of four years. Due to the electoral system, the Second Chamber includes many parties from right to left. Women play an increasingly influential role in party politics, and there is now a Women's Party.

The press is free, but it generally observes unofficial limits in writing about the royal family. Broadcasting is state-owned but autonomously operated, and offers pluralistic points of view on social and political issues. Traditionally, commercials have been restricted, and banned on Sundays for religious reasons. Laws against inciting racism and expressing racist ideas limit free expression. For example, in 1992 the state prosecuted Mohammed Rasoel, a Pakistani-born author, who had described Muslims as primitive people with a mentality "that borders on insanity and blood-thirstiness." The Anne Frank Foundation, an anti-racist organization, had pressed a criminal complaint, saying that Rasoel's writing was "insulting to Muslims in Holland" and "an incitement to racial hatred."

The Netherlands has accepted immigrants from its former colonies, Suriname and Indonesia, and granted asylum to various refugees from other developing countries and Eastern Europe. However, the newcomers have encountered some discrimination in housing and employment. In order to prevent further discrimination, the Council of State, a constitutional body, overruled a proposed, compulsory national identity card in July 1992.

Religious freedom is respected. The state subsidizes church-affiliated schools based on the number of registered students. The extensive public sector regulates the private economy, and provides generous social welfare benefits. Organized labor is free. Only civil servants lack the right to strike, but they strike sometimes anyway.

The Dutch have tolerated euthanasia for twenty years. The hospitals employ guidelines requiring the patient's expressed consent, but critics charge that health professionals violate this guideline by taking lives without such consent. In June 1992, a court granted immunity to two physicians who had assisted suicides.

New Zealand

Polity: Parliamentary democracy
Economy: Capitalist
Population: 3,433,000
PPP: $11,155
Life Expectancy: 75.2
Ethnic Groups: Predominantly Anglo-Saxon, Maori and Polynesians (12 percent)

Political Rights: 1
Civil Liberties: 1
Status: Free

Overview:

Facing anxiety over sweeping cutbacks in the welfare state and over the country's growing economic isolation, New Zealanders overwhelmingly rejected their electoral system in a September 1992 referendum. Many citizens are alienated by the ideological convergence of the two major parties, and want a new system which would give smaller, more responsive parties a greater impact.

New Zealand achieved full self-government prior to World War II, and gained formal independence from Great Britain in 1947. Politics in this parliamentary democracy have been dominated by the mildly conservative National Party and the left-of-center Labor Party, both of which helped develop one of the world's most progressive welfare states. By 1984, a slow economy and lower world agricultural prices forced an incoming Labor government to begin liberalizing the economy to make it more competitive. The government deregulated the financial system, reformed the tax code, ended import protections, and privatized many industries.

Discontent over the changes and a severe recession led to a National Party landslide in the October 1990 election. The party took a record 68 seats to Labor's 28 in the unicameral parliament. The New Labor Party, a spinoff of the Labor Party, took one seat, while four others seats were reserved for Maori representation.

Rather than slow the reforms, Prime Minister Jim Bolger's government began tampering with two areas previously considered untouchable—welfare and labor relations. Welfare payments were slashed and targeted to more limited groups, and the government broke Bolger's pre-election pledge to remove a tax surcharge on state pensioners' supplementary earnings, increasing it instead. The May 1991 Employments Contract Act ended the unions' privilege to negotiate national, occupation-based awards, bringing many contracts to the factory or even individual level.

In August 1991, two National MPs quit the party in protest and revived the Liberal Party, which had been moribund since 1927. Despite the growing discontent, in early February 1992, the government ended universal free hospital care, which had been a pillar of the welfare state.

Throughout 1992 frustration over the recession and distrust of both major parties—Labor for abandoning its interventionist economic philosophy and the National for cutting social welfare—became evident. Although the National Party managed to win a close by-election on 15 February, the Alliance coalition, consisting of the discontents from both main parties, the Green Party, and the Maori Mana Motuhake party, ran a strong second. Formed in 1989, the Alliance favors increasing the maximum tax rate from 33 to 40 percent, and returning to 1960s-style free education and medicine and subsidized housing.

In a 19 September referendum, 85 percent rejected the first-past-the-post system electoral system, which has fostered the growth of the two major parties. In a choice among four alternatives, 70 percent favored a Mixed Member Proportional (MMP) system. The MMP gives each citizen two votes. The first is for a geographical constituency seat, and the second goes towards filling the other half of parliament through proportional representation. The MMP would allow small parties to win seats if they passed a certain threshold. At the next general election, due by November 1993, voters will face a second referendum pitting the existing system against the MMP. A third referendum will decide on reconvening the upper house, last used in 1951.

Although unemployment hovered around 10 percent most of the year, the austerity measures have begun to pay off. Economists predict sustainable 3 to 4 percent annual growth through 1995. Productivity has risen in many sectors, most notably among longshoremen.

A successful conclusion to the current world trade talks would boost agricultural exports by ending tariffs and other barriers. If the talks fail, New Zealand may eventually apply to the North American Free Trade Area to avoid economic isolation. To do so, it will have to improve relations with the United States, which deteriorated in 1985 when New Zealand refused to allow potentially nuclear-armed warships to dock. Although the U.S. began removing nuclear weapons from surface ships in July 1992, some groups favor continuing a ban on nuclear-powered ships.

Political Rights and Civil Liberties: New Zealand's citizens can democratically change their government. Although there is no written constitution, fundamental freedoms are fully respected in practice. An independent judiciary provides full due process rights for the accused. Freedoms of the press, speech and association are respected and fully practiced by citizens. All religious faiths are allowed to practice freely. The 1991 Employment Contracts Act ended compulsory union membership and the system of national awards, in which a single contract covered all workers. Since the ECA came into effect, unions have lost 20 percent of their membership, have not mounted any significant job actions, and have been excluded from negotiations in half the contracts signed.

A tribunal established in 1975 hears land claims and other matters brought by the Maori and other Pacific Island groups. The Maori base their land claims on the disputed 1840 Treaty of Waitangi, which they say gave up only governership but not sovereignty over the land. In September 1992, Maori tribes reached an agreement with the government to share fish resources, as required under the Treaty.

Nicaragua

Polity: Presidential-legislative democracy (military influenced)
Economy: Capitalist-statist
Population: 4,096,000
PPP: $1,463
Life Expectancy: 64.8
Ethnic Groups: Complex, with mestizo (approximately 70 percent), Caucasian (16 percent), black (9 percent), and indigenous (5 percent)

Political Rights: 4
Civil Liberties: 3
Status: Partly Free

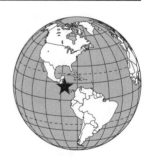

Overview: The government of President Violeta Chamorro remained locked in an ill-considered embrace with the Sandinistas, allowing General Humberto Ortega to emerge as a strongman in the tradition of the former Somoza dynasty. The coalition that had supported Chamorro's 1990 election challenged the legitimacy of her rule, increasing the likelihood of renewed political upheaval.

The Republic of Nicaragua was established in 1838, 17 years after gaining independence from Spain. Power struggles between the Liberal and Conservative parties dominated politics until General Anastasio Somoza Garcia took over in 1937.

Authoritarian rule under the Somoza family lasted until the 1979 revolution that brought the Marxist Sandinista National Liberation Front (FSLN) to power.

The FSLN suspended the 1972 constitution and ruled by decree. Daniel Ortega became president in 1985 after an election best described as a state-controlled plebiscite. In 1987, the FSLN produced a new constitution providing for the election every six years of a president, vice president, and a 96-member National Assembly.

In 1987, the Sandinistas, under increasing pressure from the Contra insurgency, signed the Arias peace accord, which called for democratization in all Central American nations. In 1989, the National Opposition Union (UNO), a coalition of 14 political parties ranging from left to right, nominated Violeta Chamorro, the publisher of opposition newspaper *La Prensa*, to run for president.

On 25 February 1990, 55 percent of the electorate voted for Chamorro, 40 percent for Ortega. UNO won 51 Assembly seats, with the FSLN taking 39 and two seats going to smaller parties. UNO won in nearly two-thirds of the municipal races.

Before Chamorro's inauguration, Antonio Lacayo, her son-in-law and campaign chief, negotiated a transition agreement with General Humberto Ortega, Daniel's brother and commander of the Sandinista military. With Daniel threatening the FSLN would "govern from below," Lacayo agreed, over the heads of UNO leaders, to let Humberto remain as military chief. In exchange, Humberto agreed the defense and interior ministries would be headed by civilians, and the state security apparatus would be dismantled.

But the new interior minister had limited authority, and the defense minister, President Chamorro herself, practically none. Before leaving office, Daniel Ortega decreed a military law that makes it virtually impossible to remove General Ortega from his command and grants him complete control over the military's internal and external affairs. The national police remained under the direct command of a longtime Sandinista militant. Moreover, General Ortega secretly transferred the state security apparatus from the interior ministry to the army.

Lacayo, the minister of the presidency and power behind the throne, believed the transition agreement would allow the new administration to establish itself on the strength of a market-oriented, economic reform program. But in 1990 the FSLN exercised veto power over government policy through violent extortion. The government, with the stated goal of "national reconciliation," regularly caved in to FSLN demands in order to stop the seizure of state enterprises and government ministries by armed FSLN militants.

By the end of 1990, the FSLN had leveraged the Chamorro government into a power-sharing arrangement. Left on the sidelines were UNO, private business and independent labor—the three pillars of the coalition that had supported Chamorro for president.

In 1991, UNO prepared a bill requiring the return of an estimated $1 billion in government property appropriated by the FSLN before leaving office. The so-called "Pinata" included homes, cars, land, businesses, and media outlets and made the FSLN business empire one of the largest in Nicaragua.

In response, Daniel Ortega called for armed rebellion, and FSLN cadres occupied farms and factories and rampaged through Managua and three other cities. Following the established pattern, Lacayo invited the FSLN for private talks, then announced that "national reconciliation" remained the government's goal.

By December 1991, it was evident the FSLN had usurped UNO's position as the government party. UNO's property bill and another cutting the Sandinista army's budget were opposed by Lacayo and defeated in the Assembly by the 39-member Sandinista bloc and eight UNO votes. Months later, the comptroller-general charged that the eight UNO deputies, calling themselves the Center Group, had been bribed by the government with foreign aid funds.

In 1992, day-to-day cooperation between Lacayo and General Ortega grew closer and communication between Lacayo and Alfredo Cesar, the National Assembly president and head of the UNO opposition bloc, broke off. A number of key cabinet ministers resigned and joined UNO in demanding the resignation of General Ortega. In September, when the FSLN and Center Group deputies boycotted the Assembly, Cesar brought in substitute legislators to obtain a quorum and pass legislation targeting the FSLN. The Supreme Court, controlled by the FSLN, invalidated Cesar's actions. The FSLN hinted it might seek to re-establish the Assembly under separate leadership, opening the possibility of two dueling legislatures.

In October, with UNO calling for a plebiscite to decide the legitimacy of the Chamorro administration, General Ortega stated that the military would resist all attempts to destabilize the government and that he would remain in his post at least until 1997.

UNO charged that General Ortega's declaration amounted to a "technical coup d'état." Chamorro tried to downplay the general's statement, repeating her vow that the general would be replaced before the end of her administration in 1996. But she failed to stem the anger of UNO, independent labor unions, private business, rights groups, and the Catholic Church. Tensions increased in November when Arges Sequiera Mangas, a leader of an organization demanding the return of confiscated property, was assassinated by a shadowy group that UNO claimed was linked to the FSLN.

Guerrilla actions by a number of Contra bands that took up arms again in 1991 added to the instability. Because of the devastated economy, the government could not fulfill its commitment to aiding former Contras, part of the 1990 demobilization agreement mediated by the OAS. The economic outlook dimmed further after conservative senators in the U.S. Congress blocked U.S. aid disbursements in mid-1992.

Political Rights and Civil Liberties:

Nicaraguans have the right to change their government through elections. However, the Chamorro government's authority has in large part been usurped by the Sandinistas, who retain control of the military and the police.

The 1987 constitution permits the organization of political parties, civic groups and labor unions. But because the FSLN prepared the document with the expectation of holding power indefinitely, individual rights, civil liberties, and the right to free expression are so narrowly defined and qualified as to often make them inapplicable in practice. In effect, the 1987 constitution does not guarantee political rights and civil liberties. Rather, it guarantees the right of the government to restrict them.

The Chamorro government nonetheless committed itself to full respect of political rights and civil liberties. But it has been unable to guarantee effectively these rights because the Sandinista army and the police operate with impunity.

In 1992 there were continued reports by Nicaragua's independent human rights groups of intimidation, false arrest, and torture during interrogation. Abuses are directed mostly against demobilized Contras and UNO supporters, particularly in rural areas. Many violations are committed by former members of state security transferred to the national police in 1990. More than 200 people have been killed as a result of political violence since 1990—over 100 demobilized Contras, with the remainder including FSLN supporters, UNO sympathizers, peasants, and independent labor leaders. The army has also committed abuses during the campaign to disarm the civilian population of tens of thousands of weapons left over from the Contra war.

The army has stonewalled the investigation of the October 1990 murder of Jean Paul Genie who, according to a group of Venezuelan jurists working at the request of UNO, was killed on a highway by members of General Humberto Ortega's armed escort. In 1992, a criminal court ruled that the bodyguards should be tried for murder and Ortega be prosecuted for a cover-up for the killing. But under current law, criminal cases involving the army are handled by a military court, which has the authority to annul the civil court charges.

The police rarely protect people and property from the armed actions of FSLN labor unions or rural paramilitary units. Since 1990, there have been virtually no arrests in response to the bombings, takeovers of government buildings and private property, and other incidents of FSLN violence. The cases of nine former Contra leaders murdered since 1990 have not been resolved, nor have the 1992 killings of two government auditors investigating charges of government corruption.

At the same time, the FSLN demands full freedom for its own activities, and justifies the action or inaction of police as necessary for the protection of its rights. The FSLN claims the police do not intervene during the armed occupation of ministries and state enterprises because it would impinge on the right to strike. Under FSLN rule, labor strikes were outlawed.

The judiciary is headed by a Supreme Court stacked by the FSLN before it left office. It is inefficient and politicized, and ineffectual in dealing with a surging crime wave fueled by a decade of economic deterioration. Prisons are overcrowded and conditions deplorable, with hundreds of detainees held for months, and in some cases, years before being brought to court.

Nicaraguan human rights organizations continue investigating long-standing charges of systematic, summary executions by the FSLN when it was in power. Since 1990, more than a dozen clandestine mass graves have been uncovered, but according to the military law decreed by the FSLN before leaving office, the army alone is responsible for investigating charges of rights violations against its members. Moreover, in December 1991, the Chamorro government issued an amnesty granting immunity for all human rights violations and acts of political violence committed prior to that date.

All points of view are represented in the print and broadcast media. Before leaving office, the FSLN dismantled the 17-station state radio network and "privatized" it to mostly FSLN loyalists; the move was part of the massive, illegal transfer of state resources to the FSLN party. They left behind two television channels, which are operated by the government. The first private television station went on the air in 1992. Attacks by the FSLN against non-FSLN media diminished in 1992.

There are no restrictions on religious expression. The Catholic Church has been outspoken in its concern over the Chamorro government's relationship with the Sandinistas.

Niger

Polity: Transitional   **Political Rights:** 5
Economy: Capitalist   **Civil Liberties:** 4
Population: 8,319,000   **Status:** Partly Free
PPP: $634
Life Expectancy: 44.5
Ethnic Groups: Daza, Fulani, Hausa, Kanuri, Kawar,
Songhai, Tuareg, Zerma, other

Overview: In 1992, the government of Niger continued a slow transition
to democracy while struggling to avoid inter-ethnic war
between northern Tuaregs and the rest of Niger.

A large, land-locked West African country, Niger gained independence from
France in 1960. The military overthrew a civilian, one-party government in 1974.
General Ali Seibou was named head of state by a supreme military council in 1987.
In late 1988, President Seibou announced plans to return Niger to constitutional one-
party rule. A few months later, Seibou was re-elected without electoral opposition to a
seven-year term. In December 1989, the government reported that voters overwhelmingly approved a constitution confirming the ruling National Movement of the Society
for Development (MNSD) as the sole legal political party. Nonetheless, the President
announced in November 1990 that the country would adopt multi-partyism based on
the recommendations of a special commission set up earlier in the year to assess the
country's political structure. He indicated that a national conference would be convened sometime in 1991 to take up the issue of political change.

In March 1991, the National Assembly approved a new constitution formalizing
the end of one-party rule and purportedly establishing civilian authority over the
military. The national conference was convened the following July. The conference
suspended the constitution and dissolved the National Assembly. The conferees also
created the position of transitional prime minister and appointed Amadou Cheiffou to
the post. Cheiffou assumed most of President Seibou's powers, including formal
control of the armed forces. André Salifou was elected chairman of the High Council
of the Republic (HCR), the new interim legislature. The democratic transition was
scheduled to last fifteen months.

In 1992, the HCR began operating with the complaint that reforms mandated by the
national conference, such as dissolution of the presidential guard, were not being
implemented. Numerous political parties were legalized throughout the year. In late
February and March, mutinous troops briefly seized the government radio station on
three occasions and detained HCR Chairman Salifou once. Foremost among the
mutineers' demands was release of a popular army captain imprisoned on charges of
having led the May 1990 massacre of 63 Tuaregs in the town of Tchin-Tabaradene.
The troops also demanded payment of salary arrears. Salifou and another hostage were
freed unharmed, the captain was provisionally released and the military was granted the
pay concessions sought. The civilian population held a two-day general strike in protest.

Meanwhile, the Tuareg revolt against the government continued. In January 1992,
armed rebels of the Front for the Liberation of Aïr and Azawad (FLAA) struck towns

scattered across northern Niger, kidnapping civilians and military personnel. The government has long dismissed the Tuareg revolt as mere banditry, but the interior minister acknowledged the political basis for the rebellion in January. Demands from FLAA spokesmen included withdrawal of army forces in the north, an end to persecution of the Tuaregs, and an independent investigation into accusations of human rights abuse. The FLAA also insisted on greater regional autonomy and more government spending in the Tuareg's resource-rich but drought-stricken portion of the country.

The government responded by calling upon the rebels to disarm and enter into negotiations. In early April, the executive branch granted police powers to the army in northern Niger. The regime and the FLAA negotiated a fifteen day truce to take effect on 15 May, but there were attacks during and afterward by bands of armed Tuaregs. These attacks were often followed by army and police reprisals against unarmed Tuareg civilians. Targeting trans-Saharan tourist convoys as well as isolated Nigerien villages, the FLAA abducted and held 30 prisoners. Negotiations broke off in May because FLAA refused to release its hostages. Talks resumed in August, but the army unilaterally seized 186 Tuareg civilians as hostages between 27 and 31 August. Responding, the FLAA refused to meet with the government until the detained Tuaregs were freed.

The major foreign policy issue during 1992 was the Prime Minister Cheiffou's 19 June decision to restore diplomatic recognition with Taiwan in exchange for US$50 million in development assistance. He suspended the decision a week later after heavy pressure from André Salifou and the HCR, most Nigerien political parties, and demonstrating Nigerien students. But others, particularly civil servants, sprang to Cheiffou's defense with the argument that foreign aid was critical to the cash-starved administration. In the end, the government went forward with the decision to recognize Taiwan, and the People's Republic of China suspended relations with Niger.

On 13 August, the government indefinitely postponed a constitutional referendum scheduled for 4 October. It based its decision on an inability to finance the electoral exercise, the incompletion of voter registers, and the delay in adopting a new electoral code. The referendum was later rescheduled for 28 November and then for 26 December. The constitution was approved by 89 percent of the vote, but voter turnout was low. Legislative, presidential, and municipal elections were first set for November and December of 1992, but later were put off until 1993.

Political Rights and Civil Liberties:

Citizens of Niger cannot yet change their government democratically, but 40 political parties have been legalized. Traditional chiefs remain the dominant powers in rural areas.

Civil and criminal cases are generally conducted fairly. In the past, security cases have been tried by the State Security Court, which functions outside the normal legal framework. Special courts handle civil servant corruption cases. Political detainees, particularly Tuaregs, have been held indefinitely without charge or trial.

The Nigerien media are increasingly independent, and criticism of government policy is no longer unusual. The right of assembly is respected, and freedom of religion in this overwhelmingly Muslim country is generally respected. Intolerant religious fundamentalism poses a growing threat to the creation of a liberal and democratic society.

The Federation of Niger Trade Unions, long linked to the ruling MNSD, is now effectively independent. A significant force in the struggle for democratization, it has resisted austerity measures imposed as a part of a structural adjustment program.

Nigeria

Polity: Military
(transitional)
Economy: Capitalist-
statist
Population: 90,122,000
PPP: $1,160
Life Expectancy: 51.5
Ethnic Groups: Hausa, Fulani, Ibo, Yoruba, Kanuri, other

Political Rights: 5
Civil Liberties: 4
Status: Partly Free

Overview:
In July 1992 Nigeria held its first parliamentary elections in 12 years as part of a democratic transition that had been expected to lead to civilian control by January 1993.
However, massive fraud in the ensuing presidential primaries led to a postponement of the December presidential elections, and the military government of General Ibrahim Babangida delayed the return to civilian rule until mid-1993.

Since gaining independence from Britain in 1960, Nigeria has been under periods of military rule for 22 of the past 32 years. Differences between the Muslim-dominated north and the mostly Christian south, as well as among the country's 250 tribal groups, have frequently led to violence. Tribal animosity led the Eastern Region to secede in May 1967 as the Republic of Biafra. When the resulting civil war ended in January 1970, more than 1 million people had died through starvation and fighting. An oil boom in the 1970s created high economic expectations in this resource rich country, but corruption and extravagant spending led to hyperinflation and rising unemployment in the 1980s.

Babangida took power in an August 1985 coup and established the Armed Forces Ruling Council (AFRC), acting as both head of state and chief executive. Although Babangida pledged to clean up corruption and return the country to civilian rule by 1990, the democratic transition has repeatedly been pushed back. The AFRC continues to rule by decree, corruption remains rampant, and the president's 1986 economic Structural Adjustment Program has shown few results.

As part of the transition program, the government lifted a ban on political parties in May 1989, but by October 1989 the government had nullified the applications of all 50 parties. Instead, authorities created two groups—the Social Democratic Party (SDP) and the National Republican Convention (NRC)—and provided them with platforms, financing and offices. Babangida described the two as "one a little to the left, and the other a little to the right," but their manifestos differed only marginally. The government hoped that these secular parties would help bridge religious and tribal differences.

In August 1991, after the government created nine new states to redress regional grievances, riots broke out in areas where residents did not get new states. In elections in November and December 1991, the NRC took 16 of 30 gubernatorial races, and the SDP held a slight advantage in the state legislative voting.

In January 1992, the country seemed to be on course for the scheduled transfer to civilian power on 3 January 1993. The civilian governors elected in December replaced their military predecessors, and Nigerian Electoral Commission (NEC)

Chairman Humphrey Nwosu announced that National Assembly elections would be held on 7 November, followed by the presidential elections on 5 December. The Assembly elections were later moved up to 4 July.

In May, the transition appeared threatened as a series of economic and religious riots hit the country. Discontent had been building since March, when the government devalued the currency by 43 percent, leading to higher prices. The government also shut three of the country's four refineries for maintenance; and the country, which exports more than $13 billion of oil each year, inexplicably had to import up to 20 percent of its oil needs. The ensuing shortages, exacerbated by gasoline smuggling to neighboring countries where the price per gallon is several times higher, sent transportation prices soaring 400 percent. On 5 May, and again on 13 May, riots erupted in the capital of Lagos and several other cities across the country. Many demonstrators called on Babangida to resign. The latter riots came after both the banned National Association of Nigerian Students and the Nigerian Labor Congress called for 48 hours of protests and strikes.

In unrelated violence, in mid-May upwards of 300 Muslims and Christians died in the Northern Kaduna state in fighting that began over land dispute. Even more chilling were the emerging details of several months of intense fighting between the Tiv and Jukun peoples in Taraba state, where by some accounts 5,000 people have been killed. Wary of these escalating tensions, on 20 May the government banned all associations based on tribal, ethnic, and religious ties.

Despite the unrest, on 4 July the country held parliamentary elections for the first time in 12 years. Given the lack of clear ideological differences between the parties, elections for the 91-seat Senate and the 598-seat House of Representatives mostly turned on differences in individual personalities. To guard against fraud, voters lined up before pictures of their preferred candidates to allow for public counting. Critics say this denial of a secret ballot leads to lower voter turnout. Despite the government's fear that the NRC would emerge as a northern, Muslim party and the SDP as a southern, Christian party, much of the voting crossed religious and geographic lines. Overall, the SDP took 47 seats in the Senate and 310 in the House.

On 1 August, the final phase of the transition began with primaries in 5 out of the 30 states for the December presidential elections. The primaries were marred by massive fraud; in some states the turnout far exceeded the number of registered voters. On 6 August, the government voided the results. The primaries were attempted for a second time in September, but were again characterized by blatant vote-rigging, and on 7 October Babangida suspended party activity. By some accounts the 23 candidates had spent up to $815 million, most of it illegally. During the month, the President nullified the results of the primaries and replaced the national and local leaderships of the parties with appointed caretaker committees.

On 17 November, Babangida announced that the presidential elections would instead be held on 12 June 1993, with the power transfer taking place on 27 August. Under a new plan, both parties will nominate a presidential candidate via congresses in each of the 30 states plus the capital district, for a total of 62. One candidate from each party will then be elected at national party conventions. Babangida also disqualified all 23 candidates who took part in the earlier primaries, and said all cabinet ministers would be fired on 2 January 1993, to be replaced by a civilian-led National Defense and Security Council that would guide the transition.

In another major issue, the government in March released the results of a census taken the previous November, which had avoided questions on religion or tribal allegiances to prevent animosity over federal funding and political representation. The final count showed 88.5 million people, 20 million fewer than previously assumed. Also, South African President F.W. de Klerk visited the country in April, but there were no signs that the two nations would establish diplomatic relations in the near future.

Political Rights and Civil Liberties:

Nigerians cannot change their military government. The government has micromanaged the democratic transition process, creating and supervising the only two legal parties and, under Decree 48, banning numerous individuals from running.

Civilians now run the state governments, but the junta, backed by the military, the State Security Service and the police, runs the federal government. The regime has been accused of numerous rights violations, including extrajudicial killings, police brutality, arbitrary detentions and press restrictions. Decree Two, issued in 1984, gives the government broad powers to detain suspects without charge and suspend their civil liberties. In 1990, the government shortened the maximum detention time from six months to six weeks and required the Vice President to sign all detention orders, but in practice these changes are frequently ignored, and a panel created at the time to review detentions rarely meets to do so.

In addition to the regular court system, special tribunals hear cases involving matters such as corruption and armed robbery. Many of the tribunals presume defendants guilty and hand down harsh sentences. Death sentences are issued without appeal, and conviction rates in the tribunals average over 90 percent. The regular courts generally observe due process rights, but suspects are often held for months and even years without going to trial, and judicial independence is suspect in cases where government is a party. The Civil Liberties Organization estimates 2,000 prisoners die each year from poor conditions.

The government has a monopoly on radio and television broadcasting, although there are no restrictions on press ownership. A fair amount criticism of the government is tolerated in the private press, but journalists are frequently warned against overstepping boundaries, and the threat of sanction leads to self-censorship. In the spring, the government closed the Concord Press for two weeks after its news magazine included a critical survey of the economy. In May, the government arrested prominent human rights leader Dr. Beko Ransome-Kuti and several of his associates a week after Ransome-Kuti's Committee for the Defense of Human Rights called for the government to resign. They were detained for two months before being release on bail.

A permit requirement for outdoor meetings is generally not enforced. The National Association of Nigerian Students remains banned, and in recent years the government has temporarily closed a number of universities and summarily expelled or suspended hundreds of students for political activism.

There is no official religion, and all groups worship freely, but tensions between Muslims and Christians have led to frequent clashes. Citizens can generally travel freely but the government has prevented people from leaving the country for political reasons. Workers, except for government employees in essential services, may join unions and strike. However, the government has the power to supervise union accounts, merge unions and mandate compulsory arbitration prior to strikes.

Norway

Polity: Parliamentary democracy
Economy: Mixed capitalist
Population: 4,276,000
PPP: $16,838
Life Expectancy: 77.1
Ethnic Groups: Norwegian, Finnish, Lappic (Sami), and small immigrant groups

Political Rights: 1
Civil Liberties: 1
Status: Free

Overview:

A major national debate over joining the European Community (EC) dominated politics in 1992. Labor Party Prime Minister Gro Harlem Brundtland won her own party's support for the EC, and parliament approved the Community application on 19 November by 104 votes to 65, with six absent or abstaining. Most voters, especially in fishing and agricultural areas, the Socialist Left Party, and the Center Party, remain opposed to joining Europe. Norway made its EC application official on 25 November.

Anne Enger Lahnstein, the Center leader, has used her traditionally agrarian party's anti-EC stance to recruit members in urban areas. The Center's opposition stance includes hostility towards the European Economic Area, a common market associated with, but not in, the EC. The Labor government made a gesture to anti-EC maritime communities when it announced a decision to resume whaling despite a world ban. Whaling and fishing will be major issues when Norway and the EC discuss terms of admission to the Community.

The present government of Norway formed at the end of 1990 following the collapse of a Conservative-led cabinet. The next elections to parliament will be in 1993. The present Norwegian constitution, known as the Eisvold Convention, dates from 1814 and is one of the oldest written constitutions in the world. The largely ceremonial head of state is King Harald V. The parliament, referred to as the "Storting," consists of 165 members elected by proportional representation every four years. Once the Storting is elected, one fourth of its members are elected from within the parliament to serve in the upper chamber (*Lagting*). The remaining parlia-mentarians remain in the lower chamber (*Odelsting*). The two chambers consider legislative proposals separately although most other matters are handled by the Storting as a whole. In 1992, seven political parties held seats in the Storting. The Labor Party held 63 seats, the Conservative Party occupied 37 seats, the Party of Progress occupied 22 seats and other parties occupied the remaining seats.

Political Rights and Civil Liberties:

Norwegians can change their government democratically every four years in free and fair elections. The Lappic (Sami) minority has political autonomy and its own assembly.

There are few restrictions on free speech, free press, free assembly, or free association. Major restrictions, other than laws against slander and libel, include the prohibition of racist and sexist comments either printed or spoken in public. The police routinely grant permission for public demonstrations.

The Lutheran Church is the established church of Norway and is financed by the state. Approximately 96 percent of all Norwegians are members of the established church. However, there are alternative churches available to Norwegians. Although there is significant freedom of worship, there are some minor restrictions on religion. For example, by law the King and half of the cabinet must be members of the state church. In some circumstances, employers have the right to ask job applicants whether they respect Christian beliefs.

It is illegal to discriminate on the basis of gender, language, social status and race in Norway. There are instances of racially motivated violence committed by civilians against recent non-Nordic immigrants in Norway. However, the police and other authorities have dealt firmly with such cases.

The press is free and vibrant. The state subsidizes many of the newspapers in Norway in order to support pluralism of political thought. The state funds television and radio broadcasting corporations but does not interfere with editorial concerns of the corporations. A commercial cable television channel and small private radio stations are available to the public. Censorship is minimal in Norway, but the Film Control Board has the right to prevent the public from viewing films that it deems blasphemous, overly violent or pornographic. However, the blasphemy clause has not been employed in over twenty years. Workers have the right to organize and strike. More than half of the workforce is affiliated with a union.

Oman

Polity: Traditional monarchy
Economy: Capitalist-statist
Population: 1,588,000
PPP: $10,573
Life Expectancy: 65.9
Ethnic Groups: Arab, Baluchi, Zanzibari, Indian

Political Rights: 6
Civil Liberties: 5
Status: Partly Free

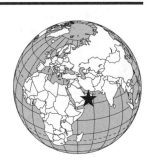

Overview: The Gulf War and its aftermath have had a substantial impact on both Omani domestic and international policy. The war prompted Oman to reform its system of governance and to develop foreign economic and security relations. Sultan Qabus ibn Sa'id al Sa'id has ruled this small, oil-rich country since 1970, when he assumed the throne by overthrowing his father in a palace coup.

In December 1991, the government launched a 2-year experimental *Majlis al-Shura*, or Consultative Council, replacing the former appointed Council that advised the monarch but had no legislative function. In each of Oman's 59 provinces, three candidates were popularly elected in spring 1991 to serve in the new Majlis. The names of the winners were then passed to a nominating committee of leading families, who selected representatives according to their "qualifications." Representatives are responsible for reviewing and proposing legislation, preparing development plans, investigating matters concerning the public sector and voicing citizens' concerns in a public forum. Their decisions are subject to the approval of the Sultan; nevertheless, the debates have been lively and have raised considerable controversy for criticizing the behavior of government ministers.

Any disagreement between the Cabinet and the Majlis is referred to the Sultan directly. At the end of two years, the process will be reviewed to determine its effectiveness. In addition, a census will be taken to ascertain the number of representatives needed to represent the population. Locally, the Ministry of the Interior continues to appoint and supervise the tribal chiefs, who function as governors.

Oman has been strengthening relations both with its Gulf Cooperation Council (GCC) partners and with Iran. As of April 1992, citizens can freely cross the Omani-UAE border without passports. In October, the country ended a border dispute with Yemen that had led to occasional skirmishes by agreeing to cede a few kilometers of desert.

Since the Gulf War, Oman has also worked to increase regional security. Sultan Qaboos appealed to the Gulf Cooperation Council (GCC) for a 10,000 strong all-Gulf army in December 1991. This would avoid the problems of the June 1991 Damascus Declaration, signed by the GCC, Syria and Egypt, which proposed an all-Arab security pact. The Declaration excluded Iran, which is imperative for free navigation and a balance of power in the Gulf, and included Syria contrary to the desires of the U.S. Due to these conflicts, the GCC refused the security component of the Declaration but is still considering the economic aspects.

The Sultan's internationalist views and desires for rapid development are in sharp contrast to the reigns of his predecessors. His goals for the country include diversification of the economy, assimilation or repatriation of foreigners (who make up 45 percent of the labor force), and intensive infrastructure development. While Oman is not a member of OPEC, it does adhere to OPEC's export quotas.

Political Rights and Civil Liberties:

Omanis cannot change their government democratically. The Sultan receives consultation from his Council of Ministers and from the Majlis al-Shura in this absolute monarchy. There is no constitution, and neither civil nor political rights are codified. The judicial system is rudimentary with no requirement for legal counsel. *Shari'a* (Islamic law) is the law of the land. Cases may be appealed in a Court of Appeals and finally brought to a higher level or Grievance Committee, whose decisions are final. Amputation and stoning are permissible but were not being practiced in 1992. There are also civil courts that treat misdemeanor and criminal felony cases, a committee for the resolution of commercial disputes, and a military tribunal. A special security court system is infrequently invoked for internal security matters.

As part of the government's efforts to preserve Omani culture, it has engaged in an "Omanization" process. This includes restructuring the education system to provide training for Omanis and to prepare them for replacing the current 300,000 expatriates. A 1986 law forbids marriage between foreigners and Omanis. In addition, more current policies ban babysitting and require maternity leave and set aside hours for breast feeding.

The government censors the press for what it considers politically, culturally or sexually offensive material. The state permits no criticism of the Sultan and only infrequent press criticism of government agencies or individuals. Government sensors screen foreign publications. The government owns and operates all electronic media.

The law does not guarantee freedom of assembly. All organizations must have government sponsorship. While Oman is an Islamic state, it does not prohibit the practice of other religions. In accordance with Islamic law, the Sultan donates land to Christian and Hindu communities for houses of worship. All Omanis are free to travel internally. Male Omanis may travel abroad freely, but females must receive the authorization of the husband or the father.

The law requires equal pay for equal work and is enforced. Female circumcision is still practiced in the rural regions. Labor unions and strikes are strictly forbidden. Workers may file grievances.

Pakistan

Polity: Parliamentary democracy (military influenced)
Economy: Capitalist-statist
Population: 121,665,000
PPP: $1,789
Life Expectancy: 57.7
Ethnic Groups: Punjab, Baluchi, Sindhi, Pathan, Afghan

Political Rights: 4
Civil Liberties: 5
Status: Partly Free

Overview:　The ruling coalition, the Pakistan Democratic Alliance (PDA), led by Prime Minister Nawaz Sharif's Islamic Democratic Alliance (IDA), began to crumble in the summer of 1992. Member parties deserted over the government's corruption and ineffectiveness. However, the most important factor was the June military action to rid Sindh province of hoodlums and political opposition. The government also faced religious and factional violence.

Formed in 1947 through the partition of India, Pakistan warred with India over the Kashmir province in 1947-48 and again in 1965. In 1971, East Pakistan separated to form Bangladesh, leading to a third war in which India defeated Pakistan. In 1971 Zulfikar Ali Bhutto became president and, subsequently, prime minister under a new constitution. General Mohammed Zia Ul-Haq seized power in 1977, imposed martial law, and outlawed political parties. Zia's government hanged Bhutto in 1979, on charges of complicity in an assassination. In 1985, martial law was repealed and political parties were legalized again. Zia died in a mysterious airplane crash in August 1988, and elections brought Bhutto's daughter, Benazir, to power as prime minister in November 1988. The parliament chose Ghulam Ishaq Khan as President for a five-year term.

The seemingly ceremonial presidency has some significant power over the parliamentary government. In 1990, Ishaq Khan dismissed Bhutto for alleged corruption, nepotism, and abuse of authority, and dissolved the 237-seat National Assembly. In the 1990 elections for a new Assembly, the conservative Islamic Democratic Alliance (IDA) defeated Bhutto's Pakistan People's Party (PPP) and formed a new government under Mian Mohammed Nawaz Sharif. Of the 217 directly elected seats, the IDA won 105, and the PPP, in a coalition called the People's Democratic Alliance, won just 45. Despite Bhutto's claim of massive vote-rigging, in January 1991 an international team released a report concluding that the election was generally free and fair. However, the international observers also urged reforms in the electoral process, including the removal of corrupt officials.

In 1991, the IDA strengthened its control of the 87-seat Senate, which has 76 members chosen by the country's four provincial assemblies, and eleven members chosen by the National Assembly from the tribal region and the capital, Islamabad. The Senate has the power to block lower house legislation. In March 1991, elections for 46 Senate seats, the IDA won 23 seats, the PPP took five, and smaller parties and independents captured 18. Prior to the election, Bhutto had accused Sharif of "brutal dictatorship," and warned that the IDA would attempt to sabotage the vote, although there was no evidence of large-scale vote-rigging .

The government's military operations in Sindh province began in January 1992 with police rounding up Sindhi nationalists after a speech supporting an independent Sindhi homeland. The government's actions targeted the nationalist Jiye Sindh Movement (JSM) and anyone speaking "against the integrity of Pakistan." In April, Sindhi local elections were marked by severe corruption, police harassment of party workers and journalists, violence and ballot fraud.

Historically, the government has been concerned with political opposition in Sindh. The region has been plagued by politically organized bandits committing kidnappings, looting and rape. President Ishaq Khan cited Bhutto's inability to maintain order in Sindh as a rationale to dismiss her from office. On 2 June, the federal government invoked Article 147 of the constitution, providing the army with six months to clear Sindh of outlaws, under the supervision of the civilian government. The army unsuccessfully requested invocation of Article 245 which gives the military absolute control and utilizes military justice to try offenders. The political opposition feared that Article 245 would lead to a witch hunt, because the PPP dominates Sindh's rural population and the MQM (Mohajir Quami Movement, comprised of Urdu-speaking migrants from India), controls Karachi.

The government imprisoned hundreds of PPP workers. In an effort to appear impartial, the army went after the MQM and inadvertently unearthed MQM torture cells. Their discovery led to fighting between MQM factions in Karachi. MQM-Haqiqi, a splinter faction of MQM claiming innocence of torture, allied with the military to attack MQM. Altaf Hussein, leader of MQM, ordered MQM-Haqiqi members killed. By 28 June, MQM quit both the Sindhi and National Assemblies; many members either resigned or changed parties. By July, the military chafed at long delays in civilian court procedures and requested parallel military courts. The government denied the request. MQM set conditions to quell the fighting: disarm MQM dissidents, return its torture cells, and desist from MQM arrests. The government refused. On 8 July, the government offered retroactive immunity to the military for any infringements of civil rights and offered broad discretion in search and seizure.

The discovery of MQM torture cells raised questions about whether the major parties had ignored massive human rights abuses. These questions provoked a political crisis, as PDA members threatened to pull out of the coalition. President Ishaq Khan promised to hold by-elections to fill vacant seats in the assemblies. While fear of martial law loomed, the prospect of Ishaq Khan's dissolving the National Assembly was unlikely, because he and Sharif shared political views and dislike for Bhutto. Additionally, Ishaq Khan feared his own political future after reports surfaced about crimes of his son-in-law, the former Home Minister of Sindh.

By the mid-July, opposition forces demanded Sharif and Ishaq Khan's resignations. They accused Ishaq Khan of undermining the judiciary, executive and military, rigging elections and unleashing a reign of terror.

In August, the Minister for Religious Affairs declared Bhutto a "Kafir" (unbeliever), upon penalty of death, for not advocating the Federal Shariat (Islamic Law) Court as supreme. The death threat produced pandemonium in the National Assembly. The opposition claimed that the government was trying to avoid Pakistan's real problems by diverting attention to religious affairs and destroying pluralism. The threat was rescinded.

On 14 August, Sunni-Shiite violence erupted during religious celebrations. The government deployed troops and declared curfews to quell the violence in Lahore and Peshawar.

By 27 August, the National People's Party, Sunni Islamic fundamentalist Jamaat-i-Islami (JI) and MQM had all left the PDA coalition. The various crises caused IDA dissidents to form the Functional Muslim League. Sharif invoked Islamic legislation to garner support from the Islamic parties, forcing them to vote with the IDA in the National Assembly or lose their mandate. To deny Bhutto power, fundamentalists mounted an unsuccessful campaign to forbid women as prime minister.

In September, the Sharia (Islamic) Court upheld a decision banning interest on loans. The ruling shook Pakistan's financial markets and encouraged international aid donors to withdraw from constructing a hydroelectric plant. The government appealed the decision unsuccessfully. Without interest, foreign investment will dissipate and the economy will collapse.

In October, Bhutto's brother Murtaza admitted being the leader of the Syrian-supported Al-Zufikar Organization, a terrorist group operating out of Sindh and responsible for hijackings and bombings. He announced that he would stand trial, if the army were tried for human rights abuses.

Benazir Bhutto, who is still under investigation for corruption during her tenure as prime minister and whose husband is still in prison for fiscal mismanagement, longed to return to power. Bhutto gained credibility with the discovery of thirteen internal security agency tapes, which implicated Sharif in bribing parliamentarians to vote no-confidence against her government. The Supreme Court voted in a split decision that her government's dismissal was justified. Bhutto, who has had problems with the military since they pressed for her ouster, began to curry their favor, hoping to break the Ishaq Khan-Sharif-army troika.

Sharif and Ishaq Khan's ire against Bhutto erupted on 11 November. She planned a cross-country march to encourage Pakistanis to rebel against the government, corruption and repression and to demand free and fair elections. Sharif banned Bhutto and her mother from Islamabad, for defying a national ban on public demonstrations. The government imprisoned them on 18 November for holding the illegal rally.

Hundreds of Bhutto's supporters were also arrested. Violence between the police and PPP supporters occurred in Peshawar and Lahore. On 30 December, the government bowed to public pressure and dropped a law aimed at Bhutto's husband that would have forbidden his bail appeal to the Supreme Court.

Pakistan finally agreed to a phased repatriation of 250,000 Bihari refugees from Bangladesh (East Pakistanis who opted for West Pakistan after the 1971 war between them). Many Afghan refugees returned to Afghanistan, following that country's Muslim guerrilla overthrow of the Communist government. On 26 August as conditions worsened in Kabul and thousands of new refugees arrived, Pakistan sealed its borders and provided only cross-border assistance. The 3,500 Iraqi refugees in Baluchistan are restricted to the city of Quetta.

Political Rights and Civil Liberties: Pakistanis can change their government democratically. However, widespread corruption, vote fraud, and the military's political role undermine the formal democracy.

In July 1992, the Supreme Court banned student involvement in politics and political discussions on campuses. Other restrictive measures include a requirement that female television personalities cover their hair. Conversely, the Court declared recent prohibitions against the marriage of flight attendants and military nurses as unconstitutional. The judicial system invokes Islamic punishments including stoning, public whipping, execution and amputation.

The media offer lively debate and pluralistic points of view. Although Pakistanis have some freedom of speech, a law passed in 1991 mandates the death sentence for anyone defaming Mohammed, and laws prohibit strong criticism of the army and the constitution. The government owns electronic media and controls their news content. CNN is broadcast live, although the government often blacks portions out. A government-operated trust runs four large newspapers, but privately owned papers exceed their circulation. Although editors frequently practice self-censorship, they do print statements critical of the government. This limited freedom does not preclude government attacks on journalists. After the government charged three reporters with sedition, journalists threatened a national media strike. The government dropped the charges.

Women do not have equal rights in Pakistan. They are either underrepresented or non-existent in public activities across the country. In the north, local and Islamic customs circumscribe women's behavior. Anti-female violence is common, but underreported. Laws stipulate that a woman may be imprisoned and stoned for being the victim of rape (considered fornication, if she cannot produce four male witnesses). Women's testimony is not admissible in court.

Despite legal prohibitions, some Pakistanis are bonded laborers. Due to grave poverty, most children receive little or no schooling and many begin work before adolescence. Persian Gulf countries buy Pakistani children for camel races. The children die as a result of the game.

The government generally respects freedom of association, but magistrates can ban gatherings if they suspect violence.

The population is 97 percent Muslim. The Sharia Act stipulates that minorities may practice their religion and that Sharia will not affect non-Muslims. In practice, non-Muslims suffer economic and political discrimination with no legal redress. Shiite and Ahmadi Muslims also suffer from discrimination is this predominantly Sunni nation.

Hindus complain of violence by Islamic fundamentalists. After Hindus destroyed an Indian mosque in December 1992, Islamic mobs destroyed several Hindu temples in Pakistan.

Citizens are generally free to travel internally and abroad, although students and government officials must obtain special permission to leave the country. Many of the country's Afghan refugees reside outside camps and may hold jobs. Large sectors of the work force may not bargain collectively. The government restricts state-sector union activity and often bans strikes under the pretext of community or national interest.

Business is heavily influenced by clan ties. The political and business elite control the markets leaving only small business to others.

Panama

Polity: Presidential-legislative democracy
Economy: Capitalist-statist
Population: 2,431,000
PPP: $3,231
Life Expectancy: 72.4
Ethnic Groups: Mestizo (70 percent), West Indian (14 percent), white (10 percent), Indian (6 percent)

Political Rights: 4
Civil Liberties: 3
Status: Partly Free

Overview: Most citizens failed to benefit from an economic rebound and President Guillermo Endara's popularity ratings dropped to single digits as Panama was beset by social unrest, bomb attacks and a wave of drug-related criminal activity. The weakness of the political system was underscored by polls showing that a large majority of Panamanians did not want the U.S. to end its military presence.

Panama was part of Colombia until 1903, when a U.S.-supported revolt resulted in the proclamation of an independent Republic of Panama. Until World War II, the government was dominated by small groups of family-based, political elites. During the next two decades public discontent mounted over U.S. control of the Panama Canal. A 1968 military coup resulted in the coming to power of General Omar Torrijos and a renegotiation of the treaty that granted the U.S. control of the Canal Zone in perpetuity.

After the 1977 canal treaties were signed, Torrijos promised Panama would become a democracy. The 1972 constitution was revised, providing for the direct election of a president and a Legislative Assembly for five years. But after Torrijos' death in 1981, General Manuel Noriega emerged as Panamanian Defense Force (PDF) chief. Noriega rigged the 1984 election that brought to power the Democratic Revolutionary Party (PRD), the political arm of the PDF.

The May 1989 elections were unfair in every aspect. Even so, Guillermo Endara, the presidential candidate of the Democratic Alliance of Civic Opposition (ADOC), defeated Carlos Duque, Noriega's candidate, by nearly 3-to-1. Noriega annulled the election, abolished the legislature and declared himself head of state.

On 20 December 1989, after Noriega's removal during a U.S. military invasion, Endara was sworn in as president. His running mates, Ricardo Arias Calderon and Guillermo "Billy" Ford were sworn in as first and second vice-presidents. In February 1990, the electoral tribunal confirmed the winners of 58 of 67 legislative seats. Fifty-one seats went to the ADOC coalition: 27 to Arias's Christian Democrats, 15 to Ford's Molirena coalition, five to Endara's Arnulfista party and four to the Authentic Liberal party. Seven seats went to the PRD.

Overseen by the U.S., the PDF was transformed into a police force and renamed the Public Force (PF). Over a hundred PDF officers were retired and a civilian chief was appointed. After the departure of the U.S. invasionary forces in 1990, the PF assumed responsibility for public order. However, it remains weak, poorly disciplined, and retains within its ranks former PDF members with questionable loyalties. A coup attempt led by a retired officer in December 1990 had to be put down by U.S. troops. The PF has also been ineffectual against the drug trade as Panama continues to be a major transshipment point for both cocaine and illicit arms.

Hundreds of pro-Noriega former officers remain underground and some have carried out terrorist attacks against government, U.S. and other foreign targets. The most active group is the 20 December Movement (M-20) which claimed credit for more than a dozen attacks in 1992. The Endara government claimed the M-20 and others have been behind a half dozen coup attempts since 1991, but many Panamanians believe Endara was only seeking sympathy as his popularity plummeted.

The economy has grown significantly since 1991, although some analysts say it is due to the country's reemergence as a drug-trafficking and money-laundering center. However, unemployment has remained at 20 to 25 percent, fueling unrest and violent crime. The government's free-market program, which is undermined by corruption and mismanagement, led to a series of paralyzing labor strikes in 1991 and 1992. Popular discontent was also evident in the January 1991 elections for the nine legislative seats left in dispute in 1990. Five of the seats were won by the PRD and its allies, only four by ADOC.

In 1992, Endara became increasingly isolated. The Christian Democrats, having split from ADOC, went into formal opposition. Left with a minority bloc in the legislature, Endara was enticed by the PRD into a *de facto* alliance, although both denied it. The maneuvering seemed to leave the traditional political parties discredited in the eyes of most citizens. With the next election due in May 1994, singer-actor Ruben Blades, an 18-year resident in the U.S., appeared the favorite for president. But even he was running second to "Nobody" in most polls.

On 15 November, voters rejected by 2-to-1 a package of constitutional reforms proposed by the government. It was a major defeat for Endara, as the special vote was widely seen as a referendum on his government. One of the reforms would have prohibited the re-formation of a national army, but most of those who voted—60 percent stayed home—appeared more concerned with expressing opposition to Endara than with the threat of renewed militarization.

People also appeared to have little confidence the government could stand on its own. Since 1991, polls have indicated that more than two-thirds of Panamanians want the ten U.S military bases—with a contingent of 10,000 U.S. troops—to remain after 1999, the year they are to be dismantled according to the 1977 treaties.

Political Rights and Civil Liberties:

Upon Noriega's removal, decrees restricting the constitutional rights of freedom of expression, organization, assembly and religion were rescinded. No limitations were imposed on political parties or media that supported the former regime. In 1992, parties from across the political spectrum were gearing up for the 1994 election.

There are a number of independent human rights organizations that operate without interference. The government has been open to investigations by international human rights organizations, and has accepted the jurisdiction of the Inter-American Human Rights Court.

Independent rights groups and opposition parties have criticized the Endara government for creating new security branches—the Judicial Police and the Anti-Terrorism Police. There have been frequent charges that these units have been used by the government to intimidate and spy on political opponents.

The judiciary, cowed into submission under Noriega through bribery and intimidation, was revamped in 1990. President Endara replaced all nine Supreme Court judges, who in turn appointed thirteen new members to the 19-seat Superior Court and replaced two-thirds of the 48 lower court justices.

But the judicial system has been overwhelmed, and its administration remained inefficient, politicized, and undermined by corruption. During the U.S. invasion, the Supreme Court building was sacked by looters, and hundreds of thousands of court records were destroyed. The disarray was compounded by an unwieldy criminal code and a sudden influx of cases, many of them grievances against PDF officers accumulated over two decades of military rule.

In 1992, there were nearly 18,000 court cases pending, with the numbers climbing due to a drug-fueled crime wave. Less than 15 percent of the nation's prison inmates had been tried and convicted, and the penal system was marked by a rash of escapes and violent disturbances in decrepit facilities packed with up to eight times their intended capacity. The country has barely twenty public defenders.

All media shut down by Noriega reopened in 1990. Three newspapers seized under Torrijos were returned, but the Endara government continues to hold their owners liable for debts incurred during military rule. Since 1990, the media have been a raucous assortment of daily newspapers, weeklies publications, and talk shows. Broadcast media includes live coverage of Legislative Assembly debates. However, some restrictive media laws dating back to 1978 remain on the books and have been used against anti-government radio stations and a number journalists critical of the government.

In January 1992, the offices of Panama America, the publisher of two newspapers, were nearly destroyed in a bombing attack apparently carried out by the pro-Noriega 20 December Movement. In August 1992, a journalist was physically attacked by Mayin Correa, the mayor of Panama City. President Endara provoked outrage when he sided with Correa.

Labor unions are well organized and legally permitted to strike. In 1991, however, the government suspended collective bargaining rights for three years to attract foreign investment. The government also failed to comply with a recommendation by the International Labor Organization that government workers fired in a mass dismissal in 1991 be reinstated.

Papua New Guinea

Polity: Parliamentary democracy
Economy: Capitalist
Population: 3,860,000
PPP: $1,834
Life Expectancy: 54.9
Ethnic Groups: A multi-ethnic, multi-tribal state—some 700 indigenous tribes

Political Rights: 2
Civil Liberties: 3
Status: Free

Overview:

Papua New Guinea's voters, fed up with corruption and politicians who, according to one former prime minister, "come and go from one party to another like fleas switching dogs," threw out a record number of incumbents in the June 1992 parliamentary elections. Although in October the government claimed victory in a three-year battle with secessionists on Bougainville Island, it faced a possible new revolt from other island provinces after it proposed to shut down the country's provincial governments.

The country, which consists of the eastern part of New Guinea and numerous islands, won independence from Australia in September 1975. Its parliamentary democracy has been tested by extreme cultural differences between the cities and remote highlands, the presence of some 700 tribes speaking 1,000 languages, and rampant political corruption. In the outgoing parliament, 89 of the 109 MPs faced investigation on charges of misappropriating money, and 10 resigned after being prosecuted for corruption. In March 1992, the Leadership Tribunal found Labor and Employment Minister Tony Ila guilty of 43 counts of misconduct in office, including asking for money in return for remaining in the governing coalition. Several other MPs were accused of demanding money in return for voting against a no-confidence motion.

The country's fourth post-independence elections took place in June 1992, with some 1,650 candidates running for the 89 nationally-elected and 20 provincially-based seats in parliament. Although 16 parties were on the ballot, there were few if any ideological differences among them. A record 59 members lost their seats, including 15 of the 28 cabinet ministers, and the ruling Papua New Guinea United Party suffered a net loss of 11 seats and ended up with 19. On 17 July, the new parliament narrowly elected People's Democratic Movement leader Pais Wingti prime minister over incumbent Rabbie Namaliu. Wingti, who held the office from 1985 to 1988, promised to fight corruption, and said he would pressure foreign businesses to process raw materials in the country rather than merely send them abroad. After the election, Namaliu quit politics and former prime minister Michael Somare became opposition leader.

In early October, Wingti suspended four mainland provincial governments for financial mismanagement, and sparked a crisis by proposing to shut down all nineteen mainland and island-based provincial governments on the grounds that they are too costly, have done little to promote rural development, and are riddled with corruption.

Provincial heads immediately claimed this would concentrate too much power in the center. The threat diminished somewhat in November, after the opposition said it opposed the idea.

This new threat diminished somewhat days later when the government claimed victory over the rebel army on Bougainville. This insurgency began in December 1988 when miners and other islanders began staging guerrilla attacks on the Australian-owned copper and gold mine at Panguna to demand compensation for landowners and a 50 percent share of the profits. The mine closed in May 1989, and the newly-styled Bougainville Revolutionary Army (BRA) called for independence for the island. In May 1990, Government troops began blockading the island, leaving some 160,000 people without supplies or basic services.

Peace negotiations stalled in April 1992 when the BRA reportedly executed a leading negotiator, Anthony Anugu, along with several others. During the year the army launched several cross-border raids into neighboring Solomon Islands to destroy fuel depots believed to be used to supply the BRA.

On 29 October, Prime Minister Wingti announced that government troops had overtaken the provincial capital of Arawa, the BRAs last stronghold, and now controlled 90 percent of Bougainville Island. Approximately 150 people have died from direct fighting, while up to 3,000 islanders may have died from food and medicine shortages due to the blockade.

Political Rights and Civil Liberties:

Papua New Guineans have the right to democratically change their government. The June 1992 elections were generally free and fair, but irregularities occurred in the rural highlands region despite a substantial police presence. Fisticuffs broke out at several polling areas, at least 30 ballot boxes were destroyed, and police arrested MP Tom Amaiu in connection with several tampered ballot boxes. Of greater concern is political corruption and the necessity of trading favors to secure tribal backings to win elections. One opportunistic tribe leader told *Pacific Islands Monthly*, "We are a market good. Whoever wants our vote can buy it."

The judiciary is independent and the accused have due process rights. However, the police force is not firmly under civilian control. Abuse of prisoners and detainees occurs relatively frequently, often by intoxicated officers. In the past several years police reportedly harassed communities suspected of harboring criminals or participating in tribal warfare. A growing crime problem prompted parliament to approve the death penalty in 1991, but its enforcement awaits specific guidelines. Both the government and the BRA have been accused of using torture and unnecessary force on Bougainville Island.

An independent media has contributed to the country's democratic system. The state-run National Broadcasting Commission exercises full independence in its news coverage. Police approval for public demonstrations is not denied for political reasons but is occasionally refused on public safety grounds. There is full freedom of religion, and missionaries often provide essential services in remote areas. Freedom of movement is unrestricted, and workers are free to bargain collectively and strike.

Paraguay

Polity: Dominant party
Economy: Capitalist-statist
Population: 4,519,000
PPP: $2,742
Life Expectancy: 67.1
Ethnic Groups: Mostly mestizo; small Indian, white, black minorities

Political Rights: 3
Civil Liberties: 3
Status: Partly Free

Overview: A new constitution paved the way for the election of a civilian president in 1993, indicating that democracy was making headway against authoritarian traditions that date back to the Republic of Paraguay's independence from Spain in 1811. But fallout from a corruption scandal involving top military officers highlighted the continued scheming between the armed forces and the ruling Colorado Party.

Following the 3 February 1989 coup led by General Andres Rodriguez that ended the 35-year dictatorship of General Alfredo Stroessner, the new government initiated a period of dramatic liberalization. Rodriguez, promising a transition to full democracy by 1993, was hailed as a hero and easily elected on 1 May 1989 to finish Stroessner's last presidential term.

The main opposition parties—the Authentic Radical Liberal Party (PLRA), the Febrerista Revolutionary Party (PRF), and the Christian Democratic Party (PDC)—threatened to boycott the election unless Stroessner's constitution and electoral laws were reformed. But realizing that Rodriguez would win on popularity alone, they joined what turned out to be a free-wheeling campaign and won a number of seats in the legislature.

Acknowledging the structural deficiencies in the political system, President Rodriguez moved to make the reforms necessary for a democratic transition. The electoral laws were revised and the old voting list was modernized in preparation for the 26 May 1991 municipal elections, the first in the nation's history. A third of voter names were purged, largely the dead, and a system of multi-party ballots and the practice of inking voters' fingers to prevent repeat voting were introduced.

In a stunning upset, 31-year-old union leader Carlos Filizzola, a political independent who ran at the head of an anti-corruption movement, was elected mayor of Asuncion, the nation's capital. It was the first time the Colorado Party had lost a major election since 1947. President Rodriguez rankled Colorado hard-liners by personally congratulating Filizzola.

The Colorados made a comeback in the 1 December 1991 constituent assembly election after Rodriguez leaned on the party's numerous factions to present a common front. The Colorados won 123 seats in the 198-member body. The PLRA won 57 seats, the Constitution for All Movement (CPT), an offshoot of Filizzola's group, won 16, and the PRF and the PDC one each.

Despite the Colorado majority, the constituent assembly conducted itself in an independent manner and produced a democratic constitution, which went into effect in June 1992. The document designates the president as commander-in-chief of the armed forces, subordinates the military to civilian authority, and bars active-duty military personnel from engaging in any type of political activity. Under Stroessner, Colorado Party membership was a prerequisite for joining the officer corps.

The president, vice-president and a bicameral Congress consisting of a 45-member Senate and an 80-member Chamber of Deputies will be directly elected for five-year terms starting in 1993. Presidents, including General Rodriguez, are barred from running for re-election. The president is to be elected by a simple majority. The opposition parties had pressed for a second round of voting if the leading candidate fails to get an absolute majority in the first round. But the Colorado bloc wanted to forestall a scenario in which opposition forces united around a single candidate in a run-off election.

By fall 1992, as the various Colorado factions vied for the party's presidential nomination, it was clear that despite the constitutional prohibition, the old tradition of military interference in politics would be difficult to overcome. While President Rodriguez lent support to one Colorado group's candidate, General Lino Oviedo, the second most powerful officer after Rodriguez, was rubbing shoulders with other factions. When an active-duty colonel associated with Oviedo implicated a group of top officers linked to Rodriguez in a huge smuggling operation, it appeared that an old-style power play for control of the armed forces and the Colorado Party was underway.

As the accused military officers were brought before the courts and the media looked for signs of a potential coup, opposition parties voiced the anti-corruption sentiments of most Paraguayans. They also protested against the military's interference in the Colorado nominating process, and some parties threatened to boycott the 1993 election unless there were clear guarantees against government and/or military support for whomever turned out to be the Colorado candidate.

In summer 1992, the PLRA, factions of the PRF and the PDC, and the Paraguay for All Movement (formerly the CPT) joined in an electoral alliance. It remained unclear whether the PLRA's Domingo Laino, potentially the strongest opposition candidate, would be the coalition's presidential nominee. Another serious challenger was Guillermo Caballero Vargas, a well-heeled businessman running as an independent.

Political Rights and Civil Liberties:

Under the 1992 constitution, citizens are granted full democratic rights and are able to change their government through the ballot box. However, pending the 9 May 1993 general election, the ruling party still exercised inordinate power and the military continued to exert undue influence in the political process.

Since 1989, political parties and civic groups have operated freely. In 1989 political prisoners were freed and political exiles were invited to return home. Previously banned leftist parties were granted legal status. Meetings, rallies and marches are held regularly. Freedom of religion is respected.

Freedom of expression is generally respected. The independent press and radio, which were closed under Stroessner, operate freely, and new publications and radio outlets have appeared. Passionate political debate occurs regularly in all media, including state-run television. In 1992, some media finally broke the taboo against addressing allegations of corruption directly involving President Rodriguez. Still, journalists investigating official corruption remain subject to intimidation and violent attacks, and the case of a reporter murdered in 1991 remains unresolved. Also, while the 1992 constitution establishes safeguards for free expression, there are vague, potentially restrictive clauses regarding "responsible" behavior of journalists and media owners.

Over a hundred trade unions and two major union federations have been legalized. Nonetheless, labor actions have occasionally been broken up by the military and labor leaders detained. The 1992 constitution, overturning the old labor code, gives public sector workers the right to organize, bargain collectively, and strike.

In the countryside, peasant organizations demanding land have often met with violent police crackdowns, detentions, and forced evictions by vigilante groups in the employ of large landowners. Nearly a dozen peasants have been killed in the ongoing disputes. The government's promise of land reform has been largely unfulfilled, as nearly 80 percent of farm and ranch land remains in the hands of foreign companies and a few hundred Paraguayan families.

The judicial system continued to be influenced by the ruling party and the military, susceptible to corruption, and mostly unresponsive to human rights groups presenting cases of rights violations committed either before or after the overthrow of Stroessner. Allegations in recent years include illegal detention by police and torture during incarceration, particularly in rural areas.

The 1992 constitution establishes the separation of powers between the three branches of government, but the transformation of the judiciary into an independent body will be a lengthy process. One test was how it would handle the corruption charges brought against military officers in 1992, the first such case in Paraguay's history. Before the proceedings were even underway, the home of the lawyer representing the whistle-blower was machine-gunned by unknown attackers.

Peru

Polity: Presidential-military
Economy: Capitalist-statist
Population: 22,454,000
PPP: $2,731
Life Expectancy: 63.0
Ethnic Groups: Complex, Indian of Inca descent (46 percent), Caucasian (10 percent), and mixed (44 percent)

Political Rights: 6
Civil Liberties: 5
Status: Partly Free

Overview: On 5 April 1992, President Alberto Fujimori, backed by the military, dissolved the Congress and suspended the constitution. The move was widely supported because of general disdain for the political establishment and the subsequent capture of Shining Path (*Sendero Luminoso*) guerrilla leader, Abimael Guzman. Fujimori held elections for a constituent assembly in November, but the exercise was aimed more at consolidating his *auto-golpe* (self-coup) than returning to democratic rule.

The independent Republic of Peru was proclaimed in 1821. Its history has been marked by periods of civilian and military rule. The military held power most recently from 1968 to 1980. A constituent assembly was elected in 1978 and a new constitution drafted in 1979. Military rule ended when Fernando Belaunde Terry of the right-wing Popular Action (AP) party was elected president in 1980.

The 1979 constitution provides for a president and bicameral Congress elected for five years, with a 60-member Senate elected on a regional basis and a 180-member Chamber of Deputies elected on the basis of proportional representation.

Alan Garcia of the social democratic American Popular Revolutionary Alliance (APRA) won the 1985 elections and presided over five years of fiscal chaos and economic collapse. In 1988 novelist Mario Vargas Llosa formed a free-market reform movement backed by the AP and the Christian Popular Party (PPC) and led nine other presidential candidates for the April 1990 election. Economic issues were matched by concern over the mounting strength of the Maoist Shining Path, one of the most virulent, tightly organized insurgencies in the history of guerrilla warfare. The Shining Path is self-financing, earning an estimated $40 million a year from Peru's cocaine trade.

Fujimori, an agricultural engineer and the son of Japanese immigrants, was a political unknown. But his Change 90 campaign gained momentum as Vargas Llosa became identified with the mostly white political class disdained by the nation's poor majority (primarily Indian and mixed race) because of its corruption and ineptitude. In the first round of voting in April 1990 Vargas Llosa edged out Fujimori for first place, but Fujimori won with 56.5 percent of the vote in the June run-off.

Once in office Fujimori decreed a series of drastic economic austerity measures. Lacking an organized political party, he turned to the armed forces to shore up his government. The army was given control of the national police and more provinces were put under martial law, leaving over half the country under army control. In absorbing the police, the military took control of the anti-drug effort. In Peru, the world's largest coca producer, the military is the institution most often implicated in drug-related corruption.

Fujimori halted hyper-inflation but his shock program led to severe recession. By early 1992 the normally feckless Congress was uniting against his authoritarian style of rule and the Shining Path was mounting a concerted attack on urban centers. The 120,000-man army, poorly trained and ill-equipped, seemed overmatched and feared mainly by the civilian population.

On 5 April, Fujimori dissolved the Congress, shut down the judiciary and suspended the constitution. Vladimiro Montesinos, a former army captain and close Fujimori advisor, engineered the support of the armed forces. Fujimori claimed his new authority would allow him to effectively combat drug-trafficking and the Shining Path. Polls showed that a large majority of Peruvians supported the coup.

The U.S. and other industrialized democracies suspended aid and the Organization of American States (OAS) demanded the restoration of democratic rule. In May, Fujimori promised to hold elections in the fall for a constituent assembly to replace the Congress.

Fujimori's popularity dropped amid a devastating guerrilla offensive in Lima during the summer. But after the capture of Abimael Guzman and other key Shining Path leaders on 12 September, Fujimori appeared confident enough to go through with the constituent assembly election scheduled for 22 November. He placed close associate Jaime Yoshiyama at the head of a patchwork New Majority-Change 90 coalition and, over the protests of OAS observers, provided logistical assistance from the military for its campaign and millions of government dollars for political advertising.

After replacing the heads of the national election commission with people under his influence, Fujimori decreed that the 80-member Democratic Constituent Congress would be unable to reverse his executive orders and would be limited to rewriting the constitution. In response, APRA, AP, the Freedom Movement and a number of leftist parties boycotted the election. These parties, which represented a majority of the electorate in the past, stated the election was designed to "legalize the dictatorship."

On November 13, a group of retired and active army officers attempted to seize the presidential palace. The coup attempt was easily put down but indicated discontent within the armed forces over a decree law, evidently hatched by Montesinos, granting Fujimori special powers to remove any officer for purposes of restructuring the military. Just before the election, the Shining Path unleashed renewed attacks in Lima. Although not nearly as effective as the summer offensive, it indicated the guerrillas had been able to regroup to a certain extent following the capture of Guzman.

On 22 November, voters selected lists of candidates nominated by eighteen mostly new parties and political movements. New Majority-Change 90 won less than 40 percent of the vote but took 44 of 80 seats thanks to newly decreed electoral rules that heavily favored the party receiving a plurality. OAS observers said the voting process was "satisfactory," but refrained from equating the election to a return to democracy. Fujimori declared that the election was "the formalization of the 5th of April," indicating that he planned to continue governing unchallenged.

Political Rights and Civil Liberties:

With no constitution in place, Peruvians cannot change their government democratically. Limited rights of free expression, assembly and political organization are allowed but are not guaranteed by law. Moreover, political and civic activity is severely restricted by the actions of the Shining Path guerrillas and the impunity with which the military, security forces and paramilitary groups conduct repressive, indiscriminate counter-insurgency measures.

According to Peru's diligent human rights organizations, political violence caused nearly ten deaths per day in the first two years of the Fujimori government, up from four a day in 1989. The rate appeared to increase after Fujimori assumed virtual dictatorial control in April 1992.

Civilian executions, disappearances, arbitrary detentions and torture by the military and security forces are integral to counterinsurgency policy and match the barbarity of the Shining Path. The countryside is almost totally militarized and there is evidence that peasant patrols, or *rondas*, organized by the army against the guerrillas are used as cannon fodder, that the army coerces people into joining them, and that some *ronderos* are extorting money and joining in the drug trade. Since the April coup, rights groups have reported numerous disappearances of intellectuals, students and political activists not associated with the guerrillas, raising the specter of a "dirty war" against opposition to the government.

The government cannot guarantee the security of elected officials or government functionaries. The Shining Path has killed dozens of political candidates and more than 500 municipal officials in the last decade. It has also assassinated priests and nuns, foreign missionaries and aid workers, military officers, human rights activists, and journalists—in short, it is committed to eradicating anyone associated with the established order. The capture of Abimael Guzman and other key leaders weakened the Shining Path, but military commanders were untouched and the guerrillas retained the capability to carry out hundreds of terrorist actions per month.

Peru's human rights community is assailed by all sides because it investigates violations by both the government and the Shining Path. Offices have been bombed and activists attacked in an atmosphere of intimidation promoted by the government. In 1991, President Fujimori accused rights groups of "playing the game of subversion." In mid-1992, he accused them of providing cover for the Shining Path. Fujimori also continued to promote military officers responsible for serious abuses.

Prior to April, the judiciary was riddled with corruption and subject to intimidation by drug dealers, the Shining Path and the armed forces. Fujimori shut it down, overhauled it and in effect made the judicial system an arm of the executive. A draconion anti-terrorist law was decreed and judicial guarantees were eliminated in a new system of anonymous judges installed to try accused guerrillas. Defense lawyers were not allowed to call witnesses, government witnesses remained unidentified, and sentences (up to twenty years for painting subversive slogans on walls) were handed down within hours. At the same time, military courts continued to exonerate officers and soldiers accused of rights abuses, ensuring the impunity of the armed forces, and civil courts were used by the government to intimidate political opposition leaders.

After the capture of Guzman it was decreed that guerrilla leaders would be tried in summary proceedings in secret military courts. In October, the government announced its intention to withdraw from the American Convention on Human Rights in order to pave the way for introduction of the death penalty for convicted terrorists.

Labor unions remained legal after April, but a new labor code decreed in July 1992 gave the government the right to break up any strike it deemed to be endangering a company, an industry, or the public sector. Labor also remained the target of political violence. Unionists continued to be killed or disappeared at a rate of more than one per month.

The press is largely private. Radio and television are both private and public. Over 30 journalists have been killed in the last ten years—at least two in 1992—by either security forces, drug traffickers, or the Shining Path. Radio stations are frequently attacked by guerrillas and a Shining Path car bomb destroyed a television station in June 1992. After the coup, many media outlets and journalists critical of the government were pressured into self-censorship or exile by death threats, government libel suits or police harassment.

Philippines

Polity: Presidential-
legislative democracy
Economy: Capitalist-
statist
Population: 63,667,000
PPP: $2,269
Life Expectancy: 64.2
Ethnic Groups: Christian Malay (92 percent), Muslim Malay
(4 percent), Chinese (2 percent)

Political Rights: 3
Civil Liberties: 3
Status: Partly Free

Overview: The Philippines experienced its first peaceful transition of
power in 27 years in June 1992 as Fidel Ramos succeeded
Corazon Aquino as president. Notably, Ramos won the May
election largely without relying on the cronyism and patronage networks that have
been a fixture in politics since the Marcos era.

The Philippines, an archipelago of 7,100 islands in Southeast Asia, achieved
independence in 1946 after 43 years of United States colonial rule, and subsequent
occupation by the Japanese during World War II. Strongman Ferdinand Marcos ruled
for 21 years until the "people power" revolution in February 1986, when thousands
protested his "victory" over Corazon Aquino in massively rigged elections. After
several top military officials, including acting army chief of staff Fidel Ramos and
Defense Secretary Juan Ponce Enrile, declared their support for Aquino, Marcos fled
the country and Aquino took office. A new "U.S.-style" constitution approved in
February 1987 provided for a directly elected president (the vice president is elected
separately) who serves a single six-year term, and a bicameral Congress consisting of
a 24-member Senate and a House of Representatives with 200 directly-elected
members and up to 50 more appointed by the president. The president cannot impose
martial law for more than 60 days without congressional approval.

In August 1987, Aquino's government survived the first of seven coup attempts,
mostly by right-wing elements of the military. Although during her term the economy
grew 3.5 percent per year on average, and the percentage living below the poverty
line dropped slightly to 50 percent, Aquino will likely be remembered as a transitional
figure who failed to make inroads against the endemic corruption, patronage and
business oligarchies—many of which maintain private armies—that contribute to
widespread impoverishment throughout the country.

In 1991 numerous candidates began positioning themselves for the May 1992
election to succeed Aquino. In a 30 November party vote, the centrist, pro-
government Struggle of the Democratic Filipino (LDP) coalition, the nation's largest
and strongest grouping, chose House Speaker Ramon Mitra over Ramos as its
candidate. The conservative Nacionalista Party split three ways among Vice President
Salvador Laurel, Enrile, and Eduardo "Danding" Cojuangco, a former Marcos crony
who is Aquino's estranged cousin and rival.

On 25 January 1992, President Aquino announced her support for Ramos, noting
his role in ousting Marcos and quelling the coup attempts against her. By this time,

the Commission on Elections had approved eight candidates. They were: Mitra and Ramos, who ran as a member of the National Union of Christian Democrats (NUCD) after not being able to beat the deadline for registering a new party; former Senate president Jovito Salonga, backed by the two largest left-of-center parties, the Liberal Party and Filipino Democratic Party-Laban in the People's Coalition; Imelda Marcos, wife of the late president; Cojuangco, who had a huge patronage network at his disposal; former immigration commissioner Miriam Defensor Santiago, a wildcard who ran on the single issue of ending corruption; and two longshots, Laurel and onetime actor Jaime Estrada.

On 13 February, after Ramos, Mitra and Salonga rejected Aquino's call for an "anti-Marcos" coalition against both Imelda Marcos and Cojuangco, the president hinted that she might jump in the race regardless of the constitutional term limitation. Ramos, weakened by the Aquino's wavering support and lacking a patronage machine, was also stung by frequent references to his role in implementing martial law as head of the Philippine Constabulary during Marcos' reign. In addition, influential Manila Archbishop Cardinal Jaime Sin suggested on 18 February that this predominantly Roman Catholic nation should choose one of its own as president, a thinly veiled broadside at Ramos, a Protestant. Mitra, meanwhile, picked up popular former supreme court justice Marcelo Fernan as his running mate early in the month.

By the spring, political neophyte Defensor Santiago's acerbic rhetoric against traditional politics put her atop many polls. Meanwhile, the other candidates stuck to vague pledges about deregulating the economy, bringing in more foreign investment, and expanding rural political and economic power.

By the eve of the election, the field had narrowed to four leading candidates— Ramos, Mitra, Santiago, and Cojuangco. Estrada had dropped out in late March to become Cojuangco's running mate, while the other three also-rans hung on stubbornly until the end. Despite polling well, Mitra may have been doomed by the 2 May discovery of several tons of his campaign literature in the printing room of the House of Representatives, feeding his image as a traditional, machine-backed politician.

Ramos ultimately won the 11 May balloting with only 23.5 percent of the vote, beating Defensor Santiago by only 800,000 of the 23 million ballots cast. Estrada won the vice presidential race. The final results took five weeks to announce because the ballots had to pass through complex procedures designed to prevent fraud. Although Defensor Santiago claimed victory in what she called a rigged race, most observers rated the election the freest in over two decades. On 30 June, Ramos took office as the country's 12th president in the first peaceful transition of power since Marcos' election in 1965.

Ramos immediately needed to build support to compensate for having won with the smallest mandate in the country's history and to face a Congress dominated by the LDP. A loose alliance soon took shape between Cojuangco's National People's Coalition and Ramos' NUCD. On 27 July, Jose de Venecia, a key Ramos supporter, won the speakership of the 201-member House of Representatives, drawing scattered support from the NPC, the Liberal Party, and the NUCD, as well as some members of the LDP.

By August rifts were already apparent within the executive branch as four main groups of Ramos supporters battled for influence—a core of retired military officers, corporate elites from the so-called Makati Business Club, supporters of de Venecia and

Aquino appointees. On 10 August. Executive Secretary Peter Garrucho quit the top cabinet post after Ramos opposed his proposals on a number of duties and taxes. Two other top officials, National Security Advisor Jose Alamonte and Justice Secretary Franklin Drilon, clashed over the former's proposal to expand the government's security apparatus. Revelations that many kidnapping syndicates, which target the children of wealthy businessmen, operate under the protection of top-ranking police officers led to the dismissal of Philippine National Police Chief Cesar Nazareno on 22 August.

Ramos also moved quickly to end the country's 23-year-old Communist insurgency, which has stunted economic growth in rural areas. Ramos had the Congress repeal a 35-year-old law outlawing the Philippine Communist Party in order to give the rebels a chance to move from the jungle to the ballot box, and has called for a review of the cases of hundreds of political prisoners. Already the party's military front, the New People's Army (NPA), is down from a peak of 25,000 guerrillas in the late 1980's to approximately 15,000 today. In early September, the government released two top Communist leaders, Satur Ocampo and Romulo Kintanar, former head of the NPA. Exploratory talks with rebel leaders were held in the fall, but no date for negotiations was set. Additional threats come from the Reform the Armed Forces Movement, a group of right-wingers who launched several of the coup attempts against Aquino, and from Muslim separatists in the south. On 23 December, Gregorio Honasan, a rebel officer implicated in three coup attempts against Aquino, surrendered to the government.

The West Point-educated Ramos also promises to improve relations with the United States, which soured in 1991 when the Philippine Senate rejected a ten-year, $203 million per year lease agreement at the mammoth Subic Bay naval facility. The country is saddled with a $29 billion foreign debt, and Ramos has made economic growth a priority over income redistribution. Already he has rejected legislated wage increases, and plans to continue opening up the economy.

Political Rights and Civil Liberties:

Filipinos can change their government democratically. Despite some charges of irregularities, the May 1992 elections were free of the wholesale fraud of the Marcos era. Witnesses reported some transfers of food and money to voters, mostly for local races. Delays in counting the ballots were caused by power failures and a complex balloting system designed to prevent fraud. Voter's fingerprints were matched to a serial number, preserving anonymity while allowing ballots to be tracked. A team from the International Federation of Settlements in Finland said that the Catholic Church's precinct-level monitoring had helped deter fraud and violence. In the three months prior to the vote, pre-election violence claimed "only" 71 lives, less than half the total prior to the 1988 local elections.

Freedoms of speech and press are respected in practice, although journalists face intimidation and violence outside Manila from illegal logging outfits, drug smugglers and others. The press is often harshly critical of the government. Freedom of assembly is respected; the police generally follow a policy of "maximum tolerance," giving non-violent protesters substantial leeway. During the election campaign the Commission on Elections used a 1988 law to ban paid media ads and restrict political banners. Broadcasters were required to provide 30 minutes of free air time per day for distribution among candidates who requested it.

The judiciary is independent of the government, and the accused enjoy adequate due process rights. However, the military and police have been accused of torturing suspects. More frequently, prison human rights violations occur at the hands of other inmates. Freedom of religion is respected. Citizens are free to travel internally and abroad, although military action by the army and communist insurgents frequently cause areas to be cordoned off. Workers are free to bargain collectively, and can strike after a 30-day cooling off period.

Poland

Polity: Presidential-parliamentary democracy
Economy: Mixed statist transitional
Population: 38,377,000
PPP: $4,770
Life Expectancy: 71.8
Ethnic Groups: Polish , Ukrainian, Byelorussian, German, others

Political Rights: 2
Civil Liberties: 2
Status: Free

Overview:

In 1992, Poland continued its transition to a free-market economy despite a political crisis that forced two prime ministers to resign. After the October 1991 elections, the fragmented parliament, which included representatives of 30 parties, seemed unable to deal effectively with the country's problems, focusing instead on inter-party squabbles and secondary issues. This prompted President Lech Walesa to call repeatedly for strengthening of his office, which led critics to warn of his "authoritarian tendencies." In 1992, Poland also experienced the largest wave of labor unrest since the fall of communism in 1989.

Poland began 1992 with a new coalition government composed of five center-right parties. New Prime Minister Jan Olszewski was initially opposed and later reluctantly accepted by Walesa and confirmed by the 460-member Sejm (the lower house) in December 1991. Faced with implementing drastic hikes in the price of energy and public utilities, the new government issued a bleak report on the state of the economy, blasting the previous government's overly optimistic economic assessment. Despite protests and sporadic strikes the government refused to rescind the increases.

In January, the first tensions surfaced between President Walesa and the newly appointed civilian minister of defense, Jan Parys, about the forcible retirement of the previous minister of defense, General Kolodziejczyk, who had been the President's candidate for the post of inspector general of the armed forces. Another point of contention between Walesa and Parys was the appointment by the latter of the emigré Radek Sikorski to the post of the vice-minister of defense.

In February, the Democratic Union deputies in Sejm, led by former Prime Minister Taduesz Mazowiecki, presented a new electoral draft law that would require parties to pass a 5 percent hurdle of the votes before being accepted in parliament. The law also proposed changes in the constitution, including more clearly separating the powers of the president and government and giving the government the right to rule by decree in economic matters, thus bypassing the parliament. Walesa prepared another draft stressing the inadequacy of many of the existing laws and regulations left over from the Communist period. The main difference between the presidential and the parliamentary draft was in the way the constitution was to be ratified. In the presidential version, the voters in a national referendum were to approve the final draft. The parliamentary draft favored National Assembly ratification.

On 6 April, Defense Minister Parys, in a televised speech, told officers of the Army General Staff that certain unnamed politicians were attempting to manipulate high-ranking members of the military in order to overthrow the democratic system. The speech was interpreted as directed against Mieczyslaw Wachowski and Jerzy Milewski, ministers in the Bureau of National Security, subordinated to the president. At the core of the controversy was the lack of a clearly defined chain of authority over the armed forces in times of peace. According to the Communist-era constitution, amended in 1989, the president has special responsibility for the army in peacetime, and is the commander-in-chief during war. However, the day-to-day operations are to be conducted by the minister of defense, answerable to the prime minister. Since the prime minister answers directly to parliament and not the president, the situation caused ambiguity.

President Walesa, citing the need to have a good working relationship with the defense minister until the constitutional issues were cleared, asked Parys to resign. The minister refused and accused certain forces, hinting at the president and his confidants, of attempting to restore communism in Poland, and called on Poles to create "committees for national defense" to prevent his dismissal. A parliamentary commission was appointed on 25 April to inquire into the circumstances behind the speech. Walesa responded by making all files of the presidential chancellory and the national security office available to the investigative committee. Despite his objections, the prime minister remained reluctant to dismiss Parys, instead extending his vacations. In response, Walesa withdrew his support from the Olszewski government, proposing a non-partisan "government of experts" instead. For the time being, the Olszewski government was able to survive for lack of viable alternative. Parys was dismissed, however, after a special parliamentary commission found his accusations to be "groundless and harmful to state interest." Shortly thereafter, the President in a speech to parliament called for a speedy ratification of a new constitution, which would allow the President to exercise the most important powers, including the right to appoint and dismiss the prime minister.

On 28 May, another political crisis erupted, finally resulting in a no-confidence vote for the entire Olszewski cabinet. It started with the adoption of a resolution proposed by Janusz Korwin-Mikke of the right-wing Union of Real Politics (UPR), obliging the minister of interior to disclose the lists of senior public officials who had acted as informants to the Communist-era security service (SB) in the years 1945 to 1990. The resolution, hastily adopted by a large majority, was immediately criticized by the centrist Small Coalition and the small leftist Solidarity of Labor Party, as violating the laws on police, the state protection office, and state secrets. In a meeting with Interior Minister Antoni Macierewicz, Lech Walesa cautioned him to limit the terms of inquiry and respect the right of legal defense for the accused. However, on 4 June Macierewicz delivered the first pile of names of possible agents to the parliament leaders, provoking immediate denunciation by Walesa, who called the move "haphazard" and an "illegal manipulation," adding that his name might also be on the list for blackmail.

On 5 June, the Sejm reacted to Walesa's motion and dismissed Olszewski's cabinet, appointing Waldemar Pawlak, leader of the Polish Peasant Party, as prime minister. Pawlak's appointment initiated a five-week government crisis during which he was unable to form a coalition government. To right-wing parties, Pawlak represented the resurgence of the post-Communist forces, since his party was an ally of the Communist party until 1989.

Despite support from President Walesa, Pawlak resigned on 10 July. He was succeeded by Hanna Suchocka, Poland's first female premier, who headed a seven-party coalition composed of liberal, Christian, and peasant parties. Suchocka, a constitutional lawyer and member of the Democratic Union, was able to form the ideologically broad coalition due to her pro-market stance on the economy and her conservative views on abortion. In her inaugural address, she called for continuation of market reforms, swift privatization, and respect for the rule of law. Faced with the strongest labor unrest since 1989, she refused to negotiate over pay increases and gave management of state-owned companies the power to summarily lay-off workers who refuse to return to work.

In 1992, economic issues continued to be a major concern, including a lingering recession, the budget deficit, and high unemployment. Wrangling about the size of the budget deficit dominated parliament for several months in 1992, culminating in June with the final approval of a budget that limited the deficit to 5 percent of GNP, in accordance with IMF guidelines. Unemployment, which reached 13.1 percent in July, led to strikes and demonstrations. On 19 August, the government approved a mass privatization plan that distributed the majority of shares in 400 state-owned companies among 20 private stock funds.

Abortion remained a contentious and unresolved issue in 1992. In May, a new ethics code drafted by the Doctor's Guild went into effect, threatening with suspension any doctor performing abortions. The code, contravening existing law, was challenged by the Ombudsman as unconstitutional. In July, the Sejm began a debate on abortion considering three proposals, ranging from holding a referendum on the issue to punishing doctors performing abortions with jail terms.

Political Rights and Civil Liberties: Poles can change their government democratically. The last parliamentary elections in October 1991 resulted in a fractured parliament consisting of 30 parties and groups. President Walesa's attempts to vest more power in his office led to accusations of his having "authoritarian tendencies."

There were several constitutional questions brought by the Ombudsman before the Constitutional Tribunal in 1992. One involved a government decree requiring religious or ethics training in public schools, and the other the Doctor's Guild's decision to expel its members for performing abortions. On both issues the Ombudsman's efforts were unsuccessful.

Religious freedom is respected, although there were charges that the Catholic

Church exercises too much influence in public life. Freedom of the press is respected and there is a wide variety of politically diverse publications. Besides the state-owned television and radio stations, which were frequently attacked by all sides of the political spectrum as being biased, private television and radio stations are allowed to operate. Domestic and foreign travel is unrestricted. Freedom of association is respected and independent trade unions are legal.

Portugal

Polity: Presidential-parliamentary democracy
Political Rights: 1
Civil Liberties: 1
Economy: Mixed capitalist
Status: Free
Population: 10,481,000
PPP: $6,259
Life Expectancy: 74.0
Ethnic Groups: Portuguese and Africans from former Portuguese colonies

Overview: Economic stress and European policy were major issues in Portugal in 1992. With inflation running at about nine percent, Portugal struggled to raise its economic performance to European Community standards. The center-right government of Prime Minister Anibal Cavaco Silva faced waves of public sector strikes. While the government attempted to fight inflation by keeping down wages, the workers tried maintaining living standards with wage demands that anticipated more inflation.

Located on the Atlantic coast of the Iberian peninsula, Portugal was a monarchy until a republic was declared in 1910. Antonio Salazar headed a fascist dictatorship from 1932 to 1968. His successor, Marcello Caetano, held power until 1974, when the leftist Armed Forces Movement overthrew the regime. The military had become exhausted and disenchanted with fighting to retain Portuguese colonies in Africa. The transition to democracy began with the election of a constituent assembly in 1975, which adopted a democratic socialist constitution. There has been a series of governments since then, some led by the Socialists, others led by the more centrist Social Democrats.

The president is elected directly for a five-year term. The incumbent is the Socialist ex-Prime Minister, Mario Soares, who won election in 1986 and 1991. The president appoints a prime minister from the largest party or coalition in the 250-member Assembly of the Republic, the unicameral parliament. Cavaco Silva, leader of the center-right Social Democrats, heads the current government. The Assembly members are elected by proportional representation for a maximum term of four years.

The government aims to modernize and privatize the economy. For example, private shareholders will own 51 percent of Petrogal, the national oil company, by 1994. Cavaco Silva advocates budget and staff cuts and tighter labor laws for the public sector, especially after strikes shut down many public services in February and

November 1992. There is controversy over neighboring Spain's growing role in the Portuguese economy. In past decades, Portugal was the more prosperous Iberian country, but now Spain has passed Portugal in per capita national income.

The Social Democrats and the Socialists, the leading opposition party, both backed the Maastricht treaty on European integration in 1992. On 18 November, parliament passed extraordinary revisions to the constitution that backed European monetary union and local and European parliamentary voting rights for resident foreigners. The Communists, the Greens, and the Democratic and Social Center Party opposed the changes.

Political Rights and Civil Liberties:

The Portuguese have the right to change their government democratically. Voters choose both the president and the parliament through direct competitive elections.

The print media are owned by the government, political parties, and private publishers. They are generally free and competitive. Until 1990, television and radio were state-owned with the exception of a Catholic radio station. The Social Democratic government introduced legislation to establish two private television channels to supplement the public ones.

There are a few minor restrictions on freedom of expression. One may be arrested for insulting the government or the armed forces, but the state has not acted recently on these provisions. Political organization is unrestricted, except for fascist organizations. Although Catholicism is prevalent, religion is unrestricted. There are competing Communist and non-Communist labor federations. Public sector workers have gone on strike to protest the government's economic policies. Freedom of assembly is permitted. Protest organizers need to give the government one day's notice before a march or an assembly. Permission is normally granted. The economy is becoming more private as the government sells state companies, but there are some limits on non-Portuguese ownership. The number of Communist-oriented co-operative farms is declining. Many parts of the country remain economically backward and more like the Third World than Western Europe. For example, there is a growing problem of child labor. According to a report of the British-based Anti-Slavery Society, Portugal has 200,000 child laborers. Typically, they work at construction sites and in factories in the poor North.

Qatar

Polity: Traditional monarchy
Economy: Capitalist-statist
Population: 483,000
PPP: $11,800
Life Expectancy: 69.2
Ethnic Groups: Arab, Pakistani, Indian, Iranian

Political Rights: 7
Civil Liberties: 6
Status: Not Free

Overview:

In 1992, major issues in Qatar were a border dispute with Saudi Arabia and a rare challenge to the Emir's absolute authority.

Qatar is a small, oil-rich sheikdom in the Persian Gulf. Originally dominated by Bahrain, Qatar was ruled by the Ottoman Turks from 1872 until 1916, when it became a British protectorate. Qatar began exporting petroleum in 1949 and gained independence in 1971. In 1972, Sheikh Hamad ibn Khalifa al Thani came to power by deposing his cousin in a palace coup. He serves as both head of state and prime minister. A provisional constitution requires that the emir be chosen from the adult males of the al-Thani family, and provides for a Council of Ministers and an Advisory Council. The latter Council is comprised of 40 appointed members drawn from influential families. In practice, neither Council wields significant influence.

In an effort to change this system, in January 1992, 50 prominent citizens signed a petition calling for democratic reforms and an elected council under Islamic guidelines. Several were briefly imprisoned after they attempted to leave the country to attend a pro-democracy conference in Kuwait. They were detained under a broad states security law which prohibits citizens from damaging the country's image abroad, and have not had their passports returned.

Other key issues involved security matters. On 30 September, Saudi troops attacked a Qatari border post and briefly entered the country. Qatar responded by annulling a 1965 border treaty that had demarcated the disputed border between the two countries. Qatar also recalled 200 soldiers from a joint Gulf security force, which had been stationed in Kuwait since 1985.

Since the Gulf War ended, the country has begun a process of "Qatarization" of the economy designed to reduce the number of Palestinians in technical and administrative positions. Many, however, have simply been replaced by Egyptians, Syrians, and South Asians.

Political Rights and Civil Liberties:

Citizens of Qatar cannot change their government democratically. The Emir has absolute control over the country and rules by decree. There are no elections, and political parties are banned. The Advisory Council can draft legislation, but the Emir must grant approval before it becomes law. Women are barred from government positions and are limited to pursuing education and medical careers. The judiciary is not independent; judges are appointed by the Emir, and, because many are not citizens, they remain in the country at his will.

The government maintains an intrusive security apparatus to monitor the population, particularly since there are four times the number of foreigners as there are Qataris. The Interior Ministry operates two security agencies. One is concerned with subversion and the activity of expatriates. The other investigates cases of sedition, espionage, and drug trafficking. The armed forces also monitor political dissidents and terrorist suspects. The threat of being exposed by one of these groups has effectively limited public discussion of political issues. The press is heavily censored. Freedom of assembly is severely curtailed. Non-Muslims cannot worship in public. Workers are not allowed to join unions, but may associate based on professional or private interests.

Romania

Polity: Presidential-parliamentary democracy
Economy: Statist transitional
Population: 23,188,000
PPP: $3,000
Life Expectancy: 70.8
Ethnic Groups: Romanians (88 percent), Hungarians, Germans, Gypsies

Political Rights: 4
Civil Liberties: 4
Status: Partly Free

Overview:

Romania's 1992 local and national elections were characterized by growing factionalism in the ruling National Salvation Front (NSF) and increased polarization between the ruling neo-Communists and the opposition. Local elections produced significant gains for the opposition coalition, the Democratic Convention (DC), but the national elections were won by incumbent President Ion Iliescu and his newly formed Democratic National Salvation Front (DNSF). The results cast doubt on the future of economic reforms undertaken by the previous government of Prime Minister Theodor Stolojan, and exacerbated ethnic tensions with the large Hungarian-speaking minority in the western province of Transylvania.

The first local multi-party elections in 45 years were held in February. The DC, an alliance of 18 opposition parties, gained a substantial number of mayoral posts and local council seats, including that of the capital, Bucharest, and other major cities. In the election, the National Salvation Front (NSF), which had ruled Romania since the fall of the hard-line Ceausescu regime in 1989, won more than 40 percent of the vote, but the DC won almost 21 percent, a positive showing. The ultra-nationalist Romanian National Unity Party (RNUP) won only 4 percent of the vote, but its leader, Gheorghe Funar, won the mayoral contest in Cluj, the capital of Transylvania, setting the stage for conflict with ethnic Hungarians.

In preparation for national elections, the NSF held its national convention in March to prepare its platform and endorse a presidential candidate. Following NSF's poor showing in the February's local elections, the party became increasingly polarized into two factions: 1) former Communist functionaries aligned with President Iliescu;

and 2) a reformist wing, consisting of young technocrats aligned with Petre Roman, the former prime minister who had accused Iliescu of masterminding the downfall of his government in the fall of 1991.

Prior to the convention, Iliescu's supporters attempted to discredit Roman by releasing a report prepared by a special senatorial commission accusing him of mismanaging the economy during his tenure. The report backfired when acting Prime Minister Stolojan dismissed it as "hasty and contrary to reality."

During the convention, Roman was able to garner the support of a large majority of delegates to adopt a party platform committing the NSF to free-market economic reform and the ideals of a Western-style social democracy. Roman's supporters also blocked Iliescu's nomination for the upcoming presidential elections, resulting in a walkout by his supporters, who subsequently formed a new party, the Democratic National Salvation Front (DNSF), headed by Iliescu.

Following the formal split within the NSF, the Iliescu-sympathetic parliament delayed setting a date for national elections, originally scheduled to be held in spring. On 1 June, 5,000 Bucharest workers walked off their jobs to demand immediate elections. Hours later, the Chamber of Deputies voted to set the election date for 26 June, disregarding the provision of the law requiring a 60-day campaign period prior to the election. The following week, however, the date was rejected during a joint session of the bicameral parliament.

On 16 July, parliament voted to hold presidential and parliamentary elections simultaneously on 27 September. The election law required presidential candidates to submit at least 100,000 voter endorsements to the Electoral Commission. Only parties who garnered at least three percent of the votes were allowed to be represented in parliament. Of the initial 26 presidential candidates, only six were able to gather enough signatures to be registered. Incumbent President Iliescu was nominated by the DNSF and endorsed by the nationalist Greater Romania Party (GRP) and the Socialist Labor Party (SLP). The main opposition candidate was the rector of Bucharest University, Emil Constantinescu, who was chosen as a compromise candidate to represent the various parties united under the DC umbrella. Another candidate was Gheorghe Funar, the ultra-nationalist mayor of Cluj, representing the Party of Romanian National Unity (PRNU). Fully 10,620 candidates from 83 political parties competed for 199 seats in the Senate and 387 seats in the Chamber of Deputies.

The first round of presidential elections proved inconclusive as Iliescu won 47 percent, and Constantinescu 31 percent. Funar finished third with over 10 percent. In the 11 October runoff, Iliescu won a clear majority, receiving 61 percent of the votes against 39 percent for Constantinescu. In the parliamentary elections, both the DNSF and the DC won 166 of the 484 seats contested in the two houses. The NSF finished third, capturing 61 seats. Four other parties won less than 50 seats each.

Following the elections, the opposition called for a recount because of the unusually high number of votes declared invalid. According to the Election Commission, 13 percent of votes for parliament and almost 5 percent of the first round of the presidential election were declared invalid. On 14 October, the Constitutional Court validated the results, citing lack of proof of voter fraud.

After his re-election, Iliescu appealed for the formation of a government of national unity composed of all parties in parliament. Following failed talks with the opposition, Iliescu nominated Nicolae Vacaroiu, a financial expert with no party affiliation, to head the new government. Vacaroiu's cabinet consisted of DNSF members and non-party specialists. On 19 November, the new government was officially approved by a vote of 260 to 203. In his inauguration speech, Vacaroiu vowed to continue implementing political and economic reforms, while asserting that social costs had to be taken into consideration even at the price of temporarily slowing down reforms. By year's end, there were indications that the government would roll back market reforms in an effort to offset spiralling declines in social conditions brought on by unemployment and price liberalization.

In other issues, inter-ethnic relations continued to remain tense following the strong electoral showing of nationalist parties. Cluj mayor Gheorghe Funar issued a series of controversial decisions, including banning public signs in Hungarian; a quarter of the city's population is ethnic Hungarian. During the general election campaign the nationalist parties accused the DC of serving Hungarian interests. In September, the only ethnic Hungarian member of the government was dismissed without explanation.

In January 1992, parliament voted to keep the archives of the dreaded Securitate (the secret police of the Ceausescu regime) closed for 40 years. But in April, the director of Securitate's successor, the Romanian Intelligence Service (SRI), urged parliament to release the files, alleging that some opposition figures would be unmasked as informers. On 20 April, the Supreme Court overturned an earlier acquittal, and sentenced 21 former Ceausescu advisors to lengthy jail terms for their complicity in attempting to suppress the December 1989 anti-Ceausescu uprising.

The question of restoring constitutional monarchy continued to resurface in 1992 despite a lack of broad public interest in the matter. In April, former King Michael I was allowed to enter the country after a 45-year exile. After his four-day Easter visit, deemed "historic" by some opposition groups, Michael expressed his view that constitutional monarchy was the only way to finally break with Communism, reinforce democracy, and rebuild the economy. In July, the leader of the National Liberal Party, Radu Campeanu, asked the former king to accept his party's nomination as a candidate for president. Michael declined, stating that he could only accept the position of head of state in accordance with laws guaranteeing his impartial role in promoting national unity.

In foreign affairs, major issues included relations with neighboring Hungary in light of heightening ethnic tensions in Transylvania. Another key area was the issue of Moldova, the former Soviet republic with a predominantly Romanian-speaking population. Part of Moldova belonged to Romania until the Hitler-Stalin Pact of 1939. At the end of 1991, Romanian leaders talked openly about the eventual "reunification" with Moldova. The ongoing uprising by Slavs in Moldova's Trans-Dniester region was a cause of major concern in Bucharest.

Another issue was the resettlement of Gypsies (Roma) who had fled Romania citing persecution and government indifference. In September, the Romanian and German governments signed a treaty providing for the deportation from Germany of 50,000 Romanians, mostly Gypsies, who had asked for political asylum.

Political Rights and Civil Liberties:

Citizens of Romania have the right to change their government democratically. After the 1992 presidential and parliamentary elections, the opposition voiced suspicion about the high number of invalid votes, alleging widespread voter fraud. However, the Constitutional Court validated the results.

The new Romanian constitution, adopted in 1991, stipulates that the interpretation of constitutional provisions concerning the rights and duties of citizens must be in line with the Universal Declaration on Human Rights and other international treaties. Where there are discrepancies between domestic laws and international agreements, the latter should take precedence.

The 1990 penal code guarantees the right of detainees to a defense council in criminal cases and stipulates compensation for those detained illegally. The Law on Public Administration grants anyone who believes that he has been deprived his legal rights by an administrative authority the right to appeal for the review of the case, and if rejected, to sue in a court of law.

Regarding the rights of the minorities, the vagueness of the 1991 Law on National Security limits full rights of association and expression. Among activities considered to infringe on the security of the state are "initiating, organizing, committing or sup-porting...revisionist ideas," that might endanger Romania's unity and territorial integrity.

The Law on Broadcasting Media stipulates that freedom of the press is guaranteed; at the same time, however, it forbids defamation of the country, dissemination of classified information, and producing materials offending public morals. There is a variety of newspapers and magazines. Government-controlled television and radio generally reflect government policies, but there are student radio stations and an independent television station.

Freedom of religion is guaranteed, although the government exercises control over the activities of the churches. Most domestic and foreign travel restrictions were abolished following the fall of Communism.

There are three major trade union confederations, as well as organizations of employers. Unions represent an important opposition force despite government efforts to monitor union activities and co-opt union leadership.

Russia

Polity: Elected presi-
dential-parliamentary
(transitional)
Economy: Statist transitional
Population: 149,299,000
PPP: na
Life Expectancy: 70.0
Ethnic Groups: Russian, over 100 ethnic groups

Political Rights: 3
Civil Liberties: 4
Status: Partly Free

Overview: In its first year as an independent country, the Russian Federation faced an ongoing political struggle between the reformist government of President Boris Yeltsin and a legislature dominated by ex-Communist hardliners. The struggle culminated in the December 1992 ouster by parliament of Yegor Gaidar, the main architect of the reforms, who had been designated acting prime minister by Yeltsin in June. Gaidar was replaced by Viktor Chernomyrdin, a Soviet-era manager.

Stretching from the Baltics across Eurasia to the Pacific, Russia was the political center of two mighty empires. With the collapse of Tsarism after the 1917 Russian Revolution, Russia became the power-base of the Bolshevik revolution, and the nucleus of the Union of Soviet Socialist Republics (USSR), formed in 1921-22. Its capital, Moscow, was the seat of a vast, multinational Communist empire that included 14 other republics and dozens of autonomous regions, and its language and culture eventually dominated the Soviet Union.

With the collapse of the USSR in December 1991, Russia—the only constituent republic not to declare sovereignty from the Soviet Union—gained *de facto* independence under President Yeltsin, the charismatic leader directly elected in June 1991. In the subsequent power struggle with Soviet President Mikhail Gorbachev, Yeltsin banned Communist Party (CPSU) organizations from government offices and workplaces in Russia. When hardliners launched a coup against Gorbachev on 19 August, Yeltsin's heroic stand against the junta further undermined the Soviet president's remaining authority, and power shifted irrevocably from the center to the republics. As head of the largest republic, Yeltsin oversaw the takeover by Russia of major Soviet institutions, thus sealing the USSR's demise. He was also the driving force behind the formation of the Commonwealth of Independent States (CIS), which initially included only the Slavic republics—Russia, Ukraine and Belarus—but was later joined by all but one of the newly independent republics.

The key political dynamic in 1992 was the ongoing struggle between President Yeltsin and the 1,046-member Congress of People's Deputies, which had been elected in 1990 under Soviet rules that set aside a majority of seats for CPSU members and Party organizations. The primary issue was the fate of Yeltsin's economic reforms, but a corollary conflict was over the future of the *nomenklatura*, entrenched bureaucrats committed to blocking reform, maintaining their positions, and the principle of strong, central leadership. In the fall of 1991, Yeltsin had been granted emergency powers to run the economy by decree and appoint cabinet ministers without parliamentary approval. The post of prime minister, however, needed parliamentary approval, and for the time being, Yeltsin held the post as head of government.

In April 1992, the Russian Congress of People's Deputies held its first session since the dissolution of the Soviet Union. During the first week, it passed an amendment requiring the president to nominate a prime minister within 90 days, and called for increased social spending and subsidies to large state enterprises. Reform-minded deputies opposed these measures as inflationary and supporting unproductive industrial enterprises. Yeltsin's government also attempted to push through a constitutional amendment allowing for unrestricted sale and purchase of land, but the effort failed to gain the required two-thirds majority because of conservative opposition. On 30 May, the Supreme Soviet (the smaller standing parliament) refused to pass a law on privatization and bankruptcy. Despite these setbacks Yeltsin underscored his commitment to market reforms by appointing Gaidar acting prime minister on 15 June.

The same month, President Yeltsin faced a new challenge with the emergence of a new centrist political bloc in parliament. On 21 June, leaders of three influential conservative Russian parties—the Democratic Party of Russia led by Nikolay Travkin; the People's Party of Free Russia founded by Vice President Aleksandr Rutskoy; and the All-Russian Renewal Union, headed by industrialist and former CPSU official Arkady Volksy—formed the Civic Union (CU), which represented the largest single block of seats in parliament. The Renewal group, composed of powerful old-time industrial directors, also played an important role in the CU. While professing loyalty to Yeltsin, the CU maintained that radical economic reforms pursued by Gaidar were too harsh for conditions in Russia and could provoke a social explosion.

With political gridlock exacerbating a badly faltering economy, tensions increased. In July, Foreign Minister Andrei Kozyrev warned of an "anti-democratic coup...either through another congress of the Soviet Communist Party or by a reversal on the part of the apparat," the still-powerful state bureaucracy. Meanwhile, economic distress and public discontent also led to fears of a right-wing, ultra-nationalist resurgence sprearheaded by several anti-Western, xenophobic organizations. Prominent right-wing organizations included: the National Salvation Front; *Nashi* (Ours), headed by the so-called "black colonels" Viktor Alksnis and Nikolay Petrushenko; and the Liberal Democratic Party led by the demagogic anti-Semite Vladimir Zhirinovsky. Even some long-time "radical democrats" began questioning the adaptability of a free market in Russia, given its entrenched socialist economy. In July, Sergei Stankevich, former liberal deputy mayor of Moscow, called on Russia to abandon the "liberal dream" of a market economy and democratic institutions, and focus on creating a strong central government. Meanwhile, Democratic Russia, a mass movement organized by liberal deputies and intellectuals in 1990, which had scored important electoral gains in parliamentary elections that year and secured Yeltsin's election to the presidency in 1991, also lost momentum and support.

In August, the first anniversary of the coup attempt against Soviet leader Gorbachev, there were indications that the Gaidar government was in serious trouble. Civic Union's Volsky announced he and his supporters would be able to win a vote of no-confidence in the prime minister. Meanwhile, Ruslan Khasbulatov, the speaker of parliament and a strong critic of radical reforms, took control of the so-called Russian Property Fund, which nominally controlled the stake in privatized firms that would remain in state hands after shares had been sold to the public.

In the fall, President Yeltsin struck back at hardliners, but it became apparent toward year's end that he would have to seek compromise before the session of the Congress of People's Deputies slated for December. On 28 October, Yeltsin outlawed the National Salvation Front and banned the 5,000-strong armed guard under direct control of conserva-tive parliamentary Speaker Khasbulatov. In banning the guard, Yeltsin prevented Khasbulatov from taking control of the liberal daily *Izvestia*, which supported the president.

In late November, to appease hard-line legislators before the opening of the Seventh Congress of People's Deputies on 1 December, Yeltsin dismissed two key liberal supporters: Mikhail Poltoranin, deputy prime minister in charge of information, and Yegor Yakovlev, chairman of the Russian state radio and television company.

Yeltsin's conflict with hardliners came to a head during the Seventh Congress. The legislature criticized Yeltsin's economic program and voted down all his major proposals. A major setback came on 9 December, when the Congress rejected Gaidar as prime minister. In a fiery speech, Yeltsin accused legislators of trying to "carry out a creeping coup" and threatened to take the matter to the people holding a referen-dum on who should be vested with ultimate power in Russia.

New Prime Minister Chernomyrdin stressed his willingness to continue reforms, but said priorities would change, with a concentration on restimulating industrial production. The new cabinet, which retained key reformers, was announced on 23

December. Throughout the year, the economy continued to deteriorate. Production fell by 24 percent and inflation reached 25 percent a month, shriveling the living standards of most Russians. Pensioners and those on fixed incomes were hardest hit by steep price hikes on food and consumer goods.

Other major issues facing Russia were de-communization, adopting a new constitution, increased ethnic unrest within its borders, and friction with Ukraine.

Following the 1991 coup attempt, Yeltsin banned the CPSU. Its vast assets were taken over by the Russian state or, in some cases, by worker collectives. The CPSU splintered into new parties, among them the neo-Stalinist All-Union Bolshevik Party and the Russian Communists Workers Party.

In February 1992, after a four-month investigation into the CPSU's financial affairs, a special investigative committee headed by Deputy Prosecutor Yevgeny Lisov revealed that former Soviet President and CPSU General Secretary Gorbachev had authorized channeling Party funds into secret bank accounts and property. It also revealed that the Party had routinely transferred money to foreign Communist parties. On 30 November, the Constitutional Court ruled on Yeltsin's three decrees banning the Party. The suit was initiated by 36 hard-line Communist legislators who contended that Yeltsin had exceeded his authority. A countersuit filed by 52 Yeltsin supporters argued that the Party was never a true political party, but an unconstitutional organization that seized control during the 1917 revolution, sent millions to their deaths, and hid behind a phantom government. Chief Judge Valery Zorkin announced the court upheld Yeltsin's ban, but ruled grassroots Communist groups could exist, leaving open the possibility that the Communist party could rebuild a national structure.

Adoption of a new constitution was a critical issue in determining the future structure of the state. During its April session, the Congress of People's Deputies failed to endorse any of the four constitutional drafts. It accepted the basic concepts of the official draft prepared by parliament's Constitutional Commission, which called for a bicameral arrangement. The uneasy relationship between the executive and legislative branches of the government was reflected in debates on the new draft constitution, with each trying to wrest more power. After numerous conciliatory sessions between Yeltsin's and parliament's constitutional advisers, on 12 December the Congress issued a decree titled "On the Stabilization of the Constitutional Structure of the Russian Federation." The decree outlined 10 major concepts of the draft constitution that will be cited in a national referendum on 11 August 1993.

Also of concern in 1992 were rising ethnic tensions in several parts of Russia, a multi-ethnic state with 16 republics and 30 autonomous regions. On 1 April, the central government and leaders of the autonomous republics signed a treaty specifying the division of power. The only republic not to sign was Tatarstan, whose residents approved a referendum in late March declaring the region a sovereign state. Following the Constitutional Court's ruling declaring the referendum a violation of federal law, Tatarstan's leaders indicated a willingness to sign a separate treaty with Russia.

A volatile situation continued in the northern Caucasus region, where a year earlier, the Chechen part of the Chechen-Ingush Autonomous Republic declared independence. In 1992, fighting broke out between the Ingush and their neighbors from the North Ossetian Republic, which claimed more than 300 lives. In November, Yeltsin dispatched military units to the region, in an effort to separate the two sides. However, some independent journalists reported Russian troops assisted the Ossetians.

The year also saw friction with Ukraine, the second-most populous of the former republics and Russia's neighbor. On 22 May, the Supreme Soviet adopted a resolution declaring illegal the 1954 transfer of the Crimean Peninsula to Ukrainian jurisdiction. Another area of contention was the fate of the Black Sea Fleet. After a "war of decrees," in which both sides attempted to take control of the fleet, President Yeltsin and Ukrainian President Leonid Kravchuk signed an agreement on 3 August placing it under joint command for three years.

Moscow also remained concerned for Russian minorities living outside Russia. In July, the Supreme Soviet passed a resolution calling for economic sanctions against Estonia for its refusal to grant automatic citizenship rights to Russian residents. In August, Russia and Lithuania signed an agreement on the withdrawal of Russian troops, but two months later Yeltsin declared that he was suspending troop withdrawal from the Baltics because Russian minorities needed protection and because proper housing for the military and their families was not available in Russia.

Political Rights and Civil Liberties: Russians have a limited right to change their government democratically. President Boris Yeltsin was elected in a direct and fair popular election in June 1991. However, the Congress of People's Deputies was elected in 1990 under Soviet rules, with the majority of the seats reserved for members of the Communist party and other "public organizations." The Congress meets twice a year to deliberate on constitutional issues and approve personnel changes in the government. The smaller standing legislature, the Supreme Soviet, is elected from among Congress members. The current term of the legislature expires in 1995.

Parliament prepared a new draft constitution and legal system to replace the 1977 Soviet constitution still in effect, although about 200 amendments have been added. The working draft states that "the Russian Federation is a sovereign, legal, democratic federal...state," and provides for a multi-party system, free elections for president, vice president, and legislature, and includes other Western democratic concepts. Russians are scheduled to vote on the constitution in a referendum slated for August 1993.

There are a multitude of parties, as well as non-political civic, cultural, social, business, youth and other organizations.

In February, President Yeltsin pardoned the last known political prisoners from labor camps. However, in October, Vil Mirzayanov, a scientist who objected to Russia's ongoing development of chemical weapons, was imprisoned for allegedly revealing state secrets.

In the spring, parliament adopted a new law on the print media, which prohibited censorship and the formation of monopolies. There is a wide-range of independent newspapers and periodicals printing diverse views. A draft on television and radio broadcasting was submitted to parliament.

Freedom of religion was generally respected in this primarily Russian Orthodox country, with increased activities by Protestant, Jewish, and Islamic groups.

Restrictions on freedom of movement have been lifted, and at the end of the year a new law granted all adult citizens the right to travel abroad. Freedom of movement was curtailed in some areas, however, because of flare-ups of separatist violence.

There are numerous independent trade unions and labor associations, among them the Independent Trade Union of Miners (NPG), the Confederation of Labor, and numerous unions of pilots, flight controllers, and railroad workers.

Rwanda

Polity: Dominant party (military dominated)
Economy: Mixed statist
Population: 7,718,000
PPP: $680
Life Expectancy: 49.5
Ethnic Groups: Hutu (84 percent), Tutsi (15 percent), Twa pygmy (1 percent)

Political Rights: 6
Civil Liberties: 5
Status: Not Free

Overview: In 1992, Rwanda's ruling party admitted four recently legalized opposition parties to the government, but a power-sharing agreement with the insurgent Rwanda Patriotic Front (RPF) foundered when President Juvenal Habyarimana dismissed it as "scraps of paper."

Rwanda, which gained independence from Belgium in 1962, is a poor and landlocked country in central-east Africa. It is led by Juvenal Habyarimana, head of the National Republican Movement for Democracy and Development (MRNDD). Habyarimana seized power in a bloodless coup in 1973. The National Revolutionary Movement for Development (MRND), established in 1976, was the only legal party under a 1978 constitution. Running unopposed in 1988, Habyarimana was re-elected to a third five-year term as president with 99 percent of the vote. After opposition parties were legalized in 1991, the ruling party was re-named the MRNDD. On 23 April 1992, the president resigned from the armed forces.

In October 1990, a force of 5,000 Rwandan Patriotic Front (RPF) insurgents invaded the country from neighboring Uganda. Many of the insurgents are exiles of the Tutsi ethnic group that have served in the Ugandan army. The invasion was another episode in an often violent inter-tribal rivalry between Rwanda's numerically dominant Hutu ethnic group and the minority Tutsis, who had dominated national life until 1959, when the Tutsi king was overthrown by Hutu rebels. Tutsi refugees, numbering as many as a half million, have been the source of manpower for those dedicated to the overthrow of the successive Hutu regimes that have governed Rwanda since the 1959 coup.

The army beat back the October 1990 invasion with the aid of Zairian troops, but the RPF mounted subsequent offensives the following two years. Negotiated ceasefire agreements between the parties failed to keep the peace for long. The regime asserted that refugees were free to return to Rwanda peacefully and participate in multi-party politics. The RPF responded that its movement's followers would be in danger if they entered politics in opposition to the regime. Instead, the insurgents demanded that a government of national unity replace the existing regime, and that institutionalized ethnic and regional discrimination cease. The regime has stated that political change will be limited until the RPF is disarmed and hostilities cease.

In November 1990, the president announced his intention to move Rwanda to multi-partyism. The regime promulgated a new constitution in mid-1991 that legalized political parties, but most opposition parties fear that President Habyarimana and the

MRNDD retain enough power to manipulate the transition to competitive elections.

On 14 March 1992, the legal political opposition announced that it had reached agreement with the regime to form a coalition government. In mid-April, President Habyarimana replaced MRNDD member Sylvestre Nsanzimana as prime minister with Dismas Nsengiyaremye of the Republican Democratic Movement (MDR). Nsanzimana had been unable to form an all-party transitional government because opposition parties refused to participate in his cabinet. The MDR joined the MRNDD, the Liberal Party (PL), the Christian Democratic Party (PDC), and the Social Democratic Party (PSD) in the new cabinet. The new administration announced goals of negotiating peace with the RPF, organizing elections, and drawing up a new constitution.

In June, the government and RPF announced that they would convene full peace talks in Tanzania. The parties signed a ceasefire accord on 14 July that went into effect two weeks later. In August, negotiators met again and signed a preliminary agreement to form a new, all-party transitional administration to share power until elections. Ominously, the MRNDD refused to participate in the peace talks.

The negotiations reached an impasse in September after the RPF demanded the creation of a seven-member "council" to rule Rwanda for four years. The rebel movement rejected the counter-proposal that President Habyarimana head the council, demanding instead that he either serve as a ceremonial head of state or resign as president. In early October, the ceasefire briefly broke down in renewed fighting between the army and RPF forces in northern Rwanda. At the same time, the MDR, PL, and PSD demonstrated in the capital of Kigali, charging that the MRNDD and Habyarimana were trying to block a final agreement with the RPF.

Negotiators agreed in October to form an all-party commission to draft a new constitution and prepare for new elections, but the MRNDD voiced its opposition to the agreement almost immediately. Officials questioned the authority of the prime minister's negotiators to commit the regime to any accord, and President Habyarimana dismissed the agreement as "scraps of paper." The prime minister and his cabinet allies in turn criticized the MRNDD and the president for undermining the negotiated agreement.

Political Rights and Civil Liberties:

Rwandans do not have the power to change their government democratically. The constitution allows for competitive multi-party elections, but Rwanda remains a military-dominated one-party state. Although the regime has allowed its non-violent political opposition to organize, Africa Watch reported in February 1992 that officials have harassed members of the recently legalized parties.

The security apparatus in Rwanda is pervasive and intrusive. Security laws allow for the preventive detention of persons suspected of undermining national interests and public safety. Police, soldiers, and local officials have rounded up and imprisoned alleged RPF accomplices and supporters. Members of the Tutsi ethnic groups face beatings and torture, and hundreds of Tutsis have been extrajudicially executed. Authorities have encouraged Hutu civilians to launch attacks on Tutsis in their communities. The RPF is also responsible for violence toward its civilian opponents, and has driven over 300,000 Hutus from the territories it has seized. The judicial system makes little effort to bring human rights abusers to justice.

Discriminatory quotas have limited the level of Tutsi participation in public employment and education. The state requires citizens to carry identification cards specifying their ethnic group. Authorities arrested Fidèle Kanyabugyi of the human rights group Kanyarwanda in March 1992 and charged him with endangering the security of the state for investigating a massacre of Tutsi civilians by Hutu gangs incited by officials.

In February 1992, a court sentenced a newspaper editor-in-chief to four years in prison for "insulting the head of state" by publishing a cartoon criticizing Habyarimana. The regime has charged journalists of the independent press with sedition for various political offenses, including contacts with the RPF and publication of articles criticizing the regime's discriminatory policies. Authorities have arrested, imprisoned, and occasionally tortured journalists who accused those in power of corruption. Yet the independent press continues to thrive. The regime controls broadcasting, and presently allows opposition parties limited air time.

Although the constitution guarantees freedom of religion, the regime has a record of harassing Jehovah's Witnesses. The single-party state severely restricted freedom of assembly in the past, but opposition parties have often held demonstrations without incident. The regime restricts freedom of movement by requiring that those traveling within Rwanda obtain official permission and documents. The ruling MRNDD controls the Central Union of Rwandan Workers. By law, the government-controlled executive committees must approve all strikes.

St. Kitts-Nevis

Polity: Parliamentary democracy
Economy: Capitalist
Population: 40,000
PPP: $3,150
Life Expectancy: 67.5
Ethnic Groups: Black, mulatto, other

Political Rights: 1
Civil Liberties: 1
Status: Free

Overview:　This Caribbean nation, consisting of the islands of St. Kitts and Nevis, became an independent state with a federal constitution in 1983. The British monarch is represented by a governor-general who appoints a prime minister as leader of the parliamentary majority. The governor-general also appoints a deputy governor-general for Nevis.

There is a unicameral National Assembly, whose members are directly elected for five years from single-member constituencies, eight on St. Kitts and three on Nevis. Senators, not to exceed two-thirds of the elected members, are appointed, one by the leader of the parliamentary opposition for every two by the governor-general.

The current People's Action Movement (PAM) government of Prime Minister Kennedy Simmons came to power in the parliamentary election of 1980 with the support of the Nevis Reformation Party (NRP) and led the country to independence in

1983. The center-right PAM-NRP coalition increased its majority in early elections in 1984; the PAM won six of the eight seats on St. Kitts and the NRP took all three seats on Nevis. The Labour Party (LP), a left-leaning party that once dominated the political scene, lost all but two of its seats.

Simmons was sworn in for a third term after the PAM retained its six seats in the 1989 elections. The NRP retained two seats on Nevis, losing one to the newly organized Concerned Citizens' Movement (CCM). The LP retained its two seats. Denzil Douglas, a parliamentary newcomer, was elected the LP leader following the elections and replaced Lee Moore as the parliamentary opposition leader. The LP has been conducting an anti-corruption campaign against the government as it gears up for the next general elections, constitutionally due by the end of 1994.

Nevis is provided with its own island Assembly consisting of five elected and three appointed members. The deputy governor-general appoints a premier and two other members of the Nevis Assembly to serve as a Nevis Island Administration. Nevis is also accorded the right to secession from St. Kitts if approved by two-thirds of the elected legislators and endorsed by two-thirds of those voting on the matter in an island referendum.

In the Nevis Assembly elections held on 1 June 1992, the CCM won three of five seats, unseating the NRP, which was seeking a third consecutive five-year term. The CCM leader, businessman Vance Amory, became Premier, replacing the NRP's Simeon Daniel. Amory is also the CCM member of the National Assembly.

Political Rights and Civil Liberties: Citizens are able to change their government through free and fair elections. Constitutional guarantees regarding the right of free expression, the free exercise of religion and the right to organize political parties, labor unions and civic organizations are respected. The main labor union, the St. Kitts Trades and Labour Union, is associated with the opposition LP. The right to strike, while not specified by law, is fully recognized and respected in practice.

Television and radio on St. Kitts are owned by the government but offer different points of view. There is no daily newspaper, but each of the major political parties publishes a weekly or bi-weekly newspaper. The opposition publications are free to criticize the government and do so vigorously. There is a religious television station and a privately owned radio station on Nevis.

Rule of law, based on the 1983 constitution, is respected. The judiciary is independent and the highest court is the West Indies Supreme Court (based in St. Lucia), which includes a Court of Appeal and a High Court. In certain circumstances, there is right of appeal to the Privy Council in London.

St. Lucia

Polity: Parliamentary democracy
Economy: Capitalist
Population: 156,000
PPP: $3,361
Life Expectancy: 70.5
Ethnic Groups: Black, mulatto, other

Political Rights: 1
Civil Liberties: 2
Status: Free

Overview:

Prime Minister John Compton and the United Workers Party (UWP) retained power with a convincing win in the April 1992 elections. However, Compton suggested that he might step down before the end of his third consecutive five-year mandate.

St. Lucia, a member of the British Commonwealth, became internally self-governing in 1967, and achieved independence in 1979. The British monarchy is represented by a governor-general whose emergency powers are subject to legislative review. Under the 1979 constitution, there is a bicameral parliament consisting of a seventeen-member House of Assembly elected for five years, and an eleven-member Senate, with six senators appointed by the prime minister, three by the leader of the parliamentary opposition, and two by consultation with civic and religious organizations. The prime minister must be a member of the House and command a majority therein. Since 1985, the island has been divided into eight regions, each with its own elected council and administrative services.

The leftist St. Lucia Labour Party (SLP) won a landslide victory in the 1979 elections, but factional disputes between SLP radicals and moderates led to new elections in 1982. The radical faction led by George Odlum broke off to form the Progressive Labour Party (PLP). The 1982 elections saw the return to power of Compton and the UWP.

In the 1987 elections, the UWP won a narrow 9 to 8 victory over the SLP, which had declared a social democratic orientation under the new leadership of Julian Hunte, Compton's brother-in-law. The PLP won no seats. Compton, hoping to increase the UWP majority, called new elections a few weeks later, but there was no change in the distribution of seats. However, an SLP representative switched parties later in the year, giving the UWP a 10-7 majority.

The 1992 election campaign was a bitter one, accompanied by some violence, a dispute over boundaries between electoral districts, and an exchange of personal accusations, including one by *The Star*, an anti-Compton weekly, that said the 65-year-old prime minister had an affair with an 18-year-old student. But the electorate evidently was not distracted from the core issue, the economy. St. Lucia has experienced economic growth and development in recent years, at a time when many of its Caribbean neighbors have been struggling. Despite the need for improved social services, one of the SLP's main campaign planks, voters on 27 April returned the UWP to power, increasing its parliamentary majority to 11 to 6 over the SLP.

In the aftermath, Compton denied that the UWP was a one-man show, saying new leaders were being groomed in the UWP and hinting that he might step aside before the end of his mandate. For his part, Julian Hunte had to fend off a series of challenges during an SLP convention in July before retaining the party leadership.

Political Rights and Civil Liberties: Citizens are able to change their government through free and fair elections. Constitutional guarantees regarding free expression and the right to organize political parties, labor unions and civic groups are generally respected as is the free exercise of religion. Opposition parties have complained of difficulties in getting police permission for demonstrations and charge the government with interference. Newspapers are mostly private or sponsored by political parties. The government has been charged with trying to influence the press by withholding government advertising. Television is privately owned; radio is both public and private.

Civic groups are well organized and politically active. The labor unions, which represent a majority of wage earners, are free to strike. The competition among political parties and allied civic organizations is heated, particularly during campaign periods when there is occasional violence and mutual charges of harassment.

The judicial system is independent and includes a High Court under the West Indies Supreme Court (based in St. Lucia), with ultimate appeal under certain circumstances to the Privy Council in London. Personal security is generally respected under the rule of law, although the recent appearance of drug-related violence has become a cause for concern. Also, in September 1992, the government ordered an investigation into two reports of police brutality.

St. Vincent and the Grenadines

Polity: Parliamentary democracy
Economy: Capitalist
Population: 115,000
PPP: $3,420
Life Expectancy: 70.0
Ethnic Groups: Black, mulatto, other

Political Rights: 1
Civil Liberties: 2
Status: Free

Overview: St. Vincent and the Grenadines has the status of "special member" of the British Commonwealth, with the British monarchy represented by a governor-general. St. Vincent became internally self-governing in 1967 and achieved independence in 1979, with jurisdiction over the northern Grenadine islets of Beguia, Canouan, Mayreau, Mustique, Prune Island, Petit St. Vincent, and Union Island.

At the time of independence, the constitution provided for a unicameral House of Assembly with thirteen members directly elected for five years. Six senators are appointed, four by the government and two by the opposition. The prime minister is the leader of the party or coalition commanding a majority in the House. In 1986, the House approved a constitutional amendment raising the number of elected members to fifteen.

In the May 1989 elections, Prime Minister James Mitchell won a second term when his centrist New Democratic Party (NDP) swept all fifteen seats. The three opposing parties were the moderate socialist St. Vincent Labor Party (SVLP), which had held power from 1979 to 1984, and two leftist parties, the United People's Movement (UPM) and the Movement for National Unity (MNU). Despite failing to win any seats in the "first past the post" system, the opposition garnered over 30 percent of the vote.

In 1991, charges of misconduct by the national police commissioner, and a scandal involving the seizure by U.S. authorities of a St. Vincent-registered vessel allegedly carrying a large quantity of hashish, led the three opposition parties to form the National Council in Defence of Law and Order. The council, backed by trade unions and some private sector and civic groups, became the main opposition vehicle for criticizing the Mitchell government. It continued to be active in 1992 and previewed a possible coalition for the next elections, due by 1994.

Political Rights and Civil Liberties: Citizens can change their government democratically. Constitutional guarantees regarding the right to free expression, freedom of religion and the right to organize political parties, labor unions and civic organizations are respected. Labor unions are active, politically involved, and permitted to strike. Political campaigns are hotly contested, with occasional charges from all quarters of harassment and violence, including police brutality. In 1990, the government admitted during United Nations Human Rights Committee hearings that prison conditions were poor, but denied allegations by the St. Vincent and the Grenadines Human Rights Association of prisoner beatings.

The press is independent, with one privately owned independent weekly, the *Vincentian*, and two weeklies and a fortnightly run by political parties. The *Vincentian* has been charged with government favoritism by the opposition and the Caribbean Association of Media Workers. In August 1992, the labor ministry began investigating charges by two *Vincentian* editors that they were unfairly dismissed for publishing articles calling for reforms in the management of the newspaper. Radio and television are government owned. Differing points of view are presented, but there is evidence of government interference in radio programming.

The judicial system is independent. The highest court is the West Indies Supreme Court (based in St. Lucia), which includes a Court of Appeal and a High Court, one of whose judges is resident on St. Vincent. The Human Rights Association has criticized judicial delays and the large backlog of cases caused by a shortage of personnel in the local judiciary.

San Marino

Polity: Parliamentary
democracy
Economy: Capitalist
Population: 24,000
PPP: na
Life Expectancy: 76.0
Ethnic Groups: Sammarinese (Italian)

Political Rights: 1
Civil Liberties: 1
Status: Free

Overview:
San Marino became a full member of the United Nations in March 1992. Previously an observer member of the world body, San Marino has become more diplomatically active. In 1992, the tiny nation granted diplomatic recognition to Croatia and Slovenia before the European Community did.

According to tradition, a Christian stonecutter named Marinus founded San Marino in 301 A.D. Surrounded entirely by Italy, San Marino is the world's oldest republic. The country signed the first of several friendship treaties with Italy in 1862. Italy handles many of San Marino's foreign and security affairs and utilities, but otherwise San Marino has its own political institutions.

The republic has a lively multi-party system. In recent years, Socialists, Communists, Christian Democrats, and Social Democrats have participated in coalition governments. Cabinets have changed frequently, due to a lack of consensus on policy. In the May 1988 election, the Christian Democrats and Communists won enough seats to continue their coalition government. After the collapse of Communism in Eastern Europe, the Sammarinese Communists renamed themselves the Progressive Democratic Popular Party. In February 1992, the Christian Democrats broke up the coalition with the ex-Communists and formed a new one with the Socialists. There are two other parties: the Socialist Unity Party and the Democratic Movement, a moderate social democratic party. The next general election is due in 1993. The Sammarinese foreign ministry is offering travel subsidies so that some of the 16,000 citizens abroad can come home to vote.

The government extends official recognition to seventeen groups of Sammarinese living elsewhere. Recognized communities receive government subsidies for office space and communications, including fax machines. In autumn 1992, the government organized a *consulta*, a gathering of recognized Sammarinese communities from around the world that discussed the country's future.

Since 1600, San Marino's Grand and General Council has served as the legislature. Its 60 members serve for a maximum term of five years. The Council chooses the State Congress, which functions as a cabinet. Chosen by the Council for six-month terms, two Captains Regent supervise the State Congress. One Captain Regent represents the city of San Marino, and the other stands for the surrounding area.

Political Rights and Civil Liberties:
Sammarinese living at home and abroad have the right to change their government democratically. The media are free, and Italian newspapers and broadcasts are freely available.

Political parties, trade unions, and the government publish newspapers, periodicals, and bulletins. The country has a vibrant, largely private-enterprise economy that depends heavily on tourism. San Marino claims never to have refused asylum to people in need.

Sao Tome and Príncipe

Polity: Presidential-parliamentary democracy
Economy: Mixed statist (transitional)
Population: 127,000
PPP: 616
Life Expectancy: 65.5
Ethnic Groups: Black Africa, Mestiço/Mulatto, European

Political Rights: 2
Civil Liberties: 3
Status: Free

Overview: The new democracy of São Tomé and Príncipe experienced its first political crisis when President Miguel Trovoada dismissed the government of Prime Minister Daniel Daio in April 1992.

Located in the Gulf of Guinea 130 miles off the coast of Gabon, the Republic of São Tomé and Príncipe consists of two main islands and several smaller islets. The islands gained independence from Portugal in 1975. From independence until 1991, Manuel Pinto da Costa served as the nation's president and leader of the sole legal party, the Movement for the Liberation of São Tomé and Príncipe (MLSTP). The transformation of the state from a leftist, single-party political structure into a multi-party democracy formally began at the end of 1989. A national MLSTP conference recommended constitutional amendments to allow for multi-party elections and term limitations for the office of the presidency. Opposition figures were granted amnesty and opposition movements were legalized.

On 20 January 1991, in the first multi-party parliamentary elections in the country's independent history, the MLSTP came in second place to the opposition Democratic Convergence Party-Group of Reflection (PCD-GR). The PCD-GR won 55 percent of the vote and 31 seats in the 55-seat national assembly. The MLSTP gained only 30 percent of the vote and 21 seats. The Democratic Opposition Coalition (CODO) finished in third place, with 5 percent of the vote and 3 seats. On 3 March 1991, independent candidate Miguel dos Anjos Trovoada was elected president after the incumbent, Manuel Pinto da Costa, and two other aspirants withdrew from the race.

By April 1992, the new government of Prime Minister Daniel dos Santos Daio faced significant public disenchantment. Citizen complaints focused on the Daio administration's structural adjustment program, which included substantially reduced public spending, a devaluation of the currency, as well as hiring freezes and moves toward cutting the number of civil servants in half.

In early April, President Trovoada criticized the Daio administration for attempting to thwart the holding of a demonstration against its economic policy. The president's criticism brought to a head a year of increasing tension between himself and Daio. Each had struggled to claim a preponderance of power for his own office. On 3 April 1992, Daio publicly accused the president of attempting to destabilize the country, but the government allowed the demonstration to be rescheduled. On 8 April, two thousand protesters took to the streets of the capital to denounce the adjustment program and demand the immediate resignation of Daio and his cabinet.

Responding to what he perceived to be a national crisis, the president summoned the National Assembly into an extraordinary session. In an address broadcast to the nation, Trovoada warned that gaps in the 1990 constitution concentrated power in the legislative branch. He further charged that Daio was intentionally misinterpreting the document in order to amass even greater power. The MLSTP and CODO opposition in the Assembly declared their support for the president, calling for him either to dissolve the PCD/GR-majority legislature and set an early date for elections, or dismiss the government and press for a new "government of national unity." In response, the leadership of the ruling PCD/GR announced its support for Daio. It accused opposition parties of exploiting the economic situation and the strained relations between president and prime minister for partisan advantage.

On 22 April, President Trovoada dismissed the Daio government and threatened to call legislative elections if the PCD/GR refused to nominate a new candidate for prime minister. Although the party denounced the president's action as a "constitutional coup d'état," it nominated former finance minister Norberto Costa Alegre as the new prime minister. Trovoada agreed. Difficult negotiation followed over the list of proposed ministers drawn up by Costa Alegre.

In early August, the capital was briefly rocked by an armed clash between army troops and the paramilitary police. Similar to the conflict between Daio and Trovoada, there is uncertainty over the jurisdiction and authority of the police and army under the new constitution. Local elections on 6 December resulted in a victory for the former-ruling MLSTP in five of seven districts. The PCD-GR managed only a tie in one of the seven districts.

Political Rights and Civil Liberties: Citizens of São Tomé and Príncipe can change their government democratically. In August 1990, voters approved a multi-party constitution that called for a mixed economy, freedom of expression, and labor rights.

Until quite recently, the judiciary has not been fully independent from executive interference, particularly in security and political cases. Radio, television, and a periodic newspaper are government-controlled, but there is now more latitude to criticize government policies. However, the opposition MLSTP accuses the new government of persecuting journalists and monopolizing the media. Leaders of the new regime have promised to respect freedom of association and religion, allow diverse opinions in the media, respect judicial independence and depoliticize the military.

Saudi Arabia

Polity: Traditional monarchy
Economy: Capitalist-statist
Population: 16,057,000
PPP: $10,330
Life Expectancy: 64.5
Ethnic Groups: Arab tribes, other Arab and Muslim immigrants

Political Rights: 7
Civil Liberties: 7
Status: Not Free

Overview:
In 1992, Muslim extremists continued to pressure King Fahd ibn Abdul Aziz to implement stricter Islamic Law in Saudi Arabia. The King warned the extremists of "harsher treatment" if they persisted, and had several dozen militants arrested. During the year, the King introduced a series of limited political reforms, including a Consultative Council, which did little to undermine his near-absolute authority.

King Fahd has ruled this traditional monarchy since 1982. Full power is vested in the King, who as prime minister rules by decree and appoints all other ministers. On 1 March 1992, the King introduced a modest political reform plan. At its core was a new 60-member Consultative Council, which would have the authority to consult with the King, and review laws and government policies. The Council members were to be appointed by the King and serve four-year terms. Another decree provided for the creation of a formal government system for each of Saudi Arabia's fourteen provinces within one year. In addition, the King announced that his successor would be chosen by a system equivalent to an electoral college, composed of royal family princes. The Crown Prince would no longer be automatically entitled to the throne. However, in late March, the King also said the country would never hold free elections, calling western-style democracy unsuited to traditional Arab and Islamic culture in the Gulf. The King hoped that this latter announcement would placate the religious establishment by assuring it predominance in all governmental and legal affairs.

During the year, extremist Muslim groups continued to criticize the government in speeches outside mosques and in clandestinely-distributed audio tapes. The attacks by young, well-educated clerics, known as Ulema, focused on official corruption, opposition to any negotiations with Israel, as well as banks which pay interest (forbidden by the Koran). They also criticized the government for suspending some aspects of Islamic law, such as public executions, during the Gulf War. The government, fearing a rise in fundamentalism, arrested some 50 Muslim clerics in January. However, in a move to appease the extremists, the government reintroduced executions as a punishment. In February, three men were beheaded for armed robbery; and in September a 23-year-old was beheaded for allegedly insulting the Prophet Muhammad and the Koran. In December, seven convicted criminals were publicly beheaded by sword, including a Nigerian, a Filipino, and a Sudanese-born Saudi. In October a large group of Muslim militant clergymen in Saudi Arabia submitted a petition to King Fahd criticizing his internal and external policies, and asking for stricter Islamic rule and more clerical authority to enforce the rule of Islam.

In 1992, territorial disputes continued along Saudi Arabia's ill-defined borders with Yemen and Qatar. In April, the Saudi government warned foreign oil companies operating in Yemen to stay clear of the border region. On 30 September, Saudi troops attacked a Qatari border post, killing two soldiers and taking a third prisoner. However, Saudi officials claimed the incident was merely an inter-Bedouin tribal clash. In an odd shift of policy, the Saudis joined the Middle East peace process, participating in the negotiations started by the 1991 Madrid talks. In addition, in January members of the American Jewish Congress met with Foreign Minister Prince Saud for the first time on Saudi soil. Jewish visitors or anyone with Israeli visas in their passports are rarely permitted entry to the kingdom.

Political Rights and Civil Liberties: Saudi citizens cannot change their government democratically. Full power is vested in the King, political parties are prohibited and there are no organized opposition groups. The modest reforms announced by King Fahd in March 1992, including the introduction of a Consultative Council, only marginally reduce the King's near-absolute rule.

Traditionally, citizens have expressed their opinions through interest groups such as tribes, families and professional hierarchies. The primary forum for expression is the open-door majlises that the King, princes, and all important officials hold regularly and openly. However, since the assassination of King Feisal in 1975, access to the King has been more difficult.

Public demonstrations are prohibited. There is no freedom of association, and non-political clubs and professional groups must receive permission to organize. Freedoms of press and speech are severely limited. Criticism of Islam, the ruling family or the government is not allowed. Television and radio are state-owned and controlled, and there is extensive censorship of all media, press, and cultural expression. All materials with reference to politics, religion, pigs, alcohol, or sexual innuendo are removed. The Ministry of Information must approve all editorial appointments. Foreign publications are available but subject to censorship. Academic freedom is also curtailed, and the government prohibits the study of Marx, Freud, and western philosophy. Movie theaters, public musicals and theatrical performances are prohibited.

Despite the country's efforts to aid approximately 33,000 Iraqi refugees by providing shelter and assisting in relocating them, in April, the American Lawyers' Committee for Human Rights cited "oppressive" conditions and cases of physical abuse at the two Iraqi refugee camps. Dozens have reportedly been forcibly repatriated.

The judicial system is based on *Shari'a* (Islamic Law). Trials are closed and are normally held without legal counsel. Judges, appointed by the King, act in accordance with the will of the royal family. Saudi security forces have unchecked rights and freedoms to arrest and detain both citizens and foreigners, and surveillance is routine. Torture is common and widespread as a means of extracting confessions out of suspected criminals and dissidents.

Women have minimal political and social rights in Saudi Arabia, and are not equal members of society. They may not drive cars, are restricted in using public facilities when men are present, and cannot travel alone without permission. They are restricted to special designated areas in public transportation, and are required to wear the *abaya* (a black garment covering the entire body and face). Furthermore, they are discriminated through the Islamic legal system in matters such as inheritance and divorce. Employment and educational opportunities for women are limited. There are also societal prejudices based on ethnic and national origin. Asian and African foreign workers are subject to various forms of discrimination, and Jordanians, Palestinians and Yemenis suffer from discrimination stemming from the Gulf War.

The Shiite population is also discriminated against in government and industrial employment. Shiites face several limitations on their access to social services and have been subject to surveillance and limitations on travel abroad. They suffer systematic persecution by security forces and have minimal legal rights.

Islam is the official religion, and all citizens must be Muslims. Islamic practice is limited to that sanctioned by the Wahabi sect's interpretations of the Hanbali jurisprudence school of Islam. Any practice contrary to these interpretations, even the use of Shiite call to prayer, is prohibited. The government seldom permits private construction of Shiite mosques, Shiites are not allowed to celebrate their Muslim holidays, and those found practicing are usually arrested and imprisoned. Persons wearing non-Islamic religious symbols in public may be arrested by the *Mutawwai'* (religious police). Non-Muslims cannot own businesses in Saudi Arabia.

All male citizens over the age 18 may usually travel freely within and outside the country; but government officials require the permission of the royal court. Exit visas are occasionally denied as a form of punishment. Shiites believed to have pro-Iranian sympathies may not be allowed to travel abroad. Travel within and outside Saudi Arabia for foreign workers is limited.

Labor unions, collective bargaining, and strikes are prohibited. Foreign workers suffer from systemic abuse. Mostly notably, Asian maids are frequently physically and sexually abused and have little recourse through the government and legal system.

Senegal

Polity: Dominant party (transitional)
Economy: Mixed capitalist
Population: 7,947,000
PPP: $1,208
Life Expectancy: 48.3
Ethnic Groups: Wolof (36 percent), Mende (30 percent), Fulanai (17 percent), Serer (17 percent), other

Political Rights: 4
Civil Liberties: 3
Status: Partly Free

Overview: The West African republic of Senegal, independent from France since 1960, has one of Africa's liveliest (if not always the most competitive) multi-party systems. The broad-based Socialist Party (PS) established by Leopold Senghor, the country's renowned poet and first president, has dominated political life since independence. Senghor led the country until his retirement in 1980, when his prime minister Abdou Diouf succeeded him as president and head of the PS. Elections have consistently given the PS large majorities, but these contests have historically sparked opposition charges of fraud, episodes of unrest, and high voting abstention rates. This was particularly the case in the 1988 elections. There are now sixteen opposition parties, though only the Senegalese Democratic Party (PDS) is represented in the legislature. The next presidential elections are scheduled for February 1993, and parliamentary elections will be held the following May.

Two parties apart from the PS were a part of the government coalition until late October 1992: the liberal PDS and the leftist Independence and Labor Party (PIT). In 1991, the three parties formed the first government in post-independence Senegal to include ministers of parties other than the PS. On 18 October 1992, Abdoulaye Wade of the PDS quit this national unity government; he had served as minister of state for nineteen months. Three other members of his party holding ministerial portfolios left the cabinet with him. Only a single PIT minister remained in the otherwise solidly PS government. In August, Wade had proposed a joint Diouf-Wade ticket for the 1993 presidential race, but withdrew the suggestion after a resounding rejection by the PDS membership. His only alternative was to join six other announced candidates for the 1993 presidential race.

In 1992, the government continued to face a separatist rebellion in the fertile southern Casamance province. The current rebellion began in 1992, when secessionists formed the Casamance Democratic Forces Movement (MFDC) after a Christmas day confrontation with police in which the Senegalese flag was burned. Members of the Diola ethnic group, which forms a majority in the Casamance region, make up most of the movement. Many Diolas resent the dominance in national political life of the northern Wolof elite, who are generally Muslim, and the presence of northern settlers in the Casamance. The government has responded to armed attacks by the MFDC with an often-brutal counter-insurgency campaign. Thousands of citizens from the region, which has a population of approximately 400,000, have fled to neighboring Guinea-Bissau and Gambia in the face of military repression, including torture, extrajudicial execution, beating, and indefinite detention of anyone suspected of having separatist sympathies.

In May 1991, the government signed a ceasefire agreement with the MFDC. But fighting renewed that December, when gunmen killed a legislator and a local leader in the Casamance. The victims were on their way to a political gathering of northern Senegalese two days after the MFDC announced it would forcibly stop any such meetings. In 1992, MFDC attacks targeted northern Senegalese residents in the Casamance. Approximately twenty people were killed in fighting between MFDC secessionists and northern Senegalese in early July 1992. A thousand villagers fled to neighboring Gambia. Violence continued until the end of the year as the MFDC struck at villages attempting to participate in national politics. Rebel spokesmen warned tourists to avoid vacationing in coastal Casamance after assailants killed 40 people in two fishing villages during October and November.

In the past, Senegalese officials accused neighboring Mauritania of supplying logistical support to the rebellion. Senegal and Mauritania have fought sporadic border skirmishes since April 1989, but on 23 April 1992, both countries announced the resumption of full diplomatic ties.

Political Rights and Civil Liberties: Although Senegal has a multi-party system and a vocal political opposition, the ruling Socialist Party has never faced a serious challenge to its hold on power. The opposition has repeatedly charged that elections are not fair. Despite new electoral laws passed in 1989, undemocratic electoral practices persisted, fueling continued charges of fraud. In early 1991, the government announced it intended to draw up a voters' register and provide identity cards to avoid the possibility of repeat voting. In mid 1992, the legislature passed a new electoral code that provided for secret ballots, opposition monitors at voting sites, and other reforms. In 1992, the government also created regional assemblies for each of the country's ten provinces.

The judiciary is considered independent, despite allegations of sensitivity to government pressure. Though public demonstrations require government authorization, freedom of assembly is generally respected. Unionized workers, a small percentage of the work force, are politically important.

The press is diverse and free. However, radio and television are government-controlled. In 1992, the government created a new agency to ensure equal access for all parties to state-owned media. Senegalese have complete freedom of religion; Islamic law does not apply except by consent, and discrimination based on religion does not normally occur. Some Muslim fundamentalists have agitated for an Islamic state, a demand rejected by Senegal's secular leadership.

Seychelles

Polity: Dominant party (transitional)
Economy: Mixed-statist
Population: 71,000
PPP: $3,892
Life Expectancy: 70.0
Ethnic Groups: Mixed African, South Asian, European

Political Rights: 6
Civil Liberties: 4
Status: Partly Free

Overview:

In 1992, Seychelles legalized opposition parties, but in November, voters rejected a new multi-party constitution that catered to the ruling party.

Seychelles is an archipelago of 115 islands situated in the Indian Ocean east of Tanzania. The country gained independence from the British in 1976. Prime Minister France Albert Rene installed himself as head of state after overthrowing elected President Sir James Mancham in 1977. Rene declared his Seychelles People's Progressive Front (SPPF) the only legal party the following year. Only SPPF-approved candidates stood for the 25 seats in 1987 National Assembly elections. Rene was re-elected to a third five-year term as president in 1989, again without facing an opponent.

In December 1991, President Rene promised to legalize opposition parties and invited political exiles to return to the Seychelles to participate in a transition to multi-party democracy. The opposition was quick to take advantage of a 27 December constitutional amendment permitting new parties—the government registered eight parties by April 1992. Former President Mancham, leader of the Democratic Party and Rene's strongest political opponent, returned to Seychelles for a brief visit in April. It was his first time in the country since the 1977 coup.

Rene announced a three-stage democratic transition: election for a constitutional commission, a constitutional referendum, and general elections. Although the DP argued that the 1976 multi-party constitution should be re-instated, the president stated his electoral schedule was non-negotiable. In July, Seychellois voters selected a 22-member commission to draw up a new constitution. It was the first multi-party election in eighteen years; the SPPF officially received 58.4 percent of the vote, and the DP received 33.7 percent. The other six registered parties picked up the remaining votes. The vote left the SPPF with fourteen seats on the constitutional commission and the opposition with eight seats. Although British Commonwealth observers judged the balloting free and fair, the DP accused the SPPF of widespread intimidation and vote-buying. The opposition also pointed out there was significant scope for electoral fraud: while the registration rolls listed about 50,000 voters, a recent census showed only 42,000 voting-age Seychellois.

DP commissioners pushed for a constitutional provision allowing citizens living overseas to vote, but the SPPF majority rejected the proposal. This disenfranchised up to 12,000 Seychellois, the majority of whom were probably Mancham supporters. The commission completed a draft constitution in time for a constitutional referendum in November. Voters surprisingly rejected the commission's proposed multi-party constitution. Rene reconvened the commission after the referendum to prepare another draft, and he postponed general elections until 1993.

Despite opposition charges of economic mismanagement and corruption, there is little poverty on these naturally endowed islands. Per capita income exceeds $2,000 and there is free health care and education. Tourism is a major industry, but the government has sought to preserve the natural beauty of the islands by allowing only 100,000 visitors per annum.

Political Rights and Civil Liberties:

Citizens of the Seychelles cannot change their government democratically. Until 1992, the leftist Seychelles People's Progressive Front was the only legal political party.

A state of emergency proclaimed in 1981 was in effect throughout the 1992 election for a constitutional commission. In addition, the police banned public meetings eleven days before the balloting—a clear violation of an electoral law permitting campaign activity up to three days before the election. Authorities did allow private meetings on private property. The police used tear gas to break up opposition gatherings during the 1992 series of elections. The DP accused the police of beating and temporarily detaining over 100 opposition supporters on 27 July during a "squabble" with SPPF partisans. Civil and criminal cases are generally adjudicated fairly, but regime-appointed judges are still susceptible to manipulation in political cases. The ruling SPPF maintains a system of informers in every village to identify opposition supporters.

In April 1992, the opposition protested President Rene's control of the Seychelles Broadcasting Corporation. The protests arose from fears that the Board would restrict opposition access to state-owned broadcasting during the July election. In the end, the opposition did have significant access. Opposition parties launched newspapers after the December 1991 political opening, and were free to criticize the SPPF regime.

Freedom of religion is respected. There are no restrictions on internal travel, but until recently there were restrictions on citizens traveling abroad. The National Workers' Union is associated with the ruling SPPF. Strikes are permitted by law, but other regulations inhibit workers from exercising that right.

Sierra Leone

Polity: Military
Economy: Capitalist
Population: 4,436,000
PPP: $1,061
Life Expectancy: 42.0
Ethnic Groups: Temme (30 percent), Mende (30 percent), Krio (2 percent), other

Political Rights: 7
Civil Liberties: 6
Status: Not Free

Overview: Sierra Leone's shaky transition toward democracy was aborted when a military coup in late April 1992 sent civilian President Joseph Momoh into exile. He was replaced as head of state by Captain Valentine Strasser.

The democratic transition appeared to get under way when Momoh appointed a review committee in late 1990 to study the 1978 constitution. This much-criticized document enshrined the All People's Congress (APC) as the sole legal political party. The APC came to power in 1967 when it defeated the ruling Sierra Leone People's Party (SLPP) in the general election. The SLPP never won another general election, but despite the APC's own slipping popularity, in 1978 former President Siaka Stevens declared Sierra Leone to be a one-party state. Momoh, Stevens' anointed successor, became president and leader of the APC in 1985.

Until his creation of the constitutional review committee, Momoh made clear his personal opposition to multi-partyism. Nevertheless, a growing public chorus of demands for abandoning the one-party system seemed to force his hand. The demands, made primarily by university students, arose out of growing popular dissatisfaction both with the APC and the deteriorating state of the economy. Momoh's constitutional review committee released its recommendation for a move to multi-partyism in March 1991, and by the following October, an amended constitution allowed new opposition parties to register.

Of the seven parties formed, all but the National Democratic Party were formed around figures associated at some point with APC regime. The Momoh regime agreed to opposition demands that new voters lists be drawn up to replace those alleged to have been fraudulently altered by the APC.

In early 1992, the Momoh government continued struggling to contain an insurgency born out of the civil war in neighboring Liberia. In March 1991, the armed forces of Charles Taylor's National Patriotic Front of Liberia (NPFL) had made an initial incursion into Sierra Leone to flush out guerrillas of the anti-Taylor United Liberation Movement for Democracy (ULIMO). ULIMO was using Sierra Leonean territory as a staging ground for attacks against the NPFL. NPFL attacks into Sierra Leone were temporarily stopped by Momoh's troops with the armed assistance of

Guinea and Nigeria. Controversy grew over whether the defenders of Sierra Leone's territory were solely up against an invasion from Taylor's Liberia, as the Momoh government claimed, or were increasingly dealing with an indigenous force of insurgents. The native Sierra Leone Revolutionary United Front (RUF) declared itself responsible for all attacks on government forces, stating its intent was to overthrow Momoh. Its leader, Foday Sankoh, dismissed the on-going transition to multi-party democracy as mere show.

Meanwhile, Momoh indicated his deadline for holding multi-party elections before the end of 1992 could not be met if the state of war in the country's eastern third continued. The regime also proposed to declare a state of emergency.

As fighting continued in 1992, the Sierra Leonean military grew increasingly frustrated with their civilian government. On 29 April, truckloads of unpaid and hungry troops from the war front entered the capital to protest the lack of logistical support. The troops ended up ousting the Momoh regime. A group of junior officers led by Captain Strasser formed the National Provisional Defense Council—later renamed the Supreme Council of State (SCS)—to rule the country. Despite promises to end official corruption and make a rapid transition to democracy, the junta banned multi-party politics. Some civilian cabinet ministers were appointed in July. In early December, the SCS set up a fifteen-member national advisory committee to "work out the modalities for the return to multi-party democracy."

National sentiment initially appeared to favor the coup. But popular opinion began to shift as the new military regime began to clamp down on civil liberties. The SCS prosecuted the war in the east with renewed effort. By year's end, the government seemed to be getting the upper hand, pushing its opponents close to the Liberian border. However, it is doubtful peace will be achieved in Sierra Leone until a settlement is reached in neighboring Liberia.

An estimated 300,000 Sierra Leoneans are internally displaced due to war, and another 200,000 are reportedly refugees in neighboring countries.

On 29 December, the Strasser regime announced that it had quelled a coup attempt mounted by military supporters of ex-President Momoh. Nine alleged plotters were condemned to death only days after seventeen others reportedly involved in what the government called a "subversive meeting" in November were convicted of treason. Since their sentences were non-appealable, all 26 were executed.

Political Rights and Civil Liberties: Citizens of Sierra Leone are cannot change their government democratically. The military regime has dissolved parliament, banned independent political activity, and suspended all provisions of the 1991 democratic constitution inconsistent with its decrees. The rights of free association, assembly, and expression, which had finally begun to be respected during the last months of the Momoh government, are no longer recognized by the military regime.

The judiciary have been generally free from executive interference, though the Momoh administration often failed to promptly charge political detainees in accord with the law. Local chiefs administer customary law. In 1992, Amnesty International accused all sides in the conflict in eastern Sierra Leone of carrying out gross human rights violations, including the use of torture and extrajudicial execution against noncombatants. Fifty former officials of the Momoh government have been imprisoned. A new special military tribunal was set up in late 1992 to punish treason and other capital crimes. Both civilians and soldiers may be tried, verdicts cannot be appealed, and those convicted can be executed.

The APC regime had revoked the publishing licenses of critical independent newspapers and detained their out-spoken editors. Despite its initial promises to distinguish itself from the prior regime by respecting freedom of expression, the SCS later issued Decree Number 6 "to keep the press in line." The measure provides for fine and imprisonment for those who publish or possess material that threatens "public tranquillity." There are some restrictions on domestic travel, but foreign travel is generally permitted. Freedom of religion is respected. Trade unionism is an integral part of society, and workers have customarily had the right to strike. Strikes for higher wages continued in 1992 after the military coup. Most unions belong to the Sierra Leone Labor Congress.

Singapore

Polity: Dominant party
Economy: Mixed capitalist
Population: 2,765,000
PPP: $15,108
Life Expectancy: 74.0
Ethnic Groups: Ethnic Chinese (76 percent), Malay (15 percent), Pakistani and Indian (7 percent)

Political Rights: 4
Civil Liberties: 5
Status: Partly Free

Overview:

In 1992, Prime Minister Goh Chok Tong, who had been considered a transitional figure when he replaced Lee Kuan Yew in 1990, strengthened his position by winning a special by-election and taking over as secretary general of Singapore's ruling People's Action Party (PAP). The moves came after the government announced that Lee's son, who had been groomed to inherit the leadership of the country, is being treated for cancer and will be out of politics indefinitely.

Originally established as a trading station, Singapore became a British colony in 1867. The country became self-governing in 1959, and after two years in the Malaysian Federation became fully independent in 1965. Since then the conservative People's Action Party (PAP) has dominated politics and social affairs, spreading its Confucian-based values and policies through the media, public advertising campaigns, labor associations, local organizations and the military, even though political activities within such non-political entities are illegal. The party completely swept elections from 1968 to 1980 before losing a by-election in 1981. Under Prime Minister Lee's paternalistic, authoritarian rule, the PAP transformed the squalid island into a miniature economic power.

In October 1990, Lee stepped down after 31 years as the country's first and only premier. His handpicked successor, Goh Tok Chong, called a snap election for 31

August 1991 to get a popular mandate for his somewhat more liberal leadership. Though the opposition only contested 40 of the 81 seats, the PAP had its worse showing ever, winning 77 seats with 61 percent of the overall vote. The Singapore Democratic Party took three seats, and the center-left Worker's Party one. After the election, Goh admitted that the government had become too elitist, and had neglected the economic needs of the working-class Chinese voters who form its traditional base. Many citizens complained that the government has not used enough of their mandatory contributions to the Central Provident Fund for social programs.

The opposition may have won more seats if not for changes to the electoral law prior to the vote. The government increased the number of Group Representation Constituencies (GRC) from thirteen to fifteen, and increased the number of seats in each from three to four. Opposition groups have trouble contesting GRC's because they must come up with four credible candidates, one of whom must be non-Chinese, for each one. The government may eventually turn the remaining 21 seats into GRC's.

The timing of the elections prevented the country's most outspoken opposition figure from running. Workers' Party secretary-general J.B. Jayaretnam had been banned from parliament until November 1991 following his controversial conviction in a 1986 court case involving irregularities in collecting party funds. Goh has denied claims that the government held the election when it did to prevent Jayaretnam from running.

In November 1992, the government announced that two of the country's senior politicians, deputy prime ministers Ong Teng Cheong and second prime minister Lee Hsien Loong, the son of Lee Kuan Yew, are suffering from cancer. Both are expected to recover, but the announcement raised anxiety because Lee is widely expected to be the next prime minister, and the PAP has no other obvious successor. Prime Minister Goh clearly had the most to gain from the news. On 3 December, the PAP unexpectedly named Goh as its secretary-general on the advice of the elder Lee, who had held the post for 38 years and still calls the shots in the party. On 19 December, Goh further strengthened his authority after he and three other candidates won a special by-election in a GRC. Goh had resigned from his seat to personally contest this by-election, which he called in order to give voters a fresh chance to renew his mandate.

The younger Lee had also been considered a possible candidate for the January 1993 election for a new, expanded presidency. The next president will be able to veto parliamentary decisions regarding the country's financial reserves and key civil service and judiciary appointments. A three-member panel, including two members of the government, will screen potential candidates, who can be rejected for having poor character. Opposition leaders, some of whom have been arrested in the past, fear this will be used to bar them from running.

Political Rights and Civil Liberties: Citizens of Singapore nominally have the right to change their government through free elections, although the ruling People's Action Party (PAP) maintains its virtual political monopoly through various means.

Opposition figures have frequently been held under the Internal Security Act (ISA), which allows the president to detain suspects considered to be a threat to national security for an unlimited number of two-year periods. Judicial review is limited to procedural matters, and trials under the ISA do not have to be public.

Many former detainees continue to face restrictions on residence, travel, and the right to make public statements or publish. In August, the government admitted that some 1,000 suspected drug traffickers and gangsters are being held without trial.

The independence of the judiciary is questionable. Lower court judges are appointed by and serve at the discretion of the president, while higher court judges are considered to be closely aligned with the government.

Public meetings of six or more people require a police permit, and the Societies Act requires organizations of more than 10 people to register with the government. Registration has been denied on broad grounds to a variety of groups. Freedom of expression is heavily restricted. Public statements that could incite ethnic or religious antagonism, or disrupt public order or security, are illegal. These restrictions are frequently used directly or as threats against opposition politicians. In November 1991, Worker's Party candidate Gopalan Nair was fined $4,800 for having questioned the independence of the judiciary during the August election campaign. Academics have been refused tenure because of their views.

The government tightly controls the written press. Key "management shares" in the Singapore Press Holdings, which publishes all the major newspapers, must be held by government-approved people. The Official Secrets Act bars the unauthorized release to the media of official information. In August 1992, investigators searched the offices of the *Business Times* and questioned journalists after suspecting that the 29 June issue had published leaked economic data.

The foreign press has been hampered by a 1986 amendment to the Newspapers and Printing Presses Act allowing the government to restrict circulation of any foreign newspaper it feels interfered with domestic politics. The government limited the distribution of the *Asian Wall Street Journal* to 400 per day in February 1987, and suspended all sales in October 1990. Since then, the Journal's allotment has been incrementally increased, most recently to 3,500 in July 1992. Distribution of the *Far Eastern Economic Review (FEER)*, and to a lesser extent *Asiaweek*, is also limited. In addition, *FEER* is prohibited from having a correspondent in the country, and the *Journal* can only post a correspondent in the country 7 days per month. The government also owns all three television channels and all but one of the ten radio stations. Editorials and domestic news coverage strongly favor the government.

Freedom of religion is generally respected in practice, although the Jehovah's Witnesses and the Unification Church are banned. Citizens must carry identification cards, and can be prevented from traveling internally and abroad. Approximately 98 percent of unionized workers belong to unions affiliated with the pro-government National Trades Union Conference. Workers have the right to strike but rarely do so, in part because labor shortages give them increased leverage.

Slovenia

Polity: Presidential-par-
liamentary democracy
Economy: Mixed-statist
(transitional)
Population: 1,925,000
PPP: na
Life Expectancy: 71.0
Ethnic Groups: Predominantly Slovenian

Political Rights: 2
Civil Liberties: 2
Status: Free

Overview: Bordering Austria and Italy, this former constituent republic
of Yugoslavia declared independence in June 1991, and its
well-armed defense forces secured the nation's borders by
staving off subsequent intervention by the Yugoslav People's Army (YPA).

Ethnically homogeneous and without significant minority groups, Slovenia, which
for centuries was part of the Hapsburg empire before being incorporated into the
newly created Yugoslavia after World War I, managed to avoid being dragged into
the protracted inter-ethnic war launched in Croatia and Bosnia by indigenous Serbian
irregulars supported by Serbia. It was formally recognized by the European Community (EC) in January 1992, and later by the United States.

The major political issue in 1992 was the 6 December national election. Milan
Kucan, the popular leader of the (former Communist) Party for Democratic Renewal
(LCS-PDR) was re-elected president with 63 percent of the vote. The centrist Liberal
Democratic Party (LDS) led the vote for a new 130-seat bicameral parliament, with
23 percent. The new body replaced the cumbersome tricameral Assembly consisting
of the Socio-Political Chamber, the Chamber of Municipalities, and the Chamber of
Associated Labor. The Christian Democrats got 14.9 percent in the new parliament,
and the Untied Left, which included the former Communists, trailed with 13.26
percent. Incumbent Prime Minister Janez Drnovesk said a coalition government would
be organized by 1993.

Slovenia's independence drive began in earnest in 1989 when the most prosperous
of Yugoslavia's six republics took steps toward greater economic reform,
democratization and political autonomy. With the approval of Kucan, the reform-
minded leader of Slovenia's Communist Party, the tricameral Assembly (parliament)
overwhelmingly approved a set of constitutional amendments that strengthened its right
to secede from the federation. In April 1990 elections, the first multi-party vote since
1938, the opposition six-party coalition, DEMOS, won an absolute majority. DEMOS,
composed of the Liberal Democrats, Social Democrats, Christian Democrats, the
Farmers' Alliance, the Greens and the Slovene Tradesmen's Party, campaigned for
independence within a year, and won 55 percent of the Assembly seats, but failed to
get a majority in the Chamber of Associated Labor. The former Communists, the
Party for Democratic Renewal (LCS-PDR), came in second with 17.3 percent, and
Kucan, the popular LCS-PDR presidential candidate, won in a runoff.

As Yugoslavia's political crisis intensified in 1991, Slovenia and Croatia declared
independence on 25 June following respective republic-wide referenda. Within days,

YPA tanks were sent to Slovenia. As defense forces beat back the YPA, Yugoslavia's collective presidency ordered units to withdraw by 18 July. The withdrawal was part of the EC-brokered Brioni accord, which called for Slovenia to impose a three-month moratorium on the implementation of its independence.

In 1992, Slovenia faced the difficult challenge of consolidating independence, strengthening government institutions and dealing with a sagging economy. The task was made difficult by a cumbersome legislative system, a lack of coordination among 27 government ministries, and friction within DEMOS.

As the year began, economic reform bills were bottle-necked in the Assembly, whose structure made pushing draft legislation politically difficult and time-consuming. Most acts required a two-thirds majority vote from among all three chambers. The government's property and ownership laws, which required a simple majority vote, included 240 amendments, and the amendments had to be voted upon in each of the three chambers.

Internal rivalries splintered the DEMOS coalition. In February, a group of independent deputies called for a vote of no-confidence against the incumbent government of Prime Minister Lozje Peterle, head of the Christian Democratic Party, the largest party in DEMOS. The prime minister was accused of footdragging on economic reform and had lost several ministers because of disagreement over economic policies. The attempt to bring down the government failed, but the government was polarized between the Christian Democrats and the Farmers' Alliance on one side, and the liberals grouped around the Democratic and Liberal Democratic parties on the other side.

On 22 March, legislators did oust Prime Minister Peterle's government and chose 42-year-old Janez Drnovsek, a former head of the collective, eight-member Yugoslav presidency and a member of the Liberal Democrats, to head the government. Some 126 of 240 legislators supported the no-confidence vote. Several days later, the new prime minister promised presidential and parliamentary elections by year's end.

In July, hopes for an autumn election were dashed when an election law for parliament failed to gain the two-thirds majority in each chamber. Much of the opposition came from right-wing deputies who opposed the post-independence regime because of the large-scale participation of former Communists in the government. As parliament continued to block legislation, the government began issuing decrees.

Political stagnation also slowed economic reforms and the institutionalization of certain fundamental civil liberties. With independence, Slovenia lost its market share in the former Yugoslav republics, which previously accounted for more than 30 percent of exports and imports. Industrial production, compared to 1991, fell 4 percent to 15 percent, and unemployment rose to 12 percent of Slovenia's 750,000-member workforce. Nearly 45 percent of Slovenian workers were employed in money-losing companies. Gross Domestic Product (GDP) fell 30 percent. In May, a general strike and political infighting scuttled several early privatization plans.

In late July, the government presented a comprehensive plan titled "Restructuring and Privatization of the Slovene Economy." The proposal contained five closely interconnected plans: the restructuring of banks and the restructuring and privatization of enterprises; financial rehabilitation and privatization; revitalization of the public sector; social programs; and Slovenia's inclusion in European integration. However, the Assembly continued to drag its feet on implementation.

In other issues, the government kept a wary eye on the escalating war in Bosnia-Herzegovina, signing mutual security agreements with Hungary and other countries. In June, the government announced that over 70,000 refugees from Bosnia had entered Slovenia. About 45,000 had found refuge with relatives or friends, and the remainder were located in 59 refugee camps set up in former YPA barracks. In mid-August, citing financial considerations and difficulties in providing food and accommodation, the government announced a formal ban on refugees from Bosnia who did not have immediate family in Slovenia.

Political Rights and Civil Liberties: Slovenes have the right to change their government democratically. The judiciary is being restructured to conform to democratic principles. Freedom of speech is respected. There are several independent newspapers, but media freedom is compromised by the state-run radio and television system. With a bloated administrative staff of 2,500, it is run by the old Communist bureaucracy which only allows broadcasts reflecting government views. The only competition to state television is a small, undercapitalized station, Kanal A, in Ljubljana, the capital. Most major dailies are beholden in one way or another to parliamentary or political party pressures.

Freedom of assembly and association are guaranteed and respected in practice. Freedom of religion is respected; the Roman Catholic Church is the predominant denomination. There are no significant restrictions on domestic and international travel. Independent trade unions have been established.

Solomon Islands

Polity: Parliamentary democracy
Economy: Capitalist
Population: 360,000
PPP: $2,626
Life Expectancy: 69.5
Ethnic Groups: Melanesian (93 percent), small Polynesian, Micronesian and European minorities

Political Rights: 1
Civil Liberties: 1
Status: Free

Overview: A collection of ten large islands and four groups of smaller islands in the Western Pacific Ocean, the Solomon Islands has been an independent member of the British Commonwealth since 1978. The 38-seat unicameral parliament is elected by universal suffrage for a term of up to four years. Executive power is held by the prime minister, who is elected by parliament and appoints a cabinet. Solomon Mamaloni has been prime minister since March 1989, a month after his People's Alliance Party (PAP) won an 11-seat plurality to form the country's first one-party government. Other parties taking seats were the Nationalist Front for Progress, with 5; the Liberal Party, 4; the United Party, 3; and the Labor Party, 2, along with 13 independents. Mamaloni resigned from the PAP in October 1990 after opposition leader Andrew Nori, along with several PAP members, accused him of ruling in a non-consultative fashion; but Mamaloni remained prime minister to form a "national unity" government. His new cabinet featured four opposition members and a PAP backbencher. In November 1991, Joses Tuhanuku took over as leader of the 16-member opposition, which includes seven former PAP members who are now independents.

The key issue in 1992 was a pair of cross-border raids by Papau New Guinea (PNG) security forces as part of their operations against rebels on PNG's Bougainville Island. In March, troops attacked a fuel depot allegedly used to supply the rebels, and on 12 September, two Solomon citizens were killed and a 3-year-old was wounded after a raid that the PNG claims was to pursue two "hard-core" rebel members. The Solomons demanded compensation, and said it would consider recognizing the rebel army and the government it has declared on Bougainville. Many people in the country feel the Bougainvilleans are culturally and geographically Solomon Islanders.

Political Rights and Civil Liberties: Citizens of the Solomon Islands can change their government democratically. Party affiliations tend to be based on personal loyalties rather than ideology. In August 1991 Prime Minister Solomon Mamaloni called for the country to leave the British Commonwealth and draw up a new constitution, calling the old one "lousy and inadequate." The judiciary is independent of the government and provides procedural protection for the accused. Freedoms of speech and press are respected in practice. The country has two private weekly newspapers and several government publications. State radio provides diverse viewpoints. The country does not have television broadcast facilities, and the government controls the use of satellite dishes because it feels that outside programming containing sex and violence could have a negative effect on the population. Permits are required for demonstrations but they have never been denied on political grounds. Christianity is the established religion, but there are no restrictions on other groups. Citizens may travel freely inside the country or abroad. The Trade Disputes Act of 1981 provides for collective bargaining, but only private sector workers can strike. However, public school teachers did successfully strike in 1989.

Somalia

Polity: Rival warlords (partly foreign-occupied)   **Political Rights:** 7
Civil Liberties: 7
Economy: Mixed-statist   **Status:** Not Free
Population: 8,325,000
PPP: $861
Life Expectancy: 46.1
Ethnic Groups: Somali (Hawiye, Darod, Isaaq, Isa, other), Gosha, Bajun

Overview: Fighting between rival clan leaders plunged Somalia into a state of chaos and created the deadliest human-rights crisis in the world. Civil war, drought and famine claimed over 300,000 Somali lives in 1992, including more than 25 percent of Somali children under the age of five. The United Nations responded to the disaster slowly, reluctant to intervene without assurances of safety for those distributing food aid. In December, the United States sent 28,000 troops to Somalia to protect famine relief efforts.

Major General Siad Barre seized power from an unpopular elected government in a bloodless coup nine years after Somalia won independence in 1960. Over the years, his rule devolved into a repressive and dynastic form of crypto-Marxism that strongly favored his own minority sub-clan, alienating majority clans and fueling several clan-based insurgencies. In January 1991, Siad Barre and remnants of the regime were dislodged from the capital of Mogadishu by the insurgent United Somali Congress (USC) of the Hawiye clan, one of six clans all Somalis trace their lineage through. Various ethnic Somali clans and sub-clans struggled to expand their enclaves by force during the rest of 1991 and into 1992. In May 1991, the Somali National Movement, made up of insurgents from the Isaaq clan, unilaterally declared an independent "Republic of Somaliland" in northwestern Somalia.

Within a few days of Siad Barre's flight from Mogadishu, one USC faction appointed Ali Mahdi Mohamed, a Hawiye businessman and former member of parliament, as "interim" president of Somalia. In July 1991, Ali Mahdi was confirmed as transitional president for two years at a conference attended by all Somali insurgent movements but the SMN. At the same time, General Mohamed Farah Aidid, whose USC troops had ousted Siad Barre from Mogadishu, was elected chairman of his movement.

Both Ali Mahdi and Aidid claimed to be the rightful leader of Somalia and asserted they represent "democracy." Ali Mahdi, from the Abgal sub-clan of the Hawiye, and Aidid, from the Habar Gedir sub-clan, capitalize on sub-clan loyalty to inveigle unemployed young men to join their militias. Offered weapons, some food, and the narcotic *kat*, the undisciplined fighters were encouraged to steal more food and other loot from Somali civilians and relief workers. Their weapons came from the enormous Soviet and American-supplied stockpile left behind by the fleeing Siad Barre.

On 17 November 1991, rival armed factions aligned with Ali Mahdi and Aidid began a protracted and bloody struggle in the capital. Because each man was from a separate sub-clan of the Hawiye, most observers saw the fighting as the latest manifestation of long-traditional feuds. Gunfire ripped through Mogadishu as forces of the two men occupied different portions of the city. Mortars devastated civilian dwellings while snipers indiscriminately killed noncombatants. The level of violence was so high by year's end that most U.N. agencies charged with relief services finally refused to jeopardize the lives of their personnel to provide emergency food or medical assistance.

The conflict between Aidid and Ali Mahdi drastically cut the inflow of emergency relief into Mogadishu. Though the U.N. Security Council called for the Secretary General to draw up a plan for massive assistance to Somalia in late January 1992, the council president said the aid was contingent upon the end of fighting in the capital. Relief groups argued that food could be distributed without a ceasefire only if the international community was prepared to inundate the country with food, giving it to combatants and noncombatants alike. Conflict over scarce food would dwindle only if food scarcity was eliminated.

In early January, U.N. Under Secretary-General James O.C. Jonah flew into Mogadishu to see if a truce could be arranged between Ali Mahdi and Aidid. Jonah said on his return to Nairobi that Aidid had rejected U.N. efforts, a statement that prejudiced the general against future U.N. peacemaking attempts for months afterward. Soon after Jonah's visit, the Security Council adopted a resolution imposing an arms embargo on

Somalia. Aidid publicly responded on 26 January that he would agree to a U.N.-mediated ceasefire, but demanded that any transitional government to follow exclude Ali Mahdi and his partisans. The general added that outside intervention in the form of an international peacekeeping force was unnecessary and unwanted, because it would only act to bolster Ali Mahdi's claims to be president. Welcoming that very prospect, Ali Mahdi reacted to Jonah's announcement that Aidid was an obstacle to peace by encouraging the deployment of a U.N. force—a position he maintained throughout 1992.

On 14 February, representatives of the two USC factions agreed in New York to an immediate ceasefire in Mogadishu and environs. Aidid took advantage of the impending ceasefire announcement by mediator Jonah to launch an attack on Ali Mahdi's section of Mogadishu. The interim president's forces repelled the offensive. When Jonah traveled to Somalia in early March to obtain Aidid and Ali Mahdi's own signatures on the ceasefire agreement, the conflict was still raging. By then, more than 40,000 people were estimated killed and wounded since the two warlords had begun battling in November. The ceasefire finally took effect by the end of March; mortars and other heavy-artillery bombardments ceased in the airport and port areas. However, automatic arms fire continued until the end of the year.

In April, the forces of Mohamed Siad Hersi, the son-in-law of Siad Barre, pushed within 40 miles of the capital before being driven back by a temporarily united USC. Siad Barre himself was finally chased out of his Marehan clan refuge near the Kenyan border, seeking safety in Nairobi. Aidid's forces then went on to expand their control through much of southern Somalia. The forces of Siad Hersi again went on the offensive in mid-October, seizing the key southern town of Bardera from General Aidid and disrupting relief efforts there.

Food relief began to be received in Mogadishu again in early May, but most of it was taken by looters and militia members. Armed Somali guards hired by the international organization often helped hijackers divert truckloads of food being driven to feeding stations. The food was taken to warehouses owned by powerful Hawiye merchants, and Mogadishu shopkeepers were soon offering the donated food for sale. Food not stolen was made available for free at food distribution centers in the capital. In the Somalian interior, other distribution centers attracted the famine-stricken from the countryside. Some made it into town only to die, others died on the way. Many were farmers whose livestock and crops had been looted by armed militiamen.

On 24 April, the Security Council voted to send 50 military observers to Mogadishu to monitor the truce. But the Council temporarily suspended an expanded plan to send a battalion of 500 armed U.N. troops to protect relief workers and aid convoys when the United States signaled its disapproval. Fearing it would be assessed for a costly peacekeeping plan, the U.S. sought the commitment of oil-producing Arab countries to foot the bill. The Security Council finally approved the use of force at mid-year after televised images of starving Somalia's prompted a world-wide outcry in favor of a sizable relief effort for Somalia.

Although Aidid finally agreed to the 500-man battalion of peacekeeping troops in mid-August, he balked when the Council approved an additional 3,000 troops on 28 August. He threatened to shell the battalion on its arrival in the capital. Six of the 50 military observers arrived in Mogadishu on 5 July, but for a few weeks Aidid refused to allow the rest to land in Mogadishu. Other warlords warned they would attack any international troops entering into their territory without their authorization. Five hundred Pakistani peacekeeping troops entered the capital in October and sat in their camp at the airport. By late October, Secretary General Boutros Ghali's special envoy for Somalia was harshly criticizing the U.N. for its inability either to deploy its troops or deliver substantial food aid to famine victims without permission from warlords. The envoy, Mohammed Sahnoun, was forced to resign.

The U.S. announced a humanitarian airlift of food on 17 August. By the time "Project Relief" began ferrying assistance to Somalia from its base in neighboring Kenya, Washington had agreed with the Red Cross not to insist the relief be accompanied by armed American troops. That relief agency and others tried to arrange transportation and protection within Somalia from clan elders in exchange for food. But up to one-third of all relief convoys were still being attacked and looted.

In late November, the Bush administration proposed the use of U.S. troops under the U.N. flag to protect food distribution. When the U.N. voted on 3 December to accept the American precondition that the U.S. maintain control over the mission, the way was open for rapid deployment. The U.S. insisted its primary job was to deliver food, but the U.N. secretary-general insisted the troops needed to disarm Somali combatants. On 9 December, American soldiers began arriving in Somalia.

Political Rights and Civil Liberties: Somalians cannot democratically choose their government at any level. Ali Mahdi of the United Somali Congress (USC) was confirmed as the country's "president" by the leaders of Somalia's principal armed movements soon after his faction of the USC seized control of Mogadishu in early 1991. Ali Mahdi's government now only has effective control over the northern part of the capital and its environs. The rest of the country is dominated by unelected warlords who battle each other to expand territory. There is no elected legislature.

Since fighting first broke out in 1988, hundreds of thousands of civilians and combatants have either been extrajudicially killed or have starved to death. Militiamen have indiscriminately murdered their rivals, unarmed civilians and relief workers. Villages of agrarian Somalis and non-Somali ethnic Bajun and Gosha have been subjected to raids by Somali pastoralists from other clans; and food and animals have been confiscated and the villagers left to starve. The famine and fighting have forced thousands of to seek sanctuary elsewhere within Somalia or in neighboring Kenya, Ethiopia. Djibouti, or Yemen.

Most Somalis are Muslims. Punishments based on Somali customary law and a rough concept of Muslim penalties is summarily applied by mobs to those who violate social norms. For example, in December a Somali women narrowly escaped being stoned to death by a crowd convinced that she had sexually consorted with French soldiers. Women traditionally suffer clitorectomy at birth and gender-based discrimination throughout their lives.

Some warlords control broadcasting facilities, and all direct the media in areas they control. The various armed movements do not tolerate dissent within their respective territories; freedom of assembly, association, and speech are not permitted.

Commerce in many areas has devolved to the buying and selling of stolen relief food and looted property. Official corruption is commonplace; local authorities usually facilitate the traffic in stolen goods. Since industry has broken down in most urban centers, organized labor barely operates.

South Africa

Polity: Transitional   **Political Rights:** 5
Economy: Capitalist-statist   **Civil Liberties:** 4
Population: 41,688,000   **Status:** Partly Free
PPP: $4,958
Life Expectancy: 61.7
Ethnic Groups: Black (Zulu, Xhosa, Swazi, Sotho, other;
69 percent), white (Afrikaner, English; 18 percent),
Coloured (10 percent), Indian (3 percent)

Overview: Multilateral negotiations between the white minority government of President F.W. de Klerk and 18 opposition parties at the Convention for a Democratic South Africa (Codesa II) broke down in May 1992 over minority veto power and the percentages required to adopt a new constitution. However, by year's end, there were prospects for a power-sharing agreement in 1993 between the government and the African National Congress (ANC) led by Nelson Mandela. The government also took steps to bring the black nationalist Pan Africanist Congress (PAC), the pro-apartheid Conservative Party (CP) and the black consciousness Azanian People's Organization (Azapo) into a restructured Codesa process.

The Union of South Africa became an independent republic outside the British Commonwealth in 1961 and has been ruled by the Nationalist Party (NP) since 1948. Despite the dismantling of all apartheid laws requiring the separate development of the races, South Africa remains a *de facto* segregated society. A third of the black majority, and most mixed-race Coloureds and Indians, live in racially segregated areas in and near large cities, although certain suburbs and many private schools are absorbing large numbers of middle-class blacks. An additional 10 million blacks live in ten tribal homelands.

The government's stated policy of negotiating power-sharing with the black majority continued throughout 1992 despite several serious setbacks. In December 1991, the opening round of Codesa had ended on a hopeful note. The convention approved a Declaration of Intent and agreed to draw up the outlines of a new constitution and a time frame for a peaceful transition.

However, in February 1992, the government experienced a potential political setback when it lost a parliamentary seat to the CP in a hotly-contested mid-term election. De Klerk immediately announced an extraordinary referendum for whites only to establish whether he had a mandate to negotiate further reforms. The NP, the progressive Democratic Party and the business sector campaigned for a "yes" vote, while the CP and the Afrikaner Resistance Movement (AWB) urged a "no." The "yes" forces presented the electorate with the stark choice of economic decline and black insurrection or growing abundance and national accord. Eighty-five percent of the white electorate turned out on 17 March, and 69 percent endorsed further negotiations. In October, the NP-controlled parliament did away with mid-term elections as a way to prevent the CP from increasing its parliamentary representation.

On 15 May, Codesa II deadlocked when the government demanded that a three-fourths majority of a proposed regionally elected upper house be required to adopt and amend certain elements of the proposed new constitution. The ANC rejected the demand, estimating at most it could only gain a 70 percent legislative majority. Frustrated by the government's seeming intransigence, the ANC Alliance—which included the ANC, Cosatu (Congress of South African Trade Unions), and the South African Communist Party (SACP)—threatened to institute a mass action campaign to force the government's hand.

The threat—called "the Leipzig Option" and based on the populist-led downfall of the East German government in 1989—was overtaken by a massacre on 17 June, when Zulu workers from the KwaMadala hostel struck Boipatong township near Johannesburg, killing 45 people. The ANC responded to the massacre by calling for U.N. involvement and withdrawing from both bilateral talks with the government and Codesa. In late July, U.N. Secretary General Boutros Boutros-Ghali appointed Cyrus Vance as his special representative to South Africa with the task of making recommendations on stopping the violence and resuming multi-party talks.

In early July, De Klerk and Mandela publicly exchanged memoranda reiterating their political bottom lines: a federation of strong regional and local governments (NP) versus a unitary state with a strong central government (ANC). Mass action rallies and marches, which began in late July and continued through August, were capped by a general strike on 3 August and a Mandela-led march on parliament.

On 7 September, a government-scheduled pro-federation summit was attended by representatives of the NP, the CP, and the Inkatha Freedom Party (IFP), led by KwaZulu Chief Minister Mangosuthu Gatsha Buthelezi. The meeting was also attended by homeland leaders President Joshua "Oupa" Gqoco of Ciskei and President Louis Mangope of Bophuthatswana (BOP). Also on 7 September, the SACP/ANC led a march on Bisho, the capital of Ciskei, which ended in the death of 29 demonstrators when the Ciskei Defence Force opened fire. The march on Bisho was a warning that the government's intended alliance with black homeland leaders was not acceptable to the ANC/SACP.

Bilateral negotiations between the government and ANC got back on track at a 26 September summit between de Klerk and Mandela. The two leaders signed a Record of Understanding (ROU), which stated: an elected constituent assembly (CA) would draft and adopt a new constitution; a transition executive council would be appointed alongside the CA; the existing Tricameral parliament would be dissolved; a government of national unity would be elected following the adoption of a new constitution.

On 27 September, Buthelezi rejected the ROU and announced the IFP's withdrawal from Codesa. In October, he met with the leaders of the CP, the conservative Afrikaner People's Union (AVU)—a CP splinter group—the Ciskei and BOP. The meeting ended in the formation of a new group, the Concerned South Africans Group (Cosag), which strongly rejected the ROU and Codesa.

In a special session of parliament mid-October, de Klerk for the first time used the NP-controlled President's Council to push through a Further Amnesty Bill. The bill had been opposed by all parties, including elements in the NP, because it would allow perpetrators of violence to admit their guilt without public censure. Another measure, a Constitution Amendment Bill, allowed de Klerk to appoint blacks to his Cabinet.

On 18 November, the ANC published a document—"Negotiations: A Strategic Perspective"—that stated its reluctant willingness to share power with the government and other parties after the adoption of a new constitution. On 26 November, de Klerk announced the government's transition timetable: multilateral talks could resume in February or March; a transition executive council could be appointed in June; elections for a constituent assembly could be held in April 1994. The ANC had called for elections in late 1993.

On 28 November, the Azanian People's Liberation Army (APLA), the military wing of the PAC, claimed responsibility for a black-on-white attack in King Williamstown and another attack on December 4 in Queenstown. While PAC officials denied any advance knowledge of the attacks and refused to condemn them, statements by APLA members indicated they had been carried out for two major reasons: to prevent the pro-negotiations faction in the PAC from entering the Codesa process and to caution the government and ANC against concluding a "secret" power-sharing deal. With the exception of Azapo, all black groups strongly condemned the attacks. The white right called for the government's resignation and promised white-on-black attacks, and the government announced it would conduct "hot pursuits" into the Transkei should more attacks occur.

On 1 December—the eve of a "secret" *bosberaad* (bush council) between the government and the ANC—Buthelezi announced a constitution that would join KwaZulu and Natal into an autonomous region with its own tax base and the authority to override the central government. On the same day, Ciskei's President Gqoco called for a Kei region, incorporating large areas of the Cape Province but excluding the Transkei.

Another major issue in 1992 was black-on-black violence, which worsened in 1992, particularly between the supporters of the IFP and ANC. Pitched battles and political assassinations ripped through urban townships and rural settlements, with revenge attacks by both sides fueling the increasingly brutal cycle. The power struggle between the ANC and IFP continued to be centered mainly in Natal, KwaZulu and the Vaal Triangle south of Johannesburg. Three potential new trends emerged: the formation of combatant Self-Defence Units (SDUs) in townships; disillusioned members of the ANC's military wing, Umkhonto We Sizwe (MK), were reported to assume dominance of some SDUs, to become informants to the South African Defence Force (SADF), to join IFP ranks or to turn to crime; the ANC claimed that Renamo mercenaries from Mozambique were fighting alongside IFP forces. There were also unconfirmed reports that President Bantu Holomisa of the Transkei had provided weapons to MK and APLA.

Since the IFP-ANC fighting began in 1984, the ANC has alleged that the South African police and security forces instigate and abet IFP forces. Despite government denials, evidence of a "Third Force" continues to accumulate. In April, a white policeman and four black constables were convicted of killing 11 blacks at a funeral in 1988. In May, the pro-ANC Johannesburg newspaper *New Nation* published an alleged electronic order authorizing the 1985 murders of three ANC activists. The order purportedly was given by the head of the Eastern Cape Command. In November, intelligence files seized by the government-appointed Goldstone Commission revealed two planned anti-ANC "smear" campaigns. On December 19, de Klerk admitted for the first time that elements of the SADF and Directorate of Military Intelligence (DMI) had been involved in anti-ANC activities.

While the government declined to move strongly against its own security forces or the IFP, Pretoria did take action against extremist groups from the far left (black) and the far right (white). Members of the neo-Nazi AWB and other armed white-separatist groups were detained for a succession of bombings, and activists from Azapo and the PAC were arrested following attacks on people and buildings.

Political Rights and Civil Liberties: Only white South Africans have the power to democratically change the government. Blacks do not yet have the vote, but the government continued negotiations with the representatives of most black parties to reach a power-sharing agreement. The Coloured and Indian communities are represented in the Tricameral parliament.

The judiciary is independent of the executive. Civil and criminal cases are generally handled. In 1992, Amnesty International charged that the South African police and security forces continue to carry out extrajudicial execution and torture either as agents of the government or without its consent. In October, an ANC-appointed committee published a report acknowledging the movement's history of torturing political prisoners in exile bases in Angola, Tanzania, Uganda and Zimbabwe. Amnesty International followed the ANC's report with a detailed account of ANC human rights abuses.

An estimated 25,000 political exiles have returned or will be allowed back under a bilateral amnesty agreement between the government and the ANC. In September, the government agreed to release all remaining ANC political prisoners by mid-November. And, in October, President de Klerk sought to push through a Further Amnesty Bill for all perpetrators of political violence after they had come forward and admitted their violations of the law. The measure was approved by the NP-controlled President's Council, which suggested that confessions be public rather than private. The bill will be re-introduced in the next parliamentary session in 1993 and would apply to all political parties as well as the security forces and the police.

Direct censorship has ended, but regulations giving police powers to bar reporters from covering street clashes continue. In May, the police sought an injunction barring the *Vrye Weekblad* and *Weekly Mail* from reporting allegations concerning police instigation of township and rural black-on-black violence. Journalists also face intimidation and life-threatening violence from militants of the PAC, Azapo, IFP, ANC and white supremacist groups.

Legalized in 1979, black trade unions play an increasingly important role in political, economic and social life. The two main black labor federations are the pro-ANC Congress of South African Trade Unions (Cosatu) and the National Council of Trade Unions (Nactu).

Spain

Polity: Parliamentary
democracy
Economy: Capitalist
Population: 38,554,000
PPP: $8,723
Life Expectancy: 77.0
Ethnic Groups: Various regional cultures (Castilians, Basques, Catalans, Galicians, Valencians, Andalusians), Gypsies, and various immigrant groups, notably North Africans and Latin Americans

Political Rights: 1
Civil Liberties: 1
Status: Free

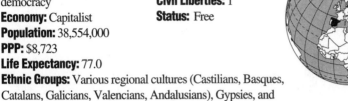

Overview: In 1992, the Socialist government of Prime Minister Felipe Gonzalez faced high unemployment, labor strife, financial scandals, and separatist pressures. The country's mounting troubles raised questions about Gonzalez's chances for victory in the 1993 general election.

Spain is a constitutional monarchy that has had democratic parliamentary government since 1977. The country became a monarchy again in 1975, following four decades of right-wing dictatorship by Generalissimo Francisco Franco and a brief transitional government headed by Adolfo Suarez, a moderate conservative. King Juan Carlos, the largely ceremonial head of state, used his personal prestige to support the transition to democracy in the 1970s and to stave off attempted coups.

The Socialists have been in power nationally since 1982, having won re-election in 1986 and 1989. In the 1989 general election, the Socialists won 176 of the 350 seats in the lower house of parliament. That was just enough for an absolute majority for Gonzalez. The Communist-led United Left won 17 seats, a gain of 10, while the right-wing Popular Party garnered 106 seats, a gain of one. Jose Maria Aznar, the Popular Party leader, expects the Socialists to lose the 1993 elections, but a Socialist-regionalist coalition could keep Gonzalez in power. The rest of the lower house is held by various centrist, regional, and nationalist parties. The government has a four-year mandate. The less powerful upper house, the Senate, has 208 directly elected members who serve for four-year terms. Each province sends four members. Outlying territories send from one to three members each. Spain has seventeen regions with varying degrees of autonomy.

As the unemployment rate climbed over 18 percent in 1992, the government maintained austerity policies that included job cuts in the steel industry and unemployment benefits for only a fragment of the jobless. The government's response to the recession deepened the split between the Socialists and their onetime ally, the General Union of Workers (UGT). In May, the trade union federations staged a general strike in protest, but it was only partially effective. The strike did not cause a change in unemployment policy, because Gonzalez believed that Spain had to adhere to European Community (EC) guidelines on labor markets and deficit spending. Parliament approved the Maastricht Treaty on EC integration in November 1992. However, problems remained between Spain and the EC over the Community's borders, because Spain claims neighboring Gibraltar, a long-time British colony.

After a decade in office, the Socialists found themselves in the midst of scandals. There were several cases of official bribery in the provinces, central bank mismanagement, and a railroad real-estate scam, among others. These followed the deputy prime minister's resignation over campaign finance scandals in 1991. The growing record of corruption has tarnished the image of the Gonzalez government and has caused some disillusionment with the political process in this relatively young democracy.

In 1992, regionalist·and separatist forces continued to press Madrid for more autonomy or outright independence. Of Spain's seventeen regions, four (Andalucia, the Basque country, Catalonia, and Galicia) have more autonomous rights than the others. In September 1991, the central government began talks with the thirteen other regions about expanding their rights. Catalans, who are concentrated in the northern and eastern parts of Spain, gained nationalist inspiration from the break-ups of Yugoslavia and the Soviet Union. They have become increasingly assertive about advancing Catalan as a language distinct from Spanish. During the 1992 Olympics in Barcelona, Catalonia advertised itself internationally as the *country* hosting the games, and it succeeded at making Catalan an official Olympic language. Unlike some radical Catalan nationalists, Catalonia's head of government, Jordi Pujol, favors as much autonomy as possible within Spain, not complete independence. However, a growing minority of Catalans favors breaking away.

ETA (the Basque acronym for Land and Liberty), the Basque terrorist group, carried out numerous violent incidents around Expo '92, the world's fair in Seville, and during the run-up to the Olympics. French security forces arrested Francisco Garmendia, the alleged leader of Basque terrorism, in March. Further arrests followed in Spain, but the threat of violence continues.

Political Rights and Civil Liberties: Spanish voters have the right to change their government democratically. Under democratic rule since 1977, Spain has switched from governments of the center-right to the center-left. In 1992, the parliament extended local voting rights to European Community immigrants under the terms of the Maastricht Treaty. Regional cultures have significant autonomy, but Basque separatist terrorism remained a problem in 1992. Approximately 700 people have died in ETA attacks since 1968. Basque prisoners have charged the government with mistreatment. Under new rules, Spain requires visas for visitors from North Africa; the government punishes employers for hiring illegal aliens; and immigration quotas now favor the groups the state believes are easiest to integrate. Latin Americans require no visa to enter Spain, which they use as an entry point to the rest of Europe. This has raised problems with other EC countries. Ethnic minorities, especially immigrants, have complained about mistreatment, but Spain still lacks a law dealing with racial discrimination. In November 1992, gunmen killed one Dominican immigrant and wounded another at a disco. This incident raised fears about anti-immigrant violence spreading to Spain from elsewhere in Europe.

The print media are free and competitive, but the opposition has charged that state television has a pro-government bias. There are also three private commercial stations on the air.

Two labor federations exist, one traditionally Socialist, the other Communist. They have cooperated in general strikes in recent years. The General Union of Workers (UGT) broke its formal ties to the Socialists in late 1990. Enterprise is increasingly free and modern as Spain becomes more closely linked with the more advanced countries of the European Community.

Religious freedom is protected under the 1978 constitution. Roman Catholicism is the majority faith, but there is no state religion. The government has signed religious accords in recent years, that took complete effect in 1992, placing Protestantism, Judaism, and Islam on par with Roman Catholicism. The agreement recognizes the legitimacy of non-Catholic weddings, allows for non-Catholic religious education in the state schools, and mandates the armed forces to respect the rights of these minority faiths to observe their holy days. The Roman Catholic Church still benefits from contributions designated on tax returns, but non-Catholic institutions have secured tax-exempt status. As the government's liberal proposals on birth control and abortion indicate, the influence of Catholicism on the state has declined sharply since Franco's death.

Sri Lanka

Polity: Presidential-parliamentary democracy
Economy: Mixed-capitalist statist
Population: 17,632,000
PPP: $2,253
Life Expectancy: 70.9
Ethnic Groups: Sinhalese, (74 percent), Tamil (18 percent), Moor (7 percent), others

Political Rights: 4
Civil Liberties: 5
Status: Partly Free

Overview:
In 1992, Sri Lankan president Ranasinghe Premadasa survived a series of no-confidence motions and rejected opposition charges that he has become too authoritarian. Meanwhile, the government lost approximately 900 soldiers and several top officers at the hands of Tamil rebels fighting for a homeland in the north and east.

Located off southeastern India, Sri Lanka (known until 1972 as Ceylon) achieved independence from the British in 1947. Since then, political power has alternated between the centrist United National Party (UNP) and the nationalist, leftist Sri Lanka Freedom Party (SLFP). The 1978 constitution established a powerful presidency and a 225-member legislature. The president can serve two six-year terms, appoints the prime minister and other top officials, and can dissolve parliament following a no-confidence motion or the rejection of an appropriations bill. In the 1988 presidential election, the UNP's Ranasinghe Premadasa won with 50.43 percent of the vote against 44.94 for former prime minister Sirima Bandaranaike of the SLFP.

The legislature serves up to six years, with 198 seats elected through proportional representation from 22 electoral districts, and the remainder distributed according to national vote totals. In the February 1989 parliamentary elections, the UNP won 125 seats, with the opposition vote split between the SLFP with 67, the Tamil United Liberation Front with 10, the Sri Lanka Muslim Congress with 4, United Socialist Alliance with 3, and the People's Front with 3, along with 13 seats for independent Tamils.

The opposition has called for the current "Gaullist" presidency to be replaced by a Westminster parliamentary system. In August 1991, up to 120 MPs, including many from the UNP, signed an impeachment motion charging that Premadasa had become too authoritarian and had intimidated political opponents through wiretapping and other means. The president's supporters claimed the dissidents merely resented the strict discipline Premadasa placed on ministers, as well as the removal of various privileges for MPs. Premadasa responded by prorogueing parliament and throwing eight UNP members out of the party. In October, the speaker of the parliament ruled some of the signatures on the impeachment petition invalid, and dismissed the motion. The eight expelled UNP members joined the new Democratic United National Front (DUNF).

In 1992 Premadasa's opponents continued to try to bring down the government. On 5 May, the opposition filed its third no-confidence motion of the year, this one accusing the government of supporting death squads that were allegedly responsible for 1,079 political killings against Marxist insurgents of the People's Liberation Front (JVP). The JVP first attempted to overthrow the government in 1971, and renewed their attacks in the south in 1987 before being crushed in 1990. Parliament defeated the motion in August.

Premadasa won another victory on 1 September, when the Supreme Court dismissed a motion to invalidate the 1988 presidential elections, ending a three-year legal challenge. The Court ruled that former prime minister Bandaranaike had failed to prove that threats of violence from right-wing groups had been a decisive factor in the low 55 percent turnout or in Premadasa's victory.

Premadasa has also faced severe criticism for his failure to end—by force or through peace negotiations—the separatist war in the north and east which has killed 20,000 people. Since 1983, the Liberation Tigers of Tamil Eelam (LTTE) have been fighting for an independent homeland, claiming that the Hindu Tamil minority is discriminated against in housing, jobs, and education. In 1987, after the government captured the strategic Jaffna Peninsula, where the group's headquarters is located, India began airlifting supplies to the rebels. Sri Lanka agreed to a treaty which brought in an Indian peacekeeping force (IPKF) to maintain a ceasefire.

Refusing to disarm, the LTTE temporarily abandoned its war against the government and fought the numerically superior IPKF to a standstill. In May 1990, the last Indian troops were withdrawn. Fighting between the LTTE and the government resumed in June 1990, with some of the heaviest fighting in the civil war coming in the summer of 1991.

In January 1992, India began repatriating some 200,000 Tamil refugees who had fled to the southern Indian state of Tamil Nadu to escape the fighting. In May, India banned the LTTE, which had used Tamil Nadu as a safe-haven and staging ground, because of the group's links to the May 1991 assassination of Rajiv Ghandi.

In June, as fruitless peace negotiations continued, the army failed for the second year in a row to capture Jaffna Peninsula. Meanwhile, the rebels continued to target leading military figures. On 8 August, a landmine killed 10 top army officers including Major General Denzil Kobbekaduwa, who headed the campaign against the rebels, and Jaffna security forces commander Brigadier Vijaya Vimalaratne. A similar attack killed Deputy Defense Minister Ranjan Wijeratne in March 1991.

A wave of attacks in November prompted the government to take emergency action. On 3 November, 23 soldiers and nine rebels were killed when the LTTE ambushed a patrol, and on 16 November, a Tamil suicide bomber killed navy commander Clancy Fernando in the capital of Colombo. On 23 November, the government passed an emergency law requiring all citizens to register with police, seek police permission before allowing visitors to stay at their homes, and notify the authorities if anyone moves out. The move came amidst reports that the Tigers were preparing a major attack to mark the 38th birthday of leader Velupillai Prabhakaran.

During the year, the LTTE also continued its attacks on Muslim Tamils, who initially fought on the rebels' side but later deserted them following Muslim purges in Jaffna. In April, rebel raids on villagers in Aanchipathan and Muslim counterattacks left more than 100 dead. In October, the LTTE raided four villages in the northern Polonnaruwa district, reportedly killing 190 Muslims.

Political Rights and Civil Liberties:

Sri Lankans can change their government democratically. Separatist violence has prevented elections for the northeast provincial council from being held. Tamils claim discrimination in government-controlled processes such as university admission, the civil service, and educational funding.

In January, an unofficial Canadian delegation reported that arbitrary arrests and torture continues, while a U.N. Working Group on Enforced or Involuntary Disappearances blamed the army, police and right-wing death squads for 12,000 disappearances since 1983, particularly during the anti-JVP offensive.

The 1979 Prevention of Terrorism Act (PTA) and the Emergency Regulations (ER), renewed monthly since 1983, grant the government broad powers. Under the ER confessions to police officers are admissible in court, and defendants must prove they were given under duress. Suspects may be held incommunicado for preventive reasons for up to 18 months under the PTA and are frequently beaten by police. Defendants in ordinary cases generally receive due process rights.

Freedom of speech and of press can be constitutionally restricted in the interest of national security. On 5 April, former police deputy inspector-general Premadasa Udugampola told reporters that the Black Cat death squads used against the JVP had been supported by the government. Four days later the Attorney General filed charges against both Udugampola and newspaper publisher Lokubanda Wanigasekera for fomenting tension between ethnic groups and inciting hatred against the government. Wanigasekera's left-wing *Sinhalese Aththa* paper had published a list of victims allegedly killed by the Black Cats.

The country's independent newspapers publish diverse opinions on political and human rights issues, but small papers claim they are often coerced by various groups, particularly by the LTTE in the north. The government owns the radio and television networks, and approves all news broadcasts. In August 1992, thugs attacked 10 foreign and domestic journalists covering an anti-Premadasa rally, and in a separate incident stabbed political cartoonist Jeffrey Yoonis, who frequently lampooned the president. Freedom of association can be restricted under the ER and PTA.

Although Buddhism is the official religion, other groups practice freely. Citizens are free to travel internally, although certain areas are restricted due to fighting. State workers are prohibited from striking, and labor activists say the Public Service

Commission, to which state workers can appeal, is biased against them. The Essential Services Act allows the president to declare a strike illegal in any industry.

Sudan

Polity: Military
Economy: Mixed capitalist
Population: 26,477,000
PPP: $1,042
Life Expectancy: 50.8
Ethnic Groups: Arab, sub-Saharan African (Dinka, Nuer, Shilluk, Nuba, Fur, other)

Political Rights: 7
Civil Liberties: 7
Status: Not Free

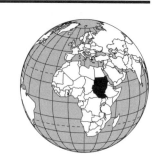

Overview:

In 1992, the Sudanese military government carried out a major offensive against the insurgent Sudan People's Liberation Army (SPLA), a Christian and animist guerrilla group which is seeking greater autonomy for the south and protection from the application of Islamic law. The fighting displaced up to one million people, and an ensuing rebel siege on the southern garrison town of Juba blocked relief flights and left 300,000 residents in danger of starvation.

Sudan, Africa's largest country by area, won independence from Britain and Egypt in 1956, and functioned as a parliamentary democracy for 13 years. Violence between the Muslim north and Christian south has plagued the country for decades. Following the 1969–72 *Anya Nya* separatist war, the southern third of the country achieved a high level of autonomy. Jafar Numeiri, who took power in a 1969 coup, ended this arrangement in 1983 by breaking up the southern region into three smaller states and introducing *Shari'a* (Islamic law). Southern Christians and animists, led by Dr. John Garang, a United States-educated renegade colonel, formed the Sudan People's Liberation Army (SPLA) and began fighting for greater autonomy. This insurgency continued even after the military toppled Numeiri in a 1985 coup, and returned the country to civilian rule with elections in 1986.

In June 1989, General Omar Hassan Ahmad al-Bashir led a another military coup that overthrew the pro-Western, elected government, suspended the constitution, dissolved the elected constituent Assembly, and banned all political parties. In July al-Bashir took over as prime minister, although actual power rests with Hassan al-Turabi, a Western-educated fundamentalist. Within a year, the military government placed fundamentalist supporters of al-Turabi's National Islamic Front (NIF), a political party ostensibly banned with others in 1989, in control of the security apparatus, the judiciary and universities, and declared an Islamic state. In March 1991, the government approved the Shari'a for the entire country, although in practice has thus far exempted the south.

In the south, the 40,000-strong SPLA has been weakened by the May 1991 fall of the Mengistu regime in Ethiopia, which had provided it with bases and funds, and by an August 1991 split in its ranks. A breakaway faction headed by Reik Machar challenged Garang's autocratic leadership and charged him with summary executions of rivals and other abuses. The dispute runs along tribal lines, as the main SPLA is supported by the Dinka people, while the so-called Nasir faction, which calls for complete independence from the north, is dominated by the Nuer. Fighting between the two factions continued into early 1992, and resulted in more than 2,000 civilian and military casualties. The government army, meanwhile, has been augmented by $300 million in weapons from China and by training from Iranian military advisors. The government has also created an 85,000-man Popular Defense Force of ill-equipped but highly motivated Islamic militants.

In late February 1992, the civil war intensified as the government began a major dry-season offensive on four fronts in the south. Many of the attacks were launched from Ethiopian territory, and were mostly focused on the main SPLA forces. From 24 May to 3 June, as the fighting continued, the two sides met for negotiations in Abuja, Nigeria. Although the SPLA, which had until recently controlled 90 percent of the south, was now cornered in the southeast, the government had faced heavy casualties, and there were reports of mutinies in some northern barracks. At the talks, the two SPLA factions reconciled and jointly called for a referendum on "self–determination." However, after the government rejected any discussion of independence, the SPLA dropped this demand, and both sides agreed to review a Nigerian proposal on federalism. Garang's faction then indicated that it continued to consider secular democracy more important than self-determination, thus continuing the rift between the factions.

In June, with the SPLA in retreat, the government re-opened river and rail links from the north to Juba and Wau, two of the south's largest cities. On 13 July, the army captured the town of Torit where the SPLA had its main base, driving much of the rebel army into the bush. It marked the 14th town captured by the government since March. In late October, the SPLA's Nasir faction launched an offensive on Malakal, a provincial capital in the south, in the process capturing six Iranian military advisors. There were also reports of new fighting between the SPLA factions.

The fighting has led to severe refugee problems. By September, the U.N. estimated that one million people had fled their homes in the latest offensive, joining 2 million people previously displaced by the war. Many were threatened with starvation as the government offensive cut the overland supply routes from Kenya and Uganda that relief groups use to supply the south. Although on 17 September the U.N. won approval from both sides to fly aid to 21 towns in the south, by year's end 300,000 people continued to face starvation in Juba, a government-held garrison town besieged by SPLA shelling. Within the town there were widespread reports of torture and summary executions by the army.

During the year, the government also pushed an estimated 750,000 refugees, who had fled the fighting in the south, out of the capital of Khartoum and into squalid, ill-equipped camps in the outlying desert. One U.S. official referred to the deportations as a virtual "death sentence." The government has also relocated tens of thousands of non-Arab Nuba tribesmen to camps on the pretense of giving them shelter from the civil war, although relief agencies said the relocation was part of a campaign to destroy the group's cultural identity.

The military regime's future plans are unclear. In early January 1992, Bashir announced plans for an appointed 300-member parliament which would have the power to propose and pass legislation, and veto RCC decisions. This Transitional National Assembly convened on 24 February, and included the entire RCC, a number of RCC advisors, and all cabinet members and state governors. Bashir said the Assembly would eventually yield to an elected parliament, and hinted at the possibility of presidential elections, but refused to give a timetable for either, saying only that the civil war was the principal obstacle to elections. However, there are reports of rifts within the NIF, with many civilians calling for an end to military rule. Meanwhile, a loose anti-government coalition known as the National Democratic Alliance, composed of union leaders, heads of banned political parties and SPLA representatives, met in London in early 1992 to call for a transitional government, which would lay plans for a multiparty system.

Political Rights and Civil Liberties:

Citizens of Sudan cannot change their government democratically. The military junta, which seized power in 1989, gave itself control over the constitution and all laws. Both the government and the rebel Sudan People's Liberation Army have committed grave rights abuses, including extrajudicial killings and torture. In 1992, martial law and a state of emergency, in place since the 1989 coup, remained in effect.

The government has set up a system of neighborhood "popular committees" ostensibly to serve as the local government. In reality, these committees monitor households and control the rationing of basic goods. Surveillance of suspected dissidents is routine, and numerous dissidents, including Christian clergymen, have been arrested. The 1991 Criminal Act permits the possible future application of the Shari'a to the south, and although this has not been done as of yet, in 1992 southern schools were ordered to teach Arabic and the Koran.

The judiciary is under the direct control of the Ministry of Justice, and is subservient to the government. All judges are linked to the National Islamic Front and favor application of Shari'a. On 27 July, the government announced the release of an unspecified number of prisoners serving less than 15 years for their role in four coup attempts, and halved the sentences of prisoners serving life terms. Others who had been involved in the coup attempts had been summarily tried and executed. The government also said that trials involving security violations would now be open to the public, although it gave no other guarantees of due process rights.

Freedom of speech is severely limited, and all private publications have been banned. The government controls all radio and television broadcasts, which reflect state views. Protests are banned, and have been forcibly broken up. Non-religious groups and associations are also banned. Internal travel is limited by the civil war, and some security suspects have been prevented from leaving the country. Workers cannot unionize, and a violation of the ban on strikes is punishable by death.

Suriname

Polity: Presidential-
parliamentary democracy
Economy: Capitalist-
statist
Population: 437,000
PPP: $3,907
Life Expectancy: 69.5

Political Rights: 3
Civil Liberties: 3
Status: Partly Free

Ethnic Groups: East Indian (approximately 40 percent), Creole
(approximately 30 percent), followed by Javanese, Bush Negroes,
Amerindians, Chinese and various European minorities

Overview:

President Ronald Venetiaan made significant progress toward the full restoration of democratic rule during his first year in office. The constitution was amended to remove any political role for the military, which had seized power in December 1990, and a peace agreement was signed between the government and the country's two main rebel groups. The resignation of Colonel Desi Bouterse as head of the military appeared to enhance the prospects for stronger civilian rule.

The Republic of Suriname achieved independence from the Netherlands in 1975 and functioned as a parliamentary democracy until a military coup in 1980. Bouterse emerged as the strongman of the ruling National Military Council that brutally suppressed all civic and political opposition. In 1985, Bouterse announced a program for a "return to democracy" and appointed an assembly to draft a new constitution.

The 1987 constitution provided for a system of parliamentary democracy, but gave the military the right to intercede in political affairs. A 51-member National Assembly, elected for a five-year term, selects the nation's president. The president is nominally the head of the armed forces, but civilian authority was undercut by the Military Council, which by law retained a tutelary role as the "vanguard of the people."

The Front for Democracy and Development, a three-party coalition, won the November 1987 general elections, taking 40 of 51 seats in the Assembly. The National Democratic Party (NDP), the army's political front, won three seats. The assembly elected Ramsewak Shankar president.

During its three years in office, the Shankar government was hamstrung by the military on most policy issues, including its efforts to negotiate a peace agreement with the Bush Negro-based Jungle Commando insurgency. At the same time, the military deepened its involvement in cocaine trafficking and remained unaccountable for human rights violations. In December 1990 Shanker was ousted by the military in a bloodless coup and replaced by a government controlled by Bouterse.

Under intense international pressure, the puppet government scheduled elections for 25 May 1991 and invited the Organization of American States (OAS) to observe. The leader in the opinion polls was the New Front (NF), essentially the same coalition of Hindustani, Creole and Javanese parties that had been ousted in 1990. Also contending were the NDP, and the newly formed Democratic Alternative 91

(DA 91), an ethnically mixed coalition led by young professionals who campaigned for establishing a commonwealth-type relationship with the Netherlands as a means of limiting the power of the military.

In the election, the NF won 30 seats in the National Assembly, the NDP won 12, and DA 91 won nine. But the NF lacked the two-thirds majority needed to elect its presidential candidate, educator Ronald Venetiaan. An electoral college was convened, formed by members of the Assembly and representatives of district and municipal councils. Venetiaan won 80 percent of the 817 electoral college votes.

After taking office in September 1991, President Venetiaan began a process of constitutional reform to bolster civilian rule (amendments require a two-thirds majority vote in the Assembly), and moved to strengthen ties with the Netherlands, the U.S. and neighboring Venezuela as a means to preclude a recurrence of military intervention. With an OAS observation team still posted in the country, Bouterse kept a low profile as the reform process gathered momentum.

On 25 March 1992, the National Assembly unanimously approved amendments restricting the role of the military to national defense and combating "organized subversion." Despite arguments in favor of preventing members of the military from engaging in political activity as individuals, the new clauses merely restrict soldiers from holding representative public office. Further amendments abolished conscription and the People's Militia.

Responding favorably to these reforms, the Hague reinstated in June the substantial Dutch economic aid program frozen since 1982. A month later Bouterse, in his first public appearance since the passage of the constitutional reforms, accused the Venetiaan government of selling out to foreign powers and warned it not to "go too fast and too far" in reorganizing the military.

Bouterse backed off after the Dutch media reported how he had amassed great wealth at the expense of the state over the last decade. In November, when some in the ruling coalition started discussing disciplinary action against him, Bouterse suddenly announced his resignation as military commander.

A peace accord was signed on 8 August 1992 between the government and the two main rebel groups, the Jungle Commando and the indigenous-based, military-linked Tucuyana Amazonas. The guerrillas agreed to disarm under the supervision of the OAS and the government committed itself to new economic and social programs in the country's interior.

Political Rights and Civil Liberties: Citizens are able to choose their government in relatively free elections. The constitution guarantees the right to organize political parties, civic organizations and labor unions. Aside from the parties in the government coalition, there are at least a half dozen other parties, including a number of labor-based organizations. Labor unions are well-organized and legally permitted to strike, but other civic institutions remain weak.

The constitution also guarantees the right of free expression. Radio is both public and private, with a number of small commercial radio stations competing with the government-owned radio and television broadcasting system. All broadcast in the various local languages and offer pluralistic points of view. There are a number of independent newspapers. Although intimidation by the military has lessened, some outlets still appear to practice a degree of self-censorship.

The constitution provides for an independent judiciary but the judicial system is weak and the military generally ignores its authority. Much of the country's interior still remains under army control and there is evidence that it continues to provide a base for the military's drug-trafficking activities. The peace agreement between the government and the two main rebel groups calls for the integration of former guerrillas into the police force. The formal cessation of hostilities also paved the way for 10,000 refugees, who fled to neighboring French Guiana during the 1980s, to start returning to Suriname.

There are a number of well organized human rights organizations. With the return to civilian rule in 1991 and the lessening of rights violations, they have been aiming to achieve justice for violations committed under military rule. Stanley Rensch, the leader of Mooiwana '86 who was frequently exiled in the 1980s, expressed strong opposition to the terms of the peace agreement, in which former rebels and the military were granted amnesty for rights violations committed during the conflict.

Because of the weakness of the Surinamese judiciary, some rights cases have been brought before the Inter-American Court of Human Rights, whose authority has been recognized by the Venetiaan government. In December 1991, the government accepted responsibility for the murder of seven Bush Negroes by the military in 1987 and agreed to pay damages to the victims' families. A number of other cases were in the process of being heard at the Court in 1992.

Swaziland

Polity: Traditional monarchy
Economy: Capitalist
Population: 825,000
PPP: $2,405
Life Expectancy: 56.8
Ethnic Groups: Swazi, European, Zulu

Political Rights: 6
Civil Liberties: 5
Status: Partly Free

Overview: Swaziland is a small, land-locked monarchy tucked into an eastern corner of South Africa. In 1968, it became an independent state with a Westminister-style parliament. However, in 1973, the first monarch in independent Swaziland, King Sobhuza II, abolished the multi-party system.

In 1978, Sobhuza set up a *tinkhundla* legislative system based on tribal councils. Chiefs' committees select two members of each council to form an 80-member electoral college. The college, in secret session, designates 40 of the 50 members of the legislative House of Assembly. The king appoints the remaining 10 members of the House. In turn, the House and the king each appoints 10 members to the Senate. The king also designates the prime minister. The bicameral legislature passes legislation that it must submit to the king for approval. In effect, the king retains ultimate political power. He delegates significant decision-making to members of his long-serving Central Committee.

Responding to criticism of the *tinkhundla*, Sobhuza's successor, King Mswati III, declared in 1990 that he would appoint a review committee to assist him in evaluating the system. Formed in September 1991, the committee reported to him in February 1992. It passed on popular complaints that the unaccountable Central Committee enjoyed apparent life tenure, that the members of the legislature were corrupt and unrepresentative, and that the 60-day detention law was oppressive.

Critics of the government, such as those writing for *The Independent Review*, suggest that the regime appointed this *tinkhundla* review committee to deflect demands for real political change. Throughout the review process the opposition stuck to its central demand: that an interim government abolish the *tinkhundla* system and pave the way for for multi-party elections. Regime detractors have dismissed any reform of the existing system. However, in January 1992, the king announced that he would appoint a second review committee to propose such reforms. Launching the second committee on 26 February, Mswati stated that he would permit parliamentary elections sometime in the future.

In 1992, the regime continued to reject the legalization of political parties. However, it seemed to abandon a policy of arresting multi-party advocates publicly agitating for pluralism. On 1 February, members of the Swaziland Youth Congress ostensibly marched to raise funds after receiving permission from Prime Minister Obed Dlamini. Police had earlier banned the walk by the highly politicized opposition group, but they were over-ruled by Dlamini. Later that month the illegal People's United Democratic Movement (Pudemo) decided to defy the ban on parties and go public. Minor parties soon followed in Pudemo's wake. The opposition movements have sought dialogue with the regime on democratization but have refused to be co-opted into participating in the second *tinkhundla* review committee.

On 9 October, King Mswati dismissed parliament. He stated that a new constitution would be drafted and parliamentary elections would follow sometime in 1993. He added that he and his advisers would rule directly until legislative balloting took place.

The second *tinkhundla* review committee presented its report to the king in late October 1992. Mswati endorsed its recommendations as the basis for a new constitution. Pudemo was quick to reject the report, even though the committee had recommended several reforms, including the end of the 60-day administrative detention law. The committee did not propose multi-partyism; rather, it proposed that candidates in future elections compete as individuals rather than as party representatives. By year's end the regime and the opposition were still unable to agree on the form Swaziland's "democracy" should take.

Political Rights and Civil Liberties: Swazis cannot change their government democratically. King's Decree No. 12 (1973) formally prohibits political parties as well as organization or attendance at political meetings. The legislature has tended to function as a rubber-stamp for the king, and the prime ministership is always filled by someone from the Dlamini princely family. Although the regime usually allows citizens to express political opinions, government remains almost exclusively the domain of the country's aristocracy.

Most of the opposition parties are committed to the establishment of a constitutional monarchy.

A state of emergency, declared in 1973, is still in effect. There is an independent judiciary composed of a High Court, a Court of Appeal, district courts and several other courts for tribal and customary issues. Special tribunals hear cases dealing with political offenses "against the king." Until the end of 1992, police could hold prisoners incommunicado without charge or trial for a renewable 60-day period.

The media practice a measure of self-censorship, but the private press increasingly presents diverse views on controversial issues. The Sedition and Subversive Activities Act prohibits the printing, publishing and distribution of literature considered to be "subversive." The state requires the media to funnel all inquiries touching on government operations through a director of information, who may respond at his discretion. The police allow gatherings, although they usually deal harshly with overtly anti-government demonstrations and meetings. Professional and business associations function openly. Workers can freely organize unions. The leading labor federation is the Swaziland Federation of Trade Unions, which is independent of government interference to the extent it stays clear of politics.

Sweden

Polity: Parliamentary democracy
Economy: Mixed capitalist
Population: 8,669,000
PPP: $14,817
Life Expectancy: 77.4
Ethnic Groups: Native (Swedish, Finnish, Lappic or Saami), 88 percent, immigrant groups, 12 percent

Political Rights: 1
Civil Liberties: 1
Status: Free

Overview:

In 1992, the government dealt with rising unemployment, a currency crisis, violence against immigrants, and questions about Sweden's future membership in the European Community (EC).

Sweden is a constitutional monarchy governed by a parliamentary democracy. The head of state is King Carl Gustaf XVI. The head of government is Prime Minister Carl Bildt, the Moderate Party leader, who heads the majority coalition in the unicameral, 349-member parliament (*Riksdag*). Voters elect 310 parliamentarians directly, and the parties receiving at least four percent of the nationwide vote divide 39 seats. There is a three-year term.

In the parliamentary election in 1991, a four-party coalition defeated the Social Democrats, who had governed Sweden for 53 of the previous 59 years. The conservative Moderate Party, the Liberals, the Center Party, and the Christian Democrats captured a combined 170 of the 349 parliamentary seats. The coalition depends on the right-wing populist New Democracy Party, which gained 25 seats after less than a year of existence. New Democracy had campaigned to make life "simpler, cheaper, and more fun," and specifically for cheap alcohol, lower immigration, and no foreign aid to Africa. This platform was too harsh for some of the other center-right politicians, so the new party stands outside the coalition. The Social Democrats took only 138 seats, while the Left Party, the successor to the Communists, holds sixteen.

Prime Minister Bildt's initial domestic program included: encouraging private business; lifting restrictions on foreign ownership; allowing private childcare facilities; privatizing state holdings; and making criminals serve longer prison terms. In late 1992, Bildt also proposed deregulating transportation and communications; raising the retirement age; forcing competitive purchasing on local governments; and instituting a family doctor system. In the 1991 election, the Social Democrats campaigned for their traditional welfare state and interventionist economic policies, but they have adopted more market-oriented policies. As of 1991, about 57 percent of gross domestic product went to taxes, but the socialists had implemented lower national income tax rates before the center-right victory.

A major reason for the Social Democrats' defeat was the state of the economy. Rising inflation and unemployment undermined the party's image as a successful economic manager. Joblessness has worsened under the Bildt government. In 1992, unemployment more than doubled in a year, reaching 6.5 percent, the highest figure in half a century. Government retraining schemes keep thousands of jobless people out of the labor market, making the unemployment figure artificially low. The Bildt government has proposed abolishing the state monopoly on employment agencies and limiting government training activities.

Increasing economic problems have led to hostility between Swedes and the immigrant population. Since August 1991, there have been several episodes of Swedes shooting immigrants. The government condemned the violence and supported a day-long protest strike against the trend. The King denounced the attacks as "frightening and unworthy of a democracy. In February 1992, the Stockholm police commissioner advised immigrants not to go out alone at night. By later in the year, racist activities expanded, including desecration of Jewish cemeteries. Nazi groups clashed with anti-racist demonstrators on 30 November, the anniversary of the death of King Karl XII, the eighteenth-century warrior whom the extreme right-wingers have adopted as a nationalist symbol.

Under the Social Democrats, Sweden applied to join the European Community (EC) in 1991. This was a significant break from the country's previously cool attitude towards the EC, which neutral Sweden had identified with NATO.

With the end of the cold war, Sweden pegged its currency, the krona, to the ECU (European Currency Unit), the forerunner of a common European currency. However, when Britain suspended the pound from the European exchange-rate system in September, a currency panic ensued, endangering the value of the krona. Sweden's central bank responded by setting a record-high lending rate of 500 percent. The crisis set the stage for the government and the opposition Social Democrats to negotiate extraordinary economic packages. Under the deals, the government reduced the number of holidays and raised food taxes in exchange for slowing down privatization. In addition to those measures, employers and unions will assume payments for sick leave and occupational injury insurance from the government. However, employers will bear lower social security costs, while individual taxpayers will pay higher income taxes. The central bank responded to the austerity plan by lowering interest rates to double-digit figures. Sweden had to let the krona float downwards on the exchange markets by 19 November.

Despite the misgivings of some members of the coalition parties, the government has continued the push for EC membership. In July 1992, the EC Commission issued a report strongly supportive of EC membership. The body concluded that Sweden's neutrality would not be an insurmountable obstacle to EC membership. However, the commission noted that Sweden would have to give "specific and binding" assurances that it would accept an integrated EC security policy, which could include a common defense. Prime Minister Bildt insists that these details will be worked out and that Sweden will hold a referendum on EC membership in 1994, leading to membership in 1995. In November 1992, the parliament voted 308 to 13 to join the European Economic Area, a trading zone including the EC and non-EC member countries of the European Free Trade Association.

As part of the government's reassessment of policy, it has promised to modernize the armed forces. The Bildt government also released information that called Sweden's neutrality into question. According to the records, Sweden co-operated with NATO planners during the 1950s and widened its landing strips so that NATO fighters could have landed in the event of hostilities with the Soviet Union.

Political Rights and Civil Liberties:

Swedes have the right to change their government democratically. Parliamentary elections take place at least once every three years. Aliens resident for three years have the right to participate in local elections. In 1992, the Lappic (Saami) ethnic minority won the right to its own parliament and significant powers over education and culture.

The judiciary is independent. The rights of the accused are generally respected. Sweden increased the rights of foreign suspects in 1991 by reforming the Terrorism Act. That law had allowed the state to confine alleged terrorists to their communities of residence. The government may still require that such suspects report periodically to the police. An underground racist group, the Aryan Resistance Front, has carried out sporadic terrorist attacks in recent years. There is growing concern about anti-Semitism, anti-foreigner violence, and Nazi demonstrations.

With a few minor exceptions, freedom of expression is guaranteed, and the press is unrestricted. The government subsidizes daily newspapers regardless of their politics. Publications or videotapes that contain excessive violence or national security information are subject to censorship. Following the success of private satellite television channels, a land-based commercial television station won a license in 1991. Freedom of assembly and association are guaranteed and respected in practice. Lutheranism is the state religion, and the church gets public funding. However, other religions are free to practice.

Emigration and domestic and foreign travel are unrestricted. Workers have the right to form and join trade unions and to strike. The trade union federation has been traditionally strong and well-organized. Despite its historical links with the Social Democrats, the labor movement has become more structurally independent from the party.

Switzerland

Polity: Parliamentary democracy
Economy: Capitalist
Population: 6,868,000
PPP: $18,590
Life Expectancy: 77.4
Ethnic Groups: German, French, Italian, Romansch

Political Rights: 1
Civil Liberties: 1
Status: Free

Overview:

In 1992, Switzerland sent the world mixed signals on changing its international role. The country also suffered from its highest unemployment since the 1930s.

In February, the government approved a deal between the European Community (EC) and the European Free Trade Association (EFTA) creating the free-trade European Economic Area (EEA). Both domestic and international economic actors assumed that Swiss participation in the EEA would presage EC membership. In May 1992, the government announced that it would make a formal application to join the EC. However, Swiss farmers were concerned that they would lose their subsidies under a common European agricultural policy. They staged large demonstrations around the country on 1 September to express their fears about being driven off the land. In a referendum on 6 December, the Swiss rejected the EEA 50.3 percent to 49.7 percent. The French-speaking areas voted for the EEA, and the German-speaking ones opposed it. Older voters had reservations about how European integration would affect immigration.

This landlocked, mountainous country began as a small confederation in the Middle Ages. Internationally recognized as a neutral country since 1815, Switzerland combines 23 territories called cantons. There are twenty full cantons and six half-cantons. Each canton has its own political system, customs, and dominant ethnic group. Swiss Germans predominate, but French, Romansch, and Italian groups are concentrated in some areas. Switzerland is the home base of numerous international organizations and resorts that have attracted people from all over the world.

The Federal Assembly (parliament) is bicameral. The voters elect the 200-member lower house, the National Council, to four-year terms by proportional representation. The various parties have the following numbers of seats: Christian Democrats, 37; the conservative Radicals, 44; the conservative People's Party, 25; Social Democrats, 41; Greens, 14; the anti-immigrant Auto Party, 8; the liberal Independents' Alliance, 6; the conservative Liberals, 10; the anti-immigrant Swiss Democrats, 5; the Evangelical People's Party, 3; the historically Communist Swiss Party of Labor, 3; the Swiss-Italian Ticino League, 2; and independents, 2. Using various local methods, the cantons elect two members each to the 46 member Council of States, the upper house. The executive branch is called the Federal Council, whose members function as a cabinet. Since 1959, the governing coalition has consisted of the Social Democrats, the Christian Democrats, the Radicals, and the People's Party. Drawn from the Federal Assembly, one of the seven cabinet executives serves as president each year. The small cabinet's composition must reflect the country's parties, regions, and language groups, leaving little room for any sector to dominate. The parliament sits for only four three-week sessions per year. Its lack of constant activity became a matter of national debate in 1992. The Federal Council's ministers end up carrying out many trivial tasks of legislation and regulation, such as defining speed limits.

The government had major economic concerns in 1992. Unemployment more than tripled since 1990, and stood over 3 percent, the highest figure since the 1930s. The Swiss attempted to adjust their infrastructure to suit their neighbors' economic needs. For example, the government planned two tunnels through the Alps to resolve a dispute with the EC over trucking rights. Since intense economic development (e.g., resorts and dams) in the mountains had already raised environmental concerns, the Greens collected enough signatures to force a referendum in September on the project. The voters approved it with 63.5 percent.

As the country debated its place in the world economy, the government applied to join the World Bank and the International Monetary fund (IMF). On 17 May, the voters agreed to join these institutions 55.8 to 44.2 percent. On another international issue, the Swiss parliament approved jet fighter purchases from America, but left-wing opponents triggered a referendum on banning such purchases through the year 2000. That vote will take place in 1993, and will raise many questions about what remains of Switzerland's traditional neutrality.

Political Rights and Civil Liberties:

The Swiss can change their government democratically. However, the Swiss system produces coalition governments, which mitigate the chances for radical changes in policy. The voters have substantial powers of initiative and referendum, which allow them to change policies directly. Voters can trigger a plebiscite with 100,000 signatures.

The political parties have the right to organize freely, and cover the entire political spectrum. The cantonal system allows considerable local autonomy, which helps to preserve the linguistic and cultural heritage of the localities. However, the Italian and Romansch communities believe that their linguistic and cultural resources are underfunded.

The government's postal ministry operates radio and television, which are linguistically and politically pluralistic. Switzerland has freedoms of discussion, assembly, demonstration, and religion. However, the country has a history of prosecuting conscientious objectors who disagree with universal military service for males. Those in military service favoring long hair got good news in 1992 when the army announced that troops could wear ponytails, as long as they were in hairnets. Women's rights improved gradually in the 1980s, but a few local government assemblies still exclude women. The Swiss Trade Union Federation staged a partially effective women's strike in June 1991. The labor movement protested against anti-female economic and social discrimination.

In March 1992, Switzerland suspended its investigation of the assassination of Iranian dissident Kazem Rajavi. Alleged agents of the Iranian government killed him in Switzerland in 1990. Iran would not co-operate with the Swiss investigation.

Syria

Polity: Dominant party
(military-dominated)
Economy: Mixed statist
Population: 13,730,000
PPP: $4,348
Life Expectancy: 66.1
Ethnic Groups: Arab (90 percent), Kurdish, Armenian and
others (10 percent)

Political Rights: 7
Civil Liberties: 7
Status: Not Free

Overview: In September 1941, the French declared Syria a republic, and
granted it full independence in January 1944. As part of the
pan-Arab movement, the state merged with Egypt to form
the United Arab Republic in February 1958, but withdrew in September 1961, re-
establishing itself as an independent state. A March 1963 military coup brought the
pan-Arab, socialist Baath party to power. Leadership struggles continued within the
Baath party until November 1970, when the military wing, headed by Hafez al-Assad,
took power. Assad became president in February 1971. The party's greatest internal
threat has been from the Muslim Brotherhood, a fundamentalist sect from the Sunni
Muslim majority which began a series of anti-government attacks in the late 1970s. In
February 1982, soldiers killed approximately 20,000 of these militants and civilians
after an armed rebellion in Hama. The government justifies spending more than 50
percent of its national budget on state security by citing this fundamentalist unrest and
an alleged threat of Israeli attack. Syria has fought Israel three times, losing the
strategic Golan Heights in 1967. Syrian troops were stationed in Lebanon since 1975
to ostensibly quell the civil war, increasing the troop levels after the Israeli invasion in
1982. Assad views Lebanon as part of "Greater Syria."

Assad serves as head of state and government, commander in chief of the armed
forces and secretary general of the Baath Party. A former fighter pilot and a member
of the Alawite Muslim minority, he has shrewdly given key government positions to
members of the Sunni majority and played up his devotion to Islam, while using the
army and up to a dozen intelligence and security units to keep a close watch on the
population. A 250-seat People's Assembly is elected for four-year terms and
nominally approves legislation and the budget, but holds little actual power. On 2
December 1991, Assad, running unopposed after being nominated by the Assembly,
won a fourth seven-year term with a reported 99.982 percent of the popular vote.
Government officials closely watched the voters, who had a "yes" or "no" choice.

On 29 June 1992, Assad reshuffled the cabinet, but as usual the move carried
little significance. Assad returned Prime Minister Mahmoud Zubi to the cabinet, along
with the defense and foreign ministers. A second woman attained ministerial level as
Minister of Higher Education; the other is Minister of Culture.

Although in December 1991 Assad released more than 1,000 political prisoners,
along with several hundred more in April 1992, the government continues to crack
down on dissidents. In March, workers from the Committee for the Defense of
Democratic Freedom and Human Rights (CDF) were tried for violating martial law

and the state of emergency regulations. The state accused them of distributing information without permission, circulating criticism of the government and belonging to an illegal organization. More than 50 workers from the CDF are currently in prison. The group monitors human rights conditions, which is strictly prohibited without governmental approval. Seventeen activists were sentenced to 10 years in prison under a 1965 government decree that outlaws actions "opposing any of the goals of the revolution, or advocating disorderly acts or publishing false news with the aim of causing disorder."

Abroad, Assad has been frustrated in recent years on several fronts. Syrian participation in the Allied effort against Iraq during the 1991 Gulf War did not yield the level of Western foreign aid it desired; and with the Soviet collapse in 1991, the country's dependence on the West for aid and trade is growing. Syria was also disappointed that several Gulf states tabled the 1991 Damascus Declaration between the Gulf Cooperation Council members, Syria and Egypt. The Declaration intended to link the states in trade and defense. In April 1992, Assad made a rare visit to the Gulf to attempt to revive the Declaration and encourage support against the U.N.-sponsored embargo on Libya.

In August, Syria rebuffed an Israeli offer of partial territorial concessions of the Golan Heights, and said that even if a peace agreement is ever signed, there would be neither diplomatic nor economic relations between the countries. In September, Syria for the first time requested discussion on all "security concerns," but by year's end little progress had been made.

In November, Syria refused to withdraw its 40,000 troops from Lebanon, which were brought in under a 1989 accord, claiming that although elections there had been held according to schedule, the new government failed to scrap the system of setting aside government posts according to religion. The Taif Accord had only authorized the troops to stay in the Bekka Valley until September.

In another foreign policy issue, in April the government arrested 500 Turkish Kurdish Workers' Party (PKK) members, and banned PKK activities in the country. The PKK has used Syria as a launchpad for terrorist attacks in Turkey for the last decade. Recently, the government has launched currency reforms and policies to increase entrepreneurial activity to bolster the sagging economy. The discovery of oil and gas in the north has yielded $2 billion annually. Despite declining unemployment, the gap between rich and poor continues to widen.

Political Rights and Civil Liberties:

Syrians cannot change their government democratically. President Hafez al-Assad maintains absolute authority, and all important decisions are made by him and his advisors. Candidates for all offices are approved by or affiliated with the Baath Party. The Parliament is elected every four years but has no independent authority. Political opposition is suppressed by force. Emergency laws have been in effect since 1963.

Members of the Baath Party receive privilege in educational and civil service opportunities. Governmental corruption is commonplace. Jews suffer discrimination and the state security apparatus closely monitors the Jewish community.

The government severely curtails freedom of the press and speech. Citizens may not criticize the President, the government, and the Baath Party, which owns and operates all media and publishing houses and strictly controls all information. The state censors all domestic and foreign news. All associations must be non-political and must register with the government. The law provides for equal rights of development, pay and education for women. However, traditional custom tends still to delineate gender roles in civil affairs. Religious authorities maintain the right to intercede in social and interpersonal matters.

Although there is no officially preferred religion, most key government positions are occupied by members of the minority Alawite sect, which is considered heretical by most Sunni Muslims. The state forbids Jehovah's Witnesses and Seventh-Day Adventists from practicing or owning church property; some members have been arrested. On 27 April, Syria lifted the travel ban on all of its 4,500 Jews, although they still may not travel to Israel. Previously, the law forbade Jews from traveling 4 km from their homes without official permission. In August, the government ceased indicating on identity cards that the citizen was Jewish.

The government restricts most travel near the borders with Israel, Lebanon, Jordan and Iraq. Individuals who have not completed required military service cannot travel abroad.

The government enforces and controls a single trade union system, and uses it to dominate nearly all aspects of union activity. Strikes are prohibited.

Taiwan (Rep. of China)

Polity: Dominant party
Economy: Capitalist-statist
Population: 20,830,000
PPP: na
Life Expectancy: 74.5
Ethnic Groups: Chinese (native majority, mainland minority, 98 percent), Aboriginal (2 percent)

Political Rights: 3
Civil Liberties: 3
Status: Partly Free

Overview:

On 19 December 1992, Taiwan held its first full direct legislative elections since the Nationalist government fled from mainland China in 1949. The ruling Nationalist Party, or Kuomintang (KMT), maintained its majority but received just 53 percent of the popular vote, giving it 96 seats in the 161–member parliament to 50 seats for the main opposition Democratic Progressive Party (DPP). During the year, the government also eased the highly restrictive Sedition Law, but hardliners in the KMT stalled further political reform by shelving proposals for a directly-elected presidency.

The island, located 100 miles off the Chinese coast, came under the control of the Nationalist government in China after World War II. Following the communist victory on the mainland in 1949, the Nationalist leadership fled to Taiwan and established a government-in-exile under Chiang Kai-shek. For most of the next four decades, the KMT ruled in an authoritarian manner while providing one of the highest living standards in the region. Both Taiwan and China officially consider Taiwan to be a province of China, and both claim to be the legitimate government of all of

China. Today, approximately 15 percent of the population consists of mainlanders or their descendents, as opposed to the numerically dominant native Taiwanese.

The 1947 constitution is a holdover from the KMT's rule on the mainland. It provides for a National Assembly, which elects and can recall the president and vice-president, and has the power to amend the constitution. The president serves a six-year term, can declare war and appoints numerous officials. The government has five specialized yuan (branches), each with its own head. The Executive Yuan runs most of the ministries; the Legislative Yuan, headed by premier Hau Pei-tsun, enacts laws; the Judicial Yuan interprets the constitution; the Examination Yuan holds civil service examinations; and the Control Yuan serves as an administrative and fiscal check on the other branches.

In recent years, the government has responded to calls from the growing middle class for political and social reform. The government ended martial law in 1987, and in 1988 Lee Teng-hui became the first native-born Taiwanese president following the death of Chiang Ching-kuo. Lee was elected for a full term in 1990. The National Assembly met in April 1991 to consider a total renewal of the country's three parliamentary bodies. At the time, the Assembly consisted of mostly aging mainlanders elected in 1947 or 1969 whose terms had been frozen to maintain the KMT's monopoly on politics and legitimize their claim to the mainland. The deputies agreed to hold elections for a new Assembly in December 1991, a new Legislative Yuan in 1992, and a new Control Yuan in 1993. These aging deputies, along with 81 veteran representatives from the Legislative Yuan, stepped down by the end of 1991. In addition, on 1 May the government unilaterally ended the state of war with the mainland.

In December 1991, Taiwanese elected a new National Assembly. Direct elections were held for 325 of its 403 seats (the remainder were held over from the 1986 elections), with 225 seats representing constituencies and the other 100 allotted through proportional representation. The main opposition came from the Democratic Progressive Party (DPP), led by Hsu Hsin-Liang, which violated the Sedition Law by calling for Taiwan to declare independence from the mainland, but received no sanction. The KMT, running on a theme of stability and prosperity, won 254 seats and the DPP 66, with five seats going to independents. This put the KMT above the three-quarters majority needed to pass constitutional amendments.

Continuing his efforts at political reform, in March 1992 President Lee backed proposals for direct presidential elections, having already said he has no intention of running in 1996. The idea is opposed by KMT hardliners, who are mostly mainlanders or their descendents, and fear that direct elections will lead to another native Taiwanese president.

A KMT Central Committee plenum in mid-March agreed to implement some form of popular elections in the future, although hardliners were able to block an outright endorsement of direct elections. In late March, the debate shifted to the 70-day National Assembly session, where KMT conservatives successfully kept the issue off the agenda. As in the past, fistfights and melees marred the session. DPP-organized street demonstrations in mid-April drew up to 20,000 people to demand discussion of the issue, and on 4 May the party's delegation walked out of the Assembly in protest. The Assembly shelved the issue issue until an extraordinary session to be called before May 1995.

The Assembly took a major step towards freeing up the political climate by amending the sedition law to apply only to acts advocating violence. Advocating formal independence from China is no longer an offense. The Assembly also gave the president the power to appoint officials to the Judicial, Executive and Control Yuans, and granted itself the power to approve the appointments. It also reduced the terms of the president and assembly deputies from six years to four, while increasing terms for members of the Legislative Yuan from three to four years.

Despite boasting one of the highest standards of living in Asia and some $100 billion in foreign reserves, many key areas of the economy, including finance, transportation, and energy, are dominated by state-run firms. The government has announced a multi-year, $300 billion infrastructure investment plan, although investors say this must be complemented by an easing of government regulations.

The government has shown a new openness in dealing with the "2-28" incident, a massacre of civilians which began on 28 February 1947. In February, it published a report suggesting up to 28,000 people may have been killed. For decades the incident, and the KMT's suppression of any discussion of it, had contributed to a pervasive distrust of the government.

Abroad, the country lost a key diplomatic relationship in August, when South Korea decided to recognize China. In early September, the United States government angered China by announcing a $4 billion sale of F-16 fighters to Taiwan.

Political Rights and Civil Liberties: Taiwanese have been granted greater power to democratically change their government. With the December 1991 elections for the National Assembly and the December 1992 elections for the legislative Yuan, the ruling Kuomintang has given up its monopoly on power. However, the president is still not directly elected, and the KMT maintains its position through control of the media and the government apparatus, as well as through a number or barriers on opposition parties. For example, the July 1991 legislative code, which prevents candidates who lost races for constituency seats from being named by their party to at-large seats, favors large parties with numerous capable candidates.

In 1992, the government eliminated several restrictions on civil liberties. In January it ended a requirement for mainlanders arriving in Taiwan to formally renounce their Chinese Communist Party (CCP) membership. In April, the National Assembly amended the Sedition Law, making only advocating violence punishable. In May, the government released seven dissidents including Huang Hwa, a former DPP presidential candidate who had received a ten-year prison term in 1990 for advocating independence. In June, the government abolished the "thought police" system, in which special units were stationed in government offices to monitor civil servants. They will be replaced with special offices to check corruption and maintain discipline.

In June, the government also announced plans to eliminate the Garrison Command, the military agency responsible for internal security. The Command had the authority to censor and ban publications, conduct surveillance and detain dissidents. It has frequently tortured prisoners to extract confessions, and has been accused of murdering opponents of the KMT. However, functions such as phone tapping and mail checks have reportedly been taken over by the Ministry of Transportation and Communications, and opposition leaders and dissidents claim they are still harassed. In November, the government ended martial law on Quemoy and Matsu, two islets near the Chinese coast it controls.

The Publications Law allows police to censor or ban publications. Although such censorship rarely occurs, the threat can have a chilling effect on political discussion. Electronic media remain highly regulated by the government, which maintains major shares in Taiwan's three television stations. Numerous radio stations are controlled by the government or the KMT-controlled Broadcasting Corporation of China, and no applications to start new stations have been approved since 1969. Political reporting is often biased against the opposition. The Parade and Assembly Law requires that demonstrations do not advocate either communism or independence, and that organizers are responsible for the conduct of participants. Opposition leaders have been charged with harming public order stemming from misconduct at demonstrations they organized.

The accused generally receive a fair trial, although in sensitive cases the judiciary is not considered fully independent. Police occasionally abuse suspects in custody. Freedom of religion is fully respected. The country's tiny aboriginal minority suffers from social and economic alienation, but are ensured representation in parliament through reserved seats. Citizens can travel freely within the country, and in June the government revised the National Security Law to allow 282 of 287 barred dissidents to return to the country.

The right to strike is subject to numerous restrictions, including government-required approval of strike vote meetings. Unions must be approved by the government, and can be disbanded if deemed to disturb the public order.

Tajikistan

Polity: Communist-dominated (in flux)
Economy: Statist
PPP: na
Life Expectancy: 70.0
Ethnic Groups: Tajiks (58 percent), Russians and Ukrainians (11 percent), Jews, Armenians, Gypsy, others (7 percent)

Political Rights: 6
Civil Liberties: 6
Status: Not Free

Overview:
In 1992, the first year of independence for the former Soviet republic of Tajikistan, the country continued to spiral toward civil war and anarchy. During the year, the nominal government shifted from the hard-line Communist government of President Rakhmon Nabiev, to the Islamic-democratic coalition headed by Akbarsho Iskandarov, and by the end of the year back to the ex-Communists. The civil war also involved regional, ethnic, and clan disputes, raising fears that the country might disintegrate along ethnic as well as political lines. Meanwhile, Russia, Iran, and Afghanistan vied for influence in this Central Asian country.

Tajikistan, the poorest of the former Soviet republics, was carved out of the Uzbek Soviet Republic on Stalin's orders in 1929. The boundaries of the republic angered the Tajiks by leaving Samarkand and Bukhara, the two main centers of Tajik culture, outside of the republic's boundaries.

The momentum for political change after decades of Soviet rule began to accelerate in 1990, when the newly formed national movement Rastokhez (Rebirth) sparked a wave of protests demanding redress for long-neglected social and economic problems. During the protests, a number of demonstrators were killed and hundreds injured. Following the disturbances, the Communist rulers declared a state of emergency and launched a crackdown against the opposition. In February, only Communist Party candidates were permitted to run in elections to the 250-member unicameral Supreme Soviet (parliament).

In 1991, the Democratic Party and the Islamic Renaissance Party (IRP) were formally registered. In November presidential elections, old-style Communist functionary, Rakhman Nabiev, was elected president, with the opposition claiming election fraud. With the disintegration of the Soviet Union, Tajikistan joined the Commonwealth of Independent States (CIS) in December 1991. Opposition groups formed an umbrella organization, the Movement for Democratic Reforms, which included the Rastokhez Movement, the Democratic Party, and the IRP.

In early 1992, Lali Badakshan, a movement advocating autonomy for the eastern Badakshan region, joined the coalition. In March, Maksud Ikramov, a parliamentary deputy and mayor of the capital, Dushanbe, was arrested in parliament on charges of corruption. According to the opposition, the real motive behind Ikramov's arrest was his pro-opposition, anti-Communist sympathies, which included granting permission to remove Lenin's statue from Dushanbe.

Following Ikramov's arrest and attempts by the hard-line parliament to dismiss independent-minded Minister of Internal Affairs Mamadaev Narzuhuhanov, the opposition organized demonstrations demanding a new constitution, new parliamentary elections, and an end to prosecution of political dissidents.

In April, the opposition stepped up its protests, and threatened to call a "national congress" to create an alternative power center. The legislature of the Badakshan region, which comprises 40 percent of the country's territory, supported the demonstrators' demands, and also voted to declare the region an autonomous republic. Many opposition figures came from this eastern region, while members of government were almost exclusively from the northern Leninabad region.

On 17 April, parliament accepted demands for a new constitution and parliamentary elections in return for a three-week moratorium on demonstrations. Protesters responded by issuing an ultimatum insisting on the resignation of Parliament Speaker Safarali Kenjaev. The demand was not met initially, leading some protesters to form armed groups, which included rebellious members of the National Guard. Several members of parliament were taken hostage. On 22 April, Speaker Kenjaev resigned and the hostages were released. Parliament also agreed to abolish censorship, and President Nabiev granted amnesty to those who participated in demonstrations prior to 23 April.

The subsequent appointment of Kenjaev to head the National Security Committee sparked a new wave of protests. In response, parliament granted Nabiev the right of direct presidential rule for six months.

Following more than two weeks of demonstrations in which 70 protesters were killed, both sides reached an agreement on 11 May specifying the formation of a coalition government. Eight of 24 ministerial posts were to be reserved for the opposition, and parliament was to be equally divided between the former deputies and opposition members. Nabiev was to remain President until December presidential elections. An 80-member transitional Assembly (*Majilis*) was established, containing Supreme Soviet deputies and members of the opposition parties. The body was to serve until the December elections for a multi-party People's Assembly.

In June, following the formation of the government of national reconciliation, President Nabiev issued a decree authorizing the disarmament of armed groups. The implementation of the decree met with widespread resistance from armed opposition groups as well as supporters of Nabiev opposed to the power-sharing scheme.

By the end of June, armed clashes between the groups loosely connected with the Communists and the opposition were reported in the southern Kulyab and Kurgan-Tyube districts. In July, an attempted truce failed, leaving the crisis unresolved. In August, parliament stripped Nabiev of the power of direct presidential rule. Violence escalated, and on 24 August, Prosecutor General Nurullo Khuvaidullaiev, one of Nabiev's staunchest supporters and opponents of reforms, was murdered. Three days later, eight members of the opposition were killed in retaliation for Khuvaidullaiev's assassination.

Following the outbreak of violence in the capital, the opposition presented Nabiev an ultimatum: either stop the fighting and resolve the issue of refugees from the two embattled regions, or resign. On 31 August, protesters stormed the presidential palace, taking 33 top government officials hostage. Nabiev escaped, reportedly hiding in a CIS army base near Dushanbe. On 3 September, the hostages were released, and the parliamentary presidium and cabinet passed a no-confidence vote on the Nabiev government.

Nabiev attempted to flee to his home base in the Leninabad district, but his column was intercepted on 7 September, and he was forced to resign. The same day, parliamentary Chairman Akbarsho Iskandarov was elected as acting president.

Instability in Tajikistan prompted alarm in Russia and the neighboring Central Asian republics. With Uzbeks making up almost one-quarter of Tajikistan's population, the Communist-holdover governments in Uzbekistan and other newly independent states in the region feared an escalation of the conflict. The increased support of Islamic opposition by Iran, and the massive arms smuggling from Afghanistan, led to a Tajik-Russian agreement on the deployment of CIS peacekeeping troops in August. Russian President Boris Yeltsin ordered CIS border guards, under the Russian jurisdiction, to patrol the Tajik-Afghan border.

On 3 September, the presidents of Russia, Uzbekistan, Kazakhstan and Kyrgyzstan issued a warning to the government and political organizations in Tajikistan, and agreed to send more troops to the Tajik-Afghan border region to prevent the arms smuggling. Iran and Afghanistan were warned not to interfere in Tajikistan's affairs. By the end of September, Russian troops took control over Dushanbe airport, and responded with tanks and artillery against groups intending to seize arms and ammunition.

With the takeover of the government by opposition forces dominated by the IRP, acting President Akbarsho Iskandarov said Tajikistan would not become an Islamic state. Parliamentary elections, he announced, would be held in December.

However, forces loyal to Nabiev refused to recognize the new government, staging an unsuccessful coup in the capital on 24 October. On 6 November, amid a growing unrest, Iskandarov urgently asked Russian troops to directly intervene in the conflict by enforcing curfews and disarming groups. But a week later, bowing to pressure from Nabiev's supporters, the coalition government resigned, leaving Iskandarov as the head of an intermittent State Council until new elections.

On 19 November, pro-Nabiev gunmen killed Jarubek Aminov, the pro-Islamic deputy security chief and one of the most effective leaders of the former coalition government. On 10 December, pro-Nabiev forces took control of the capital, forcing coalition troops to retreat. A week later, the new leader, Emomali Rakhmonov, issued an ultimatum to opponents to hand over their weapons or face annihilation. On 25 December, Rakhmonov asked for a U.N. team to monitor the situation in the country.

Political Rights and Civil Liberties: Citizens of Tajikistan do not have the right to change their government democratically. The parliamentary elections scheduled for December were not held due to the fighting and subsequent violent change of government from the democratic-Islamic coalition to the Communist forces.

In this ethnically and regionally fragmented country, fighting and social unrest continued throughout 1992. At least 250,000 people remained internally displaced by the end of the year. Following the change of government in December, approximately 50,000 people fled to the neighboring Afghanistan. Most ethnic Russians, who held most of the skilled jobs, either left or intended to leave, causing another blow to an already ravaged economy.

Most of the repressive Soviet era laws remain in place. In March, the Communist-dominated parliament passed a restrictive law on assembly, prompting criticism by independent journalists. Subsequent demonstrations and the formation of the government of national unity, rendered the law irrelevant in practice.

Independent newspapers and periodicals of various political orientations exist in the country, but the government controls television and radio. In 1992 the civil war curtailed freedom of movement.

Islam was revived after many decades of atheist indoctrination, although religious leaders publicly opposed the establishment of a religious state. There are no independent trade unions.

Tanzania

Polity: Dominant party (transitional)
Economy: Statist
Population: 27,432,000
PPP: $557
Life Expectancy: 54.0
Ethnic Groups: African (coastal Swahili, Sukuma, Gusii, other), with significant South Asian and Arab minorities

Political Rights: 6
Civil Liberties: 5
Status: Partly Free

Overview: In 1992, the Tanzanian government legalized independent political parties. At the same time, however, the government opted to maintain the 27-year-old one-party rule of the Revolutionary Party of Tanzania, or Chama Cha Mapinduzi (CCM), until multi-party elections in 1995.

The East African United Republic of Tanzania was formed in 1964 with the merger of mainland Tanganyika and the islands of Zanzibar and Pemba. President Ali Hassan Mwinyi, running as the only candidate, was re-elected in 1990 to a second five-year term. He succeeded to the leadership after Julius Nyerere, the still-influential first president of post-independence Tanzania, stepped down as president in 1985. Mwinyi was re-elected CCM party chairman at a party conference on 21 December 1992.

Nyerere, considered one of Africa's leading elder statesmen, was the architect of *ujamaa*, a Swahili word for a "cooperative-socialist" system that stresses self-reliance. Launched in the famous Arusha Declaration of 1967, *ujamaa* was characterized in part by the establishment of communal villages practicing collectivized agriculture and the creation of state-owned marketing boards. The regime set up vast domestic industries in pursuit of an import-substitution scheme, and private banks, commerce and factories were nationalized. Although there were some gains in social equity, the economy was plagued by inefficiency, bureaucratic mismanagement, and rampant corruption.

In early 1990, after regimes in Eastern Europe had toppled, Nyerere made several statements criticizing the CCM's stagnation and corruption. By mid-year, however, he had reaffirmed his commitment to the Arusha Declaration and urged the continuation of the country's one-party system.

Amid continuing national discussion and intra-Party debate about the single-party system, Mwinyi appointed a presidential commission in March 1991 to investigate the matter formally. He assigned the commission to move through the country for one year, taking public testimony and proposals, and presenting its findings to him in early 1992. The opposition accused commission members of using the interviews to re-inforce the regime's long-held position that political pluralism outside the CCM would lead to social unrest. In the end, however, the Commission's report recommended that opposition parties be allowed to register. On 20 January 1992, the CCM executive committee officially endorsed the commission's proposal, though it rejected the suggestion for a switch to federalism to give Tanganyika and the islands more autonomy. Former President Nyerere, who joined other committee members in the action, successfully urged that single-party rule be continued until Parliament's term ended in 1995. The regime has also continued to reject opposition calls for a sovereign national conference to revise the constitution.

In November 1991, opposition leaders had founded two groups: the Civic Movement and the Union for Multi-party Democracy. They called for a general amnesty for political prisoners and exiles, the creation of a national conference to draft a new constitution, and an end to human rights abuses by the regime. The government briefly detained the would-be party leaders and charged them with attempting to form unconstitutional political organizations. The regime gave the go-ahead on 17 June 1992 for opposition parties to petition for legal status. The opposition party ranks were soon swollen by the formation of the Democratic Party, the Tanzanian Democratic Alliance Party, and twenty other parties. The government has banned foreign assistance for opposition parties and asserted that international monitoring of the country's projected 1995 multi-party elections will be unnecessary. The CCM has responded to the challenge of multi-partyism by seeking to increase its membership massively.

Former Foreign Minister Oscar Kambona returned to Tanzania on 5 September after 25 years of political exile. An opponent of *ujamaa* when it was first launched by Nyerere, Kambona returned to the country vowing to form a new political party to challenge the CCM in 1995 elections.

The islands of Zanzibar and Pemba experienced continuing unrest in 1992. Advocates of independence for the islands struggled against the Tanzanian leadership's determination to keep the mainland and islands united as one country. Pro-independence activists were stymied by the requirement that any new opposition party be a national and not a regional organization. After government warnings that secessionists would be arrested, fifteen activists were briefly detained without charge in late February. One pro-independence group, *Kamahuru*, officially merged with the Civic Movement to form the Civic United Front.

Political Rights and Civil Liberties: Tanzanians cannot change their government democratically. Opposition parties are legal, but one-party government remains. Candidacy for elections has been limited to members of the Party. Zanzibar enjoys a measure of political autonomy, with a directly elected president and House of Representatives. Tanzania's legal system is based on the British model, with modifications to accommodate Islamic and customary law.

The judiciary is generally free from government interference in non-political cases. The Preventative Detention Decree allows for indefinite detention without bail of persons considered a threat to national security or public order. Under the Deportation Act, political offenders may also be internally exiled. Local law enforcement authorities reportedly torture criminal suspects to extract confessions.

Independent newspapers such as the *Business Times*, and the *Family Mirror* have begun to appear in the past few years, and government-owned periodicals have begun to reflect a greater diversity of opinion. For example, during the on-going national debate on political liberalization, the viewpoint of multi-party advocates has been accurately reported in the government-owned *Daily News*. The president is permitted by law to require that any periodical cease publication if he determines that it is not "in the interest of the people."

Internal travel is controlled. In an effort to prevent mass migration to the cities, there are residency and employment requirements. In late 1991, Tanganyikan activists advocating multi-partyism were banned from visiting either Zanzibar or Pemba. Travel abroad is constrained by the onerous and time-consuming regulations of an over-staffed bureaucracy. Freedom of religion is officially respected, but there are reports of growing intolerance among Muslim fundamentalists and Christian evangelicals. In mid-1992 the government banned all religious demonstrations and open-air sermons in the capital of Dar-es-Salaam to alleviate tension.

There are significant restrictions on the rights of association and assembly. Opposition parties wishing to hold public rallies must be legalized first; activists of the still-illegal DP were arrested in July 1992 for holding an illegal gathering in the town of Dodoma. Government critics charge that it is difficult to register new parties. Independent non-political organizations are allowed to function if they avoid politicization. Neighborhood committees of informants have monitored political dissent in the past. Advocates of independence for Zanzibar are not permitted to form political parties. These dissidents charge that they are subjected to persistent police harassment for their views.

All unions must belong to the government-controlled Organization of Tanzanian Trade Unions (OTTU). In 1992, the teachers' union boldly announced that it would cut its links with the OTTU labor federation. Workers have and use the right to strike.

Thailand

Polity: Parliamentary
democracy
(military influenced)
Economy: Capitalist statist
Population: 56,340,000
PPP: $3,569
Life Expectancy: 66.1
Ethnic Groups: Thai (84 percent), Chinese (12 percent),
Malaysian, Indian, Khmer, Vietnamese minorities

Political Rights: 3
Civil Liberties: 4
Status: Partly Free

Overview:

Over a year after the military took power in a coup,
Thailand returned to full civilian rule following parliamentary
elections in September 1992. Earlier elections in April had
resulted in a pro-military parliament that named coup leader Suchinda Kraprayoon as
prime minister, touching off massive street demonstrations in Bangkok. In May, the
army fired on the protesters, killing dozens before the King intervened and called for
fresh elections.

The Kingdom of Thailand is the only Southeast Asian country never colonized by
a European nation. A bloodless military coup in 1932, the first of seventeen attempted
military coups this century, limited the power of the monarchy. Since World War II,
a succession of pro-Western military and civilian governments have ruled.

Following a period of military rule, Major General Chatichai Choonhaven took
office in 1988 as the first directly elected prime minister since 1976, and appeared
committed to reducing the military's role in civilian affairs. In February 1991,
however, the army staged a bloodless coup, claiming that Chatichai's administration
was riddled with corruption. More likely, the coup leaders believed Chatichai was
seeking to limit the army's power, and particularly the influence of graduates of
Chulachomklao Royal Military Academy's Class Five, from which most of the
military elite hails.

In March 1991, the army named Ayand Panyarach, a widely respected former
diplomat and successful businessman, as interim prime minister. The generals also
formed an interim National Assembly, consisting mostly of active or retired military
officers, along with businessmen, bureaucrats and journalists who had openly
supported the coup. In December 1991, this pro-military National Assembly approved
a controversial new constitution. The constitution allowed the military to appoint the
270-seat Senate, which meant that in a no-confidence motion, a unified Senate could
bring down the government if it was joined by only 46 pro-military votes from the
360-seat House of Representatives. In addition, it provided the Speaker of the House
the option of recommending to the King a non-elected prime minister.

The 22 March 1992 elections for the 360-seat lower house were expected to lead
to a full return to civilian government. Three pro-military parties won a slim 190-seat
majority, and joined with two centrist parties in naming Narong Wongwan, an ethnic
Chinese businessman, as its candidate for prime minister. On 26 March, the U.S.
State Department told reporters that Narong had been denied a visa to enter the U.S.

in July 1991 because of alleged ties to drug trafficking. In early April, the coalition switched its support to coup leader Suchinda, even though he had stated in the past that he did not want the position, and had not run for a seat in parliament. King Bhumibol Adulyadej approved the appointment on 7 April, and Suchinda immediately surrendered all his military posts.

Thai civilians immediately protested the former coup leader's appointment, and called for the government to name an elected MP to the position. For weeks, thousands of people demonstrated in Bangkok, and some opposition MPs wore black to the opening sessions of parliament. On 17 April, Suchinda announced a 48-member cabinet, which included many holdovers from Chatichai's administration. They included eleven who had been investigated for corruption, three of whom had been found guilty.

By mid-May, Palang Dharma (Moral Force) party leader Chamlong Srimuang had emerged as the leader of the protest movement, which now topped 100,000 people. The military-man-turned-Bhuddist ascetic appealed to the masses because of his spartan lifestyle and reputation for honesty during his tenure as Bangkok governor. Chamlong inspired the crowds by beginning a hunger strike, and declared himself prepared to die if Suchinda did not resign. Notably, many of the protesters were members of Bangkok's increasingly prosperous middle class, which coordinated their moves via cellular telephone.

Near midnight on 18 May, Chamlong, backed by thousands of protesters, began a march towards the prime minister's residence at Government House. Soldiers opened fire randomly into the crowd, beginning three days of confrontations between police and protesters which left several dozen protesters dead, although the actual number will probably never be known. Thousands, including Chamlong, were arrested. The violence ended on 20 May when King Bhumibol called Suchinda and Chamlong to the palace, and ordered them to broker a compromise. Weeks later, hundreds of people remained missing, and unconfirmed reports circulated around the city that the army secretly buried dead bodies in mass graves.

Suchinda resigned on 24 May after just 48 days in office, and two days later the government lifted the state of emergency in Bangkok and surrounding areas. Both the opposition and the government coalition demanded the new prime minister come from within their ranks. Wary of further violence, parliamentary president Arthit Urairat delayed nominating a new prime minister until a compromise could be worked out.

On 10 June, Arthit informed the King that his efforts to find a candidate acceptable to both sides had failed. Instead, he nominated Anand for a second stint as interim prime minister. Although he had not stood in the March elections, all sides approved of Anand since he had run a smooth and competent administration following the February 1991 coup. The same day, the parliament amended the constitution to ensure that future prime ministers would come from among the elected MPs. Anand took a bold step towards reform on 10 July in eliminating the Internal Peace-Keeping Force, which had been formed in 1978 to stifle internal disorder. Soldiers from the Force had been involved in the May shootings in Bangkok.

Fresh elections were held on 13 September. The Democrat Party, headed by Chuan Leekpai, took 79 seats, along with Chart Thai, 77; Chart Pattana, 60; the New Aspiration Party, 51; Palang Darma, 47; and the Social Action party 22. Twenty-four seats went to smaller parties. The Democrats joined with Palang Darma, New

Aspiration, and the small Solidarity party in a non-military coalition, giving the non-military parties the numbers to elect Chuan as prime minister on 23 September. Six days later, Chuan named a 48-member cabinet, which included experienced politicians and top bankers.

On 7 October, the new parliament unanimously voted to overturn an amnesty Suchinda had granted to generals who had ordered soldiers to fire at the demonstrators in May. However, in a final ruling on 10 November, a government tribunal upheld the amnesty, meaning that no charges can be brought against the generals.

In 1992, Thailand ended 17 years of border tension with Laos by signing a treaty of friendship and cooperation in February. The Thai army had been embarrassed in brief border fights in 1987 and 1988.

Political Rights and Civil Liberties:

With the September 1992 elections, citizens of Thailand can again change their government democratically, although the army continues to have a pervasive influence in politics.

Freedom of speech and of press is generally respected, except in several areas—legal restrictions exist on defaming the monarchy (*lese majeste*), advocating a communist government, and inciting disturbances or insulting religion. Prominent social critic Sulak Sivaraksa remains in self-imposed exile abroad after a warrant was issued for his arrest in 1991. Sivaraksa had suggested that the monarchy should be subject to fair and honest criticism. The press is generally outspoken except in these proscribed areas. The government or the military control each of the five national television networks, and prior to the installation of the civilian government, reporting had frequently been biased. The judiciary is considered independent of the government. The accused are presumed innocent and receive adequate due process safeguards, although a closed trial can be ordered for cases involving the royal family or defamation of religion. Separate military and Islamic courts exist. Freedom of religion is unhindered. Freedom of internal travel and residence is restricted for some Chinese and Vietnamese aliens, and the government must approve passports for single Thai women. The 1975 Labor Relations Act allows private sector workers to join unions, although civil servants may only join "employee associations." The 1975 Act also grants the government the right to "restrict the right to strike whenever a strike would affect national authority or cause severe negative repercussions for the population at large," but this power is used infrequently. In April 1991, the government prohibited state enterprise workers from forming unions and denied their right to strike.

Togo

Polity: Transitional   **Political Rights:** 6
(Military dominated)   **Civil Liberties:** 5
Economy: Mixed statist   **Status:** Not Free
Population: 3,814,000
PPP: $752
Life Expectancy: 54.0
Ethnic Groups: Aja, Ewe, Gurensi, Kabyé, Krachi, Mina, Tem

Overview: In 1992, Togo's planned multi-party legislative and presidential elections were delayed amidst a series of bombings and assassination attempts against several prominent politicians opposed to strongman President Gnassingbe (originally Etienne) Eyadéma. Although voters approved a multi-party constitution in September, the army continued to dominate politics.

This West African country on the Gulf of Guinea became independent in 1960, and has been ruled since 1967 by President Eyadema as a one-party state under the Rally of Togolese People (RPT). Togo was a multi-party democracy until 1963, when Eyadema assassinated the sitting president in the first military coup in post-independence West Africa to overthrow an elected civilian government. The president's northern Kabyé ethnic group has held most positions of power in the regime, a departure from earlier governments dominated by southern Ewes.

Following pro-democracy protests in October 1990, Eyadéma set up a commission to draft a multi-party constitution. Completed within two months, the draft constitution provided for a system with a strong president limited to two seven-year terms. Rejecting popular calls for a national conference, the regime further announced it would not hold a constitutional referendum until the end of 1991.

Following widespread student protests which led to violent clashes with security forces in March 1991, the president agreed to permit the formation of opposition parties, issue a full amnesty, and allow a national conference to be convened. A coalition of ten legalized opposition groups set up in May, called the Union of Forces of Change (FAR), demanded a truly sovereign national conference, which would appoint a transitional government to lead the country to multi-party elections. After initially resisting, Eyadéma agreed, and a conference was convened in July. It appointed an interim High Council of the Republic (HCR), as well as a prime minister, Kokou Koffigoh, to lead the transitional government. It also froze RPT funds, and barred Eyadéma from running for re-election.

Refusing to participate in the conference, the army threatened the proceedings by surrounding the hall, occupying the state radio station to make demands, and even trying to kidnap Koffigoh himself. Throughout the remainder of the year, the "dialogue of the streets" between Ewe protesters and Kabyé soldiers was carried on in Lomé with truncheons, tear gas, Molotov cocktails, and rocks. Finally, in November, the HCR voted to ban the RPT for alleged provocations.

In December 1991, army troops responded by assaulting the prime minister's palace and seizing Koffigoh after killing at least a dozen of his guards. Koffigoh was then brought to the president, where he agreed under duress to dissolve the transitional government. In its place, a new "national unity government" was formed to bring back Eyadéma supporters into administration. Much of the 79-member HCR and other opposition representatives went underground after the assault. Bowing to power politics, a number of opposition parties conceded to Eyadéma's demand for a national unity government. In turn, the HCR was allowed to come out of hiding to approve a Koffigoh-sponsored charter of social reconciliation.

In 1992, the complicated and violent struggle for power continued between Eyadéma and the political opposition, delaying the municipal, legislative, and presidential elections that had been scheduled in stages from May to June. Koffigoh was the most prominent opposition moderate, stressing reconciliation and compromise. Western threats to cut off economic aid prevented the president from decisively rooting out the interim government. Nevertheless, Eyadéma's soldiers attacked numerous opposition figures, prompted counter-assaults on buildings owned by Eyadéma associates. In July, gunmen assassinated Tavio Amorin of the Pan-African Socialist Party, a harsh critic of the president.

In May, the government postponed elections indefinitely after an assassination attempt on a prominent opposition figure. Meanwhile, political maneuvering continued. On 2 July, the HCR adopted a draft constitution setting the minimum age for a presidential candidate at 45, thus disqualifying Koffigoh. A constitutional referendum set for 23 August was postponed after last-moment negotiations between Eyadéma partisans and their opponents. Under continuing pressure, on 26 August, the opposition agreed to constitutional provisions allowing Eyadéma to run for re-election and guaranteeing significant Kabyé representation in a future parliament. In mid-September, Koffigoh dissolved his cabinet and appointed Eyadéma supporters to the most powerful ministries. The constitutional referendum was finally held on 27 September, and between 80 and 90 percent of the electorate voted in favor of the new constitution, which had been endorsed by most parties.

However, the turmoil continued as soldiers took all HCR members hostage on 22 October. The opposition called a strike in response, demanding the creation of a armed force to protect the transitional government. France and the U.S. responded by cutting off military aid. On 9 November, Koffigoh tried to dismiss two Eyadéma supporters from his cabinet, a move rejected by the president. The Interior Minister, one of the two, threatened to arrest the prime minister, and troops surrounded the affected ministries. Another strike, this time indefinite, was called to back demands that the military stop interfering in the transition and that a new cabinet be formed. A transition that was to end 20 August 1992 was again paralyzed.

Political Rights and Civil Liberties:

Citizens of Togo cannot democratically change their government. In the past, citizens were only able to vote "yes" or "no" for one candidate. Multi-party elections originally scheduled for 1992 were canceled.

The court system is subject to direct control by the executive. Opponents of the military regime are subject to indefinite detention without charge, and torture of political prisoners is common. The new constitution guarantees freedom of assembly, but military troops beat and occasionally shoot and kill demonstrators. In 1991, soldiers killed 28 demonstrators.

Despite the passage of a more liberal press code, the regime has a record of prosecuting independent journalists. The state-controlled broadcast media have been exhibiting greater independence, but the Eyadéma supporters have emphasized freedom of expression does not give license to "slander" the head of state. Those convicted of the offense can be imprisoned for up to five years.

Religious activity is no longer hindered as a matter of official policy. Discrimination against women is commonplace. Although the regime-linked National Confederation of Workers of Togo (CNIT) once held a virtual monopoly on union activity, the anti-Eyadéma Coordinating Committee of Independent Trade Unions has more recently attempted to mobilize workers on labor and political issues. Authorities have repressed strike action in the past.

Tonga

Polity: Monarchy and partly elected legislature
Economy: Capitalist
Population: 103,000
PPP: na
Life Expectancy: 67.5
Ethnic Groups: Tongan (98 percent), other Pacific Islanders and Europeans (2 percent)

Political Rights: 3
Civil Liberties: 3
Status: Partly Free

Overview: In November 1992, nearly 1,000 Tongans crowded into the capital's Basilica Hall to call upon the country's 73-year-old monarch to change the constitution and give up his near-absolute powers. However, this unprecedented pro-democracy conference failed to produce any clear strategy or consensus among opposition leaders and provoked no response from the King.

This Polynesian South Pacific kingdom became an independent member of the British Commonwealth in June 1970. King Taufa'Ahau Tupuo IV has reigned since 1965. The constitution, drafted in 1875, is the product of an era in which the chiefs had unlimited power over commoners, who were referred to as "eaters of the soil." The King appoints and heads the Privy Council, which makes the major policy decisions. The unicameral Legislative Assembly consists of 9 nobles selected by the 33 hereditary nobles of Tonga, 12 cabinet ministers from the council, and only 9 representatives elected by universal suffrage, thus ensuring a two-thirds majority for the King and the nobility. There are no political parties.

On 24 November 1992, Akilisi Pohiva and other commoner members of the Assembly, calling themselves the Pro-Democracy Movement, convened a four-day conference on changing the constitution to limit the King's powers. Many of the nearly 1,000 people who attended were members of the country's growing middle class. The most poignant attacks came from the clergy. In his address, Pastor Siupeli Taliai noted that the King has almost absolute power. This "allows a despot to be a despot" and is "designed to preserve old Tongan inequality, entrenched power and position."

The government allowed the conference to proceed as planned, but did try to limit any publicity. Foreigners were banned from entering the country to attend, and police dragged a Tongan-born United States politician back onto his airplane when he attempted to enter. The organizers applied to the broadcasting board of the state-owned radio station to advertise the conference's opening and to secure an hour of coverage each day, but both requests were denied. Police questioned a Reuters correspondent about a report that was being filed with Radio Australia, and allegedly took names and notes of the proceedings.

The conference ended on 27 November with few clear answers about how to proceed. Many participants concluded that the monarchy is important for preserving stability, and that the problem is corruption and inefficiency among the nobles and government, rather than with the King himself. The country depends almost entirely on squash sales to Japan for income, and pressure on the King could increase if a failed harvest worsens economic conditions, or if New Zealand limits immigration further, shutting down an important social safety valve.

Political Rights and Civil Liberties: Tongans cannot change their government democratically. The King and the hereditary nobles can make major policy decisions without the popularly elected representatives, and hold a pre-eminent position in society through substantial landholdings. Although nine members of the Legislative assembly are elected, unelected nobles and appointed cabinet ministers hold a permanent majority and generally vote as a bloc.

Citizens receive due process safeguards, and a Court of Appeal created in 1990 is independent of the government. Freedoms of speech and press are generally respected in practice, and government media regularly include opposition opinions. Freedom of assembly is respected, and there are no restrictions on travel. Freedom of religion is respected. Workers have the right to form unions, but none exist.

Trinidad and Tobago

Polity: Parliamentary democracy
Economy: Capitalist-statist
Population: 1,263,000
PPP: $6,266
Life Expectancy: 71.6
Ethnic Groups: Complex, black (41 percent), East Indian descent (41 percent), mixed (16 percent), white (1 percent)

Political Rights: 1
Civil Liberties: 1
Status: Free

Overview: A strong performance in the September 1992 local elections showed that the ruling People's National Movement (PNM) of Prime Minister Patrick Manning had retained popular support since returning to power in late 1991.

The Republic of Trinidad and Tobago, a member of the British Commonwealth, achieved independence in 1962. The state is composed of two islands, with Trinidad accounting for nearly 95 percent of the country's area and population. Under the 1976 constitution, Trinidad and Tobago became a republic with a president, elected by a majority of both houses in parliament, replacing the former governor-general. However, executive authority in the parliamentary system remains invested in the prime minister.

The bicameral parliament consists of a 36-member House of Representatives elected for five years, and a 31-member Senate, with 25 senators appointed by the prime minister and 6 by the leader of the parliamentary opposition. The prime minister is the leader of the party or coalition commanding a majority in the House. Local government (counties and major municipalities) is elected.

In 1980, the House approved a bill establishing a 15-member House of Assembly for Tobago, with twelve members directly elected for four years and three named by the majority party. In January 1987, Tobago was granted full internal self-government.

In the December 1986 elections, the opposition National Alliance for Reconstruction (NAR), led by A.N.R. Robinson, defeated the black-based People's National Movement (PNM), which had ruled for 30 years, by taking 33 of 36 seats. Robinson had forged the first solid opposition coalition, including both black and East Indian elements, against the PNM. The NAR was composed of Robinson's Democratic Action Congress (DAC), the East Indian-based United Labour Front (ULF) led by Basdeo Panday, Karl Hudson-Phillip's Organization for National Reconstruction (ONR), and the Tapia House Movement.

After taking office, Robinson's coalition unraveled. By 1988, the Tapia House Movement had withdrawn and Panday, the NAR deputy leader, had been expelled. Panday formed a new East Indian-based party, the United National Congress (UNC), and became the official opposition leader in 1990. Robinson also encountered labor strikes against the government's economic austerity program and the declining standard of living.

On 27 July 1991, the radical Muslim group Jamaat-al-Muslimeen, led by Yasin Abu Bakr and numbering less than 300 members, seized the nation's parliament and the state-run television facility. A five-day stand-off marked by rampant looting in the capital city of Port of Spain left nearly two dozen dead and more than 300 wounded according to official sources. The siege ended when the government made Bakr believe the insurgents would receive amnesty if they surrendered.

The incident delivered a shock to an already ailing economy, causing tens of millions of dollars in damages and setting back an anticipated tourist boom. It also left the Robinson government struggling to restore confidence amid increasing animosity between the roughly equal black and East Indian communities. By fall 1991, opinion polls showed the PNM, resurgent under the new leadership of geologist Patrick Manning, with a commanding lead.

On 16 December 1991, the PNM, with a slate featuring many younger members, won 21 of 36 parliamentary seats and Manning became Prime Minister. Panday's UNC won 13 seats and became the official opposition. The NAR retained only its two Tobago seats, and Robinson resigned as party leader. The voter turnout was 66 percent.

In 1992, the 46-year-old Manning made good on a number of his "people-oriented" campaign promises by granting a public sector pay raise and higher state pensions. At the same time, he was under pressure from international financial institutions to continue with economic restructuring. His ability to balance competing national needs, at least during the first year, was rewarded when the PNM won 10 of

14 municipal and regional council elections on 28 September 1992. The UNC won in the other four. The PNM had not won in local elections in ten years.

Political Rights and Civil Liberties: Citizens can change their government through free and fair elections. Constitutional guarantees regarding the right to free expression and the right to organize political parties, civic organizations and labor unions are respected.

There are a number of human rights organizations. Traditionally active in addressing allegations of police brutality, more recently they have criticized government anti-narcotics initiatives as threatening to civil rights. Following the 1990 coup attempt, these groups reported scattered charges of harassment by security forces against the Muslim community, which comprises 6 percent of the nation's population. Freedom of religion, however, is generally respected.

Labor unions are well organized, powerful and politically active. They have the right to strike and have done so frequently in recent years. An independent industrial court plays a central role in arbitrating labor disputes.

Newspapers are privately owned, uncensored and influential. There are independent dailies and party publications. Radio and television are both public and private. Trinidad and Tobago's new media giant, Caribbean Communications Network (CCN), launched the country's second television station in 1991. The other station is run by the state-owned Trinidad and Tobago Television Company.

An independent judicial system is headed by a Supreme Court, which consists of a High Court and a Court of Appeal, with district courts operating on the local level. Under the constitution, there is a right of ultimate appeal to the Privy Council of the U.K.

In the aftermath of the 1991 coup attempt, Jamaat-al-Muslimeem leader Bakr and 113 others were arrested and charged with treason, murder and kidnapping. Defense lawyers challenged the validity of the charges, claiming that Bakr had given up the rebellion in exchange for amnesty. In a June 1992 decision that aroused a wave of public indignation, a high court judge ruled for the defense, and all defendants were released. Soon after, the Manning government initiated an appeal, a process that was expected to extend into 1993.

Tunisia

Polity: Dominant party
Economy: Mixed capitalist
Population: 8,424,000
PPP: $3,329
Life Expectancy: 66.7
Ethnic Groups: Arab

Political Rights: 6
Civil Liberties: 5
Status: Partly Free

Overview: In 1992, the Tunisian government continued its repression of Islamic fundamentalists, culminating in a mass trial in which more than 250 alleged anti-government plotters were convicted. Following the passage of a new law on associations, the Tunisian Human Rights League was dissolved, leading to the resignation of two Constitutional Court judges.

Tunisia is a one-party state governed by the Democratic constitutional Rally (RCD), whose leader, General Zine el-Abedine Ben Ali, is the President of the country. Although six other political parties were officially registered in 1992, all parliamentary deputies were RCD members, and the major political force capable of opposing the RCD monopoly on power, the Islamic Al-Nahda or Renaissance Party, continued to be banned, and its leader, Rachid Ghannouchi, forced into exile.

During 1991, the government stepped up measures to suppress the dissemination of radical Islamic thought, using censorship, detention of suspected Al-Nahda activists, and harassment of those who have beards or wear veils.

In February 1992, the Minister of Interior, Abdallah Kallel, expressed his appreciation for the Algerian government's crackdown against Islamic fundamentalists in that country. He reiterated the Tunisian government's refusal to conduct any dialogue with Al-Nahda, and called their leaders and supporters "sick-minded people."

In March, Amnesty International issued a report describing the Tunisian government's violations of human rights, including the use of torture. The government described the report as "tendentious" but admitted that some abuses were committed by individual security officers, and charged 74 of them with the violations.

In late March, the security forces reported having uncovered a secret arms depot, said to belong to Islamic Jihad, a militant group with ties to Al-Nahda.

At the same time, the rubber-stamp parliament passed a new law on associations, aimed at undermining the position of the influential Human Rights League. The new law stipulated that associations could not reject anyone applying for their membership. The League rejected the legislation, saying that it violated Tunisian and international law, and that its intention was to infiltrate the organization, the oldest of this type in the Arab world, with government supporters thus eliminating its independence. Shortly thereafter, the League was dissolved due to its refusal to bow to the new law. In a protest, two Constitutional Court judges resigned stating that the new law violated the provisions of the Constitution.

In July, two trials of Islamic fundamentalists began; the fundamentalists were charged in connection with the disturbances in the spring of 1991. One of the trials involved 171 members of Al-Nahda, and the second trial, 108 members of Talaa el Fida (Commandos of Sacrifice), a dissident group within Al-Nahda. The government accused the members of the two groups of preparing to overthrow the government violently, attempting to shoot down the presidential plane with a Stinger missile. Among the accused were members of the police, the armed forces, and customs officials. During the trial, the accused denied any attempts to overthrow the government by force; instead, they said, that the government was using the threat of violence as a pretext to delay democratic reforms the president had promised to implement after seizing power in 1987. Many of the accused, and international human rights observers present at the trial, accused the government of using torture to extract confessions and denying defense lawyers access to the defendants. Although the prosecutors asked for the death penalty for twenty of the 279 accused, surprise came on 29 August, when the military tribunals pronounced 46 sentences of life imprisonment as the highest form of punishment. In reaction to the verdicts, the Politbureau of the Social Democratic Movement, the most influential of the tolerated opposition groups, issued a statement praising the independence of the judiciary from the government pressure.

Shortly after the end of the trials, the security forces arrested twenty Islamic underground activists and confiscated weapons and explosives in their possession.

In December, the Interior Minister Kallal claimed that the security forces completely dismantled the network of militant Islamic groups within the country.

Political Rights and Civil Liberties: Although Tunisia is constitutionally a parliamentary democracy, in practice the right of its citizens to democratically change their government is limited. The ruling RCD holds a monopoly on power and the parliament essentially reaffirms policy made by the president. The tolerated opposition includes the Social Democratic Movement, the New Democratic Progressive Party (formerly the Communist party), the Popular Unity Party, and the Unionist Democratic Union. The fundamentalist Al-Nahda Party is denied recognition, however. All political parties require government authorization, and only groups that are authorized may be allowed to hold public meetings, which call for further government approval. Islamic fundamentalists are subject to government harassment, delays in passport renewal, phone taps, mail opening, searches without warrant, arbitrary arrest and detention and physical abuse by unidentified plainclothesmen. The government maintains a heavy police presence in universities to oversee student demonstrations and Islamic groups. The government also runs the mosques and may appoint and dismiss all imams.

Cases of torture of dissidents were reported in 1992. Under the law, suspects may be held incommunicado for up to ten days before being brought before the judge. Tunisian law permits arrests and searches without a warrant.

The Tunisian press is both publicly and privately owned. Self-censorship is frequently practiced because most printing houses are dependent on government money and all written material must have prior authorization to be published. Specific issues of newspapers have been confiscated for articles critical of the government. Writers, editors, and publishers are often arrested, imprisoned, or fined on charges of defamation. Television and radio are state-owned and coverage heavily favors the government.

Islam is the state religion, and while small Christian and Jewish communities are generally free to practice, the Baha'i may not worship. Tunisians are relatively free to travel within and outside of the country, but passports have been withheld from fundamentalists. Twenty percent of workers are unionized and almost all belong to the General Union of Tunisian Workers (UGTT), which has increasingly become independent. The legal and social position of women has significantly improved in recent years.

Turkey

Polity: Presidential-par-
liamentary democracy
Economy: Capitalist-
statist
Population: 58,500,000
PPP: $3,900
Life Expectancy: 65.1
Ethnic Groups: Turks, Kurds (12 million), Armenians,
Jews

Political Rights: 2
Civil Liberties: 4
Status: Partly Free

Overview: The ongoing Kurdish insurgency in the southern part of the
country, economic recession and relations with the new
Turkic countries of former Soviet Central Asia, were among
the chief concerns facing the government of Prime Minister Suleyman Demirel in
1992.

Mustafa Kemal Ataturk proclaimed the Turkish republic in 1923. The country has
maintained a pro-Western foreign policy and been a member of NATO since 1952.
Free elections were held in 1950, although the military has intervened several times to
maintain public order. A military coup ousted the elected government in 1980 and
imposed martial law until 1983. One month after the November 1983 elections, the
Motherland Party (ANAP) formed a government under Prime Minister Turgut Ozal,
who used a parliamentary majority to become president in 1989. After his election in
1991, Demirel, who had been premier six times previously and ousted twice by the
military, promised to improve the economy and address the problems of the Kurds,
whose ranks had been swelled by an estimated 500,000 Iraqi Kurds who fled Saddam
Hussein's terror after the end of the Gulf War.

In 1991, Demirel's True Path Party defeated ANAP, which had ruled for eight
years. On 20 October, elections for the unicameral 450-member parliament, Anap won
24 percent of the vote, with the True Path gaining 27 percent. Demirel formed a
coalition with Erdal Inonu's left-of-center Social Democratic Party.

Guerrillas of the outlawed Marxist Kurdish Labor Party (PKK), who had been
waging a war for Kurdish independence in southeastern Turkey since 1984, intensified
their campaign. Over 5,000 people have been killed in the eight-year insurgency,
including 2,000 in 1992 alone.

In March, the Turkish military stepped up bombing on PKK camps in Turkey
and in Northern Iraq (six miles from the Turkish border). Guerrillas had been
preparing a spring offensive during the Nevroz—the long-banned traditional Kurdish
New Year's festival celebrated on March 21. Several explosions shook Istanbul, after
the urban guerrilla group Dev-Sol (Revolutionary Left) planted bombs to protest the
violence in southeast Turkey. According to Abdullah Ocalan, the PKK leader based in
Lebanon, the guerrilla army numbered about 10,000 people. The March violence was
considered to be some of the heaviest since the beginning of the 1984 war.

A serious rift with Germany, Turkey's chief supplier of military aid, developed
when Bonn suspended all arms shipments because German-supplied weapons were

used against Kurds. In 1991, Germany had sent Turkey $900 million in weapons from the arsenal of former East Germany, including 300 armored personnel carriers, 250,000 Kalashnikov machine guns and ammunition. In effort to find new supplies of weapons, Turkey asked Russia for support.

Clashes with Kurdish guerrillas continued in April. At the same time, Syria arrested 500 Turkish Kurdish rebels based on its territory and pledged to shut down the group's training camps. New attacks against the Kurds in southeastern Turkey broke out just two days before Iraqi Kurds voted on 17 May for a paramount leader and parliament in Northern Iraq. In August, the PKK marked its eighth anniversary of armed struggle with an attack on military police stations in Eruh and Semdinle. After two days, 100 people had died and hundreds more were injured. The Turkish military bombed the town of Sirnak, and the government banned all press coverage of the conflict. In an effort to control the region, the PKK declared an embargo on all Turkish trade with Northern Iraq and blocked traffic crossing the border. At a November meeting in Ankara, Turkey, Iran and Syria agreed to cooperate against Kurdish self-determination in Northern Iraq. In the fall, Turkey sent aircraft, helicopters, and 20,000 troops into Iraq to fight the Turkish Kurds operating from bases in Iraqi Kurdistan.

In another issue, Turkey—under growing domestic pressure to side with the Muslims in the sectarian conflict the former Soviet republic of Azerbaijan—in May called for the U.N. Security Council to intervene in Nagorno-Karabakh, the Christian Armenian enclave in Azerbaijan. President Ozal called for immediate military action against the Armenians. Turkey sought to establish close diplomatic and economic relations with the Turkic-Muslim republics in Central Asia.

The civil unrest in southern Turkey adversely affected the economy. More than 40,000 municipal workers in five cities went on strike in July after an unresolved five-month pay dispute. The average daily wage is around $3 in state industries. Despite growth in export and production and a drop in the country's trade deficit and inflation rate, Turkey's economy remained in recession. While population grew at an annual rate of 2.2 percent, gross national product in 1991 grew by only 0.3 percent, the slowest rate in more than a decade. At the same time, Turkey took a leading economic role in the region with the creation in June of the Black Sea Economic Cooperation Pact in Istanbul, which grouped eleven European and Asian countries. Also in June, foreign ministers of the Organization of the Islamic Conference (OIC) gathered in Istanbul to discuss their support for the besieged Muslims in Bosnia-Herzegovina. Turkey was a strong supporter of Bosnian Muslims, and the government met frequently with Bosnian President Alija Izetbegovic to discuss aid to the war-torn country.

Political Rights and Civil Liberties: Turks have the right to change their government democratically, but the military continues to be a major factor in political life. In 1991, the government passed an anti-terror act, which human rights groups assailed for broadening the definition of terrorism, lengthening prison sentences, adding restrictions on press and political activity and making it difficult to bring legal action against police for torture. Turkish lawyers reported to Human Rights Watch that police torture up to 90 percent of political prisoners and about 50 percent of criminal suspects in the country. The torturers are rarely investigated, tried or sentenced. The Turkish government consistently denies charges that it uses torture. President Ozal said in 1989 that "inexperienced interrogators might use torture as a means of obtaining information, but when that happens, an investigation is opened and the necessary punishment is meted out." In January 1992, Helsinki Watch reported about a dozen cases of children being tortured in Turkey over the last two years.

Political violence and terrorism threatened to derail government efforts to introduce and implement human rights reforms. In early February, five security officials were killed, including the Istanbul state prosecutor. Dev-Sol, an urban left-wing group active in the 1970s, claimed responsibility. They also took responsibility for the February bombing at the Istanbul Chamber of Commerce, which killed two and injured 20. In March, two unidentified attackers threw hand grenades at the Neve Shalom synagogue in Istanbul, a city which has a Jewish population of approximately 22,000. In March, a car bomb killed a senior Israeli Embassy security officer.

Although privately-owned media criticize the government and reflect a variety of opinions, there are significant restrictions on speech and the press, particularly on coverage of events in southeastern Turkey and action against the Kurds. The criminal code provides penalties for those who "insult" the president, parliament and the army. Fifteen journalists, writing for radical publications, were reportedly killed in 1992. Confiscation of left-wing and pro-Kurdish periodicals was common during the year. In the first six months, police confiscated at least 41 issues of newspapers and magazines. Book publishing is restricted and there were several cases of restrictions on the use of the Kurdish language, including the closing of a school.

In early 1992, the government permitted distribution of Kurdish films and music cassettes, and two Kurdish newspapers were launched. The Social Democratic Party, part of the government coalition, contains many Kurdish parliamentarians. Since the inception of the modern Turkish state, Kurds have attempted to gain greater autonomy over their affairs and the right to express their cultural identity. Turkey recognizes Armenian and Jewish citizens as distinct minorities, but not Kurds. For a long time, Kurdish schools, publications, associations, and until recently, even the word "Kurd," were banned.

Jews and Christians can practice their religion, but there are some restrictions on Christian missionaries. Islamic religious instruction is compulsory for Muslims. The government severely restricts trade union activity, but there were several strikes in 1992.

Turkmenistan (Turkmenia)

Polity: Presidential -parliamentary (Presidential-domination)
Economy: Statist
Population: 3,856,000
PPP: na
Life Expectancy: 66.0
Ethnic Groups: Turkmen (68.4 percent), Russian (12.4 percent), Uzbeks (8.5 percent), Kazakhs (2.9 percent)

Political Rights: 7
Civil Liberties: 6
Status: Not Free

Overview:

During its first year as an independent state, the former Soviet republic of Turkmenistan, bordering Iran and Afghanistan, remained in the authoritarian grip of President Saparmurad Niyazov, a former first secretary of the Communist party. Rejecting calls for greater political democratization and market-style economic reforms, Niyazov concentrated power in his office and, in many ways, had become as powerful as the Khan of Merv, whom the Bolsheviks destroyed in the 1920s.

Niyazov ran unopposed in January 1990 for the chairmanship of a new, largely conservative Supreme Soviet (parliament), 90 percent of which was comprised of Communist party members. At the end of October—after the Supreme Soviet amended the republic's constitution in order to introduce an executive presidency—Niyazov, unanimously nominated by parliament, again became the sole candidate in the presidential elections. The main opposition group, known as Agzybirlik, formed in 1989 by leading intellectuals, was banned and its leaders harassed.

During the hard-line coup attempt against Soviet President Mikhail Gorbachev on 19 August 1991, Niyazov refused to condemn the plotters until it was clear that the putsch had failed. With the imminent collapse of the Soviet Union, Turkmenistan held an independence referendum on 26 October, with 94 percent of voters opting for a break with the USSR.

In 1992, Niyazov continued to consolidate his authority. The opposition was all but muzzled by a 1991 decree banning all liberal publications from outside Turkmenistan and making private ownership of photocopiers a criminal offense. The president further ensured control by appointing his own judiciary and arrogating all legislative, executive and juridical powers. He has also managed to win over the old Party *nomenklatura* and check Muslim fundamentalism despite a largely Sunni Muslim population. His chief lieutenants were Valeri Otsersov, the ethnic Russian trade minister, and investment-committee director Atah Charoiv, who has ancestors from one of the major five tribes that continue to play an important role in Turkmen life. The 16-member ruling council became largely superfluous.

On 18 May, parliament granted itself the sole right of nominating presidential candidates, and not surprisingly, President Niyazov was the only nominee. For its part, on 29 May Agzybirlik nominated Nuberdy Nurmamed, who had been tried three times on trumped-up political charges and spent a short time in prison. Agzybirlik's request that elections be postponed until the autumn to give the opposition time to mount an effective campaign was ignored. On 22 June, the day after the vote, the official Central Election Commission announced that Niyazov won 99.5 percent of the vote, and that the turnout was over 98 percent.

In his inauguration address on 26 June, President Niyazov said Turkmenistan would be "neither communist, nor Islamic," and pledged to implement market reform and privatization over the next several years. In fact, the government has resisted market restructuring. Bucking the trend in the rest of the former Soviet Union, Niyazov declared that no dwelling in Turkmenistan would be sold for a decade, and that the state would relinquish no share of its enterprises.

Nevertheless, Western and regional business interest has been high. With the world's third-biggest natural gas production and 213 million tons of oil, Turkmenistan had been negotiating with Ukraine and other former republics to sell oil for hard currency and with Italy to barter oil for the building of a modern refinery. A joint venture with Iran would build a railway to provide a final link of track from Beijing to Istanbul. Nevertheless, widescale graft and corruption, as well as the country's go-slow attitude toward development has frustrated many Western investors.

In other issues, Turkmenistan announced in June that it would build its national armed forces under a joint Turkmen-Russian command, the only former republic to make such an arrangement. A June decree also granted citizenship to Turkmen living in other former republics and in Iran.

Political Rights and Civil Liberties: Citizens of Turkmenistan cannot change their government democratically. Power has been concentrated in the hands of the president, and only the parliament—which is 90 percent Communist—has the right to nominate presidential candidates. Agzybirlik and other opposition groups face intimidation and repression. Early in the year, following a visit from an Australian TV crew, three Agzybirlik members were taken to court and fined several hundred rubles. The militia appears to act on personal whim, without legal sanction, and there have been numerous reports of beatings and kidnappings, particularly of young women family members of activists. The judiciary remains in the control of the presidency.

Western observers report an atmosphere of fear and intimidation. Few citizens dare criticize the president, even privately. There are reportedly no political prisoners. The state confiscates the few opposition publications. Opposition groups have virtually no access to the media. The press law insists on the registration of every publication, irrespective of print run. Most applications are refused.

Freedom of association is also circumscribed. Public organizations not only have to submit their charter for approval before registration, but must find support from at least two-thirds of parliamentary deputies, most of them members of the ex-Communist *nomenklatura.*

Although the population is overwhelmingly Sunni Muslim, the government has kept a tight reign on religion in hope of averting the rise of Islamic fundamentalism. Travel restrictions do exist, and families of opposition activists who do travel abroad are often harassed at home.

The state-run Trade Union Federation is little more than a rubber-stamp for the government. On 15 June, President Niyazov and the chairman of the federation council signed an agreement on social partnership, with the unions apparently pledging not to raise the issue of increasing wages and not to allow strikes.

Tuvalu

Polity: Parliamentary democracy
Economy: Capitalist
Population: 9,000
PPP: na
Life Expectancy: 61.0
Ethnic Groups: Polynesian

Political Rights: 1
Civil Liberties: 1
Status: Free

Overview:

This tiny Polynesian country became a "special member" of the British Commonwealth (participating in all Commonwealth affairs except heads-of-government meetings) upon achieving independence in October 1978. The constitution provides for a governor general, who is a Tuvalu citizen appointed by the British monarch for a four-year term. Real executive power is invested in a prime minister who is elected by the 12-member parliament. The governor general, currently Toaripi Lauti, appoints the four-member cabinet on the advice of the prime minister. Political parties are legal but none exist. Local government on the eight permanently-inhabited islands is run by six-person island councils, which are elected by universal suffrage to four-year terms, and are often influenced by hereditary elders wielding traditional authority.

The tiny country has a poor resource base and is dependent on food imports. Agricultural output consists mainly of the cocoa palm and its derivatives. Much of Tuvalu's revenue comes from remittances from some 1,500 countrymen working abroad, as well as from the sale of stamps and coins. Since taking office in September 1989, Prime Minister Bikenibeu Paeniu has sought to reduce dependence on foreign aid. Interest from the Tuvalu Trust Fund, established in 1987 by contributions from major aid donors, covers a fourth of the annual budget. Scientists say the country is slowly sinking into the Pacific Ocean, as most of the islands are only a few feet above sea level and have been eroded by frequent storms. Numerous experts have been to the islands to assess the possibility of building some form of sea wall.

Political Rights and Civil Liberties:

Citizens of Tuvalu can change their government democratically. The judiciary is independent of the government, and citizens generally receive fair public trials. Freedom of speech is fully respected. There are no restrictions on the right to form associations or hold public assemblies or meetings. There is complete freedom of religion, and in 1990, the prime minister rejected a request by the Protestant Church of Tuvalu, which represents 70 percent of the population, to recognize it as the official religion in the country, citing his belief in the separation of church and state. The government promotes a family planning program out of concern that a rapidly growing population will overwhelm the densely-packed country's already strained resources. Citizens can travel freely internally and abroad. Workers are free to organize into unions. Strikes are legal but none have occurred.

Uganda

Polity: Military
Economy: Capitalist
statist
Population: 17,477,000
PPP: $499
Life Expectancy: 52.0
Ethnic Groups: Acholi, Baganda, Kakwa, Lango, Nkole, Soga,
Teso, other

Political Rights: 6
Civil Liberties: 5
Status: Not Free

Overview: In 1992, unelected President Yoweri Museveni's constitutional review committee spent its third year assessing
public opinion about political reform. However, opposition
party activity remained illegal.

In early 1986 Museveni seized control of Uganda as leader of the guerrilla
National Resistance Army (NRA). He then retained power as the head of the
purportedly "interim" National Resistance Council (NRC). In 1990, he extended the
life of the NRC and his own term in office until at least 1995.

Inter-ethnic warfare, insurrection, intermittent coups, and brutal dictatorships have
been a sad fact of life in Uganda virtually since its independence in 1962, and have
led to the deaths of an estimated 800,000 Ugandans. After the ouster of strongman Idi
Amin by Tanzanian troops in 1979, Milton Obote ruled the country for six years. His
regime was marked by military atrocities, further economic disintegration, corruption,
and civil strife. In July 1985, Obote was deposed by Lieutenant General Tito Okello,
who was overthrown six months later by Museveni's NRA.

Since taking control as NRA commander-in-chief and NRC chairman, President
Museveni has become one of the most powerful leaders in Uganda's history. He has
asserted a commitment to democracy, but has made clear that "democracy" does not
necessarily mean multi-partyism. Rather, the president has said a no-party, "mass
democracy" is more appropriate until the country is economically developed. His
National Resistance Movement (NRM) organized "Resistance Council Committees" on
local and regional levels in 1987 to administer their respective jurisdictions and to
encourage popular participation in support of the regime. Elections for resistance
committees at the local and district level were held on 29 February 1992.

The NRM formed a constitutional review committee in March 1989 to travel
throughout the country and consult with Ugandans. A new constitution, however, will
not be completed until 1995. The regime says it intends to give NRA officers an
important role in drafting the constitution.

The NRM regime has worked to undermine Uganda's traditional political parties,
dismissing them as antiquated and only representing narrow, elite interests. There have
been calls both within and outside the country for a national referendum on multi-
partyism. Others demand the appointment of a transition government by a national
conference to pave the way for multi-party elections. In late November 1991,
President Museveni said that the regime would allow the opposition to contest the
January 1995 elections if the constitutional review committee endorsed multi-partyism.

However, in July 1992, he reaffirmed that even though the government would not ban political parties in the interim, open political party activity would be prohibited.

In January 1992, authorities arrested four high officials of the Democratic Party and an official of the Uganda People's Congress, charging them with treason for allegedly plotting the overthrow of the NRM regime. Those detained joined three other imprisoned opposition activists similarly charged in 1991 but not yet brought to trial.

Despite government claims to have routed insurgent groups in northern and northeastern Uganda in 1991, rebels continued sporadic attacks in 1992. The army detained 14,000 people in military camps in January 1992 for allegedly sympathizing with either the rebel United Christian Democratic Army or the Uganda People's Army.

In March 1992, the government pledged to cut military spending by 25 percent. The 100,000-man military accounts for nearly 50 percent of the budget. *Africa Confidential* noted the regime apparently fired Uganda's minister of finance in late March for urging greater cuts in the army's budget.

Tens of thousands of refugees fled into Uganda from drought and civil strife in neighboring Sudan and Zaire during 1992. Another serious crisis facing the country is the rapid spread of AIDS, which has devastated significant areas of the country, particularly in the south.

Ugandans of South Asian descent have been returning to their country in small numbers at the invitation of President Museveni. Idi Amin had expelled all "Asians" in 1972. Despite the regime's invitation, a widely distributed statement by a so-called Uganda African Trade Movement threatened in January 1992 to "harm, maim and cause enormous suffering" to anyone returning to reclaim lost properties. The group is probably composed of Ugandans who took advantage of the expulsion to appropriate the Asians' unwillingly abandoned properties.

In September 1991, a senior aide to President Museveni, Innocent Bisangwa-Mbuguje, and four others were indicted in Washington for attempting to illegally export antitank missiles and launchers to Uganda. The Ugandan Ambassador to the United States was detained and questioned by Customs Service officials; the ambassador had been videotaped inspecting the missiles in Florida. Although U.S. officials released the ambassador after he asserted diplomatic immunity, the aide was only released after he posted $1 million bond.

Political Rights and Civil Liberties:

Ugandans cannot change their government democratically. Voters are forced to line up publicly behind the local candidate they prefer. Citizens can only vote directly for local officials.

Freedom of assembly is curtailed for political groups; the government frequently breaks up demonstrations and party meetings. The government manipulates the legal system to intimidate and punish non-violent political opponents; it can detain those charged with seditious activity for years without trial. In August 1992, Chief Justice Wako Wambuzi ordered the release of all prisoners detained without charge or trial beyond the legal limit. According to the Red Cross, the government complied. In September 1992, Amnesty International asserted that the army engages in torture and extrajudicial execution of its perceived enemies. Personal security within the capital city of Kampala has increased significantly over the past five years due to better police protection.

The press has covered a broad range of topics, including guerrilla fighting and human rights abuses by the army. Journalists do face harassment, however. The regime arrested four news editors in early 1992 and variously charged them with sedition for criticizing new regime programs or with criminal defamation for accusing a government minister of corruption. President Museveni has denounced "those in the habit of putting out seditious publications or statements against the state and the army."

Nonpolitical associations and independent human rights groups must register with the government. Their members are often subject to official intimidation. The regime does not interfere with religious practice. Rebel activities have put certain restrictions on domestic travel. Workers are organized under the National Organization of Trade Unions (NOTU).

Ukraine

Polity: Elected presidential parliamentary
Economy: Statist-transitional
Population: 52,103,000
PPP: na
Life Expectancy: 71.0
Ethnic Groups: Ukrainian (72.6 percent) ; Russian (22 percent); others (5.4 percent)

Political Rights: 3
Civil Liberties: 3
Status: Partly Free

Overview:

In 1992, Ukraine, the former Soviet Union's second-largest republic and a major agricultural-industrial center, marked its first year of independence faced with serious economic problems, and nagging tensions with neighboring Russia over territory and nuclear arms. In September, pressure from the democratic parliamentary opposition demanding faster economic and political reforms forced Prime Minister Vitold Fokin and his cabinet to resign. Nevertheless, unlike Russia and other former republics, Ukraine was spared ethnic strife and political turmoil, as Leonid Kravchuk, the former Communist Party ideologist elected president in 1991, steered a cautious path between democrats, nationalists, and the large Russian minority.

Ukraine declared independence, subject to a referendum, on 24 August 1991, five days after the abortive hard-line coup attempt against Soviet President Mikhail Gorbachev. During a 1 December referendum and presidential vote, 90 percent of voters voted "yes" to independence and Kravchuk was elected president with 62 percent of the vote, defeating runner-up Vyacheslav Chornovil (25 percent), the Rukh nominee who spent 12 years in a labor camp, and five other candidates. Even in heavily Russian areas like Donetsk and the Crimea, the pro-independence vote was 77 and 54 percent, respectively. In mid-December 1991, Ukraine joined with Russia and Belarus to form the Commonwealth of Independent States (CIS).

The country's 450-seat legislature was elected on 4 March 1990, and although it was dominated by former Communists (the party was effectively banned 31 August 1991), the Democratic Bloc of over 100 deputies proved a formidable parliamentary faction, particularly in pressuring hardliners to adopt a sovereignty declaration in July 1990.

At the end of September 1992, President Kravchuk finally gave in to opposition criticism of the government's non-reformist economic policy, and on 30 September he announced the resignation of Prime Minister Fokin, an unpopular leader who opposed free-market reforms. On 1 October, the parliament adopted a resolution expressing no confidence in the entire government, forcing President Kravchuk to name a new cabinet head within 10 days. First Deputy Prime Minister Valentyn Symonenko was named interim prime minister, and on 13 October, Kravchuk proposed Leonid Kuchma, a former plant director, who was approved by a large majority. In his early pronouncements, the new prime minister pledged to implement free-market reforms, but said he would avoid the "shock therapy" approach favored by some radical reformers.

The cabinet crisis followed several months of inconclusive attempts to launch an economic reform program against a background of political infighting between radicals and traditionalists. Meanwhile, the country's economy continued to deteriorate. Despite a solid industrial base and among the most fertile agricultural land in the world, industrial production continued to plummet, manufacturing of consumer goods fell off drastically, and production of agricultural goods fell by 36 percent early in the year. Meanwhile, the government continued to waffle on the extent of reforms. On 24 March, parliament approved a moderate plan to introduce a Ukrainian currency and withdraw from the ruble zone. The plan came under heavy attack from radical reformers like Minister of Economics Volodymyr Lanovoy, who charged that the government plan was a conservative reaction to price liberalization in Russia. President Kravchuk dismissed Lanovoy in July, replacing him with Symonenko, a moderate.

In June and July, parliament attempted to pass several no-confidence resolutions before recessing until the fall. More than 20 political groupings formed a coalition, a New Parliament for an Independent Ukraine. The group called for the government to resign, new parliamentary elections, and a referendum of the dissolution of parliament. In September, with the economic crisis worsening and still no cogent government plan for action, the Fokin government was forced to resign.

At the end of November, parliament granted new Prime Minster Kuchma extraordinary powers for six months to facilitate his economic reform program of tight budget and wage controls combined with accelerated privatization and the elimination of corruption.

In other domestic political developments, 1992 saw the split of the Rukh opposition movement at its Congress on 28 February. The Rukh movement was the multi-ethnic umbrella group formed in 1989 by reform Communists, intellectuals and former dissidents. The main point of contention was support of President Kravchuk, whom even many in the opposition saw as a professional politician capable of guaranteeing Ukrainian statehood and security despite his Communist past and some authoritarian tendencies. The other faction, led by Chornovil, maintained that Ukraine's democratic evolution was far from consolidated, and criticized President Kravchuk's reliance on the old Communist apparatus and his reluctance to push effective economic reforms. In December, Chornovil assumed full control of Rukh and converted it to a political party. Earlier, on 2 August, the other faction coalesced around the Congress of National

Democratic Forces (CNDF). A third coalition that emerged was New Ukraine, spearheaded by the center-left Party for Democratic Rebirth of Ukraine, which included many reform Communists, trade unions, Green organizations and industrial groups. In June, it announced that it opposed Kravchuk and parliament. It joined forces with Rukh to collect signatures for a petition demanding a referendum on early parliamentary elections. However, the effort to gather 3 million signatures sputtered by the 21 December deadline due to political apathy and disillusionment.

The key foreign issues in 1992 were relations with Russia and the ultimate disposal of Ukraine's nuclear arsenal. Early in the year, tensions between Ukraine and Russia, which controlled much of Ukrainian territory for some 400 years, were heightened by Russian threats to retake the Crimea, which had been given to Ukraine by Khrushchev in 1954. Controversy also continued over the fate of the Black Sea fleet. Moreover, many Russian political figures in the Yeltsin government and in the hard-line opposition frequently voiced their opposition to an independent Ukraine. Two summits between Presidents Kravchuk and Yeltsin lessened tensions, because it was agreed to place the Black Sea Fleet under joint Russian-Ukrainian command. But a Russian draft of a new Ukraine-Russia treaty made public in September indicated that Russia still had difficulty fully accepting Ukrainian sovereignty. The Ukraine-Russian relationship also had an effect on the CIS, with Russia supporting a more tightly integrated body and Ukraine opposing a CIS "superstate." Most opposition groups in Ukraine called for its withdrawal from the CIS.

In terms of nuclear policy, Ukraine's wariness after years of Russian domination led the government to withhold the transfer of short-range nuclear arms to Russia. Ukraine objected to the notion that Russia was somehow a successor state to the Soviet Union and would be the only country in the region to possess nuclear weapons. Even when transfers were resumed in May, Ukraine balked at surrendering its strategic nuclear weapons, and by year's end had not signed any START agreements. Ukraine also focused on building its own army, and Ukrainian peacekeepers were part of the U.N. forces deployed in Bosnia.

In other issues, Ukraine was asked in February to join NATO's Cooperation Council. In September, the European Bank for Reconstruction and Development announced a major program of aid for Ukrainian privatization. In November, the World Bank extended a $40 million loan to Ukraine, pledging additional assistance if the Kuchma government implements an economic reform program. With Ukraine's energy supplies limited by the reduction of supplies of cheap oil and gas from Russia, two nuclear reactors at the infamous Chernobyl plant—scene of the world's worst nuclear accident in 1986—were restarted despite strong objections by the European Community.

Political Rights and Civil Liberties: Ukrainians can change their government democratically, but have not yet held post-Soviet parliamentary elections. Steps have been taken to finalize judicial reform, implement the rule of law and draft a final constitution. Citizens are free to organize in political groupings and associations, and there are scores of political parties and other independent organizations. There are numerous independent newspapers and magazines that offer diverse views. But the price and availability of newsprint and adequate distribution has forced many smaller publications to cease production in the last few years. Freedom of assembly is recognized and generally respected, but in August President Kravchuk threatened to expel several Ukrainian political activists from the West who were openly critical of the government, parliament and the president. However, no one was expelled.

While the previously outlawed Ukrainian (Uniate) Catholic and the Ukrainian Autocephalous Orthodox churches are legal, conflicts between the two churches arose in 1992 concerning buildings and church property in western Ukraine. Disputes also arose over the leadership and authority of the Orthodox Church in eastern Ukraine. A schism occurred between the U.S.-based Ukrainian Autocephalous Church, headed by 94-year-old Patriarch Mstyslav, and the Ukrainian Orthodox Church of Kiev headed by the Communist-appointed Metropolitan Filaret. Several new synagogues were opened for Ukraine's substantial Jewish population. In late October, the first Jewish Congress of Ukraine was held in Kiev.

There are few restrictions on domestic and foreign travel. Ukrainian workers are organized in several independent trade unions, and there were several strikes in 1992.

United Arab Emirates

Polity: Federation of traditional monarchies
Economy: Capitalist-statist
Population: 2,522,000
PPP: $23,798
Life Expectancy: 70.5
Ethnic Groups: Native Arabs, Arab and other immigrant groups

Political Rights: 6
Civil Liberties: 5
Status: Partly Free

Overview: Established in 1971, the United Arab Emirates (UAE) is a federation of seven emirates. Each emirate maintains extensive control over matters such as mineral and oil wealth, and over some aspects of defense and internal security. There are both federal- and emirate-level budgets. The emirates are governed by a seven-member supreme council of rulers, made up of the rulers of the seven emirates, which elects a president every five years. Sheikh Zayid bin Sultan al Nahayan, ruler of Abu Dhabi, has been president since 1971. Decision-making at the federal level is done through consensus of the seven emirates.

In September 1992, the government launched an austerity program to decrease budget deficit, which was caused by falling oil prices and the country's financial contribution to the Gulf War effort. The economy, based on oil and gas production and light manufacturing, has provided citizens with one of the highest per capita incomes in the world. The country produces two million barrels of oil daily and can afford generous family, housing, medical, education and social benefits for its citizens. Although the economy is mostly privatized, the government owns the majority share (to 88 percent) of the oil revenues, and petroleum provides 60 percent of the national income. Due to the reality of future declining oil reserves, the emirate governments are engaging in diversification, development and expansion. In 1985, Dubai created a free-trade zone dedicated to diversification of and foreign investment in the economy.

In 1992, UAE was engaged in a dispute with Iran over the control of the three islands in the Persian Gulf. The islands have been ruled for two decades by Iran and Sharja, one of the seven emirates, under a 1971 agreement that also allowed an Iranian garrison to be stationed on one of the islands. In March, Iran expelled UAE citizens and only allowed expatriates with Iranian permits to remain. Iranian police reportedly harassed residents. On 30 September, the UAE brought the case to the U.N. General Assembly, but by year's end no action had been taken. The conflict pushed Iranian-Arab relations to their lowest level since the Iran-Iraq war.

Political Rights and Civil Liberties:

Citizens of the United Arab Emirates cannot change their government democratically. There are no democratically elected institutions and political parties are illegal. Although there are consultative councils on the federal and national level, executive and legislative power lies in the hands of the rulers of the seven emirate's and their extended families. Male citizens may express their grievances and opinions in *majlis* held by the rulers of each emirate.

The judicial system consists of both *Shari'a* and civil courts, each of which deals with criminal and civil cases. The Shari'a courts are administered by each emirate, but the civil courts are part of the federal system. Due process is generally respected in both courts, which are usually independent of the government. In response to a growing drug problem, in 1992 the Ministry of Justice permitted capital punishment for drug dealers.

Despite constitutional guarantees on freedom of speech, most citizens practice self-censorship on sensitive political issues. Many of the local English and Arabic newspapers are privately owned, but receive government subsidies. The press is cautious in reporting on government policy, the ruling family, national security, religious matters, and relations with other countries. All television and radio stations are government-owned and controlled. Cable News Network is available.

The Ministry of Information reviews all literature, films, and foreign publications and occasionally bans material that does not conform to their guidelines. Academic freedom is also restricted. In May, the government threatened Indian actors performing in the country with the death penalty after they illegally staged a play considered offensive to the Prophet Mohammad and Jesus Christ. Organized public demonstrations require government permits, and guidelines vary among the emirates. Private organizations are free to form.

Women still play a traditionally limited role in society, but opportunities for women are increasingly available in government services, the media, education, and health. The UAE military service is the only one in the Gulf region that accepts women volunteers. Citizens are free to travel internally and abroad, although women require the permission of their husbands to travel with their children.

Islam is the official religion. Non-Muslims are free to practice their religion, but may not proselytize and distribute religious literature. Christians are permitted to teach their religion in their schools and are allowed to engage in private charitable activities.

There are no trade unions, no collective bargaining, and it is a criminal offense for public workers to strike. Workers only have recourse to conciliation committees organized by the Ministry of Labor and Social Affairs. Over the last 4 years, more than 20,000 Pakistani and Bangladeshi children have been smuggled into the emirates (and other Gulf countries) for mortal games of camel racing.

United Kingdom

Polity: Parliamentary democracy
Economy: Mixed capitalist
Population: 57,763,000
PPP: $13,732
Life Expectancy: 75.7
Ethnic Groups: English, Scottish, Welsh, Irish, and various Asian, African, and Caribbean immigrant groups

Political Rights: 1
Civil Liberties: 2
Status: Free

Overview:
Prime Minister John Major's Conservative Party won the general election on 9 April 1992. However, intra-party divisions over the economy and the European Community (EC) dogged the government for the rest of the year.

The United Kingdom of Great Britain and Northern Ireland combines two formerly separate kingdoms (England and Scotland), an ancient principality (Wales), and six counties of the Irish province of Ulster. *(See Northern Ireland section under Related Territories.)* Parliament has an elected House of Commons with 651 members chosen by plurality vote from single-member districts, and a House of Lords with over 1,000 hereditary and appointed members. The Lords have a suspensive veto, under which they can delay legislation for six months. If the House of Commons backs the bill again, it becomes law. A section of Lords serves as a supreme court. Parliament has a maximum term of five years.

Queen Elizabeth II is the largely ceremonial head of state who nominates for prime minister the party leader who has the highest support in the House of Commons. Two of her children, Prince Charles and Prince Andrew separated from their wives, Diana and Sarah, respectively, in 1992. Their marital difficulties and cost to the taxpayers undermined public support for the monarchy. After a public outcry over rebuilding Windsor Castle (which burned in 1992), the Queen agreed to pay income taxes and a larger share of expenses.

The Conservative Party has been in power since 1979. In 1990, the Conservative parliamentary caucus unseated Prime Minister Margaret Thatcher and replaced her with the more moderate John Major. Despite a recession, Major won his own mandate with the 1992 election. The campaign concentrated on the economy, taxes, and healthcare. In Scotland, pre-election polls had shown 50 percent support for an independent Scotland, but the the Scottish National Party (SNP) failed to make a breakthrough. Both Labour and the Liberal Democrats campaigned for a Scottish regional legislature.

Although public opinion polls had forecast a Labour Party victory, the Conservatives won 41.9 percent of the vote and 336 seats. Led by Neil Kinnock, Labour improved its showing from 1987, but received only 34.4 percent and 271 seats. Paddy Ashdown's Liberal Democrats finished third with 18 percent and 20 seats. The remaining 24 seats went to regionalist and nationalist parties. Due to Labour's loss, Kinnock resigned the party leadership. John Smith, a moderate, replaced him.

Major endured a European currency crisis in September 1992. After intense speculative pressure, the government tried backing the pound with higher interest rates, but then withdrew the British pound from a system that links European currencies. After this episode, Smith called Major "devalued." However, the government survived a confidence vote by a margin of 330 to 288.

In October, Conservative parliamentarians rebelled against government plans to close 31 coal mines and cut 30,000 jobs. The government back-tracked, and decided to close only 10 mines with 7,500 jobs. On 21 December, High Court judges ruled that the pit closure plan was illegal, because it ignored workers' rights. The judges ordered detailed consultations with the miners.

Major also faced severe pressure from anti-EC Conservatives. On 4 November, Conservative rebels joined with Labour to oppose a symbolic motion stating that Britain should play a leading role in the EC. With the help of the Liberal Democrats, Major eked out a 319 to 316 victory. He put off a vote on final approval of the Maastricht Treaty on European integration until 1993.

Political Rights and Civil Liberties: Citizens can change their government democratically. A government survey handles voter registration. Irish and Commonwealth (former British Empire) citizens resident in Britain have the right to vote. British subjects abroad have voting rights for twenty years after their emigration. Wales, Scotland, and Northern Ireland have no regional legislatures, but they elect members to the House of Commons. Many rights and liberties are well-established by custom and precedent in Britain's largely unwritten constitution. However, Britain's contact with Europeans who have codified freedoms has influenced a growing movement for a written constitution with a bill of rights.

The lack of a written constitutional right to press freedom is raising increasing concerns about government interference. Tough libel laws may have a chilling effect on some kinds of publishing and entertainment. In 1992, National Heritage Secretary David Mellor ordered a study of the need for legal press restraints. However, he resigned from the government in September following press revelations about his extramarital activities and acceptance of a free vacation from a Palestine Liberation Organization supporter.

The Official Secrets Act provides the government with a tool to attempt halting publication of intelligence activities and other official matters. The media can deal with this restraint through appeals in the courts and publication overseas.

The British Broadcasting Corporation (BBC) is an autonomous public body. It responds to government pressure to censor controversial items. However, the BBC offers pluralistic points of view, and airs political broadcasts of both government and opposition parties. There are also private electronic media. They are subject to government interference. For example, a 1992 High Court ruling allowed the Prevention of Terrorism Act to compel Channel Four and Box Productions to reveal their sources for a report on collusion between the security forces and Protestant paramilitaries in Northern Ireland. The court held the television producers in contempt for refusing to reveal their informants, and fined the two companies. Police arrested a news researcher in the case.

Since 1989, the courts have had to overturn several convictions in cases of alleged terrorism. For example, an appeals court ruled in 1992 that Judith Ward had suffered a wrongful conviction in a 1974 bus-bombing case. In overturning the earlier decision, the court held that officials involved in the case had lied and withheld evidence concerning a mental disorder that made her give false confessions. In a report on the Maguire Seven, a case with doctored scientific evidence and an overturned conviction, Sir John May, a retired appeals judge, recommended creating a new, independent tribunal to review alleged miscarriages of justice. In 1992, responding to public criticism of botched investigations, the government announced a plan to videotape interrogations of suspects in criminal cases. However, this procedure would specifically exclude alleged Irish Republican Army (IRA) terrorists, a category prone to miscarriages of justice, as in the Ward and Maguire cases.

The IRA carried out extensive attacks and bomb threats in Britain in 1992. The London subway system was the target of over 1,600 bomb threats, including hoaxes intended to paralyze the system. Terrorists bombed government buildings, rail stations, and London's financial district, among other targets. The most notable explosion took place in London on 10 April, when the biggest bomb in Britain since World War II killed three people and injured 91. Other IRA attacks coincided with the Conservatives' election victory and the 1992 Christmas season.

In 1992 there were increasing attacks on foreigners in Britain. Frequently, young, unemployed white skinheads attacked Black and Asian immigrants. In December, Hindu-Muslim clashes in India spread to immigrant communities in Britain, where Hindu temples and community centers were targets.

There is generally freedom of movement, but the government has barred more than 100 people from travelling between Britain and Northern Ireland. Despite the free movement promised in the Maastricht Treaty, Britain will continue passport checks on European travellers.

Britain has free religious expression, and the Church of England and the Church of Scotland are established. The Queen is head of the Church of England. There is some possibility for political interference in religion, because the Queen appoints Anglican bishops on the advice of the prime minister. The government finances some Christian denominational schools, but denies subsidies to Muslim academies because Islamic educators reject state curriculum guidelines that include sex education.

Trade unions and business groups are powerful and active. Union membership has fallen from 53 to 38 percent of the workforce since 1979. In 1991, the government proposed several new restrictions on labor. If adopted, these rules would mandate: cooling-off periods before strikes; advance notice stating the precise kind of industrial action a union would take; and frequent individual re-authorization of union dues.

United States of America

Polity: Federal presidential-legislative democracy
Economy: Capitalist
Population: 255,570,000
PPP: $20,998
Life Expectancy: 75.9
Ethnic Groups: Various white, black, Hispanic, Asian, native American (Indians, Eskimos/Inuit, Aleuts), and others

Political Rights: 1
Civil Liberties: 1
Status: Free

Overview:

In the 1992 presidential election, Democrat Bill Clinton defeated Republican President George Bush 43 percent to 38 percent of the popular vote. Clinton became the first Democrat to win a presidential election since 1976. His vice presidential running mate was Senator Albert Gore. The Republicans, the more conservative of the two major parties, had won seven out of the previous ten presidential elections. Independent candidate H. Ross Perot, a billionaire businessman, captured 19 percent, the best third-party performance since 1912. Popular discontent with the recession and with the government's domestic performance undermined the Bush campaign and caused a 20 percent turnover in Congress. Voters chose a House of Representatives with 258 Democrats, 176 Republicans, and one independent; and a Senate with 57 Democrats and 43 Republicans. Voters had expressed outrage with a scandal in the House of Representatives' private bank. Many members had written checks on insufficient funds for years. Although the accounts of other members, not public funds, covered the overdrafts, most Americans believed the checking practice typified abuse of privilege in high office. Reflecting the country's anti-politician mood, 14 states passed referenda limiting terms for members of Congress.

The U.S. federal government has three branches: executive, legislative, and judicial. The constitution leaves significant powers with the state governments and the citizenry.

The electoral college is the technical device for electing the president and vice president for four-year terms. The voters in each state and Washington, D.C., vote for slates of electors who usually cast their votes in the electoral college for the candidates with the most support in their jurisdiction. Occasionally, individual electors have voted for someone other than the candidates to whom they were pledged. In 1992, the Clinton-Gore team won 370 electoral votes to 168 for Bush and Vice President Dan Quayle. Perot and his running mate, James Stockdale, won no electoral votes.

The U.S. Congress is bicameral. There are 435 members of the House of Representatives, not counting delegates from Washington, D.C. and U.S.-related territories. In late 1992, the House Democratic Caucus proposed allowing the D.C. and territorial delegates to vote on all matters except final passage of legislation. Republicans may challenge the move in court. Each state is guaranteed at least one representative. The rest are apportioned on the basis of population. Representatives have two-year terms. The 100-seat Senate has two members from each state regardless of population. Senators have six-year terms.

The Supreme Court is the ultimate arbiter of the constitutionality of government actions. On occasion, the federal courts have ruled against the decisions of the legislative and executive branches of the federal government.

Political Rights and Civil Liberties: Americans can change their government democratically. However, voter turnout is comparatively low. In most recent presidential elections, scarcely 50 percent of the voting age population has turned out. The 1992 contest brought out approximately 55 percent, a gain over recent contests. A few localities grant resident aliens the right to vote. The party system is competitive, but members of Congress seeking re-election win in overwhelming numbers. Members spend an increasing amount of their time raising campaign funds from wealthy individuals and special interest groups. This undermines the quality of representation and reduces the chances for the opposition to increase its support.

In presidential election years, an ideologically unrepresentative minority chooses Democratic and Republican presidential nominees through a chaotic, complicated, and debilitating series of primary elections and local party meetings called caucuses. The early caucus and primary states play a disproportionately powerful role in reducing the field of presidential contenders. Voters in states holding later contests often have little influence in deciding the nominations, even if their populations are larger or more representative of the nation as a whole. The news media and political advertising consultants have taken over most of the traditional informational and organizational functions of parties. Federal Communications Commission (FCC) guidelines require television stations and networks to broadcast advertisements for candidates for federal office regardless of content, but the rules allow broadcasters discretion to accept or reject other kinds of political advertisements.

Several states, such as New York, have daunting petitioning hurdles that make it difficult for small parties or major party insurgents to receive a place on the ballot. In June 1992, the Supreme Court ruled that states may prohibit write-in votes as long as they provide reasonable ballot access for those who are not official candidates of established parties. In many states, the rights of initiative and referendum allow citizens to place issues on the ballot, and to decide questions directly, sometimes overturning the decisions of their elected representatives. California is especially noted for a high number of referenda.

The American media are generally free and competitive. However, there are some worrisome trends towards monopolization. As literacy rates fall, most Americans get their news from television. Broadcast news is highly superficial, and is becoming increasingly difficult to distinguish from entertainment.

In December 1992, the FCC fined Infinity Broadcasting $600,000 for "indecency" in the programs of Howard Stern, a radio host known for his vulgarity. However, a federal judge ruled in a separate matter that the National Endowment for the Arts standards were too vague when they required arts grant policy to "take into consideration general standards of decency."

Public and private discussion are very open in America. However, a trend in universities to ban allegedly racist and sexist language is subject to broad interpretation, and may have a chilling effect on academic freedom. There also has been a growing recognition that a tendency towards left-wing conformism among university faculties resulted in a pressure on independent thinkers to mouth "politically correct" views.

Large corporations may have a chilling effect on free speech when they hit their activist opponents with lawsuits, which are known as SLAPP suits (special litigation against public participation). Several states and localities have passed legislation outlawing hateful expression. The Supreme Court ruled in June 1992 that those governments may not ban cross burnings and similar forms of hate speech and bias crimes.

Since the early 1980s, the Supreme Court has made increasingly conservative rulings, generally reversing the pattern of more liberal decisions in the 1960s and 1970s. Court systems at all levels of government suffer from a severe backlog of cases, delaying the course of justice in countless criminal and civil cases. The high crime rate and growing public demand to punish criminals have led to severe overcrowding in American prisons. Federal and state prisons and local jails hold about 1.1 million people, a rate of 455 prisoners per 100,000 population.

Riots broke out in Los Angeles and other cities in April and May 1992 after a jury found police officers not guilty in the Rodney King beating case. The nation had been shocked in 1991 when it saw a televised videotape of several Los Angeles policemen repeatedly beating and kicking King, a black suspect. The original incident and the subsequent verdict gave credence to complaints from racial minorities about police brutality. More than 50 people died in post-verdict violence. Attacks on Korean store owners during the riots in Los Angeles formed part of an emerging trend of violence and harassment against Asian-Americans. In response to the King case verdict and the riots, the federal government initiated a separate civil rights case against the officers.

In May 1992, Americas Watch issued a report detailing the U.S. Border Patrol's physical abuse of both legal and illegal residents along the U.S.-Mexican border. According to a 1992 survey by the National Alliance for the Mentally Ill and the Public Citizen Health Research Group, 29 percent of American jails admitted to holding mentally ill people without charge and an additional 23 percent of jails acknowledged holding the mentally ill on such minor charges as vagrancy and disorderly conduct.

Several death penalty cases, including 31 executions, continued the long-running dispute over capital punishment in 1992. For example, the state of Arkansas executed Ricky Ray Rector, a brain-damaged convict. His lawyer argued that Rector lacked the mental capacity to understand the permanence of death.

A federal judge ruled in December 1992 that former Panamanian strongman Manuel Noriega, a convicted felon, was a prisoner of war under the Geneva Convention, and that he was entitled to POW treatment in U.S. prisons.

The U.S. has freedom of association. Trade unions are free, but the labor movement is declining as its traditionally strong manufacturing base shrinks. Due to management's increasing use of replacement workers during strikes, the strike has become a less effective weapon. In recent years, the federal government has used anti-racketeering laws to place some local and national unions under federal trusteeship, in order to remove corrupt officers and end patterns of criminal activity.

The country has a regulated, largely free-market economy, with a growing number of service jobs and declining manufacturing employment. The entrepreneurial spirit remains strong. Most job growth takes place in small enterprises in the private sector.

There is religious freedom and a constitutional separation of church and state. The Supreme Court has issued rulings limiting religious displays on public property and prohibiting organized prayer in the public schools. In an upcoming decision, the high court will determine the constitutionality of a law in Hialeah, Florida, that bans animal sacrifices for religious purposes.

Most poor people in the U.S. are white, but there is a large, disproportionately black underclass that exists outside the economic mainstream. Characterized by seemingly permanent unemployment, the underclass lives to a great extent on welfare payments. Heavy drug use, high crime rates, female-headed households, and large numbers of poorly fed, badly educated, illegitimate children characterize underclass neighborhoods. The quality of life in America's older cities is in decline. In Washington, D.C., 42 percent of young black males are in the court system as defendants, prisoners, or parolees.

Despite Supreme Court rulings against school segregation, some American school districts are experimenting with deliberately all-black or all-black male schools with special black curricular emphases. These are desperate attempts to motivate black youngsters who have poor skills and low self-esteem. There is also a black middle class, which has made significant gains in housing, education, and employment since the civil rights legislation of the 1960s.

American women have made significant gains in social and economic opportunities in recent decades, but still lag behind men in income. Affirmative action programs have increased the number of women in business and the professions, but they remain concentrated in low-paying occupations.

During the presidential campaign, candidate Clinton promised to lift the military's ban on homosexuals. On 3 November 1992, the state of Colorado approved a referendum denying homosexuals civil rights protections, but the state of Oregon rejected a referendum to allow anti-homosexual discrimination and to require the state to discourage homosexuality.

In 1991-92, the U.S. turned away many Haitian asylum-seekers, dismissing them as economic refugees from a poor country. Critics charged that the policy was racially motivated.

Environmentally, many parts of the U.S. have serious problems. Unacceptably high levels of air, water, and ground pollution threaten inhabitants with higher disease rates, and may lead to personal restrictions, including limits on business activity and the use of automobiles and water supplies.

The U.S. government seems largely indifferent to the plight of the American Indians. Many descendants of the first Americans live in poverty on reservations. Several tribes have cases in court against the federal government, charging violation of treaty provisions relating to control over land and resources.

Uruguay

Polity: Presidential-legislative democracy
Economy: Capitalist-statist
Population: 3,131,000
PPP: $5,805
Life Expectancy: 72.2
Ethnic Groups: White, mostly Spanish and Italian, (89 percent), Meztizo (10 percent), Black and Mulatto (1 percent)

Political Rights: 1
Civil Liberties: 2
Status: Free

Overview:
President Luis Alberto Lacalle came under increasing fire in 1992 as his program for overhauling Uruguay's statist economy antagonized labor unions and left-wing political groups, as well as right-wing, nationalist sectors of an increasingly restive military.

After achieving independence from Spain in 1825, the Republic of Uruguay was established in 1830. The Colorado Party dominated the relatively democratic political system until it lost in the 1958 elections. It returned to power in 1966, the same year voters approved a constitutional amendment returning the political system to a one-man presidency. An economic crisis, student and worker unrest, and the activities of the Tupamaro urban guerrilla movement led to a military takeover of the government in 1973.

The government was returned to civilian hands in 1985 after negotiations between the right-wing military regime and civilian politicians joined in the so-called *Multi-partidaria*. Jose Sanguinetti of the Colorado Party won the presidential election in November 1984 and took office, along with a newly elected Congress, in March 1985.

The current political system is based on the 1967 constitution. The president and a bicameral Congress consisting of a 99-member Chamber of Deputies and a 31-member Senate are elected for five years through a system of electoral lists that allows parties to run multiple candidates. The leading presidential candidate of the party receiving the most votes overall is the winner; in essence, party primaries are conducted simultaneously with the general election. Congressional seats are allocated on the basis of each party's share of the total vote. Municipal and regional governments are elected.

During the transition to democratic rule, the military backed down from demands for a permanent say in national security matters. Its defense actions and the declaration of a state of siege are now subject to congressional approval. In turn, the Sanguinetti government in 1986 pushed through Congress an amnesty for officers accused of human rights violations during military rule.

The constitution permits a referendum on laws passed by the legislature, provided that 25 percent of the electorate sign a petition requesting it. An effort by mostly leftist opponents of the amnesty led to the collection of enough signatures, and a plebiscite was held on 16 April 1989. Uruguayans voted, 57 percent to 43 percent, to confirm the amnesty law.

In the November 1989 elections, there were eleven presidential candidates from seven parties and coalitions. The ruling right-wing Colorado Party had three candidates. The centrist National Party, the other traditional party, also had three. The Marxist Broad Front coalition had one.

The leading National candidate was Luis Alberto Lacalle and the leading Colorado candidate was Jorge Batlle. The Broad Front candidate was Liber Seregni. Lacalle was elected president as the National Party obtained 37.4 percent of the vote, against 28.8 percent for the Colorados. The Broad Front obtained only 8 percent of the vote; but in municipal voting, it captured Montevideo, the nation's capital and home to nearly half the country's population. In congressional races, the National Party won 51 of 129 seats, with the Colorados taking 39, the Broad Front 29, and the remaining 10 going to smaller, predominantly social-democratic parties.

Upon taking office in 1990, Lacalle secured a co-governing agreement with the Colorados, giving him the parliamentary majority necessary to pass legislation in 1991 for privatizing inefficient state enterprises and attracting foreign investment. The program was opposed by Uruguay's powerful labor unions and the Broad Front administration in Montevideo under Mayor Tabare Vasquez. By mid-1992, the country had endured six general strikes, Lacalle was plummeting in opinion polls and losing the support of the Colorados, and the Broad Front was spearheading a drive to overturn the privatization program.

In a non-compulsory "consultation" held on 1 October 1992, nearly one-third of the electorate turned out, forcing the government to schedule a formal referendum to ratify or scrap key elements of the 1991 privatization law. A similar poll in July had failed to attract the necessary 25 percent of registered voters. The referendum was expected to be held in December.

In the spring of 1992, two shadowy groups with links to middle-ranking and junior military officers claimed credit for two bomb attacks, one against the office of former President Sanguinetti. One group, the previously unknown *Guardia de Artigas* (named after a hero of Uruguayan independence), said its actions were "against the traitors to the Fatherland who serve foreign interests and support an economic plan to starve the people." At the same time, the newly formed National Movement of Retired Officers (MNR) assailed the government's economic policies, while expressing solidarity with the military-backed coup by President Alberto Fujimori in Peru and the junior officers who had attempted to overthrow the elected government of Venezuela.

The military high command remained aloof from these apparent attacks against democratic rule, but continued to make veiled warnings against a possible victory by the Broad Front in the 1994 general elections. Opinion polls in 1992 showed that Tabare Vasquez was by far the country's most popular politician.

Political Rights and Civil Liberties:

Citizens are able to change their government through free and fair elections. Constitutional guarantees regarding free expression, freedom of religion and the right to organize political parties, labor unions and civic organizations are respected. Elections and referendums are overseen by an independent electoral commission.

After the return to civilian rule in 1985, legal status was restored to all outlawed political organizations. The Sanguinetti government released all political prisoners and permitted the return of an estimated 20,000 exiles.

Political expression is occasionally restricted by violence associated with hotly contested political campaigns and government-labor disputes. Labor is well organized, politically powerful, and frequently uses its right to strike.

The judiciary is independent and headed by a Supreme Court. The system includes courts of appeal, regional courts and justices of the peace.

In recent years, several police detainees alleged they had been tortured, and a number of police personnel have been prosecuted for ill-treatment or unlawful killings. New measures to prevent such practices, which did not appear to be widespread, were implemented by the Lacalle government. But there was a lack of effective investigation in some cases.

Human and legal rights organizations are active and played a key role in the 1991 decision by the Inter-American Commission on Human Rights of the Organization of American States that the 1986 Amnesty Law violated key provisions of the American Convention on Human Rights.

A long tradition of press freedom was restored with the return of civilian rule. The press is privately owned, and broadcasting is both commercial and public. There is no censorship. There are numerous daily newspapers, many associated with political parties, and a number of weeklies, including the influential *Busqueda*. However, because of the government's suspension of tax exemptions for the import of newsprint, a number of publications have gone out of business. Television has become an important part of the political landscape. The 1989 campaign featured presidential debates and news coverage was extensive on the four channels that service the capital. In 1992, the Catholic church protested the government's refusal to grant it a radio license.

Uzbekistan

Polity: Dominant party
Economy: Statist-transitional
Population: 21,301,000
PPP: na
Life Expectancy: 69.0
Ethnic Groups: Uzbeks (70 percent), Russians (10 percent), Ukrainians, Meshketian Turks, others

Political Rights: 6
Civil Liberties: 6
Status: Not Free

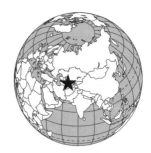

Overview:

In 1992, the increasingly authoritarian regime of President Islam Karimov intensified a crackdown on the opposition while facing a sagging economy, catastrophic environmental issues and ethnic tensions in this populous Central Asian republic.

President Karimov, a former first secretary of the Communist party, was elected president on 29 December 1991 as head of the People's Democratic Party (the Communist party changed its name after the abortive hardline coup against Soviet President Mikhail Gorbachev on 19 August). He received 86 percent of the vote, defeating well-known poet Mohammed Saleh of the Erk (Freedom) Democratic Party, who got 12 percent. The largest opposition group, the nationalist Uzbek Popular Front

(Birlik), was barred from registering as a party, and the Islamic Renaissance Party (IRP) was banned entirely. Voters also overwhelmingly approved a referendum calling for independence from a rapidly disintegrating Soviet Union. Uzbekistan's Supreme Council (legislature), elected in early 1990, continued to be dominated by old-line Communists.

Just two weeks after President Karimov was sworn in on 4 January 1992, the capital of Tashkent exploded in violence, as 10,000 students protested increases brought on by price liberalization. At least six students were killed in several days of rioting. The students were supported by Birlik, which accused the government of ruling by "dictate and terror." Birlik leader Abdul Rakhman Pulatov told U.S. Secretary of State James Baker in February that "the totalitarian regime has been destroyed in Moscow, but in Tashkent it continues to exist."

Shortly after his inauguration, President Karimov consolidated his power by abolishing the office of vice president held by rival Shukrulla Mirsaidov, who was accused of ties with organized crime and inciting the student riots to destabilize the government. Mirsaidov was named a "state secretary," and Karimov created the office of prime minister, appointing Abdulkhashim Mutalov, his former deputy in the Cabinet of Ministers, to the post.

Throughout the year, the government tightened repression of the opposition. The Erk newspaper continued to be censored, and a February hunger strike by Birlik activists to try to force authorities to register the movement's newspapers failed. In April, police evicted Birlik from its Tashkent headquarters. Scores of opposition figures were beaten and arrested. In late June, Birlik leader Pulatov was severely beaten after leaving the prosecutor's office, where he had been brought for questioning. On 2 July, internal affairs ministry troops blocked areas of Tashkent to prevent a joint Erk-Birlik demonstration, subsequently cancelled for fear of violence. Protests in Samark were broken up by police, and sixteen Erk leaders arrested. As a result, Erk Chairman Saleh resigned from parliament. By mid-year, over twenty Birlik members had been charged with criminal offenses, and many were taken into administrative detention for interrogation.

With Erk's withdrawal from parliament, the government sponsored several new puppet political parties to maintain the illusion of a multi-party system, among them the Party of the Heirs of Timur and the Social Progress Party (PSP). Both received wide coverage in the official press.

Partly to deflect attention from his repressive measures and to undercut the nationalist and Islamic opposition, Karimov launched a campaign to blame Moscow and ethnic Russians for Uzbekistan's economic, ecological and social woes. To this end, the government sought to rehabilitate the late Sharaf Rashidov, first secretary of the Uzbek Communist Party from 1959 until his death in 1983, who—along with dozens of high Uzbek officials—had been implicated in a massive corruption scandal during the Brezhnev years known as the "Uzbek cotton affair." In late 1991, the government amnestied former Party First Secretary Inamjon Usmankhojaev, who had been arrested on bribery and embezzlement charges in 1989 and sentenced to 12 years' imprisonment. In early 1992, the attempt to transform the leaders implicated in the "cotton affair" into victims of Russian-Bolshevik aggression was intensified.

The government's anti-Russian tone spurred a further exodus of Russians, who had previously supported President Karimov as a bulwark against the Uzbek nationalists and Islamic fundamentalists. Approximately half a million Russians, many of them badly needed professionals and skilled workers, left Uzbekistan between 1979 and 1989, and in 1992 the brain-drain continued. Many cited escalating harassment and the language law that required the use of Uzbek. And while the government managed to avoid the kind of inter-ethnic violence that erupted in 1989 between Uzbeks and Meshketian Turks in the Fergana Valley, ethnic tensions remained high in 1992.

Uzbekistan's economic outlook remained bleak, despite the discovery of oil reserves in March. Although the country was the world's third-largest cotton grower and seventh-largest gold producer, the collapse of Soviet markets, as well as decades of corruption and mismanagement, left it among the former Soviet Union's poorest nations. Although an extensive series of laws passed by the Supreme Council— including the legalization of private property, private banks, foreign investment, and commodity and stock exchanges—laid a legislative foundation for a market economy, little had changed in the structures of economic control or in economic institutions. Privatization of state assets had not been implemented.

Productivity and investment continued to plunge, and unofficial estimates put unemployment at close to 2 million. The country's skyrocketing population growth put further pressure on the government to find long-term solutions. President Karimov dismissed the need for "shock therapy," and continued a policy of deficit spending and government subsidies. Russia's decision to free most retail prices in January affected Uzbekistan, which imported over 60 percent of its consumer goods and 80 percent of its grain from Russia. Prices for basic foodstuffs were capped and subsidies to school cafeterias were doubled in an effort to soften the blow. Controls on prices for most basic social services remained in place. With most state enterprises beset by financial problems, the government continued a soft-credit policy, further fueling the deficit.

Even as the government actively sought foreign investors, a lack of a stable currency and continued government intervention in the economy created barriers to foreign investment. Under the country's privatization laws, land and natural resources remained the property of the state. The strategy for reforming the large agricultural sector included the expansion of private (leased, not owned) plots of land; the development of small-scale food processing plants to ease unemployment; and the closure of unprofitable state farms and collectives. Few of the measures were implemented, and central control of farm output remained substantial.

The ongoing ecological impact of the receding Aral Sea continued to be a major issue. An ill-conceived project diverting water from two rivers that fed the huge inland sea led to a 65 percent decrease in the sea's volume, creating large quantities of oversalianated dust from emerging banks that destroyed soil already poisoned by pesticides. Fishing was ruined, and infant mortality and illness rose in adjoining regions.

Political Rights and Civil Liberties: Citizens nominally have the right to change their government democratically. Although the 1991 presidential elections were deemed generally free and fair, there were significant irregularities. A draft constitution, published in late September, declared Uzbekistan a "sovereign, democratic republic" where "no ideology or religion can be established as the official state ideology or religion." The head of state would be elected for a term of five years, during which he must suspend membership in any political party. Under the provisions, the president cannot be subjected to impeachment. The constitution, which has yet to be adopted by referendum, clearly gives the president almost dictatorial powers.

In 1992, the government cracked down on the political opposition, harassing and detaining leaders and activists from Birlik and Erk. Overtly political laws remain on the books, thus limiting political activities, press freedom and freedom of expression. The Islamic Renaissance Party remains banned, and Birlik still cannot register as a political party.

In March, the editor of *Khalk Suzi*, the official organ of the Supreme Council, was fired, provoking a strike by journalists. In response, the presidium shut down the newspaper. The Erk newspaper has been denied access to newsprint, and issues have been consistently censored. The Uzbek-language *Ozbekistan avazi* is officially controlled by the ruling party, and presents one-sided coverage. Birlik has been prohibited from publishing a newspaper in Uzbekistan. A charitable organization set up by Birlik in Russia—Aloqa—does publish a newspaper, *Nezavisimyi ezhenedelnik*, which is transported from Russia into Uzbekistan. In June, police arrested one of the paper's reporters, who was charged with "offending the honor and dignity of the president," a crime since 1990. Later, the charge was increased to "spying for a foreign government." The press law forbids publishing anything which promotes war, fascism, the incitement to ethnic violence, or contains "non-objective" attacks on individuals.

Other opposition activists were charged under political statutes. Poet Yadgar Obid, charged with "agitation for the overthrow of the existing order by force," received political asylum in Azerbaijan. New measures passed by the Supreme Council gave the state security apparatus more powers to tap telephones, and punish anti-government activities. A new provision for registering political parties was likely passed to allow the government to deprive Erk of its legal status.

While freedom of religion is nominally respected in this largely Muslim nation, the government controls aspects of religious life. The autonomy of the official Muslim establishment remains limited. The Muslim Religious Board for Central Asia is still under secular control. When a group of Muslim clergymen tried to unseat the head of the Muslim Religious Board, Mufti Muhammad-Sadiq Muhammad-Yusuf, charging he was corrupt and excessively subservient to the state, only the corruption charges were investigated. In January 1992, the mufti was accused of having cooperated with the KGB. Nevertheless, the government continued to resist calls for the mufti's resignation.

Travel restrictions have been placed on opposition activists, and there are no independent trade unions.

Vanuatu

Polity: Parliamentary
democracy
Economy: Capitalist-
statist
Population: 175,000
PPP: $2,054
Life Expectancy: 69.5
Ethnic Groups: Indigenous Melanesian (90 percent), French,
English, Vietnamese, Chinese, and other Pacific Islanders

Political Rights: 2
Civil Liberties: 3
Status: Free

Overview: Located in the Western Pacific, this 800-mile-long archipelago
of some 80 islands, formerly called the New Hebrides, was
an Anglo-French condominium until receiving independence
in 1980. The condominium arrangement divided the islanders into English and French
speakers, creating rifts which continue today. The francophones were largely excluded
from authority in the first post-independence government, and a number of islands
initially faced secessionist movements.

Following a repeat victory by the anglophone Party of Our Land (VP) in the
1987 election, cabinet minister Barak Sope began mounting a challenge to Prime
Minister Father Walter Lini's leadership. In May 1988, a demonstration called by
Sope to protest the government's management of traditional lands turned into a riot.
In the aftermath, Lini threw Sope out of the cabinet and ultimately the parliament. In
December 1988, President Ati George Sokomanu, Sope's uncle, called on the support
of the armed forces and attempted to dissolve parliament and replace it with an
interim administration headed by Sope and opposition leader Maxime Carlot. All three
were arrested and charged with inciting mutiny, although an appeals tribunal
overturned their conviction in April 1989. An increasingly insecure Lini assumed
several top cabinet posts in late 1990, and in April 1991 he fired most of his
ministers for refusing to sign loyalty pledges, replacing many with friends and
relatives. In August 1991, the VP dumped Lini as its leader, and in September
parliament replaced Lini with Donald Kalpokas.

In the 2 December 1991 elections, Carlot's francophone Union of Moderate
Parties, formed in the 1970s to delay British-supported plans for independence, won
42 percent of the vote and 19 of the 46 seats in parliament. Both Lini's new National
United Party and the VP gained 10 seats, with 4 seats going to Sope's Melanesian
Progressive Party, one to the tiny Fren Melanesian Party, along with two independents. In late December, Lini and new Prime Minister Carlot, who beat out Kalpokas
for the top spot in a parliamentary vote, shunted aside traditional Anglo-French
animosities and joined their parties in a governing alliance.

In 1992, the new government quickly assumed a pro-French slant, causing doubts
over how long the alliance would last. In January, the government received $300,000
in goodwill aid from the French territory of New Caledonia, which Lini castigated as
"selling the nation's sovereignty." The government also announced plans to increase
French education and replace more than 40 senior civil servants with French-speaking

appointees. In October, full diplomatic ties were restored with France. Relations were broken in 1987 when Lini expelled the French ambassador for alleged interference in the country's affairs.

Political Rights and Civil Liberties: Citizens of Vanuatu can change their government through free and fair elections.

The judiciary is independent of the government, and citizens receive fair trials. On Christmas Day 1991, the incoming government released the entire prison population of some 200 inmates in a general amnesty, setting free at least one murderer and several rapists. Freedoms of speech, press and association faced various restrictions under the Lini government. There are no independent newspapers or radio stations, and the government often did not allow opposition viewpoints to be aired and attempted to censor news of the VP's leadership struggle. In August 1991, the High Court issued an order against further restrictions. Restrictions were also placed on the timing and location of opposition rallies. Freedom of religion is respected in practice, although a constitutional review committee is considering placing limits on the activities of non-established religious groups. Citizens have full freedom of movement internally and abroad.

Twenty trade unions are grouped under Vanuatu Trade Union Congress, which is independent of the government. Strikes are infrequent due to the high rate of unemployment.

Venezuela

Polity: Presidential-legislative democracy
Economy: Capitalist-statist
Population: 18,883,000
PPP: $5908
Life Expectancy: 70.0
Ethnic Groups: Mestizo (69 percent), White (Spanish, Portuguese, Italian, 20 percent), Black (9 percent), Indian (2 percent)

Political Rights: 3
Civil Liberties: 3
Status: Partly Free

Overview: President Carlos Andres Perez barely survived an attempted coup by mid-level military officers in February 1992. After months of street protests demanding he resign and attempts by the Congress to cut short his mandate, rebellious air force and navy units failed in a second coup attempt in late November. Amid increasing political uncertainty, Perez vowed to remain in office until the end of his term in February 1994.

The Republic of Venezuela was established in 1830, nine years after achieving independence from Spain. A history of political instability and long periods of military rule culminated with the overthrow of the General Marcos Perez Jimenez regime in 1958. The election of President Romulo Betancourt and the promulgation of a new constitution in 1961 established a formal democracy.

The 1961 constitution created a federal system consisting of twenty states and the federal district of Caracas. The eastern territory of Delta Amacuro became the twenty-first state in 1991. The president and a bicameral Congress are elected for five years. The Senate has at least two members from each of the states and from the federal district. All former presidents are life members of the Senate and additional seats are awarded to minority parties. There are currently 201 seats in the Chamber of Deputies. State legislatures and municipal councils are elected.

Politics is dominated by the social-democratic Democratic Action (AD) party and the Christian Social Party (COPEI). The AD has won the last two national elections. In December 1988, former President Carlos Andres Perez (1974-79) defeated COPEI's Eduardo Fernandez.

After Perez took office in February 1989, Caracas was torn by a series of violent street protests—remembered as the *caracazo*—against the government's austerity program intended to stabilize the debt-strapped economy. The riots left over 300 people dead, according to official sources.

In the 1989 local elections, the AD lost in over half the country's 20 states and 269 municipal districts. Three governorships went to left-wing parties that ran anti-corruption campaigns. Despite the first-ever opportunity to elect local officials, voter abstention was more than 70 percent.

The government's optimism about its economic liberalization program was undercut in 1991 by corruption scandals, labor strikes and the penetration of the nation's institutions by the region's expanding drug trade. And while the economy grew by 10 percent in 1991, official figures showed that more than half the population lived in poverty. Opinion polls and renewed social unrest reflected disillusionment not only with the government but with the political establishment generally.

On 4 February 1992, Perez was nearly overthrown by mid-level officers representing almost ten percent of all army units. Widespread popular support for the nationalist rebels and their call for an end to government corruption was expressed in the mass anti-Perez demonstrations and labor and student strikes that continued until the summer.

To shore up his tottering government, the 70-year-old Perez gave cabinet positions to the opposition COPEI and to military commanders who led the successful counterattack against the insurrection. He also increased army salaries. But with popular anger toward Perez increasing, COPEI joined with left-wing parties in a series of legislative maneuvers to cut short Perez's mandate. During the summer, Perez was able to marshal barely enough support in the legislature to avoid a national referendum on his rule. In mid-November, after the Senate passed a non-binding resolution calling for a referendum to be held at the time of state and municipal elections scheduled for 6 December 1992, Perez went on national television surrounded by the military high command to reject the proposal.

Throughout the year polls showed that Lieutenant Colonel Hugo Chavez, the imprisoned leader of the February coup attempt, remained the most popular political figure in the country, while Perez's disapproval rating reached 90 percent in some surveys. After a summer lull, street protests and strikes resumed, punctuated by the first acts of political terrorism in decades. A shadowy group called the Bolivarian Liberation Forces (FBL) took credit for armed attacks on an AD legislator accused of corruption and the home of former President Jaime Lucinchi, also of AD. Although there was no concrete evidence of a connection to Chavez's Bolivarian Military Movement, the FBL expressed support for Chavez and called for a "civilian-military insurrection."

On 27 November, air force and navy units allied with Chavez and backed by apparently left-wing civilian insurgents made a second attempt to overthrow the government. After a day and a half of fierce fighting, the rebels were repulsed by armed forces loyal to Perez. Most Venezuelans ignored the rebel calls for a popular insurrection. Polls indicated that despite antipathy toward Perez, most people did not want military rule.

In the aftermath, Perez vowed again to complete his term and to continue the economic reform program despite growing opposition to it within his own party, which suffered a major defeat in the 6 December municipal and regional elections. By the end of the year, with twelve months to go before the next presidential election, Perez was increasingly dependent on the military high command for political support and to forestall renewed unrest within the officer corps.

Political Rights and Civil Liberties:

Citizens are able to change their government through elections. Constitutional guarantees regarding freedom of religion and the right to organize political parties, civic organizations and labor unions are generally respected. Political parties occupy the spectrum from right to left, but the two major parties are autocratic organizations which have become increasingly detached from the citizenry.

Freedom of expression and freedom of political and civic activity have been threatened in recent years. After the attempted coup in February 1992 and in response to the wave of anti-government protests that followed, the government suspended a series of constitutional guarantees. Free expression, freedom of movement and the right to strike were restored after two weeks. Freedom of assembly and the right to protection against detention without due process and unwarranted searches of private property were not restored until 9 April. The government temporarily suspended most civil liberties again after the November coup attempt.

Human rights abuses have risen dramatically as the police and security forces have cracked down on a growing crime wave and against the series of protests and demonstrations against the Perez government. There are numerous independent human rights organizations. Since the February 1989 riots and following the 1992 coup attempt, these groups have recorded thousands of abuses, including intimidation, arbitrary arrest, torture during detention and summary executions. In 1992 rights monitors charged the government with interfering in their international communications, especially to the United States.

The judiciary is headed by a Supreme Court whose members are elected by the Congress. Although nominally independent, the judicial system is overly politicized and weakened by the chronic corruption that permeates the entire political system. It is also slow, ineffective and generally unresponsive to charges of rights abuses by police and security forces. Less than a third of the prison population, which totals over 30,000, has been convicted of a crime. Military courts investigating abuses by members of the armed forces are slow to cooperate with the civil court system, if at all. Military court decisions cannot be appealed in civilian courts. The judiciary has also been undermined by drug-related corruption, with growing evidence of bribery and intimidation of judges.

The press is privately owned. There are nearly a dozen independent daily newspapers. Radio and television are mostly private, supervised by an association of broadcasters under the government communications ministry. Censorship of the press and broadcasting media occurs during states of emergency. Under the Perez government, numerous journalists investigating corruption and rights abuses have been arrested, interrogated or otherwise threatened. The media in general has faced a pattern of intimidation from official and unofficial sectors. The government has also been accused of spying on journalists covering politics. In 1992, a number of radio news programs and call-in shows were suspended after interviewing officers involved in the February coup attempt or their sympathizers.

Labor unions are well organized but prone to corruption. A new labor law in 1991 reduced the work week from 48 to 44 hours and made it illegal for employers to dismiss workers without compensation. However, the law is often disregarded and a number of labor leaders were detained during strikes broken up by security forces in 1992.

Vietnam

Polity: Communist one-party
Economy: Statist
Population: 69,212,000
PPP: $1,000
Life Expectancy: 62.7
Ethnic Groups: Predominantly Vietnamese, with Chinese Khmer and other minorities

Political Rights: 7
Civil Liberties: 7
Status: Not Free

Overview: The Vietnamese government revamped the constitution in April 1992 to formally allow private enterprise, foreign investment and land inheritance, reflecting a six-year shift away from central planning. However, the new constitution maintains the country's nominal commitment to socialism as well as the Vietnamese Communist Party's (VCP) monopoly on power.

The French colonized Vietnam's three historic regions of Tonkin, Annam and Cochin-China from 1862 to 1884. During World War II, a resistance movement led by Ho Chi Minh fought the Japanese occupiers, and later battled the returning French. The country won independence in 1954, and was divided between a French-installed government in the south and a Communist one in the north. Planned free elections were never held, and military forces and insurgent groups from the North eventually overtook the South, re-uniting the country in 1976 as the Socialist Republic of Vietnam.

As the nation struggled with mounting poverty, the Seminal VCP Sixth Party Congress in 1986 began a reform program called *doi moi* (renovation), which has decentralized economic decision-making, encouraged small-scale private enterprise and largely dismantled agricultural collectivization. Farmers were allotted land and permitted to sell output at market prices, transforming the country into a rice exporter. Despite this, living standards remain dismally low. Malnutrition and health problems are widespread, and the government has eliminated the system of free health care. The education system is in poor shape—teachers are underpaid, and schools are severely understaffed and under-equipped.

The VCP renewed its commitment to socialism at its Seventh Party Congress in June 1991, but it also acknowledged that private enterprise was needed to build up what newly elected party leader Do Moi candidly referred to as "a poor and backward country." The Congress filled a new politburo with educated reformers who could apply modern economic principles while maintaining the party's power. In August 1991, veteran revolutionary fighter turned economic reformer Vo Van Kiet was named prime minister.

On 15 April 1992, the National Assembly approved a new constitution that codified many of the economic changes of the past six years. Heated debates pitting young reformers against hard-line military representatives and veteran revolutionaries forced a four day delay in the ratification. The new document explicitly recognizes the right of citizens to run private businesses and allows foreigners to own capital and assets. However, conservatives blocked proposals to allow farmers, who make up three-fourths of the population, to own land outright. Instead, the constitution allows them to transfer state-allotted land to their children.

Although the constitution nominally prohibits the VCP from interfering in day-to-day government affairs, the party remains the "leading force of the state and society." In addition, the document kept the party-controlled "people's committees" which supervise daily life at the village level. The constitution streamlined government in several areas. A single presidency replaced the Council of State, which had been the parliamentary standing committee and had served as a collective presidency. The president will be elected from within the National Assembly, will nominate candidates for prime minister and chief justice, and will command the armed forces. The constitution also scrapped the Council of Ministers in favor of a cabinet. Overall, 138 of the 148 articles of the 1980 constitution were revised.

A new 395-seat National Assembly elected on 19 July epitomized the VCP's continuing control of political life. Of the 601 candidates, 89.5 percent were VCP members, and nearly all the rest were backed by the umbrella Vietnam Fatherland Front. Although the new constitution allows anyone over 21 to run as an independent, only 2 candidates out of some 40 hopefuls managed to be accepted. The government disqualified many for late or incorrect forms, while the rest were "rejected" by the neighborhood and workplace units which had to approve them.

Prior to the vote, candidates heard surprisingly candid criticisms of the government from government-selected voter representatives, who were mainly retired bureaucrats and military officers. These representatives repeatedly mentioned rampant corruption, high unemployment, and the high price of electricity. Ultimately, both independent candidates lost their races, as did numerous sitting deputies. Most of these defeated deputies were from the older generation of revolutionary leaders, and they were replaced by relatively young technocrats with university degrees.

In late September, the Assembly elected conservative general Le Duc Anh as president, and re-elected Vo Van Kiet as prime minister. The Assembly also elected Nong Duc Manh, the politburo's first ethnic member, as its chairman. A new cabinet announced in October indicated the government's commitment to ending corruption. Of the four ministers dropped, at least three had been linked to corruption and inefficiency within their departments.

During the year, the government continued to call upon the United States to end its 17-year-old boycott, which bars American investment and prevents international lending institutions from granting development assistance. The U.S. has pegged a normalization of relations to the political situation in Cambodia, where a Vietnamese-installed government is scheduled to hold free elections in mid-1993, and to receiving a full accounting of the fate of the over 2,000 Americans listed as "Missing in Action" in Indochina. In November, several U.S. senators were given access to previously secret areas and documents, and in December, the U.S. said it would allow firms to sign contracts with Vietnam to be executed after the embargo is lifted.

Despite the country's vaunted natural resources, the expected windfall in investment after the U.S. embargo is lifted may take years to materialize. Investors face a decaying infrastructure, electricity shortages, bureaucratic corruption, and political ossification. Few of the 700 state enterprises are likely to turn a profit. Nearly $3 billion from abroad has already flowed to the formerly capitalist south.

Political Rights and Civil Liberties: Vietnamese citizens cannot change their government democratically. The July 1992 National Assembly elections were open almost exclusively to members of the Vietnamese Communist Party (VCP) and affiliated independents. Only two truly independent candidates managed to clear the bureaucratic and political hurdles towards getting clearance to run for office, and neither were elected.

The apparatus to monitor the population, including mass organizations and village and work units, has reportedly become more relaxed in recent years, although dissidents remain under surveillance. Ordinary citizens have become more open in criticizing government corruption and inefficiency, although questioning the one-party system or the government's commitment to socialism is illegal. Several notable crackdowns occurred in 1992. Police arrested a man who attempted to display the former South Vietnamese flag in front of reporters at the start of the inaugural Ho Chi Minh City Marathon in February; the police also seized negatives from foreign reporters attempting to photograph the scene. *Far Eastern Economic Review* reported the unpublicized April arrest of 17 activists of a People's Action Party in Ho Chi Minh City; the activists called for an overthrow of the government. The government magazine *Phap Luat* (The Law) reported on 5 March that six dissidents had been sentenced to terms ranging from 3 to 14 years for anti-government activities—one for forming an opposition organization called To Hach Tam (The Nucleus), and the others for belonging to an anti-Communist group. On 24 May, a court sentenced dissident Nguyen Ngoc Dat to 20 years in jail for "subversive activities" and sentenced several of his followers up to 12 years.

Defendants lack procedural safeguards and are at the whim of a judiciary subservient to the government. Prisoners often face brutal conditions, including torture and food deprivation. The government says it released its last "political re-education" camp prisoners on 30 April.

The government controls all media, which increasingly criticize bureaucratic inefficiency and economic inertia. Freedom of assembly is limited to state-approved gatherings or organizations. The government discourages, but generally does not prohibit, adherence to religion. Publication of religious materials is limited, and clergy members have been detained for alleged anti-regime activities. Many religious leaders, including several leading Buddhist monks, are under house arrest or in prison. Government plans to run the funeral in May for Buddhist patriarch Thich Don Hau were dropped following an international appeal and threats of immolation by at least one monk.

Citizens need permission to relocate, and travel abroad is restricted. Hong Kong's policy of repatriating Vietnamese refugees in its camps has largely stopped citizens from leaving Vietnam to seek asylum abroad. Ethnic minority groups living in rural areas continue face even worse economic conditions than the rest of the population—a study released in January 1992, for example, indicates that 40 percent of the Hmong suffer from goiter and 80 percent are illiterate.

All workers must belong to the state-controlled Confederation of Vietnamese Workers. Strikes are prohibited.

Western Samoa

Polity: Elected parliament and family heads
Economy: Capitalist
Population: 195,000
PPP: $1,981
Life Expectancy: 66.5
Ethnic Groups: Samoan (88 percent), mixed race (10 percent), Europeans, other Pacific Islanders

Political Rights: 2
Civil Liberties: 2
Status: Free

Overview:

In 1992, Western Samoa continued to recuperate from a devastating cyclone that hit in December 1991, causing upwards of $300 million in damages to houses and food crops.

Located 1600 miles northeast of New Zealand, the western Samoan islands became a German protectorate in 1899. New Zealand claimed the islands during World War I and administered them until granting independence in 1962. Malietoa Tanumafili II is head of state for life and must approve all legislation passed by parliament. Recent changes have limited the authority of traditional rulers. Future heads of state will be elected by the parliament for five-year terms. In an October 1990 referendum, 53 percent approved universal suffrage for all citizens over 21, although due to low participation rates, only 22.9 percent of the eligible voters actually backed the measure. Previously, only the *matai*, traditional tribal chieftains who represent villages of extended families, could vote. However, seats in the 47-

member *fono* (parliament) are still restricted to *matai*, with the exception of two seats set aside for citizens of non-Samoan descent. In the same referendum, voters rejected creating an upper house both restricted to and selected by the *matai*.

Roughly 90 percent of the electorate turned out for the country's first direct elections on 5 April 1991, held several weeks later than planned due to the difficulty of registering approximately 80,000 newly franchised voters. Several MPs shifted alliances after the election, leaving the Human Rights Protection Party with 30 seats, up 3 from the 1988 vote, and the opposition Samoan National Development Party with 14, along with three independents. The new parliament assembled for the first time on 7 May and re-elected Tofilau Eti Alesana as prime minister. A new nine-member cabinet included Fiami Naomi, the country's first female cabinet minister.

Ceremonial gifts were banned in the lead-up to the vote because of the difficulty in distinguishing between bribery and traditional gift-giving. In the ensuing confusion, post-election petitions were filed against eleven members of parliament for charges ranging from illegally distributing food and drinks, to receiving votes from people dead or out of the country.

In 1992, the country continued to repair the damages caused by violent cyclones in February 1990 and December 1991. The cyclones destroyed cocoa and coconut crops, all but eliminating a crucial revenue source.

Political Rights and Civil Liberties: Western Samoans can change their government democratically. Although two competing parties exist, politics are conducted largely according to individual loyalties.

The judiciary is modeled on the British system and is independent of the government. However, many disputes are handled at the local level by the 362 village *fonos* (councils of tribal chieftains) through traditional law. The 1990 Village Fono Law affirmed this authority but gave recourse in certain cases to the Lands and Titles Courts. Fonos occasionally order harsh punishment, including stonings and the burning of houses. There are no restrictions on speech, press or association. Although the government grants full freedom of religion in this predominantly Christian country, village leaders often choose the religion of their followers. There is generally full freedom of movement, although citizens are occasionally banished from villages as punishment. Workers can strike and join unions of their own choice, although no unions have formed in the private sector.

Yemen

Polity: Military-civilian ruling council and parliament (transitional)
Economy: Capitalist-statist
Population: 10,395,000
PPP: $1,560
Life Expectancy: 51.5
Ethnic Groups: Arab majority, African and Asian minorities

Political Rights: 6
Civil Liberties: 4
Status: Partly Free

Overview: In 1992, the recently unified Republic of Yemen postponed its first free elections until April 1993 amidst a wave of assassination attempts. In addition, there were rifts between the leaders of the former North and South republics stemming from their starkly different political backgrounds.

Located at the southern end of the Arabian peninsula, the Republic of Yemen was formed on 22 May 1990 through the merger of the northern, conservative Yemen Arab Republic (YAR) and the southern, Marxist People's Democratic Republic of Yemen (PDRY). The two countries had fought border skirmishes in 1971-72 and a one-month war in 1979. Reunification efforts began in the early 1970s, continued after the war, and increased in the late 1980s, reportedly with the backing of the Soviet Union.

A constitution ratified by an announced 98.3 percent in a popular referendum on 15-16 May 1991 provides for a transitional Presidential Council, composed of a president, vice-president and three other officials, who were scheduled to serve pending free parliamentary elections in November 1992. The elected parliament will draft a permanent constitution. The transitional constitution also established an interim 301-seat House of Representatives led by prime minister Haydar Abu Bakr al-Attas, a former DPRY president. All but 31 of the MPs are from the YAR's General People's Congress (GPC) and the DPRY's Yemen Socialist Party (YSP). Under arrangements made prior to reunification, the YAR's Ali Abdallah Salih serves as president, and the DPRY's Ali Salim al-Biedh is vice-president.

Since the reunification, there been constant signs of a split along north-south lines in the coalition government, owing to prior political differences as well as centuries-old tribal and regional animosities. A key issue has been the demand of many northern groups, particularly the fundamentalist Al Islah party of Sheik Hussein Abdullah al-Ahmar, that the new constitution place the country under the *Shari'a*, or Islamic law. The YSP rejects this, but worries that it will lose to the northern-based GPC in the elections. To ease this latter concern, in February President Salih assured al-Bieidh of a continued role in the government for himself and his party regardless of the election outcome.

A series of assassination attempts further stoked the tensions between the parties. The violence began soon after reunification, when the YSP attempted to extend its influence in the north by opening offices there to increase its membership. The violence increased in September 1991 when unknown assailants killed Hassan Huraibi and wounded Omar al Jawi, leading members of the new Yemeni Unionist Alliance party. In the first half of 1992, there were 15 reported assassination attempts, including the wounding of the justice minister and the killing of the prime minister's brother. Although two members of the GPC were killed, the majority of the attacks were against leading figures of the YSP. Many accused Saudi Arabia of instigating the attacks in order to disrupt the country's democratic transition. Despite the unrest, on 22 May, the second anniversary of reunification, Salih pledged to push ahead with the elections.

The attacks continued in the latter half of the year with attempts on the prime minister, the speaker of the parliament, and two members of the ruling Presidential Council. Newspapers also reported new rifts between the president and vice-president and between their parties, particularly regarding influence among the country's powerful tribal groups. The GPC accused the YSP of provoking tribal disputes, while the YSP accused the GPC of marshalling tribal groups against it. On 5 November, the joint leadership postponed parliamentary elections until 27 April 1993. The president and vice-president said they had resolved their differences, but felt the violence must be controlled before elections are held.

The economy continues to be affected by the government's support of the Iraqi invasion of Kuwait in 1990. In September 1990, Saudi Arabia cut off aid and expelled one million expatriate Yemenis, ending the country's largest source of hard currency and leaving the government hard-pressed to repay a $7.8 billion debt. In June 1992, Saudi Arabia warned foreign oil companies working in Yemen to avoid a several-thousand square mile area near the two countries' disputed border where there have been recent oil discoveries, jeopardizing Yemen's attempt to increase oil output to 800,000 barrels per day within five years. The economic conditions led to anti-government riots in October, and on 9 December, shootouts in the southern city of Taiz between riot police and demonstrators protesting runaway inflation left 10 dead. Despite the difficulties, the government has accepted tens of thousands of Somali refugees in danger of starvation.

Political Rights and Civil Liberties: Yemeni citizens cannot change their government democratically. An interim government composed of leading figures from the former North and South states postponed elections planned for November 1992 until April 1993. Upwards of 40 parties ranging from the radical left to the far right have formed.

A combined security force from the two states functions as part of the Ministry of the Interior, and has broad powers against suspected security threats. This force has abused detainees to extract confessions and routinely monitors civilians.

The judiciary is in the process of being reformed, and the lower courts of the two former republics continue to operate according to the laws in their respective areas. In August 1991, the government appointed a 48-member Supreme Court with judges drawn from the north and south, although there are still jurisdictional disputes arising from the differing legal systems. In the former YAR, there are Islamic and commercial courts, both of which are considered generally independent. In the former DPRY, the judiciary continues to function without adequate due process rights.

During the transition period, citizens have been cautious in expressing criticism of the government, although newspapers have been more vocal. Professors at Sanaa

University are required to pass a security clearance before being hired. All organizations must be registered with the government, but freedom of association appears relatively unrestricted. Citizens have been free to demonstrate against the government.

Islam is the state religion, and other faiths face restrictions. The tiny Jewish community in the rural north is not allowed to build synagogues, but can practice in their homes and meet with foreign Jewish groups, who have distributed religious materials. In August 1992, the *New York Times* reported on a major effort by several Western Jewish organizations to discreetly relocate the remaining 1,600 Jews. Indian Hindus maintain temples in Aden, but the small Christian community is not permitted to build churches. Citizens can travel freely internally and abroad. During the transitional period, the labor codes of the former republics remain in effect. In both unions were closely controlled by the government, and workers rights were restricted.

Yugoslavia (Serbia and Montenegro)

Polity: Dominant party (military-influenced)
Economy: Mixed statist
Population: 9,965,000
PPP: na
Life Expectancy: 72.6
Ethnic Groups: Serbs (80 percent), Montenegrin (7 percent), Muslim Slavs (Sanjak, 4 percent) Gypsies, Albanians, others

Political Rights: 6
Civil Liberties: 5
Status: Partly Free

Overview: After four of six constituent republics that used to make up Yugoslavia declared independence, Serbia and Montenegro declared a truncated, rump-Yugoslavia in April 1992, but the new state faced diplomatic isolation and international sanctions because of Serbian aggression in Croatia and Bosnia-Herzegovina. Internally, the new Federal Republic of Yugoslavia (FRY) saw friction between Serbian strongman Slobodan Milosevic, a hard-line nationalist, and Milan Panic, the Serbian-American businessman who was asked to take over as prime minister of the FRY in June. In December parliamentary and presidential elections, Panic challenged Milosevic for the Serbian presidency, but was defeated in a vote fraught with irregularities and fraud. By year's end, the FRY risked becoming superfluous, as Milosevic consolidated his power, hopes for lifting the embargo faded and the U.S. and Europe were considering stiffer measures or intervention against Serbia.

Rump-Yugoslavia was largely a Serbian-prompted creation to maintain the illusion of a federated state after the secession of Slovenia, Croatia, Macedonia and Bosnia-Herzegovina left Serbia—together with its putatively autonomous provinces of Kosovo and Vojvodina (*See reports in Related Territories section*)—and tiny, impoverished Montenegro as the only republics that had not seceded from Yugoslavia in 1991-92. Under a new constitution, accepted by the Serbian and Montenegrin republican assemblies on 23 April, the FRY was declared as a "sovereign federal state based on the principle of equality of its citizens and its member republics." The new constitution gave the republics sovereignty over issues not within the competence of the FRY and transformed the Yugoslav People's Army (YPA) into the Army of the Republic of Yugoslavia. Elections for the bicameral federal Assembly (parliament), consisting of the 42-member Chamber of Republics (divided evenly between Serbia and Montenegro) and 138-seat Chamber of Citizens, were scheduled for late in the year.

The key political dynamic throughout 1992 was the power struggle between Milosevic, whom most blamed for fueling the 1991 war in Croatia and the outbreak of war in Bosnia-Herzegovina in March 1992, and Panic, who many felt would be easily manipulated by the Serbian president but who began to use his FRY post as a forum to criticize Serbian policies and to seek ways to lift the international sanctions and bring an end to the fighting in Bosnia. However, the international community's reluctance to recognize the FRY made it difficult for Panic, whose efforts were often snubbed by world leaders until he decided to challenge Milosevic for the Serbian presidency late in the year.

The power struggle was framed by the escalating war in Bosnia and the May United Nations Security Council vote imposing tough economic sanctions on the Yugoslav government. Two days earlier, the European Community (EC) imposed a partial trade embargo on Serbia and Montenegro. The U.N. vote imposed a trade embargo, froze Yugoslav assets abroad, ended air traffic, reduced diplomatic relations and called for a general ban on Serbian-Montenegrin participation in all international cultural, sports and scientific events.

On 15 June, 71-year-old Dobrica Cosic, a politically independent, well-known author, was elected president by the Assembly for a four-year term. Milosevic, leader of the Socialist Party of Serbia (formerly the Communist Party) who was elected in a fraud-marred election in 1990, remained the powerful president of Serbia. Momir Bulatovic, also elected in 1990, remained president of Montenegro.

In June, the ruling Socialist Party of Serbia invited Panic to be prime minister, with one leading party member noting, "With Mr. Panic's selection as prime minister, our country would come out of this economic and social crisis much quicker." Most observers saw Panic as a tool to be used by Milosevic to convince the U.N. to lift sanctions. But upon his arrival in Belgrade, the capital, in early July, Panic declared that his mission was to "stop the war." On 7 July, Panic asked the 52-nation Conference on Security and Cooperation in Europe (CSCE) to delay any action against Belgrade. A week later, in a statement that put him on a collision course with Milosevic and other hard-line Serbian nationalists, he said his government recognized Bosnia-Herzegovina as an independent state and that the most important thing "for all Serbs is to stop shooting." At the end of the month, he flew to Sarajevo, the besieged Bosnian capital, to bolster a ceasefire that ultimately failed.

To undermine Panic, Serbia's Communist-dominated republican parliament handed Milosevic sweeping powers to regulate every facet of the republic's economy. And while Panic promised freedom of the press, Milosevic sought direct control of the republic's largest and most influential newspaper, *Politika*, and obtained legislation imposing severe limits on demonstrations and awarding new powers to the police. Moreover, even as Panic promised to breakup the Serb paramilitary groups fighting in Bosnia, free military training was offered every night in Belgrade's largest sports stadium, less than a mile from Milosevic's office.

By September, Panic faced a no-confidence motion in the Assembly in a showdown with Milosevic, but President Cosic threw his support behind the beleaguered prime minister. The motion against Panic was supported by 68 Socialist and ultra-nationalist Serbian Radical Party parliamentary deputies. Panic survived the no-confidence motion partly because deputies from Montenegro, which resents the war and the concomitant international isolation, supported the prime minister.

On 19 October, President Cosic met in Geneva with Bosnian President Alija Izetbegovic. The two issued a joint statement after six hours of negotiations with U.N. negotiator Cyrus Vance and EC representative Lord Owen in which they called for an end to the siege of Sarajevo and for the city's demilitarization. The announcement was undercut by the seizure that same day of the Yugoslav Interior Ministry by troops loyal to Milosevic. The Serbian president had become increasingly angry with Cosic for signing an agreement in September with Croatian President Franjo Tudjman, which called for an end to "ethnic cleansing," the Serbian-initiated policy of forcibly removing non-Serbs from areas in Bosnia controlled by Serb militias.

Prime Minister Panic faced another crisis on 2 November, when the Serbian nationalists who controlled the Yugoslav parliament pushed through a motion of no-confidence in the lower house. The chamber, backed by Milosevic, accused Panic and President Cosic of unilaterally acting to improve ties with Croatia and Muslim Albanian minorities in Serbia. The no-confidence motion, which was approved by a 93-to-24 vote, was not decisive because the upper house narrowly voted to retain him, again because of Montenegro's support. Meanwhile, President Cosic called for new elections for 20 December, hoping that opposition parties could defeat the Socialists in the federal and Serbian parliaments and pave the way for sanctions to be lifted.

President Cosic's increasingly outspoken opposition to Milosevic, and the somewhat surprising surge in Panic's popularity among voters in mid-November, led a key adviser to the Yugoslav president, Svetoar Stojanovic, to predict, "if the opposition unites, it could form a coalition with Socialist splinter groups." But five weeks before the vote, the opposition, which included the Serbian Renewal Movement led by Vuk Draskovic, the Democratic Party (SP) and several others had not decided whether to take part in the elections.

By mid-November, the United States, which for months had refused to take Panic seriously, began to publicly support the prime minister. Even as the U.N. approved a naval blockade in the Adriatic to toughen sanctions, the U.S. was seeking an exemption to import communications equipment to the independent television stations in Belgrade and TV-Politika, which were openly critical of Milosevic. The effort was aimed at offsetting Milosevic's control of Yugoslavia's main television stations, which reached 9 million viewers around the country. The U.S. move appeared to come at the request of Prime Minister Panic, who wrote the 15-member U.N. Sanctions Committee asking the right to import television equipment.

In November, Panic announced that he would challenge Milosevic for the Serbian presidency in the 20 December elections. On 9 December, the Supreme Court reversed an earlier decision by the republic's electoral commission that denied the prime minister, a naturalized American, the right to run because he failed to meet the one-year residency requirement enacted in November by Milosevic supporters. On 16 December, the U.S. increased pressure on Serbian voters by announcing that Milosevic was a possible war criminal who should be tried some day by a "second Nuremberg" tribunal.

Meanwhile, the strategy seemed to backfire as Milosevic stepped up his appeal to the Serb's traditional defiance toward foreign pressure, warning during campaign stops that major powers were attempting to set up a "puppet regime" in Belgrade.

Prime Minister Panic, campaigning on a peace platform, said that he could restore Serbia's international standing by negotiating an end to the war and to sanctions. Early polls indicated that Panic held a slight lead over Milosevic. Moreover, most opposition groups, though decidedly nationalistic, threw their support behind Panic, with several well-known figures such as Vuk Draskovic choosing not to run. By election night, independent polls were showing Milosevic and Panic in a dead heat, but both with under 50 percent of the vote needed to avoid a run-off. However, international observers monitoring the elections cited instances of fraud, particularly in the countryside, tampering with voter registration lists that left eligible voters, particularly pro-Panic students, off the rolls, and such irregularities as dead people voting. Shortly after the election, Milosevic announced that he had won 57 percent and Panic 33 percent, a dubious figure given the fact that Panic was expected to easily win Belgrade and other major cities. On 29 December, former Communist and nationalist allies of Milosevic voted to oust Panic as prime minister. The vote in the upper house was 30 to 5, with Montenegrins essentially cowed by Milosevic's victory, and 95 to 2 in the lower house. Vojislav Seselj, leader of the Radicals who has been accused of being a war criminal for leading a militia group in Bosnia, accused Panic of embezzling state funds and sabotaging the economy.

According to official results published by the Election Commission, Milosevic's Socialists won 101 seats in the 250-seat Serbian parliament. The extreme nationalist Radicals won 73 seats.

In the 138-seat Yugoslav Federal Assembly, the Socialists won 47 seats, the Radicals, 34, and the DEPOS opposition coalition, 20. In Montenegro, President Bulatovic faced a 10 January 1993 run-off against Milosevic ally Branko Kostic, after failing to win 50 percent of the vote. The vote, combined with the fact that Serbia-backed militias and former army forces controlled over 70 percent of Bosnia, presaged possible intervention by the West.

In economic issues, rump-Yugoslavia felt the pinch of economic sanctions, but their impact was not as drastic as some Western leaders had hoped. Fuel was getting through via Greece, Bulgaria and Romania. Goods were also coming across the Albanian border and through Macedonia. In fact, the price of gasoline actually dropped before the election, and Belgrade shops were stocked with goods and food in December, reflecting the region's status as a major food-producer. And while some Montenegrin ports were idle and the naval embargo was put into force in November, only a small amount of the strategic trade to Serbia and Montenegro covered by the U.N. embargoes arrived by sea.

Yet, international sanctions did have an impact, as shortages fueled hyperinflation. Several large manufacturing enterprises had to be closed, but to cushion the blow of unemployment and its possible destabilizing effects, the government—by printing money—kept many workers on at least partial salary. As a result, inflation, which ran at an annual rate of 786 percent from January to May, was likely to exceed 100,000 percent by year's end.

In foreign affairs, the rump-Yugoslavia remained something of a pariah throughout the year. On 22 September, after months of effort by the United States and the EC, the U.N. General Assembly overwhelmingly voted to expel the Belgrade government from the seat once occupied by the defunct Yugoslav federation.

Political Rights and Civil Liberties: Yugoslav citizens cannot freely elect their representatives; both the president and the prime minister are appointed by a parliament dominated by former Communists and nationalists loyal to Serbian President Slobodon Milosevic. Reports of widespread fraud and irregularities plagued the Serbian presidential and parliamentary races, as well as races for the Yugoslav Federal Assembly. The federal judiciary, headed by a Constitutional Court and a Federal Court (the latter hears appeals from the republican and provincial supreme courts), is in effect subordinate to Serbian and Montenegrin systems, which still contain elements antithetical to the rule of law.

Freedoms of expression and assembly are generally respected, but Serbian authorities have frequently threatened to ban demonstrations. Freedom of association is virtually forbidden for the Albanian majority in Kosovo. There are a plethora of parties in Serbia, but most are, to varying degrees, nationalistic, with the exception of one or two small parties that are genuinely democratic. Montenegro has three main parties: the Democratic Party of Socialists of Montenegro, a successor to the Communist party; the pluralist-oriented Democratic Coalition; and the pan-Serbian National Party. Independent newspapers in Serbia are uncensored, and both *Vreme* and *Borba* are often stridently anti-Milosevic. Independent TV station Studio-B and TV-Politika offer views divergent from the government, but their signals do not go beyond Belgrade. Independent radio station B-92 also does not reach past Belgrade. On the other hand, the Milosevic government controls the three government-run channels, and their ability to reach viewers in the vast rural areas was a decisive factor in the 1992 elections.

Freedom of movement is restricted by international sanctions, which forbid foreign airlines from flying into or out of Yugoslavia. Domestic travel is generally unrestricted, although Kosovo is an exception.

Serbs are overwhelmingly Eastern Orthodox, and are free to practice their religion. As for Catholics and Muslims, political realities have made public worship for them difficult, if not impossible, in some areas. Minority rights are also a key issue, particularly in Kosovo and Vojvodina, which has a large Hungarian minority. Thus far, Hungarians have not been the subject of persecution, and there are Hungarian newspapers and schools. In Kosovo, however, Serbia banned the elected parliament and most Albanian political activity has been forced underground.

The independent trade union movement in Serbia and Montenegro has been adversely affected by the war, sanctions, and government resistance.

Zaire

Polity: Presidential-
military (transitional)
Economy: Capitalist-
statist
Population: 37,928,000
PPP: $380
Life Expectancy: 53.0
Ethnic Groups: Some 200, including Azande, Bemba, Kasai,
Kongo, Luba, Lunda, and Pygmy

Political Rights: 6
Civil Liberties: 5
Status: Not Free

Overview:

In 1992, Zairian President Mobutu Sese Seko continued to evade challenges to his 27-year monopoly on power. The year ended in a stand-off between Mobutu and a newly established transitional government attempting to assert authority.

Known as the Belgian Congo until it gained independence in 1960, Zaire has been ruled since 1965 by Mobutu and his Popular Movement of the Revolution (MPR). Internecine blood-letting and attempted secessions following independence took the lives of 100,000 people and only ended with Major General Mobutu's consolidation of power. The trade-off for a quarter-century of political stability under Mobutu—with occasional help from foreign troops—has been an impoverishing level of official corruption and frequent repression of political opposition.

Before the legalization of independent political parties in 1990, the regime only allowed MPR-approved candidates to compete in elections to the unicameral National Legislative Council. The Council is subservient to the Mobutu-appointed Political Bureau. Zaire has held no elections since the legalization of political parties.

In 1990, facing growing popular pressures for political reform, Mobutu announced a series of changes ostensibly meant to introduce a multi-party system in the country. In 1991, however, it became clear the legalization of opposition parties had little to do with limiting the president's hold on power. Mobutu has refused to cede significant authority to a prime minister. Accusing his political opponents of trying to seize control through a "civilian *coup d'etat*," the President has emphasized he would retain control of the national treasury and the military even if the government included members of the opposition. Mobutu spends most of his time ruling from his yacht on the Zaire River outside the capital of Kinshasa.

In July 1991, approximately 200 opposition groups formed the Sacred Union of Forces for Change. A national conference was convened in the capital the following month. The conference was suspended two weeks later, however, when opposition groups called a boycott to protest the regime's attempt to stack it with Mobutu supporters. It was not until December 1991 that the opposition was able to seize control of a reconvened conference by ensuring it had a majority of the 2,000 conferees. President Mobutu called for immediate elections in 1992, but the opposition resisted elections before the national conference could appoint a transitional administration to organize balloting without the president's interference. Meanwhile, Mobutu announced he would stay on as head of state until the presidential election was eventually held.

On 25 November 1991, Mobutu appointed as prime minister Nguza Karl-i-Bond of the Union of Federalists and Independent Republicans (UFERI), an expelled member of the Sacred Union. One week later, the reconvened National Conference elected the archbishop of Kisangani, Monsignor Laurent Monsengo Pasinya as its president. He decisively defeated a Mobutu supporter for the position, an indication that control of the conference had escaped the president. Five months of procedural wrangling over conference membership and agenda had ended with a clear-cut opposition victory. The conferees then turned to the substantive tasks of launching the democratic transition.

The regime reacted by suspending the conference indefinitely on 19 January 1992. Delegates from Prime Minister Nguza's UFERI had already walked out, complaining it was now stacked with supporters of Etienne Tshisekedi, a Mobutu opponent and leader of the Union for Democracy and Social Progress (UDPS). France, Belgium, and the United States officially condemned suspension of the conference. There were clashes in Kinshasa and elsewhere in Zaire between UFERI supporters, mainly from Nguza's province of Shaba, and UDPS supporters, mainly from Tshisekedi's home province of Kasai.

The Sacred Union announced a general strike for 23 January to protest the conference suspension, but a small group of soldiers pre-empted the strike when they purportedly seized the national radio station the evening before. For three hours, they broadcast demands for a resumption of the national conference and for Mobutu and Nguza to step down. Opposition leaders distanced themselves from the action, and afterward claimed it was a regime ploy to ensnare them in a phony insurrection.

On 16 February, Catholic priests and opposition leaders led hundreds of thousands of anti-regime demonstrators in a protest against suspension of the national conference. Security police violently attacked the peaceful but banned march, shooting 40 of the protesters dead and injuring hundreds. The regime claimed that the "rioters" provoked the police, that the march was part of a plot to overthrow Mobutu, and that only seventeen died. According to an Africa Watch report issued in July, every claim was patently false.

Foreign pressure on Mobutu to reopen the national conference continued. He finally permitted it to be reconvened on 6 April. The conference quickly proclaimed its decisions "sovereign." The regime responded by reiterating that the conference had no authority to revise the constitution, appoint a transitional prime minister and cabinet, or take any other far-reaching measures. Yet the conferees officially moved in August to resume use of Zaire's former name—Congo—and re-adopt the country's former flag, thus reversing unilateral actions taken by the president in the early 70s.

Angered by this symbolic rejection of his rule, Mobutu demanded that these measures be submitted to referendum. After conceding on that point, on 15 August the conference chose the UDPS's Tshisekedi as transitional prime minister. Nguza Karl-i-Bond resigned, but not before declaring that his Shaba province would not recognize Tshisekedi's authority. Bloody ethnic clashes re-erupted in Shaba between supporters of the two men. Before Monsignor Monsengo Pasinya adjourned the national conference on 6 December, it had drafted a transitional charter to replace Mobutu's constitution and formally dissolved the regime's parliament. It also elected the Monsignor president of the new legislative body, the High Council of the Republic (HCR). Mobutu responded by suspending the HCR on 11 December.

Mobutu soon challenged Tshisekedi's authority. In early October, when the prime minister tried to fire the central bank governor, troops and tanks surrounded the bank, preventing Tshisekedi's new governor from assuming office. At the same time, members of Mobutu's supposedly dissolved national assembly defied the work of the national conference. The assembly met in its building, also protected by the military, in order to come up with a new Mobutuist constitution. Mobutu demanded on 1 December that Tshisekedi dissolve his cabinet and appoint new ministers with closer ties to the president. Mobutu also ordered top civil servants to take over control of all ministries. Days later Mobutu declared that he was suspending the HCR.

The American, Belgian and French governments have all cut off financial aid to the regime. Mobutu rejects demands for political reform in return for economic aid, asserting "nobody dictates policy to me." Hyperinflation squeezed the resources of the average Zairian; less than 25 percent of the population was employed in 1992. After the government imposed stringent rationing in the face of a nationwide fuel shortage, it announced in early June 1992 that it was seizing the petroleum supplies of every foreign oil company in Zaire. Meanwhile, Mobutu himself is reputed to have amassed a fortune of up to $6 billion.

Political Rights and Civil Liberties: Citizens of Zaire cannot change their government democratically. Although President Mobutu legalized opposition parties in 1990, he still wields absolute power.

The executive firmly controls the judiciary. Arbitrary arrest and detention are commonplace, and corruption and abuse are rife in the security forces. Opposition activists and human rights workers continued to be harassed and detained in 1992. Opposition headquarters have been attacked; in August 1992, the UDPS headquarters were fire-bombed. Security police and paramilitary squads violently break up opposition gatherings; in February, the police killed 40 people while breaking up "the March of the Christians."

In 1990, a number of independent newspapers critical of the regime began publication. Parties unknown have ransacked and bombed the offices of some. In November 1992, soldiers torched a printing company that published most Zairian opposition newspapers. Authorities can and have detained journalists for "insulting the head of state." State-run papers provide only pro-regime views, and ignored news about upheaval in 1992. Despite promises of opposition access to the state-owned broadcast media, dissent is almost nonexistent on the airwaves.

The regime does not recognize the right of assembly. Government officials routinely refuse to authorize opposition meetings and rallies, and nonviolent gatherings without permit are subject to brutal dispersal. Nonpolitical associations must register with the government. Churches need government permission to operate. Travel is often restricted and citizens must carry identification cards. Most Zairian women are subjected to traditional forms of subordination. The MPR formally controls the umbrella National Union of Zairian Workers; membership is compulsory for state employees. However, the regime has lost control over workers, who repeatedly struck for wage hikes and payment of salary arrears in 1992.

Zambia

Polity: Presidential par-   **Political Rights:** 2
liamentary democracy   **Civil Liberties:** 3
Economy: Mixed statist   **Status:** Free
Population: 8,385,000
PPP: $767
Life Expectancy: 54.4
Ethnic Groups: Bemba, Lozi, Lunda, Ngoni, other

Overview: **U**nder the leadership of democratically elected President Frederick Chiluba, Zambia completed its first full year of multi-party democracy in 1992.

The Republic of Zambia, which gained independence from Britain in 1964, is located in south-central Africa. The 1972 constitution institutionalized "one-party participatory democracy" under the leadership of President Kenneth Kaunda and his United National Independence Party (UNIP). Running as the sole candidate, Kaunda was re-elected in October 1988 to a sixth five-year term. Until 1991, all candidates for the unicameral National Assembly had to be UNIP members.

After the fall of communism in Eastern Europe, Zambia Congress of Trade Unions Chairman Frederick Chiluba publicly called for multi-partyism in late 1989. After growing public pressure, Kaunda announced in late 1990 that the country would hold multi-party parliamentary and presidential elections sometime in 1991. By December 1990, he signed the necessary constitutional amendments legalizing opposition political parties.

On 31 October 1991, Chiluba, standard-bearer for the opposition Movement for Multi-party Democracy (MMD), was elected president with an estimated 80 percent of the vote. The election was described by international observers as generally free and fair. The MMD also gained some 125 of 150 parliamentary seats. Kaunda conceded defeat gracefully, even though he had earlier warned that a civil war was possible if the UNIP lost.

Chiluba lost no time in firing prominent officials linked to Kaunda's regime. But Chiluba faced harsh criticism of his new appointees from within his party. MMD dissidents asserted that several of the president's new cabinet ministers were just as self-serving and autocratic as those in the Kaunda regime. The critics, many from the dissident Caucus for National Unity, complained in 1992 that Chiluba favored those of his own ethnic Bemba group for senior positions, and that too many appointments were rewards for assisting the MMD financially. The critics were invited by an irritated Chiluba to leave the MMD and form a new opposition party.

Meanwhile, the UNIP split in June 1992, when Enock Kavindele formed the United Democratic Party. Kavindele had led a brief challenge to Kaunda's role as party leader before the October 1991 election. Kaunda retired as opposition leader less than a year after he led the UNIP to defeat in the election. UNIP Secretary-General Kebby Musokotwane was elected president of the party on 1 October.

In August 1992, the Sport, Youth, and Child Development Minister and the Science, Technology, and Vocational Training Minister resigned from the cabinet, alleging growing government corruption. Their detractors charged that they had resigned because of unhappiness over their low-profile ministerial portfolios. Two weeks later, Chiluba dismissed the Minister of Works and Supply after reports that the latter had misappropriated substantial sums.

Local government elections marked by a 20 percent turnout were held on 18 November 1992; the ruling MMD dislodged the UNIP from almost every district council except those in Kaunda's east Zambia.

The new government inherited a devastated economy. Soon after his inauguration, the president called for the country's creditors to forgive or re-schedule the over $7 billion Zambia owed. Foreign creditors responded in 1992 by forgiving almost one-half. The new regime has pledged to remove trade barriers, encourage foreign investment, decrease state regulation of business, dismiss redundant state employees, privatize more than one hundred parastatals, and reduce or eliminate budget-busting subsidies for food staples. One of its early moves upon taking office was to pay more than $50 million in arrears to the World Bank, qualifying Zambia for renewed funding by the lending organization. It has also devalued the currency.

The trade union federation and university student groups have criticized the new government's willingness to sell off parastatals and accept an externally mandated structural adjustment program. A student demonstration in late September was violently dispersed by police; one student was killed and another severely injured. With the removal of price controls and the end of subsidized maize meal, popular dissatisfaction with the MMD is growing. Despite government attempts to expand agricultural exports, particularly as revenues from Zambian copper decline, the regional drought is causing massive crop failures.

Political Rights and Civil Liberties: Zambians can change their government democratically. Although parliamentary sessions are marked by free and open debate, critics allege that the constitution gives the executive overwhelming power.

The court system is independent of executive interference. The 27-year-old state of emergency was lifted by the new government in November 1991. Freedom of speech is generally respected by the new government. The press frequently publishes diverse views and may openly criticize actions by the MMD without fear of reprisal. Police permits for demonstrations and rallies are needed and are usually granted, although over-restrictive permit requirements may infringe on the right of free assembly. Former President Kaunda was detained in August 1992 for convening a political meeting without having obtained the necessary permit.

There have long been many autonomous cultural, professional, and civic associations. Freedom of religion is constitutionally guaranteed, although members of Chiluba's government have emphasized Zambia is a "Christian" nation. The Minister of Information briefly banned Muslim programs from being broadcast on state-owned radio in late 1991 until adverse public reaction forced him to reverse his action. He was eventually dismissed. Zambia has a strong industrial trade union tradition, and Chiluba's administration has not been spared strikes despite the new president's long-time links with labor. All large unions belong to the independent and democratic ZCTU, the only legal confederation.

Zimbabwe

Polity: Dominant party
Economy: Capitalist-statist
Population: 10,339,000
PPP: $1,469
Life Expectancy: 59.6
Ethnic Groups: Shona, Ndebele, white, and others

Political Rights: 5
Civil Liberties: 4
Status: Partly Free

Overview:
In the midst of economic decline and food shortages, President Robert Mugabe's government faced increasing public discontent 1992.

The Republic of Zimbabwe, formerly white-ruled Rhodesia, was established in 1980 after fifteen years of guerrilla activity and diplomatic negotiations forced Prime Minister Ian Smith to accept black majority rule. A Declaration of Rights in the new constitution specified that certain fundamental rights could not be modified by less than the full Parliament until ten years after independence. Following parliamentary elections in February 1980, Mugabe, leader of the ethnic Shona-dominated Zimbabwe African National Union (ZANU), was asked to form a government as prime minister. ZANU was one of two main guerrilla groups of the rebel Patriotic Front coalition, which fought for majority rule. After some post-independence armed conflict between ZANU and the smaller Ndebele-dominated Zimbabwe African Peoples Union (ZAPU), the two groups merged in December 1987, forming the ZANU-PF. With the approval of the ZANU-PF controlled House of Assembly, Mugabe became president of the country and the position of prime minister was dropped.

President Mugabe was re-elected in 1990 in an election characterized by an aggressively negative tone and acts of physical intimidation by partisans of both the ZANU-PF and the opposition Zimbabwean Unity Movement (ZUM). ZANU-PF won over 75 percent of the vote. Three parties are represented in the legislature: the ZANU-PF with 147 seats, the ZUM with two seats, and the remnant of a pre-Mugabe ZANU (now ZANU-Ndonga) with one seat. New legislative and presidential elections are scheduled for 1995.

In 1992, portions of the fragmented opposition attempted to revive themselves by forming coalitions. Most notably, the liberal Forum for Democratic Reform (TRUST), which will likely try to transform itself into a political party by 1995, came together on 30 May 1992. This multi-racial organization's trustees include prominent churchmen, jurists, and businessmen. TRUST pledged support free-market reform, proportional voting, paring down a bloated military, return to a two-chamber legislature, and limits on the executive president's power. In July 1992, Ndabaningi Sithole joined with former Prime Minister Smith, representatives of ZUM, and another small party to plan the creation of a separate, conservative opposition front. Sithole, head of ZANU-Ndonga, recently returned to Zimbabwe after seven years of self-imposed exile.

In its election manifesto of 1990, ZANU-PF stated it intended to introduce a land acquisition bill in Parliament that would allow for massive redistribution of land and the resettlement of peasant farmers. Approximately 4,500 white farmers own one-half of Zimbabwe's best agricultural land, much of it confiscated from blacks while the country was still a British colony. In December 1990, with ten years after independence, the ZANU-PF majority in the House of Assembly voted to address the problem of peasant landlessness. It amended the Declaration of Rights to ensure that neither the sum offered in compensation for the land taken for redistribution nor the confiscation itself could be judicially appealed.

In March 1992, the government moved to redistribute nearly half of all white-owned farmland. It decided to allow affected landowners to contest whether authorities had accurately applied their own pricing formula. However, Minister of Agriculture Witness Mangwende announced that farmers would not be compensated for the value of any improvements to land. The list of initial properties slated for purchase included the largest dairy farm in eastern Zimbabwe as well as some farms owned by blacks, though none owned by government officials. At mid year, however, the minister was replaced and his substitute revoked some of the takeovers.

In 1992, inflation worsened, unemployment increased, bureaucratic inertia and corruption continued, and the country suffered serious food shortages. The regional drought has forced Zambia to import grain from abroad. Under pressure from the IMF and World Bank, the government had sold grain reserves in 1991 to pay foreign creditors. Excessive government regulation was another factor that kept food prices artificially low.

Political Rights and Civil Liberties: ZANU-PF domination places limits on the people's ability to change the government democratically. However, other parties exist and manage to win a few parliamentary and local council seats. Parliament consists of the 150-mem-ber unicameral Assembly, with 30 seats reserved for chiefs and nominated members.

The judiciary is generally independent, and the president cannot dismiss judges. President Mugabe has been accused of obstructing justice in order to protect ZANU-PF officials from conviction. In 1991, the government moved to amend the constitution to sharply limit the scope of judicial review of legislative actions. These actions include allowing for capital punishment, tightening govern-ment control over universities, and restricting private property rights. With the expiration of the ten-year-old British brokered Lancaster House constitution in 1991, the House of Assembly is empowered to overturn by a two-thirds majority any clause in the bill of rights. Freedom of association, while still respected, is no longer constitutionally guaranteed.

The Law and Order Maintenance Act grants virtually unrestricted power and impunity to the regime's Central Intelligence Organization (CIO). CIO operatives frequently harass ZANU-PF's suspected "enemies." In October 1992, the regime asserted that it may deal with dissidents as internal security threats.

The major print media, television, and radio are government-owned. All reflect a ZANU-PF point of view in their coverage and presentation of the news. Small, private print media, such as the *Daily Gazette,* are freer to offer critical assessments of the government.

Political and non-political organizations are permitted, although the former face some restrictions. Political meetings and rallies require police permits, which may be denied on "security" grounds. In 1992, police broke up legally convened meetings of the political opposition and temporarily detained attendees.

Freedom of religion is respected. There are no restrictions on travel. Unions belong to the Zimbabwe Congress of Trade Unions, but there are increasing restrictions on the right to strike in services and industries deemed essential. Unionists were forbidden from holding nation-wide protests against the government's economic policies in 1992. Private human rights groups are permitted to operate in the country.

Australia
Christmas Island (Kiritimati)

Polity: Appointed administrator
Economy: Capitalist-statist
Population: 2,000
Ethnic Groups: Chinese and Malay

Political Rights: 3
Civil Liberties: 2
Status: Free

Overview:
Located in the Indian Ocean, Christmas Island is the home of a disappearing phosphate industry, which is owned by the Australian government's Australian Phosphate Corporation. Under Australian administration since 1958, Christmas Island has a government run by an administrator appointed by the Governor General, Queen Elizabeth's representative in Australia. Australia classifies the island as an external territory, but residents have the right to opt for Australian citizenship or residency status. Due to the near exhaustion of phosphate, the chief source of employment, many islanders have moved to Western Australia, Singapore, and Malaysia. The Australian government proposed laying off 150 phosphate miners in 1986. This caused labor and ethnic strife. The government decided to reduce the mine labor force gradually during 1986-89.

To reinvigorate the economy, Australia approved construction of a gambling resort complex. Pacific Consultants International of Japan suggested in 1989 that the island needed a new resort hotel, recreational and marine facilities, harbor facilities, and a better airport. A Melbourne-based consulting firm began studying the airport and tourism issues in 1990.

Two weeks after the 1987 election, the Australian government dismissed Christmas Island's democratically elected nine-member assembly, citing fiscal mismanagement. However, the islanders retain the right to vote in Australian national elections as part of the mainland's Northern Territory.

Cocos (Keeling) Islands

Polity: Appointed administrator and elected council
Economy: Capitalist-statist
Population: 1,000
Ethnic Groups: Malay

Political Rights: 1
Civil Liberties: 2
Status: Free

Overview:
Located in the Indian Ocean and discovered by Captain William Keeling in 1609, the Cocos Islands were a personal fiefdom of the Clunies-Ross family until 1978. An Austra-

lian-appointed administrator is the chief executive. An elected local council began functioning in 1978. In a 1984 referendum, the inhabitants voted to integrate with Australia. They are now part of Australia's Northern Territory, which elects members of the Australian Parliament. The population is mostly Malay.

Norfolk Island

Polity: Appointed administrator and elected assembly
Economy: Capitalist
Population: 2,000
Ethnic Groups: *Bounty* families, Australians, New Zealanders

Political Rights: 2
Civil Liberties: 1
Status: Free

Overview: Located in the South Pacific, Norfolk Island is the home to many descendants of *Bounty* mutineers. An Australian-appointed administrator is the chief executive, but there has been a freely elected, nine-member assembly since Australia's passage of the Norfolk Island Act in 1979. This legislation provided for substantial self-government. The assembly executive committee acts like a cabinet on the island.

Chile
Rapanui (Easter Island)

Polity: Appointed governor and elected local government
Economy: Capitalist-statist
Population: 2,000
Ethnic Groups: Spanish-speaking Polynesian natives (70 percent), and Chilean settlers (30 percent)

Political Rights: 3
Civil Liberties: 2
Status: Free

Overview: Rapanui (Easter Island) held democratic municipal elections in June 1992. Chilean President Patricio Aylwin had announced the vote during a visit in 1991, when he also expressed the need to update local laws to protect the native culture. Located in the Pacific Ocean, 2,360 miles from Chile, the island is the home of an ancient Polynesian culture. Under Chilean ownership since 1888, the island is isolated from the world with the exception of twice-weekly airline flights and twice-yearly cargo ships. There are no newspapers, but there is a local radio station. Tourism is the main source of income. Visitors come to see the island's hundreds of giant, long-faced statues. However, these attractions are crumbling. Islanders hope to save them with foreign funding.

Formerly run by the Chilean navy, the island became a Chilean municipality with voting rights in 1966. The territory has its own local government. Islanders have many social rights and economic advantages. Every family has the right to a house and five hectares of land. The government subsidizes energy and utility costs. Island students are eligible for government university scholarships in Chile.

China
Tibet

Polity: Communist one-party
Economy: Statist
Population: 3,000,000*
Ethnic Groups: Tibetans, Han Chinese

Political Rights: 7
Civil Liberties: 7
Status: Not Free

(*3 million Tibetans live under Chinese control, including 1.9 million in the Tibetan Autonomous Region)

Overview:

In 1992, China launched a new development policy for Tibet, including upgraded road and air links, which critics charge will only facilitate the settlement of ethnic Chinese into the area and further submerge the Tibetans' cultural identity.

Prior to the Chinese invasion in 1949, Tibet was a sovereign state for the better part of 2,000 years. The Manchus exerted influence on Tibet from the 18th century until their overthrow in 1911, although they never incorporated it into China. Between 1911 and 1950, Tibet functioned as a fully independent state. In late 1949, China invaded with 100,000 troops. China quickly defeated the small Tibetan army, occupied half the country, and established military and political control by 1951. That year, China forced a Tibetan delegation to sign a "17-Point Agreement for the Peaceful Liberation of Tibet," which purported to legitimize the occupation, guarantee religious freedom and largely exempt Tibet from Communist "reforms." At the time, there were 40,000 Chinese troops in Tibet, and the Tibetan spiritual and temporal leader, the 14th Dalai Lama, Tenzin Gyatso, feared the entire country would be overrun. Because the agreement was signed under duress, it lacks validity under international law.

Throughout the 1950s, the Chinese intensified their repression of Tibet and violated the Agreement on virtually every count. In 1959, popular uprisings culminated in massive independence demonstrations in Lhasa. China crushed the uprising over several months, killing an estimated 87,000 Tibetans in the Lhasa region alone. The Dalai Lama fled to India with 80,000 supporters.

In 1960, the International Commission of Jurists called the Chinese rule genocidal, and said that prior to the Chinese invasion Tibet had possessed all the attributes of statehood as defined under international law, including a defined territory and an independent government. During the Chinese Cultural Revolution from 1966 to 1976, the Chinese government banned Tibetans from enjoying basic cultural rights, such as wearing traditional clothes. By the late 1970s, more than one million Tibetans had died as a result of the occupation, and all but 11 of Tibet's 6,200 monasteries had been destroyed.

Although the repression eased somewhat after Mao's death in 1976, China continues to deny Tibetans basic political and cultural rights, and has often curtailed freedom of expression violently. Between 1987 and 1990, Chinese soldiers brutally broke up demonstrations throughout the country. Hundreds were killed and thousands were arrested. China placed Lhasa under martial law from March 1989 to May 1990.

In May 1992, China began a drive to transform Tibet "from a closed or semi-closed economy to active participation in domestic and international commerce." The government said it would offer incentives for foreign investment, and would establish a new economic and technical development zone in Lhasa. The Chinese have already ecologically destroyed parts of Tibet through massive deforestation. The latest plans include expanded road and air connections with China. Exiled Tibetans say this will facilitate the mass settlement of Chinese into Tibet.

Political Rights and Civil Liberties:

Tibetans cannot change their government democratically. China appoints all top government officials, and continues to systematically suppress the Tibetans' cultural identity and stifle calls for independence. The Chinese government has pursued a Sinification policy which includes curtailing the teaching of the Tibetan language in schools, sending several thousand Tibetan students to study in China, and settling ethnic Chinese into Tibet through special incentives. Tibet now has more Chinese than Tibetans.

Because monasteries have historically been the centers of education, authority and national identity in Tibet, the Chinese government has sharply curtailed religious freedom and stationed monitors in monasteries. The government limits the number of new monks, forbids religious leaders from giving large public teachings, and has canceled Tibetans' most sacred religious holiday, the Monlam prayer festival. Hundreds of monks have been detained in recent years for offenses such as chanting certain "forbidden" religious prayers and for carrying a photo of the Dalai Lama.

Tibetans are particularly discriminated against in education; according to official statistics they have a 25 percent literacy rate compared to 77 percent for China. Freedom of expression is severely limited. Several monks and nuns were reportedly arrested after staging demonstrations in May 1992.

There are credible reports that Tibetan prisoners are frequently tortured. On 29 May 1992, Western diplomats said they had been told by the Labor Reform Bureau in Lhasa that 1,000 people were serving in one prison camp and two "reform-through-labor" camps in the area. They included 70 who had been sentenced for counterrevolutionary crimes, although the authorities claimed none had been tortured. The actual number of political prisoners is believed to be in excess of 200. The London-based Tibet Information Network announced on 20 February that Dorje Wangdu had been sentenced without trial recently to three years in a labor camp, allegedly for suggesting that his friends wear Tibetan clothes on a Chinese national holiday. Prison conditions are brutal, and nuns are reportedly raped.

Tibetans who live outside Lhasa cannot visit the capital without going through an arduous task of obtaining permits. Although China's draconian family planning policy ostensibly does not extend to minorities such as Tibetans, sources indicate the one-child rule is stringently enforced in Tibet.

Denmark
Faeroe Islands

Polity: Parliamentary democracy
Economy: Mixed capitalist
Population: 49,000
Ethnic Groups: Faeroese

Political Rights: 1
Civil Liberties: 1
Status: Free

Overview:

The Faeroe Islands hosted a conference of whaling nations in September 1992. Along with Greenland, Iceland, and Norway, the Faeroe Islands decided to form a pro-whaling commission to manage whale and seal harvesting in the North Atlantic. The Faeroese had become frustrated with the whaling ban imposed by the International Whaling Commission.

The Social Democratic Party and the People's Party formed a coalition government in January 1991. Atli Dam, the Social Democratic leader, was named premier for the sixth time. His People's Party predecessor, Jogvan Sundstein, remained in the cabinet as the Minister of Finance.

Since 1948, the Faeroe Islands have had substantial autonomy within the Kingdom of Denmark. The Danish Government maintains authority over foreign affairs, defense, finance and justice. A high commissioner (ombudsman) represents Denmark. The Faeroese government has responsibility for communications, culture, and industry. It shares responsibility with Denmark for education, health, and social services, but the Faeroese administer these areas locally. The islands send two representatives to the Danish parliament, but pay no Danish taxes. The territory has the right to opt out of Denmark's European Community membership. There are 50 local authorities. Presently, six political parties with diverse ideological perspectives compete in elections. The parliament, the *Løgting*, is composed of 27 members chosen by proportional representation in seven districts, plus up to five supplementary members.

Fishing and agriculture dominate the economy. The territory has a chronic trade deficit, but Denmark subsidizes the economy. The Faeroese have a full range of political rights and civil liberties. Eight newspapers publish freely. There are public radio and television stations. Although the established Lutheran Church represents almost 90 percent of the population, religious freedom is respected, and there are several independent churches.

Greenland

Polity: Parliamentary
democracy
Economy: Mixed-
capitalist
Population: 57,000
Ethnic Groups: Inuit (Eskimo), native whites, Danish

Political Rights: 1
Civil Liberties: 1
Status: Free

Overview: Greenland's legislature consists of 23 members chosen by ·
proportional representation and up to an additional four
members for parties failing to win seats in districts. Jonathan
Motzfeldt was premier of Greenland (1979-91) and head of the socialist Forward
(*Siumut*) Party. Although his party remained dominant after the 1991 elections, he was
replaced by Lars Emil Johansen after allegations of financial mismanagement. The
Forward party won eleven seats in the election and formed a coalition with the Marxist-
Leninist Eskimo Brotherhood (*Inuit Ataqatigiit*) Party, which won five seats. The new
government is expected to seek increased independence from Denmark and adopt a new
tax system favoring lower income groups. The opposition parties in the legislature are:
the conservative Feeling of Community or Solidarity (*Attasut*) Party with eight seats;
the new Center Party with two seats; and the pro-business Polar (Issittrup) Party with
one seat.

Located in the North Atlantic, Greenland has had substantial autonomy from
Denmark since 1979. Denmark still controls Greenland's foreign and defence policy,
but the local authorities handle most other matters. Greenland sends two representatives to the Danish parliament in Copenhagen. Although Denmark has European
Community membership, in 1985 Greenland used its right to opt out of the EC.

Political Rights   Political rights and civil liberties are generally respected.
and Civil Liberties: There is full freedom of expression and association. However, published reports suggest evidence of discrimination
against Inuits in a contraception program. Doctors administer a disproportionately high
number of contraceptive injections to Inuits, and fail to explain side-effects and other
implications of the shots. In Denmark, doctors give these same shots only to those
who cannot take care of themselves.

Ethiopia
Eritrea

Polity: One-party
(transitional)
Economy: Mixed-statist
Population: 3,200,000
Ethnic Groups: Afar, Arab,
Beja, Bilin, Jabarti, Kunama, Saho, Tigrawi

Political Rights: 6
Civil Liberties: 4
Status: Partly Free

Overview: With a referendum on independence scheduled for April 1993, at the end of 1992 Eritrea was on the verge of becoming the first territory in post-colonial Africa to secede successfully from an African country. The interim administration has been the Provisional Government of Eritrea (PGE), headed by Issaias Aferwerki, secretary-general of the Eritrean People's Liberation Front (EPLF).

Eritrea extends from Djibouti to Sudan along the Red Sea in northeastern Africa. It bases its claim for independence on the assertion that it is a territory related to, but distinct from, Ethiopia. Italy colonized Eritrea in 1890. Mussolini's officials administered Eritrea and Ethiopia from 1936 to 1941 as part of the Italian colonial holdings in northeastern Africa. After the British routed local Italian forces during World War II, Britain governed Eritrea under a U.N. trusteeship until federation with Ethiopia in 1952.

During the federal period, Ethiopia banned Eritrea's trade unions and pro-independence political parties despite constitutionally guaranteed autonomy. The Ethiopian government also illegally imposed Amharic, a non-Eritrean language, as the language of administration. In 1962, Eritrea lost its formal autonomous status when the Ethiopian government exerted heavy pressure on the Eritrean legislative assembly to approve the assimilation of Eritrea into a unitary Ethiopia, making it another Ethiopian province.

The Eritrean Liberation Front (ELF) began an armed struggle for secession in 1961. It was supplanted by the EPLF, a politically more radical movement that arose in the 1970s. The EPLF drew financial support from Arab regimes in Iraq and Sudan and from some Communist European states.

In 1974, Ethiopian emperor Haile Selassie was overthrown by a Marxist-Leninist military clique (the Dergue), which also opposed Eritrean independence. Military control of Eritrean territory see-sawed between the EPLF and the Dergue during the next 17 years. During occasional peace negotiations, the Ethiopian government repeatedly stated that it would consider some form of arrangement for Eritrea short of independence, while the EPLF demanded a referendum within Eritrea that would have independence as one of its options.

In February 1990, the EPLF captured the port of Massawa after penetrating Ethiopian army defenses. In early 1991, a coordinated offensive waged by the EPLF in Eritrea and the rebel Ethiopian People's Revolutionary Democratic Front (EPRDF) in Ethiopia forced Ethiopian troops back on all fronts. The Dergue's troops finally capitulated in May 1991, with the EPLF seizing Asmara and the port of Asab, and the EPRDF emerging victorious in Ethiopia proper.

Although the EPLF had earlier indicated that Eritreans would be allowed to choose between federation with Ethiopia, integration into Ethiopia, or independence, the PGE announced in April 1992 that voters would only be able to vote yes or no for independence. The EPRDF, still running Ethiopia, stated in 1992 that it does not intend to block the U.N.-sponsored independence referendum in Eritrea. When Eritreans opt for independence, as it is virtually certain that they will, the strength of Greater Ethiopia nationalism among some Ethiopians will not be enough to seriously threaten Eritrea and its well-armed EPLF. An independent Eritrea would mean a land-locked Ethiopia, although the EPLF has agreed that the port of Asab can be a free port for Ethiopia.

The EPLF's rhetoric was Marxist-Leninist until the 1980s, when its party program began to claim that the movement had become social democratic. Until its victory over the Dergue, the EPLF had little tolerance for other Eritrean political factions. Several ELF leaders in exile have returned to Eritrea to participate in reconstruction, but others are staying abroad until the EPLF allows open political activity by opposition groups.

Struggling with a devastating drought, up to 85 percent of Eritreans now subsist on international food aid. The crisis has been exacerbated by the gradual return from neighboring countries of hundreds of thousands of refugees.

Political Rights and Civil Liberties: Although the Eritrean people have achieved *de facto* independence, they do not yet have the opportunity to change their government democratically. Elections for a national assembly are projected to follow the internationally supervised April 1993 referendum on independence. Local and provincial assemblies have already been elected under EPLF auspices.

EPLF's Issaias Aferwerki stated in late 1991 that there is no justification for political groups other than the EPLF in a liberated Eritrea. The Provisional Government of Eritrea announced in November 1992 that it will allow no political parties to operate in Eritrea prior to the referendum. The EPLF does not consider itself a political organization, but rather a "liberation front." Political movements like the Eritrean Liberation Front-Unified Organization have accused the EPLF of repressing all opposition to its rule during the pre-independence period. Other Eritrean political movements include the EPRDF-linked, anti-independence Eritrean People's Democratic Organization.

The Provisional Government has published a civil and criminal code that includes judicial remedies such as *habeas corpus* and limits on detention without charge. It has also created a court system and provided formal safeguards of judicial independence. However, because Eritrea's provisional government has not yet adopted a constitution, there are no formal civil liberties guarantees. A new constitution is to be drafted after the referendum.

Finland
Aland Islands

Polity: Parliamentary
democracy
Economy: Mixed
capitalist
Population: 24,000
Ethnic Groups: Aland Islanders (Swedish)

Political Rights: 1
Civil Liberties: 1
Status: Free

Overview:
The major political debate in the Aland Islands in 1992 concerned membership in the European Community (EC). Because the Alands have autonomous status within Finland, the islands could choose to remain outside the EC even if Finland were to become a member.

The Alands are an archipelago located between Sweden and Finland. Sweden lost the territory to Russia in the 1808-09 war. The Alands became part of the Grand Duchy of Finland within the Russian Empire. Russia, France, and the United Kingdom recognized the Alands as a demilitarized zone in 1856. When Finland proclaimed its independence from Russia in 1917, it rejected a petition from Alanders requesting reunion with Sweden. In 1921, the League of Nations recognized the islands as an autonomous Swedish-speaking province within Finland.

The Alanders elect a 30-member, multi-party parliament for four-year terms. The parliament can pass laws on internal affairs such as health and medical services, education, and culture. Finnish laws apply in areas where the Alanders have no legislative power. The Finnish president has veto power over local legislation only if the bill exceeds the parliament's authority or when there is a threat to national security. Alanders also elect a member of the Finnish parliament. A county governor represents Finland.

The Swedish language and local land ownership have special legal protection. There are competing newspapers and a public radio station.

France
French Guiana

Polity: Appointed commissioner and elected
assembly and council
Economy: Capitalist-statist
Population: 105,000

Political Rights: 2
Civil Liberties: 2
Status: Free

Ethnic Groups: Complex, black (66 percent), Caucasian
(French) (12 percent), East Indian, Chinese and Amerindian (12
percent), and other (10 percent)

Overview: As one of four French Overseas Departments, French Guiana
is ruled according to French law and the administrative
establishment is headed by a commissioner of the Republic
who is appointed by the French Ministry of the Interior. Representatives to the French
parliament are elected. A 19-member General Council is elected for six years with
councilors representing individual districts. Since 1982 the Council has been given
increased powers, particularly in financial matters.

At the most recent General Council elections in fall 1988, the Guianese Socialist
Party (PSG) retained control by taking twelve seats against seven for the rightist Rally
for the Republic (RPR) and other right-wing parties.

When French Guiana was given regional status in 1974, a Regional Assembly was set up, distinct from the General Council, with limited control over the
economy. This control was expanded under the Mitterrand reforms of 1982-83.
The first direct elections to the Regional Assembly, on the basis of proportional
representation, were held in February 1983. Mayors and municipal councils are
also directly elected.

In the Regional Assembly elections held on 22 March 1992 the PSG won 16 out
of 31 seats, followed by the Guianese Democratic Front (FDG) with ten and rightist
parties with the remainder. In the 20 September 1992 French referendum on the
Maastricht treaty defining European unity, only 11.4 percent of eligible French
Guianese voters cast valid ballots, with a majority of those voting "yes."

In recent years there has been concern about the condition of the estimated
10,000 Bush Negro and Amerindian refugees who fled into western French Guiana
because of guerrilla conflict in neighboring Suriname. Local and international human
rights groups charged the refugees were denied basic rights in camps controled by the
French army, allegations denied by the French government. With the end of the
conflict in Suriname, a fifth of the 6,000 refugees registered by the French government returned home in the first half of 1992, but only after after France offered them
cash incentives to leave.

Pluralistic points of view are presented in the media including two major
newspapers and several radio and television stations. A general strike carried out by
the United Trade Union Movement (MSU) briefly paralyzed French Guiana in
October 1992, reflecting mounting worker concerns over increased unemployment, low

European investment and the drain on the economy by a growing influx of immigrants from Haiti and neighboring Brazil.

French Polynesia

Polity: Elected Assembly **Political Rights:** 2
Economy: Capitalist- **Civil Liberties:** 2
statist **Status:** Free
Population: 199,000
Ethnic Groups: Polynesian (83 percent), French and
other European (11 percent), and Chinese and other
Asian (6 percent)

Overview:
French Polynesia consists of 120 South Pacific Islands, the most populous of which is Tahiti. A High Commissioner represents the French government. France controls justice and the security forces, some education, immigration, and international airline traffic, but the territory has significant autonomy. Polynesians elect a member of the French Senate and two National Assembly deputies.

The Polynesian Territorial Assembly consists of 41 members elected for a maximum term of five years. The Assembly elects the President, who selects the ministers with the Assembly's approval.

In the 1991 election, Gaston Flosse's People's Rally Party, an affiliate of the French Gaullist Rally for the Republic, won 18 of the 41 Assembly seats. An alliance between supporters of outgoing President Alexandre Leontieff and Assembly President Jean Juventine captured only fourteen seats, and three smaller groups won the remaining seats. Flosse and Vernaudon formed a governing coalition. Subsequently, their coalition picked up two more seats.

France's suspension of nuclear testing in April 1992 could have a severe economic impact, because the program generated about 10,000 jobs and 20 percent of the territory's net worth. Flosse denied the program caused environmental damage. Instead, his concern was French compensation for the economic damage resulting from the testing's suspension.

Economic problems have mounted since 1991. That year, Flosse instituted an audit of territorial finances, significant budget cuts, and higher consumption taxes. In July 1991, striking workers blocked roads and manned barricades in an anti-tax protest. The French High Commissioner and religious leaders negotiated a solution. Flosse agreed to roll back taxes, and France agreed to make up the difference in with subsidies. France and the territory each provide about half the expenses of running the Polynesian government.

The budgetary problems of 1991 increased in 1992, leading France to intervene and cut one billion francs from the unbalanced budget. This limit on autonomy outraged Flosse who believed it could have been a French Socialist attack on his French Gaullist affiliations. However, leading politicians with other affiliations faced charges of "passive corruption" or financial scandals.

Both Flosse and the pro-independence Liberation Front of Polynesia urged islanders to boycott the French referendum in the territory on the Maastricht Treaty on European integration. On 20 September 1992, about 70 percent of the few Polynesians participating voted yes. That same month, a group of pro-independence pearl farmers settled on the island of Mopelia after previous evacuations, and proclaimed a free and independent state. After security forces put down the uprising, the participants went on a hunger strike until they won a promise of negotiations. The confrontation highlighted the issue of conflicting local land claims.

Peaceful advocates of independence have freedom of expression and association. The islanders are largely Christian. There are three daily newspapers and a public broadcasting service. The Chinese minority prospers in business, and enjoys much greater acceptance than Chinese communities on other Pacific islands.

French Southern and Antarctic Territories

Polity: Appointed administrator and consultative council
Economy: Capitalist-statist
Population: 180
Ethnic Groups: French

Political Rights: 3
Civil Liberties: 1
Status: Free

Overview: The French Southern and Antarctic Territories consist of the Indian Ocean islands of St. Paul, Amsterdam, the Kerguelen and Crozet archipelagos, and the French-claimed sector of Antarctica. Due to the small population and scattered locations of these territories, the French administrator is based in Paris, where the consultative council meets twice annually. The administrator also appoints heads of the territories' four districts. Kerguelen's 100 inhabitants comprise the largest population of the territories. The chief activities are scientific research and fishing. Since 1977, Port-aux-Francais (Kerguelen) has served as a registry point for supply ships and bulk cargo ships. This registry allows French shippers to use non-French seafarers to sail under the French flag.

Guadeloupe

Polity: Appointed commissioner and elected
assembly and council
Economy: Capitalist-statist
Population: 389,000
Ethnic Groups: Predominantly black with white French
minority

Political Rights: 2
Civil Liberties: 2
Status: Free

Overview: As one of four French Overseas Departments, the Department of Guadeloupe is ruled according to French law and
the administrative establishment is headed by a commissioner
appointed by the French Ministry of the Interior. In the wake of Hurricane Hugo,
which ravaged Guadeloupe in 1989, the interior ministry appointed a new commissioner, Jean-Pierre Truce. Representatives to the French parliament are elected.

A General Council is directly elected to a five-year term, with each member
elected to represent individual districts. Since 1982, the Council has been given
increased powers, particularly in financial matters.

When Guadeloupe was given regional status in 1974, a Regional Assembly was
set up, parallel to the General Council, with limited control over the economy. This
control was expanded under the Mitterand reforms of 1982-83. The first direct
elections to the Regional Assembly, on the basis of proportional representation, were
held in February 1983. Mayors and municipal councils are also directly elected.

In the 1988 General Council elections the Socialist Party (PS) increased its
majority by one seat, defeating opponents 26-16. The Communist Party of
Guadeloupe (PCG), which normally secures a quarter of the vote, is pro-independence
but non-violent. Since the late 1960s, there have been a number of militant pro-
independence groups. Those that resorted to armed tactics were outlawed. Since 1985
violent activity has nearly died out. Labor unions are legal and there are two main
labor federations.

In the Regional Assembly elections held on 22 March 1992 the right-wing
Guadeloupe Objective gained 15 of 41 seats. The PS and another socialist group won
16, the Communists regrouped under the Progressive Democratic Party eight, and the
pro-independence Popular Union for the Liberation of Guadeloupe (UPLG) two.

In the 20 September 1992 French referendum on the Maastricht treaty defining
European unity only 9.6 percent of eligible voters cast valid ballots, with a majority
of those voting "yes."

There is one daily newspaper and a handful of radio and television transmitters.
International news agencies maintain local offices. In November 1992 banana planters
on Guadeloupe and Martinique blocked highways and airports, ending their four-day
shutdown of the islands when France pledged to maintain subsidies.

Martinique

Polity: Appointed com-
missioner and elected
assembly and council
Economy: Capitalist-statist
Population: 370,000
Ethnic Groups: Predominantly black with French minority

Political Rights: 2
Civil Liberties: 1
Status: Free

Overview: As one of four French Overseas Departments, the department of Martinique is ruled according to French law, and the administrative establishment is headed by a commissioner appointed by the French Ministry of the Interior. Representatives to the French parliament are elected.

A 44-member General Council is directly elected to a five-year term, with each member elected to represent individual districts. Since 1982, the Council has been given increased powers, particularly in financial matters.

Martinique was given regional status in 1974 and a Regional Assembly was set up, parallel to the General Council, with limited control over the economy. This authority was expanded under the 1982-83 Mitterand reforms. The first elections to the Regional Assembly on the basis of proportional representation were held in February 1983. Mayors and municipal councils are also directly elected.

In 1988 the left-wing Martinique Progressive Party (PPM), the Socialist Federation of Martinique (FSM), and the Martinique Communist Party (PCM) formed an electoral alliance, the Left Union (UG). Both the PCM and PPM advocated autonomy for the island as the first step toward independence. The UG obtained a one-seat majority in the 1988 General Council elections.

In Regional Assembly elections held on 22 March 1992 the right-wing Union for a Martinique of Progress gained 16 of 41 seats. The pro-independence Martinique Patriots and the PPM each won nine seats, the PCM, four, and the New Socialist Generation, three. The presidency of the Assembly was won by Emile Capgras, one of the four Communists, after three rounds of balloting.

In the 20 September 1992 French referendum on the Maastricht treaty to define European unity only 13.5 percent of eligible voters cast valid ballots, with a majority of those voting "yes."

A number of militant separatist groups resorted to violence in the mid-1980s and were banned. Separatist violence has nearly disappeared in recent years. Labor unions are legal and permitted to strike. There are two main labor federations.

The media are varied and reflect pluralistic points of view. There are several radio and television stations. There are one daily and several weekly newspapers. In November 1992 banana planters on Martinique and Guadeloupe, supported by teachers, and civil servant unions, blocked highways and airports, ending their four-day shutdown of the islands after France pledged to maintain subsidies.

Mayotte (Mahore)

Polity: Appointed com-
missioner and elected
council
Economy: Capitalist
Population: 87,000
Ethnic Groups: A mixture of Mahorais, French, Comoran, and
Malagasy speakers of African and European descent

Political Rights: 2
Civil Liberties: 2
Status: Free

Overview:

Part of the Comoran archipelago, Mayotte is an overseas
French possession located in the Indian Ocean east of
Mozambique and northwest of Madagascar. On 20 Septem-
ber 1992, most of the electorate failed to turn out for a referendum on whether
France and its overseas territories ought to ratify the Maastricht treaty advancing
European union. The island's ruling Mahorais Popular Movement (MPM) had called
for boycott of the vote to register popular disapproval of the French government's
policy of not requiring that Comoran nationals have entry visas. The Comoros, once
united with Mayotte as a French colony, is now an independent republic of three
islands immediately to the north of Mayotte.

In two referenda, the Mahorais population has rejected joining the adjacent
Federal Islamic Republic of the Comoros. Nonetheless, the Comoran government has
continued to claim Mayotte, rejecting the referenda supporting continued association
with France. The French prime minister stated in 1991 that France would not turn
Mayotte over to the Comoros against Mahorais wishes.

The French government appoints a commissioner as chief executive, and the
residents elect a seventeen-member general council. The MPM controls the general
council. Mayotte sends one member to the French Senate and elects one deputy to the
National Assembly. Residents enjoy the same rights as French citizens. The government-
owned radio station broadcasts in French and Mahorais. The economy is based largely
on tourism and primary products such as ylang-ylang, vanilla, copra, and coffee.

Monaco

Polity: Prince and
elected council
Economy: Capitalist-
statist
Population: 30,000
Ethnic Groups: French, Monegasque, Italian, and others

Political Rights: 3
Civil Liberties: 1
Status: Free

Overview:

The Principality of Monaco is located on the French
Mediterranean coast. Prince Rainier is the hereditary chief of
state, but the French government nominates the Minister of

State (the prime minister) and has the right to veto the heir to the throne. Monaco has a customs union with France, which controls the principality's foreign relations. However, Monaco belongs to several U.N. agencies and intergovernmental organizations. The voters elect an eighteen-member National Council for a five-year term. In the 1988 election, the National and Democratic Union won all eighteen seats. There is an elected sixteen-member municipal council, headed by a mayor and assistants appointed by the council.

Monaco's political future is uncertain, because Prince Albert, Rainier's heir, shows no interest in marriage. If the monarch dies without a male heir, France may incorporate Monaco into its territory.

Newspapers in nearby Nice print Monaco editions, which they distribute freely in the principality. Radio and television are government-operated. The French government has a controlling interest in Radio Monte Carlo. A tax haven, Monaco is the home of gambling casinos and light industry. Roman Catholicism is the state religion, but the constitution guarantees religious freedom. There is freedom of association, including trade unionism.

New Caledonia

Polity: Appointed commissioner and elected congress and assemblies
Economy: Capitalist-statist
Population: 176,000
Ethnic Groups: Kanaky, Wallisian-Futunians, Javanese, French, Tahitians, Vietnamese, other Asian/Pacific groups

Political Rights: 2
Civil Liberties: 2
Status: Free

Overview: New Caledonia, a group of islands located in the South Pacific 1,000 miles east of Australia, became a French territory in 1853, and gained internal autonomy in 1976. A major issue in recent years has been a drive for independence led by the indigenous Melanesian Kanaky people, who make up 43 percent of the population. Of the remainder, 37 percent are French and the rest are Pacific Islanders and Asian. The 1988 Matignon Accords, agreed to by pro- and anti-independence groups, called for Paris to administer the territory for a year, during which a referendum would be held on dividing New Caledonia into three autonomous regions, one dominated by settlers, and two dominated by Kanaks. The Accords also called for pro-independence areas, which are the least developed parts of the territory, to get a greater share of the wealth, much of which is derived from the world's largest nickel reserves. The Accords were ratified in 1988 by the settler-dominated Territorial Assembly, by the pro-independence Kanaka Socialist National Liberation Front (FLNKS), and approved in referendums held in New Caledonia and France. A referendum on independence will be held in 1998.

Elections to the new provincial councils were held on 11 June 1989. The anti-independence Rally for Caledonia in the Republic (RPCR) took 27 of the 54 total seats in the three regions, and the FLNKS took 19. In May 1991, RPCR leader Jacques LaFleur called for the 1998 referendum to be abandoned in favor of a "consensual solution" that would give the territory greater autonomy while maintaining its links to France. The FLNKS ignored the proposal. In November 1992, FLNKS president Paul Neaoutyine said his party faction favored a FLNKS boycott of the upcoming 1993 legislative elections, in part because of the "assumption of control by the RPCR of the main sectors of economic activity" in the territory.

Reunion

Polity: Appointed commissioner and elected assembly and council
Economy: Capitalist-statist
Population: 618,000
Ethnic Groups: Creole (Afro-European), French, Malagache, Malay, South Asian, and Vietnamese

Political Rights: 2
Civil Liberties: 2
Status: Free

Overview:

Located in the Indian Ocean east of Madagascar, Reunion has been in French hands since the seventeenth century. The population is multi-racial and largely Catholic. Sugar cane is the most important crop. A French commissioner carries out executive functions. There is a competitive, multi-party system, which ranges from pro-French conservatives to pro-independence Communists. Reunion has a bicameral legislature, consisting of an elected 36-member General Council and an elected 45-member Regional Assembly. The territory elects three National Assembly deputies and one Senator to the French Parliament. There are three daily newspapers and a government radio and television system.

The working class quarter of Saint-Denis, the capital, was rocked in early 1991 by three days of rioting; more than 50 people were injured and 11 killed. The disorders were precipitated by the government's seizure of the transmitters of a pirate television station that was popular among the poor Creole-speaking portion of the population. Government troops soon quashed the disturbance. High unemployment, insufficient opportunities, and a lack of diversions are abiding problems on the island, all leading to enforced idleness and frustration.

St. Pierre and Miquelon

Polity: Appointed
commissioner
and elected council
Economy: Capitalist
Population: 6,000
Ethnic Groups: French

Political Rights: 2
Civil Liberties: 2
Status: Free

Overview:
Located south of Newfoundland in the North Atlantic, the islands of St. Pierre and Miquelon are the only remaining French possessions in North America. Fishing is the mainstay of the economy. A quota agreement governing French and Canadian fishing in the area expired at the end of 1991. The International Court of Arbitration settled a long-running Canadian-French dispute over the territory's boundaries in June 1992. The panel awarded Canada most of the disputed area with the best fishing stocks. However, the arbitrators also gave France a corridor through the ocean south to international waters. Now France must negotiate for access to the Canadian fishing zone.

The French government appoints a commissioner, and local residents elect a fourteen-member general council and municipal councils. The islanders also choose a National Assembly deputy and a senator to the French Parliament. The islanders also have the right to vote in French referenda. On September 20 1992, voter turnout was low for the vote on the Maastricht Treaty on European integration. St. Pierre's Mayor, Albert Pen, had recommended abstention as a protest gesture against the French government's position on Canadian fishing rights. There is freedom of association. The unionized workers belong to *Force Ouvriere* (Workers' Force). The only newspaper is a bulletin of government announcements. There is a medium-wave radio transmitter and a government radio and television station.

Wallis and Futuna Islands

Polity: Appointed
administrator
and elected council
Economy: Capitalist-statist
Population: 14,000
Ethnic Groups: Polynesian

Political Rights: 3
Civil Liberties: 2
Status: Free

Overview:
Located in the South Pacific, Wallis and Futuna Islands have almost completely Polynesian populations. The islands voted to become a French territory in 1959. There is a French-appointed administrator and a locally elected twenty-member assembly. Three traditional chiefs are council members. The territory elects a National Assembly

deputy and a senator to the French Parliament. In 1989, local leaders criticized the administrator for governing without their participation. The parties include local affiliates of the French center-right, but the current Assembly deputy is a leftist. In 1991, there were talks on the islands' future between the French and the local leadership. In 1992, islanders voted for the Maastricht Treaty on European integration despite the Gaullist senator's plea for a "No" vote. The only radio station broadcasts in both French and Wallisian.

France-Spain Condominium
Andorra

Polity: Co-Princes and parliament
Economy: Capitalist
Population: 54,000
Ethnic Groups: Andorran (Catalan), Spanish, Portuguese, French, other European

Political Rights: 2
Civil Liberties: 1
Status: Free

Overview:

Andorra began 1992 in political deadlock. Oscar Ribas Reig, the head of government, had been unable to pass a budget for eleven months. Although the General Council had decided in 1990 to draft the territory's first constitution, conservatives blocked Ribas's attempt to codify rights in a written constitution. The French and Spanish governments had pressed Andorra to legalize trade unions and to establish other rights. Ribas had only 12 supporters in the 28-member General Council (parliament). After a technically illegal demonstration by 300 people, the parliament voted to dissolve itself. In elections on 5 and 12 April, reformist Ribas backers won 17 of the 28 seats. The new majority has the task of drafting the promised constitution and presenting it for approval in a referendum.

Located in the Pyrenees Mountains between France and Spain, Andorra has been a joint territory of the French government and the Bishop of Urgel, Spain since 1278. Before 1981, there was no clear power structure to rule the country. As Co-Princes, the French President and the Spanish Bishop had representatives there, but Andorra had no locally chosen head of government. The Co-Princes' representatives (vicars) still play a role, especially in the court system. Since 1981, there has been a head of government (*cap del govern*), chosen by the parliament. In 1982, Andorran voters approved a system of proportional representation in a referendum, but the French and Spanish sides have not enacted this reform, due to 48 percent voter abstention. There are some limitations on voting rights for young, first-generation Andorrans. Otherwise, there is universal suffrage at age 18. Only a minority of the population is Andorran.

In 1991, Andorra joined the European Community customs union. Its neighbors are forcing the principality to modernize and liberalize the economy.

The number of Spanish and Portuguese immigrants is growing faster than the native population. The government has proposed easing citizenship requirements.

Technically, there are no political parties, but there are factions and associations which have effective party functions. The French have generally handled Andorra's foreign relations. There are two competing, private weekly newspapers. There is a local public radio and television service. French and Spanish media are easily available. In 1990, the co-princes issued the first Andorran penal code, which eliminated the death penalty.

India
Kashmir

Polity: Indian-
administered
Economy: Capitalist-
statist
Population: 6,200,000
Ethnic Groups: Kashmiris (Muslim majority, Hindu minority)

Political Rights: 6
Civil Liberties: 6
Status: Not Free

Overview: During 1992, violence between Muslim separatist groups and the Indian government continued in the Indian-administered portion of Kashmir. The current round of unrest began in January 1990. Kashmir is the only Muslim-majority state in predominantly Hindu India. Over 200,000 Indian troops line the tense border with Pakistan, which is predominantly Muslim. Muslim militants raised the specter of war with two attempted border crossings between Indian Kashmir and Pakistani-controlled Azam or "Free Kashmir" in 1992. The countries moved together to defuse the situation.

Until 1947, all of Kashmir was an integral part of the British-ruled Indian territories. Headed by a Hindu ruler, the Maharajah of Kashmir, the area had a Muslim majority that did not wish to join India after the British decided to partition the region into Muslim Pakistan and Hindu-dominated India. Caught in the subsequent fighting in the 1947-48 partition war, the Maharajah opted for India. The Indian government announced that it would hold a referendum to settle the territory's fate, but the plebiscite has never taken place. Under Article 370 of India's constitution, the Indian government retains the right to legislate for Kashmir. Following the first Indo-Pakistani war, the U.N. divided Kashmir into Indian- and Pakistani-administered areas in 1949. In 1957, India officially annexed Kashmir into its territory as the state of Jammu and Kashmir. Following Indian-Chinese clashes in 1962, India ceded a portion of Kashmir to China. India and Pakistan warred over Kashmir in 1965 and in 1971-72. The two countries agreed in principle to accept the "line of actual control" as the *de facto* border and as a truce line under the terms of the 1972 Simla Agreement.

Kashmiris in the Indian-held areas have become increasingly anti-Indian since the late 1980s. India's central government appointed a new Kashmiri government in January 1990 and the elected government of Chief Minister Farooq Abdullah resigned. Following the senior religious leader's assassination and deadly clashes at his funeral between mourners and the Indian military, the Indian government imposed direct rule over Kashmir in July 1990. The Indian government also passed the Armed Forces Special Powers Act, which permitted search and seizure without warrant, granted the use of force against anyone suspected of contravention of any law, and offered immunity from prosecution to the armed forces. After increasing violence, the government enacted a series of laws further curtailing civil rights. More than 8,000 people have been killed as a result of the violence since 1990.

In January 1992, the Pakistani-backed Hizbollah movement took Amunallah Khan hostage in Pakistan. Khan is leader of the Jammu Kashmir Liberation Front (JKLF). Hizbollah wanted to stop a JKLF-threatened march to Indian-controlled Kashmir. JKLF, which also receives support from Pakistan, desires an independent Kashmir while Hizbollah wants Kashmir to join Pakistan. Throughout the year guerrilla groups attacked each other's members and civilians. Intermittently, the groups declared solidarity, only to rupture the accords with violence.

In February, the Indian and Pakistani prime ministers, P.V.N. Rao and Nawaz Sharif, met at an unrelated conference in Switzerland and discussed Kashmir. Sharif lauded 1992 as a "year of reconciliation." The following day, he announced a general strike in Pakistan for 5 February to show solidarity for the Muslims in Kashmir. The JKLF planned a storming of the Indian border from bases in Pakistani Kashmir to observe the eighth anniversary of the hanging of former JKLF president Maqbool Butt. Pakistan and India girded up for a new war in the event that the militants crossed. The Pakistanis deployed 40,000 troops to the border and set up blockades. After the troops fired, killing a few of the 7,000 marchers, Khan called off the march. Several thousand demonstrated in solidarity in Indian Kashmir. Tensions heated again as Khan called for a second border crossing in March. Pakistan banned rallies and jailed militants including Khan. It built barricades at the border and dispersed crowds with tear gas. Indian troops sealed the border and threatened to shoot anyone who tried to cross. In August, India and Pakistan held their first talks in twenty years over the fate of Kashmir. Discussions will continue.

India extended direct rule over Kashmir twice for six month periods in March and again in August 1992. Governor Girish Chandra Saxema of Kashmir discussed increased autonomy within the framework of the Indian constitution and offered dialogue with the separatists. He mentioned bringing Kashmir back to its 1953 status when New Delhi controlled only defense, communications, and foreign affairs. Rao extended this offer in August by promising elections and greater autonomy if guerrillas laid down their arms. The militants rebuffed the government's offers as empty promises.

Problems in Kashmir were futher complicated by September floods that caused the deaths of 2,500 people and destroyed 400,000 acres of crops.

Political Rights and Civil Liberties: Kashmiris cannot change their government democratically. Kashmir has been under direct rule from New Delhi since 1990; and Kashmiris were not permitted to vote in the 1991 Indian elections. The Indian government postponed scheduled 1992 elections indefinitely. Elections were last held in Kashmir in 1987 and were alleged to have been rigged by the victorious National Conference/Congress Party. Political parties are allowed, but the government bans militant organizations. The autonomy of Kashmiris in domestic matters, although protected by the terms of Kashmir's accession to India in 1947, is not respected by New Delhi.

Kashmiris suffer under the constant threat of violence from both the government and more than one hundred guerrilla organizations. More than 5,000 people have been killed since the beginning of the current unrest in 1990. Attacks on government and guerrilla sympathizers are common. The Indian government frequently detains sympathizers without trial.

Both the government and the militants restrict the media. Both commit acts of violence against journalists and ban the press. Government troops attacked journalists in March 1992 during a demonstration over censorship regulations. The JKLF banned the circulation of the *Kashmir Times* for five days to protest anti-guerrilla bias. BBC journalists were reprimanded for similar reasons. Pakistan detained journalists for breaking emergency laws and meeting with a "wanted man" near the Kashmiri border in March. Indian security forces frequently disperse peaceful demonstrations violently fire. Courts are theoretically sovereign and their decisions are not subject to appeal in Indian courts. Under the Army Act, the army can try cases in military court.

The insurgency and the government's military activities touch all aspects of life. Curfews are frequent. Army patrols limit freedom of movement. Emergency acts limit freedom of association. The government banned participation in separatist conventions. Militant Islamic groups limit women's freedom in dress, movement and activity. Security forces subject separatists and suspected sympathizers to torture, extra-judicial execution and incommunicado detention. The military also stands accused of gang rapes, village razings, attacks on children, and sealing residents in their homes and then setting the dwelling ablaze.

Indonesia
East Timor

Polity: Dominant party (military-dominated)
Economy: Capitalist-statist
Population: 750,000
Ethnic Groups: Timorese, Javanese, others

Political Rights: 7
Civil Liberties: 7
Status: Not Free

Overview: **A** year after the Indonesian army killed dozens of peaceful protesters in the East Timorese capital of Dili in November 1991, only token punishments have been handed out to the soldiers involved, while Timorese accused of being involved in pro-democracy demonstrations have received harsh terms, including life imprisonment.

In 1974, Portugal agreed to allow its colony of East Timor to conduct a referendum on self-determination in 1975. In August 1975, the Democratic Union of Timor, which had advocated independence, launched a military coup against the colonial administration, while the leftist Revolutionary Front for an Independent East Timor (Fretilin) mounted its own insurrection. On 28 November, Fretilin declared an independent republic, and on 7 December, Indonesia invaded, formally annexing East

Timor in July 1976 as the country's 27th province. As many as 200,000 people died from 1975 to 1979 as Indonesia strove to crush the Fretilin resistance. Periodic skirmishes and military abuses have continued ever since.

In 1991, the situation received international attention after Indonesian soldiers fired on thousands of East Timorese in the capital of Dili on 12 November. The victims were fired on as they engaged in a peaceful march to the burial site of Sebastian Gomes, a supporter of East Timorese independence killed by internal security forces in October. Several marchers had held pro-independence banners. On 26 December, the government said troops had "overreacted" to the situation and that 50 people had been killed, although eyewitness accounts placed the number at up to 200. Two generals in the region were removed from their posts.

In a series of court-martials in the spring of 1992, ten officers were given light terms ranging from eight to eighteen months. Meanwhile, eighteen East Timorese were sentenced to terms ranging from six months to life imprisonment for alleged anti-government activities proceeding or during the 12 November demonstration, or for subsequent protests in the Indonesian capital of Jakarta. An August report by the International Commission of Jurists said that while the trials appeared fair, the length of the sentences showed the "grim reality of raising a voice in dissent" against Indonesia's rule in East Timor.

In other major issues, in September 1992, the legislature elected Abilio Jose Osorio Soares as the new governor of East Timor, although Portuguese newspapers called him a puppet of the Indonesian government. In New York on 27 September, Portugal pressed Indonesia to allow the territory to hold a referendum on self-determination. On 20 November, soldiers captured Fretilin leader Jose Gusmao, dealing a serious blow to the rebel movement which has waged a low-grade independence campaign since the 1976 annexation. At least seven others were also arrested.

Political Rights and Civil Liberties: Since the 1976 Indonesian annexation, there have been persistent reports of rights abuses by the Indonesian government. In the aftermath of the November 1991 killings, the security situation in East Timor remains tense. The government has placed a ban on demonstrations, prohibited foreign reporters, and, in the lead-up to the first anniversary of the event, police stepped up security checks on civilians. Police are also said to tolerate bands of right-wing thugs who terrorize people in urban areas. The mostly Catholic population is generally allowed to worship freely.

Irian Jaya

Polity: Dominant Party (military dominated)
Economy: Capitalist-statist
Population: 1,200,000
Ethnic Groups: Mainly Papuan

Political Rights: 7
Civil Liberties: 6
Status: Not Free

Overview:

In 1992, the tiny guerrilla independence movement in Irian Jaya suffered serious setbacks as the Indonesian military killed one rebel leader in a raid, and another top commander surrendered. Meanwhile, the government is reportedly relocating villagers in the Central Highlands region away from a potentially lucrative mining area, in some cases by withholding food, medicine and other services.

In 1848, the Dutch colonized Irian Jaya, located on the western half of the island of New Guinea. In 1963 Indonesia assumed administrative responsibility for the territory under a U.N. agreement, which mandated that a referendum on self–determination be held by 1969. The mostly Papuan population seemed to favor independence. However, instead of a free referendum, Indonesia held a sham "act of free choice" in the summer of 1969, convening eight regional assemblies which all voted for annexation with Indonesia.

Since the 1960s, the guerrilla Free Papua Organization (OPM) has fought for Irian Jaya's independence. The Indonesian army carried out an offensive against the OPM in 1984 which sent hundreds of villagers into neighboring Papua New Guinea. The army also mounted significant cross-border raids in 1988 and 1989. Since then, the OPM threat has been greatly diminished, with only about 200 members still hiding in jungles near the border. On 31 May 1992, the Indonesian government raided a hideout and killed 48-year-old M.L. Prawar, an OPM commander. In August, veteran rebel leader David Jebleb surrendered to the military.

Indonesia's controversial transmigration program, under which residents from overcrowded parts of the country have been settled in areas such as Irian Jaya, appears to have slowed in recent years. There had been fears that the settlers would submerge the indigenous Papuan cultural identity on Irian Jaya. However, residents in some parts may be facing a more insidious threat. The April 1992 *Pacific Islands Monthly* reported that since 1989, government teams have attempted to relocate the populations of a number of villages in the Kurima district in the Central Highlands area by offering material incentives. More ominously, government educational and health workers have abandoned several villages, and officials have let food shipments sit in warehouses, causing hardships for several thousand villagers who refuse to leave. The affected villages are in the new exploration area of Freeport Indonesia Inc., a mining outfit.

Political Rights and Civil Liberties:

Residents of Irian Jaya face mistreatment by both the military and the OPM. Several dozen Irianese political prisoners remain incarcerated under Indonesia's anti-subversion laws, and many have been beaten or tortured. Trials under the subversion law lack due process safeguards. In July 1992, a court jailed a civil servant for 66 months for supplying food, ammunition, and a typewriter to the OPM. The government continues to restrict both access to and movement within Irian Jaya for both Indonesians and foreigners.

Iraq
Kurdistan

Polity: Dual leadership-elected parliament
Economy: Capitalist-statist
Population: 4,000,000
Ethnic Groups: Kurdish majority

Political Rights: 4
Civil Liberties: 5
Status: Partly Free

Overview: In May 1992, Kurdistan held presidential and legislative elections that were deemed free and fair by international observers. Coalition forces created a safety zone in the face of continued attacks by the Iraqi government, which fears growing Kurdish autonomy. The leaders of the two democratic parties, Massoud Barzani of the Kurdistan Democratic Party (KDP), and Jalal Talabani of the Patriotic Union of Kurdistan (PUK), split the vote, and established a joint leadership. Their parties also split the legislative vote.

Iraqi Kurds have fought with successive Iraqi goverments to end repression and to attain a level of autonomy. Saddam Husein granted limited cultural and political expression in the 1970s, but reneged on his agreements. During the 1980s, the Iraqi government engaged in genocide against the Kurds, including systematic mass murder, rape, torture, detention, forced deportation, and chemical bombing.

Iraqi Kurdistan gained international recognition after the abortive Kurdish uprising following the Gulf War. Under U.N. auspices, coalition forces of the U.S., UK, France and the Netherlands established a secure region above the 36th parallel, which protects some traditional Iraqi Kurdish areas. Consequently, more than 1.5 million Kurdish refugees returned from the Iraqi mountains and neighboring Turkey and Iran. The Iraqi government refuses to recognize the zone.

In December 1991, the Iraqi Kurds planned popular elections to elect a single leader and end traditional tribal and political divisions. On 17 May 1992, four candidates competed for the presidency, or "Leader of the Kurdish National Movement": Barzani, Talabani, Mahmoud Osman of the United Socialist Party of Kurdistan, and Sheikh Othman of the Islamic Movement. Barzani and Talabani virtually tied for the post. After backroom deliberations, they cancelled run-off elections and decided to share power.

On a separate ballot, one Islamic and six nationalist party lists vied for the 100 seats in the new Kurdish National Assembly (five seats were reserved for Christians). Party leaders avoided post-election conflict by agreeing on 15 May not to contest the election outcome. Despite some minor irregularities, international observers termed the elections free and fair. However, some Kurds criticized the system on the grounds that the party leaders had chosen the candidates for the lists. The Kurds accused the Iraqis of planting car bombs near the voting booths to disrupt the elections. Saddam Hussein termed the elections "a farce and a crime organized by their American masters and implemented by their Kurdish lackeys." The Kurds countered that the 1974 Law of Autonomy guaranteed elections.

One million voters, or 88 percent of the electorate, voted, and men and women turned out in nearly equal numbers. The direction for Kurdistan remained elusive: the KDP and PUK split the seats, 51 to 49. To avoid conflict, the two parties decided to split the seats evenly. No other party received the requisite 7 percent to attain a seat. The Islamic Movement received five percent; the others less than two percent. The PUK's Fuad Ma'sum, elected by parliament as Prime Minister, took office on 5 July.

In September the PUK and KDP decided to merge their *peshmergas* (guerrillas, literally "those who face death") into one force. In addition, sporadic violence continued throughout the year. Several aid personnel were killed or injured by car bombs and sniper fire, and snipers frequently shot at smugglers. During a July visit a car bomb narrowly missed the First Lady of France, Danielle Mitterand. In December, because of increasing violence, the U.N. suspended aid operations until the Iraqi government provided assurances of safety.

Turkish, Iranian and Syrian fears over growing Kurdish autonomy resulted in meetings between the leaders of those countries and several agreements to stop the formation of an independent Kurdistan. In September, the Turkish government announced that its airbases in Incirlik could only be used to protect the Kurds and not to install a Kurdish state. In an effort to gain the good will of the Turkish government, the Iraqi Kurds agreed to battle the terrorist Turkish Kurdish Workers' Party (PKK) camps located in northern Iraq.

Due to the U.N.'s economic embargo of Iraq, instituted at the close of the 1991 Gulf War, and Iraq's embargo of Kurdistan, prices soared during the year. Petroleum siphoning and smuggling into Kurdistan occur regularly.

In November 1992, Kurdistan hosted the first ever meeting on Iraqi soil of all Iraqi opposition groups. The groups reached an unprecedented agreement, devising a model for a federated Iraq and electing a Sunni, a Muslim, a Kurd and a Shiite to work for a unified Iraq.

Political Rights and Civil Liberties: Under Western protection, the Iraqi Kurds elected a National Assembly in 1992. Some media are party-controlled. The PUK owns and operates four television stations; the KDP one. The other parties are limited to newspaper and radio transmissions for lack of funds. The stations air foreign films. News perspectives are clearly party-oriented. Traditional practices curtail the role of women in decision making, education and the private sector, although to a lesser degree than in neighboring Muslim countries. Religious groups practice relatively freely with no official intervention.

Israel
Occupied Territories

Polity: Military-
administered
(West Bank and Gaza)
Economy: Capitalist
Population: 1,538,000
Ethnic Groups: Palestinian Arab, Jewish

Political Rights: 6
Civil Liberties: 6
Status: Not Free

Overview: The June 1992 election in Israel bringing Yitzhak Rabin's
Labor-led coalition to power raised the prospect of new
flexibility in negotiations over the status of the West Bank and
Gaza Strip. In August, the new Israeli government presented Palestinian delegates at the
Mideast peace talks detailed plans for an elected administrative council in the territories.
This would give Palestinians relatively high autonomy in running their daily affairs.

The West Bank, Gaza Strip, Golan Heights and East Jerusalem were occupied by
Israel following the 1967 Six Day War. Gaza, which has never been legally recognized as
part of any state, had been held by Egypt since 1948 but never annexed. The West Bank,
often referred to by the Biblical name, Judaea and Samaria, had been part of the Jorda-
nian-held portion of Palestine. Israel annexed East Jerusalem in 1967 and the Golan
Heights in 1981. In July 1988, Jordan's King Hussein abandoned his country's claim to
the West Bank, saying it would respect the wishes of Palestinians to establish an independent state in the territory. The Israeli Defense Ministry currently governs the territories
through the Civilian Administration. Jordanian and Egyptian laws (plus British regulations), as modified by the military authorities, are applied in their respective areas. However, Israeli Jews, who make up 5 percent of the population, are subject to Israeli law.

Since 1987, Palestinians living in the territories have participated in an uprising
(*intifada*) against Israeli rule. These largely spontaneous and uncoordinated attacks
included stone-throwing and violent acts against Israeli soldiers, who at times responded with lethal force. More than 900 Palestinians have been killed by the Israeli
Defense Forces (IDF) since the *intifada* began. Palestinian attacks on the IDF have
become increasingly more violent. In 1992, at least 11 Israeli soldiers were killed,
including 3 who were attacked by Islamic militants in Gaza in December.

In addition, in recent years many Palestinians have been killed by other Palestinians,
often because of alleged cooperation with Israeli authorities. Others were killed in
factional disputes, particularly between supporters of Fatah, the mainstream Palestine
Liberation Organization (PLO) movement, and those of Hamas, an Islamic fundamentalist rival that opposes the PLO's support for the Mideast peace talks. In 1992, the bulk
of the killings were Palestinian on Palestinian. Death squads from various factions,
which have killed approximately 800 people in the past five years, continued to terrorize
the population. By mid-November, Palestinians had killed more than 200 unarmed
Palestinians throughout the year, while 100 Palestinians had been killed by the IDF.

Throughout 1992, the status of the territories continued to be an issue at the
multilateral Mideast peace talks, which began in October 1991. On 25 August, Israel
presented Palestinian negotiators plans for Palestinian self-rule in the West Bank and

Gaza Strip. Under the plan, Palestinians would have a high degree of autonomy in running daily affairs through an administrative council, which could be elected as early as the spring of 1993. Talks on the final status of the territories would occur within three years of the council's formation. Palestinian negotiators had called for a 180-member parliament with full legislative powers. However, the Israeli plans required the council to consult with Israeli authorities on several matters, such as taxation. Rabin's government has also reduced government housing incentives for Jews in the territories. In December, however, the peace process received a setback after Israel deported more than 400 Palestinians suspected of terrorism. The moves followed the shooting death of an Israeli policeman in the West Bank, presumably by Islamic militants.

Political Rights and Civil Liberties: Palestinians living in the West Bank and Gaza cannot change their government democratically. Municipal and local elections in the West Bank have not been held since 1976, and some elected officials have been since dismissed. There have been no elections in the Gaza since 1946, dating back to the Egyptian occupation. Political parties are banned. Palestinians also have little control over economic planning, which frequently favors Israelis.

In February 1992, in response to a new wave of shootings of Jews in the West Bank, the Israeli Army relaxed the rules under which soldiers could use their weapons. The new guidelines allowed soldiers to fire on Palestinians who are armed, or who are being sought on suspicion of violent offenses. In May, the commander of Israeli forces in the West Bank said these new regulations allowed troops to shoot armed suspects without warning. Although the Israeli government does not officially condone extrajudicial killings, non-uniformed security agents have killed unarmed Palestinians in recent years, many of whom were wanted by or fleeing from the authorities.

There are credible reports of physical and psychological abuse by security forces of Palestinian detainees. In April 1992, the Israeli human rights group *B'Tselem* (In the Image) claimed that 5,000 prisoners had been tortured or mistreated in the previous year. Palestinians are frequently subject to administrative detention on alleged security grounds without formal charge. Administrative detention orders are valid for a maximum of six months. Each detention order is subject to judicial scrutiny and must be approved by the Minister of Defense. Orders can be renewed indefinitely, but are subject to judicial scrutiny each time. The military can enter homes without warrant for security reasons, provided there is authorization by an officer with the rank of lieutenant colonel or higher. Israeli security forces have also destroyed or sealed homes on security grounds.

Palestinians accused of ordinary crimes are tried in local courts by Israeli-appointed Palestinian judges. However, since the *intifada* began, many of these judges have resigned, resulting in a case backlog. Those accused of security offenses are tried in Israeli military courts. Security offenses include non-violent political acts deemed likely to be linked to violent acts. Attorneys are often not allowed to see a suspect until a confession has been obtained. Roughly 95 percent of the defendants are convicted in security cases.

The display of Palestinian flags or other political symbols is prohibited, as is public expression of support for the Palestine Liberation Organization or Islamic fundamentalist groups. In recent years, numerous Palestinian journalists have been arrested, detained or interrogated, and press offices have been raided. Both Israeli and Palestinian journalists are censored. Gatherings of ten or more people require a permit. In April, the authorities reopened Bir Zeit University, the last of six schools that had been shut down in 1988 in response to student protests and violence. Following violence in Gaza in May, Israel prevented Gazans from entering Israel to work. In June, Israel relaxed the ban, requiring instead that Palestinians from Gaza entering Israel be at least 25 and be employed in places where at least 10 Gazans work together. Although Palestinians are free to emigrate, the authorities often make it difficult to obtain travel permits.

Freedom of religion is respected. In the West Bank, workers are free to join unions, although some labor groups have been banned for suspected political affiliations. In Gaza, unions can organize on a craft or workplace basis, and are restricted as to the election of leaders and the opening of branch offices. Israeli authorities discourage much union activity through arrests and searches of offices, citing political links.

Morocco
Western Sahara

Polity: Appointed governors
Economy: Capitalist
Population: 201,000
Ethnic Groups: Arab, Sahrawi

Political Rights: 7
Civil Liberties: 5
Status: Not Free

Overview: In 1992, it appeared less likely that a referendum on self-determination for Western Sahara will ever be held. The Polisario rebel group fighting for territorial independence continued to fall apart, while sharp differences remained between the group and Morocco over voter eligibility for the referendum.

Spain annexed the coastal area of this region in 1884 and the interior in 1934. In 1957, Morocco renewed its centuries-old claim to the territory, and in 1960 newly independent Mauritania also staked a claim. These bids intensified in 1963 with the discovery of substantial phosphate deposits in the area. In 1966, the U.N. made the first of several calls for a territorial referendum.

In the face of increasing Moroccan-backed guerrilla attacks, in May 1975, Spain said it intended to give up the colony. In November, Morocco's King Hassan ordered 300,000 unarmed citizens into the territory in what was later called the "Green March." The territory ceased to be a Spanish province at the end of 1975, and a 1976 bilateral agreement gave Morocco the northern two-thirds of Western Sahara and Mauritania the remainder.

Native Saharans resisted this takeover, and organized the Popular Front for the Liberation of Saguia el Hamra and Rio de Oro (Polisario), a Marxist, Algerian-backed guerrilla group. Polisario formed a political wing, the Saharan Arab Democratic Republic (SADR) government-in-exile. In August 1979, after Mauritania signed a peace pact with Polisario, Morocco annexed the remaining southern third of the territory. In 1985, in the face of repeated Polisario attacks, Morocco began constructing 1,200 miles of fortified sand walls to hamper the rebels.

In August 1988, Morocco and Polisario agreed to a plan calling for a cease-fire and the presence of a U.N. force which would supervise a self-determination referendum. Both sides agreed that the voter rolls would be drawn from the last official census, which had been taken by the Spanish colonial authorities in 1974 and showed 74,000 residents. In April 1991, the U.N. formally agreed to sponsor all aspects of the referendum. A ceasefire took effect 6 September, and shortly afterward a 375-member U.N. peacekeeping force took up positions in advance of a January 1992 referendum.

However, in December 1991, the dispute over the electoral rolls caused the referendum to be postponed indefinitely. After the Moroccans argued that the Spanish count took no mention of nomadic herdsmen, many of whom have settled in neighboring countries for political and economic reasons, the U.N. agreed to include non-resident Saharans in the referendum. However, Polisario immediately vetoed the idea.

In 1992, it appeared less likely the referendum will be held at all. Polisario lost a key leader in August when Ibrahim Hakim defected. Hakim, the most senior of the 1,000 soldiers who have quit since the early 1980s, said the struggle was hopeless, largely because backing from Libya and Algeria had nearly dried up. He called on other Polisario guerrillas to quit. With the continuing Polisario decline, Morocco has taken administrative control over all the towns and phosphate mines, and continues to build new schools, hospitals and houses in the 80 percent of the territory it controls. By allowing residents of the Western Sahara to vote in a Moroccan constitutional referendum on 4 September, King Hassan effectively sealed Morocco's claim to the territory. In December a planned meeting of 38 tribal chiefs in the territory fell through after Polisario objected to seven of the chiefs nominated by Morocco. The U.N. had earlier convinced Morocco and Polisario that the chiefs could best decide who should vote.

Political Rights and Civil Liberties: In 1992, Western Saharans were again denied the opportunity to vote on self-determination. The territory has ten seats in the Moroccan parliament, and King Hassan appoints governors for the territory's four provinces. The majority of the population lives in areas administered by Morocco, and has similar civil liberties as those in Morocco proper. Moroccan authorities monitor and reportedly torture Saharans suspected of supporting Polisario.

Netherlands
Aruba

Polity: Appointed governor and parliamentary
democracy
Economy: Mixed capitalist
Population: 65,000

Political Rights: 1
Civil Liberties: 1
Status: Free

Ethnic Groups: Black majority with Carib Indian and European
minorities

Overview: Aruba was part of the Netherland Antilles from 1954 until
1986 when it achieved formal parity with the Netherlands
and Netherlands Antilles under the Dutch crown. Under the
assumption of domestic autonomy, Aruba agreed to retain economic and political links
to the Netherland Antilles until 1996.

The Netherlands is represented in Aruba by an appointed governor, but the island
is largely self-governing. Domestic affairs are the responsibility of the prime minister
appointed by the freely elected unicameral Staten (legislature). Full freedom of party
organization and expression is respected. The Council of Ministers at the Hague
remains responsible for foreign affairs and defense.

The 21-member Staten is directly elected for four-year terms. The social democratic People's Electoral Movement (MEP) won the 7 January 1989 election, taking
ten seats against the incumbent, center-right Aruba People's Party (AVP), which won
eight seats. Three smaller parties obtained one seat each. Following the election, a
three-party government was formed, headed by the MEP's Nelson Oduber.

The MEP has traditionally been the major force for independence. In 1989,
however, Prime Minister Oduber shifted in favor of commonwealth status to ensure a
full defense commitment from the Netherlands against the threat of the Colombian
cocaine cartels, and to guarantee certain forms of financial assistance. During discussions in July 1990, the Oduber and the Dutch governments agreed that a new
constitutional relationship, to be negotiated in the future, would not involve transition
to full independence in 1996.

The press, radio and television are private, free and varied. Three daily newspapers are published, one in Dutch, one in English, and one in the local Papiamento.
There are five privately run radio stations and one commercial television station.

Netherlands Antilles

Polity: Appointed governor and parliamentary democracy

Political Rights: 1
Civil Liberties: 1
Status: Free

Economy: Mixed capitalist
Population: 192,000
Ethnic Groups: Black majority with Carib Indian and European minorities

Overview:

In 1954 the Netherlands Antilles was granted constitutional equality with the Netherlands and Suriname (which became independent in 1975). In 1986, Aruba split off and was given formal parity with the Netherlands and the Netherlands Antilles. The Netherlands Antilles currently consists of two groups of two and three islands each, the southern (Leeward) islands of Curacao and Bonaire and the northern (Windward) islands of St. Maarten, St. Eustatius, and Saba.

Although the Netherlands is represented by an appointed governor, the Netherlands Antilles is largely self-governing. Domestic affairs are the responsibility of the prime minister appointed by the unicameral Staten (legislature) of twenty-two deputies (fourteen from Curacao, three each from Bonaire and St. Maarten, and one each from St. Eustatius and Saba) elected for four years. Full freedom of party organization and expression is respected. Foreign affairs and defense remain the responsibility of the Council of Ministers at the Hague.

Coalition governments have been highly unstable given the geographical range of the islands and island-based political differences, particularly over the issue of island independence. There have been seven governments since 1977 as eight different political parties have entered in and out of a variety of coalitions. The two main parties are the center-right National People's Party (NPP), which formed the government in 1988 under Maria Liberia-Peters, and the social democratic New Antilles Movement (MAN) headed by former prime minister Dom Martina.

The Liberia-Peters government retained office in new elections held on 16 May 1990. The PNP increased its representation to seven seats, and its coalition partner, the Workers Liberation Front (FOL), won three seats. With 10 out of 14 seats on Curacao, the PNP also had the support of the Democratic Party (St. Eustatious) and the Windward Islands Patriotic Movement (Saba), both of which retained their seats, and the Bonaire Patriotic Union, which took all three seats on Bonaire. Claude Wathey, the leader of the Democratic Party (St. Maarten) and powerbroker of most federation governments over the last three decades, lost his seat.

Local government on each of the islands is constituted by freely elected Island Councils.

Since 1990 the Netherlands has shifted on its long-held policy of encouraging full independence. In 1990 the Dutch government announced that it would begin considering a new constitution governing relations between the Netherlands, the Netherlands Antilles, and Aruba. In the Netherland Antilles, there continued to be great differences of opinion between political parties and islands alike over the issue.

The press, radio and television are private, free and varied. The islands are serviced by six daily newspapers, two in Dutch and four in the local Papiamento. Privately owned radio stations operate on all islands except St. Eustatius. There is a television station on Curacao.

New Zealand
Cook Islands

Polity: Parliamentary democracy
Economy: Capitalist-statist
Population: 18,000
Ethnic Groups: Polynesian majority, European and mixed race minorities

Political Rights: 2
Civil Liberties: 2
Status: Free

Overview:
Located in the South Pacific, the Cook Islands are in free association with New Zealand and have the right to independence at any time. Aside from defense and foreign affairs, they are largely self-governing. The inhabitants have New Zealand citizenship rights. The governor-general of New Zealand appoints a Queen's representative who appoints the prime minister. The 24 seat parliament has a maximum term of five years. There is also an advisory council of chiefs. Prime Minister Geoffrey Henry of the Cook Islands Party has been in power since the 1989 election. The previous coalition government had banned politics from the media in 1988, but lifted the ban for the 1989 campaign.

The government took control of telecommunications from the British Cable and Wireless Company in 1991, in order to fulfill its campaign promise to develop inter-island communications. In 1992, the Henry administration signed an agreement with France for nearly $1 million in water and electricity supply programs.

The arrival of lotto from Australia changed island life significantly in 1992. The game did a booming business on the islands, and began to subsidize the Cook Islands Sports and Olympic Association, which gets 35 percent of the take. Opposition legislators charged that lotto would cause social disturbances and lead to gambling casinos. A more immediate problem was the time difference between the Cook Islands and lotto headquarters in Australia. A Cook woman who thought she had won $1 million had not won; because Australia and the islands are on opposite sides of the international dateline, she was a loser by one day.

Since 1991, Hong Kong companies have used the islands as an offshore locus of incorporation. Many companies may switch their registration in advance of Hong Kong's accession to China in 1997.

Niue

Polity: Parliamentary democracy
Economy: Capitalist-statist
Population: 3,000
Ethnic Groups: Polynesian, other Pacific Islanders, Europeans

Political Rights: 2
Civil Liberties: 2
Status: Free

Overview:
Niue's top news story in 1992 was the announcement that long-time Prime Minister Sir Robert Rex would retire in 1993. Because New Zealand cut economic aid in 1992, Sir Robert attempted to get new assistance from Australia before his retirement.

Located northeast of New Zealand in the South Pacific, the island is in free association with New Zealand, which gives Niueans full citizenship rights. The small population is more than 90 percent Polynesian. The island has a very poor economy, and endures such natural disasters as long droughts and cyclones. Subsidies from New Zealand sustain the relatively large local government and the declining population. In 1992, however, New Zealand's Foreign Minister, Don McKinnon, announced a 21 percent cut in assistance to Niue. As a result, Sir Robert Rex flew to Australia and sought aid from Prime Minister Paul Keating. It is not clear whether Australia is willing to make up for New Zealand's declining subsidy. Niue is attempting to promote such natural resources as rock pools and volcanic caves. The island hopes to build links to Fiji as an alternative market to New Zealand. If all economic plans fail, some or all of the remaining Niueans could move or be moved fairly cheaply to New Zealand. About 12,000 Niueans live there already.

The island's politics are characterized by shifting alliances of personalities and family squabbles. The twenty-member Assembly is elected every three years. Sir Robert Rex has been the political leader since the 1950s. Many islanders grew tired of his longevity, and elected six new members of the Assembly in the 1990 election. Many candidates on both sides were members or in-laws of the Rex family. The only formal party, People's Action, led by Young Vivian, won the most votes in the 1990 election, but Sir Robert was able to take advantage of splits on the People's Action side and secure a twelve to eight majority in the Assembly. Young Vivian and the voters were stunned.

After a few months in office Rex dumped two of his ministers, charging that they "stabbed me in the back." The pair had sought to replace Sir Robert. Then the leader named two new ministers including his electoral opponent, Young Vivian. Following the announcement of Sir Robert's retirement, the other politicians began jockeying to succeed him in 1993.

There is only one newspaper. Most islanders belong to the Christian Council of World Missions, but other groups have freedom of worship.

Tokelau

Polity: Administrator, elected leaders and elders
Economy: Capitalist-statist
Population: 2,000
Ethnic Groups: Polynesian

Political Rights: 2
Civil Liberties: 2
Status: Free

Overview:

Tokelau is a collection of Polynesian islands in the south Pacific. New Zealand appoints the territorial administrator. Each village elects a Faipule, who represents the community and presides over the council of elders, and a Pulenuku, who is responsible for village administration. Elections take place every three years. The next one is due in January 1993. Land may not pass to non-indigenous people. Some land belongs to families, while some is common property. There are no newspapers or broadcast media. There is freedom of worship. Islanders belong to various Christian groups. New Zealand subsidizes the local economy. In 1991, the U.N. Decolonization Subcommittee on Small Territories examined the question of independence for Tokelau, but its status is unchanged.

Norway
Svalbard

Polity: Appointed governor and advisory council
Economy: Capitalist statist
Population: 3,942
Ethnic Groups: Russian majority, Norwegian minority

Political Rights: 3
Civil Liberties: 1
Status: Free

Overview:

Svalbard, "Cold Rim," is a collection of islands and skerries which extends across 24,000 square miles. Two-thirds of the area is covered by glaciers. The population of Svalbard consists primarily of mine workers and their families.

In 1920, under the Treaty of Svalbard, nineteen signatories and twenty adherents agreed to place the islands under Norwegian sovereignty, accepting that all the islands and its waters were equally accessible for maritime, mining, and other commercial operations. The treaty requires that Svalbard have no permanent defense installations. Since 1925, Svalbard has been a part of the Kingdom of Norway.

Norwegian law and legislation apply to Svalbard. Norwegian legislators may introduce regulatory measures if these provisions do not discriminate against non-

Norwegians. The government instituted strict environmental regulations and tourist controls to protect the delicate ecosystem. The main industry is coal mining.

The King of Norway appoints a governor who serves as the local head of administration and chief of police. He has certain other functions connected with the administration of justice. The local Svalbard council has existed since 1971. The fifteen-member council serves as an advisory body for the central and local administrations.

Portugal
Azores

Polity: Elected assembly
Economy: Capitalist-statist
Population: 269,000
Ethnic Groups: Portuguese

Political Rights: 1
Civil Liberties: 1
Status: Free

Overview:

In 1992, the Azores developed a free trade zone and European offshore business center. The territory consists of three groups of islands located 800 miles west of Portugal in the Atlantic Ocean. After the 1974 revolution in Portugal, separatist sentiment increased. Subsequently, the Lisbon government surrendered administration of the islands to local political leaders. A multi-party, 43-seat Assembly was established in 1976, and a regional government formed under the Popular Democratic Front, currently called the Social Democratic Party. Statutes passed by the Azorean regional assembly remain subject to the approval of the Portuguese parliament, which has Azorean representatives. Islanders have the same civil liberties as Portuguese mainlanders.

Macao

Polity: Appointed governor and partially elected legislature
Economy: Capitalist-statist
Population: 474,000
Ethnic Groups: Chinese, Mecanese, Portuguese

Political Rights: 3
Civil Liberties: 3
Status: Partly Free

Overview:

Pro-Chinese candidates swept all eight directly-elected seats in Macao's September 1992 legislative elections. The Portuguese established Macao in 1557 as the first European trading station on the Chinese coast. Consisting of two islets and a peninsula at the mouth of the Canton River, it has been a major entrepôt for trade with China as well as a gambling mecca. Under a May 1987 agreement, Portugal agreed to surrender

Macao to China on 20 December 1999, with China agreeing to retain the territory's capitalist system for 50 years afterwards. China will honor dual citizenship for all residents born in Macao before 1979, and for children of Portuguese passport holders.

In the 20 September legislative elections, pro-China parties won all eight of the directly elected seats. Two communist parties, the Union for the Promotion of Progress and the Development Union each took two seats, and four smaller parties each took one seat. Another eight seats were elected by landowners, labor and cultural and educational associations, and seven were subsequently chosen by Governor Vasco Rocha Viera.

During the year, Portuguese and Chinese negotiators continued to hammer out the Basic Law, which will govern Macao after the transfer. The thorniest issue has been Portugal's refusal to accept Chinese demands to allow for the death penalty in Macao.

Political Rights and Civil Liberties: Citizens of this "Chinese territory under Portuguese administration" have the full range of rights granted by the Portuguese constitution. In 1992 two free expression issues arose. In June, the administration attempted to prevent a public assembly marking the third anniversary of the Tiananmen Square crackdown in Beijing. Activists ignored a police warning and held the demonstration anyway. In May, the media leaked an administration plan to introduce legislation forbidding public assemblies within 50 meters of any government building or office of any social organization. In small, densely packed Macao, this could effectively ban all assemblies. The government said it is unlikely that the law, when introduced, will be so restrictive.

Madeira

Polity: Elected assembly
Economy: Capitalist-statist
Population: 290,000
Ethnic Groups: Portuguese

Political Rights: 1
Civil Liberties: 1
Status: Free

Overview: The Madeira Islands are located 500 miles southwest of Portugal in the Atlantic Ocean. Although an independence movement proclaimed a provisional government in 1975, the regional government functioning since 1976 is committed to autonomy within Portugal. Statutes passed by the elected assembly are subject to Portuguese parliamentary approval. However, Madeira may spend tax revenue as it wishes. The territory has legislative representation in Lisbon. Civil liberties are the same as those on the mainland.

Madeira is prospering as an offshore business and banking center. Under the Social Democratic government of Alberto Joao Jardim, Madeira has won substantial subsidies from the European Community (EC), to which it belongs. EC grants have helped with a variety of health, training, and educational programs. Per capita income is less than 30 percent of the EC average, but it is rising along with economic development.

South Africa
Bophuthatswana

Polity: Dominant party
Economy: Capitalist-
statist
Population: 1,959,000
Ethnic Groups: Tswana majority,
Pedis, Shangaans, Xhosas, South Sothos, and Swazis

Political Rights: 6
Civil Liberties: 5
Status: Not Free

Overview:
Located in north-central South Africa, Bophutatswana consists of seven arid and noncontiguous territories. South Africa granted the territory nominal independence in 1977, but no other country has recognized this status. Kgosi (Chief) Lucus Mangope has been president since 1977, and was re-elected for a third seven-year term in 1991. Under a 1984 constitution amendment he has the right to run any government ministries. In February 1988, the army attempted to force Mangope from power and install the opposition Progressive People's Party (PPP) in power. South African troops put down the rebellion within 15 hours. The Bophutatswanan regime then used its Internal Security Act to ban the PPP, an ally of South Africa's ANC. The Mangope's ruling Bophutatswana Democratic Party currently holds all the seats in parliament. Despite homeland income derived from tourism and platinum mines, the South African Institute of Race Relations estimates that Bophutatswana depends on the South African government for 60 percent of its budget.

In 1992, President Mangope continued to reject proposals for the re-incorporation of Bophutatswana into South Africa. He has called instead for autonomy within a new South African confederation. In late 1991, the government of Bophutatswana joined multilateral negotiations in the Convention for a Democratic South Africa. On 29 September 1992, Mangope joined Ciskei's ruler Oupa Gqoza and KwaZulu's Mangosuthu Buthelezi in publicly objecting to bilateral agreements reached by the ANC's Mandela and South African President de Klerk. All three homeland leaders fear the government and ANC will agree to do away with homeland autonomy without bothering to consult with them.

Supporters of the Bophutatswana Broad Front (BBF) have called Mangope's regime illegitimate and have demanded an immediate end to the territory's autonomous status. The BBF is made up of local branches of the ANC, the Congress of South African Trade Unions, and the South African Communist Party. The BBF called off a massive march on the homeland planned for September when Mangope threatened to turn it back with armed force.

Although a Declaration of Fundamental Rights formally permits freedom of association, assembly, and speech, the regime commonly restricts civil liberties. The Electoral Act of 1979 prohibits political organizations not registered with the government from holding rallies or marches without express permission. The ANC has never received official permission to hold a gathering in Bophutatswana. The South African newspaper *Vrye Weekblad* reports that there are at least five political prisoners in the homeland.

Ciskei

Polity: Military
Economy: Capitalist-
statist
Population: 844,000
Ethnic Groups: Xhosa-speaking south Nguni tribes

Political Rights: 6
Civil Liberties: 6
Status: Not Free

Overview: In 1992, the power struggle between the homeland government headed by Brigadier Oupa Gqozo and partisans of the
African National Congress (ANC) continued. On 7 Septem-
ber, 29 people died and hundreds were wounded when Ciskei Defense Force fired on
a crowd of ANC and South African Communist Party (SACP) protesters attempting
to cross over from South Africa with the express goal of forcing Gqozo's overthrow.
     Located in south-central South Africa, Ciskei is composed of two noncontiguous
territories and is considered the poorest of the country's nominally independent black
ethnic homelands. Ciskei's "independence" was granted in 1980 by South Africa, which
still provides some two-thirds of the homeland's budget in the form of direct aid. An
eight-member Council of State headed by Gqozo has ruled Ciskei since the military
overthrew the civilian one-party regime of President Lennox Sebe in March 1990. The
African Democratic Movement (ADM), founded in mid-1991, is Gqozo's ruling party.
     In 1991, the homeland gave up some of its sovereignty when it yielded four of
its ministries to South Africa. At the time, Gqozo characterized the move as "the first
step on the road to incorporation into a new, non-racial South Africa." In 1992, the
Ciskei government indicated that it favored autonomy for the homeland within a
confederated South Africa. Both the head of the homeland police and defense force
are on loan from the South African military.
     The ANC favors reincorporation of all the homelands into a unitary South Africa with a
strong central government. It has accused Gqozo of trying to "impose" himself on Ciskei
and called upon South Africa to replace him with an interim administrator, a suggestion that
Pretoria has rejected. In the past Gqozo has attempted to restrict ANC organizing efforts and
has detained ANC activists. Local community residents associations often linked to the ANC
have been banned by the regime. In return, ADM organizers have been targeted for violence
by ANC partisans. At the end of 1992, the government stepped back from greater confrontation by provisionally giving the ANC permission to organize within Ciskei.
     On 4 August, as part of a mass action campaign against the governments of South
Africa and its allies among the homelands, 30,000 protest marchers organized by the ANC
and South African Communist Party demanded entry to Ciskei to hold a rally. After briefly
confronting Ciskeian troops at the border, the demonstrators were turned back. A month later
a similar march ended in deaths and injuries when soldiers drove off 70,000 protesters by
firing into the crowd. Gqozo had refused to allow the group to enter the homeland and
warned that those who tried to cross the border did so at their own risk. Protesters dismissed
Gqozo as a South African puppet and declared that they planned to march to the nearby
Ciskeian capital of Bisho to press for his ouster. While ANC officials were negotiating at the

border to resolve the impasse, a group of marchers suddenly crossed into Ciskei and the massacre followed. All sides disclaimed responsibility for the carnage. In a wave of retaliations that followed within Ciskei, three local leaders were reported killed and the homes of police and soldiers were burned down.

Ciskei was represented at the Convention for a Democratic South Africa (Codesa) talks convened in late December 1991. In early September 1992 Ciskei attended a Federal Alliance summit in South Africa convened by President F.W. de Klerk. On 29 September 1992, Gqozo joined Bophutatswana's ruler Lucus Mangope and KwaZulu's Mangosuthu Buthelezi in publicly objected to bilateral agreements reached by the ANC's Mandela and South African President de Klerk. All three homeland leaders fear that the government in Pretoria and the ANC will agree to do away with homeland autonomy without bothering to consult with them.

Transkei

Polity: Military
Economy: Capitalist
Population: 3,301,000
Ethnic Groups: Xhosa

Political Rights: 6
Civil Liberties: 5
Status: Not Free

Overview: In 1992, Transkei's military government turned back a possible coup. It was also accused by South Africa of allowing radical black terrorists to use Transkeian territory as a sanctuary from which to launch attacks against whites. The regime, ruled by Major General Harrington Bantubonke Holomisa at the head of a five-man Military Council, continues to project a militantly pro-ANC (African National Congress) stance.

Located in southeastern South Africa, Transkei is a nominally independent black homeland consisting of three noncontiguous territories. It has been self-governing since 1976, but its independence has only been recognized by the South African government. The Transkei army seized power from a civilian government in 1987, and successfully defeated a coup attempt in late 1990. On 1 September, 1992 four members of the Military Council were arrested by 2,000 soldiers that surrounded military headquarters in the homeland's capital of Umtata. The regime later denied that it was a coup attempt, asserting that the troops involved were only demanding salaries equal to those received by members of the South African Defense Force.

The homeland provides a secure base for Chris Hani, the ANC's former military chief of staff and now general-secretary of the South African Communist Party (SACP). Although the ANC and the SACP have launched campaigns of disruption against homelands with unrepresentative governments, the unelected regime in Transkei remains untouched. Transkei denies reports that it has allowed the ANC's military wing, Umkhonto we Sizwe, to store arms and ammunition on its territory. After the Azanian People's Liberation Army the (APLA), military wing of the left-wing Pan-Africanist Congress, claimed responsibility for the deaths of five white civilians in two attacks in neighboring South Africa, the government in Pretoria accused Transkei of also providing safe haven for the APLA. President Holomisa denied the allegation, and counter-charged that the South African Defense Force was training subversives in neigboring areas to overthrow his regime.

The Holomisa's regime states that it is willing to be re-incorporated into South Africa after transition to majority rule; in 1991 and 1992, representatives of Transkei attended meetings of the Convention for a Democratic South Africa, stages one and two. The Military Council has indicated that it would support armed activities of the ANC's military wing if negotiations with the de Klerk government fail.

Venda

Polity: Military
Economy: Capitalist-statist
Population: 518,000
Ethnic Groups: Venda majority, Sangaan and Pedi minorities

Political Rights: 6
Civil Liberties: 5
Status: Not Free

Overview:
In 1992, the military regime in power in the South African homeland of Venda continued to align itself with the African National Congress (ANC) in multilateral negotiations to create a non-racialist and unified South Africa.

Brigadier Gabriel Ramushwana, chairman of the ruling Council of National Unity, has promised that his regime would create a broad-based forum in the homeland to set the terms for any re-incorporation of Venda into a united, post-apartheid South Africa. Negotiations between the South African government and other parties on the shape of such a regime are likely to be prolonged, but the Council of National Unity has stated that there will be no general elections prior to the end of Venda's separate political status. Political parties such as the African National Congress have been free to organize in Venda.

Situated in northeastern South Africa along the Limpopo River, Venda was granted nominal independence in 1979. Only the Republic of South Africa recognizes the homeland as "independent." The homeland was created in accordance with the South African project for setting up separate political entities for various indigenous African ethnic groups in their historical territories. The object was to deprive the black majority in South Africa proper of the right to claim citizenship. Under its original form of government, the territory of Venda had a legislative assembly with a combination of elected and appointed members. By the time Ramushwana overthrew the civilian government of President Frank Ravele in 1990, it had devolved into a closely controlled one-party state

In mid-December 1992 Venda police used tear gas to disperse thousands of civil servants protesting against the privatization of their pension fund. A similar gathering four days previously was also broken up by police.

Spain
Canary Islands

Polity: Regional
legislature
Economy: Capitalist
Population: 1,578,000
Ethnic Groups: Racially mixed, mostly Hispanic

Political Rights: 1
Civil Liberties: 1
Status: Free

Overview: The Canary Islands are located off the northwest coast of Africa.
The islands have the status of a Spanish autonomous region
with an elected legislature that chooses the regional president.
Although the people are mostly Hispanic, they are of diverse origins and maintain pre-
Spanish customs. There have been periodic separatist movements, but the development of
regional autonomy has reduced such sentiments. The population enjoys the same rights
and guarantees as residents of mainland Spain. The Federation of Canaries Independent
Groupings (FAIC) has one elected member in each house of the Cortes, the Spanish
parliament. The FAIC has supported Spanish Prime Minister Felipe Gonzalez.

Ceuta (Places of sovereignty in North Africa)

Polity: Municipal
administration
Economy: Capitalist-
statist
Population: 80,000
Ethnic Groups: Moroccan, Spanish

Political Rights: 2
Civil Liberties: 1
Status: Free

Melilla

Polity: Municipal
administration
Economy: Capitalist-
statist
Population: 65,000
Ethnic Groups: Moroccan, Spanish

Political Rights: 2
Civil Liberties: 1
Status: Free

Overview: Ceuta and Melilla, located on the coast of Morocco, are
governed as municipalities of two Spanish provinces. Both
areas have Muslim populations with Moroccan roots who
have lived there for generations. Some other small areas nearby also fall under
Spanish control. In 1985, there was a violent controversy over Spain's residency law

that required all foreigners to reapply for residence or face expulsion. This law raised questions about the status of ethnic Moroccan Muslims in Ceuta and Melilla. In 1986, the government created a commission to examine how to integrate the Muslims into Spanish society. After demonstrations in 1986, the Spanish government made a move to give most Muslims citizenship over time. Both cities have Muslim political parties. Since 1985, the Party of Muslim Democrats has functioned in Melilla. Its leader, Aomar Mohamedi Dudu, a former official of Spain's ruling Socialist Workers' Party, became a special advisor to the Interior Ministry on the Muslim communities of Spain in 1986. In 1990, Ahmed Subaire formed a party called Incentive for Ceuta. In 1992, area residents gained legal protection when Spain placed Islam on par with the other major religions.

Turkey
Cyprus (T)

Polity: Presidential-par-
liamentary democracy
(Turkish-occupied)
Economy: Mixed capitalist
Population: 176,000
Ethnic Groups: Turkish Cypriot, Turkish, Greek Cypriot,
Maronite

Political Rights: 3
Civil Liberties: 3
Status: Partly Free

Note: See Cyprus (Greek) under country reports

Overview: In 1992, the first face-to-face meeting occurred between the leaders of the Greek and Turkish Cypriot communities. Despite the U.N. mediation efforts and threats to withdraw its peacekeeping forces reunification, no major breakthrough in negotiations occurred.

In 1974, after a group of army officers seeking Cypriot unification with Greece staged an unsuccessful coup, the Turkish military invaded the northern portion of the island, justifying it as protection of Turkish-speaking population. Following the invasion some 200,000 Greeks fled the Turkish-occupied area. Some 40,000 Turks left the Greek Cypriot-administered areas. Subsequently, some 50,000 immigrants from Turkey entered the island. There are also 35,000 Turkish troops.

In 1983 the Turkish Cypriot administration declared independence, calling itself the "Turkish Republic of Northern Cyprus" (TRNC). Turkey became the only country to recognize the new entity.

In early 1992, during a meeting of the Turkish and Greek Prime Ministers, both sides announced their intention to normalize relations and move towards signing a friendship treaty, causing Greek Cypriots to fear a lessening of Greek support.

Turkey's enhanced regional role following the Gulf War and the emergence of independent Turkic republics in Central Asia boosted the Turkish Cypriots. The position of TRNC was closely linked to that of Turkey, on which it was dependent for military and financial support.

On 4 March 1992 over 20,000 Greek Cypriot women had demonstrated, along the U.N. buffer zone between two sides, demanding the withdrawal of Turkish troops, reunification of the island, and the return of refugees to their homes. The Turkish Cypriot authorities arrested and imprisoned several demonstrators for several days for border violations.

On 10 April the U.N. Security Council adopted a resolution urging both parties to cooperate with the U.N. efforts to reach a settlement, and warning that the U.N. peacekeeping forces could not remain on the island indefinitely. The resolution came after Canada and Denmark, two of the six countries contributing to the U.N. troops, warned that they might withdraw their military units by the end of 1992.

In June the TRNC President Rauf Denktash met with the U.N. Secretary General Boutros-Ghali to discuss the reunification of the island as a federation. The talks centered on the issue of territorial changes in the planned federation, which would reduce the extent of the Turkish Cypriot area. Another topic was the problem of repatriating the refugees to their homes lost in the 1974 conflict.

The talks continued in July, with Denktash becoming more intransigent following revelations of a strong U.S. pressure on Turkey to exercise its influence in order to achieve a compromise.

Despite the first-time meeting of the Greek and Turkish Cypriot presidents on 17 July, there was little progress.

On 14 August the intensive talks were adjourned following a deadlock over the contents of the proposed new constitution, and the extent of area to be returned to the Greek Cypriots. Denktash rejected the U.N. Secretary General's proposal to return the agriculturally rich area around the town of Morphue, and insisted that his side be able to retain at least 29 percent of the land area, from the current 37 percent. The U.N. proposal limited the Turkish-administered area to 28.2. percent. In addition, he demanded a 50:50 parity ratio in government for the 18 percent of the Turkish Cypriot population, and a unilateral right of Turkey to intervene in Cyprus's affairs.

The talks reconvened on 28 October. However, the deadlock over constitutional and territorial issues could not be broken, resulting in a suspension of negotiations until March 1993.

In a report released by the U.N. Secretary General, Boutros-Ghali blamed Denktash for the deadlock, accusing him of introducing positions beyond the parameters of U.N. resolutions.

Political Rights and Civil Liberties:

The TRNC is a presidential-legislative system dominated by President Denktash, the National Unity Party (NUP), and Turkey. The popularly elected president serves a five year term and appoints a prime minister, chosen from the party being able to muster the majority of votes in the fifty-member unicameral legislature. Legally, the president must be independent of political parties, but the NUP is his former party.

Following the 1990 general elections, the opposition parties boycotted the legislative assembly to protest an electoral law which gave the NUP 34 out of 50 seats, despite winning only 34 percent of the vote.

Despite its self-proclaimed independence in 1983, the TRNC remains heavily dependent on Turkish military and economic support. A large influx of rural migrant workers from Turkey prompted the opposition to complain about Turkish Cypriots becoming a minority in their own country.

About 1,000 remaining Greeks and Christian Maronites do not vote in TRNC general elections, but have the right to elect their village councils. They may vote in Greek Cypriot elections, but must travel to the south in order to exercise that right.

The judiciary is independent and fair trials are provided for in law, and accorded in practice. Freedom of speech and the press is guaranteed, and there are newspapers representing differing viewpoints. Citizens and foreign residents are able to practice their religion freely.

The workers have the right to strike, and independent trade unions exist.

There is a general freedom of movement, although the government regulates the travel in and out of the Greek Cypriot area.

United Kingdom
Anguilla

Polity: Appointed governor and elected assembly
Economy: Mixed capitalist
Population: 7,000
Ethnic Groups: Relatively homogeneous, black majority

Political Rights: 1
Civil Liberties: 1
Status: Free

Overview:

Following the establishment of the Associated State of St. Kitts-Nevis-Anguilla, Anguillans rejected governmental authority from St. Kitts and in 1969 a British commissioner was appointed. A separate constitution was provided in 1976 giving the commissioner (now governor) authority over foreign affairs, defense, civil service and internal security. In January 1990 the governor also assumed responsibility for international financial affairs. All other governmental responsibilities are carried out by a freely elected seven-member House of Assembly. The first House elections were held in 1976. In December 1980, the dependent status of the territory was formally confirmed.

In the 27 February 1989 elections, the incumbent Anguilla National Alliance (ANA) headed by Chief Minister Emile Gumbs retained control of the House over the opposition Anguilla United Party (AUP) led by Hubert Hughes.

Anguillans enjoy all civil rights common to the homeland. The press is government owned and operated. Radio is both government owned and private. There is no television.

Bermuda

Polity: Appointed governor and parliamentary democracy
Economy: Mixed capitalist
Population: 61,000
Ethnic Groups: Black (approximately 60 percent), large British minority

Political Rights: 1
Civil Liberties: 1
Status: Free

Overview:

Under a constitution approved in 1967, Bermuda was granted the right of internal self-government in 1968. A British-appointed governor (currently Lord Waddington, former Conservative Party leader in Britain's House of Lords) exercises responsibility for external affairs, defense, internal security and police. A premier is appointed by the governor but is responsible to a freely elected 40-member House of Assembly for all internal matters.

In the 9 February 1989 general election the incumbent center-right, multiracial United Bermuda Party (UBP) of Premier John Swan retained control of the House over the left-wing, predominantly black Progressive Labour Party (PLP). The UBP won 23 seats, the PLP fifteen, and the National Liberal Party (NLP) and an independent environmentalist, one each. Poverty, race and immigration were the main issues; the question of independence has diminished in importance as most of the electorate has demonstrated its support for the status quo. The next general election is due by 1994.

A non-binding referendum on the future of capital punishment, held on 28 August 1990, produced a 78.4 percent vote for its retention, on a turnout of less than a third of the 33,330 registered voters. The turnout at general elections is usually around 70 percent. The decision to hold the referendum was taken by the House of Assembly in 1989, after a tied vote on a motion to abolish the death penalty. The last executions were in December 1977. Capital punishment is limited to cases of premeditated murder.

Bermudians enjoy all civil rights common to the homeland. There are several newspapers, all privately owned. There are over half a dozen radio stations and two television stations. Labor unions, the largest being the 6,000-member Bermuda Industrial Union, are well organized. The right to strike is recognized by law and in practice.

British Virgin Islands

Polity: Appointed governor and elected council
Economy: Mixed statist
Population: 13,000
Ethnic Groups: Relatively homogeneous with black majority

Political Rights: 2
Civil Liberties: 1
Status: Free

Overview:

The 1977 constitution granted the government of the British Virgin Islands greater responsibility over internal affairs. A British-appointed governor retains responsibility for external affairs, civil service, defense and internal security. On other matters the governor acts on the advice of the Executive Council whose members are the governor, the chief minister, four members of the legislature and the Attorney General. The chief minister, representing the majority party in the elected nine-member Legislative Council, is appointed by the governor.

The 1986 Legislative Council elections were won by the Virgin Islands Party (VIP) headed by the chief minister H. Lavity Stoutt. In October 1990 the legislature was dissolved and campaigning began for new elections. A total of 36 candidates were announced by the ruling VIP, the People's Progressive Democratic Party, and the British Virgin Islands United Party, as well as independents. On 12 November 1990, Stoutt was re-elected to a second term as the VIP won six of nine legislative seats.

Residents enjoy all civil liberties common to the homeland. There is one weekly newspaper, one radio station and one television station. A spate of shooting incidents in 1992, apparently the work of drug dealers, raised concerns about whether the 136-member police force should remain unarmed.

Cayman Islands

Polity: Appointed governor and elected assembly
Economy: Capitalist
Population: 31,000
Ethnic Groups: Mixed (40 percent), Caucasian (20 percent), black (20 percent), various ethnic groups (20 percent)

Political Rights: 2
Civil Liberties: 1
Status: Free

Overview:

Previously governed from Jamaica, the Cayman Islands were placed under a British administration in 1962. A British-appointed governor (currently Michael Gore) chairs an Executive Council composed of four elected members plus an appointed Chief Secretary, Financial Secretary and Attorney-General. The Executive Council is drawn from the Legislative Assembly consisting of fifteen elected members, with a new Assembly elected every four years.

In the Legislative Assembly elections held on 18 November 1992, the newly formed National Team of government critics led unofficially by Thomas Jefferson swept twelve of fifteen seats, with the other three going to independents. The three members of the Executive Council who were seeking re-election were all defeated. Jefferson and three other National Team members were appointed to the Executive Council.

The result cast doubt over a constitutional reform, proposed by a team appointed by the Foreign and Commonwealth Office in 1991, that would abolish the "collective responsibility" of the Executive Council and replace it with a ministerial government headed by a Chief Minister. The reform, which the National Team campaigned against, would require a majority vote in the Assembly.

Residents enjoy all civil liberties common to the homeland. There is one daily newspaper and a weekly publication. There is at least one radio and one television station.

Channel Islands

Polity: Appointed executives and legislatures (varies by island)
Economy: Capitalist
Population: 143,000
Ethnic Groups: British, Norman French

Political Rights: 2
Civil Liberties: 1
Status: Free

Overview: The Channel Islands, located in the English Channel, include the islands of Jersey and Guernsey and their dependencies. They are Crown fiefdoms and are connected to Britain through the person of the monarch. The Queen appoints her representatives, who are called lieutenant governors and commanders-in-chief. British laws do not apply unless the parliamentary legislation specifies that they do or unless the British Privy Council extends coverage of the laws to the islands. Islanders can make certain legal appeals directly to the Privy Council. In Jersey and Guernsey the appointed bailiffs preside over the royal courts and legislatures. Jersey's legislature, the States, is elected directly by universal suffrage. Guernsey's legislature, the States of Deliberation, has a mixture of directly and indirectly elected members.

In 1992, the major controversy in Jersey involved the dismissal by the Lieutenant Governor Sir John Sutton of Deputy Bailiff Vernon Tomes. The alleged reason for the dismissal was Tomes's backlog of undecided court cases. Most of the residents, however, viewed this as a conspiracy by the local establishment to remove Tomes, a farmer's son, from office, and an unacceptable interference of Britain in the island's affairs. Following his dismissal, Tomes vowed to remain in public life and work towards changing Jersey's contract with the Crown so that the Bailiff and Deputy Bailiff could be elected directly by the States.

Falkland Islands

Polity: Appointed governor and partly elected legislative council
Economy: Capitalist-statist
Population: 2,000
Ethnic Groups: British

Political Rights: 2
Civil Liberties: 1
Status: Free

Overview:

On 2 April 1992 the Falkland Islands observed uneventfully the tenth anniversary of the Argentine invasion. In February UK and Argentine officials convened to discuss seismic studies for petroleum. In September the local authorities granted two companies the authority to begin the studies. As a diplomatic gesture, the Falklands will make the survey results available commercially to companies operating in Argentina.

Since the invasion, economic development has exploded in this British outpost. The early 1980s discovery of squid and the local authorities' decision to grant fishing permits in 1986 brought wealth and massive infrastructure development, including its first telephone system and roads. Revenue from squid subsidizes the traditional sheep farming.

Britain opened the waters around the islands for oil exploration, and Argentina issued a decree claiming its continental shelf, including the Falklands, for commercial development. Sovereignty remains a difficult issue. Early in 1991, the two countries reached a fishing agreement to control squid fishing exploitation and to determine water boundaries. The United Kingdom and Argentina reestablished diplomatic relations in February 1990. Relations remain strained but improving.

The British first came to these islands in 1610. Spain and Britain clashed over ownership of the Falklands in the eighteenth century. In 1820 Britain rejected Argentina's claim to the territory. Britain and Argentina negotiated over the Falklands' status in the 1960s and 1970s, but never reached agreement. In 1982, Argentina's military government decided to invade and seize control of the islands. Britain defeated Argentina after several weeks of fighting.

Britain appoints a governor to represent the Queen. A chief executive assists in administering the islands. The Legislative Council consists of six members elected by the people, the chief executive, and the financial secretary. The latter two officials, nominees of the governor, and two nominees of the Legislative council form an Executive Council. There are two newspapers, one of them government-published. The public Falkland Islands Broadcasting Service operates two radio stations.

Gibraltar

Polity: Appointed
governor and mostly
elected assembly
Economy: Capitalist-statist
Population: 30,000
Ethnic Groups: Italian, English, Maltese, Portuguese,
and Spanish

Political Rights: 1
Civil Liberties: 1
Status: Free

Overview:

On 16 January 1992 Gibraltar returned Prime Minister Joseph Bossano (Gibraltar Socialist Labor Party) to office by 73.3 percent with 71 percent of the electorate voting. His campaign platform stressed greater autonomy from the United Kingdom and self-determination. He rebuffs criticism that the GSLP is anti-Spanish.

Located at the southern tip of the Iberian peninsula, Gibraltar came under British control in 1704 after the War of the Spanish Succession. Due to its strategic location between the Atlantic and the Mediterranean, Gibraltar is a key British naval base. Spain still claims sovereignty over the territory. British-Spanish tension over ownership is relaxing. In 1964 the colony gained some self-government and in 1967 voted to remain under British control. A new constitution established an Assembly in 1969. Spain blocked land access to Europe, but lifted the ban in 1984. In 1990, the two countries announced closer cooperation in civil aviation and extended a 1985 extradition treaty and a 1989 anti-drug agreement. However, Spain refused to sign a European Community border treaty by 1 January 1992 which Madrid argued would have implicitly recognized Gibraltar as British. In June Spain refused to implement the "Toaster" solution for immigration which required Spanish officials to monitor immigration documents via an electronic relay.

Britain appoints a territorial governor. A Council of Ministers advises him. Chosen through competitive, multi-party elections, the House of Assembly handles domestic affairs. Britain determines defense and foreign affairs. Association is free. There are 7 newspapers and a public broadcasting corporation. The government encourages Gibraltar's use as a tax haven.

Hong Kong

Polity: Appointed
governor and
partly elected legislature
Economy: Capitalist
Population: 5,748,000
Ethnic Groups: Chinese (98 percent)

Political Rights: 4
Civil Liberties: 3
Status: Partly Free

Overview:

In October 1992, new Hong Kong Governor Christopher Patten unveiled plans to make the 1995 Legislative Council elections more democratic. Although Patten said the proposals are compatible with prior Sino-British agreements, China responded by threatening to scrap any changes after it takes over the colony in 1997, and hinted it would renege on its commitment to maintain Hong Kong's political and economic autonomy.

Located on the southern coast of China, the Crown Colony of Hong Kong consists of Hong Kong Island and Kowloon Peninsula, both ceded in perpetuity to Britain by China following the Opium Wars in the mid-1800s, and the mainland New Territories, leased for 99 years in 1898. Long an important naval port and transshipment hub, Hong Kong became a booming manufacturing and later financial center in the post-War period. Executive power rests with a British-appointed governor who provides over an advisory Executive Council (Exco). A 60-seat Legislative Council (Legco) approves all legislation and the colony's budget.

In October 1982, Britain and China began talks on transferring Hong Kong to China. Because the New Territories includes 365 of Hong Kong's 404 square miles, it was inevitable from the outset that China would take control of the entire colony when the New Territories lease expired in 1997. On 26 September 1984, the two countries signed the Joint Declaration, which gives China sovereignty on 1 July 1997. Under the slogan "one country, two systems," China agreed to maintain Hong Kong's *laissez faire* economy for 50 years by turning the territory into a Special Administrative Region with financial and monetary autonomy. China also agreed to maintain Hong Kong's political and judicial independence. Beijing would only be responsible for defense and foreign affairs. The Declaration also established the Sino-British Joint Liaison Group (JLG) to consult periodically on matters leading to a smooth transfer of power.

In 1990, Britain and China agreed that 18 Legco seats would be directly elected in 1991, 20 in 1995, 24 in 1999, and 30 in 2003. These plans were incorporated into the Basic Law, Hong Kong's post-1997 constitution, which China's National People's Congress approved in April 1990.

In September 1991, the colony held its first ever direct Legco elections. Pro-democracy liberals won 16 of the 18 of the contested seats, led by Martin Lee's United Democrats of Hong Kong (UDHK) with 12. Of the other 42 seats, 18 were appointed by Governor David Wilson, and 21 were chosen by "functional constituencies" representing professionals and industries, along with three ex-officio members.

In 1992, the colony's liberal politicians, bolstered by this surprising success, pressed Britain to put more seats up for direct election in 1995. China claimed that this would contravene the Basic Law, which it said could not be amended prior to 1997. The first sign of a more aggressive British policy came on 24 April, when Prime Minister John Major appointed Christopher Patten as the colony's 28th and probably last colonial governor. The 47-year-old Patten's reputation as a political heavyweight raised hopes among the colony's liberals that he would be more assertive with China than his predecessors, who were mostly career diplomats interested in appeasing Beijing.

China went on the offensive even before Patten was sworn in on 9 July. In the first of many blatant Chinese interferences in the colony's affairs, on 18 June Guo Feng Min, head of the Chinese side of the JLG, warned Patten not to appoint any liberals to Exco. Over the summer, the liberals suffered a pair of setbacks. On 24 June, Legco rejected a motion calling for more directly elected seats in 1995. On 30 August, the UDHK lost a by-election seat to a pro-China independent.

On 7 October, Governor Patten outlined his plans for the 1995 elections in a much-awaited speech at the opening Legco session. His blueprint kept the number of directly elected seats at 20. However, it greatly expanded the franchise for the remaining 40. The most controversial aspect involved the makeup of the Election Committee, which will select 10 seats. China envisioned an 800-member appointed body. Instead, Patten proposed to make the Committee an electoral college, drawn from the colony's 230 district and urban council seats. At present, a third of these 230 local seats are appointed, but Patten proposed that all of them be elected by 1995.

The remaining 30 Legco seats will still be chosen by functional constituencies. However, Patten proposed that the franchise be widened for the 21 existing constituencies. Currently, only the leaders of each constituency vote. More importantly, the nine new constituencies would be broad enough to give almost everybody in the workplace a direct vote for an interest group seat. The electoral rolls would be further expanded by lowering the voting age from 21 to 18. In addition, the Governor proposed to drop the current double-seat, double-vote system in favor of single-seat, single-vote constituencies.

To resolve the contentious issue of placing liberals on Exco, Patten simply closed Exco to all party politicians, fully separating Exco from Legco. Exco will now consist entirely of appointed business and community leaders. At the same time, he instituted a new monthly governor's question time, pledged to give Legco financial and administrative autonomy, and encouraged it to establish a system of committees that would oversee and challenge the government on policy. The Governor also proposed increasing social and environmental spending.

China immediately claimed the plans violated the Basic Law. On 23 October, Lu Ping, the top Beijing official in the colony, warned that China might have to sack Legco, Exco and the judiciary in 1997 if the proposals were adopted. The same day, China claimed that in secret negotiations in January and February 1990, Britain had agreed to Beijing's plan for an appointed Election Committee. On 28 October, Britain, faced with the prospect of losing credibility over the Chinese claims, released the transcript of the negotiations. Diplomats who reviewed the documents said that contrary to China's claim, Britain had never agreed to any specific outline for the Election Committee.

On 11 November, Legco voted by a comfortable 32 to 21 margin to offer "general support" to Patten's proposals. Just five days later, Chinese Deputy Prime Minister Zhu Rongji sent a chill throughout the territory by suggesting that China might have to scrap the 1984 Joint Declaration if Hong Kong went ahead with the proposals. On 30 November, China gave already jittery investors further cause for concern when it warned that after the transfer it would not be obligated to honor any existing business contracts signed by the colonial government. Despite the Chinese threats, on 1 December Patten said he would submit the proposals to Legco for approval in February 1993.

Throughout the year, the political situation closely affected bilateral negotiations over the planned multi-billion Chek Lap Kok airport and related projects. China has delayed granting approval of the financing, ostensibly because it wants assurance that it will not be saddled with the debts. In reality, it has used the airport project to gain leverage on political issues. On 27 November, Legco voted 27 to 25 to start building the airport anyway. The political and economic uncertainties in the colony caused the stock market to drop sharply in December, although it still closed up 28.3 percent for the year.

In another major issue, in April the police were faulted for abandoning a Vietnamese detention camp for more than an hour during a riot on 3 February. The ensuing melee left 24 dead and 119 injured, many after a hut the Vietnamese had taken refuge in was torched. Hong Kong camps hold more than 50,000 Vietnamese hoping to emigrate to the West, although fewer have arrived since authorities began forcibly repatriating refugees in late 1991. In May 1992, Britain and Vietnam signed an agreement allowing forced repatriation of all "economic refugees." Only a few thousand political refugees will be allowed to remain.

Political Rights and Civil Liberties: Hong Kong citizens cannot change their government democratically. Residents, who live in what is essentially a free but undemocratic society, had no say in the 1984 agreement transferring sovereignty to China in 1997. An April 1992 report by the International Commission of Jurists condemned Britain for denying Hong Kong the right to self-determination, and recommended that it expand democracy before 1997 and extend the right of abode to the 3.2 million Hong Kong residents who have British Dependent Territory Citizen status.

The colony has an independent judiciary, and defendants receive fair trials. In June 1991, Legco passed a Bill of Human Rights patterned after the International Covenant on Civil and Political Rights, although China said it reserves the right to review the Bill after the 1997 takeover. Liberals have criticized an agreement by Britain and China to allow only one foreign judge to sit on the post-1997 Court of Final Appeal. A free and lively press criticizes both the government and China, although self-censorship is often practiced to avoid overly antagonizing China. The Public Order Ordinance requires permission for public assemblies of more than 20 people. On 4 June, the authorities allowed 50,000 people to gather in Victoria Park on the third anniversary of the Tiananmen Square military crackdown, but required protesters marching to the office of China's Xinhua News Agency to proceed in groups of 19 or less. Workers are free to join independent unions and strike. Only 16 percent of the work force is unionized.

Isle of Man

Polity: Appointed executive and elected legislature
Economy: Capitalist
Population: 70,000
Ethnic Groups: Mostly Manx (of mixed Celtic and Scandinavian descent)

Political Rights: 2
Civil Liberties: 1
Status: Free

Overview: The Isle of Man is located west of Britain in the Irish Sea. Like the Channel Islands, it is a crown fiefdom, tied to Britain through the monarch. The Queen appoints an executive, the lieutenant governor. The Court of Tynwald is the bicameral legislature. Claiming to be the world's oldest functioning legislature, it consists of a twelve-member Legislative Council, of which the lieutenant governor is a member, and an elected twenty-four-member House of Keys. For most matters, the two houses sit in joint session. There is a ten-member Council of Ministers, headed by the chief minister. The Isle has its own laws. Acts of the British Parliament apply to Man only if they state so specifically.

Effective April 1992, the government reduced the tax rate on the fees earned by fund management companies from twenty to five percent. The island is attempting to become Europe's leading offshore funds center. In 1990 the government proposed legalizing homosexual acts. Britain's acceptance of the European Human Rights Convention on behalf of its territories had put the island in breach of continental rights standards on this issue. The island is the only European territory of the U.K. where people do not have the right of individual petition to the convention. Some supporters of Manx autonomy opposed the homosexual reform measure, because they feared it would jeopardize the territory's special legal status. The Isle of Man owes its success as a tax haven to its freedom from British tax laws. Manx economic interests feared that the homosexual reform would set a precedent that would undermine the island's ability to write its own tax laws, but the change in the fund management tax suggested otherwise.

Montserrat

Polity: Appointed governor and partly elected council
Economy: Capitalist
Population: 13,000
Ethnic Groups: Mostly black with European minority

Political Rights: 2
Civil Liberties: 1
Status: Free

Overview: **A** British-appointed governor (currently David George Pendleton Taylor) presides over an appointed Executive Council. Local legislative matters are the responsibility of an eleven-member Legislative Council. Of the eleven members, who serve five-year terms, seven are directly elected, two are official members, and two are nominated. The chief minister is the leader of the majority party in the Council.

In the 25 August 1987 Council elections, the People's Liberation Movement (PLM) headed by incumbent chief minister John Osborne retained its four-seat majority.

In December 1989 negotiations in London between Osborne and the British government led to an agreement on a new constitution. The new constitution, which was instituted on 13 February 1990, consolidates the provisions of the Montserrat Letters Patent of 1959 and other legislation, and adds a statement on the fundamental rights and freedoms of the individual. On disputed matters, Osborne agreed that the chief minister would relinquish to the governor responsibility for international financial affairs, as proposed by the British government in the wake of a banking scandal in 1989. In exchange, the British government agreed to add a provision recognizing

Montserrat's right to self-determination, and to eliminate the governor's power to overrule the Legislative Council on certain types of legislation.

In elections held on 10 October 1991, Osborne and the PLM were swept out of office after thirteen years by the newly formed National Progressive Party (NPP) which won four of seven legislative seats. The PLM won one seat, the NDP one seat, and the last seat was taken by an independent, Ruby Wade-Bramble. NPP leader Reuben Meade, a 37-year-old former civil servant, was named chief minister.

In 1992 Meade came under increasing criticism for failing to devise a plan to re-develop the island which was devastated by Hurricane Hugo in 1989. Nonetheless, Wade-Bramble failed in November to gain majority support for a no-confidence motion in the legislature.

Residents enjoy all civil liberties common to the homeland. There are at least two newspapers, including the opposition Montserrat Reporter, several radio stations and one television station. Labor unions are well organized and the right to strike is recognized by law and in practice. In October 1992 former chief minister Osborne and a former cabinet official were ordered to stand trial on charges of conspiracy and corruption involving the solicitation of bribes from a U.S. real estate investor.

Northern Ireland

Polity: British administration and elected local
councils
(military-occupied)
Economy: Mixed capitalist
Population: 1,578,000
Ethnic Groups: Irish Protestants, Irish Catholics

Political Rights: 3
Civil Liberties: 3
Status: Partly Free

Overview: Failed negotiations for a political settlement of Northern Ireland's sectarian strife dominated the news in 1992.

Northern Ireland consists of six of the nine counties of the Irish province of Ulster. At the insistence of the locally dominant Protestants, these counties remained within the United Kingdom after the other 26 counties, which are largely Catholic, gained home rule in 1921. Protestants comprise over 60 percent of the general population, but Catholics form a majority of the youth under age fifteen. Generally, Protestants favor continued political union with Britain and thus have the political labels "Loyalist" and "Unionist," while the "Nationalist" or "Republican" Catholic population favors unification with the Republic of Ireland. Britain's Government of Ireland Act (1920), which partitioned Ireland, set up a Northern Irish parliament which functioned until the British imposed direct rule from London in 1972. Subsequent attempts at power-sharing failed in 1974, 1976, and 1986.

Until the late 1960s, electoral regulations favored the economically dominant Protestants by according business property owners voting rights for both their residential and commercial addresses. A non-violent Catholic civil rights movement in the 1960s met with limited success and a violent response from the Protestants. Attempting to impose order in 1969, the British government sent in the army, which originally appealed to some Catholics as a preferable security force to the Protestant-controlled local police. However, Catholics soon viewed the troops as an army of occupation. The violently confrontational situation of the late 1960s and 1970s led to divisions in both the Unionist and Nationalist communities. There are now several Unionist and Nationalist parties. The most important of these are: the conservative Official or Ulster Unionist Party, led by James Molyneaux; the hard-line Democratic Unionist Party, led by Rev. Ian Paisley; the moderate, pro-Nationalist Social Democratic and Labour Party (SDLP), led by John Hume; the militant, pro-Nationalist Sinn Fein, led by Gerry Adams; and John Alderdice's moderate, interdenominational Alliance Party. Sinn Fein is the political wing of the Irish Republican movement, whose military wing is the Provisional Irish Republican Army (IRA).

In 1990-91, Britain's Secretary of State for Northern Ireland, Peter Brooke, organized negotiations on power-sharing involving major political parties (except Sinn Fein) and the British and Irish governments. Sinn Fein's refusal to renounce violence kept it out of the discussions. The talks bogged down in procedural wrangling, and broke down altogether in July 1991. The Nationalists charged the Unionists with being more interested in scuttling the Anglo-Irish Accord than in sharing power. The Unionists feared that more negotiations would have led to a greater role for Dublin in the North.

Under Sir Christopher Mayhew, Brooke's replacement, the negotiations revived in April 1992. Their highlights included the first talks in eighteen years between the Dublin government and the Unionists, an official visit of the Unionists to Dublin, and several constitutional proposals. The SDLP advocated a Northern Irish legislature plus a cabinet consisting of three elected executives and three appointed by the European Community and the Irish and British governments. However, the talks collapsed in October after reaching an impasse on the Irish constitution. Its Articles II and III claim the North for the Republic. Unionists insisted that Dublin would have to make a serious offer to amend the Articles before more negotiations. Additionally, the Unionists objected to holding talks when the British and Irish governments were resuming their consultations under the Anglo-Irish Accord in November 1992.

In the British general election on 9 April 1992, Gerry Adams lost Sinn Fein's seat in the House of Commons, because some Protestants cast tactical votes for Dr. Joe Hendron, the successful SDLP candidate. Prior to the election, a policeman killed three Sinn Fein headquarters workers and Protestant gunmen killed a Sinn Fein campaign worker. In the vote, Unionist parties won a combined thirteen Commons seats and the SDLP took four, its highest ever. After the campaign, a constituent challenged Hendron's election in court, charging that he had exceeded campaign spending limits. A court decision could deprive Hendron of the seat.

Political Rights and Civil Liberties: The people of Northern Ireland have the right to elect members of the British House of Commons and local government bodies. However, the regional parliament remains suspended. Nationalists argue that they lack the right of self-determination, because Britain has effectively granted the Unionists a veto over the six counties' entrance into a united Ireland. Unionists, on the other hand, insist that the Irish Republic should have no role in governing them, and they resent Dublin's consultative role in Northern Ireland under the terms of the 1985 Anglo-Irish Accord. Elections appear to be conducted fairly, and have allowed Sinn Fein to win both parliamentary and local council seats.

British law bans broadcast appearances by members or supporters of terrorist organizations. Censorship has the effect of making non-terrorists appear subversive. For example, in 1992 former Nationalist parliamentarian Bernadette Devlin McAliskey, a victim of terrorism, recorded a discussion for a televised documentary, but the BBC replaced her voice with subtitles on their lawyers' advice. The British lifted the broadcast ban on Sinn Fein for the parliamentary campaign, because it is a legal party. The government has banned several violent organizations including: the IRA, the Irish National Liberation Army (INLA), the Irish People's Liberation Organization (IPLO), the Ulster Volunteer Force (UVF), the Ulster Freedom Fighters (UFF), the Ulster Defense Association (UDA), and the Red Hand Commandos. In late 1992, the IRA killed an IPLO leader and wounded eight others, thereby forcing IPLO to disband. Reports persist that elements of the security forces share information with Loyalist paramilitaries, leading to the deaths of Catholics. In 1992, Britain's Channel Four and Box Productions broadcast a documentary demonstrating this collusion. After Channel Four and Box refused to reveal their sources, the British government fined the companies, and the police arrested a news researcher.

Trial by jury does not exist for suspected terrorists in Northern Ireland. A judge tries such cases, and there is an extremely high conviction rate. Under the Prevention of Terrorism Act, the security forces may arrest suspects without warrants. The authorities may prevent suspected terrorists from entering Britain from Northern Ireland and may keep non-natives out of Northern Ireland.

In 1992, 84 people died in political and sectarian violence. The death toll since the start of "the troubles" in 1969 exceeds 3,000. Unlike some earlier years, in which Republican terror was responsible for the highest portion of the death toll, in 1992 the combined UFF-UDF forces killed 33, while the IRA killed 29. Of the 84 victims, 55 were Catholics. Republican or Nationalist terrorists tend to attack policemen, soldiers, alleged Protestant paramilitaries, and alleged Catholic informers and collaborators. Loyalist or Unionist terrorists target alleged IRA members and sympathizers. Both sides often kill innocent, unintended victims.

The Provisional IRA is a major economic force. Through protection rackets, drug-dealing, and other enterprises, the IRA reaps a $14 million annual profit, according to police estimates. Other terrorist groups (including the older Official IRA) have degenerated into pure rackets, almost totally devoid of their original political purposes.

In March 1992, male officers conducted forcible strip searches of female Republican prisoners at Maghaberry jail. The women reported injuries and alleged sexual abuse. In May, the British army suspended an officer after soldiers attacked a crowd of civilians at Coalisland. Catholics charge that security forces often use a shoot-to-kill policy. For example, in November 1992 the Royal Ulster Constabulary shot an unarmed IRA activist in the back, killing him in Belfast.

In August 1992, the British government denied IRA prisoner Joe Doherty credit towards parole for the nearly nine years he spent in U.S. prisons. Doherty, convicted of killing a British captain, had escaped to America in 1981. He won several rounds of court cases in the U.S. where he tried unsuccessfully to win political asylum. After losing in the U.S. Supreme Court, Doherty returned to an Ulster prison in 1992.

Traditionally, Protestants have discriminated against Catholics throughout the economy. The British Parliament passed the Fair Employment Act of 1989, which set up a commission to monitor discrimination. Numerous organizations around the world have campaigned for the MacBride Principles, a set of standards designed to direct investment only to Northern Irish firms which adopt affirmative action hiring practices. Catholics are two and a half times as likely as Protestants to be unemployed. According to a British government report, this situation will take more than a decade to improve.

Pitcairn Islands

Polity: Appointed governor and partly elected council
Economy: Capitalist-statist
Population: 52
Ethnic Groups: *Bounty* families (Mixed Anglo-Tahitian)

Political Rights: 2
Civil Liberties: 1
Status: Free

Overview: Located in the South Pacific, the territory consists of Pitcairn and three uninhabited islands. The inhabitants are descended from the *Bounty* mutineers and Tahitian women. In 1990 the island observed the bicentennial of the community's founding. In 1790 mutiny leader Fletcher Christian and his fellow muntineers settled there with a dozen Tahitian women.

In 1990 was the withdrawal of Japan Tuna's trawlers from the colony's waters after a three-year trial. The island had hoped to profit from selling fishing licenses, but the Japanese found the local catch insufficient to justify continuing fishing there. Aside from fishing, the local economy is based on plant life, postage stamp sales, and crafts. Islanders make money by carving ornaments to sell to passing ships. In 1989, the island's gross income was 958,733 Pitcairn dollars, but the outgo was 923,355 Pitcairn dollars, leaving a surplus of 35,378 Pitcairn dollars.

The appointed governor is the British High Commissioner in New Zealand. Ten residents serve on the Pitcairn Island Council. They include the elected magistrate, Brian Young, and three other elected members; the island secretary; one member appointed by the governor; two members appointed by the elected members; one non-voting member appointed by the governor; and one non-voting member named by the council. The council controls immigration by issuing licenses to land only in rare circumstances. Magistrate Young and his wife visted London in July 1990, and met with Queen Elizabeth at a Buckingham Palace garden party. "We pay no taxes but we all do some form of public works," Young said. Among other tasks, the island's twelve able-bodied men maintain 17.5 miles of mud roads. Local law forbids public displays of affection. The islanders are Seventh-Day Adventists, and observe a strict Sabbath on Saturdays.

St. Helena and Dependencies

Polity: Appointed governor and elected council
Economy: Capitalist-statist
Population: 7,000
Ethnic Groups: British, Asian Africa

Political Rights: 2
Civil Liberties: 1
Status: Free

Overview:

St. Helena, Ascension Island, and the Tristan da Cunha island group are scattered across the South Atlantic between Africa and South America. The British governor administers the islands with an executive council of two *ex officio* members and the chairmen of the council committees. Residents elect a twelve-member Legislative Council for a four-year term. The Legislative council started in 1967. Political parties are legal, and took part in earlier elections, but have become inactive. Tristan da Cunha and Ascension have appointed administrators who are responsible to the governor of St. Helena. Advisory councils assist them. The Ascension advisory council includes representatives of the BBC, South Atlantic Cable Company, Cable Wireless Ltd., the U.S. National Aeronautics and Space Administration, and the U.S. Air Force, all of which have facilities there. Ascension has no native population. In 1981 the governor appointed a constitutional commission to determine desired constitutional changes, but the commission found too little interest among the population to draw any conclusions. The island economies are dominated by British and American bases. There are also local fishing, timber, craft, and agricultural industries. The colony has a government-run broadcasting service and a weekly newspaper. The trade union is the St. Helena General Workers Union.

Turks and Caicos

Polity: Appointed governor and elected council
Economy: Capitalist
Population: 13,000
Ethnic Groups: Relatively homogeneous with black majority

Political Rights: 2
Civil Liberties: 1
Status: Free

Overview:

Previously governed from Jamaica, the islands were placed under a British administration in 1962. A constitution adopted in 1976 provides for a governor, an eight-member Executive Council, and a Legislative Council of thirteen elected, four ex-officio, and three nominated members. The chief minister is the leader of the majority party in the Legislative Council.

In 1985, chief minister Norman Saunders of the conservative Progressive National

Party (PNP) was arrested in Miami on drug trafficking charges and forced to resign. He was replaced by his deputy Nathaniel Francis, who was forced to resign in 1986 on corruption and patronage charges. The British government then imposed direct rule under the governor and established a commission for making constitutional reforms designed to inhibit corruption.

In the 3 March 1988 elections that marked the return to constitutional rule, the People's Democratic Movement (PDM), formerly in opposition, took nine of eleven seats and Oswald Skippings became chief minister. In the 3 April 1991 elections, the PNP returned to power by winning eight legislative seats to the PDM's five and PNP leader Washington Missick became chief minister.

Residents enjoy all the civil liberties common to the homeland. There are at least one weekly newspaper and several radio stations.

United States of America
American Samoa

Polity: Elected governor and legislature
Economy: Capitalist
Population: 51,000
Ethnic Groups: Samoan (Polynesian)

Political Rights: 1
Civil Liberties: 1
Status: Free

Overview:

American Samoa is located in the South Pacific. The U.S. ruled the territory through an appointed governor for most of this century, but Samoans have elected their governor directly since 1977. The bicameral legislature is called the Fono. It consists of a twenty-member House of Representatives and an eighteen-member Senate. The House is elected by popular vote for two-year terms. The *matai*, the chiefs of extended Samoan families, elect senators from among themselves for four-year terms. Peter Tali Coleman is governor. There are local affiliates of the U.S. Democratic and Republican parties. The territory sends a delegate to the U.S. House of Representatives. Tourism, fishing, and agriculture are major industries. There are free and competing newspapers. There is a private radio station and a government-owned television station.

In 1992, efforts to raise the wages of tuna workers to make them compatible with those prevailing in the United States continued, with vigorous opposition on the part of the employers and public officials. There is a special provision for American Samoa in the U.S. wage laws. A subminimum wage prevails, subject to periodic review by a six-member joint Samoan-American comission. Most tuna workers are Western Samoan citizens who lack an electoral voice in the territory, so there was little political pressure from them to raise their pay.

The territory receives $ 80 million in U.S. grants, and received an additional $30 million in response to the hurricane Val, which hit the island in December 1991.

Guam

Polity: Elected gov-
ernor and legislature
Economy: Capitalist-
statist
Population: 142,000
Ethnic Groups: Guamanian or Chamorro (Micronesian)
majority, U.S. mainlanders, Filipinos

Political Rights: 1
Civil Liberties: 1
Status: Free

Overview: The leading issues on Guam in 1992 were Guam's political
status, abortion legislation and natural disasters.

An unincorporated territory of the U.S., Guam has
lobbied Washington in recent years for commonwealth status. In 1982 the voters
chose commonwealth, but the U.S. has not passed the required enabling legislation.
The Guamanians want to end the U.S. Congress's theoretical right to abolish the
island's constitution. They also want direct access to the federal Supreme Court in any
plan for commonwealth. There was commonwealth enabling legislation in Congress in
1992, but it did not pass. Consequently, Guam's delegate to the U.S. House of
Representatives lost his seat. His successor announced plans to introduce enabling
legislation again in 1993.

In the 1992 legislative elections, for the unicameral legislature, the Democrats won
fourteen seats to seven for the Republicans.

In 1992, a federal appeals court judge declared Guam's abortion law unconstitutional. The legislation would have prohibited abortion, even in cases involving rape,
incest, and fetal abnormality. The only exceptions to the abortion ban would have
been situations involving medically certified threats to the mother's life or health. The
law also forbade open discussion of abortion rights. The U.S. Supreme Court let the
appeals court's ruling stand by refusing to hear the case in November 1992.

Typhoon Omar hit Guam in October 1992, and caused damage to most buildings
on the island. Property damage ran over $500 million. The U.S. government declared
Guam a disaster area, making it eligible for federal reconstruction funds.

Located west of Hawaii, Guam became American territory as a result of the
Spanish-American War in 1898. Since 1970 the territory has had an elected governor
who serves a four-year term. Former two-term, Democratic Governor Ricardo
Bordallo, who was found guilty of corruption, killed himself in January 1990. Shortly
before his scheduled trip to prison in California, Bordallo chained himself to a statue
of an island chief, covered himself with the territorial flag, and shot himself. Despite
Bodallo's departure from office in 1987 and his death in 1990, the White House sent
him a perfunctory thank-you note in 1991. This letter caused islanders to complain
about Washington's ignorance of their situation.

American bases and U.S. subsidies contribute significantly to the local economy.
During summer 1992, the legislature moved to raise the minimum wage to $7.00 per
hour, well above the U.S. level. There are free and competitive print and broadcast
media.

Northern Marianas

Polity: Elected governor and legislature
Economy: Capitalist
Population: 47,000
Ethnic Groups: Highly diversified populations of Pacific Islanders, Asians, Europeans, and Americans

Political Rights: 1
Civil Liberties: 1
Status: Free

Overview:
Major news stories in 1992 involved a court's rejection of an appeal by former officials convicted in a corruption case, and a settlement of a wage dispute.

Situated west of Hawai in the Pacific, the Northern Marianas formed part of the former U.S. Trust Territory of the Pacific. The U.N. recognized the end of the trusteeship in 1990. The islands have commonwealth status, and residents have U.S. citizenship. The U.S. has responsibility for the islands' defense. The territory has no representation in the U.S. Congress, but in 1991 the commonwealth's representative in Washington suggested that he should be elected as a non-voting member of Congress. The directly elected governor serves for four years. The Senate has a four-year term, while the House of Representatives has a two-year term. The Commonwealth government has responsibility for immigration. There is a very high number of Asian workers, possibly the majority of labor force. Reportedly, many are illegal aliens. Handicrafts, fishing, tourism, and agriculture are significant industries. In March 1992, a U.S. federal court rejected an appeal by the former Senate President Ponciano Cruz Raza, his brother, and another defendant, convicted of receiving kickbacks from a Japanese company while in office.

In May, following a U.S. Department of Labor crackdown against exploitive labor practices, major employers agreed to pay $9 million to 1,500 former employees, most of them from mainland China.

There are three competing newspapers, three radio stations, and several cable television channels.

Palau (Belau)

Polity: Elected president and legislature
Economy: Capitalist
Population: 16,000
Ethnic Groups: Palauan (a mixture of Micronesian, Malayan and Melanesian) and mixed Palauan-European-Asian

Political Rights: 1
Civil Liberties: 2
Status: Free

Overview:
Palau (Belau) became part of the U.N. supervised Trust Territory of the Pacific after World War II. In 1980, Palau adopted its constitution and changed its name to Republic of

Palau. Under the constitution, executive power is vested in a President who is elected in a nationwide election for a period of four years. Legislative power is vested in the Olbiil Era Kelulau (National Congress of Palau) consisting of a House of Delegates and a Senate. Judicial power is vested in a Supreme Court, a National Court and other inferior courts. Palau is the only remaining U.S. trust territory.

Since 1983, Palau has held several plebiscites in an attempt to terminate its status as a trust territory and enter into a compact of free association with the U.S. Concerned about potential militarization and wary of U.S. nuclear tests in the Marshall Islands, Palau incorporated a non-nuclear clause into its constitution which requires a 75 percent approval of any agreement that involves the testing, use, storage, or stationing of nuclear forces on the island. Several plebiscites have failed to reach this mark.

During the unsuccessful attempts to settle its constitutional arrangements, two of Palau's presidents have died, and the territory experienced some political violence. In 1988, President Salli committed suicide, apparently over a bribery scandal. His predecessor, President Romelli had been assassinated in 1985. In the spring of 1992, the police arrested a suspect in the assasination, who claimed that it was orchestrated by the ex-minister of state.

Palau is very clannish and traditional. Historically, the main chief was selected by the highest ranking woman, the Bilung, and behind the scenes women held real power on the islands, although their influence has dwindled since the implementation of the Constitution. Social rank depends on the family's standing in the home village. Non-Palauan citizens and firms may not own land, but leases are available. Tourism, fishing, and agriculture are the major industries. The only newspaper is government-owned.

Puerto Rico

Polity: Elected governor and legislature
Economy: Capitalist
Population: 3,721,000
Ethnic Groups: Relatively homogeneous, Hispanic

Political Rights: 1
Civil Liberties: 1
Status: Free

Overview: Following approval by plebiscite, Puerto Rico acquired the status of a commonwealth in free association with the U.S. in 1952. Under its terms, Puerto Rico exercises approximately the same control over its internal affairs as do the fifty U.S. states. Residents, though U.S. citizens, do not vote in presidential elections and are represented in the U.S. Congress only by a delegate to the House of Representatives who can vote in committee but not on the floor.

The Commonwealth constitution, modeled on that of the U.S., provides for a governor and a bicameral Legislature, consisting of a 27-member Senate and a 51-member House of Representatives, directly elected for four-year terms. An appointed Supreme Court heads an independent judiciary and the legal system is based on U.S. law.

On 3 November 1992 Pedro Rosselló of the pro-statehood New Progressive Party

(PNP) was elected governor, defeating Victoria Munoz Mendoza, the candidate of the incumbent Popular Democratic Party (PPD). Outgoing Gov. Rafael Hernandez Colon decided not to seek re-election after two terms in office.

With 83 percent of registered voters participating, Rosselló took 49.9 percent of the vote against 45.8 percent for Munoz, 3.8 percent for environmentalist Neftali Garcia and 3.3 percent for Fernando Martín of the Puerto Rican Independence Party (PIP). The PNP won 36 of 51 seats in the House and 20 of 27 Senate seats, and was victorious in 54 of the island's 72 municipalities. The PNP's Carlos Romero Barceló, a former governor, won in the race for the non-voting delegate to the U.S. Congress.

Although the island's relationship with the U.S. remains a fundamental political issue, the election reflected an anti-incumbency fever and immediate concerns over rising crime, high unemployment, government corruption and education. Nonetheless, Rosselló promised in his campaign to hold a plebiscite in 1993 in which voters would choose between statehood, independence or retaining commonwealth status.

In recent years, polls have shown voters almost evenly divided between remaining a commonwealth and becoming a state, with less than ten percent favoring independence. But the 1992 election suggested a tilt toward statehood. A vote to change the island's status would have to be approved by the U.S. Congress.

Rosselló also vowed to reinstate English as one of the island's two offical languages. Polls showed that only about a quarter of Puerto Ricans supported the Spanish-only law passed under Hernandez Colon.

As U.S. citizens, Puerto Ricans enjoy all civil liberties granted in the U.S. The press and broadcast media are well developed, highly varied, uncensored and critical. In June 1992 television Channel 2 of Telemundo of Puerto Rico received a series of threats, apparently from hard-line elements of the island's Cuban exile community, after airing a series of live reports from Cuba.

In July the Puerto Rican Supreme Court upheld a lower court's ruling that it is unconstitutional for police to maintain dossiers on prominent figures of the island's independence movement. In late 1992 dozens of pro-independence politicians, labor activists and journalists filed a class action suit seeking damages after being the targets of police intelligence over the last four decades.

United States Virgin Islands

Polity: Elected governor and senate
Economy: Capitalist
Population: 99,000
Ethnic Groups: Relatively homogeneous with black majority

Political Rights: 1
Civil Liberties: 1
Status: Free

Overview: The U.S. Virgin Islands, consisting of St. Croix, St. Thomas, St. John and four dozen smaller islands, are governed as an unincorporated territory of the U.S. The inhabitants were made U.S. citizens in 1927 and granted a considerable measure of self-government in 1954. Since 1970, executive authority has resided in a governor and lieutenant governor directly elected for a four-year term. There is also a unicameral 15-member Senate elected for two years; each of the three main islands are proportionately represented. Since 1973 the territory has sent one non-voting delegate to the U.S. House of Representatives.

In September 1989, the islands were ravaged by Hurricane Hugo, with St. Croix the hardest hit. After looting broke out, President Bush ordered U.S. troops and federal marshals onto St. Croix for twenty days to keep order. Governor Alexander Farrelly of the Democratic Party was criticized in some quarters for his handling of the crisis. Nonetheless, in November 1990, he scored a landslide victory over his main challenger, former governor Juan Luis, to secure a second term. The other main political party is the Independent Citizens' Movement.

As U.S. citizens, island residents enjoy all civil liberties granted in the U.S. There are at least two newspapers and several radio and television stations. Alleged mistreatment of workers and the beatings of several supervisors led to an August 1992 lockout of 2,000 workers at the Hess Oil refinery on St. Croix, the largest private employer on the island. The lockout ended after unions and management negotiated an agreement to establish a joint committee to ensure worker safety and arbitrate racial disputes.

Yugoslavia
Kosovo

Polity: Serbian administration
Economy: Mixed-statist
Population: 1,700,000
Ethnic Groups: Albanians (90 percent), Serbs and Montenegrins (10 percent)

Political Rights: 7
Civil Liberties: 7
Status: Not Free

Overview:

In 1992, Kosovo, an Albanian enclave within Serbia that used to be an autonomous region in Yugoslavia, remained a tinderbox as fears rose that Serbian repression could escalate to war. Despite pressure by Serbia, which took over administration of the region in 1991, Albanians elected a shadow president and parliament to underscore the illegitimacy of the Serb-imposed administration.

Although Kosovo has neither strategic nor economic importance and is one of the poorest areas of former Yugoslavia, the region is the historic cradle the Serbian medieval state and culture. It was the site of the Battle of Kosovo Fields in 1389 between Serbian Prince Lazar and the Turks, which solidified Ottoman control over the Serbs for the next 500 years. Serbian President Slobodan Milosevic rose to power in 1987 over the issue of Kosovo's status. The central plank in his platform was the subjugation of the then-autonomous Yugoslav province (autonomy was granted by Tito's 1974 Constitution) to Serbian authority, which was imposed in mid-1990 when

Milosevic abolished the provincial government and legislature and introduced a series of amendments to the Serbian constitution that effectively removed the legal basis for Kosovo's autonomy.

With Serbian gains in the war in Bosnia-Herzegovina, tensions in Kosovo rose in 1992. On 27 April, Montenegro and Serbia (including the provinces of Kosovo and Vojvodina) declared the formation of a new, rump-Yugoslavia. Under a new constitution, the status of Vojvodina and Kosovo remained unchanged.

On 24 May, Albanians held elections (branded illegal by Belgrade) for new members of a clandestine government. Ibrahim Rugova, leader of the Democratic League of Kosovo, was elected president of an "independent" Kosovo. Delegates to the 130-member legislature also were elected.

Despite Serbian provocations, Albanians followed the instructions of their leaders to resist violence. In November, Albanian students organized demonstrations demanding Albanian-language education and the right to set their own curriculum. Serbian police officers clashed with thousands of demonstrators, leaving several people hurt and 15 arrested.

On 20 December, Kosovars boycotted the Serbian elections despite pleas that they participate by Yugoslav Prime Minister Milan Panic, who opposed Milosevic for the Serbian presidency. With over one million voters, it was believed that Kosovar support for Panic could have had an impact on the elections.

Political Rights and Civil Liberties:

Kosovars cannot democratically change the *de jure* government imposed by Serbia. The main Albanian political group is the outlawed Albanian League of Democracy Party headed by Ibrahim Rugova, which claims 700,000 members. Other parties include the Parliamentary Party, led by Veton Surroi, and the Social Democratic Party, under Shkelzin Maliqi. Personal as well as political differences account for the proliferation of parties, but all of these groups agree on the need at least to restore the rights taken away by Milosevic. Kosovo's democratically elected legislature and government remained underground following the elections, which was not recognized by Serbia.

Albanian cultural identity was also under siege in 1992. Albanian monuments have been torn down, streets have received Serbian names, and signs in the Cyrillic alphabet have replaced those in the Latin script. Serbian has supplanted Albanian as the official language of Kosovo, and a Serbian curriculum has been used in schools since 1991, the year at least 6,000 Albanian teachers were dismissed. A network of private Albanian schools was set up by unemployed teachers. During the year, Serbian police confiscated the Albanian-language stamps, seals, and teaching materials in Kosovo schools. Searches were often followed by beatings, arrests and prison sentences.

Rugova's shadow government claims that some 105,000 Albanians out of a total work force of 240,000 have been fired since 1990. According to official Serbian sources 23,000 Serbian and Montenegrin workers have been hired in Kosovo over the same period to replace the dismissed Albanians.

Albanian TV and radio were recognized, then abolished. A single Albanian newspaper was due to be taken over by a Belgrade conglomerate in January 1993. Albanian judges have been replaced, and no Albanian police remain. Freedom of movement for Albanians has been curtailed. Each month for the last two years, the *Official Gazette of Serbia* (a record of the Serbian parliament similar to the U.S. *Congressional Record*) has published an average of 18 decrees curtailing Albanian rights in Kosovo.

The Independent Trade Unions of Kosovo (BSPK), an outlawed Albanian-language confederation, was also a subject of repressions. In May and June, the Serbian police performed two raids on the BSPK headquarters in Pristina, the capital, and members were arrested, beaten and tortured. The building and union documents and equipment were destroyed. The BSPK has refused to affiliate with the official Serbian unions or to sign collective bargaining agreements approved by these unions.

Vojvodina

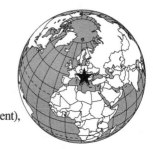

Polity: Serbian adminis- **Political Rights:** 6
tration and provincial **Civil Liberties:** 5
assembly **Status:** Not Free
Economy: Mixed-statist
Population: 2,000,000
Ethnic Groups: Serbians (57 percent), Hungarians (17 percent),
Slovakians, Bulgarians, Romanians, others.

Overview: In 1992, Vojvodina, northern Serbia's agriculturally rich and most ethnically diverse province, managed to avoid the type of violent ethnic strife that gripped most of former Yugoslavia.

Like the Albanian-dominant province of Kosovo, Vojvodina enjoyed political autonomy within Yugoslavia until 1990, when the nationalist Serbian government under Slobodan Milosevic abolished most of its constitutional privileges. Vojvodina had enjoyed relative autonomy under the Austrian-Hungarian empire, and at the end of World War I, it—along with Slovenia, Croatia, Montenegro, Serbia and Bosnia-Herzegovina—formed Yugoslavia. Under Communist leader Josip Borz (Tito) Yugoslavia granted greater autonomous status to Vojvodina and Kosovo, though they were not made constituent republics.

In 1992, Vojvodina hoped to regain a measure of autonomy. In August, represent-atives from Vojvodina at the London peace conference on Yugoslavia offered a proposal to turn Serbia into a federal republic consisting of Serbia, Vojvodina and Kosovo. The plan, drawn up with leaders of the Albanian majority in Kosovo, would have given all three federation members equal rights; each would have their own government, parliament, supreme court, education system, and other institutions. The plan met serious opposition among Serbs in Vojvodina, who made up 57 percent of the province's inhabitants.

Vojvodina's independence drive was spearheaded by the League of Social Democrats of Vojvodina/Yugoslavia (LSVY). An August opinion poll by an indepen-dent newspaper showed that if elections were held at the time, the LSVY would garner up to 30 percent of the vote, more than any other party. The same poll found that some 65 percent of Vojvodina voters wanted autonomy restored.

In 1992, Vojvodina was affected by Serbia's war against Bosnia-Herzegovina. Several Serbian paramilitary groups used Vojvodina as a base for operations in Croatia and in Bosnia. Some 150,000 men in Vojvodina—about one in three—were drafted. In Serbia, the figure was one in eleven. Since 1991, thousands of conscripts of Hungarian, Slovakian, Romanian and Bulgarian descent fled to escape military service.

Vojvodina's relative peace made it an oasis for a steady stream of refugees from Bosnia-Herzegovina and Croatia. By September, 200,000 refugees had been registered, most living in camps or with local families. In some instances, the influx led to ethnic tensions and displacements. In the spring, Serbian refugees forcibly ejected Croats from their houses in the village of Hrtkovci. In May, Hrtkovci's population of 4,000 was about 80 percent Croatian; in two months, however, it became about 75 percent Serbian. Serbian newcomers replaced the local government and renamed the town Srbislavci. Serbian refugees gave local families days, or sometimes hours, to sign over their homes in exchange for property in Croatia that Serbs had abandoned. The forced exodus from Hrtkovci began after Vojislav Seselj, an ultranationalist Serbian militia leader accused of war crimes, rallied supporters in Hrtkovci and denounced 17 non-Serbs as traitors. By year's end, only 400 Croats from the original 1,800 were still living there.

Hungarians are a majority in many towns. Some 80 percent of 22,000 residents in Ada, site of ethnic tensions in June, are ethnic Hungarians holding Yugoslav citizenship. Janos Vekas, vice president of the Democratic Alliance of Hungarians in Vojvodina, said that, with Serbia internationally isolated for its role in Yugoslavia's civil war, Hungarians felt it especially important to make Vojvodina a separate entity.

In February, Vekas' party won a promise from Milosevic to look into its demands of "territorial or cultural autonomy." But by year's end, nothing had been done. Demands also included Hungarian-language media, an ethnic Hungarian quasi-parliament, and expansion of Hungarian-language education through high school.

At the end of May, the Serbian parliament approved the government's proposal concerning minority-language secondary schools, under which teaching in secondary schools would be in the minority language, or even in two languages if at least 15 students so desire.

On 30 July, the Vojvodina assembly elected a provincial government, comprised of a prime minister, two deputy prime ministers and seven secretaries. Seventy-five deputies voted for prime minister-designate, Dr. Koviljko Lovre, and 16 against, with one ballot invalidated. The new government planned to focus on agricultural development and rebuilding infrastructure. It also promised to focus on social services, information, and the protection of the rights of national minorities.

Political Rights and Civil Liberties:

In 1990, Vojvodina lost its status as an autonomous region within Yugoslavia when it was taken over by neighboring Serbia.

Citizens can elect a provincial government and take part in Serbian elections, as well as those for rump-Yugoslavia. However, the 20 December Yugoslav parliamentary elections, as well as those for Serbian president and parliament, were marred by fraud and irregularities. There is no truly independent judiciary.

Tensions continued throughout the year between Serbs and the large Hungarian minority, though the Serbian government did take steps toward allowing Hungarian-language and bilingual education. Hungarians faced threats in several cities. In addition, Hungarians also worried about the latest large-scale conscriptions into the Serbian army. In December, all directors of primary and secondary schools, who were to be appointed directly by the Belgrade Education Ministry, were re-selected. Similar purges of non-Serbs occurred in the police, customs, and, allegedly, the judiciary.

Prior to the 20 December elections, a broad coalition of democratic opposition parties in Vojvodina organized to take the power from the neo-Communist Socialist Party of Serbia. An alliance made up of the Democratic Party, the Reformist Democratic Party, and the Civic Party, signed an agreement on joint participation in the elections with the Democratic Movement of Serbia (DEPOS), the main Serbian opposition coalition, whose candidates for the Vojvodina Assembly and municipal assemblies represented the Serbian Renaissance Movement, the Democratic Party of Serbia, and the National Radical Party.

To date, all institutions operating in Vojvodina are essentially under control of the Serbian government in Belgrade. Freedoms of expression and speech are curtailed, and while there are a few small independent publications in Vojvodina, the media are dominated by Serbia's government-controlled television and radio, which generally reflect the official views from Belgrade. Freedom of domestic movement and international travel are generally unrestricted. Although freedom of religion is nominally accepted, Catholics, especially Croats, face intimidation and harassment by Orthodox Serbs. Trade unions are not truly independent.

Tables and Ratings

Table of Independent Countries
Comparative Measures of Freedom

Country	PR	CL	Freedom Rating
Afghanistan	6▲	6▲	Not Free
Albania	4	3▲	Partly Free
↓ Algeria	7▼	6▼	Not Free
Angola	6	6▼	Not Free
Antigua and Barbuda	3	3	Partly Free
Argentina	2▼	3	Free
↑ Armenia	4▲	3▲	Partly Free
Australia	1	1	Free
↓ Austria	1	1	Free
Azerbaijan	5	5	Partly Free
Bahamas	1▲	2▲	Free
Bahrain	6	5	Partly Free
Bangladesh	2	3	Free
Barbados	1	1	Free
Belarus	4	3▲	Partly Free
Belgium	1	1	Free
Belize	1	1	Free
Benin	2	3	Free
Bhutan	7▼	6▼	Not Free
Bolivia	2	3	Free
↓ Bosnia-Herzegovina°	6	6	Not Free
Botswana	1	2	Free
Brazil	2	3	Free
Brunei	7▼	6▼	Not Free
Bulgaria	2	3	Free
Burkina Faso	5▲	5	Partly Free
↑ Burma (Myanmar)	7	7	Not Free
↑ Burundi	6▲	5▲	Partly Free
Cambodia	6	6	Not Free
Cameroon	6	5▲	Not Free
Canada	1	1	Free
Cape Verde	1▲	2▲	Free
Central African Republic	6	5	Partly Free
Chad	6	6	Not Free
Chile	2	2	Free
China (P.R.C.)	7	7	Not Free
↓ Colombia	2	4	Partly Free
Comoros	4	2▲	Partly Free
Congo	3▲	3▲	Partly Free
Costa Rica	1	1	Free
Croatia	4▼	4	Partly Free
Cuba	7	7	Not Free
Cyprus (G)	1	1	Free
Czecho-Slovakia*	2	2	Free
Denmark	1	1	Free
Djibouti	6	6▼	Not Free
Dominica	2	1	Free
↓ Dominican Republic	2	3	Free
↓ Ecuador	2	3	Free
↓ Egypt	5	6▼	Partly Free
El Salvador	3	3▲	Partly Free
Equatorial Guinea	7	6▲	Not Free
Estonia	3▼	3	Partly Free
Ethiopia	6	4▲	Partly Free
Fiji	4▲	3▲	Partly Free
Finland	1	1	Free
France	1	2	Free
Gabon	4	4▼	Partly Free
The Gambia	1▲	2	Free
Georgia	4▲	5	Partly Free
↓ Germany	1	2	Free
Ghana	5▲	5▲	Partly Free
Greece	1	2	Free

Country	PR	CL	Freedom Rating
Grenada	1	2	Free
Guatemala	4▼	5	Partly Free
Guinea	6	5	Partly Free
Guinea-Bissau	6	5	Partly Free
Guyana	3▲	3▲	Partly Free
Haiti	7	7	Not Free
↓ Honduras	2	3	Free
Hungary	2	2	Free
Iceland	1	1	Free
India	3	4	Partly Free
Indonesia	6	5	Partly Free
Iran	6	6▼	Not Free
Iraq	7	7	Not Free
Ireland	1	1	Free
Israel	2	2	Free
Italy	1	2▼	Free
Ivory Coast	6	4	Partly Free
Jamaica	2	2	Free
Japan	1	2	Free
Jordan	3▲	3▲	Partly Free
Kazakhstan	5	5▼	Partly Free
Kenya	4	5▲	Partly Free
Kiribati	1	2	Free
Korea, North	7	7	Not Free
Korea, South	2	3	Free
Kuwait	5▲	5	Partly Free
Kyrgyzstan	4▲	2▲	Partly Free
Laos	7▼	6▲	Not Free
Latvia	3▼	3	Partly Free
Lebanon	5▲	4	Partly Free
Lesotho	6	4	Partly Free
↓ Liberia	7	6	Not Free
Libya	7	7	Not Free
Liechtenstein°	1	1	Free
Lithuania	2	3	Free
Luxembourg	1	1	Free
↓ Macedonia°	3	4	Partly Free
↑ Madagascar	4	4	Partly Free
Malawi	6▲	7▼	Not Free
Malaysia	5	4	Partly Free
Maldives	6	5	Not Free
Mali	2▲	3▲	Free
Malta	1	1	Free
Marshall Islands	1	1	Free
Mauritania	7	6	Not Free
Mauritius	2▼	2	Free
Mexico	4	3▲	Partly Free
Micronesia	1	1	Free
↓ Moldova	5	5▼	Partly Free
Mongolia	3▼	2▲	Free
Morocco	6▼	5	Partly Free
Mozambique	6	4	Partly Free
Namibia	2	2▲	Free
Nauru	1	2	Free
Nepal	2	3	Free
Netherlands	1	1	Free
New Zealand	1	1	Free
Nicaragua	4▼	3	Partly Free
↑ Niger	5▲	4▲	Partly Free
Nigeria	5	4	Partly Free
Norway	1	1	Free
↑ Oman	6	5▲	Partly Free
↓ Pakistan	4	5	Partly Free
Panama	4	3▼	Partly Free
Papua New Guinea	2	3	Free

Table of Independent Countries
Comparative Measures of Freedom

Country	PR	CL	Freedom Rating
Paraguay	3	3	Partly Free
Peru	6▼	5	Partly Free
Philippines	3	3	Partly Free
Poland	2	2	Free
Portugal	1	1	Free
Qatar	7	6▼	Not Free
Romania	4▲	4▲	Partly Free
Russia	3	4▼	Partly Free
Rwanda	6	5▲	Not Free
St. Kitts and Nevis	1	1	Free
St. Lucia	1	2	Free
St. Vincent and the Grenadines	1	2	Free
San Marino°	1	1	Free
Sao Tome and Principe	2	3	Free
Saudi Arabia	7	7▼	Not Free
Senegal	4	3	Partly Free
Seychelles	6	4▲	Partly Free
Sierra Leone	7▼	6▼	Not Free
Singapore	4	5▼	Partly Free
Slovenia	2	2▲	Free
Solomon Islands	1	1	Free
Somalia	7	7	Not Free
South Africa	5	4	Partly Free
Spain	1	1	Free
Sri Lanka	4	5	Partly Free
Sudan	7	7	Not Free
Suriname	3▲	3▲	Partly Free
Swaziland	6	5	Partly Free
Sweden	1	1	Free
Switzerland	1	1	Free

Country	PR	CL	Freedom Rating
Syria	7	7	Not Free
↑ Taiwan (Rep. of China)	3	3	Partly Free
↓ Tajikistan	6▼	6	Not Free
Tanzania	6	5	Partly Free
Thailand	3▲	4	Partly Free
Togo	6	5	Not Free
Tonga	3	3	Partly Free
Trinidad and Tobago	1	1	Free
↓ Tunisia	6▼	5	Partly Free
Turkey	2	4	Partly Free
Turkmenistan	7▼	6▼	Not Free
Tuvalu	1	1	Free
Uganda	6	5▲	Not Free
Ukraine	3	3	Partly Free
United Arab Emirates	6	5	Partly Free
United Kingdom**	1	2	Free
United States	1	1	Free
Uruguay	1	2	Free
Uzbekistan	6	6▼	Not Free
Vanuatu	2	3	Free
Venezuela	3▼	3	Partly Free
Vietnam	7	7	Not Free
Western Samoa	2	2	Free
Yemen	6	4▲	Partly Free
Yugoslavia (Serbia and Montenegro)	6	5	Partly Free
Zaire	6	5	Not Free
Zambia	2	3	Free
Zimbabwe	5	4	Partly Free

Notes for Table of Independent Countries

↑↓ Arrows up or down indicate a general trend in freedom. PR and CL stand for Political Rights and Civil Liberties. 1 represents the most free and 7 the least free category.

▲▼ Triangles up or down indicate a change in Political Rights or Civil Liberties caused by real world events since the last survey. The Freedom Rating is an overall judgment based on *Survey* results. See the "Methodological Essay" for more details. The table does not indicate changes made for purely methodological reasons since last year.

o New as a country in this *Survey*.

* Through December 1992.

** Excluding Northern Ireland

Table of Related Territories
Comparative Measures of Freedom

Country	PR	CL	Freedom Rating
Australia			
Christmas Island	3	2	Free
Cocos (Keeling) Islands	1	2	Free
Norfolk Island	2	1	Free
Chile			
Rapanui (Easter Island)	3	2	Free
China			
Tibet	7	7	Not Free
Denmark			
Faeroe Islands	1	1	Free
Greenland	1	1	Free
Ethiopia			
† Eritrea	6	4▲	Partly Free
Finland			
Aland Islands*	1	1	Free
France			
French Guiana	2	2	Free
French Polynesia	2	2	Free
French Southern and Antarctic Territories	3	1	Free
Guadeloupe	2	2	Free
Martinique	2	1	Free
Mayotte (Mahore)	2	2	Free
Monaco	3	1	Free
New Caledonia	2	2	Free
Reunion	2	2	Free
St. Pierre and Miquelon	2	2	Free
Wallis and Futuna Islands	3	2	Free
France-Spain Condominium			
Andorra	2	1	Free
India			
Kashmir	6	6	Not Free
Indonesia			
East Timor	7	7	Not Free
Irian Jaya	7	6	Not Free
Iraq			
Kurdistan*	4	5	Partly Free
Israel			
Occupied Territories	6	6	Not Free
Morocco			
Western Sahara	7▼	5	Not Free
Netherlands			
Aruba	1	1	Free

Country	PR	CL	Freedom Rating
Netherlands	1	1	Free
Antilles			
New Zealand			
Cook Islands	2	2	Free
Niue	2	2	Free
Tokelau	2	2	Free
Norway			
Svalbard*	3	1	Free
Portugal			
Azores	1	1	Free
Macao	3	3	Partly Free
Madeira	1	1	Free
South Africa			
Bophuthatswana	6	5	Not Free
Ciskei	6	6▼	Not Free
Transkei	6	5	Not Free
Venda	6▲	5	Not Free
Spain			
Canary Islands	1	1	Free
Ceuta	2	1	Free
Melilla	2	1	Free
Turkey			
Cyprus (T)**	3▼	3▼	Partly Free
United Kingdom			
Anguilla	1	1	Free
Bermuda	1	1	Free
British Virgin Islands	2	1	Free
Cayman Islands	2	1	Free
Channel Islands	2	1	Free
Falkland Islands	2	1	Free
Gibraltar	1	1	Free
† Hong Kong	4	3	Partly Free
Isle of Man	2	1	Free
Montserrat	2	1	Free
Northern Ireland	3	3	Partly Free
Pitcairn Islands	2	1	Free
St. Helena and Dependencies	2	1	Free
Turks and Caicos	2	1	Free
United States of America			
American Samoa	1	1	Free
Guam	1	1	Free
Northern Marianas	1	1	Free
Palau (Belau)	1	2	Free
Puerto Rico	1	1	Free
U.S. Virgin Islands	1	1	Free
Yugoslavia			
↓ Kosovo*	7	7	Not Free
Vojvodina*	6	5	Not Free

Notes for Table of Related Territories

* New in this *Survey*

**New as a related territory in this *Survey*

Table of Social and Economic Comparisons

Country	PPP ($)	Per Capita GNP ($)	Life Expectancy	Country	PPP ($)	Per Capita GNP ($)	Life Expectancy
Afghanistan	710	na	42.5	Ecuador	3,012	1,020	66.0
Albania	4,270	na	72.2	Egypt	1,934	640	60.3
Algeria	3,088	2,230	65.1	El Salvador	1,897	1,070	64.4
Angola	1,225	610	45.5	Equatorial	706	330	47.0
Antigua and	3,940	na	72.0	Guinea			
Barbuda				Estonia	na	11,711 GDP	71.0
Argentina	4,310	2,160	71.0	Ethiopia	392	120	45.5
Armenia	na	7,202 GDP	69.0	Fiji	4,192	1,650	64.8
Australia	15,266	14,360	76.5	Finland	14,598	22,120	75.5
Austria	13,063	17,300	74.8	France	14,164	17,820	76.4
Azerbaijan	na	5,640 GDP	70.0	Gabon	4,735	2,960	52.5
Bahamas	11,293	11,320	71.5	Gambia	886	240	44.0
Bahrain	10,804	7,424 GDP	71.0	Georgia	na	7,751 GDP	72
Bangladesh	820	180	51.8	Germany	14,507	20,440	75.2
Barbados	8,351	6,350	75.1	Ghana	1,005	390	55.0
Belarus	na	10,340 GDP	72.0	Greece	6,764	5,350	76.1
Belgium	13,313	16,220	75.2	Grenada	3,673	1,900	71.5
Belize	2,662	1,720	69.5	Guatemala	2,531	910	63.4
Benin	1,030	380	47.0	Guinea	602	430	43.5
Bhutan	750	na	48.9	Guinea-	820	180	42.5
Bolivia	1,531	620	54.5	Bissau			
Bosnia-	na	na	70.0	Guyana	1,453	340	64.2
Herzegovina				Haiti	962	360	55.7
Botswana	3,180	1,600	59.8	Honduras	1,504	900	64.9
Brazil	4,951	2,540	65.6	Hungary	6,245	2,590	70.9
Brunei	14,590	15,390	73.5	Iceland	14,210	21,070	77.8
Bulgaria	5,064	2,320	72.6	India	910	340	59.1
Burkina Faso	617	320	48.2	Indonesia	2,034	500	61.5
Burma	595	na	61.3	Iran	3,120	3,200	66.2
(Myanmar)				Iraq	3,510	na	65.0
Burundi	611	220	48.5	Ireland	7,481	8,760	74.6
Cambodia	1,000	na	49.7	Israel	10,448	9,790	75.9
Cameroon	1,699	1,000	53.7	Italy	13,608	15,120	76.0
Canada	18,635	19,030	77.0	Ivory Coast	1,381	790	53.4
Cape Verde	1,717	780	67.0	(Cote D'Ivoire)			
Central African	770	390	49.5	Jamaica	2,787	1,260	73.1
Republic				Japan	14,311	23,810	78.6
Chad	582	190	46.5	Jordan	2,415	1,640	66.9
Chile	4,987	1,770	71.8	Kazakhstan	na	7,497 GDP	70.0
China (PRC)	2,656	350	70.1	Kenya	1,023	360	59.7
Colombia	4,068	1,200	68.8	Kiribati	na	529 GDP	54.0
Comoros	732	460	55.0	Korea			
Congo	2,382	940	53.7	North	2,172	na	70.4
Costa Rica	4,413	1,780	74.9	South	6,117	4,400	70.1
Croatia	na	na	70.0	Kuwait	15,984	16,150	73.4
Cuba	2,500	na	75.4	Kyrgyzstan	na	5,522 GDP	68.0
Cyprus	9,368	7,040	76.2	Laos	1,025	180	49.7
Czecho-Slovakia	7,420	3,450	71.8	Latvia	na	12,727 GDP	71.0
Denmark	13,751	20,450	75.8	Lebanon	2,250	na	66.1
Djibouti	730	1,049 GDP	48.0	Lesotho	1,646	470	57.3
Dominica	3,399	1,680	76.0	Liberia	937	na	54.2
Dominican	2,537	790	66.7	Libya	7,250	5,310	61.8
Republic				Liechtenstein	na	22,500 GDP	69.5

Notes: Freedom House obtained the figures for purchasing power parities (PPP), per capita GNP, and life expectancy from the U.N.'s *Human Development Report 1992* (Oxford University Press, 1992). PPP's are real GDP per capita figures which economists have adjusted to account for detailed price comparisons of individual items covering over 150 categories of expenditure. In a few cases the U.N. report does not list GNP figures. For these countries, the chart lists GDP data from the Rand McNally *World Map and Facts* (1993 edition). The U.N. life expectancy figures represent overall expectancy, not differentiated by sex. In some cases not covered by the U.N., the chart lists a combined average of male and female life expectancy obtained from Rand McNally. For several countries the chart lists these combined averages.

Table of Social and Economic Comparisons

Country	PPP ($)	Per Capita GNP ($)	Life Expectancy	Country	PPP ($)	Per Capita GNP ($)	Life Expectancy
Lithuania	na	10,703 GDP	72.0	Saudi Arabia	10,330	6,020	64.5
Luxembourg	16,537	24,980	74.9	Senegal	1,208	650	48.3
Macedonia	na	na	70.0	Seychelles	3,892	4,230	70.0
Madagascar	690	230	54.5	Sierra Leone	1,061	220	42.0
Malawi	620	180	48.1	Singapore	15,108	10,450	74.0
Malaysia	5,649	2,160	70.1	Slovenia	na	na	71.0
Maldives	1,118	420	62.5	Solomon	2,626	580	69.5
Mali	576	270	45.0	Islands			
Malta	8,231	5,830	73.4	Somalia	861	170	46.1
Marshall Islands	na	1,575 GDP	72.5	South Africa	4,958	2,470	61.7
Mauritania	1,092	500	47.0	Spain	8,723	9,330	77.0
Mauritius	5,375	1,990	69.6	Sri Lanka	2,253	430	70.9
Mexico	5,691	2,010	69.7	Sudan	1,042	343 GDP	50.8
Micronesia	na	1,389 GDP	70.5	Suriname	3,907	3,010	69.5
Moldova	na	7,313 GDP	68.0	Swaziland	2,405	900	56.8
Mongolia	2,000	1,021	65.0	Sweden	14,817	21,570	77.4
Morocco	2,298	880	62.0	Switzerland	18,590	29,880	77.4
Mozambique	1,060	80	47.5	Syria	4,348	980	66.1
Namibia	1,500	1,030	57.5	Taiwan (China)	na	7,412 GDP	74.5
Nauru	na	10,000 GDP	66.0	Tajikistan	na	4,654 GDP	70.0
Nepal	896	180	52.2	Tanzania	557	130	54.0
Netherlands	13,351	15,920	77.2	Thailand	3,569	1,220	66.1
New Zealand	11,155	12,070	75.2	Togo	752	390	54.0
Nicaragua	1,463	478 GDP	64.8	Tonga	na	860 GDP	67.5
Niger	634	290	45.5	Trinidad and	6,266	3,230	71.6
Nigeria	1,160	250	51.5	Tobago			
Norway	16,838	22,290	77.1	Tunisia	3,329	1,260	66.7
Oman	10,573	5,220	65.9	Turkey	4,002	1,370	65.1
Pakistan	1,789	370	57.7	Turkmenistan	na	5,986 GDP	66.0
Panama	3,231	1,760	72.4	Tuvalu	na	575 GDP	61.0
Papua New	1,834	890	54.9	Uganda	499	250	52.0
Guinea				Ukraine	na	8,372	71.0
Paraguay	2,742	1,030	67.1	United Arab	23,798	18,430	70.5
Peru	2,731	1,010	63.0	Emirates			
Philippines	2,269	710	64.2	United	13,732	14,610	75.7
Poland	4,770	1,790	71.8	Kingdom			
Portugal	6,259	4,250	74.0	United States	20,998	20,910	75.9
Qatar	11,800	15,500	69.2	Uruguay	5,805	2,620	72.2
Romania	na	3,012 GDP	70.8	Uzbekistan	na	5,040 GDP	69.0
Russia	na	10,708 GDP	70.0	Vanuatu	2,054	860	69.5
Rwanda	680	320	49.5	Venezuela	5,908	2,450	70.0
St. Kitts-Nevis	3,150	2,390 GDP	67.5	Vietnam	1,000	232 GDP	62.7
St. Lucia	3,361	1,810	70.5	Western Samoa	1,981	700 GDP	66.5
St. Vincent and	3,420	1,168 GDP	70.0	Yemen	1,560	650	51.5
the Grenadines				Yugoslavia	na	2,920	72.6
San Marino	na	16,375 GDP	76.0	Zaire	380	260	53.0
Sao Tome and	616	340	65.5	Zambia	767	390	54.4
Principe				Zimbabwe	1,469	650	59.6

Combined Average Ratings—Independent Countries

FREE

1
Australia
Austria
Barbados
Belgium
Belize
Canada
Costa Rica
Cyprus (G)
Denmark
Finland
Iceland
Ireland
Liechtenstein
Luxembourg
Malta
Marshall Islands
Micronesia
Netherlands
New Zealand
Norway
Portugal
St.Kitts-Nevis
San Marino
Solomon Islands
Spain
Sweden
Switzerland
Trinidad and Tobago
Tuvalu
United States of America

1.5
Bahamas
Botswana
Cape Verde
Dominica
France
The Gambia
Germany
Greece
Grenada
Italy
Japan
Kiribati
Nauru
St. Lucia
St. Vincent and the Grenadines
United Kingdom
Uruguay

2
Chile

Czecho-Slovakia
Hungary
Israel
Jamaica
Mauritius
Namibia
Poland
Slovenia
Western Samoa

2.5
Argentina
Bangladesh
Benin
Bolivia
Brazil
Bulgaria
Dominican Republic
Ecuador
Honduras
Korea, South
Lithuania
Mali
Mongolia
Nepal
Papua New Guinea
Sao Tome and Principe
Vanuatu
Zambia

PARTLY FREE

3
Antigua and Barbuda
Colombia
Comoros
Congo
El Salvador
Estonia
Jordan
Guyana
Kyrgyzstan
Latvia
Paraguay
Philippines
Suriname
Taiwan (Rep. of China)
Tonga
Turkey
Ukraine
Venezuela

3.5
Albania
Armenia

Belarus
Fiji
India
Macedonia
Mexico
Nicaragua
Panama
Russia
Senegal
Thailand

4
Croatia
Gabon
Madagascar
Romania

4.5
Georgia
Guatemala
Kenya
Lebanon
Malaysia
Niger
Nigeria
Pakistan
Singapore
South Africa
Sri Lanka
Zimbabwe

5
Azerbaijan
Burkina Faso
Ethiopia
Ghana
Ivory Coast (Cote D'Ivoire)
Kazakhstan
Kuwait
Lesotho
Moldova
Mozambique
Seychelles
Yemen

5.5
Bahrain
Burundi
Central African Republic
Egypt
Guinea
Guinea-Bissau
Indonesia
Morocco
Oman

Peru
Swaziland
Tanzania
Tunisia
United Arab Emirates
Yugoslavia

NOT FREE

5.5
Cameroon
Maldives
Rwanda
Togo
Uganda
Yugoslavia
Zaire

6
Afghanistan
Angola
Bosnia-Herzegovina
Cambodia
Chad
Djibouti
Iran
Tajikistan
Uzbekistan

6.5
Algeria
Bhutan
Brunei
Equatorial Guinea
Laos
Liberia
Malawi
Mauritania
Qatar
Sierra Leone
Turkmenistan

7
Burma (Myanmar)
China
Cuba
Haiti
Iraq
Korea, North
Libya
Saudi Arabia
Somalia
Sudan
Syria
Vietnam

Combined Average Ratings—Related Territories

FREE

1
Aland Islands (Finland)
American Samoa (U.S.)
Anguilla (U.K.)
Aruba (Netherlands)
Azores (Portugal)
Bermuda (U.K.)
Canary Islands (Spain)
Faeroe Islands (Denmark)
Gibraltar (U.K.)
Greenland (Denmark)
Guam (U.S.)
Madeira (Portugal)
Netherlands Antilles (Netherlands)
Northern Marianas (U.S.)
Puerto Rico (U.S.)
U.S. Virgin Islands (U.S.)

1.5
Andorra (France-Spain)
British Virgin Islands (U.K.)
Cayman Islands (U.K.)
Ceuta (Spain)
Channel Islands (U.K.)
Cocos (Keeling) Islands (Australia)
Falkland Islands (U.K.)
Isle of Man (U.K.)
Martinique (France)
Melilla (Spain)
Montserrat (U.K.)
Norfolk Island (Australia)

Palau (Belau) (U.S.)
Pitcairn Islands (U.K.)
St. Helena and Dependencies (U.K.)
Turks and Caicos (U.K.)

2
Cook Islands (New Zealand)
French Guiana (France)
French Polynesia (France)
French Southern
    and Antarctic Territories (France)
Guadeloupe (France)
Mayotte (Mahore) (France)
Monaco (France)
New Caledonia (France)
Niue (New Zealand)
Reunion (France)
St. Pierre and Miquelon (France)
Svalbard (Norway)
Tokelau (New Zealand)

2.5
Christmas Island (Australia)
Rapanui (Easter Island) (Chile)
Wallis and Futuna Islands (France)

PARTLY FREE

3
Cyprus (Turkey)
Macao (Portugal)
Northern Ireland (U.K.)

3.5
Hong Kong (U.K.)

4.5
Kurdistan (Iraq)

5
Eritrea (Ethiopia)

NOT FREE

5.5
Bophutatswana (South Africa)
Transkei (South Africa)
Venda (South Africa)
Vojvodina (Yugoslavia)

6
Ciskei (South Africa)
Kashmir (India)
Occupied Territories (Israel)
Western Sahara (Morocco)

6.5
Irian Jaya (Indonesia)

7
East Timor (Indonesia)
Kosovo (Yugoslavia)
Tibet (China)

National Elections and Referenda

Country	Date/Type	Results and Comments
Albania 22 March 1992 29 March 1992	general legislative run-offs	The Democrats won 92 seats to 38 for the Socialists (formerly the Communist Party of Labor). The Social Democrats took 7 seats; the Unity Party of Human Rights, 2 seats; and the Republicans, 1 seat.
Algeria 16 January 1992	run-off general (cancelled)	After a military coup, the junta cancelled the election.
Angola 29-30 September 1992	general	President Jose Eduardo Santos (Popular Movement for the Liberation of Angola-MPLA) won 50.9% of the vote, defeating nine candidates including Jonas Savimbi (National Union for the Total Independence of Angola-UNITA), who took 39.4%. The MPLA won control of parliament with 56% of the vote to UNITA's 33%. There were at least forty election-related deaths during the last month of the campaign. Savimbi accused the government of widespread fraud. The election results renewed the armed conflict between UNITA and the MPLA.
Austria 26 April 1992 24 May 1992	presidential (first round) presidential run-off	Thomas Klestil (People's Party) defeated Rudolph Streicher (Social Democrat) by 57% to 43% in round two after voters eliminated Heide Schmidt (right-wing Freedom Party) and Robert Jungk (Green) in round one.
Azerbaijan 7 June 1992	presidential	Abulfez Elchibey (Popular Front) took 59.5% of the vote, defeating Nizami Suleymanov, his nearest rival, who received 33%. Two of the original seven candidates charged widespread fraud. International observers found a mixture of well-organized polling in some areas and disorganization and irregularities in others. Voting could not take place in Armenian-occupied Nagorno-Karabakh. However, refugees from there could vote at other polling stations.
Bahamas 19 August 1992	general	Hubert Ingraham's Free National Movement won 33 of 49 parliamentary seats, defeating longtime Prime Minister Lynden O. Pindling's People's Liberation Party. Pindling had ruled for twenty-five years.
Bosnia-Herzegovina 29 February-1 March 1992	referendum	Residents voted by a 2-1 margin for independence from Yugoslavia. There were boycotts in Serbian districts. Almost two-thirds of eligible voters participated. This vote led to war between the Serbs and the Bosnian Moslems.
Bulgaria 12 January 1992 19 January 1992	presidential (first round) presidential run-off	President Zhelyu Zhelev (Union of Democratic Forces) won with 52.85% to 47.15% for Velko Valkanov (the ex-Communist Socialist Party) in round two. Nineteen other candidates had competed in round one.
Burkina Faso 12 January 1992 24 May 1992	legislative (postponed) legislative (rescheduled)	Voters chose 107 members of parliament. The government front won the majority of seats.
Burundi 9 March 1992	referendum	Voters approved a new, multi-party constitution with 97.05% of the vote.
Cameroon 1 March 1992	legislative	The Social Democrats and other major opposition parties boycotted the contest, citing the government's refusal to reform electoral laws and to have an independent interim government supervise the vote. Thirty-two parties fielded candidates for the National Assembly. President Biya's Cameroon People's Democratic Movement won about half the seats.
11 October 1992	presidential	Using obvious fraud, Biya won the presidential election, defeating Fru Ndi (Social Democrat) and other candidates. International observers concluded the election was unfair.
Canada 26 October 1992	referenda	With a "No" vote of 56 %, Canadian voters rejected a proposed package of constitutional reforms that would have granted more autonomy to Quebec.
Central African Republic 25 October 1992	general (cancelled)	Claiming vote fraud, the government asked the Supreme Court to nullify the election, and delayed presidential and legislative elections until further notice. The C.A.R. President, General Andre Kolbinga, cited unauthorized and threatening election observers, illegal registers, and stolen ballot boxes and voting cards as evidence of fraud.
Comoros 22 and 29 October 1992	legislative	Pro-presidential candidates won an apparent majority, but disturbances and irregularities led to a rescheduling of some races for December. Some opposition parties boycotted.

National Elections and Referenda

Country	Date/Type	Results and Comments
Congo 15 March 1992	constitutional referendum	Voters approved the new constitution with 96.32% of the vote. Turnout was 70.93%. Incompetence and a lack of equipment delayed the report of the vote for five days.
24 June and 19 July 1992	legislative	The Pan African Union for Social Democracy won 39 of 125 seats. The Congolese Movement for Democracy and Integral Development came in second with 29 seats. The previously ruling Congolese Party of Labor won 19 seats. The Democratic Rally for Social Progress took nine seats. The Rally for Democracy and Development garnered five seats. Others won 24 seats.
2 August 1992 16 August 1992	presidential presidential run-off	General and President Denis Sassou-Nguesso (Congolese Party of Labor), Pascal Lissouba (Pan African Union for Social Democracy), Bernard Kolelas (Congolese Movement for Democracy and Integral Development), Andre Milong, and others faced each other in this race. Nguesso finished third. In the run-off, Lissouba (61.3%) defeated Kolelas. Sassou-Nguesso backed Lissouba in the run-off.
30 December 1992	legislative (postponed)	Following disagreements with the legislature, Lissouba dissolved it and called new elections, but then postponed them until March 1993.
Croatia 2 August 1992	general	Croatians voted for president and for all 124 parliamentary seats. President Franjo Tudjman (Democratic Union) won re-election over the Liberal and Party of Rights candidates. No party won a parliamentary majority, and Tudjman had to form a coalition. Croatians abroad were eligible to vote. The war situation made voting difficult in some areas.
Czecho-Slovakia 10 June 1992	general	Czech voters gave Vaclav Klaus's center-right Civic Democratic Party a plurality in the Czech regional and federal parliaments. Slovaks gave Vladimir Meciar's separatist Movement for a Democratic Slovakia a plurality of seats in the Slovak regional parliament and in the Slovak seats in the federal parliament. The election results led to the break-up of the country into two internationally recognized states.
Denmark 2 June 1992	referendum	Danes voted 50.7% to 49.3% to reject the European Community's Maastricht Treaty.
Djibouti 18 December 1992	legislative	Only three parties were allowed to register under the government's stringent requirements. The government party won a majority. One opposition party boycotted. There were charges of fraud.
Ecuador 17 May 1992 5 July 1992	general presidential run-off	In the first round of the presidential contest, Sixto Duran (Republican Unity Party) led with 33.2%. Jaime Nebot Saadi (Social Christian Party) finished second with 25.4%. Sixto Duran defeated Jaime Nebot Saadi in round two. In the 77 legislative races, the Social Christians won 21 seats; the Roldoists, 13; the Republicans, 12; the Democratic Left, 7; and nine other parties, a combined 24 seats.
Estonia 28 June 1992	referendum	Estonians voted for a new constitution and for regulations concerning the admission of citizenship applicants to the assembly. The citizenship laws had the effect of excluding most non-Estonian ethnics, especially Russians, from the vote. Russians constitute more than one-third of the population.
20 September 1992	general	Former Communist leader Arnold Ruutel (Secure Home Coalition) placed first in the presidential election, but failed to win an outright majority, thereby throwing the election to the new parliament. Lennart Meri, a leader of the conservative Fatherland Coalition, placed second. The new parliament elected Meri. Fatherland won the largest parliamentary bloc. The Fatherland Coalition announced its intention to form a coalition with the Moderates and the militantly nationalistic Estonian Independence Party. The Popular Front and the Royalists are in the opposition. Due to strict citizenship laws, about 40% of the population, consisting mostly of ethnic Russians, had no right to vote.
Fiji 23-30 May 1992	general	Former coup leader Sitiveni Rabuka's Fijian Political Party won 30 out of 70 seats in the new House of Representatives. Rabuka became prime minister after forming a coalition with the five-seat General Voters' Party and several independents.
France 20 September 1992	referendum	Voters backed the Maastricht Treaty by a margin of 51.04%-48.95%, excluding blank and spoiled ballots. This result prevented a major crisis in the European Community. Turnout was 69.69%. Metropolitan France, the French overseas territories, and French voters abroad outside French territories participated in the vote.

National Elections and Referenda

Country	Date/Type	Results and Comments
The Gambia 29 April 1992	general	President Sir Dawda Jawara won with 58.5%. Sherif Mustapha Dibba placed second with 22%. Three other candidates took the rest. The ruling People's Progressive Party lost 6 of its 31 legislative seats. The National Convention Party won 6 seats; the Gambia People's Party 2; and independents, 3.
Georgia 11 October 1992	general	Eduard Shevardnadze, the only candidate, won 90% support in his campaign for the Speakership of Parliament, Georgia's de facto presidency. Thirty-six parties competed for parliamentary seats. Liberal parties won the largest number of seats. Due to separatist violence, no voting took place in northern Abkhazia.
Ghana 28 April 1992	referendum	Ghanaians voted 92.6% "yes" for the new constitution.
3 November 1992	presidential	President Jerry Rawlings won with 58.7% of the vote. Albert Adu Boahen placed second with 30%. The opposition parties had agreed to the election despite a grossly inaccurate voter registration list. There were credible reports of ballot box stuffing and other irregularities. Violent clashes erupted just after the vote between opposition and security forces.
29 December 1992	parliamentary	Citing vote-rigging, the opposition parties boycotted the election. Of the 200 legislators elected, 189 are members of President Rawlings' National Democratic Congress, 9 members of other pro-Rawlings parties, and 2 independents.
Guinea 27 December 1992	general (postponed)	There were pre-election irregularities with voter registration lists, ethnic violence, etc. The government postponed elections until 1993.
Guinea-Bissau 15 November/ 13 December 1992	general (postponed)	The government postponed elections at least until March 1993, continuing frustration among the opposition.
Guyana 5 October 1992	general	In the presidential election, Cheddi Jagan defeated President Desmond Hoyte. Several parties competed for the 65-seat legislature. In Georgetown, the capital, a rampaging progovernment mob stormed through the streets, demanding to be added to the voter registration lists. Police fired on rioters on 6 October, killing two. Hoyte supporters claimed irregularities in the voting, but international observers said the process seemed fair.
India 19 February 1992	general (partial-Punjab-postponed from 1991)	The Congress Party won a majority of Punjab's national parliamentary seats. Sikh militants and most local parties boycotted the election. Militants intimidated 72% of voters into staying at home.
Indonesia 9 June 1992	general	Indonesians chose candidates for the House of Representatives from three government-approved parties (the government's Golkar Party, the Indonesian Democratic Party, and the Muslim United Development Party). Golkar won with 67% of the vote, down from 73% in 1987.
Iran 10 April 1992 8 May 1992	legislative (first round) legislative (second round)	Screened candidates competed for parliament. The government excluded radical incumbents and "spiritually incorrect" candidates, and allowed only limited campaigning. There were disputes over the number of ballot box observers and various irregularities. Turnout was about 30%, at most. Most oppositionists boycotted the election. The Society of Militant Clergymen and other candidates aligned with President Rafsanjani won well over 200 of the 268 seats with official victors. The Council of Guardians declared results in 2 of the 270 seats invalid, and ordered new elections there. The hard-line opposition charged the government with vote-rigging and shooting and flogging demonstrators.
Ireland 18 June 1992	referendum	Voters approved the terms of the Maastricht Treaties of the EC by a margin of 69% to 31%.
26 November 1992	general	Prime Minister Albert Reynolds' Fianna Fail party and Fine Gael, the largest opposition party, both lost significant ground. The Labour Party doubled its parliamentary representation. A Fianna-Fail-Labour coalition resulted.
26 November 1992	referenda	Voters approved two constitutional amendments on abortion: one dealing with the right to travel to other countries for abortion; a second legalizing the availability of information on abortion services in other countries. They rejected a third proposed amendment prohibiting abortion in Ireland except to save the mother's life in cases other than threatened suicide.

National Elections and Referenda

Country	Date/Type	Results and Comments
Israel 23 June 1992	general	Labor, the chief opposition group, became the largest party, winning 44 of 120 parliamentary seats. Likud, the dominant party in the outgoing government, took 32 seats. The left-wing Meretz, a three-party coalition, won 12 seats. Arab parties (Hadash and the Democratic Arab group) took 5 seats. Religious parties (Shas, United Torah Judaism, and the National Religious Party) carried 16 seats. Far-right parties (Tsomet and Moledet) won 11 seats. Labor leader Yitzhak Rabin became Prime Minister after negotiating a coalition arrangement with Meretz and other parties.
Italy 5 April 1992	general	The governing four-party coalition (Christian Democrats, Socialists, Liberals, and Social Democrats) lost significant ground, but managed to form a new government. Among the opposition parties, the Party of the Democratic Left (the reformed Communists) received 16.1% of the vote and 107 seats. The new, hardline Communist Refoundation took 5.6% and 35 seats. The regionalist Northern Leagues captured 8.7% and 55 seats. The neo-Fascist Italian Social Movement won 5.4% and 34 seats. The Republicans took 4.4% and 27 seats. The Greens increased their showing marginally to 2.8% and 16 seats. The new La Rete (The Network) received 1.9% and 12 seats. Other parties won a combined 6.3% and 13 seats. There were similar results in the Senate.
Japan 26 July 1992	legislative	Half of the parliament's 252-seat upper house was up for election. The ruling Liberal Democratic Party won a plurality, but the LDP did not win enough to control the house alone.
Kenya 29 December 1992	general	Profiting from fraud and a divided opposition, President Daniel arap Moi won with 37% of the vote. The opposition parties won a significant minority of parliamentary seats.
South Korea 24 March 1992	legislative	The opposition charged that the government gained votes by interfering with soldiers' rights to cast ballots freely. There were also reports that government intelligence agents campaigned against the opposition. The ruling Democratic Liberal Party took 149 seats with 38.5% of the vote. The Democratic Party, the leading opposition group, received 29.2% of the vote and 97 seats. The new Unification National Party captured 17.3% of the vote and 31 seats. The Party for New Political Reform captured 1 seat, and independents took 21.
18 December 1992	presidential	Kim Young Sam (Democratic Liberal Party) won with 42% of the vote, defeating Kim Dae Jung (Democratic Party) and Chung Ju Yung (Unification National Party).
Kosovo/Yugoslavia and Macedonia 24 May 1992	general	Ethnic Albanians in the Kosovo region and other parts of current and former Yugoslavia held an unofficial, multiparty election for president and legislators. Ibrahim Rugova (Democratic League of Kosovo) won the presidency.
Kurdistan/Iraq 17 May 1992 19 May 1992	general (postponed) general (rescheduled)	Iraqi Kurds chose a legislative assembly of 105 members. There were a few violent incidents during the campaign, but voting was peaceful. Election organizers delayed the vote for two days over alleged problems with German indelible ink, a measure against repeat voting. The Democratic Party of Kurdistan (DPK) and the Patriotic Union of Kurdistan (PUK) won 50 seats each, and 5 seats went to the Syrian Christians. The two leading presidential contenders, Massud Barzani (DPK) and Jalal Talabani (PUK), established a joint leadership.
Kuwait 5 October 1992	legislative	Opposition groups won 31 seats to 19 for government supporters. Islamists won 19 of the opposition seats. Only a fragment of Kuwaitis could vote.
Lebanon 23, 30 August 1992 6 September 1992	general	These were Lebanon's first parliamentary elections since 1972. Voters were to have elected 128 members, divided evenly between Muslims and Christians. However, Christian leaders objected to holding the vote before a Syrian withdrawal. There were several irregularities reported, including ballot box-stuffing and vote-rigging. Voting lists included Palestinians and Syrians who had no right to vote. There were at least four deaths linked to the elections. Turnout was extremely low in boycotting Christian areas. Resulting from the boycott, five Maronite Christian seats were vacant, pending by-elections. Amal, the Syrian-backed Shiite movement, won the most seats. Amal's slate included members of the Baathist Party and National Social Party. Hezbollah (Party of God), the Iranian-backed Shiite party also won seats. Three personalistic blocs won seats: supporters of former Prime Minister Selim al-Hoss; backers of former Prime Minister Omar

National Elections and Referenda

Country	Date/Type	Results and Comments
		Karami; and allies of Defense Minister Michel al-Murr. Most of the 59 Christians elected are independent or ran on Muslim tickets.
11 October 1992	by-elections	Resulting from the Maronite Christian boycott of elections for five seats in the general election, five Christian independents won seats. Turnout was extremely low.
Lesotho 28 November 1992	general (postponed)	The government postponed the election until January 1993.
Liechtenstein 11-13 December 1992	referendum	The country voted for the principle of joining a united Europe.
Lithuania 13 May 1992	referendum	Voters did not pass a plan to strengthen the presidency.
14 June 1992	referendum	Lithuanians voted overwhelmingly to demand the withdrawal of the troops of the former Soviet Union from the Baltics.
25 October 1992 15 November 1992	legislative (first round) legislative (run-off) and referendum	The Democratic Party of Labor (formerly the Communists) won a two-round total of 79 seats out of 141. Sajudis took 17 seats, for a grand total of 35. Others won a combined 36. Voters also approved a referendum setting up a directly elected presidency. The first such election takes place in 1993.
Madagascar 19 August 1992	referendum	Malagasy voters approved a new constitution by a 3-1 margin.
25 November 1992	presidential (first round)	Albert Zafy (Active Forces) placed first. President Didier Ratsiraka came in second. Manandafy Rakotonirina finished third. There will be a run-off in January 1993.
Malawi 26-27 June 1992	legislative	There was a one-party legislative election.
Mali 12 January 1992	referendum	98.35% of those turning out approved the new constitution. Turnout was 43.5%.
26 January 1992 23 February 1992 8 March 1992	legislative (postponed) legislative (rescheduled first round) legislative (second round)	The combined results of the two rounds produced a solid victory for the Alliance for Democracy in Mali (ADEMA) in this transitional election. Nine other parties also won seats. Fourteen of the 22 parties disputed the results. Some losing parties charged administrative bias in favor of ADEMA, especially involving the drawing up of electoral lists and the issuing of ballot papers. Turnout was estimated at 20%.
12 April 1992 26 April 1992	presidential presidential run-off	Alpha Oumar Konare (ADEMA) won the presidency with 69.01% of the vote, defeating Tieoule Mamadou Konate (US-RDA) in the run-off. The latter alleged some vote fraud had taken place. Konare appointed a new prime minister and a multiparty cabinet.
Malta 22 February 1992	general	The governing Nationalists won with a reduced majority of 51.8% of the vote and 34 seats to 46.5% of the vote and 31 seats for the Labor Party. Democratic Alternative, a breakaway from Labor, captured 1.7% of the vote and no seats.
Mauritania 24 January 1992	presidential	Using fraud, military leader Col. Maaouiya Ould Sid Ahmed Taya won the country's first contested presidential election with 62.82% of the vote. His chief opponent, Ahmed Ould Daddah (Union of Democratic Forces), carried 32.93% of the vote. The government pre-vented blacks from registering to vote or issued them invalid identification cards. Foreign observers mentioned Taya's fraud and the country's political ineptitude as the reasons for his victory. Violence broke out after the opposition charged the government with vote-rigging.
6 March 1992	legislative	The government refused the opposition's demands for a clean election, so they boycotted the polls. Members of Taya's party won 69 of the 79 lower house seats. Pro-Taya "independents" won the other 10 seats.
Mongolia 29 June 1992	legislative	The People's Revolutionary Party (the Communists) won 70 of the 76 seats in the country's new unicameral parliament. International observers reported that various irregularities and unequal campaign opportunities marred the second

National Elections and Referenda

Country	Date/Type	Results and Comments
		multiparty elections. The Communists employed Communist Chinese consultants to help control the population.
Morocco 4 September 1992	referendum	Moroccans voted by 99.6% to back minor constitutional changes. Several opposition groups boycotted the polls. The government included Western Sahara in the referendum, thereby weakening the legal case for the territory's independence.
late 1992	legislative (postponed)	Parliamentary elections, postponed from 1990 to 1992, will allegedly take place in 1993.
Nauru 14 November 1992	general	Nauruans chose members of parliament in partyless democratic elections. After the vote, M.P.'s re-elected President Bernard Dowiyogo.
New Zealand 19 September 1992	referendum	With 85% support, New Zealanders backed a proposal to change the parliamentary electoral system from British-style "first-past-the-post" elections with single-member districts. Voters chose the mixed member proportional alternative. The new system would give the voter two votes, one for a single-member district and one for a party list. Following a second referendum in 1993, the new system would become binding for the 1996 general election.
Niger 26 December 1992	referendum	The public approved a new constitution with 89% of the vote. Turnout was 54%.
November/December 1992	presidential & legislative	Niger postponed these elections until 1993.
Nigeria 4 July 1992	legislative	In transitional legislative elections, only two parties approved by the military competed. The Social Democrats defeated the more conservative National Republican Convention for control of both the Senate and the House of Representatives. In the upper house, the Social Democrats will outnumber Republicans 47-44. In the lower house, the Social Democrats won 310 of 589 seats. Voting was not secret.
5 December 1992	presidential (postponed)	Nigeria postponed presidential elections until 1993, because fraudulent primary contests delayed party nominations.
Panama 15 November 1992	referendum	Voters rejected a package of proposed reforms that included the elimination of the army. There was a 40% turnout. Of the participating electors, 63.5% voted "no," 31.5% voted "yes," and 5% cast void ballots.
Papua New Guinea 7-27 June 1992	general	Voters threw out a record 59 MP's, including 15 cabinet ministers. Incumbent Prime Minister Rabbie Namaliu's Papua New Guinea United Party had a net loss of 11 seats, ending up with 19. Namaliu had led a six-party coalition. The new Prime Minister is Pais Wingti of the People's Democratic Movement. There was some election day violence and ballot box destruction and tampering. Traditional tribal vote-buying also took place.
Peru 22 November 1992	legislative	Most traditional parties boycotted the election out of fear that their participation would accord legitimacy to President Fujimori's seizure of power. Fujimori's allies won the majority of seats, 44 out of 80, with 38% of the vote.
Philippines 11 May 1992	general	Incidents of election-day fraud and sporadic violence marred a generally peaceful campaign. According to the National Police, 51 people died in campaign-related violence from February-May. Presidential and vice presidential candidates ran separately. The presidential candidates were: Miriam Defensor Santiago (People's Reform Party); Fidel Ramos (People Power Party-National Union of Christian Democrats); Eduardo Cojuangco (Nationalist People's Coalition); Jovito Salonga (Liberal Party); Imelda Marcos (New Society Movement); Ramon Mitra (Struggle of the Democratic Filipino); and Salvador Laurel (Nationalist Party). Ramos won the presidency with 23.5% of the vote. Running separately, Joseph Estrada (National People's Coalition) won the vice presidency. No party won control of Congress. Mitra's Struggle of the Democratic Filipino won 87 of 201 seats in the house of Representatives and 16 of 24 senators. President Ramos's People Power Party-National Union of Christian Democrats won only 51 House seats and only 2 senators. Other parties won the remaining seats.

National Elections and Referenda

Country	Date/Type	Results and Comments
Romania 27 September 1992 11 October 1992	general presidential run-off	President Ion Iliescu (Democratic National Salvation Front) won re-election against Emil Constantinescu (Democratic Convention Alliance) with 61.4% of the vote in the run-off. Parliamentary results: The Democratic National Salvation Front won 148 seats; the Democratic Convention Alliance, 117; nationalist parties, 68; others, including the National Salvation Front, 84. International observers believed the elections to have been apparently fair.
St. Lucia 27 April 1992	general	Prime Minister John Compton's United Workers' Party carried 11 of 17 parliamentary seats to 6 for the opposition Labour Party.
Seychelles 26 July 1992	constitutional assembly	In the first multi-party elections in eighteen years, supporters of President Albert Rene won 58.4% of the vote and 14 of 20 seats. Opposition leader Sir James Mancham charged that the elections were unfair.
15 November 1992	constitutional referendum	The voters rejected the proposed constitution that the pro-government constitutional commission had written.
Sierra Leone November 1992	presidential	As a result of the military coup, this election did not take place.
Slovenia 6 December 1992	presidential	President Kucan won re-election with 63% of the vote.
South Africa 17 March 1992	referendum	By 68% of the vote, whites supported negotiations for a political settlement with blacks. Violence marred the campaign, but there was an 80% turnout.
Switzerland 16-17 May 1992	referendum	The Swiss voted by a margin of 55.8% to 44.2% to join the International Monetary Fund and the World Bank.
September 1992	referendum	The Swiss approved a plan for constructing transportation routes through the Alps.
6 December 1992	referendum	The Swiss rejected joining the European Economic Area, a free trade zone for the European Community and the European Free Trade Association. (See country report for details.)
Taiwan (Republic of China) 19 December 1992	legislative	The ruling Nationalists won 53% of the vote and 96 out of 161 seats in the Legislative Yuan (Branch). The opposition Democratic Progressive Party won 50 seats in the freest election to date in Taiwan.
Tajikistan 6 December 1992	legislative	Elections were scheduled for a multiparty People's Assembly, but they did not take place on account of armed conflict.
Tatarstan/Russia 21 March 1992	referendum	Tatars voted by 61.4% in favor of Tatar sovereignty. Voting was generally free and fair, although there were allegations of some irregularities in ethnic Russian areas.
Thailand 22 March 1992	general	Technically, this election marked the return of formal civilian government. Three pro-military parties won the largest share of votes. Those parties (Chart Thai, Samakkhi Tham, and Social Action) won 190 of the 360 seats in the lower house. Despite vote-rigging and -buying, Palang Dharma (Power of Virtue) and two other pro-democracy parties won 152 seats.
13 September 1992	general	A coalition of four pro-democracy parties led the contest, taking a combined 185 parliamentary seats out of 360. Chuan Leekpai, leader of the Democratic Party, became Prime Minister. The Democrats won 79 seats. The other coalition parties are New Aspiration, Palang Dharma (Power of Virtue), and the Solidarity Party. The pro-military Chart Thai Party won 77 seats. The independent monitoring group, Pollwatch, said it had received 3,000 allegations of vote-buying and other electoral violations.
Togo 28 September 1992	referendum	Voters gave overwhelming approval to a new constitution that endorses multiparty elections.
late 1992	general	The government postponed elections until 1993.
Turkmenistan 21 June 1992	presidential	In a one-candidate election, voters reelected President Saparmurad Niyazov, the former Communist Party leader, with 99.8% of the vote.

National Elections and Referenda

Country	Date/Type	Results and Comments
United Kingdom 9 April 1992	general	Prime Minister John Major's Conservatives won reelection with a reduced majority of seats in the House of Commons. The Conservatives took 41.9% of the vote and 336 seats. The Labour Party received 34.4% of the vote and 271 seats. The Liberal Democrats took 18% of the vote and 20 seats. The Scottish Nationalists won 3 seats, a loss of 2. The Welsh Nationalists won 4 seats. In Northern Ireland, Sinn Fein lost its only seat. The Social Democratic and Labour Party won 4 seats, a gain of 1. The Ulster Unionist parties won the remaining 13 of Northern Ireland's 17 seats.
United States of America 3 November 1992	general	Bill Clinton (Democrat) won election with 43% of the popular vote and 370 Electoral College votes to 38% and 168 Electoral College votes for President George Bush (Republican) and 19% of the popular vote and no Electoral College votes for H. Ross Perot, independent. In the new Senate, Democrats hold 57 seats to 43 for the Republicans. In the House of Representatives, Democrats won 258 seats, Republicans 176, and one seat for an independent socialist.
Western Sahara January 1992 (postponed)	referendum	The Moroccan government postponed Western Sahara's referendum on independence several times. The occupying power disputed with the United Nations over the eligibility of Moroccan settlers to vote on the issue.
Yemen November 1992	general (postponed)	The merged Yemen will hold its first multiparty election in 1993.
Yugoslavia (Serbia and Montenegro) June 1992	general	The opposition boycotted this first election in the newly shrunken Yugoslavia. The government announced that supporters of Serbian strongman Slobodan Milosevic won 73 of the 138 parliamentary seats. The Serbian Radical Party, supporters of "ethnic cleansing" of non-Serbians, won 33 seats. Opposition leader Vuk Draskovic questioned the government's claim that there had been a 56% voter turnout.
20 December 1992	general	In federal parliamentary elections, the Socialists (the renamed Communists) won 47 of 138 seats. The nationalist Radicals won 34 seats. DEPOS, the largest opposition group won 20 seats. Others won 37. The election produced a majority for hardline Serbian President Slobodan Milosevic. Voting was not fair. Observers reported numerous irregularities such as the exclusion of numerous opposition supporters from registration lists.
Montenegro 1 March 1992	referendum	Montenegrins voted by 95.94% to remain part of Yugoslavia. About two-thirds of eligible voters turned out.
20 December 1992	general	President Momir Bulatovic faced Milosevic ally Branko Kostic and other candidates. No one received the requisite majority. There will be a run-off on 10 January 1993.
Serbia 11 October 1992	referendum	Due to an insufficient voter turnout, Serbian voters failed to mandate the government to hold presidential and legislative elections in November 1992. The proposal for elections had required the support of at least 50% of the entire registered electorate.
20 December 1992	general	President Slobodan Milosevic faced federal Prime Minister Milan Panic for the Serbian presidency. Using vote fraud, Milosevic won with 56 %. There were five other candidates. Voters also gave Milosevic's Socialists (the renamed Communists) 101 seats out of 250 in the Serbian parliament. The ultra-nationalist Radicals took 73 seats. Other extreme nationalists captured 5 seats, giving Milosevic a combined 179 supporters.

Sources: International Foundation for Electoral Systems, Associated Press, New York Times, West Africa, Irish Voice, Irish Echo

Sources

Publications, organizations

AFL-CIO *Bulletin*
Africa Confidential
Africa Fund
Africa News
Africa Report
Agence France Presse
Al Haq Report on Human Rights
American Institute for Free Labor Development
American-Jewish Committee
Amnesty International *Urgent Action Bulletins*
Amnesty International: *Report 1991*
Andean Newsletter
Anti-Censorship Action Group
Armenian General Benevolent Union Newspaper
The *Armenian Reporter*
Asiaweek
Asian Bulletin
Asian Survey
Assembly of Turkish-American Association
Associated Press
The *Atlantic Monthly*
Attacks on Justice
Austrian Information
Beijing Review
British Information Service
Caretas (Lima)
Carib News
Caribbean Affairs
Caribbean Insight
Caribbean Review
The *Carter Center News*
Catholic Standard (Guyana)
Center for Security Policy Press Release
Center for Strategic and International Studies
Central America Report
Chickasha Daily Express
China Daily
The *Chinese Free Journal*
Chinese Information and Cultural Center
Christian Science Monitor
Civil Justice Memo
Civil Rights Update
Columbia Journalism Review
Committee to Protect Journalists *Update*
Commonwealth Correspondence
Crusade for Democracy in Seychelles
Cyprus Newsletter
Dawn News Bulletin (All Burma Students Democratic Front)
Defense and Foreign Affairs Handbook 1989
Democracy Today
Deutschland Nachrichten
Droits de L'Homme
East European Reporter
Economic & Commercial Information
The *Economist*
EFE Spanish news agency
El Nuevo Herald (Miami)
The *European*
L'Express
Facts About Greenland
Far Eastern Economic Review
El Financiero (Mexico City)

Foreign Broadcast Information Service:
　FBIS Africa
　FBIS China
　FBIS East Europe
　FBIS Latin America
　FBIS Near East & South Asia
　FBIS East Asia
　FBIS Soviet Union/Central Eurasia
　FBIS Sub-Saharan Africa
The *Financial Times*
Focus
Forum
Free Angola Information Service
Free China Journal
Free China Review
Free Labour World
Freedom First
Freedom to Write Bulletin
The *Frontier Post* (Peshawar)
Frontline
The *Globe & Mail* (Toronto)
Greece Bulletin
The *Guardian*
Guatemala Watch (Guatemala City)
Gulf News
Gulf-Kuwait Newspaper
Hemisfile
Hemisphere
The *Herald Tribune*
Hong Kong Digest
Houston *Post*
Human Rights Watch:
　Africa Watch
　Americas Watch
　Asia Watch
　Helsinki Watch
　Miiddle East Watch
Immigration and Refugee Board
The *Independent*
Index on Censorship
India News
India Today
Indian Law Resource Center
The *Indochina Institute Report*
Inside China Mainland
Institute on Religion and Democracy
Inter-American Press Association
International Commission of Jurists
International Foundation for Electoral Systems
International Herald Tribune
International Organization for Migration
International Organization of Journalists
International Republican Institute
International Union of Food and Allied Workers
Internet on the Holocaust and Genocide
Iran Times (International)
Irish Echo
The Irish Emigrant Vote Campaign
Irish Voice
Issues + Views
Japan Access
The Jarkow Institute for Latin America of the Anti-Defamation
　League of B'nai B'rith
Jeune Afrique
Journal of Afghan Affairs
Journal of Commerce
Journal of Democracy
Keesing's Record of World Events

Keesing's Revolutionary and Dissident Movements
Keesing's Border and Territorial Disputes
Khaleej Times
Korea Update
Kwacha News
Latin American Perspectives
Latin American Regional Reports
Latin American Weekly Report
Lithuanian Information Center
Los Angeles *Times*
Mainstream
Middle East Economic Digest
Middle East International
Middle East Monitor
Le Monde
The *Muslim (Peshawar)*
N. Young
The *Nation*
National Catholic Register
National Council of Trade Unions
National Democratic Institute for International Affairs
National Republican Institute for International Affairs
National Spiritual Assembly for the Baha'is of the U.S.
New Arabia
New Observer
New Pittsburgh Courier
New Republic
New York
New York Newsday
New York Times
New Yorker
The News (Karachi)
The News + Courier
News Digest
News From Austria
Newsletter (Nepal)
Newsweek
North-South Magazine
Norwegian Information Service
Le Nouvelle Observateur
Organization of American States
The Other Side of Mexico
Pacific Islands Monthly
People's Mojahedin of Iran
Le Point
Political Handbook of the World: 1991
Political Handbook of the World: 1992
Portuguese Tourist Office of Publications
Proceso (Mexico City)
Problems of Communism
Radio Free Europe/Radio Liberty: RFE/RL Report on
 Eastern Europe
  RFE/RL Report on Soviet Union
  RFE/RL Soviet/East European Report
Rand McNally World Facts & Maps, 1993 edition
Red Cross/Red Crescent
Record

Religion-Economics Quarterly
Report on Science
Respekt (Czechoslovakia)
Response
Roundup
Royal Danish Ministry of Foreign Affairs
Select Committee on Hunger
The Seychellois International
South
South Africa Briefing Paper
South Africa Institute on Race Relations
South Africa Update
South East Asia Monitor
Sri Lanka News Bulletin
State Department Country Reports on Human Rights Practices for 1991
The Statesman
Strategic World
Sudan Democratic Gazette
The Sunday Tribune
Survey on Refugees
Swedish Information Service
Swiss Press Review
Swiss Review of World Affairs
Taiwan Communique
Tampa Florida Tribune
Third World Quarterly
The Tico Times (Costa Rica)
Time
Time & Money
The Times of Oman
The Times Atlas of the World
The Times of the Americas
Togo Information Service
Transcaucasus: A Chronology
U.S. News and World Report
Ukrainian Press Agency
Ukrainian Reporter
Ukrainian Weekly
Uncaptive Minds (Institute for Democracy in Eastern Europe)
UNDP Human Development Report
UNICEF
Universal Almanac 1991
Vanity Fair
Vietnam Insight
The Vietnamese Resistance
Voice of Democracy in China
Wall Street Journal
Washington Post
The Washington Report on Middle East Affairs
Washington Times
The Week in Germany
Week in South Africa
West Africa
Whaleej Times
World Almanac 1993
World Population Data Sheet 1992 (Population Reference Bureau)
World Press Review

Human Rights Organizations

Americas Watch
Amnesty International
Andean Commission of Jurists
Caribbean Institute for the Promotion of
 Human Rights
Caribbean Rights
Center for Democracy

Chilean Human Rights Commission
Committee of Churches for Emergency Help
 (Paraguay)
Cuban Commission for Human Rights and
National Reconciliation
Cuban Committee for Human Rights
Group for Mutual Support (Guatemala)

Guyana Human Rights Association
Haitian Center for Human Rights
Helsinki Watch
Honduran Committee for the Defense of Human Rights
Human Rights Commission (El Salvador)
International League for Human Rights
Institute on Religion and Democracy
Inter-American Commission on Human Rights,
Organization of American States
International League for Human Rights
Jamaica Council for Human Rights
Latin American Commission for Human Rights and
    Freedoms of the Workers
Lawyers Committee for Human Rights

National Coalition for Haitian Refugees
National Coordinating Office for Human Rights (Peru)
Of Human Rights
Panamanian Committee for Human Rights
Permanent Commission on Human Rights
(Nicaragua)
Permanent Committee for the Defense of Human Rights
(Colombia)
Puebla Institute
Runejel Junam Council of Ethnic
    Communities (Guatemala)
Tutela Legal (El Salvador)
Vicaria de la Solidaridad (Chile)

Delegations/visitors to Freedom House

Africa/Middle East
Algeria
Angola
Benin
Burkina Faso
Cameroon
Cote D'Ivoire
Egypt
Ethiopia
Iran
Israel
Mauritius
Mozambique
Niger
Nigeria
Rwanda
South Africa
Tanzania
Tunisia
Turkey
Zaire

Asia/Southeast Asia/Pacific
Australia
Bangladesh
Burma (Myanmar)
Cambodia
China (PRC)
Hong Kong
Indonesia
(South) Korea
Malaysia

Eastern Europe
Bulgaria
Czechoslovakia

Hungary
Poland
Romania
Yugoslavia

former USSR
Belarus (Byelorussia)
Estonia
Latvia
Lithuania
Russia
Ukraine

Western Europe
European Community
Netherlands

Western Hemisphere
Argentina
Brazil
Canada
Chile
Costa Rica
Cuba
Dominican Republic
Ecuador
El Salvador
Guatemala
Guyana
Haiti
Mexico
Nicaragua
Panama
Peru
Suriname
Venezuela

Delegations from Freedom House to:

Cuba
Czechoslovakia
Dominican Republic
Ecuador
El Salvador
Guyana
Hong Kong
Hungary
India

Indonesia
Japan
Mexico
Poland
Romania
South Africa
USSR (former)
    Kazakhstan
    Russia